THE CHINA ALTERNATIVE

CHANGING REGIONAL ORDER
IN THE PACIFIC ISLANDS

THE CHINA ALTERNATIVE

CHANGING REGIONAL ORDER IN THE PACIFIC ISLANDS

EDITED BY GRAEME SMITH AND
TERENCE WESLEY-SMITH

Australian
National
University

PRESS

PACIFIC SERIES

ANU PRESS

Published by ANU Press
The Australian National University
Acton ACT 2601, Australia
Email: anupress@anu.edu.au

Available to download for free at press.anu.edu.au

ISBN (print): 9781760464165
ISBN (online): 9781760464172

WorldCat (print): 1238049900
WorldCat (online): 1238049886

DOI: 10.22459/CA.2021

Cover design and layout by ANU Press. Cover photograph: Shaun Gessler.

Contents

Opening Remarks

Delivered at The China Alternative: Changing Regional
Order in the Pacific Islands Symposium

The University of the South Pacific, Port Vila, Vanuatu

Friday 8 February 2019

Hon. Ralph Regenvanu, Member of Parliament

I feel honoured to have been invited to present a brief keynote address
on the occasion of this The China Alternative symposium, and wish
to convey my thanks at the outset to the organisers for the excellent
arrangements.

I would also like to preface my address by making the obvious point that
the dynamic and complex geopolitics that are purported to be changing
the regional order in the Pacific, and that are the subject of this symposium,
are simply reflective of international geopolitics and the paradigm and
ideological shifts that happen as the dominant world states pursue their
own national interests.

National context

For small island developing states such as Vanuatu, however, such shifts
provide opportunities, including opportunities for greater leverage,
upon which their relationship with the international community and
development partners may be predicated and adapted.

No different than for other Pacific Island countries, Vanuatu's smallness,
the smallness of our economy and our severe vulnerability to natural
disasters makes such opportunities all the more valuable.

Also no different than for any other Pacific Island country, Vanuatu's own national interests are paramount in determining our relations with the international community and other states.

Vanuatu's national interest is the successful implementation of our *National Sustainable Development Plan 2016–2030*, also known as *The People's Plan 2030*, which is the country's vision and overarching policy framework for achieving a 'Stable, Sustainable and Prosperous Vanuatu' over the next 15 years; our locally developed adaptation of the United Nations' Sustainable Development Goals or SDGs.

In launching its *Budget Policy Priorities* for 2019, for example, the Vanuatu Government also appealed to the international community and its development partners for budgetary support. This is perhaps our principle 'ask' from the international community.

To that end, it has been my key stated priority since becoming foreign minister just over a year ago to push reforms in the government's internal workings to strengthen Vanuatu's capacity to be clear in knowing what it needs from the international community, and to be able to strategically articulate these needs to the partners who will assist us. In particular, the current review of national structures, capacity and mechanisms is aimed at assisting to ensure Vanuatu's smooth transition from Least Developed Country status next year, in 2020.

To reiterate, resourcing our own sustainable development is our key national foreign policy objective.

Regional security

In spite of competing interests, Vanuatu continues to uphold a nonaligned foreign policy, which is most explicitly manifested in our advocacy and practice of principles of denuclearisation and nonmilitarisation of the Pacific region. Vanuatu became one of the first signatories to the South Pacific Nuclear Free Zone Treaty shortly after independence in 1980, and most recently signed and ratified the Treaty on the Prohibition of Nuclear Weapons in September last year.

On the other hand, in our view, the security lens oft adopted by metropolitan powers in the region can also be distorting of what we feel is the reality, and is often seen as a drawback in relations, especially by those in officialdom. There sometimes is a perception that Vanuatu is 'taking sides'.

This is notwithstanding the complex relationship that our more traditional partners like Australia, New Zealand and France have, for example, with the Pacific, especially in security and defence.

For Vanuatu, which is consistently ranked as the country in the world most susceptible to natural hazards, the adverse effects of a changing climate and natural disasters remain the greatest threat to our national security. The commitment made by Forum leaders in 2015, which is now enshrined in the Boe Declaration—reaffirming that 'climate change remains the single greatest threat to the livelihoods, security and wellbeing of the peoples of the Pacific'—confirms this.

I am here reminded of the humanitarian and economic cost in the aftermath of Tropical Cyclone Pam in 2015, amounting to over 60 per cent of the national GDP, and the ongoing Ambae volcanic disaster, which continues to cause large-scale disruption to the livelihoods of the approximately 10,000 inhabitants who are directly affected.

Less than two weeks ago, cabinet approved the establishment of our inaugural National Security Council and a draft National Security Strategy, which expands the more traditional concept of security to include climate change and disaster response, and includes the minister of climate change as a permanent member of the council and chiefs and civil society as ad hoc members.

Here I wish to acknowledge the continued support by our important bilateral partners, Australia, New Zealand, France and China, in building our national capacities to better respond to these new and emerging issues.

Political relations and development cooperation with China

Notwithstanding the perceived unorthodox means by which China's continued assistance towards Vanuatu's development priorities and aspirations continues to be manifested, the simple fact is that the assistance is meeting a development need or priority.

Also, and in spite of the recent spotlight on China's development assistance to the Pacific, including Vanuatu, China is hardly the biggest donor in the region, or in Vanuatu.

An important factor in Vanuatu's continued reliance on development assistance from China are the less stringent processes for getting large infrastructure projects implemented, which make it easier for small administrations like ours to seek direct assistance. However, our engagement with China on infrastructure projects is also stimulating us to be continually vigilant in updating and enforcing our own laws and in building our own capacities for oversight of such projects. We are pleased that this interactive aspect of our relationship on infrastructure projects is developing fast.

With China, as with our other partners, we must continue to insist on climate-proof and resilient infrastructure built according to national standards.

The party-to-party relationships between the Chinese Communist Party and many of the key political parties in Vanuatu, whilst unheard of in the history of our relations with our more traditional partners, attest to a relationship that traverses differences in political ideologies and in cultural and bureaucratic norms, and is an interesting value-add to the relationship of many of our leaders with China.

And I am pleased to announce that in addition to a growing number of scholarships for our students to study in China and ongoing discussions on air services to improve air connectivity and strengthen people-to-people links between China and Vanuatu, we also look forward to signing a visa waiver agreement in the near future to ease travel restrictions between our countries. For Vanuatu, this is a strong evidence of a joint desire by both countries to further promote friendly relations between the two countries. Conversely, this element remains a significant missing part of our longer-term relations with our other key Pacific partners.

China continues to be an important player on the international stage as a permanent member of the UN Security Council and a global leader in trade, and Vanuatu will continue to seek ways to increase cooperation with China.

Concluding remarks

To conclude, Vanuatu's engagement with the international community continues to be developmental in its focus and nature, and in ensuring that gains of the past are safeguarded and incremental steps taken to expand and diversify its trade, economic and political relations.

And Vanuatu, as with other Pacific Island countries, can only hope that this continues to be done in the spirit of mutual respect and genuine and equal partnership.

Vanuatu welcomes increased efforts by Australia and New Zealand via their respective 'Pacific Step-Up' and 'Pacific Reset' policies to reach out to the Pacific.

Vanuatu also welcomes the intention of the United Kingdom to reopen its high commission in Vanuatu, and warmly applauds the government of Japan for establishing for the very first time its permanent diplomatic presence here in Port Vila.

The geopolitical dynamics of our region, with which we are all well acquainted, provide opportunities for the region, as I have outlined in this address. However, they also pose significant potential threats to our island ways of life and cultures, and our governments need to be continually responsive to such threats by taking all necessary steps to proactively manage them.

Dame Meg Taylor, Secretary-General, Pacific Islands Forum

Thank you for the opportunity to provide remarks as part of this symposium. It is an important and timely issue for our region that requires us to explore a range of challenges and opportunities. This morning, I will aim to share some of my own reflections based on what I observe in my position as the secretary general of the Pacific Islands Forum. There are three key points that I wish to make.

Framing: The Blue Pacific

The first point I wish to stress is that the focus of the forum and its secretariat is on how to secure the future viability, prosperity and wellbeing of the 'Blue Pacific'. The forum seeks genuine partnerships with all actors who are willing to join us along the pathway towards that vision. Therefore, I reject the terms of the dilemma that presents the Pacific with a choice between a China alternative and our traditional partners. Unfortunately, this framing remains the dominant narrative in the public debate about our region in the context of today's geostrategic competition.

Such a narrative tends to portray the nations of the Pacific as passive collaborators or victims of a new wave of colonialism. In this context, it is often difficult to engage in meaningful dialogue over relations with China without being labelled pro-China, or perhaps even as naïve. Today, I want to emphasise that a key challenge for the forum is to maintain its solidarity as staunchly pro–Blue Pacific. The alternative we seek is an alternative path for development that can secure a better future for the people of our region.

Indeed, the search for alternative, more meaningful paths for development for the Pacific is not new. The founding of the Pacific Islands Forum itself can perhaps be understood in this way, with Pacific states working together to effectively exercise their newly attained sovereignty for the benefits of Pacific development. The 'Pacific Way' was perhaps the most well-known framing of an alternative approach to development at that time. Civil society, too, has often called upon each other and the leaders of the region to find alternative approaches to development that are consistent with Pacific values. In 2011, the Pacific Conference of Churches produced the short think piece 'Rethinking Oceania', or 'Rethinking the House of God', which continues to be influential amongst civil society and faith-based organisations throughout the region.

Recently, forum leaders have reinvigorated their commitment to the development of the region in a manner that reflects their shared Pacific values and concerns. In 2017, forum leaders endorsed the Blue Pacific narrative as the core driver of collective action for advancing the leaders' vision under the framework for Pacific regionalism. The narrative explicitly recognises that as the Blue Pacific, we are custodians of some of the world's richest biodiversity and marine and terrestrial resources. Through our stewardship of the Pacific Ocean, we must do all we can to protect the wellbeing of Pacific peoples, and indeed Pacific nation-states and the ocean continent they inhabit.

To date, the Blue Pacific narrative has been successful in building solidarity and shifting the prevailing narrative of the region as small, dependent and vulnerable. Going forward, we need to build on this and develop concrete strategies that leverage the increased interest in our region and secure the future of the Blue Pacific.

Last year, the theme for the Nauru forum meeting called for a stronger Pacific and the need to more assertively exercise our will in determining the Pacific we want. The theme recognises that our developmental challenges are not only due to our size and remoteness, but also are the product of the prevailing global economic system, which has undermined the health of our oceans and the safety of our climate. Through its theme, Nauru is seeking opportunities to build on the Blue Pacific narrative and reinvigorate political ownership of our regional development aspirations through rethinking development approaches and identifying, as a collective, opportunities for innovation. So, to summarise my first point: when considering the China alternative in the region, I would argue that we must do so from the perspective of securing our future as the Blue Pacific continent.

'Friends to all'

My second point: forum leaders have made it clear on a number of occasions that they place great value on open and genuine relationships and inclusive and enduring partnerships within our region and beyond. A 'friends to all' approach is commonly accepted, while some have made a more formal commitment to this principle through their nonaligned status.

China's increasing diplomatic and economic presence in the region, coupled with its growing economic and political strength globally, brings both challenges and opportunities for our Blue Pacific. In general, forum members view China's increased actions in the region as a positive development, one that offers greater options for financing and development opportunities—both directly in partnership with China and indirectly through the increased competition in our region.

Indeed, if there is one word that might resonate amongst all forum members when it comes to China, that word is access. Access to markets, technology, financing, infrastructure. Access to a viable future. For example, Australia's access to China's markets make it the former's largest trading partner in terms of both imports and exports. In 2017, China surpassed Australia as New Zealand's largest trading partner for goods and services.

To a large extent, forum Island countries have been excluded from the sorts of financing, technology and infrastructure that can enable us to fully engage in a globalised world. Many countries see the rise of China and its increasing interest in the region as providing an opportunity to rectify this. Indeed, we have seen large increases in both financing for development and trade with China over the past decade or so.

More than this, and to reiterate my first point, many Island countries see the current context as providing an opportunity for ensuring a Pacific that is (to use the words of former Kiribati president Iereme Tabai) 'a viable community in our own right and at our own standard and with a feeling of pride and self-respect'.

To be sure, we need not only think of these opportunities in relation to China specifically—their market, products, technology and so on—but also the broader range of opportunities emerging in the context of a rising China. China's presence has meant that other actors are resetting their priorities and stepping up engagement in the Pacific. We are also seeing some new partners emerging as well as the return of partners who had long left the region.

Therefore, the opportunities available to the Pacific are indeed many. Forum leaders have a keen sense of the current historical moment and the opportunities it brings to realise better development outcomes for their country and its people. We are seeing offers and counteroffers by our partners. Within this context, perhaps the key challenge facing the Blue Pacific is our ability to think through these opportunities as a collective rather than only considering bilateral gains. It is, of course, the prerogative of forum Island countries to leverage this situation for their national benefit. My point, however, is that it also provides an unprecedented opportunity to position our region for the future and secure cultural and ecological integrity, and generating our own wealth to ensure the social wellbeing of all Pacific Island people. So, to summarise my second point: our region is indeed crowded and complex. This provides immense opportunity for securing the future of the Blue Pacific.

A regional approach: Possible next steps

Finally, I wish to reflect on what might be some concrete steps that we can take as a region in the context of a rising China. Progressing the region forward towards its vision for the Blue Pacific will require long-term and focused political dialogue, both amongst the forum membership and with our partners.

More generally, the forum is already taking steps to improve its engagement with its partners. Last year, leaders called for a review of the meetings and processes of the forum so as to enable more focused and strategic engagement.

Specifically in relation to China, I think it is timely and relevant for the forum to commence dialogue on how it wishes to collectively engage with China. As I raised earlier, there is already much bilateral engagement between forum members and China, but the forum is best placed to take the lead on regional Pacific strategies for cooperation with China.

It is also appropriate to consider the merits of establishing a forum–China dialogue, perhaps in a similar manner to the PALM (Pacific Islands Leaders Meeting) with Japan or the Africa–China Dialogue. China already has its own platform for engagement with the region, the China–Pacific Islands Economic Development and Cooperation Forum, a multibilateral grouping that enables China to meet at a high level with the eight leaders of those Pacific Island countries that recognise China. While there are diplomatic issues underpinning this forum that must be acknowledged, we must not overlook the opportunities present for advancing the priorities of the Blue Pacific. This will require all forum members and a greater say in setting the agenda accordingly.

Infrastructure remains a crucial requirement for ensuring resilience in the Pacific. China's Belt and Road Initiative (BRI) claims to be an open platform supporting greater trade and investment cooperation through, in particular, cooperation in major, long-term plans for regional development. Nine forum member countries—Fiji, Samoa, Tonga, Vanuatu, Cook Islands, Federated States of Micronesia, Papua New Guinea, Niue and New Zealand—have signed MOUs to cooperate with China's BRI. Considering, the opportunities for collective engagement with the BRI merit careful analysis and discussion.

We also know that in response to China's growing influence in the region, alternative infrastructure initiatives have been announced from Japan, the US and Australia. As the Blue Pacific, rather than playing the merits of one against another, we should consider exploring the potential value of partners working together for the benefit of the region. As I have said before, I would offer that channelling such assistance through the Pacific Resilience Facility is one of the many appropriate options for strengthening our will to drive our own pathways toward resilient development.

Furthermore, through the Pacific Resilience Facility we could also consider establishing common, regional criteria to help forum members assess investments to ensure they are consistent with the long-term vision and priorities for the Blue Pacific. The issue of infrastructure quality has already been a matter of public debate. Other standards might include environmental, social and cultural protections mechanisms. For example, under the BRI, China has established an Ecological and Environmental Cooperation Plan, which could be used to hold Chinese investments to account.

Finally, 2019 presents us with an important opportunity, with Chile hosting APEC. In the secretariat's 2017 *State of Pacific Regionalism* report, we raised the potential for the Pacific to be a bridge between China and Latin America. Extending China's Maritime Silk Road through our Blue Pacific could provide opportunities for creating regional infrastructure and access that could inspire new markets of trade between Asia, the Pacific and Latin America; not to mention between Pacific Island countries themselves. It could also deliver much-needed infrastructure and technology for building Blue Pacific resilience. The 2019 APEC meeting could provide the catalyst for dialogue on such opportunities.

Conclusion

The themes from the last two forum meetings have strongly articulated leaders' desire for a shift in the development trajectory for the Pacific, through the Blue Pacific narrative and through it the opportunity to exercise our will. This is the strategic lens through which any conversation over China, and the associated geopolitical and geostrategic environment we find ourselves in, must occur. Our political conversations and settlements must be driven by the wellbeing of our Blue Pacific continent and its people, not by the goals and ambitions of others.

Introduction: The Return of Great Power Competition

Terence Wesley-Smith and Graeme Smith

The Pacific Islands region has entered a new period of uncertainty precipitated in large part by the emergence of China as a major regional actor as well as the reaction of more established powers to perceived threats to their longstanding influence. In March 2019, in the wake of a flurry of activity on the part of Australia, New Zealand and the United States aimed at countering China's growing influence in the Pacific Islands, Deputy Secretary General of the Pacific Islands Forum Cristelle Pratt declared that 'great power competition is back!' before suggesting that 'Our task is to find an appropriate balance between leveraging the *competition* between partners and ensuring peace and *cooperation* prevails in our Blue Pacific' (Pratt 2019, emphasis in original). We will argue here that although Island leaders have been remarkably successful at leveraging competition, this may not always be possible when great power strategic interests are at stake. Indeed, Pacific Island leaders may have no option but to take sides in the event that cooperation gives way to great power conflict somewhere in the vast expanses of the Pacific Ocean.

Great power competition

In 2006 Beijing signalled heightened interest in the Pacific Islands with the first China–Pacific Islands Countries Economic Development and Cooperation Forum held in Fiji. Since then, China has become firmly established as a major trade, aid, investment and diplomatic partner in the region, and Chinese companies are increasingly active in resource extraction, construction and commerce. Long-established external actors in the region first responded cautiously to China's spectacular rise, perhaps because Beijing was at pains not to confront them directly in regional or global affairs. The Chinese Communist Party (CCP), led by Hu Jintao, even backed away from the doctrine of 'China's peaceful rise' (Zheng 2005) on the grounds that 'rise' sounded threatening (Glaser and Medeiros 2007). An analysis of China's foreign policy community written at the beginning of President Xi Jinping's rule concluded that it was not monolithic, running the full spectrum of nativists and realists at one end to selective multilateralists and globalists at the other (Shambaugh 2013:13–44). While realists were thought to hold the upper hand, the author held open the possibility of a shift in either direction.

A number of recent developments mark the arrival of a new phase in the relationship, occasioned in the first instance by Xi Jinping's more assertive posture on the world stage. Since assuming leadership in 2012, Xi has consolidated his hold on domestic power and articulated a series of highly ambitious initiatives, including the nationalistic 'China Dream' that imagines China 'rejuvenated' and restored to its proper place in the world, with the Belt and Road investment and infrastructure program forging trade corridors across vast swathes of Asia, Africa, the Middle East, the Americas, Oceania and Europe (see, for example, Bradsher 2020). It is clear the nativists in China's foreign policy community now hold sway. Xi's global posture effectively marks the end of Deng Xiaoping's influential foreign policy dictum of 'hide and bide', whereby China adopted low-profile diplomacy and put aside any aspirations towards world leadership.

Beijing has also restructured its institutions to reflect a more proactive approach to diplomacy. A new aid agency (Zhang 2018) has been created to address shortcomings in the delivery of China's development assistance—and in particular to resolve tensions and coordination problems between the Ministry of Foreign Affairs, the Ministry of Commerce and more than 20 other agencies involved in China's foreign aid system (Zhang and Smith 2017). Significantly for Pacific Island nations with large Chinese populations, the organisation responsible for managing Chinese communities abroad, the Office of Overseas Chinese Affairs, was merged into the CCP's United Front Work Department (UFWD). This move to subsume a long-established government department within a party organ is both part of a broader trend of greater CCP control in matters designated as 'core' to the national interest (the offices of ethnic and religious affairs were also integrated with the UFWD) and part of more assertive and racialised nationalism that views overseas Chinese as 'all sons and daughters of the Chinese nation bounded by Chinese blood' (Groot 2017). Binding these bureaucratic shifts is a change in the CCP's framing of diplomacy as 'major country diplomacy with Chinese characteristics', which 'aims to foster a new type of international relations and build a community with a shared future for mankind diplomacy' (Xinhua 2017:6, 17). In the same report, delivered in October 2017 at the 19th CCP National Party Congress, President Xi made it clear that the 'defining feature' of 'Chinese characteristics' is 'the leadership of the Communist Party of China' (ibid.:17).

All of this puts China at odds with the United States, which for decades was prepared to facilitate China's economic rise in return for investment and trade benefits accruing to US corporations and consumers, accompanied by the tacit assumption that with prosperity China would democratise and become more 'like us'. Few hold this illusion now. Not only does China's rate of economic growth continue to outstrip the US, but structural changes in the domestic economy, away from labour-intensive manufacturing to new industries based on China-controlled technology, explicitly backed by the (now seldom mentioned) Made in China 2025 policy, pose a direct challenge to the economic and military power underpinning US global dominance since World War II. Furthermore, an accelerated military build-up under President Xi, provocative actions in the South China Sea, a more aggressive attitude to Taiwan's reincorporation with 'the motherland' as well as China's recent efforts to expand its influence overseas represent a variety of challenges to the established global order and the central role of the United States.

The Pacific Islands region is not on the geographic, strategic or economic frontlines of this new Cold War (see Wesley-Smith, Chapter 2, this volume). As argued by Zhou Fangyin in Chapter 7, there is little evidence that Beijing has attached high priority to strategic, political or economic interests in Oceania, nor has it singled out the region for special attention. This is not the case elsewhere, particularly in Asia where President Xi has explicitly challenged US leadership aspirations and where the rival powers compete fiercely over jurisdictional issues in the South China Sea and the East China Sea, the militarisation of China's 'near seas' periphery and the future status of Taiwan. Nevertheless, Western powers have exercised considerable influence in the Pacific Islands since the colonial era and in many ways this is an important characteristic—while nations in sub-Saharan Africa can be considered genuinely postcolonial, most Pacific Island nations are still strongly influenced by former (and, in some cases, current) colonial powers France, Australia, New Zealand or the US.

Each of these four metropolitan powers have announced new foreign policy initiatives explicitly or implicitly designed to counter China's growing sway in the region. These initiatives are analysed in depth in this book (see Varrall, Chapter 3; Iati, Chapter 4; Finin, Chapter 5; and Maclellan, Chapter 6). Here it will suffice to note the major characteristics of Australia's 'Step-Up' policy, New Zealand's 'Pacific Reset' plan, France's 'great power' ambitions and the renewed focus on Oceania in Washington DC, dubbed the 'Pacific Pledge' in late 2019.

The shared characteristic of these initiatives is that they reflect anxieties about regional security. Security has been a preeminent concern of the Western powers since an expansionist Japan used the Pacific Islands as stepping stones to threaten their interests in the Pacific War, and it was the central consideration during the Cold War when policy initiatives were designed to completely exclude the Soviet Union from the region. Following the collapse of the Soviet Union in 1989, Western regional security policy was recalibrated to reflect concerns about international criminal activity and, after the 9/11 attacks of 2001, the possibility that terrorist groups would become established in politically unstable or 'failing' Pacific Island states (May 2003). The concern today is not only that China has gained economic and diplomatic traction in a region long considered a Western strategic domain, but that Beijing might use its growing influence to establish a military presence. This possibility goes to the heart of long-established defence planning in the US, Australia and New Zealand, which seeks to deny adversaries the ability to project power by sea or air over the ocean spaces surrounding them.

The first public indications of renewed strategic unease came in early 2018 when Australian officials questioned the value of Chinese infrastructure projects in the region and suggested that the loans facilitating these activities had implications for the sovereignty of Pacific Island states. The essential elements of this narrative—that Beijing's lending practices reflected nefarious motives—received a boost in April 2018 when the defence correspondent for *The Sydney Morning Herald* claimed Beijing had approached officials in Vanuatu about establishing a permanent military presence (Wroe 2018). The story focused on upgrades to the Luganville wharf on the island of Espiritu Santo conducted by the state-owned Shanghai Construction Group, suggesting that the new facility could accommodate Chinese naval vessels. Officials in Vanuatu and China denied these claims and it was later revealed that the contract with the Chinese company did not contain a debt-for-equity clause as earlier claimed. Nevertheless, the idea that China has military aspirations in the region and that Chinese loans could be used to leverage that access, resonates with a wider narrative about China's activities in Djibouti, Sri Lanka, Cambodia and elsewhere, and now appears to be widely accepted by Western security analysts (see, for example, Fox and Dornan 2018).

Whatever its veracity, major elements of Australia's Step-Up policy towards the Pacific Islands region are consistent with Western suspicions of China's motives overseas. From mid-2018 Canberra moved quickly to counter an offer by the Chinese communications technology giant Huawei to construct a fibre optic cable for Solomon Islands and Papua New Guinea, extended a similar offer to Vanuatu and announced the establishment of an AU\$2 billion fund to compete with China's infrastructure development efforts. Programs designed to counter Chinese aid and construction initiatives are supported by increased diplomatic activity on the part of Australia, New Zealand, the US and the United Kingdom. Other aspects of Step-Up that make its security policy foundations clear include the establishment of the Australia Pacific Security College (DFAT 2018), a Pacific Fusion Centre to share information about unlicensed fishing, drug trafficking and other illegal activity, and a bilateral initiative with Fiji to develop the Black Rock Camp into a regional hub for police and peacekeeping training and preparedness. In addition, in late 2018 Australia signed an agreement with Papua New Guinea to develop the Lombrum Naval Base on Manus Island with support from the US. This is significant not only because it includes the planned deployment of Australian naval personnel there, but also because in his speech to APEC in November 2018 Vice President Pence explicitly linked the base to Chinese aggression in the South China Sea (Pence 2018). The Lombrum initiative is emblematic of the increased militarisation of the Pacific Islands region at a time when military aspirations attributed to Beijing are loudly condemned in Canberra. It is also worth noting that a goal of Australia's policy towards the region is further integration of Pacific Island countries 'into Australian and New Zealand economies and our security institutions' (Australian Government 2017; Dobell 2019).

If New Zealand's new policy approach to the Pacific Islands relies heavily on increased aid, diplomatic activity and people-to-people exchanges, the recent ratcheting up of interest in the region in Washington is spearheaded by the Pentagon and fuelled by strategic concerns. As Gerard Finin argues in Chapter 5, US policy in the Pacific Islands region has always been driven by strategic interests. The US maintains a large military presence in Guam, conducts training exercises in the neighbouring Commonwealth of the Northern Mariana Islands (CNMI) and tests missile systems at its Kwajalein base in the Marshall Islands. Central to the US's free association relationships with the Marshall Islands, the Republic of Palau and the Federated States of Micronesia is Washington's exclusive control of the defence of these islands and the ability to deny foreign military access to almost 6 million square kilometres of land, ocean and airspace. Finin details the increased attention in Washington to the upcoming renegotiation of the compacts of free association that tie the US to Marshall Islands, Federated States of Micronesia and Palau, and notes that in May 2019 the leaders of these entities met with President Trump, the first ever such meeting with a US president. He also highlights new outreach efforts to non-US affiliated parts of the region, including visits by senior White House officials to Vanuatu and Solomon Islands, and proposed collaborative initiatives between the Pentagon and military forces in Fiji, Papua New Guinea and Tonga.

The reemergence of the security imperative in Western foreign policy towards the region is important because such policies tend to be pursued more aggressively than would otherwise be the case. The new approach has an absolutist quality reminiscent of the 'strategic denial' policies of the Cold War, where any interaction with the Soviet Union was deemed unacceptable. Obviously, exclusion is not possible in the case of China, but Western officials have made it quite clear that any agreement between Beijing and a Pacific Island country to establish a military facility would cross a red line. They have also raised the spectre of debt-leverage to suggest that Pacific Island governments should avoid further infrastructure borrowing from China.

These priorities are at odds with the policy preferences of the leaders of many Pacific Islands states, who in recent years have worked to define a regional security approach that emphasises threats to Island societies like natural disasters and other environmental concerns. This emphasis on human security is apparent in the Boe Declaration that emerged from the 2018 Nauru meeting of the Pacific Islands Forum (PIF), which identifies climate change as the primary threat to regional security and makes no mention of foreign powers or military bases, while noting that the region is 'increasingly crowded and complex' (PIF Secretariat 2018; see also Fry 2019:264–73).

Caught in between

Before considering the implications of the reemergence of great power competition for Pacific Island nations, it is important to bear in mind that Australia and New Zealand, two of the most significant external actors in the region, are also caught in the middle of the escalating competition between the US and China. Indeed, their own attempts to manoeuvre between the conflicting demands of Washington and Beijing are already reflected in their changing policies towards the region. In other words, the ongoing efforts of policymakers in Canberra and Wellington to resolve these dilemmas will reverberate in the Pacific Islands. They suggest pressures that Pacific Island leaders also face as they walk a diplomatic tightrope between competing great powers.

Since World War II, defence policy in Australia and New Zealand has been built around the assumption of a preeminent US military presence in the Asia-Pacific region as well as an enduring alliance with Washington that would ensure US support should the need arise. Thus, Australia's *2016 Defence White Paper* identifies the US as Canberra's 'most important strategic partner' and places 'a strong and deep alliance' with Washington 'at the core of Australia's security and defence planning' (Australian Government 2016). Although New Zealand's relationship with Washington has never fully recovered from a rift over nuclear policies in the 1980s, defence statements still emphasise a commitment to the 'rules-based international order' led by the US, very close military cooperation with Australia and participation in the Five Eyes intelligence-sharing consortium that includes Canada, Australia, the United Kingdom and the US (New Zealand Government 2018).

If security policy continues to be firmly based on defence relations with the US, in recent years the economies of both countries have become heavily dependent upon China. China is now Australia's largest trading partner by far, representing 34 per cent of its exports and 24 per cent of its imports in 2018. More than 1.43 million Chinese tourists visit annually (year ending August 2018) and Australia is second only to the US as a destination for

Chinese students, making education Australia's fourth-largest export after iron ore, coal and natural gas (DFAT 2019). Unlike the US, Australia's terms of trade with China are favourable and have led to the country's first current account surplus in 44 years (Cranston 2019). China is also New Zealand's largest trading partner, providing a market for 30 per cent of its dairy products and 24 per cent of its forestry products, as well as being a significant source of investment capital, almost half a million tourists a year and over 30,000 foreign students (MFAT 2017). Both countries are in an unequal relationship with the US and China. Australia and New Zealand need the US as a military partner more than Washington needs them, and any breakdown of economic relations would hurt Australia and New Zealand more than it would hurt China.

At the heart of the debate around whether Australia needs to choose between the US and China is international relations scholar and former deputy secretary for defence Hugh White. He contends that Australia was for many years able to maintain the illusion that 'we can keep relying on China to make us rich while America keeps us safe' because neither China nor the US exerted strong pressure to choose sides (White 2017b). He argues that changed when President Obama announced his pivot to Asia in an address to the Australian Parliament in late 2011. Since the pivot was clearly aimed at containing China, and Australia had agreed to support the effort by hosting US marines in Darwin, it was no longer possible to argue convincingly in Beijing that Canberra was not taking sides in the emerging competition between the US and China. Since then, according to White, Australian officials have had to decide 'how far we can please China without risking a rebuke from Washington. Our government weighs every decision concerning each country in the light of what it will mean for our relations with the other' (White 2017a:47). Similar calculations preoccupy decision-makers in New Zealand.

At times it has been difficult to maintain the correct balance. For example, Australia has been quick to volunteer troops to support US-led conflicts in the Middle East, but was reluctant to send ships to join Washington's 'freedom of navigation' voyages designed to challenge China's maritime claims in the South China Sea. This may have helped reassure Beijing, although not enough to prevent China from sending warships to shadow Australian naval ships traversing the area on other business (Tarabay 2019). It certainly does not please the US, which, according to US Ambassador to Australia Arthur Culvahouse, 'wants Australia to embrace a power role in the Pacific' to combat China's 'payday loan diplomacy' in the region (Dayant 2019; Reuters 2019). For its part, New Zealand has struggled to reassure Beijing of its commitment to their multifaceted bilateral relationship in the face of mounting concern by its Five Eyes partners about alleged Chinese infiltration in business and domestic politics.

The cost of getting the balancing act wrong was apparent in early 2019 when Australian coal exports were held up at Chinese ports, allegedly in retaliation for, among other things, Canberra's abrupt decision to block Huawei from participating in the construction of Australia's 5G telecommunications network. Parallels have been drawn between the detention of Canadian citizens Michael Spavor and Michael Kovrig and Australian writer Yang Hengjun being held in China and charged with espionage, a crime that carries the death penalty. A senior Australian security analyst described it as 'hostage diplomacy' (Medcalf 2019). New Zealand also felt the heat from Beijing in late 2018 when the Government Communications Security Bureau denied a request by Spark, one of the country's largest telecommunications companies, to use Huawei technology in 5G infrastructure. China deferred the launch event for a major tourist promotion, turned back an Air Zealand flight to Shanghai—supposedly because of deficient paperwork—and postponed for several months a planned state visit to China by New Zealand Prime Minister Jacinda Ardern (Agence France-Presse 2018; Albert 2019; Tobin 2019a).

The increased emphasis on security in the Pacific Islands region, especially in Australia, the return of the Cold War idea of strategic denial, the explicit critique of China's regional activities by officials in Canberra and Wellington, and Australia's base initiative in Papua New Guinea suggest that, at least for the moment, these governments have decided to tilt towards Washington and attempt to manage the resulting fallout in relations with Beijing. However, this could change as US–China competition escalates. Domestic politics are a factor here. During the Australian federal election in May 2019, it was apparent that bipartisanship over China had broken down, with the ruling Coalition attempting to capitalise on remarks by former Labor prime minister Paul Keating that the government had been too hawkish on China, that 'when the security agencies are running foreign policy, the nutters are in charge', crediting this shift to former Fairfax China correspondent John Garnaut's classified report on Chinese influence in Australia. 'They've all gone berko[1] ever since then. [When] you have the ASIO chief knocking on MPs' doors, you know something's wrong' (Keating quoted in Greene and Sweeney 2019). In New Zealand, there are differences within the governing coalition, with former deputy prime minister and foreign minister Winston Peters articulating views on China that were more hawkish than those of others in cabinet, including Prime Minister Ardern (Burton-Bradley 2019).

For the Pacific and Australia, the central questions are how is US–China competition likely to evolve, what policies should be adopted and how will the strategic calculus change as events unfold. Hugh White is convinced that although war is not the inevitable outcome of the US–China struggle for leadership in East Asia, it is a likely result. He suggests that sooner or later the US will back away from an armed conflict with China that could involve nuclear weapons, largely because Washington will realise that US interests in this part of the world are not worth the human and material costs of such a conflagration (White 2019a:234–38). Critiques of White's work have run along two lines: security analysts, while agreeing with his calls to increase defence spending, maintain that he underestimates US resolve and ability to retain its influence in Asia and the Western Pacific as well as the value of alliances with other states such as India, Indonesia and Japan, while overestimating the inevitability of China's rise and its capacity to achieve its ends through military means (Goldrick and Graham 2019; Jennings 2019); and that he glosses over the nature of the CCP under Xi Jinping, misunderstands the nature of the Chinese army as an army of the party, rather than the nation, and the non-military means by which Beijing expands its influence (Garnaut 2018). White's work is remarkably silent on China, dedicating just a few pages to its motivations and including some wishful thinking: 'We might expect, and certainly hope, that China's leaders, who are keen students of history, recognise that they would be better off exercising primacy with a light touch' (White 2019a:41). All sides are remarkably silent on the Pacific itself, despite it being the focus of their threat analyses.

For analysts like White, then, Australia's immediate interests lie in reducing its strategic dependence on the US, formulating a more independent foreign policy and learning to live with China's growing power and influence in the region. Others urge Australia and New Zealand to do

---

1 Australian colloquial term meaning 'beserk' (Macquarie Dictionary, 7th edition).

whatever it takes to strengthen their relations with the US-led Western alliance and confront the CCP's attempts to infiltrate domestic politics and influence policy from within. All of this suggests that the foreign policy approaches of Australia and New Zealand towards Pacific Island countries could shift dramatically in the future depending on which school of thought gains most influence in policy circles.

Leveraging the competition?

No matter how strongly promoted, Western policies towards the Pacific Islands have always had to contend with attempts by Island leaders to exercise agency and manage outcomes. Indeed, over the years Pacific Island states have registered remarkable successes in dealing with powerful external actors, despite the apparent disadvantages of small size, lack of resources and aid dependency. Early examples include preventing Japan from dumping nuclear waste in the deep ocean; banning driftnet fishing by distant-water fishing nations; and negotiating a tuna treaty that required the US to change its stated position on the UN Convention on the Law of the Sea (UNCLOS), counter domestic legislation and take on a powerful domestic fishing industry lobby (Tarai 2015). Recent achievements are equally striking as Island countries have worked together in global multilateral settings, often in opposition to the policy preferences of their larger regional partners, to put French Polynesia back on the UN list of territories to be decolonised; include ocean management and climate change as UN Sustainable Development Goals; and make significant contributions to the final text of the 2015 Paris Accord on climate change mitigation and adaptation (Fry and Tarte 2015). As Tarcisius Kabutaulaka points out in Chapter 1, the narrative of 'our Blue Pacific' increasingly invoked by Pacific Island leaders provides a framework for this recent history of assertive diplomacy and 'is premised on the idea of responsibility and stewardship to the region, especially the Pacific Ocean, and through that, to the rest of the world'.

Pacific Island leaders have also managed to resist security policies they did not regard as appropriate, even when those policies have been afforded high priority in Washington, Canberra and Wellington. A key example here is the ultimate failure of the strategic denial imperative, the central tenet of Western policy towards the region during the Cold War, when Kiribati and Vanuatu signed fisheries access treaties with the Soviet Union despite considerable pressure not to do so (Tarai 2015). It is also worth noting that in late 2018, at the same time that Australia was promoting a new regional security agenda aimed at containing China, Pacific Island leaders agreed to the 2018 Boe Declaration, which contained a very different understanding of security and pushed back against the idea that they should curtail their dealings with Beijing to enhance the security environment.

Pacific Island states have generally welcomed China's increased regional presence and benefited materially from it. According to the Lowy Institute, in the decade after 2006 China committed a total of US$1.78 billion in aid to the eight Pacific Islands countries that recognised Beijing during this period, as well as providing financial support for regional organisations and funding scholarships for some 1,400 Pacific Island students to study in China (Lowy Institute 2019; Zhang and Marinaccio 2019). Chinese companies and individuals are significant investors in resource extraction and retail across the Pacific. Pacific economies have benefited from trade with China, now the second largest trading partner for the region as a whole. Island economies also stand to benefit from the recent increase in resources committed to the region by Australia, New Zealand and the US, even if the primary purpose of these initiatives is to counter China's influence. Papua New Guinea, for example, is to receive massive funding for rural electrification while, among other things, Solomon Islands and Vanuatu will gain improved fibre optic communications. These resources would probably not have been forthcoming without the emerging great power competition.

Some Island leaders have used China to leverage concessions from other powers. Fiji, for example, turned to China for support as part of its 'Look North' policy in the aftermath of the 2006 coup and its subsequent ostracism by members of the Commonwealth and the PIF. Sandra Tarte outlines how the relationship between Fiji and China has strengthened significantly in recent years. She argues that Fiji rather than China was instrumental in fashioning the relationship: 'Contrary to concerns about China's increasing influence in Fiji, the analysis suggests that Fiji proactively exploited opportunities within this partnership, while maintaining and exercising its autonomy and agency' (Tarte, Chapter 12). Fiji's engagement with China provided an incentive for traditional partners to return after national elections were held in 2014 and some semblance of democracy was restored. As a result, Fiji now has significantly increased foreign policy and defence options. In June 2019 Australian Minister for Foreign Affairs Marise Payne travelled to Fiji to visit the Black Rock facilities that Australia has agreed to develop; welcome Fiji into the Pacific Labour Scheme; announce an initiative to allow select Fiji athletes to train in Australia; provide a progress report on a joint study on enhanced business opportunities; and report that some Fiji infrastructure projects were under 'active consideration' for Australian funding (Payne 2019).

The China–Taiwan struggle for diplomatic recognition is one arena where the ability of island leaders to exercise autonomy and agency will continue to be tested. Before 2008, when a 'diplomatic truce' effectively suspended the competition, Pacific Island states were able to leverage significant concessions by playing Beijing and Taipei off against each other. Several Island countries, including Nauru and Vanuatu, switched recognition from one to the other in return for lucrative assistance packages. In one high-stakes case, in 2003 a new government in Kiribati successfully terminated its relationship with Beijing and recognised Taiwan despite the presence of a Chinese satellite-tracking facility on Tarawa (see Zhang, Chapter 8). At the time the so-called cheque-book diplomacy was put on hold, six Pacific Island countries recognised Taiwan. In December 2016, Beijing abandoned the diplomatic truce when China reestablished relations with the African country of Sao Tome and Principe. Since then six other countries, including two in the Pacific, have followed suit, leaving a total of only 15 countries worldwide that recognise Taiwan.

After 2016, Taipei's Pacific Island allies (Nauru, Kiribati, Tuvalu, Marshall Islands, Palau and Solomon Islands) found themselves subject to intense scrutiny. It is important to review some new factors that have come into play since the earlier round of competition. In a speech on 2 January 2019, President Xi Jinping gave the 'peaceful reunification' of Taiwan higher priority:

> We make no promise to renounce the use of force and reserve the option of taking all necessary means [to reclaim the island] … 'Taiwan independence' goes against the trend of history and will lead to a dead end (Xinhua 2019).

The strong tenor of the speech was in part a response to Taiwanese President Tsai Ing-wen's speech 24 hours earlier, where she outlined the 'four musts':

> I am calling on China that it must face the reality of the existence of the Republic of China (Taiwan); it must respect the commitment of the 23 million people of Taiwan to freedom and democracy; it must handle cross-strait differences peacefully, on a basis of equality; and it must be governments or government-authorized agencies that engage in negotiations (Focus Taiwan 2019).

In recent years the power differential between China and Taiwan has increased dramatically in favour of Beijing. Although there is debate about China's ability to use military means to force a resolution, Beijing is in a position to trump Taipei in a bidding war for recognition using aid packages and other incentives. The other new variable for Pacific Island nations emerged during the Trump administration. The US has long supported Taiwan through arms sales, but recently it has adopted a hard line towards countries that switch to China. Washington was quick to voice its displeasure and even threaten sanctions when Panama and later El Salvador, both countries with long histories of relations with the US, announced they were cutting ties to Taipei and recognising Beijing. In May 2019, the US Acting Assistant Secretary for Southeast Asia, W. Patrick Murphy, urged Pacific Island countries to maintain their relations with Taiwan. He stated that the US was eager to help countries 'protect their sovereignty and their independence, to have viable alternatives … to meet their development needs, their infrastructure needs, and their nation building needs' (Pandey and Packham 2019). The question of Taiwan recognition has become a component of wider US–China competition. Taiwan's allies in the Pacific are pressed by China to switch, while Taiwan, the US and its Western allies urge them to maintain the status quo.

One front for China's campaign to bring Taiwan's Pacific allies into the fold operates at the regional level, with Beijing bringing intense pressure on the PIF to recognise the One China policy. Although the forum is unlikely to bend to this pressure, the initiative puts Beijing's Pacific allies in a difficult position while sending a warning to countries that recognise Taiwan (Dziedzic 2019). Perhaps in an attempt to reduce the tension, PIF Secretary General Dame Meg Taylor suggests establishing a forum–China dialogue 'in a similar manner to the PALM [Pacific Islands Leaders Meeting] with Japan or the Africa–China Dialogue' that would involve all forum members not just those that recognise Beijing (see Taylor's speech in this volume).

The other, more important, dimension of China's efforts to erode Taiwan's diplomatic space in the Pacific is bilateral, with Beijing deploying a mixture of carrots and sticks to influence Pacific Island choices. Sticks were preferred in the case of Palau, where restrictions imposed by Beijing on tourists heading to this destination resulted in a 45 per cent drop in arrivals from China between 2015 and 2018, and a 31 per cent overall drop in tourist numbers during the same period (Government of Palau 2019). Yet Palau has chosen not to switch, at least for now, perhaps conscious of its many entanglements with the US and confident in the eventual renegotiation of the compact of free association with Washington on favourable terms. Like Palau, and despite a long history of protest regarding the nuclear testing legacy there, Marshall Islands relies heavily on the US for support through the compact of free association and many Marshallese take advantage of free access to the US for education, health care and work. Although there is some support for more Chinese investment in the country, particularly to create a special economic zone on Rongelap Atoll, it is not clear if that might translate into a serious move to recognise Beijing (Tobin 2019b). Such a proposal would be strongly opposed by the US, which regards the relationship as important, not least because of its missile-testing facility on Kwajalein Atoll.

Great power politics were on full display when, in April 2019, a new government was formed in Solomon Islands and announced it was considering switching diplomatic recognition from Taiwan to China (see Aqorau, Chapter 10). Solomon Islands has strong economic ties with China, which is its main export destination (nearly all of it raw logs), and the incentive to switch was an infrastructure-heavy aid package, estimated to be worth US$500 million, pitched directly to the prime minister and his close advisers by China Civil Engineering Construction Corporation (CCECC), a Chinese state-owned enterprise.[2] This was countered by the promise of enhanced development assistance from Australia, New Zealand, Japan and the US, which Taiwan's representative in the Solomon Islands referred to as the 'democratic bloc'.[3] In a break with protocol, US White House officials travelled to Honiara to lobby Prime Minister Sogavare to remain with the Republic of China, with Vice President Mike Pence adding the weight of his position by correspondence and telephone

---

2   Interviews with politicians and officials in Honiara July 2019, with second author. See also Everington (2019).
3   Oliver Liao, 12 July 2019. Deputy Head of Mission, Embassy of Taiwan, Honiara. Interview with second author.

(see Kabutaulaka, Chapter 1). Despite pressure from the US and its Western allies, in September 2019 Sogavare announced that Solomon Islands would recognise Beijing, citing the findings of the Bipartisan Task Force and a report from the Ministry of Foreign Affairs and External Trade (Sogavare 2019).

The decision to switch was made despite the reservations of some analysts concerned about Honiara's capacity to manage a relationship with Beijing. In Chapter 10, Transform Aqorau concludes that:

> China's funding support may come at the cost of further opening up natural resources to Chinese companies. Given the poor quality of government … and the poor track record of natural resource management, it is argued that a switch will only exacerbate the already weak governance setting in the Solomon Islands (see also Kabutaulaka 2019).

Similar concerns were expressed by some opposition leaders in Kiribati when the government there unexpectedly decided to recognise China less than a week after Solomon Islands did so (RNZ 2019). According to officials in Taiwan, the switch occurred after Beijing offered to provide support for transport systems, including aircraft and ferries (Lee 2019).

There are no indications that Kiribati's example will be followed in neighbouring Tuvalu, which has close ties to Taiwan in part because of a long history of illegal Taiwanese fishing in its waters (Marinaccio 2019). However, Australia has decided to open a high commission there—to join the Embassy of the Republic of China (Taiwan), the only other resident diplomatic mission in Funafuti (Pearlman 2018). It is also interesting to note that CCECC, the same Chinese company active in promoting the switch in Solomon Islands, recently set up shop in Tuvalu to undertake a refurbishment of the port. Nor is Nauru likely to contemplate recognising Beijing. Its ties to Australia run deep, not least because Canberra's offshore detention centre is located there, and its leaders expressed hostility to Beijing after heated interactions with Chinese officials when Nauru hosted the 2018 meeting of the PIF.

In his study of Pacific Islands regionalism, Greg Fry uses the idea of 'contingent power' to explain why 'Pacific island states have sometimes prevailed in shaping Pacific regionalism and at other times managed to mediate global discourses through regional action' (Fry 2019:230–322). Contingent power refers to:

Circumstances that, in certain combinations, can influence outcomes, and I am thus avoiding the conceptual trap of seeing power as a fixed capacity based on material factors and size (ibid.:320).

This concept can be applied to the issues discussed above. It might explain, for example, how Fiji was able to leverage the China factor and exercise autonomy when powerful actors were aligned against it and why some Pacific Island states are better positioned than others to resist attempts to influence their diplomatic choices. It also suggests that contingencies can place limits on a Pacific Island state's ability to leverage any particular situation to its advantage. Those Pacific Islands heavily dependent on a Western power—for example, through free association relationships—are less able to leverage competition between rival powers than those free of such entanglements. Small size or limited capacity can also be important contingent factors. For example, in retrospect, it is clear that two Chinese loans to Tonga—one to rebuild parts of Nuku'alofa destroyed by riots in 2006, and a second for road redevelopment outside the capital city—would prove problematic when it came time to repay the money. According to Rohan Fox and Matthew Dornan (2018), this debt distress and possible vulnerability to external influence was not a result of Beijing setting some kind of trap. Rather, it was a result of ill-informed or misinformed decisions by local decision-makers, egged on by Chinese companies that stood to gain from the resulting government contracts.

Peace and cooperation?

Great power competition is already impacting developments in the Pacific Islands region and the ability of Island states to manage or mediate those new forces for their own ends. But US–China competition is dynamic and how it develops in the future could alter the nature of power relations in the Pacific Islands region in profound ways. We would suggest that, in general, the more intense the US–China competition becomes the less likely that Island leaders will be able to exercise agency, preserve their independence and avoid committing to one side or the other. Here it is worth briefly exploring three areas of tension, each of which could escalate into armed conflict under certain circumstances, as well as the consequent implications for the Pacific Islands region.

The US–China stand-off in the South China Sea is likely to escalate in the short term and could even precipitate war. In large part this is because China regards its claims there to be core to its national defence and non-negotiable—and has constructed military facilities on reclaimed islands in the area to emphasise its resolve. Although it does not have any jurisdictional claims in the South China Sea, Washington sees these assertions as a direct challenge to the US-led rules-based order, to freedom of navigation principles and a significant impediment to its ability to project power in East Asia. The situation is further complicated by competing territorial or maritime claims to various parts of the area by Brunei, Taiwan, Malaysia, Indonesia, the Philippines and Vietnam. Despite its provocative freedom of navigation naval campaign, it is unclear whether the US would intervene in the event that one of the periodic altercations between Asian claimants and China turned violent. However, in March 2019, US Secretary of State Mike Pompeo invoked the mutual defence treaty to reassure Philippines leaders that the US would come to their aid if Philippine vessels or aircraft were attacked in the South China Sea (Fonbuena and Kuo 2019).

The situation regarding Taiwan is equally intractable. China has made it abundantly clear that the reintegration of what it regards as a renegade province is inevitable and President Xi has upped the ante with his nationalist China Dream rhetoric, backed by military instruments developed for this purpose. His speech on 2 January 2019 was remarkable not just for flagging a possible invasion, with the strange caveat that 'Chinese don't fight Chinese', but for what it did not say. Rather than accommodating Taiwanese aspirations for autonomy, the version of the 'one country, two systems' outlined in Xi's speech dropped any mention of preserving Taiwan's armed forces or political institutions (Bush 2019). Despite ongoing influence attempts (Huang 2019) and a buy-out of Taiwan's traditional media outlets by PRC-friendly businesses (Aspinwall 2019), anti-China sentiment has increased in Taiwan in recent years, influenced in part by ongoing protests in Hong Kong over alleged violations of the terms of its 'one country, two systems' arrangement with China. Any attempts to force the issue by military means, even using options that stop short of invasion, such as a blockade, are likely to meet with fierce resistance from the Taiwanese public as well as a well-trained and equipped military force. Most analysts agree that an all-out invasion would be logistically difficult and costly in human and material terms, even if the US were not involved (see, for example, Roy 2018). A key question is how the US would respond in the face of Chinese military aggression directed across the Taiwan Strait. Support for Taiwan has increased significantly since the Trump administration assumed power, as well as in the US Congress where, according to Denny Roy, members 'realise America's leadership position in the region would be severely if not fatally compromised' if the US declined to intervene. Yet there are few indications that the American public would support such a move. Furthermore, unlike some members of his administration, President Trump has focused almost entirely on his trade war with China, and at times seemed ambivalent about the value of US alliances in Asia (ibid.:6).

A third scenario concerns the possibility that China successfully concludes an agreement with a Pacific Island government to establish some sort of naval facility in the region. Although statements from Western allies, particularly Australia, suggest that such a development would be completely unacceptable, and the Step-Up initiative is designed to prevent it from happening, it is not clear what these powers would be prepared to do if it actually occurred. Perhaps it would depend, at least to some extent, on the nature and apparent purpose of the facility. Hugh White (2019b) argues that while establishing a Pacific base would be 'a low-cost, low-risk way for China to show off its growing military and diplomatic reach and clout', for Australia the costs of preventing it 'might simply prove impossible to bear'. He goes on to suggest that it might be more feasible to focus on building military capabilities 'that in war could neutralise Chinese bases in the South Pacific'. While White's logic for *why* China might build a Pacific base (because it can) is sound, others point out his response assumes China would only use a fraction of its military force and opt not to use ballistic missiles against Australia, a nation where more than half of its citizenry live in three cities (Shoebridge 2019).

Conflict or the likelihood of conflict over issues relating to the South China Sea or Taiwan would impact the Pacific Islands region in significant ways. Those Island entities with defence relationships with the US would be directly implicated, particularly those with significant military facilities, like Guam, Marshall Islands and, to a lesser extent, CNMI and Palau. Under the terms of its compact agreement with the US, the Federated States of Micronesia might get drawn in too, should Washington decide this was necessary. At least in these cases, choice is not an option since Island leaders are already committed to the US side of any possible conflict. As noted before, Australia has declined to participate in US freedom of navigation exercises in the South China Sea. But there would be pressure for Canberra to contribute if US–China competition escalated into armed conflict. If that were to happen, and if the redeveloped Manus Naval Base was operational, then Papua New Guinea could also be drawn in.

Escalation of US–China tensions, especially if conflict erupts, is likely to involve Pacific Island states even if they are not bound by defence agreements with a Western power. At the very least, Australia, New Zealand and the US would probably redouble their current efforts to persuade Pacific Island countries to support Western security imperatives, which, in their current form, means offering economic incentives to reduce dependency on Chinese loans and rebuff any attempts by Beijing to establish or expand military ties. It is not clear if the Western allies would adopt more drastic methods if current policies prove ineffective. After all, during the Cold War the US used some dubious tactics in the dispute with Palau over the nuclear-free clause in its constitution, delaying the passage of the compact of free association for decades until that provision was removed (see, for example, Parmentier 1991; Roff 1991). And Canberra's 2003 decision to lead the Regional Assistance Mission to the Solomon Islands (RAMSI), a massive interventionist effort, was made in the context of concerns about the regional security implications of the breakdown of law and order in that country, as well as in response to humanitarian considerations (see, for example, Kabutaulaka 2005). The establishment of a Chinese naval base in the Pacific would not necessarily lead to Australia and New Zealand reducing their involvement in the region. Instead, their outreach efforts might take radically different forms.

Despite China's impressive trade, aid and investment profile in the region, it is not clear how much influence Beijing actually has on decision-making in Pacific Island capitals. It is difficult to identify examples where China caused Island leaders to take actions they otherwise would not have taken or that were contrary to their expressed interests. Perhaps one example is Fiji's decision to close down Taiwan's trade office in Suva as a result of pressure from China (Tarte, Chapter 12). Another would be China's seizure of Chinese nationals from Fiji and Vanuatu, allegedly for internet crimes, but with apparent disregard for local legal norms and procedures. It is interesting to note that diplomatic efforts to have Pacific Island leaders speak out in favour of China's claims in the South China Sea in the aftermath of a negative decision in 2016 at the UNCLOS Permanent Court of Arbitration were largely unsuccessful. Only Vanuatu obliged and officials there suggest that it did so in the context of its own disputes with neighbouring New Caledonia over rival claims to two uninhabited islands. There is little evidence to suggest that regional leaders seek to emulate a 'China model' of political or economic development, supporting the claim that China's soft power influence in the region is limited (Herr 2019; Smith 2016). Indeed, some studies suggest that Pacific Island societies are more immediately impacted by the actions and interests of Chinese corporations than those of China's government officials (Brant 2013; Dornan and Brant 2014; Smith 2013). Nevertheless, there have been situations in Australia and New Zealand, as well as in Palau, where Beijing has employed economic tools to exert influence. Such efforts could well increase as the US–China conflict intensifies and the support of other countries becomes more important to both sides. In the event of armed conflict, more direct action cannot be ruled out if Beijing regards key strategic interests to be at stake. After all, China has pursued key interests in the South China Sea with little regard for competing claims and almost universal condemnation from the international community.

Organisation of the book

The idea for this book emerged in early 2018 in conversations between the editors about the rapidly changing nature of China's relationship with Pacific Island countries. A number of developments in the region suggested the beginning of a new, more intense, phase in the relationship and that there were numerous indications of growing unease in official circles in metropolitan countries, particularly Australia, about the political and strategic implications of China's regional activities. Despite (or perhaps because of) unprecedented media attention to China's involvement in regional affairs, we felt there was a pressing need for a rigorous reevaluation of prevailing academic and media narratives as well as policy assumptions.

We invited leading scholars to analyse key dimensions of the changing relationship between China and the Pacific Islands region and to explore the strategic, political, economic and diplomatic implications for regional actors. Draft chapters were submitted in December 2018 and authors assembled in Port Vila, Vanuatu, in February 2019 to critique each other's work in a two-day workshop and hear feedback on project themes at a one-day public symposium held at the Emalus campus of the

University of the South Pacific (USP).[4] *The China Alternative: Changing Regional Order in the Pacific Islands* consists of 16 chapters written by academics based in Solomon Islands, Fiji, Papua New Guinea, Australia, New Zealand, the United States and China, as well as an introduction by the editors. All contributions have been extensively revised in light of reviewers' comments.

The chapters in this book are framed by two keynote speeches delivered at the public symposium in Port Vila on 8 February 2019, one by Vanuatu Minister of Foreign Affairs Ralph Regenvanu, the other by Secretary General of the Pacific Islands Forum Dame Meg Taylor. These speeches serve as reminders that our focus should always be on the sovereign interests of those most directly impacted by geostrategic competition in the region. In the introduction, we attempt to place the interests and options of Pacific Island countries within a wider context of the emerging rivalry between large powers, paying particular attention to how many of the impacts of China's rise are mediated by the determination of the United States to contain that rise, as well as the policy dilemmas of Australia and New Zealand caught in between these giant rivals.

In the opening two chapters, Tarcisius Kabutaulaka discusses how Pacific leaders have developed the notion of 'the Blue Pacific' or 'the Blue Pacific Continent' as a conceptual vehicle to assert their agency in the face of competing narratives, and Terence Wesley-Smith explores the proposition that escalating US–China competition represents a new Cold War with direct and indirect implications for Pacific Island interests. The following four chapters by Merriden Varrall, Iati Iati, Gerard Finin and Nic Maclellan examine how Australia, New Zealand, the US and France, respectively, have reshaped their policies in response to China's increased profile in the Pacific Islands region. Zhou Fangyin examines

---

4   The China Alternative project was co-sponsored by the Department of Pacific Affairs (DPA), The Australian National University, and the Center for Pacific Islands Studies (CPIS), University of Hawai'i, at Manoa. We are grateful for support received from our respective institutions, as well as additional funding from CPIS National Resource Center (NRC) grant; an ANU College of Asia and the Pacific Strategic Partnership Development Grant; and an ANU Asia Pacific Innovation Program grant. The public symposium in Port Vila was generously hosted on the USP campus by Dr Joseph Foukona, who worked with Dr Tarcisius Kabutaulaka (CPIS) to plan the event. Lea Giacomelli (DPA) and James Viernes (CPIS) worked tirelessly to ensure that we all got to Vanuatu in February 2019 and that the workshop and symposium went smoothly. Special thanks to all the insightful contributors to the volume, to Sarah Jost and Cathy Johnstone who worked long and hard on copyediting all the chapters, and to Emily Tinker for shepherding the manuscript through the publication process at ANU Press under difficult circumstances.

China's regional engagement and argues against the proposition that Beijing has singled out the Pacific Islands for special attention. Denghua Zhang looks at some of China's recent bureaucratic reforms and how these might impact the delivery of aid to the region. Henryk Szadziewski rounds out this cluster of China-centred chapters by examining the implications of the inclusion of Oceania in Beijing's massive Belt and Road Initiative with its emphasis on infrastructure development along the 21st Century Maritime Silk Road.

The next two chapters examine aspects of a key challenge associated with China's regional rise and the increased pressure on Taiwan's allies in the region to switch their recognition to Beijing in the face of countervailing pressure from Western countries as well as Taipei. Transform Aqorau looks at how these factors played out in Solomon Islands, the largest of Taipei's allies, resulting in a decision to switch recognition to Beijing, and suggests that the country's governance institutions are not yet ready to effectively manage relations with the Asian giant, especially since its natural resources are already at risk through overexploitation. Jessica Marinaccio, on the other hand, examines how Taipei has emphasised an Austronesian identity to support its diplomatic relations with Pacific Island countries, with particular attention to how well this approach has worked in Tuvalu, the smallest of Taiwan's Pacific partners.

In the two country-level case studies that follow, Sandra Tarte analyses the evolving relationship between China and a key regional actor, Fiji, while Sarah O'Dowd looks at the pros and cons for Papua New Guinea of China's Belt and Road Initiative. The next three chapters focus on the Chinese communities that have sprung up in Pacific places in recent years, as well as their occasionally uneasy relationships with local populations. Fei Sheng and Graeme Smith report on their research with Chinese nationals in Vanuatu, while Patrick Matbob surveys a long history of distrust between Chinese traders and local communities in Papua New Guinea. In the final chapter, Laurentina Barreto Soares discusses how overseas Chinese have engaged with local communities in Timor Leste and how this relates to China's soft power diplomacy there. Although Timor Leste is not a member of the PIF, the fact that its leaders increasingly identify with the Pacific Islands region, and that its experience with China has many parallels in Oceania, justify the inclusion of Barreto Soares's case study in this book.

Concluding comments

This is a pivotal moment in global politics as states around the world try to understand the nature of the escalating rivalry between the US, the dominant global power since World War II, and China, by far its most formidable competitor, and identify key implications for their own national interests. The small states of the Pacific Islands region are no exception, especially given their deep entanglements with Western powers since the dawn of the colonial era. Although the region is unlikely to become a major focal point of this great power struggle any time soon, Island states are already experiencing its by-products as China's regional profile increases and traditional partners manoeuvre to maintain their influence. Furthermore, changing Western foreign policies towards the Pacific Islands reflect not just developments in the region itself, but what is happening on the front lines of the conflict, particularly in the South China Sea and the Taiwan Strait, where the US and China vie for leadership in East Asia. In a type of policy displacement or transference, Pacific Island states feel the effects of mounting anxieties in Australia and New Zealand about balancing their own relationships with the US, their main security partner, and China upon which their economies depend.

Greg Fry suggests that 'when the West sees a threat to its interests in the Pacific at a time of global rivalry, the Pacific Island states have greater bargaining power' (Fry 2019:323). As we can see from recent developments, there is much evidence to support this assertion. China's rise has given Island states more options and opportunities for trade, aid and investment, and Western powers are adding further resources in an attempt to retain their influence. Some Pacific Island states, like Fiji, have leveraged China's presence to further their own agendas, while others are enjoying material benefits they might not otherwise have received. Still others, like the freely associated states in the north Pacific, can look forward to greater leverage as negotiations with the US for compact renewal get under way. Yet the successful application of this bargaining power is contingent on a complex array of factors. Because of their strategic locations, as well as military and other connections to the US, Guam, CNMI, Palau, the Marshall Islands and Federated States of Micronesia have less room to manoeuvre when it comes to negotiating relations with China than Pacific Island entities without such entanglements. Furthermore, some Island governments may have greater capacity than others to manage relations with large external powers. This seems to have been the case when Tonga negotiated large loans from China and is certainly Transform Aqorau's major concern about Solomon Islands' switch from Taiwan to China.

A major factor in all of this, however, is the priority that larger powers give to their policies in the Pacific Islands region and it is fair to assume that strategic and defence concerns receive the most attention. For example, Australia was prepared to devote massive resources to its RAMSI initiative largely because regional security considerations were involved, and the US was determined that Palau's constitutional provisions were not going to be allowed to interfere with its ability to operate nuclear-powered or armed vessels in this strategically important part of the ocean. The current heightened engagement of the Western powers is driven by concerns about regional security and the possible establishment of a Chinese base. At the moment, the tools of persuasion are diplomatic and economic in nature and it is too early to tell how effective they will be as great power competition intensifies.

As presently constituted, Australia's Step-Up policy faces challenges given significant differences with Pacific Island leaders on regional security priorities, and divergence on climate change mitigation (Hayward-Jones 2019). How far would Western powers be prepared to go if current policies prove inadequate? What we have seen so far are mainly positive inducements to influence decisions in Island countries, but could these be turned into threats to withdraw support or even impose sanctions?

The same question might be asked about China's involvement in the region. How far would Beijing be prepared to go if strategic planners decided to make acquiring a naval base in the Pacific Islands a priority? Or to defend such a facility once it was established? Despite a recent history of effective and assertive diplomacy and the powerful symbolism of the Blue Pacific narrative, it seems unlikely that Island governments could easily resist, manage or leverage competing pressures of that nature. In other words, Fry may be correct that the bargaining power of Pacific Island states increases when larger powers compete, but there are limits to that power once the competition reaches a certain level of intensity.

Pandemic politics: An update[5]

In December 2019, a new coronavirus was detected in the city of Wuhan in central China that spread rapidly throughout the world. By early June 2020, more than 6 million cases of COVID-19 had been reported to the World Health Organization (WHO) and 370,000 deaths attributed to the virus, with the number of casualties continuing to rise. Government containment measures are likely to reduce the global gross domestic product (GDP) by a rate 'approaching the level of economic contraction not experienced since the Great Depression of the 1930s' (CRS 2020:4). The pandemic has also altered the dynamics of US–China relations and escalated strategic competition to a new and dangerous level. This has further implications for Pacific Island countries already dealing with the health and economic impacts of the COVID-19 crisis. The pandemic adds additional layers of uncertainty for the region as external competition takes new forms, the possibility of spillover from conflict zones in the broader Asia-Pacific region increases and Pacific Island countries seek to leverage additional economic support.

The pandemic has significantly impacted the economies of both the US and China and amplified the economic dimensions of their competition. The International Monetary Fund projects that the US economy will contract by 5.9 per cent in 2020, about twice the rate of decline experienced after the financial crisis in 2009, with double-digit unemployment projected to persist into 2021 (CRS 2020:6). China's economy shrank by an estimated 6.8 per cent in the first quarter of 2020, the first retrenchment since the end of the Cultural Revolution in 1976, with a real unemployment rate as high as 20 per cent (SCMP Reporters 2020a; Huifeng 2020). In his report to the annual Two Sessions high-level meetings in May 2020, Premier Li Keqiang declined to set a target for GDP growth in the coming year (SCMP Reporters 2020b). However, the ultimate result may be to further tilt the economic balance in China's favour. With the twin advantages of reopening sooner than other countries and centralised control of resources, China may be able to recover relatively quickly, though lags in overseas demand will require greater emphasis on domestic consumption. Massive government interventions

---

5   The manuscript for this collection was awaiting publication at ANU Press when the global significance of the coronavirus pandemic became apparent. This short addition to the volume's introduction was written in early June 2020 in order to identify some implications of COVID-19 for key themes dealt with in the book.

to limit the immediate damage to the US economy have ballooned the federal debt and deficit, which may hinder economic growth for years to come (Tellis 2020:2–3). If economic capacity is the essence of great-power rivalry, the real test will be China's ability to make further gains in the race for control of high technology, as Western countries accelerate efforts to decouple their economies and exclude key components, such as semiconductors, from Chinese supply chains.

COVID-19 challenged the domestic political positions of both President Xi Jinping and President Donald Trump and gave them an excuse to target each other. Xi was notably absent when the epidemic first emerged in Wuhan, only taking charge after public distress and anger had escalated significantly. Probably more important for Xi's hold on power were the economic shocks associated with the virus and their implications for the standard of living of Chinese citizens. As Minxin Pei notes, China's economy was already slowing down and 'the CCP has relied heavily on economic overperformance to sustain its legitimacy' (Pei 2020:3). Meanwhile, Trump was roundly criticised for his handling of the pandemic, which the medical journal *The Lancet* described as 'inconsistent and incoherent' (The Lancet 2020:1521). By early June, the US had recorded 1.9 million cases and 109,000 deaths, making it the epicentre of the global pandemic, and Trump's approval was dropping in the polls. Trump's efforts to hasten the reopening of the economy before the virus was contained amounted to a desperate attempt to revive his chances in the November 2020 presidential election. Both leaders tried to deflect blame, with Xi putting the focus on local party officials and Trump attempting to make state governors responsible for managing the crisis. They both also ramped up already heated nationalistic rhetoric to redirect public anger overseas.

As pro-nationalist forces gain ground within the CCP, China's military has become increasingly active in disputed parts of the South China Sea, and the US has responded with more frequent 'freedom of navigation' sorties through China's marine periphery (Starr and Browne 2020; Wu 2020). Tensions over the future of Taiwan increased in May 2020 as US Secretary of State Mike Pompeo publicly congratulated Tsai Ing-Wen on her landslide reelection as Taiwan's president, and there were reports of increased pressure on President Xi to commence military action against Taiwan, assuming that a weakened US would be unwilling to intervene (Chan 2020; Chung and Zheng 2020). Though the chances of direct US–China military conflict in the South China Sea or Taiwan Straits remain remote, opportunities for costly miscalculations have increased and the long-term impact of the economic downturn on the military budgets of both countries is unclear (Tellis 2020:3). Meanwhile, the Trump administration has weaponised the pandemic, accusing Beijing of failing to contain the Wuhan outbreak and concealing its severity. In an extraordinary move, in May 2020 Trump announced that the US would withdraw from the WHO, which he claimed had been hijacked by Beijing, further reducing the opportunity for a coordinated international response to the ongoing global health crisis. Additionally aggravating the conflict were US threats to withdraw recognition of Hong Kong's special status as Beijing 'beat the drums of Chinese nationalism' in a series of moves designed to increase its direct control of the territory in the face of the ongoing prodemocracy movement there (Fong 2020).

Rising US–China military tensions have obvious implications for those Island places essential to US strategic networks, especially Guam. They also provide further impetus for US efforts to renegotiate compacts of free association in the Federated States of Micronesia, Marshall Islands, and Palau, and for Australia to hasten the implementation of the strategic components of its Pacific Step-Up initiative. In the context of COVID-19, the Australian Department of Foreign Affairs and Trade announced it had 'paused work on a new development policy' and was placing 'a clear priority on our near neighbours, particularly the Pacific, Timor-Leste and Indonesia' (DFAT 2020). Those Island countries that continue to recognise Taipei remain firmly in the spotlight, as the struggle over Taiwan's political status and access to international organisations, such as the WHO, takes centre stage in US–China strategic competition.

Medical assistance provides a new arena for great power competition. President Trump has made no attempt to organise an international response to the pandemic, while Beijing has sought to improve its damaged global reputation through medical outreach to countries struggling to deal with the virus. Since mid-March 2020, China has deployed health workers, equipment and medical advice along a 'Health Silk Road', so-named to enhance President Xi's assertion of global leadership through his signature Belt and Road Initiative (Lancaster et al. 2020). It is unlikely that this form of diplomacy will have a lasting impact on China's image overseas, especially in the context of the more aggressive approach recently adopted by Chinese diplomats. There is no indication that the leaders accepting medical assistance will be any more attracted to a China governance model already marred by reports of human rights abuses in Xinjiang and Tibet, as well as the abrupt imposition of a national security law in Hong Kong. It is also clear that the reputation of the US has nosedived as a result of its incompetent handling of the pandemic. That there are no apparent ideological winners in this phase of the new cold war is perhaps not surprising, since both leaders are primarily focused on domestic audiences: Xi on the CCP elites and Trump on his loyal base in the Republican Party (Gill 2020).

Meanwhile, health diplomacy has been on full display in the Pacific Islands region. When the virus threat emerged, Pacific Island countries moved quickly to close their international borders, and by early June 2020 only Fiji, French Polynesia, New Caledonia and Papua New Guinea had reported cases of COVID-19 (Buhre 2020; McGarry and Newton Cain 2020). However, the economic damage to the region is severe, especially among states heavily reliant on tourism or remittances. In a somewhat belated attempt to respond collectively to the pandemic, Pacific Island leaders invoked the Biketawa Declaration on regional security and in April 2020 established the Pacific Humanitarian Pathway. The pathway's goal of 'enabling the provision of medical and humanitarian assistance … in a timely, safe, effective and equitable manner' has faced some challenges as development partners, including China, Taiwan, Australia, New Zealand and the US, tend to favour bilateral over multilateral approaches to compete for influence (Blanchard 2020; Maclellan 2020; PIF 2020).

China was quick to see the opportunity for COVID-19 diplomacy in the region, convening a videoconference in early March with leaders from the 10 Island countries that recognise Beijing in order to share medical advice and offer support. Chinese companies, philanthropic organisations and local Chinese communities have complemented government efforts with their own donations and shipments of medical supplies (Pryke and McGregor 2020; Zhang 2020). These initiatives brought a strange echo of the Luganville wharf controversy in Vanuatu, with defence sources claiming that a plane chartered by CCECC to deliver aid prevented an Australian air force plane from delivering humanitarian relief (Galloway 2020). Despite these aid efforts, travel restrictions may hurt some of China's leading contractors in the region, particularly those that have failed to localise their workforces. Many workers travelled home for Chinese New Year and have been unable to return to their project sites, putting numerous construction projects in jeopardy. The China Council for the

Promotion of International Trade has issued *force majeure* certificates to affected Chinese enterprises to assist them in avoiding liability for stalled projects, but it is doubtful these will hold up in local courts (Erie 2020).

Australia remains eager to be seen as the 'partner of choice' in the region, especially after US Secretary of State Mike Pompeo and Australian Prime Minister Scott Morrison agreed that Australia would focus its COVID-19 relief efforts on the South Pacific while the US would direct most of its aid to the American-affiliated islands in the northern Pacific (Maclellan 2020; US Department of State 2020). Australia has leaned further towards US policy positions during the pandemic, speaking out about the need for an independent inquiry into the Chinese origins of the virus and even sending a frigate to participate in a joint exercise in the South China Sea (Power 2020; Wong 2020). This has not prevented Australia from becoming collateral damage in the US–China trade war, however. In the same week Beijing announced it would be importing more beef and barley from the US under the Phase 1 trade deal, it slapped restrictions on Australia's beef and barley exports that will cost farmers over AU$2 billion. Canberra's outspokenness provided cover for these actions, helped by most Australian media outlets accepting Beijing's narrative that Australia was being punished for its temerity.

COVID-19 has demonstrated the susceptibility of Pacific Islands to global health crises and their relatively vulnerable positions in the global economy. As Island leaders contemplate the post-pandemic future, they will be looking for financial assistance to hasten the economic recovery of their countries. Their ability to win concessions by leveraging increased competition between external powers remains to be seen. Western countries are still eager to head off China's attempts to increase its regional influence, but will have to balance enhancements of their Pacific aid budgets against pressures to attend to urgent domestic needs. China faces similar tensions, and it is unclear whether it will be able to pursue its Belt and Road Initiative with the same vigor as before. Indeed, some Pacific Island countries that have borrowed heavily from China, including Tonga and Vanuatu, will probably join other countries in the Global South in requesting that existing loans be forgiven or renegotiated (Abi-Habib and Bradsher 2020). If military tensions in the South China Sea or Taiwan Strait cause protagonists to harden their positions in Pacific locations where key interests are judged to be at stake, then the strings attached to offers of support may become more explicit.

The COVID-19 pandemic has heightened existing tensions between the US and China, and, as Ashley Tellis (2020) put it, 'COVID-19 knocks on American hegemony' in the international system. While the ultimate outcome of this grand geopolitical rivalry remains unclear, states around the world, including those in the Pacific, are obliged to deal with new levels of strategic uncertainty and economic insecurity, and navigate between fiercely competing external powers as best they can. In early 2019, Dame Meg Taylor (in this volume) outlined the challenge for the region in explicit terms: 'Our political conversations and settlements must be driven by the wellbeing of our Blue Pacific continent and its people, not by the goals and ambitions of others'. COVID-19 has made that challenge more pertinent, as well as more difficult to achieve.

References

Abi-Habib, M. and K. Bradsher 2020. Poor Countries Borrowed Billions from China. They Can't Pay It Back. *New York Times*, 18 May.

Agence France-Presse 2018. Australian PM Warns China's 'Unprecedented Influence' in Pacific Is Changing the Balance of Power and Challenging US Interests. *South China Morning Post*, 1 November. www.scmp.com/news/asia/australasia/article/2171202/australian-pm-warns-chinas-unprecedented-influence-pacific

Albert, E. 2019. The Dragon and the Kiwi: New Zealand's Adern in China. *The Diplomat*, 1 April. thediplomat.com/2019/04/the-dragon-and-the-kiwi-new-zealands-ardern-in-china/

Aspinwall, N. 2019. Taiwan Shaken by Concerns Over Chinese Influence in Media, Press Freedom. *The Diplomat*, 27 July. thediplomat.com/2019/07/taiwan-shaken-by-concerns-over-chinese-influence-in-media-press-freedom/

Australian Government 2016. *2016 Defence White Paper*. Canberra: Department of Defence. www.defence.gov.au/WhitePaper/Docs/2016-Defence-White-Paper.pdf

Australian Government 2017. *2017 Foreign Policy White Paper*. Canberra: Department of Foreign Affairs and Trade. www.fpwhitepaper.gov.au/

Blanchard, B. 2020. Taiwan Wades into Hotly Contested Pacific with Its Own Coronavirus Diplomacy. *Reuters*, 15 April. www.reuters.com/article/us-health-coronavirus-taiwan-pacific/taiwan-wades-into-hotly-contested-pacific-with-its-own-coronavirus-diplomacy-idUSKCN21X0YX

Bradsher, K. 2020. China Renews its 'Belt and Road' Push for Global Sway. *The New York Times*, 15 January. www.nytimes.com/2020/01/15/business/china-belt-and-road.html

Brant, P. 2013. Chinese Aid in the South Pacific: Linked to Resources? *Asian Studies Review* 37(2):158–77. doi.org/10.1080/10357823.2013.767311

Buhre, M.L. 2020. Many Pacific Islands Are Untouched by COVID-19. Its Arrival Could Be Disastrous. *PBS*, 7 May. www.pbs.org/newshour/world/many-pacific-islands-are-untouched-by-covid-19-its-arrival-could-be-disastrous

Burton-Bradley, R. 2019. New Zealand's Government Divided Ahead of Pivotal Report on Chinese Political Interference. *ABC News*, 13 March. www.abc.net.au/news/2019-03-14/new-zealand-struggles-with-how-to-deal-with-china/10892446

Bush, R.C. 2019. 8 Key Things to notice from Xi Jinping's New Year Speech on Taiwan. *Brookings*, 7 January. www.brookings.edu/blog/order-from-chaos/2019/01/07/8-key-things-to-notice-from-xi-jinpings-new-year-speech-on-taiwan/

Chan, M. 2020. 'Too Costly': Chinese Military Strategist Warns Now Is Not the Time to Take Back Taiwan by Force. *South China Morning Post*, 4 May. www.scmp.com/news/china/military/article/3082825/too-costly-chinese-military-strategist-warns-now-not-time-take

Chung, L. and S. Zheng 2020. Beijing Warns of Action against Washington after Pompeo Congratulates Taiwan's Tsai. *South China Morning Post*, 20 May. www.scmp.com/news/china/diplomacy/article/3085190/pompeo-congratulates-taiwans-tsai-ing-wen-her-second-term

Cranston, M. 2019. Australia Posts First Current Account Surplus since 1975. *Australian Financial Review*, 3 September. www.afr.com/policy/economy/australia-posts-first-current-account-surplus-since-1975-20190903-p52nby

CRS (Congressional Research Service) 2020. *COVID-19: US Economic Effects*. 13 May. crsreports.congress.gov/product/pdf/IN/IN11388

Dayant, A. 2019. Pacific Links: Power Games, Volcanic Eruptions, and Media Blackouts. *The Interpreter*, 3 July. Lowy Institute. www.lowyinstitute.org/the-interpreter/pacific-links-power-games-volcanic-eruptions-and-media-blackouts

DFAT (Australian Government Department of Foreign Affairs and Trade) 2018. Design Summary for the Australia Pacific Security College, 1 August. dfat.gov.au/about-us/business-opportunities/Pages/design-summary-for-the-australia-pacific-security-college.aspx

DFAT (Australian Government Department of Foreign Affairs and Trade) 2019. China: Country and Trade Information. dfat.gov.au/geo/china/Pages/china.aspx

DFAT (Australian Government Department of Foreign Affairs and Trade) 2020. *Partnerships for Recovery: Australia's COVID-19 Development Response*. Barton: DFAT. dfat.gov.au/publications/aid/partnerships-recovery-australias-covid-19-development-response

Dobell, G. 2019. The Oz Pacific Policy that Can't Be Named. *The Strategist*, 22 July. Australian Strategic Policy Institute. www.aspistrategist.org.au/the-oz-pacific-policy-that-cant-be-named/

Dornan, M. and P. Brant 2014. Negotiating Chinese Development Assistance in the Pacific. *Devpolicy Blog*, 8 August. devpolicy.org/negotiating-chinese-development-assistance-the-role-of-pacific-island-governments-and-chinese-contractors-20140808/

Dziedzic, S. 2019. Beijing Intensifies Lobbying of Pacific Nations to Recognise Taiwan as Part of One China. *Pacific Beat* program. *ABC News*, 14 February. www.abc.net.au/news/2019-02-14/beijing-lobbying-pacific-nations-to-recognise-one-china-policy/10809412

Erie, M. 2020. BRI vs. COVID-19. *China, Law and Development Research Brief* No. 5/2020. Oxford: University of Oxford, 24 March. cld.web.ox.ac.uk/file/590881

Everington K. 2019. Solomon Islands Shifts Ties from Taiwan to China for US$500 Million in 'Aid'. *Taiwan News*, 16 September. www.taiwannews.com.tw/en/news/3777858

Focus Taiwan 2019. Full text of President Tsai Ing-wen's New Year's Day Speech. 1 January. focustaiwan.tw/news/acs/201901010015.aspx

Fonbuena, C. and L. Kuo 2019. US Commits to Aiding Philippines in South China Sea. *The Guardian*, 2 March. www.theguardian.com/world/2019/mar/01/us-commits-to-aiding-philippines-in-south-china-sea

Fong, B. 2020. With a New Cold War on the Rise, What's Next for Hong Kong's Autonomy? *The Diplomat*, 27 April. thediplomat.com/2020/04/with-a-new-cold-war-on-the-rise-what-next-for-hong-kongs-autonomy/

Fox, R. and M. Dornan 2018. China in the Pacific: Is China Engaged in 'Debt-Trap Diplomacy'? *Devpolicy Blog*, 8 November. devpolicy.org/is-china-engaged-in-debt-trap-diplomacy-20181108/

Fry, G. 2019. *Framing the Islands: Power and Diplomatic Agency in Pacific Regionalism*. Canberra: ANU Press. doi.org/10.22459/FI.2019

Fry, G. and S. Tarte (eds) 2015. *The New Pacific Diplomacy*. Canberra: ANU Press. doi.org/10.22459/NPD.12.2015

Galloway, A. 2020. Defence Looks at Chinese Plane Blocking Australian Aid Plane in Vanuatu. *The Sydney Morning Herald*, 15 April. www.smh.com.au/politics/federal/defence-looks-at-chinese-plane-blocking-australian-aid-plane-in-vanuatu-20200415-p54k5i.html

Garnaut, J. 2018. How China Interferes in Australia: And How Democracies Can Push Back. *Foreign Affairs*, 9 March. www.foreignaffairs.com/articles/china/2018-03-09/how-china-interferes-australia

Glaser, B.S. and E.S. Medeiros 2007. The Changing Ecology of Foreign Policy-Making in China: The Ascension and Demise of the Theory of 'Peaceful Rise'. *The China Quarterly* 190:291–310. doi.org/10.1017/s0305741007001208

Gill, B. 2020. Interview on *Killing Me Softly: The Power Dynamic*. *The Little Red Podcast*, 21 April. www.omny.fm/shows/the-little-red-podcast/killing-me-softly-the-power-pandemic

Goldrick, J. and E. Graham. 2019. A Fortress with No Water Supply: Hugh White's 'How to Defend Australia'. *The Strategist*, 18 July. Australian Strategic Policy Institute. www.aspistrategist.org.au/a-fortress-with-no-water-supply-hugh-whites-how-to-defend-australia/

Government of Palau 2019. Visitor Arrivals. www.palaugov.pw/visitor-arrivals/

Greene, A. and L. Sweeney 2019. Bill Shorten Disagrees with Paul Keating's Comments on China at Labor's Election Campaign Launch. *ABC News*, 6 May. www.abc.net.au/news/2019-05-06/federal-election-bill-shorten-disagrees-with-paul-keating-china/11082144

Groot, G. 2017. The Long Reach of China's United Front Work. *The Interpreter*, 6 November. Lowy Institute. www.lowyinstitute.org/the-interpreter/long-reach-Chinas-united-front-work

Hayward-Jones, J. 2019. Is this the End of a Beautiful Pacific Islands Relationship? *The Australian*, 13 July. www.theaustralian.com.au/inquirer/is-this-the-end-of-a-beautiful-pacific-islands-relationship/news-story/9309e662f27668646914705404f4b7bc

Herr, R. 2019. The Role of Soft Power in China's Influence in the Pacific. *The Strategist*, 30 April. Australian Strategic Policy Institute. www.aspistrategist.org.au/the-role-of-soft-power-in-chinas-influence-in-the-pacific-islands/

Huang, P. 2019. Chinese Cyber-Operatives Boosted Taiwan's Insurgent Candidate. *Foreign Policy*, 26 June. foreignpolicy.com/2019/06/26/chinese-cyber-operatives-boosted-taiwans-insurgent-candidate/

Huifeng, H. 2020. Coronavirus: China's Economic Woes Could Be Worse than Thought as Legions of Migrant Workers Return Home. *South China Morning Post*, 29 April. www.scmp.com/economy/china-economy/article/3081953/coronavirus-chinas-economic-woes-could-be-worse-thought

Jennings, P. 2019. How Not to Defend Australia. *The Strategist*, 27 July. Australian Strategic Policy Institute. www.aspistrategist.org.au/how-not-to-defend-australia/

Kabutaulaka, T. 2005. Australian Foreign Policy and the RAMSI Intervention in Solomon Islands. *The Contemporary Pacific* 17(2): 283–308. doi.org/10.1353/cp.2005.0058

Kabutaulaka, T. 2019. The Contested Trinity: Solomon Islands, Taiwan, and China. Tutuvatu blog, 15 May. tutuvatu.blogspot.com/2019/05/the-contested-trinity-solomon-islands.html

Lancaster, K., M. Rubin and M. Rapp-Hooper 2020. Mapping China's Health Silk Road. Council on Foreign Relations' Asia Unbound Blog, 10 April. www.cfr.org/blog/mapping-chinas-health-silk-road

Lee, Y. 2019. Taiwan Says China Lures Kiribati with Airplanes after Losing Another Ally. *Reuters*, 20 September. www.reuters.com/article/us-taiwan-diplomacy-kiribati/taiwan-says-china-lures-kiribati-with-airplanes-after-losing-another-ally-idUSKBN1W50DI

Lowy Institute 2019. Chinese Aid in the Pacific. Lowy Institute. chineseaidmap.lowyinstitute.org/

Maclellan, N. 2020. Geopolitics Meets Pandemic in the Pacific. *Inside Story*, 6 May. www.insidestory.org.au/geopolitics-meets-pandemic-in-the-pacific/

Marinaccio, J. 2019. Rearticulating Diplomatic Relationships: Contextualizing Tuvalu-Taiwan Relations. *The Contemporary Pacific* 31(2): 448–75. doi.org/10.1353/cp.2019.0028

May, R. (ed.) 2003. *Arc of Instability? Melanesia in the Early 2000s*. Canberra: University of Canterbury and ANU.

McGarry, D. and T. Newton Cain 2020. Coronavirus in the Pacific: Weekly Briefing. *The Guardian*, 3 June. www.theguardian.com/world/2020/jun/03/coronavirus-in-the-pacific-weekly-briefing

Medcalf, R. 2019. Arrest of Yang Hengjun Drags Australia into China's Hostage Diplomacy. *Australian Financial Review*, 25 January. www.afr.com/opinion/arrest-of-yang-hengjun-drags-australia-into-chinas-hostage-diplomacy-2019 0124-h1af6x

MFAT (New Zealand Government Ministry of Foreign Affairs and Trade) 2017. 2017 New Zealand and China: Diplomatic Milestones. Infographic. www.mfat.govt.nz/assets/Trade-agreements/China-NZ-FTA/NZ-China-2017-infographic.pdf

New Zealand Government 2018. *Strategic Defence Policy Statement 2018*. Wellington: Ministry of Defence. www.defence.govt.nz/assets/Uploads/895 8486b29/Strategic-Defence-Policy-Statement-2018.pdf

Pandey, S. and C. Packham 2019. US Official Urges Pacific Island Nations to Keep Ties with Taiwan. *Reuters*, 23 May. www.reuters.com/article/us-pacific-china/u-s-official-urges-pacific-island-nations-to-keep-ties-with-taiwan-id USKCN1SU0XE

Parmentier, R. 1991. The Rhetoric of Free Association and Palau's Political Struggle. *The Contemporary Pacific* 3(1):146–58.

Payne, M. 2019. Speech to the Fijian Press Club Lunch. Australian Minister for Foreign Affairs, 5 June. www.foreignminister.gov.au/minister/marise-payne/speech/speech-fijian-press-club-lunch

Pearlman, J. 2018. Is Australia Warning the Chinese to Back Away from Tiny Tuvalu? *Sunday Independent* (Ireland), 13 May. Available at www.pressreader.com/ireland/sunday-independent-ireland/20180513/282110637249923

Pei, M. 2020. China's Coming Upheaval: Competition, the Coronavirus, and the Weakness of Xi Jinping. *Foreign Affairs*. www.foreignaffairs.com/articles/united-states/2020-04-03/chinas-coming-upheaval

Pence, M. 2018. Remarks by Vice President Pence at the 2018 APEC CEO Summit. The White House, 16 November. kr.usembassy.gov/111618-remarks-by-vice-president-pence-at-the-2018-apec-ceo-summit/

PIF (Pacific Islands Forum) 2020. Pacific Islands Forum Foreign Ministers Agree to Establish a Pacific Humanitarian Pathway on COVID-19. Pacific Islands Forum Secretariat, 8 April. www.forumsec.org/pacific-islands-forum-foreign-ministers-agree-to-establish-a-pacific-humanitarian-pathway-on-covid-19/

PIF (Pacific Islands Forum) Secretariat 2018. Boe Declaration on Regional Security. www.forumsec.org/boe-declaration-on-regional-security/

Power, J. 2020. Australia 'Concerned' over Reports US May Have Leaked Documents to Boost Donald Trump's Wuhan Lab Claims. *South China Morning Post*, 7 May. www.scmp.com/week-asia/politics/article/3083331/australia-concerned-over-reports-us-may-have-leaked-documents

Pratt, C. 2019. Opening Remarks to the Center for Strategic and International Studies US-Pacific Dialogue, 'Strengthening the US-Pacific Islands Partnership', by Deputy Secretary General. Nadi: PIF Secretariat, 4 March. www.forumsec.org/opening-remarks-to-the-center-for-strategic-international-studies-us-pacific-dialogue-strengthening-the-us-pacific-islands-partnership-by-deputy-secretary-general-cristelle-pratt/

Pryke, J. and R. McGregor 2020. China's Coronavirus Aid to Pacific Islands is Part of Geopolitical Game. Lowy Institute, 23 April. www.lowyinstitute.org/publications/china-coronavirus-aid-pacific-islands-part-geopolitical-game

Reuters 2019. China Using 'Payday Loan Diplomacy' in the Pacific, Claims New US Ambassador to Australia. *South China Morning Post*, 13 March. www.scmp.com/news/asia/australasia/article/3001549/china-using-payday-loan-diplomacy-pacific-claims-new-us

RNZ (Radio New Zealand) 2018. Kiribati Govt Denies it's Wavering on Taiwan Support. 21 November. www.rnz.co.nz/international/pacific-news/376466/kiribati-govt-denies-it-s-wavering-on-taiwan-support

RNZ (Radio New Zealand) 2019. New Kiribati Opposition Party Says Gov't too Close to China. *Dateline Pacific,* 7 November. www.rnz.co.nz/international/programmes/datelinepacific/audio/2018721013/new-kiribati-opposition-party-says-govt-too-close-to-china

Roff, S.R. 1991. *Overreaching in Paradise: United States Policy in Palau since 1945.* Juneau: Denali Press.

Roy, D. 2018. What Would the US Do if Beijing Decided to Take Taiwan by Force? *South China Morning Post*, 22 July. www.scmp.com/week-asia/geopolitics/article/2156237/what-would-us-do-if-beijing-decided-take-taiwan-force

SCMP Reporters 2020a. China Economy: Latest Data about World's Second Largest Economy. *South China Morning Post*, 14 May. www.scmp.com/economy/china-economy/article/3084199/china-economy-latest-data-about-worlds-second-largest-economy

SCMP Reporters 2020b. Caught between China and the United States: Why Hong Kong is the Latest Battleground in the Rivalry and Article 23 Could be the Tinder to the Explosive Relationship. *South China Morning Post*, 18 May. www.scmp.com/news/hong-kong/politics/article/3084924/caught-between-china-and-united-states-why-hong-kong-latest

Shambaugh, D.L. 2013. *China Goes Global: The Partial Power*. Oxford: Oxford University Press.

Shoebridge, M. 2019. China Can't Discount America's Resolve in Asia. *The Strategist*, 6 July. Australian Strategic Policy Institute. www.aspistrategist. org.au/china-cant-discount-americas-resolve-in-asia/

Smith, G. 2013. Beijing's Orphans? New Chinese Investors in Papua New Guinea. *Pacific Affairs* 86(2):327–49. doi.org/10.5509/2013862327

Smith, G. 2016. Selling China in the South Pacific: Is Anyone Buying? *Asia Dialogue*, 29 March. University of Nottingham Asia Research Institute. theasiadialogue.com/2016/03/29/selling-china-in-the-south-pacific-is-anyone-buying/

Sogavare, M. 2019. Statement by the Prime Minister Hon. Manasseh Sogavare on Switch to China. *Solomon Times*, 20 September. www.solomontimes.com/ news/statement-by-the-prime-minister-hon-manasseh-sogavare-on-switch-to-china/9362

Starr, B. and R. Browne 2020. US Increases Military Pressure on China as Tensions Rise over Pandemic. *CNN*, 15 May. www.cnn.com/2020/05/14/politics/us-china-military-pressure/index.html

Tarabay, J. 2019. As China Looms, Australia's Military Refocuses on Pacific Neighbors. *The New York Times*, 11 June. www.nytimes.com/2019/06/11/ world/australia/china-military-asia.html

Tarai, J. 2015. The New Pacific Diplomacy and the South Pacific Tuna Treaty. In G. Fry and S. Tarte (eds), *The New Pacific Diplomacy*. Canberra: ANU Press, 237–48. doi.org/10.22459/npd.12.2015.19

Tellis, A.J. 2020. *COVID-19 Knocks on American Hegemony*. Seattle, Washington DC: The National Bureau of Asian Research. www.nbr.org/wp-content/ uploads/pdfs/publications/new-normal-tellis-050420.pdf

The Lancet 2020. Reviving the US CDC. Editorial 395(10236):1521, 16 May. doi.org/10.1016/S0140-6736(20)31140-5

Tobin, M. 2019a. New Zealand Bans Huawei from 5G, China Has Message for New Zealand. *South China Morning Post*, 17 February. www.scmp.com/ week-asia/geopolitics/article/2186402/new-zealand-bans-huawei-china-has-message-new-zealand

Tobin, M. 2019b. Explained: Why Taiwan, US and China Are Watching Marshall Islands Vote Count. *South China Morning Post*, 26 November. www.scmp.com/week-asia/explained/article/3039299/why-taiwan-washington-and-beijing-are-watching-marshall-islands

US Department of State 2020. The United States is Assisting Pacific Island Countries to Respond to COVID-19. Fact Sheet. Office of the Spokesperson. 2017-2021.state.gov/the-united-states-is-assisting-pacific-island-countries-to-respond-to-covid-19/index.html

White, H. 2017a. Without America: Australia in the New Asia. *Quarterly Essay* 68:1–81. www.quarterlyessay.com.au/essay/2017/11/without-america

White, H. 2017b. America or China? Australia Is Fooling Itself that It Doesn't Have to Choose. *The Guardian*, 27 November. www.theguardian.com/australia-news/2017/nov/27/america-or-china-were-fooling-ourselves-that-we-dont-have-to-choose

White, H. 2019a. *How to Defend Australia*. Melbourne: La Trobe University Press.

White, H. 2019b. Australia Must Prepare for a Chinese Military Base in the Pacific. *The Guardian*, 15 July. www.theguardian.com/world/commentisfree/2019/jul/15/australia-must-prepare-for-a-chinese-military-base-in-the-pacific

Wong, C. 2020. China on 'High Alert' as 'Troublemaker' US Patrols South China Sea. *South China Morning Post*, 30 April. www.scmp.com/news/china/military/article/3082376/china-high-alert-troublemaker-us-patrols-south-china-sea

Wroe, D. 2018. China Eyes Vanuatu Military Base in Plan with Global Ramifications. *The Sydney Morning Herald*, 9 April. www.smh.com.au/politics/federal/china-eyes-vanuatu-military-base-in-plan-with-global-ramifications-20180409-p4z8j9.html

Wu, W. 2020. US Air Force Ramps up Flyovers Near China in Sign of Rising Tension and Risk of Conflict between World Powers. *South China Morning Post*, 20 May. www.scmp.com/news/china/diplomacy/article/3085247/us-air-force-ramps-flyovers-near-china-sign-rising-tension-and

Xinhua 2017. Full Text of Xi Jinping's Report at 19th CPC National Congress. 3 November. www.xinhuanet.com//english/special/2017-11/03/c_136725942.htm

Xinhua 2019. Xi Says 'China Must Be, Will Be Reunified' as Key Anniversary Marked. 2 January. www.xinhuanet.com/english/2019-01/02/c_137714898.htm

Zhang, D. 2018. China's New Aid Agency. *The Interpreter*, 19 March. Lowy Institute. www.lowyinstitute.org/the-interpreter/china-s-new-aid-agency

Zhang, D. 2020. China's Coronavirus 'COVID-19 Diplomacy' in the Pacific. *DPA In Brief* 2020/10. Canberra: ANU. dpa.bellschool.anu.edu.au/sites/default/files/publications/attachments/2020-04/ib_2020_10_zhang_final_0.pdf

Zhang, D. and J. Marinaccio 2019. Chinese and Taiwanese Scholarships for Pacific Island Countries. *DPA In Brief* 2019/10. Canberra: ANU. dpa.bellschool.anu.edu.au/experts-publications/publications/6816/ib-201910-chinese-and-taiwanese-scholarships-pacific-island

Zhang, D. and G. Smith 2017. China's Foreign Aid System: Structure, Agencies, and Identities. *Third World Quarterly* 38(10):2330–346. doi.org/10.1080/01436597.2017.1333419

Zheng, B. 2005. China's 'Peaceful Rise' to Great-Power Status. *Foreign Affairs* 84:18–24. doi.org/10.2307/20031702

1

Mapping the Blue Pacific in a Changing Regional Order

Tarcisius Kabutaulaka[1]

Introduction

In the midst of increasing geopolitical competition in Oceania, Pacific Island countries are pushing back on the dominant narratives and cartographies that powerful countries use to frame how the region fits into their global agendas. Central to this resistance is the Blue Pacific narrative, which the Pacific Islands Forum (PIF) endorsed in 2017. It provides a counternarrative for Pacific regionalism and a strategy to counter the dominance of global powers. This is pertinent in a rapidly changing regional order where powerful countries compete to map Oceania into their boundaries of influence.

This chapter uses mapping as a framework to examine how the Blue Pacific narrative pushes back on the dominant cartographies by Washington DC, Beijing, Canberra, Wellington, Paris and other hubs of global power. Central to these dominant cartographies is the US-led Indo-Pacific strategy and China's Maritime Silk Road, an extension of its Belt and Road Initiative (BRI). I argue that the Blue Pacific empowers Pacific Island countries by giving them agency to frame and tell their

1   I am thankful to Greg Fry and Stewart Firth who read and provided valuable comments on an earlier draft of this chapter. However, I am the sole author and take responsibility for any errors or misrepresentations.

own narratives and map their own spaces and places—their region—in the face of overwhelming global interest by powers who want to draw Oceania into their maps and agendas. Here, I contend that since its endorsement, the Blue Pacific narrative has been successful in asserting the sovereignty of Pacific Island countries, highlighting issues that are important to them and making metropolitan powers conscious of their interests and priorities. It gives Pacific Islanders the conceptual tools to assert themselves in regional and global discussions. The Blue Pacific is therefore both a narrative and a strategy for assertive diplomacy.

Two questions underlie this chapter's discussions and are fundamental to understanding the role of the Blue Pacific in the region's contemporary geopolitics: (i) What are the tension points between the Blue Pacific as a countermap and counternarrative and the Indo-Pacific and Maritime Silk Road as the new geopolitical maps drawn by the US and China? (ii) Can the Blue Pacific, as a framework for assertive Pacific diplomacy, successfully counter the new dominant narratives and cartographies?

Geopolitical mapping in Oceania

Cartographers have long used maps to identify and claim control over geographical, economic, political and social spaces. Consequently, maps are effective tools for projecting power.

They have been deployed to claim territories for colonial control, exert geopolitical, geostrategic and geoeconomic interests, and create and maintain global order and worldviews. In mapping, the power is in the hands of the cartographers—they 'draw' the boundaries and exercise power over what is bounded, underlining the fact that maps are powerful political tools (Harley 2009; Klinghoffer 2006).

Modern states, corporations and other institutions of power deploy maps to make spaces 'legible' (Scott 1998), so that they can be appropriated and controlled. This is done through the mapping of entire regions for geopolitical control as well as locally, such as with the registration of land. But maps do not just create legibility. They also make spaces become invisible by omitting or marginalising them. As Harley points out, 'maps … exert social influence through their omissions as much as much as the features they depict and emphasise' (1992:290). For example, geoeconomic maps may emphasise resources and their economic values and omit villages, people and the cultural values of these resources (Peluso 1995). Geopolitical maps typically highlight the interests of powerful countries and marginalise or omit the interests and priorities of less powerful ones.

Oceania is not new to cartographies. Long before European contact, Pacific Islanders mapped and remapped their landscapes, seascapes and socialscapes. But since the arrival of Europeans, the region's landscapes and seascapes have been mapped and claimed by one colonial power or another. By the end of the 19th century, most of the region had been colonised as powerful countries competed for control of the Islands (Campbell 1989; Douglas 2011; Howe et al. 1994; Matsuda 2012). The colonial boundaries created in the 1800s were later adopted by present-day Pacific Island nation-states when they gained independence. The Islands were also mapped into the subregions of Polynesia, Micronesia and Melanesia, which were envisioned not only as geographical spaces, but also racialised ones (Douglas 2011; Kabutaulaka 2015a).

In the post–World War II period, geopolitical competition in the region was defined largely by the Cold War, especially the strategic denial policy adopted by the US and its allies. This policy denied communist countries, particularly the former Soviet Union, access to the region, which became an Anglo-Francophone lake (Herr 1986). Consequently, Western countries mapped the region into their sphere of influence and gave themselves the 'right' to use the region for their strategic purposes. Great Britain, France and the US used the region for nuclear testing, including Kirimati Island in Kiribati (1957–58), Moruroa and Fangataufa in French Polynesia (1966–96) and Bikini and Enewetak in the Marshall Islands (1946–62) (Firth 1986; Macllelan 2005, 2017). Furthermore, the US and France built and maintained military bases in Guåhan/Guam, Kwajalein in the Marshall Islands, French Polynesia and New Caledonia. At the end of the Cold War, Western countries, including Australia and New Zealand, continued to have a dominant influence in the region.

In the 1990s, another cartographical layer was drawn onto the region: the Asia-Pacific, which mapped the Pacific Islands as part of a broader region and with a focus on economic cooperation. Consequently, the Asia-Pacific Economic Cooperation (APEC) was established in 1989. However, it favoured the Pacific Rim countries with larger economies. Apart from Papua New Guinea (PNG), no other Pacific Island country is a member of APEC. In this Asia-Pacific map, Oceania was often treated as an empty space, or, as Hau'ofa stated, a 'hole in the Asia-Pacific doughnut' (2008:397). In the mapping of the Asia-Pacific, Oceania was drawn into this broad cartography, but at the same time was made invisible or omitted, implying that the region and its people were insignificant and had no agency, and that their places and resources were subject to the control of powerful Pacific Rim countries.

In the late 1990s, another map was drawn, especially for the western Pacific. Australian policymakers and their allies in academia described the region as part of the 'arc of instability' that stretched from Indonesia to Fiji following the conflicts in Bougainville, Timor-Leste and Solomon Islands and the coups in Fiji (Ayson 2007; Dobell 2007). This was not a neutral description of places but a subjective mapping that reflected Australia's geostrategic thinking, which in turn influenced the nature of its relationships with its neighbours—places that Canberra considers Australia's backyard, or its patch. Australia had mapped itself as being surrounded by troubled places that it had a responsibility for because they were within its sphere of influence. In essence, Australia had mapped itself as a centre of stability and power surrounded by an arc of instability.

The aforementioned illustrates how, over the past two centuries, Pacific Islands and Islanders have been drawn into numerous maps. They were never consulted or included as cartographers in these mapping exercises. These maps were not innocuous instruments. Rather, they defined global powers' geopolitical control, divided Pacific Islands and Islanders and severed preexisting relationships. The use of cartographies for geopolitical purposes continues through the present.

But Pacific Islanders have also been engaged in counter-mapping; they use the processes, instruments and power of maps to draw alternative boundaries and give visibility to their priorities. These countermaps include not only physical geographical spaces but also conceptual boundaries or ideas about relationships to spaces, places and each other. Peluso discusses counter-mapping in the forest territories of Kalimantan in Indonesia, where local communities 'appropriate the state's techniques and manner of representation to bolster the legitimacy of "custom" claims to resources' (1995:384). In the following, I discuss how Pacific Island countries utilise countermapping as a response to the geopolitical maps that have been drawn by globally powerful countries.

The Indo-Pacific and the Maritime Silk Road

In the past decade, we have seen contending cartographies used to frame geopolitical competition between global powers, especially the US and its allies on one hand and China on the other. At the centre of this are the Indo-Pacific and the Maritime Silk Road. These new terms are not innocent changes in semantics, or an objective exercise in nomenclature. Rather, they are part of a process that invokes a particular way of imagining and relating to the world, in this case to the Indian and Pacific Oceans and the countries in and around them. For powerful countries, these new and contending cartographies embody their global strategies and serve to exert their geopolitical control. They include the Pacific Islands without consulting them or acknowledging their sovereignty and agency.

The push by the US and its allies to replace the term Asia-Pacific with Indo-Pacific attempts to map a large part of the world that includes two major oceans and stretches from the west coast of the US to the east coast of Africa. This Indo-Pacific strategy is part of an attempt by the US and its allies to counter China's increasing and assertive influence in the Indian and Pacific Oceans. It is a geopolitical and geostrategic mapping that evokes interests in and control over a large part of the world.

China's increasing influence led Washington DC to 'rebalance' its foreign policy focus from Europe and the Middle East to the Asia-Pacific. This was reflected in the Obama administration's 'Asia-Pacific pivot' policy. On 17 November 2011, while addressing the Australian federal parliament, then president Barack Obama said:

> The United States is turning our attention to the vast potential of the Asia Pacific region … our new focus on this reflects a fundamental truth—the United States has been, and always will be, as Pacific nation.

Similar sentiments were expressed by then secretary of state Hillary Clinton in an 11 October 2011 article titled 'America's Pacific Century'. In it, Clinton states that 'we are also expanding our alliance with Australia from a Pacific partnership to an Indo-Pacific one, and indeed a global partnership' (2011:4). The term Indo-Pacific is not new. Japan had used it for at least a decade prior to 2010 to frame its diplomatic and development assistance to the Asia-Pacific region as the Free and

Open Indo-Pacific (FOIP). Brewster (2018) discusses how the concept of a FOIP existed alongside Japan's other programs, such as the Bay of Bengal Industrial Growth Belt (BBIGB) and the Asia–Africa Growth Corridor (AAGC). These were avenues through which Tokyo invested in new economic and transportation corridors from the Pacific across the Indian Ocean to Africa.

By the end of the Obama administration, the geopolitical thinking and language in Washington DC had shifted from the Asia-Pacific to the Indo-Pacific—a redrawing of the US's geopolitical map and which countries it had decided to draw in or out. By the time President Donald Trump took office, the idea of the Indo-Pacific as a loosely defined and panoramic perspective of the world covering the Pacific and Indian Oceans had been established. The Trump administration fleshed out the details of the Indo-Pacific. In his speech to the APEC CEO Summit in Vietnam in November 2017, President Trump outlined a 'free and open Indo-Pacific' strategy and a 'rules-based order' (Brewster 2018)—the rules being those established by the cartographers. The US has since rallied support from its allies, especially its quadrilateral partners: Australia, Japan and India (the quad). Washington DC subsequently forged a trilateral alliance with Australia and Japan that focuses on increasing influence in the Pacific Islands. Consequently, through the invocation of the term Indo-Pacific, a huge part of world was mapped and claimed as a sphere of influence. In June 2019, the acting US secretary of defence Patrick Shanahan described the Indo-Pacific as the Department of Defense's 'priority theatre' (Department of Defense 2019). But others have argued that the Indo-Pacific is more than simply a counter to China's influence, that it is not new, nor is it the exclusive preserve of the US foreign policy circle. They point to the support from other countries—not only the quad, but also Southeast Asia countries such as Indonesia and Singapore (Medcalf 2014). Pacific Island countries have been more cautious about joining the Indo-Pacific.

In the past two decades, China has established itself as a global power—at least a global economic power—that challenges the US's preeminence. This is discussed in detail elsewhere (Woodward 2017). China's increasing global influence is partly because of Beijing's own global mapping exercises. Central to this is the BRI—also referred to as the One Belt, One Road—that President Xi Jinping launched in 2013. The BRI maps China's grand strategy for geoeconomic and geopolitical expansions and influence that serve its domestic priorities. This is in line with the 2006

Central Committee of the Chinese Communist Party's announcement that its foreign policy 'must maintain economic construction as its centrepiece, be closely integrated into domestic work, and be advanced by coordinating domestic and international situations' (quoted in Wang 2011:74). The BRI integrates China's domestic priorities and international engagements (Wang 2011).

In the Pacific and Indian Oceans, the BRI is represented by the Maritime Silk Road Initiative (MSRI), which resembles the ancient Maritime Silk Road that connected China from Fuzhou in Fujian to different parts of the world, but with an emphasis on connections to Europe. Blanchard and Flint (2017) discuss the origins of the recent reiteration of the MSRI. It focuses on connectivity, including the construction of hard infrastructure projects such as ports, roads and airports. These projects involve different Chinese actors, including the state, state-owned enterprises and private companies. The MSRI underlies Beijing's establishment of itself as a territorial and economic power (ibid.). Examples of such projects in the Pacific Islands include the Santo port facility in Vanuatu, the airport terminal, sports stadium and other infrastructure projects in Samoa, and road projects in Fiji and PNG. There have also been investments in natural resource extractions, such as the Ramu Nickel mine in PNG and the bauxite mine in Bua, Vanua Levu, Fiji. The BRI and MSRI paved the way for the cooperation between China and the Pacific Island countries (Xinhua 2018). Henryk Szadziewski's chapter in this collection examines the BRI in the Pacific Islands. Elsewhere, he has discussed the BRI and anticipations for economic development in Fiji (Szadziewski 2020).

Oceania has been drawn into the contending cartographies of the US and its allies and China. While Asian influences in the Pacific Islands are not new and have increased over time (Crocombe 2007), in recent years Beijing's influence has become more prominent. This was particularly evident following the first China–Pacific Islands Development Cooperation Forum in 2006, at which then Chinese premier Wen Jiabao announced Beijing would give US$492 million (RMB3 billion) in concessional loans to the region's eight Pacific Island countries it has diplomatic relations with. Beijing has backed its assertive diplomacy with financial muscle; its aid to Pacific Island countries has increased in the past decade, making it the second largest donor in the region behind Australia (Brant 2015; Zhang et al. 2019). Most of this aid is in the form of concessional loans (Zhang 2018).

China's increasing influence has generated discussions about its challenge to the dominance of the 'traditional powers'—the US, Australia, France, New Zealand, Great Britain—in the region (see Hanson and Fifita 2011; Henderson and Reilly 2003; Windybank 2005; Yang 2011). But others have also pointed to the complexity of these relationships, Pacific Island countries' agency and how 'new powers' like China provide alternative opportunities for Pacific Island countries (see Porter and Wesley-Smith 2010; Wesley-Smith 2010, 2013). Samoa's Prime Minister Tuilaepa, in commenting on concerns about debts associated with Pacific Islands' relationships with China, said:

> Our partners have fallen short of acknowledging the integrity of Pacific leadership and the responsibility they carry for every decision made in order to garner support for sustainable development in their nations … Some might say there is a patronising nuance in believing Pacific nations did not know what they were doing (Reuters 2018).

Australia and New Zealand have also mapped their interests in the region through 'Pacific Step-Up' and 'Pacific Reset', respectively (Australian Government 2017; New Zealand Government 2018; Wallis and Powles 2018). These initiatives are supported by financial commitments, such as the AU$2 billion Australian Infrastructure Financing Facility for the Pacific (AIFFP), which aims to boost infrastructure development in the Pacific Island countries and Timor-Leste. The AIFFP is administered by the new Office of the Pacific in the Department of Foreign Affairs and Trade (Rajah 2018). Furthermore, Australia offered to pay much of the installation cost for the Coral Sea Cable System, a high-speed communications cable connecting Australia, PNG and Solomon Islands, for the specific purpose of ensuring that the Chinese company Huawei did not get the contract (Remeikis 2018). In the lead-up to the August 2019 PIF meeting in Tuvalu, the Australian Government announced it would commit AU$500 million to finance climate change adaptation efforts in the Pacific Islands (Lyons 2019a). At the same time, Australia is deepening its strategic cooperation with France in the Pacific, and increasingly views France as a counterweight to China.

Other US allies have also enhanced their presence in the region. Great Britain's 'Pacific Uplift' will see it gain a stronger presence in the Pacific by reopening its high commissions in Vanuatu and Tonga, and opening a new one in Samoa. These will add to the current offices in PNG, Solomon Islands and Fiji. The British High Commissioner in Canberra,

Vicki Treadell, stated, 'We're doubling our footprint in the South Pacific … Britain wants to be full-square alongside Australia and other partners to play our part' (Crowe 2019). Indonesia, an important US ally in Southeast Asia, launched its 'Pacific Elevation' in Auckland, New Zealand, in July 2019 (Radio New Zealand 2019c). In October 2019, Jakarta announced it will start a foreign aid program by 2021 with Pacific Island countries as potential beneficiaries (Radio New Zealand 2019d). Also in October 2019, the US announced its 'Pacific Pledge', which includes promises of millions of dollars in assistance to Pacific Island countries (Ewart 2019).

As has been the case in the past, Pacific Island countries were not included in the mapping of the Indo-Pacific and the Maritime Silk Road, or Australia's Pacific Step-Up, New Zealand's Pacific Reset, the Great Britain's Pacific Uplift, Indonesia's Pacific Elevation and the US's Pacific Pledge. But Pacific Island countries are uneasy with these geopolitical, geostrategic and geoeconomic maps. Consequently, they have drawn their own cartography—a countermap called the Blue Pacific.

The Blue Pacific

PIF leaders endorsed the Blue Pacific at their 48th meeting in Apia in September 2017. In addressing the meeting, Samoan Prime Minister and then chair of the forum Tuilaepa Lupesoliai Sailele Malielegaoi urged leaders to 'capture the essence of our Blue Pacific'. He said:

> The Blue Pacific will strengthen the existing policy frameworks that harness the ocean as a driver of transformative socio-cultural, political and economic development of the Pacific … it gives renewed impetus to deepening Pacific regionalism (2017:2).

The Blue Pacific was endorsed 'as the core driver of collective action for advancing the Leaders vision under the Framework for Pacific Regionalism', which was adopted in 2014 (PIF Secretariat 2017:3). PIF leaders also 'recognised the Blue Pacific as a new narrative that calls for inspired leadership and a long-term Forum foreign policy commitment to act as one "Blue Continent"' (ibid.). The communiqué commented on regionalism, identity, the centrality of the ocean and the responsibilities that Pacific Island governments and peoples have to the region and the world.

I propose here that the Blue Pacific has two aspects: a narrative and a strategy. Below, I examine these features, drawing from contemporary and past conversations. I also note that while the term Blue Pacific is relatively new, the ideas underlying it have a longer genealogy.

The Blue Pacific as a narrative

As a narrative, the Blue Pacific offers alternative perspectives about Oceania that are empowering and strengthen regionalism. It also places the Pacific Ocean as central to the region's shared geographies, identities, interconnections and responsibilities. It pushes back on the negative and disempowering narratives that have dominated others' representations of Oceania (Hau'ofa 2008).

First, the Blue Pacific frames the narrative for deeper Pacific regionalism, which was outlined in the Framework for Pacific Regionalism and reiterated in the Blue Pacific. These two documents provide the platform for a renewed commitment to Pacific regionalism and are the core drivers of collective actions (PIF Secretariat 2017:2–3). At the centre of this narrative is the Pacific Ocean, which connects the Pacific Islands and peoples, and is therefore the foundation for collective regional identity and cooperation. Samoa Prime Minister Tuilaepa captured the significance of the ocean:

> For the Pacific region and its island countries, the ocean is crucial. Exercising a sense of common identity and purpose linked to the ocean has been critical for protecting and promoting the potential of our shared Pacific Ocean. It is this commonality of the fundamental essence of the region which has the potential to empower the region through collective and combined agendas and actions. The Blue Pacific will strengthen the existing policy frameworks that harness the ocean as a driver of a transformative sociocultural, political and economic development of the Pacific. Furthermore, it gives renewed impetus to deepening Pacific regionalism (2017:2).

The importance of the ocean in defining Pacific identities and framing regionalism is not new. It was fundamental in the early days of establishing regional organisations such as the PIF (formerly the South Pacific Forum) and determining membership (Bryant-Tokalau and Frazer 2006; Fry 1979, 1997). More recently, Pacific Islander scholars have also pointed to the ocean as a source of inspiration, knowledge and identity. For example,

Teresia Teaiwa writes that 'we sweat and cry salt water, so we know that the ocean is really in our blood' (quoted in Hau'ofa 2008). Epeli Hau'ofa's seminal paper 'Our Sea of Islands' (2008) centres the Pacific Ocean as a source of identity and a pathway that connects the Islands and cultures.

Second, the Blue Pacific narrative presents Oceania as interconnected and vast. It pushes back on stories often peddled by metropolitan countries and their proxies that describe Pacific Island countries in largely negative ways: small, disconnected, isolated, poor and vulnerable. The alternative narrative of the Blue Pacific describes the Pacific Islands as large ocean states or a Blue Continent, rather than small island states. It highlights the fact that Oceania is large, resource rich and interconnected. This is not a mere rhetorical statement. The Pacific Ocean covers one-third of the earth's surface area and hosts rich fisheries resources, land and seabed minerals, forestry and other natural resources. Furthermore, Pacific Islanders have interacted with each other for thousands of years through trades, wars, intermarriages, etc.

Others have previously expressed these ideas about the region's vastness and interconnections. Writing in 1949, for example, Albert Norman (1949) asserted that the view that the Pacific Islands were separated and isolated from each other because of the vastness of the ocean was an illusion, created partly because the colonial powers claimed ownership of what he referred to as the 'visible peaks of the land' (the islands). He suggested that the 'first step in "reclamation" has been to free the land of these bonds, to restore the essential regional viewpoint and unity, to overlook the dividing waters, to see the land and its people as united' (Norman 1949:1). Hau'ofa (2008) also argued that the ocean connects, rather than disconnects, island countries, and that instead of thinking about the Pacific Islands as small and isolated, there is a need to think of the region as vast because it includes the entire ocean. Hau'ofa's paper has had a fundamental impact on academic discussions and has filtered into regional policy discussions as well, as exemplified by the theme of the 2017 PIF leaders meeting: The Blue Pacific—Our Sea of Islands.

Third, the Blue Pacific outlines an expanded concept of security that is inclusive of human security, humanitarian assistance, environmental security and regional cooperation in building resilience to disasters and climate change. This concept encompasses aspects of security such as geopolitics, geostrategy, geoeconomy/spatial and resources. It does not focus exclusively on strategic security.

This concept of expanded security was elaborated in the Boe Declaration, which the PIF adopted in 2018. It commits the PIF countries:

> to strengthening the existing regional security architecture inclusive of regional law enforcement secretariats and regional organisations to: account for the expanded concept of security; identify and address emerging security challenges; improve coordination among existing security mechanism; facilitate open dialogue and strengthened information sharing; further develop early warning mechanisms; support implementation; promote regional security analysis, assessment and advice; and, engage and cooperate, where appropriate, with international organisations, partners and other relevant stakeholders (PIF Secretariat 2018:11).

Within the framework of an expanded security, climate change is an issue that Pacific Island countries see as their most important existential threat. The Boe Declaration states that 'climate change remains the single greatest threat to the livelihoods, security and wellbeing of the peoples of the Pacific and our commitment to progress the implementation of the Paris Agreement' (PIF Secretariat 2018).

This is in contrast to Australia, the largest member of the PIF, but a major coal exporter that focuses primarily on strategic security, as discussed previously. Examples of this focus include the agreements between Washington DC and Canberra to a joint program to upgrade the Lombrum naval base on Manus in PNG, where it is likely Australian Navy vessels will be permanently based (BBC News 2018; Murphy 2018). In Fiji, where China had been seeking to redevelop the Republic of Fiji Military Force Black Rock facility in Nadi for police and peacekeeping training, Australia intervened with a better offer, which was accepted (Radio New Zealand 2019a; Riordan 2018). Both China and Australia presented Fiji with naval vessels in 2018. The Australians supplied the Republic of Fiji Navy Ship (RFNS) *Kikau* after an extensive refit (Singh 2018), while the Chinese gave a new monitoring vessel, RFNS *Kacau* (Talebua 2018).

Furthermore, Australia demonstrated its Pacific Step-Up with its commitment to pay for much of the installation cost of a high-speed fibre optic communications cable connecting Australia, PNG and Solomon Islands for the specific purpose of ensuring that the Chinese company Huawei did not get the contract (Remeikis 2018). The 4,700-kilometre Coral Sea Cable System was completed in September 2019. In a further sign of the Australian Government's new focus on infrastructure, it established the Australian Infrastructure Financing Facility for the Pacific, administered by the Office of the Pacific in the Department of Foreign Affairs and Trade (Rajah 2018).

Fourth, the Blue Pacific narrative highlights the responsibilities and custodianship of PIF members, especially to the health of the ocean. The Framework for Pacific Regionalism states that 'Pacific peoples are the custodians of the world's largest, most peaceful and abundant ocean, its many islands and its rich diversity of cultures' (PIF Secretariat 2014). This is reinforced in the Blue Pacific, which seeks to strengthen states with 'our shared stewardship of the Pacific Ocean and reaffirm the connections of Pacific peoples with their natural resources, environment, culture and livelihoods' (PIF Secretariat 2017:3). Embodied in this is a recognition of a shared 'ocean identity', 'ocean geography' and 'ocean resources' (Taylor 2017). The Boe Declaration also states that PIF countries 'affirm our stewardship of the Blue Pacific and aspire to strengthen and enhance our capacity to pursue our collective security interests given our responsibility to sustain our Pacific peoples and our resource' (PIF Secretariat 2018:10).

Central to Pacific Islanders' responsibility and stewardship is the issue of climate change. Pacific Island countries have taken leadership on this issue because they are at the forefront of climate change impacts, and because many global powers have not prioritised climate change. On this issue, Australia emerges as, at best, hypocritical. As a member state of the PIF, Australia signed the Boe Declaration, then soon afterwards approved the development of giant new coalfields in the Galilee Basin of Queensland, and continues as the world's largest coal exporter. Furthermore, the US withdrew from the Paris Agreement, China is the world's largest investor in coal production, Japan promotes coal-fired power and India is a significant emitter of greenhouse gas. Consequently, PIF members have a responsibility on this issue. In May 2019, during a meeting with PIF leaders in Fiji, the United Nations (UN) Secretary-General António Guterres highlighted the 'unique moral authority that Pacific Island countries have to speak out on climate change issues' (Guterres 2019). He said that 'the continued leadership of the Pacific region will be critical'.

The Pacific Island countries and metropolitan powers differ in what each regards as its central security issue. For metropolitan countries, it is geostrategic concerns, particularly China's growing influence. Pacific Island countries, on the other hand, emphasise climate change as the most important security issue. These differences came to the fore during the PIF leaders meeting in Tuvalu in August 2019. Australia was widely criticised for watering down the language in the communiqué, with Pacific Islands leaders calling for urgent action on climate change (Lyons 2019b).

The Blue Pacific as a strategy

As a strategy, the Blue Pacific does two things. First, it draws an alternative cartography by pushing back on the Indo-Pacific and the Maritime Silk Road, the dominant geopolitical maps drawn by global powers. It gives legibility and prominence to the Pacific Ocean and the Pacific Islands. The primary cartographers are the Pacific Island countries, though Australia and New Zealand are included because of their membership in the PIF. This is not just a geographical map. As discussed previously, it is also a mapping of narratives and issues.

Second, it facilitates an assertive Pacific diplomacy and empowers Pacific Island countries to be more emphatic in pushing for issues that are important to them. This is vital given the increased intensity of geopolitical competition in the region (Morgan 2018). As Prime Minister Tuilaepa states:

> The sheer fact of our geography … places the Pacific at the centre of contemporary global geopolitics … The Blue Pacific provides a new narrative for Pacific regionalism and how the Forum engages with the world (2017:4).

In such an environment, global powers often assume that their values, histories, economic and political systems, interests and security agendas are paramount and worthy of global application.

For most of the post–World War II period, Western countries dominated the region and sought to dictate Island countries' economic, political and strategic agendas. As Taylor states:

> We seem to have found ourselves in a position where some of the decisions about our region are overtly influenced by others. Overdependence on the goodwill of others has left us in a vulnerable state, particularly in relation to the climatic events (Taylor 2019).

Pacific Islanders' assertion of their collective sovereignty is not new. In 1971, the then independent Pacific Island countries established the South Pacific Forum (now known as the PIF) because of their desire to map themselves into regional and international politics and highlight issues they saw as pertinent to the region. This followed Pacific Islanders' dissatisfactions with the colonial powers' dominance of the South Pacific Commission (now the Pacific Community) (Fry 1979, 1993, 2019).

In the subsequent years, the Pacific Island countries have rallied around issues such as decolonisation, anti-nuclear weapons testing (Firth 1986; Maclellan 2017; Regnault 2005; Walker and Sutherland 1988) and resource management, especially tuna fisheries (Hanich et al. 2014). This has led to the numerous regional treaties and declarations that form the foundation of the region's security architecture: the South Pacific Nuclear Free Zone Treaty (also known as the Rarotonga Treaty) (1985); the Honiara Declaration (1991); the Waigani Convention (1995); the Aitutaki Declaration (1997); the Biketawa Declaration (2000); and the Nasonini Declaration (2002). Others such as the Niue Treaty (1992) and its Subsidiary Agreement (2012) and the Vavau Declaration (2007) focused on tuna management, a shared resource that is economically important to Pacific Island states. This illustrates how Pacific Island countries have been mapping their concerns and interests onto regional and international forums, and on issues that have national, regional and global intersections.

The Pacific Island countries have been relatively successful in their collective efforts: most have gained constitutional independence and two colonial territories—New Caledonia and French Polynesia—are on the UN's Decolonization Committee list; nuclear powers such as the US, France and Great Britain stopped their nuclear weapons testing in the region (Maclellan 2005; Regnault 2005); and there are new initiatives in tuna fisheries management, such as the Vessel Day Scheme introduced by the Parties to the Nauru Agreement (Aqorau 2007).

Despite this, Western powers and their allies continue to dominate the region. Their influence has largely been taken for granted during the post–Cold War period. It was assumed that, with the collapse of the former Soviet Union and no one to challenge the power of Western countries, the Pacific Ocean would become an Anglo-Francophone lake shared with Japan. Pacific Island countries were largely marginalised in the geopolitical discussions (Fry 1993, 2019). US influence is predominantly in the northern Pacific with the former Trust Territories—Palau, Federated States of Micronesia (FSM), Marshall Islands—Guåhan/Guam and the Commonwealth of the Northern Marianas (CNMI). This includes military bases in Guåhan/Guam, CNMI and Kwajalein in the Marshall Islands (Scott 2012). In the South Pacific, it is American Samoa, an unincorporated territory of the US. The French have influence in New Caledonia, French Polynesia and Wallis and Futuna. Australia and New Zealand are members of the PIF and have immense influence in the South Pacific, though they have some differences in the ways in which they relate to the region in terms of policies and approaches (Wallis and Powles 2018). Japan's influence has largely been through its development assistance programs (Tarte 1998). Tokyo also hosts the annual Pacific Islands leaders meeting, which gives Japan access to Pacific Island leaders. In the past decade, Indonesia has asserted itself as an emerging geopolitical and economic power in the region, especially in Melanesia, though this has often been met with resistance, primarily due to some Pacific Islands countries' concerns about the Indonesian Government's violent reprisals against pro-independence supporters in West Papua since the 1960s (Kabutaulaka 2015b; Lawson 2016). As stated previously, Indonesia has followed Australia and New Zealand by announcing its Pacific Elevation policy (Radio New Zealand 2019b, 2019c), with a plan to become an aid donor by 2021 (Radio New Zealand 2019d).

China's increasing influence has caused a renewed interest in the region. This has given Pacific Island countries the opportunity to forge and strengthen alternative relationships, including with China. In choosing to do so, Pacific Island states have asserted their sovereignty. For example, in September 2019, Solomon Islands and Kiribati severed diplomatic ties with Taiwan and established relations with the People's Republic of China (PRC). This was despite the US and Australia cautioning them not to make the switch. This caution was particularly evident in the case of Solomon Islands. On 9 September 2019, a joint mission from the US, Australia, New Zealand and Japan, headed by US ambassador Catherine Ebert-Gray, met with officials from the Solomon Islands prime minister's office. Records of the meeting indicate that then US Vice President Mike Pence had previously communicated with the Solomon Islands Prime Minister Manasseh Sogavare and that there was a mutual agreement that Solomon Islands' decision on whether or not to switch diplomatic relations to the PRC would be held off until the two leaders had met at the margins of the UN General Assembly meeting later that month. Furthermore, the US:

signaled their interest in Bina Harbour with the view to broaden the concept to a commercial and economic Centre for Malaita that goes beyond the current concept of the international wharf and fish facility to include establishment of a Centre for maritime surveillance and training for maritime security, upgrades of road links with Auki and southern part of Malaita, new access road to Aluta basing and extending the submarine cable link from Auki to Bina via terrestrial cable connection. This would be a mega investment and it would be grant funded (Office of the Prime Minister and Cabinet 2019).

Despite this, in an assertive demonstration of its sovereignty, Solomon Islands established diplomatic relations with the PRC on 21 September 2019 (Al Jazeera 2019).

Such assertive diplomacy is also being demonstrated at the regional level in what Fry and Tarte (2015) have referred to as the 'new Pacific diplomacy' and what the former Kiribati president Anote Tong calls a 'paradigm shift' (2015). It is characterised by 'a fundamental shift in the way that Pacific Island states engage with regional and world politics' (Fry and Tarte 2015:3). This assertive Pacific diplomacy has seen Island governments resisting the dominance of Western countries and the establishment of new regional organisations such as the Pacific Islands Development Forum (PIDF) in 2013. The PIDF excludes Australia and New Zealand, promotes inclusiveness of state and non-state entities in regional discussions and has taken leadership on issues such as climate change that are seen as central to Pacific Islanders' concerns (Tarte 2015).

As the PIF Secretariat (2018) stated, the Blue Pacific was part of 'responses to specific shifts in the regional or global security landscape', but also an attempt to reiterate Pacific Islands' agency and the importance of the region's own security architectures in this changing regional order. Further, 'our region has and continues to experience shifts in the security environment since the early 2000's but our regional security architecture has remained largely static' (PIF Secretariat 2018). In its 2017 communiqué, the PIF stated that the Blue Pacific 'provides a political platform that enables Forum Leaders to assert their collective sovereignty over the Pacific Vision into the future' (PIF Secretariat 2017).

Central to Pacific Island countries' diplomatic assertiveness is the issue of climate change, on which they have mapped a path that is fundamentally different from that of Australia, the US and other metropolitan powers.

Pacific Island leadership on climate change is evident not only at the regional level, but also at the international level. For example, in 2017, Fiji took on the presidency of the UN COP 23—the annual Conference of the Parties to the 1992 UN Framework Convention on Climate Change.

Pacific Island leaders have also been critical of the policies and actions of the 'traditional powers' in the region. In December 2018, for example, Tuvalu Prime Minister Enele Sopoaga called on Australia to include climate change action as part of its Pacific Step-Up. He warned that Canberra's inaction could undermine its Pacific pivot, saying:

> We cannot be regional partners under this Step-Up initiative— genuine and durable partners—unless the government of Australia takes a more progressive response to climate change … They know very well that we will not be happy as a partner, to move forward, unless they are serious (Dziedzic 2018).

Similarly, when Australian Prime Minister Scott Morrison visited Fiji on 17 January 2019, Fiji Prime Minister Voreqe Bainimarama told him, 'Here in Fiji, climate change is no laughing matter'. This was in reference to an incident in 2015 when then Australian immigration minister Peter Dutton joked about the fate of Pacific Islanders in the face of climate change, prompting laughter from then prime minister Tony Abbott (Dziedzic and Handley 2019). Bainimarama (2019) went on to highlight the seriousness of the impacts of climate change and was also critical of Canberra putting the interests of the coal industry ahead of the welfare of Pacific Islanders:

> From where we are sitting, we cannot imagine how the interest of any particular industry can be placed above the welfare of Pacific peoples—vulnerable people in the world over (Dziedzic and Handley 2019).

In the past decade, climate change has become the rallying issue for Pacific Island states and non-state entities, triggering the region to be more vocal and assertive. It has also influenced the manner in which Pacific Island countries organise themselves and participate in regional and international forums (Carter 2015; Goulding 2015). Climate change has influenced the nature and dynamics of Pacific diplomacy, similar to how, in the 1980s and 1990s, tuna fisheries influenced diplomacy between Pacific Island countries and distant-water fishing nations (Aqorau 2015). For both climate change and tuna fisheries, much of the diplomacy is about defining and asserting the interests of the Pacific Island countries and pushing back on global powers. This is similar to the assertive diplomacy seen during the height of the anti-nuclear testing era (Firth 1986).

Climate change has also influenced institutional changes within Pacific regional governance (Tarte 2014). The Pacific Small Islands Developing States Group (PSIDS) are more assertive on issues such as climate change. Fry and Tarte (2015:7) point out:

> PSIDS has taken on a dramatically new diplomatic role for the Pacific Island states since 2009, to the point where it has all but replaced the PIF as the primary organising forum for Pacific representations at the global level.

Manoa (2015) examines and discusses in detail the roles and assertiveness of PSIDS at UN forums, especially around climate change issues.

On the issue of China's increasing influence, some Pacific Island leaders view Beijing as another development partner, rather than a threat. For example, Vanuatu's Minister of Foreign Affairs and Trade Ralph Regenvanu welcomed Chinese aid and investments in his country while admitting the 'extra diplomatic pressure', saying:

> It has been good for us. The blow-up has made Australia much more interested. They have committed to build the police college for us. They have committed to picking up the national security standard. They have talked about being much more interested in improving work strategies. They have been talking about improving infrastructure. So, great (Duffield 2018).

He went on to describe China as:

> a great partner, I think far more respectful of us as government-to-government diplomatic representatives than Australia. They don't presume like Australia. They can be just as forceful, but Australia has got the gold medal for that one (ibid.).

Similarly, in response to criticism by Australia's then international development minister Concetta Fierravanti-Wells that Beijing was building 'roads to nowhere' and 'useless buildings', Samoan Prime Minister Tuilaepa called the criticism insulting to Pacific Islands leaders, saying, 'The comments seem to question the integrity, wisdom and intelligence of the leaders of the Pacific Islands' (Hill 2018).

The aforementioned demonstrates how the Blue Pacific has mobilised the Pacific Island countries and asserts their views and interests in the face of a changing regional order. As Wesley Morgan pointed out, 'if traditional powers want Pacific Islands to endorse their vision for a free and open Indo-Pacific they will need to take the concerns of island states seriously' (2018:4).

The power of the Blue Pacific

This chapter illustrates the power of the Blue Pacific as a framework for regionalism and assertive diplomacy in a changing regional order where global powers are attempting to map their geopolitical interests onto the region. The most dominant maps are the Indo-Pacific and the Maritime Silk Road. Australia, New Zealand, Great Britain, Indonesia and the US have also mapped their interests through initiatives such as the Pacific Step-Up, Pacific Reset, Pacific Uplift, Pacific Elevation and Pacific Pledge, respectively. Pacific Island countries have responded by establishing the Blue Pacific narrative, which frames regional cooperation, pushes back on the geopolitical maps imposed by the global powers and asserts the interests, concerns and priorities of the Pacific Island countries.

The Blue Pacific is both a narrative and a strategy. As a narrative, it frames Pacific regionalism by placing the Pacific Ocean at the centre of Pacific Island countries' identities and interconnections. It tells a story of empowerment, which describes Pacific Island countries as 'large ocean states' and a Blue Continent, rather than small island countries. It also outlines Pacific Island countries' responsibilities and stewardship, especially to the ocean and taking a leadership role in addressing issues such as climate change. This narrative pushes back on global powers' focus on strategic security, which has triggered geopolitical competitions, especially between the US and its allies on one hand and China on the other. Instead, it highlights climate change as the central security issue, not only for Pacific Island countries, but globally. This is articulated in the Boe Declaration, which provides for a broad and inclusive definition of security.

As a strategy, the Blue Pacific facilitates Pacific Island countries' assertion of their views at regional and global discussions. It is what I refer to here as 'assertive Pacific diplomacy'—Pacific Island countries' proactive and emphatic assertion of their agendas and priorities. This empowers them to organise as a region and push back on the dominance of metropolitan powers. Consequently, Pacific Island countries are working to strengthen existing regional organisations and establish new ones, like the PIDF.

In the midst of intense geopolitical competition and the changing regional order, Pacific Island countries have asserted their sovereignty by choosing and strengthening diplomatic relations with whomever they want. They have maintained their rapport with traditional development partners, but have also forged and strengthened relationships with new powers in the region, including China. Ten Pacific Island countries now have diplomatic relationships with China, while four have relationships with Taiwan. Beijing's increasing influence has raised concern amongst the Indo-Pacific alliance. For Pacific Island countries, the choice to have diplomatic relations with anyone is a right, an affirmation of their sovereignty and the fact that they are global players in their own rights. The Blue Pacific narrative gives Pacific Island countries the confidence and the framework to assert that sovereign right.

The Blue Pacific is an example of countermapping by Pacific Island countries, drawing their own map in the face of increased geopolitical interest. This is difficult in a region where, despite constitutional independence, Pacific Island countries are economically dependent on metropolitan countries that often use that dependence as leverage to exert political influence. It is a situation where former colonial powers still have significant influence. In some of these Island places, the colonial powers never left. These include the French territories (New Caledonia, Wallis and Futuna and French Polynesia), the US's unincorporated territories and commonwealth (Guåhan/Guam, American Samoa and CNMI) and Chile in Rapanui/Easter Island. For Palau, the FSM and the Marshall Islands, the US still has a lot of influence through the Compact of Free Association agreements. The Cook Islands and Niue are self-governing, but intricately tied to New Zealand. In this situation, where Pacific Island countries' affairs are deeply intertwined with those of metropolitan countries, the entrance of a new power like China could potentially destabilise the dominant regional order, therefore giving Pacific Island countries the opportunity to draw their own maps. In this case, they have drawn the Blue Pacific and used it as a narrative and a strategy to chart alternative futures in a changing regional order.

The power of the Blue Pacific lies in its ability to mobilise Pacific Island countries, strengthen regional solidarity and assert their sovereignty in the international arena. So far, Pacific Island countries have been able to make global powers pay attention to issues that are important to them. Consequently, these countries are mapping the Blue Pacific as an alternative geopolitical map that defines the new regional order.

References

Al Jazeera 2019. China, Solomon Islands Establish Diplomatic Relations. 21 September. www.aljazeera.com/news/2019/09/china-solomon-islands-establish-diplomatic-relations-190921111348417.html

Aqorau, T. 2007. Moving towards a Rights-Based Fisheries Management Regime for the Tuna Fisheries in the Western and Central Pacific Ocean. *Journal of International Marine and Coastal Law* 22(1):125–42. doi.org/10.1163/1571 80807781475290

Aqorau, T. 2015. How Tuna is Shaping Regional Diplomacy. In G. Fry and S. Tarte (eds), *The New Pacific Diplomacy*. Canberra: ANU Press, 223–36. doi.org/10.22459/NPD.12.2015.18

Australian Government 2017. *2017 Foreign Policy White Paper: Opportunity Security Strength*. Canberra: Department of Foreign Affairs and Trade.

Ayson, R. 2007. The 'Arc of Instability' and Australia's Strategic Policy. *Australian Journal of International Affairs* 61(2):215–31. doi.org/10.1080/103577107 01358360

Bainimarama, F. 2019. Hon. PM Bainimarama's Remarks at Welcome Dinner for Australian Prime Minister Scott Morrison. The Fijian Government, 17 January. www.fiji.gov.fj/Media-Centre/Speeches/HON-PM-BAINIMARAMA-S-REMARKS-AT-WELCOME-DINNER-FOR

BBC News 2018. US to Join Australia in Papua New Guinea Naval Base Plan. 17 November. www.bbc.com/news/world-asia-46247446

Blanchard, J.-M. and C. Flint 2017. The Geopolitics of China's Maritime Silk Road Initiative. *Geopolitics* 22(2):223–45. doi.org/10.1080/14650045.2017. 1291503

Brant, P. 2015. The Geopolitics of Chinese Aid: Mapping Beijing's Funding in the Pacific Islands. *Foreign Affairs*, 4 March. www.foreignaffairs.com/articles/143224/philippa-brant/the-geopolitics-of-chinese-aid

Brewster, D. 2018. A 'Free and Open Indo-Pacific' and What It Means for Australia. *The Interpreter*, 7 March. Lowy Institute. www.lowyinstitute.org/the-interpreter/free-and-open-indo-pacific-and-what-it-means-australia

Bryant-Tokalau, J. and I. Frazer (eds) 2006. *Redefining the Pacific?: Regionalism Past, Present and Future*. London: Ashgate Publishing.

Campbell, I.C. 1989. *A History of the Pacific Islands*. Los Angeles: University of California Press.

Carter, G. 2015. Establishing a Pacific Voice in the Climate Change Negotiations. In G. Fry and S. Tarte (eds), *The New Pacific Diplomacy*. Canberra: ANU Press, 205–22. doi.org/10.22459/NPD.12.2015.17

Clinton, H. 2011. America's Pacific Century. *Foreign Policy*, 11 October. www.foreignpolicy.com/2011/10/11/americas-pacific-century/

Crocombe, R. 2007. *Asia in the Pacific Islands: Replacing the West*. Suva: Institute of Pacific Studies.

Crowe, D. 2019. Keep Calm and Remember History, Says British High Commissioner. *The Sydney Morning Herald*, 23 July. www.smh.com.au/politics/federal/keep-calm-and-remember-history-says-british-high-commissioner-20190723-p52a09.html

Department of Defense 2019. *Indo-Pacific Strategy Report: Preparedness, Partnerships, and Promoting a Networked Region*. Washington DC: Department of Defense.

Dobell, G. 2007. The 'Arc of Instability': The History of an Idea. In R. Huisken and M. Thatcher (eds), *History as Policy: Framing the Debate on the Future of Australia's Defence Policy*. Canberra: ANU E Press, 85–104. doi.org/10.22459/HP.12.2007.06

Douglas, B. 2011. Geography, Raciology, and the Naming of Oceania. *The Globe: Journal of Australia and New Zealand Map Society* 69:1–28.

Duffield, L. 2018. Vanuatu Digs in on Chinese Presence—Foreign Minister Says It's 'Great'. *Independent Australia*, 28 July. www.independentaustralia.net/politics/politics-display/vanuatu-digs-in-on-chinese-presence--foreign-minister-says-its-great,11731

Dziedzic, S. 2018. Tuvalu Prime Minister Enele Sopoaga Says Australia's Climate Change Inaction Undermines Its 'Pacific Pivot'. *ABC News*, 4 December. www.abc.net.au/news/2018-12-04/tuvalu-pm-says-australian-pacific-pivot-undermined-by-emissions/10579424

Dziedzic, S. and E. Handley 2019. Climate Change Is 'No Laughing Matter', Fiji's PM Frank Bainimarama Tells Australia during Scott Morrison's Pacific Trip. *ABC News*, 19 January. www.abc.net.au/news/2019-01-18/climate-change-is-no-laughing-matter-fiji-pm-says/10724582

Ewart, R. 2019. US Pacific Pledge—How Does the Spin Stand Up to Scrutiny? *ABC News*, 23 October. www.abc.net.au/radio-australia/programs/pacificbeat/us-pacific-pledge-analysis/11630234

Firth, S. 1986. The Nuclear Issue in the Pacific Islands. *The Journal of Pacific History* 21(4): 202–16. doi.org/10.1080/00223348608572543

Fry, G. 1979. South Pacific Regionalism: The Development of an Indigenous Commitment. Master's thesis, Department of Political Science School of General Studies, The Australian National University.

Fry, G. 1993. At the Margin: The South Pacific and Changing World Order. In R. Leaver and J.L. Richardson (eds), *Charting the Post-Cold War Order*. San Francisco: Westview Press, 224–41.

Fry, G. 1997. The Pacific 'Experiment': Reflections on the Origins of Regional Identity. *The Journal of Pacific History* 32(2):180–202. doi.org/10.1080/00223349708572837

Fry, G. 2019. *Framing the Islands: Power and Diplomatic Agency in Pacific Regionalism*. Canberra: ANU Press. doi.org/10.22459/FI.2019

Fry, G. and S. Tarte (eds) 2015. *The New Pacific Diplomacy*. Canberra: ANU Press. doi.org/10.22459/NPD.12.2015

Goulding, N. 2015. Marshalling a Pacific Response to Climate Change. In G. Fry and S. Tarte (eds), *The New Pacific Diplomacy*. Canberra: ANU Press, 191–204. doi.org/10.22459/NPD.12.2015.16

Guterres, A. 2019. Pacific Islands Have Unique Moral Authority to Speak Out on Climate Change, Secretary-General Emphasizes at Forum Leaders Meeting. UN Secretary-General António Guterres' remarks at the Pacific Island Forum Leaders meeting in Suva, Fiji, 15 May. www.un.org/press/en/2019/sgsm19579.doc.htm

Hanich, Q., M. Tsamenyi and H. Parris 2014. Sovereignty and Cooperation in Regional Tuna Fisheries Management: Politics, Economics, Conservation and the Vessel Day Scheme. *Australian Journal of Maritime & Ocean Affairs* 2(1):2–15. doi.org/10.1080/18366503.2010.10815650

Hanson, F. and M. Fifita 2011. China in the Pacific: The New Banker in Town. *Issues & Insights* 11(5) April.

Harley, B.J. 1992. *History of Cartography, Vol. 1*. Chicago: University of Chicago Press.

Harley, B.J. 2009. Maps, Knowledge, and Power. In G. Henderson and M. Waterstone (eds), *Geographic Thought: A Praxis Perspective*. New York: Routledge, 129–48.

Hauʻofa, E. 2008. Our Sea of Islands. In E. Hauʻofa. *We Are the Ocean: Selected Works*. Honolulu: University of Hawaiʻi Press.

Henderson, J. and B. Reilly 2003. Dragon in Paradise: China's Rising Star in Oceania. *The National Interest* 72(Summer):94–104.

Herr, R.A. 1986. Regionalism, Strategic Denial and South Pacific Security. *The Journal of Pacific History* 21(4):170–82. doi.org/10.1080/0022334860 8572541

Hill, B. 2018. Samoan PM Hits Back at Australia's 'Insulting' Criticism of China's Aid Program in Pacific. *ABC News*, 12 January. www.abc.net.au/news/2018-01-12/samoan-prime-minister-hits-back-at-insulting-china-aid-comments/9323420

Howe, K.R., R.C. Kiste and B.V. Lal (eds) 1994. *Tides of History: The Pacific Islands in the Twentieth Century* Honolulu: University of Hawaiʻi Press.

Kabutaulaka, T. 2015a. Re-Presenting Melanesia: Ignoble Savages and Melanesian Alter-Natives. *The Contemporary Pacific* 27(1):110–45. doi.org/10.1353/cp. 2015.0027

Kabutaulaka, T. 2015b. West Papua: MSG's Challenge, Indonesian's Melanesian Foray. *Pacific Islands Report*, 16 June. www.pireport.org/articles/2015/06/16/west-papua-msgâ%C2%80%C2%99s-challenge-indonesiaâ%C2%80%C2%99s-melanesian-foray

Klinghoffer, A.J. 2006. *The Power of Projections: How Maps Reflect Global Politics and History*. London: Praeger Publishers.

Lawson, S. 2016. West Papua, Indonesia and the Melanesian Spearhead Group: Competing Logic in Regional and International Politics. *Australian Journal of International Affairs* 70(5): 506–24. doi.org/10.1080/10357718.2015. 1119231

Lyons, K. 2019a. Australia Will Fund a $500 Million Climate Change Package for the Pacific, PM to Announce. *The Guardian*, 12 August. www.theguardian. com/world/2019/aug/12/australia-will-fund-a-500m-climate-change-package-for-the-pacific-pm-to-announce

Lyons, K. 2019b. Australia Waters Down Pacific Islands Plea on Climate Crisis. *The Guardian*, 16 August. www.theguardian.com/world/2019/aug/15/australia-waters-down-pacific-islands-plea-on-climate-crisis

Maclellan, N. 2005. The Nuclear Age in the Pacific Islands. *The Contemporary Pacific* 17(2): 363–72. doi.org/10.1353/cp.2005.0062

Maclellan, N. 2017. *Grappling with the Bomb: Britain's Pacific H-Bomb Tests*. Canberra: ANU Press. doi.org/10.22459/GB.09.2017

Manoa, F. 2015. The New Pacific Diplomacy at the United Nations: The Rise of the PSIDS. In G. Fry and S. Tarte (eds), *The New Pacific Diplomacy*. Canberra: ANU Press, 89–100. doi.org/10.22459/NPD.12.2015.08

Matsuda, M.K. 2012. *Pacific Worlds: A History of Seas, Peoples and Cultures*. Cambridge: Cambridge University Press.

Medcalf, R. 2014. In Defence of the Indo-Pacific: Australia's New Strategic Map. *Australian Journal of International Affairs* 68(4):470–83. doi.org/10.1080/10357718.2014.911814

Morgan, W. 2018. The Indo-Pacific and the Blue Pacific. *Devpolicy Blog*, 22 August. www.devpolicy.org/the-indo-pacific-and-the-blue-pacific-20180822/

Murphy, K. 2018. America to Partner with Australia to Develop Naval Base on Manus Island. *The Guardian*, 18 November. www.theguardian.com/australia-news/2018/nov/18/america-to-partner-with-australia-to-develop-naval-base-on-manus-island

New Zealand Government 2018. *Strategic Policy Statement 2018*. Wellington: Ministry of Defence, New Zealand Government.

Norman, A. 1949. Reclamation in Oceania: Australian Smoke Signal. *The Christian Science Monitor*, 4 June.

Obama, B. 2011. Remarks by President Obama to the Australian Parliament. The White House, Office of the Press Secretary, 17 November. obamawhitehouse.archives.gov/the-press-office/2011/11/17/remarks-president-obama-australian-parliament

Office of the Prime Minister and Cabinet (Solomon Islands) 2019. Minutes of Meeting with a Joint Mission from USA, Australia, New Zealand and Japan. Secretary to Prime Minister, 9 September.

Peluso, N.L. 1995. Whose Woods Are These? Counter-Mapping Forest Territories in Kalimantan, Indonesia. *Antipode* 27(4):383–406. doi.org/10.1111/j.1467-8330.1995.tb00286.x

PIF (Pacific Islands Forum) Secretariat 2014. The Framework for Pacific Regionalism. Suva: PIF Secretariat. www.adb.org/sites/default/files/linked-documents/robp-pacific-2016-2018-ld-04.pdf

PIF (Pacific Islands Forum) Secretariat 2017. Forum Communiqué. Forty-Eighth Pacific Islands Forum. Apia, Samoa, 5–8 September.

PIF (Pacific Islands Forum) Secretariat 2018. Forum Communiqué. Forty-Ninth Pacific Islands Forum. Yaren, Nauru, 3–6 September.

Porter, E.A. and T. Wesley-Smith 2010. Introduction: Oceania Matters. In T. Wesley-Smith and E.A. Porter (eds), *China in Oceania: Reshaping the Pacific?* New York: Berghahn Books, 1–26.

Radio New Zealand 2019a. Fiji and Australia Sign Deal over Blackrock. 17 April. www.rnz.co.nz/international/pacific-news/387236/fiji-and-australia-sign-deal-over-blackrock

Radio New Zealand 2019b. Jakarta Ushering in New Era in Pacific Engagement—Marsudi. 13 July. www.rnz.co.nz/international/pacific-news/394277/jakarta-ushering-in-new-era-in-pacific-engagement-marsudi

Radio New Zealand 2019c. Indonesia's 'Pacific Elevation': Step Up or Power Play? 15 July. www.rnz.co.nz/international/pacific-news/394434/indonesia-s-pacific-elevation-step-up-or-power-play

Radio New Zealand 2019d. Jakarta Forms New Agency to Coordinate Overseas Aid. 24 October. www.rnz.co.nz/international/programmes/datelinepacific/audio/2018719037/jakarta-forms-new-agency-to-co-ordinate-overseas-aid

Rajah, R. 2018. Stepping up on Pacific Infrastructure. *The Interpreter*, 20 December. Lowy Institute. www.lowyinstitute.org/the-interpreter/stepping-pacific-infrastructure

Regnault, J-M. 2005. The Nuclear Issue in the South Pacific: Labor Parties, Trade Union Movements, and Pacific Island Churches in International Relations. *The Contemporary Pacific* 17(2):339–57.

Remeikis, A. 2018. Australia Supplants China to Build Undersea Cable for Solomon Islands. *The Guardian*, 13 June. www.theguardian.com/world/2018/jun/13/australia-supplants-china-to-build-undersea-cable-for-solomon-islands

Reuters 2018. Lenders Not to Blame for Ballooning Pacific Debts—Samoa PM. 30 August. uk.reuters.com/article/uk-pacific-debt-samoa-idUKKCN1LF1C6

Riordan, P. 2018. Australia Beats China to Funding Fiji Base. *The Australian*, 7 September. www.theaustralian.com.au/nation/defence/australia-beats-china-to-funding-fiji-base/news-story/60d05ca8eb2bec629080c2c844255bbd

Scott, D. 2012. US Strategy in the Pacific—Geopolitical Positioning in the Twenty-First Century. *Geopolitics* 17(3):607–28. doi.org/10.1080/14650045.2011.631200

Scott, J.C. 1998. *Seeing Like a State: How Certain Schemes to Improve the Human Condition Have Failed*. New Haven: Yale University Press.

Singh, A. 2018. RFNS Kikau Returned to Fiji Navy after Significant Restorative Repair in Cairns, Australia. *Fijivillage.com*, 26 July. fijivillage.com/news/RFNS-Kikau-returned-to-Fiji-Navy-after-significant-restorative-repair-in-Cairns-Australia-rsk259

Szadziewski, H. 2020. Converging Anticipatory Geographies in Oceania: The Belt and Road Initiative Look North in Fiji. *Political Geography* 77:1–10. doi.org/10.1016/j.polgeo.2019.102119

Talebua, W. 2018. Kacau Strengthens Fiji–China Ties. *Fiji Sun*, 22 December. fijisun.com.fj/2018/12/22/kacau-strengthens-fiji-china-ties/

Tarte, S. 1998. *Japan's Aid Diplomacy and the Pacific Islands*. Canberra and Suva: National Centre for Development Studies, ANU, and the Institute of Pacific Studies, USP.

Tarte, S. 2014. Regionalism and Changing Regional Order in the Pacific Islands. *Asia & the Pacific Policy Studies* 1(2):312–24. doi.org/10.1002/app5.27

Tarte, S. 2015. A New Regional Voice?: The Pacific Islands Development Forum. In G. Fry and S. Tarte (eds), *The New Pacific Diplomacy*. Canberra: ANU Press, 79–88. doi.org/10.22459/NPD.12.2015.02

Taylor, M. 2017. Secretary-General Dame Meg Taylor's Opening Remarks to the 2017 Pacific Update. University of the South Pacific, Laucala Campus, 20 June. www.forumsec.org/secretary-general-dame-meg-taylors-opening-remarks-to-the-2017-pacific-update/

Taylor, M. 2019. Blue Pacific—Reclaiming Oceanic Futures. Keynote address at the Center for Pacific Islands Studies Students Conference Blue Pacific: Reclaiming Oceania, Kamakakūokalani Center for Hawaiian Studies, University of Hawai'i, 15–16 March.

Tong, A. 2015. Charting Its Own Course: A Paradigm Shift in Pacific Diplomacy. In G. Fry and S. Tarte (eds), *The New Pacific Diplomacy*. Canberra: ANU Press, 21–26. doi.org/10.22459/NPD.12.2015.02

Tuilaepa, L.S.M. 2017. Opening Address by the Hon. Tuilaepa Lupesoliai Sailele Malielegaoi Prime Minister of the Independent State of Samoa and Chair of the 48th Pacific Islands Forum Leaders Meeting. Robert Louis Stevenson Museum, Vailima, Samoa, 5 September.

Wallis, J. and A. Powles 2018. *Australia and New Zealand in the Pacific Islands: Ambiguous Allies?* The Centre of Gravity Series. Canberra: Strategic and Defense Studies Centre, College of Asia and the Pacific, The Australian National University.

Walker, R. and W. Sutherland (eds) 1988. *The Pacific: Peace, Security & the Nuclear Issue.* Zed Books for United Nations University Studies on Peace and Regional Security.

Wang, J. 2011. China's Search for a Grand Strategy: A Rising Great Power Finds Its Way. *Foreign Affairs* 90(2):68–79.

Wesley-Smith, T. 2010. China's Pacific Engagement. In T. Wesley-Smith and E.A. Porter (eds), *China in Oceania: Reshaping the Pacific?* New York: Berghahn Books, 27–48.

Wesley-Smith, T. 2013. China's Rise in Oceania: Issues and Perspectives. *Pacific Affairs* 86(2):352–72. doi.org/10.5509/2013862351

Windybank, S. 2005. The China Syndrome. *Policy* 21(2):28–33.

Woodward, J. 2017. *The US vs China: Asia's New Cold War?* Manchester: Manchester University Press. doi.org/10.7228/manchester/9781526121998.001.0001

Xinhua 2018. BRI Paves Way for China–Pacific Islands Cooperation. *China Daily*, 18 November. www.chinadailyhk.com/articles/28/173/13/1542535066071.html

Yang, J. 2011. *The Pacific Islands in China's Grand Strategy: Small States, Big Games.* New York: Palgrave Macmillan. doi.org/10.1057/9780230339750_9

Zhang, D. 2018. China, India and Japan in the Pacific: Latest Developments and Impact. DPA Discussion Paper 2018/6. Canberra: The Australian National University.

Zhang, D., D. Leiva and M. Ruwet 2019. Similar Patterns? Chinese Aid to Island Countries in the Pacific and the Caribbean. *DPA In Brief* 2019/19. Canberra: The Australian National University.

2

A New Cold War? Implications for the Pacific Islands[1]

Terence Wesley-Smith

In 2012 former president of Kiribati Anote Tong welcomed increased interest in the Pacific Islands by external powers, commenting that it is 'nice to be relevant' (Tong 2015). He also noted significant changes in the way that leaders were dealing with outside forces impacting the region, a shift that Greg Fry and Sandra Tarte argued represented a 'new Pacific diplomacy'. Characterised by an emphasis on self-determination exercised through new institutions and focused on addressing relevant global issues, particularly climate change, Fry and Tarte identified 'a time of transformation of the regional diplomatic culture equivalent to the move from the colonial to the postcolonial era, a time that represents a transformation of regional order' (Fry and Tarte 2015:4). Yet just a few years later, the region appears to be entering another transition occasioned by the very geopolitical changes welcomed by President Tong and associated with the expanding influence of China.

Until recently, commentators have been sanguine about the impact of China's growing presence in the region, noting advantages such as new diplomatic, trade and investment opportunities for Pacific Island states (see, for example,

1   Many thanks to Greg Fry and Graeme Smith for their very useful comments and suggestions on an earlier version of this chapter.

D'Arcy 2016; Wesley-Smith 2013, 2016). These sentiments were not necessarily shared by representatives of more established external actors in the region, particularly Australia, New Zealand and the United States, worried about erosion of their longstanding influence in regional affairs. Nevertheless, officials adopted a generally pragmatic attitude, perhaps swayed by China's preference for working within established economic and political systems rather than attempting to replace them. In 2012, then US secretary of state Hillary Clinton told a news conference in Cook Islands that the Pacific 'is big enough for all of us' and went on to say, 'We think it is important for the Pacific Island nations to have good relationships with as many partners as possible, and that includes China as well as the United States' (Dziedzic 2012).

Two main factors have conspired to upset Clinton's attitude to regional developments. First, China has embarked on a more assertive and ambitious phase in its rise to global power. In 2017, five years into his tenure as Communist Party General Secretary, President Xi Jinping announced that China had 'crossed the threshold into a new era' (McCahill 2017:2). Buoyed by constitutional changes consolidating his hold on domestic power, Xi Jinping's 'Chinese Dream' imagines a proud China restored to its former status as a global actor, pursuing its interests through expanded networks of trade and diplomacy backed by a rapidly modernising military. Xi's signature diplomatic and economic program, now known as the Belt and Road Initiative (BRI), is massive in scale and aspiration. His attitude to the eventual reintegration of Taiwan has hardened considerably and his actions in the South China Sea, including building militarised artificial islands, leave no doubt about China's determination to establish 'a maritime sphere of influence with exclusive rights to resources' in what China terms its 'near seas' periphery (Roy 2014). There are clear signs in all of these developments that Beijing is now prepared to challenge a global order long dominated by the United States, at least when it considers it necessary to do so.

Second, and of more immediate importance, existing power holders have responded more forcefully to the challenges of China's rise. US President Obama's administration recognised the significance of developments in China for American power and attempted to counter them through a strategic 'pivot' to the Asia-Pacific region, as well as efforts to consolidate US relations with regional countries, particularly through the Trans-Pacific Partnership trade agreement. But the Trump administration abandoned any pretence at soft balancing and labelled China a strategic rival and evil actor. A report to the US Congress in November 2018 declared that 'many aspects of China's attempts to seize leadership have undoubtedly put at risk the national security and economic interests of the United States, its allies, and its partners' (USCC 2018:vii). In a speech to the Hudson Institute the previous month, Vice President Mike Pence roundly condemned Beijing's authoritarian domestic activities and expansionist aspirations and promised 'strong and swift action' in response to any violations of international norms (Pence 2018). As Zachary Karabell points out, Pence's remarks were reminiscent of Churchill's 1946 Iron Curtain speech signalling the start of the Cold War with the Soviet Union (2018:1). Indeed, it has become commonplace for US officials and commentators to talk of the escalating US–China contest as 'nothing less than a new cold war', even if their understanding of what that means differ (Kaplan 2019:2; see also Tarabay 2018; White 2019). Whatever its characteristics, as Stephen Walt argues, this 'will be the single most important feature of world politics for at least the next decade and probably well beyond that' (2018:3).

This chapter explores some implications of these geopolitical developments for the Pacific Islands, and particularly for president Tong's vision of a region striving to 'chart its own course' (Tong 2015:24). It is worth noting that the impacts on the region of the Cold War with the Soviet Union were profound, shaping the process of decolonisation in significant ways, and establishing patterns of 'development assistance' (and aid dependency) that persist to this day. Although Fry argues that US, British and French nuclear testing programs in the region would have proceeded regardless, Cold War dynamics enhanced their importance, with catastrophic consequences for some island populations (Fry 1993:227–29). The underlying rationale for Western foreign policy initiatives towards the region for most of this period was strategic in nature, designed to keep newly independent island states 'on side' and completely exclude the Soviet Union from regional affairs.[2]

The impact of US–China rivalry on the Pacific Islands will be different because its inherent characteristics are different, because China is already deeply involved in the region and because the region is unlikely to be a primary site of geopolitical confrontation. Nevertheless, the spillover

---

2   Even at the height of the Cold War, Pacific Islander agency helped determine regional outcomes: for example, when the Western allies were forced to modify their ideas about strategic denial after Kiribati (1985) and Vanuatu (1987) signed fisheries access agreements with the Soviet Union (Fry 1993:232–35).

effects from major zones of friction, such as the jurisdictional disputes in the South China Sea, or the struggle for control of Taiwan, are already apparent. Meanwhile, the most immediate impacts are economic and diplomatic, as the US and allies such as Australia, New Zealand, the United Kingdom, France, the EU and Japan ratchet up their own regional activities. Western interest increased dramatically in 2018 when analysts worried that China would use debt-derived leverage to establish a military presence in the region. The main impetus for Australia's 'Step-Up', New Zealand's 'Pacific Reset' and the US's 'Pacific Pledge' initiatives is again strategic. These priorities for the Western allies sets them at odds with those of their island partners who have determined that climate change, not a rising China, is the major threat to regional security. While these new levels of interest and sources of economic support are welcomed by Island leaders, the challenge will be to use them to achieve the sustainable forms of development they have espoused in recent years. Even if these domestic efforts are successful, the serious threats posed by climate change are likely to intensify, propelled in part by the race for economic growth at the heart of the US–China confrontation. If this is a new Cold War, it is taking place in and contributing to a warming world.

A new Cold War?

The US-dominated international order faces challenges on two main fronts: from Russia and its surrogates in Europe and the Middle East, and from Beijing along China's maritime peripheries, with China regarded as the more formidable opponent by far. As Hugh White notes, China 'is the strongest adversary America has ever faced, and getting steadily stronger' (2019:5). Furthermore, according to Robert Sutter, the 'partnership between China and Russia has matured and broadened … with serious consequences for US interests' (2018:3).

There are significant differences between the emerging US–China stand-off and the Cold War. Perhaps most notable is the role of ideology, a central feature of conflict with the Soviet Union. Clearly there are ideological differences between the two sides, with the US espousing liberal democratic principles and China remaining committed to Communist Party rule and a managed economy.[3] The US is the main proselytiser, constantly seeking

---

3   It is interesting to note that a group of Trump allies and leaders in conservative thought have recently revived the Cold War–era Committee on the Present Danger to counter China's 'existential and ideological threat to the United States and to the idea of freedom' (Spinelli 2019).

to promote its political values overseas aided by a dominant discourse that frames liberal ideas, such as the so-called Washington consensus for development initiatives, as self-evident. Indeed, one factor fuelling the new hostility towards China is that Beijing has not implemented the liberal reforms that Western commentators argue should accompany economic growth. Instead, the Communist Party 'has used economic growth … to strengthen its own grasp on authority … [and] advance its state-capitalist model' (USCC 2018:vii). Even if some Chinese leaders now refer to 'the China model' and President Xi routinely cites a 'community of common destiny' when discussing BRI, to date Beijing has not systematically tried to persuade its diplomatic and trade partners to adopt China's approach to governance or economic development (Callahan 2016). China has consistently refrained from commenting on the internal affairs of countries in the Global South, even if that leaves Beijing open to accusations of encouraging authoritarian or rogue regimes overseas.

Also in contradistinction to the Soviet example, China has risen to power precisely by working within the US-dominated economic and political order. Rather than two largely autonomous systems separated by an 'iron curtain', the economies of the US and China are deeply entangled, with extensive corporate and people-to-people exchanges between the countries. As Peter Frankopan notes:

> Asia and the Silk Roads are rising—and they are rising fast. They are not doing so in isolation from the West, nor even in competition with it. In fact, quite the opposite: Asia's rise is closely linked with the developed economies of the United States, Europe and beyond (2019:24).

Many countries now have significant trade, aid or investment ties to China, even those with strained political relationships to Beijing, like Japan, Vietnam or Taiwan, or firm strategic allies of the United States anxious about China's increased global influence, such as Australia and New Zealand.

Another significant difference between the emerging situation and the Cold War lies in its military dimensions. The Cold War involved an escalating arms race precipitating the 1962 Cuban missile crisis that brought the world to the brink of nuclear war, as well as bloody proxy wars in Korea, Indochina and Afghanistan (Lind 2018:2). Although China possesses nuclear weapons too, which would hopefully prevent cold war conflict becoming hot, the current situation is quite different (but see

Talmadge 2018). Beijing has devoted considerable resources to expanding and modernising its military apparatus and particularly the blue-water capacity of its navy, but it is building from a low base. The *Liaoning*, its first aircraft carrier, launched in 2012, is an older refurbished vessel of Soviet design; a second, domestically produced vessel, the *Shandong*, was commissioned in December 2019. Perhaps China's most notable achievements in military technology are the development of stealth aircraft that can reportedly match US models in performance and an increasing capacity for cyber warfare. However, it is worth remembering that in 2018 Washington devoted approximately 2.5 times more in absolute terms in support of the military than Beijing (SIPRI 2019). Western analysts acknowledge that it will be many years before China can match American military might and global reach, although they express concern about Beijing's growing digital and artificial intelligence capabilities and asymmetric ability to disrupt US military operations. In any case, given the enormous demand for resources at home, Beijing may have no immediate ambitions to mount such a global challenge. As Georgetown University's Oriana Mastro argues, 'China has no interest in establishing a web of global alliances, sustaining a far-flung global military presence, sending troops thousands of miles from its borders' (2019:2).

Unlike much of the Cold War struggle, the military dimensions of the emerging US–China rivalry are asymmetric and concentrated in key geographic areas, most notably the near seas periphery, control of which China regards as essential to its national security. Western officials are conscious of the fact that China already has the wherewithal to disrupt US naval activities and challenge the 'rules-based order' in the western Pacific; hence a new emphasis on the so-called Indo-Pacific strategy to shore up US relations with allied countries in East, Southeast, and South Asia, and the revival in 2017 of the informal Quadrilateral Security Dialogue ('the Quad') between the US, Japan, Australia and India, with a shared commitment to 'defend their vision of regional order against what they perceived as accelerating Chinese aggression' (Tarapore 2018:2; US Government 2019). As it attempts to protect itself against what Beijing perceives as US attempts to encircle and contain its rise, China seeks to displace the US as the dominant power in Asia. As Mastro puts it, 'Although China does not want to usurp the United States' position as the leader of a global order … it wants to force the US out [of Asia]' (2019:2).

In essence, then, for the moment at least, 'this is a contest … between the world's two most powerful states over the leadership of the world's most prosperous and dynamic region' (White 2019:4).

The fundamental concern among Western analysts is that China's growing economy not only enables its military expansion but also threatens US economic superiority and ability to influence global events through non-military means. As Jude Woodward argued, 'The relative decline of the US economy meant that it has less capacity to use economic leverage alone to bind countries across the developing world to its strategic priorities' (2017:5). These concerns are exacerbated by fears that US technological superiority is being eroded. The focus of the Trump regime was apparently on curbing aberrant Chinese trade practices through hefty sanctions. But the underlying worry was Beijing's rapid transition from an economy built around labour-intensive industries to one driven by China-controlled advanced technology, 'the real existential threat to US technological leadership' (Laskai 2018:2). These trends and perceptions increase the likelihood of armed conflict. As Woodward argued, 'The US's declining economic leverage means it is forced to rely more openly on military means to achieve many of its objectives' (2017:11).

In Beijing, much of this is seen as US attempts to prevent China achieving its destiny as a great power. Beijing's military build-up is understood as defensive, largely consisting of targeted efforts to establish control of vital trade routes that represent China's lifelines for continued economic growth, thereby reducing dependency on the exceptional global reach of the US navy. This need to establish control explains the establishment of Beijing's first overseas military base in Djibouti in the Horn of Africa where busy sea lanes converge, as well as the focus on China's maritime periphery—its near seas—where a large proportion of its global trade is concentrated. The renewed focus on Taiwan as a renegade province and its eventual reintegration into China is emblematic of the heightened nationalism encouraged by President Xi, but it also reflects a pragmatic recognition of the island's strategic location just a few miles off China's coast. Beijing regards its diplomatic and economic initiatives in neighbouring Asian countries as legitimate attempts to counter threats from an encircling network of US military bases in Japan, South Korea, Guam, Singapore and Australia, from staging areas in other countries such as the Philippines and a US-supported arms build-up in Taiwan.

None of this is to diminish the importance of the growing rivalry between these great powers, or potential spillover effects in the Pacific Islands, but rather to note that some of its manifestations are different from the conflict with the Soviet Union. In particular, this is not so much a zero-sum battle for ideological control of the global order as a rivalry where Beijing's challenges to the status quo are selective and where complex economic and political dimensions overlap. At least for the moment, other countries, including the Pacific Islands, find themselves dealing with both parties and attempting as best they can to balance strategic, political or commercial imperatives, although choosing one side or the other may well become necessary as the conflict intensifies (White 2017; see also Wesley-Smith and Smith, Introduction to this volume). The initial focus of the competition is on Asia, although other fronts may open up in time.[4] For most parts of the world, particularly the developing countries of the Global South, this will be a struggle for influence fought largely with trade deals, defence agreements, infrastructure projects and financial incentives.

As with the Cold War, economic growth is at the centre of US–China competition, representing the very essence of China's rise as well as the key to US attempts to retain its global power. In another similarity with the Cold War, the main instrument deployed in the competition for influence in the developing world, including the Pacific Islands, is the promise of economic development. But unlike the earlier period, all of this is playing out in the face of a mounting climate change crisis and a growing realisation that, despite the breakthrough 2015 Paris Agreement, the global community is incapable or unwilling to do enough to curb emissions (see, for example, Harvey 2019). George Monbiot argues that economic growth is the fundamental and often-ignored factor in the fight against climate change: 'Beyond a certain point, economic growth—the force that lifted people out of poverty, and cured deprivation, squalor and disease—tips us back into those conditions' (2018). After reviewing the results of recent studies about the growth–emissions relationship, economist Peter Christensen concludes that the implication is that:

---

4   In December 2018, then national security advisor John Bolton announced a new US–Africa strategy designed to counter what he described as China's corrupt and predatory practices on that continent (Bolton 2018).

> If we are producing more and consuming more, we must assume
> that emission rates will grow significantly faster than we thought.
> Our current estimates of future damages are highly sensitive
> to growth rates and the primary reason is that is what's driving
> emissions. In the absence of meaningful climate policy, higher
> baseline growth scenarios likely imply higher emissions growth
> around the world (quoted in Yale News 2018).

As will be discussed further below, in this context the emergence of US–
China competition must be regarded as a particularly ominous turn
of events.

Pacific spillover

In May 2014 President Xi Jinping sent a veiled warning to Washington
when he told a regional security forum in Shanghai that Asia's security
problems should be solved by Asians themselves (China Daily 2014).
The focus here is on the Asia part of the Asia-Pacific region and, even
if Beijing regards the Pacific Islands as part of China's 'great periphery'
or extended neighbourhood, and has included it in the BRI, there is no
strong evidence that it has been singled out for special attention even in
President Xi's 'new era' (Zhang 2018:7). China's trade, aid, investment
and diplomatic activities in the Pacific Islands region have increased
significantly in recent years, but no more so than elsewhere in the world.
Nevertheless, several overlapping sites of escalating US–China tensions in
Asia have connections with, or implications for, Pacific Island countries.
These tensions include the increased militarisation of the wider region,
the disputes in the South China Sea and the struggle over Taiwan's
political status.

The military dimensions of the US pivot to Asia include increased air
and naval capacity in the region, regular naval forays into disputed
areas along China's coastline, advanced missile systems in South
Korea, US troops stationed in Darwin, Australia, and enhanced access
arrangements in Southeast Asian countries, particularly the Philippines.
China's activities, in turn, represent what US analysts call 'Area Access/
Area Denial' (A2/AD), involving 'shore-based ground-to-air, anti-ship
and air defense missiles, improved fighter aircraft, radar and tracking'
to create a protective umbrella over its naval operations in the near seas
(Woodward 2017:72).

The most immediate impact of these developments in the Pacific Islands region is in Guam, a US territory and home to major military installations.[5] In recent years the militarisation of Guam has intensified significantly, with the planned relocation of large number of US military personnel from bases in Okinawa, the construction of facilities for these additional troops, a new deep-draft wharf to accommodate aircraft carriers and a training facility to improve Guam's capacity to intercept intercontinental ballistic missiles (Aguon 2010:65–66). Not only does all of this make Guam more vulnerable to missile attack in the event of conflict, but also it serves to deepen the social and political marginalisation of the island's indigenous people. Even before the current build-up, Chamorro represented less than 40 per cent of the resident population, a demographic disadvantage that will be exacerbated even if only a portion of the projected influx eventuates. Guam is one of the 17 remaining entities on the United Nations' (UN) list of Non-Self-Governing Territories and, despite a recent UN resolution condemning the use of such territories for military purposes, Guam's central role in the pivot must be seen as a further setback for the longstanding movement for self-determination there (Aguon 2010).

The military spillover may also have a potential impact on three US-affiliated entities, parts of which make up what strategists call the 'second island chain': the Republic of the Marshall Islands (RMI), the Federated States of Micronesia (FSM) and the Republic of Palau (ROP). These strategically significant islands were taken over by the US after the defeat of Japan in World War II and gained qualified forms of independence in 1986 (RMI and FSM) and 1994 (ROP). Their ongoing relationships with the US are defined by compacts of free association (COFA) that allow for financial support and access to the US for COFA citizens in return for complete strategic control of these entities by Washington. As a US State Department official noted in 2003, 'The most significant US interest at the time the Compact was negotiated was the value placed on the right to exercise strategic denial over half a million square miles of the Pacific between Hawaii and Guam' (in Underwood 2017:4). Although the compacts and subsidiary agreements also allow for military installations, if Washington deems them necessary, to date the only permanent military facility is the Kwajalein missile-testing facility in the Marshall Islands.

---

5   The neighbouring Northern Mariana Islands, a commonwealth in political union with the US, is also impacted but to a lesser extent.

The importance of the test site has increased with the growing emphasis on missile defence systems and two new radar systems capable of monitoring Chinese air and naval activities (as well as North Korean missiles) are being installed in Palau. Former president of Palau Johnson Toribiong recently observed that the US presence 'is more recognizable in Palau now' and describes this trend, as well as the eventual authorisation of long-delayed compact funding in the US Congress, as 'in part a reaction to the presence of China in the South China Sea' (Kerrigan 2018:2).

For RMI and FSM, the first periodic renegotiations occurred in 2003 and the new agreements, known as Compact II, entered into force in 2004. These reviews occurred in the period after the end of the Cold War and before the China threat had emerged as a major preoccupation in Washington, which may account for the relatively harsh terms insisted on by US negotiators. At the time, the Government Accounting Office concluded that the value of strategic denial was overrated in the post–Cold War world; Robert Underwood commented that a heavy emphasis on US financial oversight made Compact II 'more compact and less free' (2017:9). The funding for Palau's latest compact was agreed upon in September 2010 but not released by Congress until March 2018, also indicating lack of interest in Washington. However, in June 2018, the US–China Economic and Security Review Commission reported increased 'concern that the US Compact countries could decide to end their agreements with the United States, in part due to China's increased influence' and indeed such a move has already been proposed in the FSM legislature (Meick et al. 2018:19). This suggests that the compact states will go into the next set of negotiations, which have to occur before 2023 (2024 for Palau), with more leverage than before. A notable part of Washington's recent Pacific Pledge initiative is increased interest in the freely associated states. In May 2019, President Trump met the leaders of these states in the White House and, in another first, Secretary of State Mike Pompeo followed up with a further high-level meeting in Pohnpei in FSM in August.

Although Underwood is confident that the compacts will be renegotiated, the China factor has rendered this outcome less certain that it would have seemed just a few years ago (Grossman et al. 2019; Underwood 2017:10). It will be interesting to see whether exclusion of foreign military from the compact states continues to be the operating principle for US planners, or if further militarisation of these islands begins to replace strategic denial as US–China competition intensifies. Perhaps as a sign of things to come, in April 2019 US soldiers took part in training exercises in Palau, the first such deployment in more than 30 years (Olson 2019).

Military dimensions of the emerging conflict are also manifest elsewhere in the region. France has used the rise of China to justify maintaining a modest military presence in New Caledonia although, as Nic Maclellan argues, its possible role in the event of conflict in the distant South China Sea remains unclear (see Maclellan, Chapter 6). More significant are Australia's recent actions, triggered by concerns that China is seeking to establish a naval presence in the region. Although such speculation is not new, the narrative catapulted to prominence with a story in *The Sydney Morning Herald* in April 2018 claiming that a project to upgrade the Luganville wharf on the island of Espiritu Santo in Vanuatu, funded by Chinese loans, could accommodate Chinese naval vessels. The story quoted 'senior security officials' to suggest that this initiative might 'culminate in a full military base' (Wroe 2018). Despite emphatic denials from officials in Vanuatu and China, and the fact that the story's claims were never publicly substantiated, then prime minister Malcolm Turnbull warned that Canberra would view 'with great concern' the establishment of any military bases in the region (ABC News 2018).

Much of Canberra's Step-Up effort is economic, ostensibly designed to help Pacific Island countries avoid the 'debt trap diplomacy' associated with Chinese-funded infrastructure projects, but several initiatives are strategic in nature. Canberra has substantially increased its funding for the Australian Defence Cooperation Program in Papua New Guinea (PNG), launched a AU$2 billion Pacific Maritime Security Program, agreed to redevelop Fiji's Black Rock Camp as a regional hub for police training and proposed new security cooperation agreements with Vanuatu and Solomon Islands (Morgan 2018). Perhaps most significantly, in November 2018, Australia reached agreement with PNG to build a joint naval base on Manus Island, rehabilitating a facility used by the US in World War II. This followed reports that Chinese companies had expressed interest in helping develop the port[6] and speculation that, like the Luganville wharf, it could be used as 'an ideal logistics node for China's People's Liberation Army-Navy … as it seeks to sustain more frequent operations in the Western Pacific' (Panda 2018).

---

6   There was speculation that China Harbour Engineering, which was already developing Manus's Momote Airport, was interested in port construction on Manus (Jaipragas 2018).

The Lombrum Naval Base initiative, also supported by the US, is significant not only because it provides PNG with an upgraded facility for its coastal patrol boats, but also because Australian ships and personnel will be stationed there. While the details remain unclear, some observers have questioned the value of this investment, noting that even with upgrades the port will not be able to accommodate larger vessels (Boyd 2018). At the very least, as Mike Scrafton argued, 'the opportunity costs of building a major facility suited to military operations in a conflict in the Asia-Pacific seem largely unexamined' (2018). Apart from showing support for US hardline policies, the real objective may be to send a muscle-flexing message to Beijing. This move further militarises the conflict and complicates PNG's attempts to balance its relationship with its close neighbour and former colonial power against its significant economic relationship with China.

The Manus base agreement was concluded in the context of escalating tensions in the South China Sea as China makes increasingly clear its intentions to assert control of the area and the US responds equally forcefully (Burgers and Romaniuk 2017). There were diplomatic attempts to draw Pacific Island countries into the dispute in the aftermath of a lawsuit brought by the Philippines against China at the Permanent Court of Arbitration in The Hague. In July 2016 the court found that China's historic claims to sovereignty over most of the South China Sea had no basis in the UN Convention on the Law of the Sea, a judgment that Beijing has adamantly refused to accept (Perlez 2016). China reportedly attempted to 'whip up support' for its legal claims from its Pacific Island allies, although there is no evidence to suggest that anything more than diplomatic encouragement was involved and, in the end, only one country, Vanuatu, publicly indicated support for China's position (Flitton 2016).[7]

---

7   If conditionality were to be involved in future interactions, however, that would signal a significant change in the political dimensions of China's win–win, no-strings-attached approach to bilateral relations. Especially given their own vested interest in Law of the Sea questions, escalating Chinese pressure would increase demands on Island governments as they walk a diplomatic tight rope between competing powers.

Taiwan tensions

A major concern with implications for the Pacific Islands region is that the complex triangular relationship between China, Taiwan and the US will deteriorate further and even lead to overt conflict. The four Pacific Island countries that still recognise Taiwan (Palau, Marshall Islands, Tuvalu and Nauru) are already caught up in this dispute and the pressure to switch allegiance to Beijing is mounting. Indeed, two of Taiwan's former Pacific allies, Solomon Islands and Kiribati, decided to switch recognition to Beijing in September 2019.

Relations between Taipei and Beijing worsened after President Tsai Ing-wen and the Democratic Progressive Party came to power in Taiwan in January 2016. Although Tsai repeatedly promised not to seek formal independence, Beijing insisted that she explicitly endorse the '1992 consensus', a loose understanding anticipating eventual reunification with China, and exerted considerable economic, diplomatic and political pressure to that end. In a major speech in January 2019, President Xi Jinping claimed that reunification is inevitable, 'the great trend of history', and in the face of any independence attempts China made 'no promise to abandon the use of force, and retain the option of taking all necessary measures' (Buckley and Horton 2019). US President Donald Trump did not help matters when, after his inauguration in early 2017, he accepted a congratulatory phone call from President Tsai and indicated that he might reconsider the US's longstanding acceptance of the One China policy. In March 2018 he signed legislation that encouraged official exchanges with Taiwan and in June opened a new (unofficial) embassy in Taipei. US warships periodically sail through the Taiwan Strait, further demonstrating US support for Taipei (ibid.). Potentially significant for Pacific Island countries is the Asia Reassurance Initiative Act, signed into law in December 2018, which includes a commitment 'to counter efforts to change the status quo' regarding Taiwan.

Pacific Island countries are directly involved in the battle for diplomatic recognition as Beijing moves aggressively to reduce Taipei's international space by cutting off third-party support. Tsai's election in 2016 spelled the end of the eight-year 'diplomatic truce', an informal agreement between Beijing and Taipei to suspend competition for recognition. Since then, seven countries, including two in the Pacific (Burkina Faso, Dominican Republic, Panama, Sao Tome and Principe, El Salvador, Solomon Islands and Kiribati) have switched their recognition from Taiwan to China, leaving a total of only 15 countries supporting Taipei. As the balance of power between China and Taiwan shifted decisively in favour of Beijing in recent years, the struggle for recognition is arguably now more about symbolism than substance. Yet it continues to have real consequences, not least because of US interest in the matter. El Salvador's switch in August 2018 elicited a sharp response from the White House, which issued a statement accusing Beijing of 'apparent interference in the domestic politics of a Western Hemisphere country' and warned that it would have to re-evaluate the US relationship with El Salvador (Sands 2018).

Great power politics were very much in evidence in 2019, after it became apparent that leaders in Solomon Islands were considering abandoning their longstanding relationship with Taiwan in favour of recognising Beijing. In June 2018, a group of leaders, including two cabinet ministers, visited Beijing. Although the trip was described as private, officials in Taiwan interpreted it as 'a negative signal' for Taipei (Strong 2018). In April 2019, newly elected Prime Minister Manasseh Sogavare confirmed that a switch to Beijing was under discussion with his coalition partners (Packham 2019). The domestic debate about a possible switch revolved around the fact that China is the major market for Solomon Islands timber exports and that the economic benefits from developing the relationship further would likely far exceed those provided by Taiwan. Indeed, Prime Minister Sogavare was informed that Beijing would offer a starter aid package worth an estimated US$500 million in return for diplomatic recognition. This was soon countered by the promise of significantly increased assistance, much of it aimed at infrastructure development, from a consortium of Western countries including Australia, New Zealand, Japan and the US, with White House officials travelling to Honiara to lobby Sogavare directly. US Vice President Mike Pence was also involved in the negotiation (see Kabutaulaka, Chapter 1). Despite this political pressure, however, in September 2019 Sogavare announced that Solomon Islands would recognise Beijing, citing the findings of the Bipartisan Task Force and a report from the Ministry of Foreign Affairs and External Trade (Sogavare 2019). When Solomon Islands announced in September 2019 that it would recognise Beijing, officials in Washington DC, including Pence, were quick to register displeasure (Rampton 2019). Western interests received a further setback less than a week later when Kiribati unexpectedly decided to recognise China, apparently after receiving an offer from Beijing to help upgrade sea and air transport systems (Lee 2019).

All of this puts an intense spotlight on the Pacific Island countries that continue to recognise Taiwan and now represent more than a quarter of all Taipei's remaining diplomatic allies. The situation is further complicated by the fact that two of those countries, Palau and Marshall Islands, are bound to the US through compacts of free association, suggesting that any attempts to switch allegiance to Beijing could provoke a sharp response from Washington. The first country to feel significant pressure from China has been Palau, which has had a close relationship with Taiwan since Palau achieved independence in 1994. Concerned about its ability to cater for growing numbers of tourists, Palau's government began in 2015 to restrict the number of flights from China, which by then carried more than 50 per cent of all visitors. Beijing responded by instructing travel agents not to book tours to this destination. By 2018, the number of visitors from China had dropped by 45 per cent, with significant consequences for Palau's economy. In August 2017 Palau President Tommy Remengesau Jr said that 'it was not a secret that China would like us … to switch to them' and other officials speculated that Beijing is trying to shore up its influence ahead of the expiry of compact funding. Some business interests in Palau see the economic advantages of switching recognition to Beijing, but US counter moves seem likely given Palau's strategic location in the 'second island chain' (Lyons 2018; Master 2018).

Similar resistance in Washington might be anticipated if the Marshall Islands decides to recognise China, especially given the location of the Kwajalein missile facility there. It is interesting to note that the FSM is the only one of the compact states to recognise Beijing and has long been considered the least strategically significant of the three. Nevertheless, in light of the fact that the western extremities of the FSM constitute part of the second island chain and Chinese companies have proposed large-scale development projects in Yap, the US will probably expand its efforts to offset increasing Chinese economic influence in FSM when compact renegotiations get under way. There are few current indications that Tuvalu is inclined to move away from its recognition of Taiwan and leaders in Nauru are adamantly opposed to breaking relations with Taipei.

Economic influence and infrastructure

Existing concerns that China's growing economic ties to Pacific Island countries threaten Western influence in the region have been exacerbated by the southern expansion of the BRI. China is now the second largest trade partner in the region as a whole and the largest for some Island countries. According to the Lowy Institute's aid mapping project, China's committed aid to the region in 2016 amounted to AU$277.44 million, making it the second largest regional donor behind Australia (AU$1.02 billion) (Lowy Institute 2019). China is now Fiji's largest aid partner and the second largest for PNG, Tonga, Samoa, Cook Islands and Vanuatu. Perhaps most impressive (and visible) are Chinese commercial ventures in the region, led by Metallurgical Corporation of China's US$1.6 billion Ramu nickel-mining venture in PNG as well as a rapidly expanding number of construction contracts held by Chinese companies. Many of these contracts, estimated to be worth in excess of US$5 billion, are backed by concessional or commercial loans from China's financial institutions, including the China Export-Import Bank and the China Development Bank.

The massive economic and diplomatic BRI—first announced in 2013 and now involving some 120 countries in Asia, the Middle East and Europe—is building what Beijing calls a 'community of common destiny' based on trade and commerce. All the Pacific Island countries that recognise Beijing have signed MOUs for BRI cooperation, including Cook Islands and Niue, both in free association arrangements with New Zealand (Devonshire-Ellis 2019). Although many infrastructure projects in the region predate the launch of the Pacific leg of the BRI's 21st Century Maritime Silk Road, the significance of the initiative is clear. BRI increases incentives for Chinese companies to seek out commercial opportunities in Pacific Island countries as well as opening up new sources of funding for such projects.

Ambivalence towards the BRI in US official circles has turned to hostility in recent years. Critics express concern about development standards and practices and contribute to a narrative that highlights examples of maladministered infrastructure schemes or projects that could enable China's military expansion (Pantucci 2018). Informing many of these concerns, however, are underlying anxieties about the implications of all of this for US economic, political and military influence. Viewed through a geopolitical lens, the assumed future success of BRI is seen as a growing challenge to the current order. While officials in the Trump administration generally advocate opposition to BRI as part of the wider confrontation with China, some commentators argue that opposition is counterproductive to Western interests since many participating countries welcome this type of investment. Instead, they advocate 'alternative solutions'. Raffaello Pantucci, for example, celebrates Washington's decision to 'super-charge' the Overseas Private Investment Corporation, making more US funds available for infrastructure projects overseas (2018:4).

Western countries active in the Pacific, particularly Australia, have tended to mimic US attitudes to China's infrastructure initiatives by loudly condemning the construction of what Australia's then minister of international development, Concetta Fierravanti-Wells, called 'useless buildings' and 'roads to nowhere' and raising the possibility that some of this activity is a cover for military expansion (Wyeth 2018:1). Narratives about China's 'debt diplomacy' or 'debt-for-equity' leverage originating elsewhere, particularly in debates about the implications of a Chinese company's takeover of port facilities in Sri Lanka, have also found their way into regional discourse (Abi-Habib 2018). Such assertions persist despite a recent analysis of Chinese-funded projects by the Rhodium Group that found that 'actual asset seizures' as a result of defaults on Chinese debt 'are a very rare occurrence' (Kratz et al. 2019:5). Indeed, Barry Sautman and Yan Hairong argue that in the Sri Lankan case:

> The Hambantota port lease was not a result of any inability to service the loans, nor was it a debt-for-equity swap—the Sri Lankan government still owns the port. And funds received for the lease were not used to repay port-related debt, but to pay off more expensive loans, generally to Western entities (2019:4).

Whatever the merits of the Sri Lankan case, arbitrarily projecting generalisations about Chinese lending practices onto situations in the Pacific Islands is problematic. While China, like Western countries, undoubtedly hopes to use economic tools to exert influence, the proposition that Beijing is encouraging Pacific countries to take on unsustainable levels of debt in order to extract concessions remains unsubstantiated. Indeed, such an approach might well be counterproductive in Pacific Island countries where Chinese investment is generally welcomed and where assets sufficiently important to Beijing, including strategic ones, are difficult to identify. As Michael O'Keefe points out, if China really wanted to use economic means to undermine Western influence in the region, it has ample instruments at its disposal to do so without resorting to a roundabout scheme of debt leverage (2018:3).

Australia has also followed the US lead by attempting to provide alternatives to Chinese economic initiatives. As then foreign minister Julie Bishop put it, her government would 'compete with China's infrastructure development spree in Australia's neighborhood' ostensibly to help counter threats to their sovereignty (Wroe 2018). Among other initiatives, Australia has announced plans to establish a AU$2 billion infrastructure bank, increase incentives for Australian companies to bid for contracts in the region, build undersea fibre optic cables for Solomon Islands, Papua New Guinea and Vanuatu, and funding (with New Zealand, Japan and the US) a multibillion-dollar rural electrification project in Papua New Guinea (Packham 2018).

Implications for Pacific Islands' aspirations

China's heightened profile in the Pacific Islands has been accompanied by a significant expansion in the volume of trade with the region, as well as increased flows of aid and investment to Pacific Island countries that recognise Beijing. Heightened tensions between more established actors in the region and China promise to further accelerate the inward flow of resources. According to a statement by President Xi Jinping before his state visit to Papua New Guinea in November 2018, China's support to the region is intended to help Island countries 'in pursuing development paths suited to their national circumstances' as well as 'contributing to economic growth and people's welfare in this part of the world' (Xi 2018). Prime Minister Scott Morrison described the Step-Up in Australia's relations with the Pacific as 'a new chapter in relations with our Pacific family ... for its own sake, because it's right. Because it's who we are'. The overall goal of Australia's policy towards the Pacific, according to Morrison, is a region that is 'secure strategically, stable economically and sovereign politically' (Morrison 2018). Both these statements are laden with unexamined assumptions about, for example, Xi's link between economic growth and human welfare or Morrison's supposition that open market economies promote stability—or indeed his claim that Australia is an integral part of the Pacific family.

However, it is more important here to explore what all of this new energy might mean for the aspirations expressed by Pacific Islanders themselves. Although there is no Pacific-wide development plan, it is possible to identify some broad principles and priorities informing recent development discourse in the region. These priorities are captured in the *Draft Strategic Plan 2017–2020*, produced by the Pacific Islands Development Forum (PIDF), a regional organisation established in 2013 'out of a desire to bring transformative changes in member countries by focusing on the sustainable and inclusive development in the region' (PIDF 2017:4). Although a full analysis is beyond the scope of this chapter, it is worth noting that PIDF was formed explicitly in opposition to existing regional institutions, especially the Pacific Islands Forum (PIF), and, according to its architects, to provide a vision for the region more suited to current circumstances. Even if regional support for PIDF has waned recently, the ideas formulated there have informed changes in the priorities and practices in other regional organisations including the PIF (Fry and Tarte 2015).

Since PIDF was formed largely in opposition to the perceived dominance by Australia and New Zealand of PIF and other regional organisations, it is hardly surprising that a key principle animating the work of PIDF is self-determination. According to the PIDF charter, 'The Pacific should be governed by and for Pacific Islanders' and external powers can participate in PIDF deliberations as observers (PIDF 2015:10, 11). There is also a new emphasis on South–South partnerships in international policy initiatives. A second key value is 'a shared and enduring commitment to Green-Blue Pacific economies, sustainable development and especially poverty eradication' (PIDF 2017:8). Matthew Dornan and his colleagues note that terms like 'blue-green growth', the 'green economy' and the 'blue-green economy' are not used consistently in the region (Dornan et al. 2018). For PIDF, these terms do not suggest a rejection of economic growth per se, although there is explicit recognition of 'the valuation of critical ecological, social, spiritual/cultural assets that are not recognised by the "brown economy"' (PIDF 2017:10). Instead, the emphasis is on sustainable forms of growth and development informed by 'green' and 'blue' principles, including 'decarbonised' forms of energy and transport. Finally, the major concern that has animated PIDF from the beginning is climate change and its regional impacts. The strategic plan lists its first objective as 'advocating the very real and pressing significance of climate change for the lives and livelihoods of Pacific Islands and Pacific Islanders' (ibid.:8). This priority was echoed at the PIF meeting in Nauru in

September 2018, where the leaders adopted the Boe Declaration, which in its opening paragraph reaffirms 'that climate change remains the single greatest threat to the livelihoods, security and wellbeing of the peoples of the Pacific' (Doherty 2018).

Escalating competition for influence in the region has mixed implications for the self-determination aspirations of Pacific Island leaders. The arrival of more development partners has certainly provided leaders with more aid, trade and investment options, and transactions with China are not subject to liberal reform conditions typical of agreements with Western powers. Australia's newly discovered emphasis on infrastructure funding will also be welcomed in the region. On the other hand, and despite Morrison's appeal to Pacific Island family values, the fear is that increased Australian resources will be accompanied by an expectation of increased influence over how those resources are used. Paradoxically, if projects are funded by loans then this can only add to the debt burden routinely decried when the funds come from China. Furthermore, framing the Step-Up initiative in terms of regional security is unlikely to be seen as 'of and for' Pacific Islanders, who generally do not see the rise of China as a threat to their security even though the militarisation associated with the competition for influence may well constitute such a threat (O'Keefe 2019). As discussed above, Western strategic imperatives have already had an impact on the self-determination aspirations of colonised Chamorro communities in Guam and, under certain circumstances, could further restrict sovereign options for citizens of the compact states in Micronesia.

Whether or not the expanding flow of resources into the region associated with increasing competition for influence will help or hinder sustainable development goals prominent on the regional agenda depends to a large extent on how such development is defined and pursued. Much foreign investment flows into natural resource exploitation and large-scale mining, forestry or fishing industries are hardly known for their 'green' or 'blue' characteristics, although they might be managed to limit the resulting environmental damage. The imminent onset of seabed mining in the region raises a whole new set of environmental (and other) issues (Hunter et al. 2018).[8]

---

8   Access to some likely sites for Pacific seabed mining that lie outside the marine jurisdiction of Pacific Island states is controlled by the International Seabed Authority (ISA). As John Copley (2014) pointed out, the ISA was created 'to administer seafloor mining in international waters, not to ask the question "Is it a good idea?"'.

Sustainability in other Pacific sectors is often associated with the employment of 'green' technologies such as solar or wind energy. Given the heavy reliance on imported oil for energy generation in many Pacific Island places, as well as the large number of rural communities without access to electricity, this is clearly a desirable trend. However, it does raise questions about increased dependence on the countries where most of these technologies originate, as well as the environmental costs associated with the manufacture, transport and disposal of such equipment (UCS 2013). In a few parts of the region, like Vanuatu, there is a genuine emphasis in development planning on protecting or strengthening the long-established, sustainable and carbon-free *kastom* (traditional) economy. But even there the demands for cash incomes sometimes override concerns about resource depletion or ecological change (Dornan et al. 2018).

Implications for climate change concerns

Pacific Islands' concerns about climate change are fully justified given their relatively fragile ecosystems, as well as their vulnerability to extreme weather events and rising sea levels. Especially in the low-lying atoll states of Kiribati, Tuvalu and the Marshall Islands, salt water intrusion already endangers fresh water supplies and staple food crops, while ocean acidification damages coral reefs and degrades the marine ecosystems upon which local populations depend. Escalating great power competition is likely to increase the threat.

Pacific Island governments are actively implementing measures to adapt to the new circumstances. They have also made it a priority to lobby aggressively at the United Nations for action to mitigate the drivers of climate change, especially greenhouse gas emissions. Pacific leaders played a key role in crafting the 2015 Paris Agreement on action to counter climate change, most notably in working to add to the agreement a limit of 1.5 degrees Celsius above preindustrial global temperatures, even if this was only included as an aspirational target (Carter 2018). Their insistence on this inclusion has proved percipient as an October 2018 Intergovernmental Panel on Climate Change (IPCC) report demonstrates that limiting warming to 1.5 degrees Celsius instead of the 2.0 degrees actually targeted in the Paris Agreement makes a huge difference to the global damage caused by rising sea levels, droughts, floods, extreme weather events, reduction in biodiversity, ocean acidification and loss of coral reefs (IPCC 2018). The report also notes that a massive global effort is needed to reduce emissions enough to keep below the 1.5 degrees Celsius threshold, as well as indicating the limited time left (12 years) to do so. As a member of the IPCC working group put it, 'We have pointed out the enormous benefits of keeping to 1.5 degrees Celsius, and also the unprecedented shift in energy systems and transport that would be needed to achieve that' (Watts 2018).

The increased attention to the Pacific Islands region associated with the rise of China and efforts by other countries to contain that rise has led to more resources to support adaptation efforts by Island governments. China has supplied solar energy equipment to some Pacific Island countries and appears willing to do more, while the new Pacific policy positions announced by Australia and New Zealand in 2018 include measures to develop resilience in the face of environmental challenges. The situation regarding climate change mitigation is much less promising. The Trump administration's withdrawal from the Paris Agreement and its commitment to relaxing environmental regulations are unfortunate setbacks for global efforts to limit warming, while Australia's determination to keep exporting coal represents a major political impediment to Canberra's efforts to step up its engagement with the Pacific Islands region. And despite its leading role in the development of alternative energy technologies, and some impressive decarbonising efforts at home, China's emissions are not expected to peak until 2030. In the meantime, China remains the number one producer of greenhouse gases (Geall 2017).[9] As long as other priorities continue to supersede efforts to deal with the causes of climate change, these 'development partners' can only offer to help alleviate some of the symptoms of this existential threat to Pacific lives and livelihoods. In a report released on the eve of its annual Davos conference, the World Economic Forum (WEF) identified climate change and other environmental concerns as the top global risk for 2020 and noted that intensifying geopolitical rivalry was a major impediment to urgent multilateral mitigation efforts (WEF 2020).

---

9   For example, Sam Geall argues that 'China's shift away from coal-fired energy has proceeded at a rate that was once unimaginable', but notes that whether Beijing will replicate this success in BRI projects overseas remains unclear (2017:3).

The global competition discussed in this chapter may well aggravate the situation. China's rise is heavily dependent on capitalist-style growth, albeit with 'Chinese characters', while the US attempts to stimulate its own economic expansion in order to maintain a dominant role in the world. Meanwhile both countries seek to enhance their global influence by advocating growth-oriented development to those people on the planet not yet fully integrated into the global economy, including in Pacific Island countries. Studies show that carbon emissions are closely linked to consumption and economic growth, what Monbiot (2016:9) calls the twin 'motors of environmental destruction' (Granados et al. 2012; Rainey 2019).[10] Short of some radical rethinking of development priorities on the part of powerful global actors, this appears to be a formula destined to frustrate the chances of achieving the enormous roll back of emissions called for in the 2018 IPCC report. Veteran commentator Cary Huang notes Chinese Premier Li Kegiang's pessimistic assessment of China's recent economic performance and argues that a renewed focus on economic stability will likely overshadow efforts to combat financial risk, poverty and pollution: 'Chasing faster economic growth will inevitably come at the expense' of the three 'critical battles' identified by the leaders in 2017 (2019:6).

Although contributing relatively little to global emissions, Pacific Island countries are not entirely disconnected from the emerging crisis. The region's largest country, Papua New Guinea, is an active participant in the global carbon economy, exporting crude oil since the early 1990s and large quantities of liquefied natural gas since 2014. Together these industries represent some 60 per cent of the value of PNG's exports and contribute significant government revenue. It is also worth noting that the IPCC identifies reforestation as an essential component of all of its four identified pathways to lower emissions, but ongoing deforestation is a feature of many island countries, especially in Melanesia (IPCC 2018). In PNG an estimated 4 per cent of the total area of rainforest existing in 2002 had been cleared (some for oil palm plantations) or logged by 2014, with much higher rates in the logged areas (Bryan and Shearman 2015). Solomon Islands relies heavily on the export of unprocessed round logs,

---

10 The growth–emissions link was demonstrated in 2018 when emissions rose sharply as the US economy expanded in response to the Trump administration's stimulus measures and despite increased use of non-carbon alternatives in the energy and transportation sectors (Rhodium Group 2019). It is also worth noting that increased military spending was a significant factor in the Trump stimulus package and that the US military is the single largest institutional user of oil as well as the single largest institutional emitter in the world.

most going to China, and trees are being harvested at rates estimated to be as much as 20 times sustainable levels. Indeed, some commentators suggest that if such rates continue, rainforests in Solomon Islands will be all but gone by 2036 (Global Witness 2018).

Several years after the Paris Agreement was signed, it is hard to be optimistic about the chances of its success. The agreement clearly underestimated the speed and severity of the impacts of climate change. The 2018 IPCC report estimates that carbon pollution would have to be reduced by 45 per cent by 2030 in order to keep warming under the 1.5 degree Celsius red line, compared to a reduction of 20 per cent to achieve the 2.0 degree standard written into the agreement (IPCC 2018). And yet most signatory countries are not on track to meet even the more modest goals agreed to in 2015. The dominant discourse about the global environmental crisis assumes that current patterns of growth and consumption can not only continue but expand, as long as they are accompanied by the deployment of low-carbon energy alternatives, more efficient use of limited resources and/or the development of large-scale carbon capture technologies. However, the adequacy of any of these proposed solutions has yet to be demonstrated. For example, the authors of a recent analysis of possible climate change pathways argue that reliance on unproven technologies for large-scale carbon removal 'may well represent an irresponsible and inappropriate gamble' (Lamontagne et al. 2019).

That leaves the main focus on other carbon capture and sequestration initiatives and a radical reduction of global emissions. Some analysts suggest that a 'World War II–scale effort' would be required to implement the necessary economic, social and political changes before it is too late (Rockoff 2016). The chances of this eventuating seem remote, especially as policymakers in Washington and Beijing contemplate the emerging imperatives of a different type of war. At the core of the new Cold War, it seems, is a carbon emissions race with potentially catastrophic global consequences.

Conclusions

Pacific Island countries are facing some direct consequences of the escalating competition between a rising China and the US with its Western allies. Although most of the sites of intense military competition, such as the South China Sea or the Taiwan Strait, lie outside the region, some US-affiliated Pacific islands such as Guam, Commonwealth of the Mariana Islands, Marshall Islands, FSM and Palau are directly implicated, while others, most notably PNG, are drawn in because of their defence links to other Western powers. Meanwhile, those Pacific Island states that still recognise Taipei are under political and economic pressure from China to recognise Beijing, and from the United States and its allies not to contemplate such a shift.

However, the most significant impacts of escalating big-power competition for Pacific Island countries are neither military nor political but economic, demonstrated through increased flows of trade, aid and investment. These new resource flows increase the potential for Island leaders to exercise choice and agency, for the region to 'chart its own course', not least by breaking the monopoly of influence exercised for many years by a small number of Western powers. Yet the dominant development discourse in the region continues to emphasise economic growth, albeit using 'green' and 'blue' tools to achieve it. Whatever the perceived short-term benefits of further integration into the global economy, there are also costs associated with this type of development, including the erosion of cultural and social institutions and values, often revolving around land ownership, that have served these societies well for centuries.

A major cost of the accelerating US–China competition are additional pressures to expand a global economy, whose destructive environmental characteristics are readily apparent, and a growing political impulse to prioritise geopolitical competition over climate change mitigation efforts. In other words, the new Cold War has direct implications for what Pacific leaders have identified as the 'single greatest threat to the livelihoods, security and wellbeing of the peoples of the Pacific' (Doherty 2018).

References

ABC News 2018. Chinese Military Base in Pacific Would Be of 'Great Concern', Turnbull Tells Vanuatu. *Pacific Beat* program, 10 April. www.abc.net.au/news/2018-04-10/china-military-base-in-vanuatu-report-of-concern-turnbull-says/9635742

Abi-Habib, M. 2018. How China Got Sri Lanka to Cough Up a Port. *The New York Times*, 25 June.

Aguon, J. 2010. On Loving the Maps Our Hands Cannot Hold: Self-Determination of Colonized and Indigenous Peoples in International Law. *16 Asian Pacific American Law Journal* 47.

Bolton, J.R. 2018. Remarks by National Security Advisor Ambassador John R. Bolton on The Trump Administration's New Africa Strategy. Remarks to the Heritage Foundation. Washington DC, 13 December. td.usembassy. gov/remarks-by-national-security-advisor-ambassador-john-r-bolton-on-the-trump-administrations-new-africa-strategy/

Boyd, A. 2018. As Oz Gears Up in Manus, China Says 'Discard Cold War Thinking'. *Asia Times*, 10 November. asopa.typepad.com/asopa_people/2018/11/as-oz-gears-up-in-manUS–China-says-discard-cold-war-thinking.html

Bryan J.E. and P.L. Sherman (eds) 2015. *The State of the Forests of Papua New Guinea 2014: Measuring Change Over Period 2002–2014.* Port Moresby: University of Papua New Guinea. png-data.sprep.org/system/files/The%20 State%20of%20Forest%20in%20PNG%202014.pdf

Buckley, C. and C. Horton 2019. Xi Jinping Warns Taiwan That Unification Is the Goal and Force Is an Option. *The New York Times*, 1 January. www.nytimes. com/2019/01/01/world/asia/xi-jinping-taiwan-china.html

Burgers, T. and S. Romaniuk 2017. Will Hybrid Warfare Protect America's Interests in the South China Sea? *The Diplomat*, 30 March. thediplomat.com/2017/03/ will-hybrid-warfare-protect-americas-interests-in-the-south-china-sea/

Callahan, W. 2016. China's 'Asia Dream': The Belt and Road Initiative and The New Regional Order. *Asian Journal of Comparative Politics* 1(3):1–18. doi.org/10.1177/2057891116647806

Carter, G. 2018. Multilateral Consensus Decision Making: How Pacific Island States Build and Reach Consensus in Climate Change Negotiations. PhD thesis, ANU. doi.org/10.25911/5c7f93e2c3c08

China Daily 2014. China's Xi Proposes Security Concept for Asia. 21 May. www.chinadaily.com.cn/china/2014-05/21/content_17531900.htm

Copley, J. 2014. Shedding Some Light on the International Seabed Authority. University of Southampton blog: Exploring our Oceans, 9 March. moocs. southampton.ac.uk/oceans/2014/03/09/shedding-some-light-on-the-international-seabed-authority/

D'Arcy, P. 2016. The Chinese Pacific: An Historical Overview. In M. Powles (ed.), *China and the Pacific: The View from Oceania*. Wellington: Victoria University Press, 46–52.

Devonshire-Ellis, C. 2019. China's Belt and Road Initiative in the Pacific Islands. *Silk Road Briefing.* Dezan Shira & Associates, 23 May. www.silkroadbriefing. com/news/2019/05/23/chinas-belt-road-initiative-pacific-islands/

Doherty, B. 2018. Australia Signs Declaration Saying Climate Change 'Single Greatest Threat' to Pacific. *The Guardian,* 6 September. www.theguardian.com/ environment/2018/sep/06/australia-signs-declaration-climate-change-greatest-threat-pacific-islands

Dornan, M., W. Morgan, T.N. Cain and S. Tarte 2018. What's in a Term? 'Green Growth' and the 'Blue-Green Economy' in the Pacific Islands. *Asia and the Pacific Policy Studies. Special Issue: The Pacific Islands in the 21st Century* 5(3):408–25. doi.org/10.1002/app5.258

Dziedzic, S. 2012. US Pledges More Aid for Strategic South Pacific. *ABC News,* 1 September. www.abc.net.au/news/2012-09-01/an-us-pledges-aid-to-south-pacific-copy/4237938

Flitton, D. 2016. South China Sea Dispute: China Is Trading Aid for Support for Claims. *The Sydney Morning Herald,* 6 June. www.smh.com.au/world/south-china-sea-dispute-china-is-trading-aid-for-support-for-claims-20160606-gpc7qf.html

Frankopan, P. 2019. *The New Silk Roads: The Present and Future of the World.* New York: Alfred A. Knopf.

Fry, G. 1993. At the Margin: The South Pacific and Changing World Order. In R. Leaver (ed.), *Charting the Post-Cold War Order.* Colorado: Westview Press, 224–42.

Fry, G. and S. Tarte. 2015. The 'New Pacific Diplomacy': An Introduction. In G. Fry and S. Tarte (eds), *The New Pacific Diplomacy.* Canberra: ANU Press, 3–19. doi.org/10.22459/npd.12.2015.01

Geall, S. 2017. Clear Waters and Green Mountains: Will Xi Jinping Take the Lead on Climate Change? *Analyses,* 16 November. Lowy Institute. www.lowy institute.org/publications/clear-waters-and-green-mountains-will-xi-jinping-take-lead-climate-change

Global Witness 2018. *Paradise Lost: How China Can Help Solomon Islands Protect its Forests.* Report, 18 October. www.globalwitness.org/en/campaigns/forests/ paradise-lost/

Granados, J.A.T., E. L. Ionides and Ó. Carpintero 2012. Climate Change and the World Economy: Short-run Determinants of Atmospheric CO_2. *Environmental Science & Policy* 21:50–62. doi.org/10.1016/j.envsci.2012.03.008

Grossman, D., M. Chase, G. Finin, W. Gregson, J.W. Hornung, L. Ma, J.R. Reimer and A. Shih 2019. *America's Pacific Island Allies: The Freely Associated States and Chinese Influence*. Santa Monica: RAND Corporation. doi.org/10.7249/rr2973

Harvey, F. 2019. Richer Nations Accused of Stalling Progress on Climate Crisis. *The Guardian*, 14 December. www.theguardian.com/science/2019/dec/13/richer-nations-accused-of-stalling-progress-on-climate-crisis

Huang, C. 2019. As China Chases Economic Growth, Pollution and Poverty Will Take a Back Seat. *South China Morning Post*, 17 March. www.scmp.com/week-asia/opinion/article/3001867/china-chases-economic-growth-pollution-and-poverty-will-take-back

Hunter, J., P. Singh, and J. Aguon. 2018. Broadening Common Heritage: Addressing Gaps in the Deep Sea Mining Regulatory Regime. *Harvard Environmental Law Review*, 16 April. harvardelr.com/2018/04/16/broadening-common-heritage/

IPCC (Intergovernmental Panel on Climate Change) 2018. *Global Warming of 1.5°C. Special Report of the IPCC*. New York: United Nations. www.ipcc.ch/sr15/

Jaipragas, B. 2018. The Tiny Island with a Big Role to Play in US Plans for the South China Sea. *South China Morning Post*, 3 December.

Kaplan, R. 2019. A New Cold War Has Begun. *Foreign Policy*, 7 January. foreignpolicy.com/2019/01/07/a-new-cold-war-has-begun/

Karabell, Z. 2018. A Cold War is Coming, and it Isn't China's Fault. *Foreign Policy*, 31 October. foreignpolicy.com/2018/10/31/a-cold-war-is-coming-and-it-isnt-chinas-fault/

Kerrigan, K. 2018. Former Palau President: Compact 'The Best Deal'. *The Guam Daily Post*, 16 November. www.postguam.com/news/local/former-palau-president-compact-the-best-deal/article_60c04990-e891-11e8-a897-b3c22f850bc5.html

Kratz, A., A. Feng, and L.Wright 2019. New Data on the 'Debt Trap' Question. Rhodium Group Note, 29 April. rhg.com/research/new-data-on-the-debt-trap-question/

Lamontagne, J., P. Reed, G. Marangoni, K. Keller and G. Garner. 2019. Robust Abatement Pathways to Tolerable Climate Futures Require Immediate Global Action. *Nature Climate Change* 9(4):290–94. doi.org/10.1038/s41558-019-0426-8

Laskai, L. 2018. Why Does Everyone Hate Made in China 2025? Council on Foreign Relations, *Net Politics* blog, 28 March. www.cfr.org/blog/why-does-everyone-hate-made-china-2025

Lee, Y. 2019. Taiwan Says China Lures Kiribati with Airplanes after Losing Another Ally. *Reuters*, 19 September. www.reuters.com/article/us-taiwan-diplomacy-kiribati/taiwan-says-china-lures-kiribati-with-airplanes-after-losing-another-ally-idUSKBN1W50DI

Lind, M. 2018. Cold War II. *National Review*, 10 May. www.nationalreview.com/magazine/2018/05/28/us-china-relations-cold-war-ii/

Lowy Institute 2019. Pacific Aid Map. pacificaidmap.lowyinstitute.org/

Lyons, K. 2018. 'Palau against China!': The Tiny Island Standing Up to a Giant. *The Guardian*, 8 September.

Master, F. 2018. Empty Hotels, Idle Boats: What Happens When a Pacific Island Upsets China. *Reuters*, 18 August. www.reuters.com/article/us-pacific-china-palau-insight/empty-hotels-idle-boats-what-happens-when-a-pacific-island-upsets-china-iduskbn1l4036

Mastro, O.S. 2019. The Stealth Superpower: How China Hid Its Global Ambitions. *Foreign Affairs*, January/February. www.foreignaffairs.com/articles/china/china-plan-rule-asia

McCahill, W.C. 2017. China's 'New Era' and 'Xi Jinping Thought'. The National Bureau of Asian Research, 24 October. www.nbr.org/publication/chinas-new-era-and-xi-jinping-thought/

Meick, E., M. Ker and H.M. Chan 2018. *China's Engagement in the Pacific Islands: Implications for the United States*. Staff Research Report, 14 June. Washington DC: US–China Economic and Security Review Commission. www.uscc.gov/sites/default/files/Research/China-Pacific%20Islands%20Staff%20Report.pdf

Monbiot, G. 2016. The Zombie Doctrine. *The Guardian*, 16 April. www.monbiot.com/2016/04/15/the-zombie-doctrine/

Monbiot, G. 2018. While Economic Growth Continues We'll Never Kick Our Fossil Fuels Habit. *The Guardian*, 26 September. www.theguardian.com/commentisfree/2018/sep/26/economic-growth-fossil-fuels-habit-oil-industry

Morgan, W. 2018. The Indo-Pacific and the Blue Pacific. *Devpolicy Blog*, 22 August. www.devpolicy.org/the-indo-pacific-and-the-blue-pacific-20180822/

Morrison, S. 2018. Australia and the Pacific: A New Chapter. Speech at Lavarack Barracks. Townsville, Queensland, 8 November. www.pm.gov.au/media/address-australia-and-pacific-new-chapter

O'Keefe, M. 2018. Why China's 'Debt-Book Diplomacy' in the Pacific Shouldn't Ring Alarm Bells Just Yet. *The Conversation*, 17 May. theconversation.com/why-chinas-debt-book-diplomacy-in-the-pacific-shouldnt-ring-alarm-bells-just-yet-96709

O'Keefe, M. 2019. Morrison's Vanuatu Trip Shows the Government's Continued Focus on Militarising the Pacific. *The Conversation*, 17 January. theconversation.com/morrisons-vanuatu-trip-shows-the-governments-continued-focus-on-militarising-the-pacific-109883

Olson, W. 2019. US Soldiers Return to Palau after 37 Year Hiatus. *Stars and Stripes*. Military.com, 8 April. www.military.com/daily-news/2019/04/08/us-soldiers-return-palau-exercise-after-37-year-hiatus.html

Packham, B. 2018. Canberra to Fund PNG Internet and Electricity Boost. *The Australian*, 14 November. www.theaustralian.com.au/national-affairs/foreign-affairs/canberra-to-fund-png-internet-and-electricity-boost/news-story/652c21a086fc76a21f0c2d73b6edc8dc

Packham, B. 2019. China Eyes Pacific Alliance with the Solomon Islands. *The Australian*, 1 May. www.theaustralian.com.au/nation/politics/china-eyes-pacific-alliance-with-the-solomon-islands/news-story/7b9f0830b8d083054bb998ae22a221ff

Panda, A. 2018. Are Fears of a Chinese Port Facility on Manus Island Justified? *The Diplomat*, 29 August. thediplomat.com/2018/08/are-fears-of-a-chinese-port-facility-on-manus-island-justified/

Pantucci, R. 2018. China's Belt and Road Hits Problems but Is Still Popular. *Financial Times*, Beyond BRICS blog, 15 November. Available at raffaello pantucci.com/2018/11/28/chinas-belt-and-road-hits-problems-but-is-still-popular/

Pence, M. 2018. Remarks by Vice President Pence on the Administration's Policy Toward China. Washington DC: The Hudson Institute, 4 October. china.usembassy-china.org.cn/remarks-by-vice-president-pence-on-the-administrations-policy-toward-china/

Perlez, J. 2016. Tribunal Rejects Beijing's Claims in South China Sea. *The New York Times*, 12 July. www.nytimes.com/2016/07/13/world/asia/south-china-sea-hague-ruling-philippines.html

PIDF (Pacific Islands Development Forum) 2015. Charter of the Pacific Islands Development Forum. Suva: PIDF. www.pidf.int/wp-content/uploads/2017/07/PIDF-Charter.pdf

PIDF (Pacific Islands Development Forum) 2017. *Draft Strategic Plan, 2017–2020*. Suva: PIDF. www.pidf.int/wp-content/uploads/2017/07/PIDF-Strategic-Plan.pdf

Rainey, J. 2019. Economic Expansion Boosts Carbon Emissions, Despite Green-Tech Gains. *NBC News*, 9 January. www.nbcnews.com/news/us-news/economic-boom-spikes-carbon-emissions-despite-green-tech-gains-n956336

Rampton, R. 2019. Pence Rebuffs Solomon Islands PM after Nation Cuts Ties with Taiwan. *Reuters*, 17 September. www.reuters.com/article/us-taiwan-diplomacy-pence-exclusive-idUSKBN1W22WK

Rhodium Group 2019. Preliminary US Emissions Estimates for 2018. Rhodium Group Note, 8 January. rhg.com/research/preliminary-us-emissions-estimates-for-2018/

Rockoff, H. 2016. *The US Economy in WWII as a Model for Coping with Climate Change*. National Bureau of Economic Research Working Paper no. 22590. www.nber.org/papers/w22590

Roy, D. 2014. US–China Relations and the Western Pacific. *The Diplomat*, 16 January. thediplomat.com/2014/01/US–China-relations-and-the-western-pacific/

Sands, G. 2018. Even with US Help, Taiwan Is Fighting a Losing Battle Against China to Keep its Friends and Influence. *South China Morning Post*, 13 September. www.scmp.com/comment/insight-opinion/united-states/article/2164009/even-us-help-taiwan-fighting-losing-battle

Sautman, B. and Y. Hairong 2019. The Truth About Sri Lanka's Hambantota Port, Chinese 'Debt Traps' and 'Asset Seizures'. *South China Morning Post*, 6 May. www.scmp.com/comment/insight-opinion/article/3008799/truth-about-sri-lankas-hambantota-port-chinese-debt-traps

Scrafton, M. 2018. What War Will We Need Manus For? *The Strategist*, 4 December. Australian Strategic Policy Institute. www.aspistrategist.org.au/what-war-will-we-need-manus-for/

SIPRI (Stockholm International Peace Research Institute) 2019. World Military Expenditure Grows to $1.8 Trillion. SIPRI media release, 29 April. www.sipri.org/media/press-release/2019/world-military-expenditure-grows-18-trillion-2018

Sogavare, M. 2019. Statement by the Prime Minister Hon. Manasseh Sogavare on Switch to China. *Solomon Times*, 20 September. www.solomontimes.com/news/statement-by-the-prime-minister-hon-manasseh-sogavare-on-switch-to-china/9362

Spinelli, D. 2019. These Trump Allies Are Preparing for a New Cold War with China. *Mother Jones*, 22 April. www.motherjones.com/politics/2019/04/these-trump-allies-steve-bannon-frank-gaffney-new-china-cold-war/

Strong, M. 2018. Officials from Taiwan Ally Solomon Islands Visit China. *Taiwan News*, 16 June.

Sutter, R. 2018. *China–Russia Relations: Strategic Implications and U.S. Policy Options.* NBR Special Report no. 73. The National Bureau of Asian Research. www.nbr.org/publication/china-russia-relations-strategic-implications-and-u-s-policy-options/

Talmadge, C. 2018. Beijing's Nuclear Option; Why a U.S.–Chinese War Could Spiral Out of Control. *Foreign Affairs*, November/December: 44–50.

Tarabay, J. 2018. CIA Official: China Wants to Replace US as World Superpower. *CNN*, 21 July. www.cnn.com/2018/07/20/politics/china-cold-war-us-super power-influence/index.html

Tarapore, A. 2018. The Geopolitics of the Quad. The National Bureau of Asian Research, 16 November. www.nbr.org/publication/the-geopolitics-of-the-quad/

Tong, A. 2015. 'Charting its Own Course': A Paradigm Shift in Pacific Diplomacy. In G. Fry and S. Tarte (eds), *The New Pacific Diplomacy*. Canberra, ANU Press, 3–19. doi.org/10.22459/npd.12.2015.02

UCS (Union of Concerned Scientists) 2013. Environmental Impacts of Renewable Energy Technologies. UCS blog, 5 March. www.ucsusa.org/clean-energy/renewable-energy/environmental-impacts

Underwood, R.A. 2017. The Changing American Lake in the Middle of the Pacific. Address at Georgetown University, 16 November. www.uog.edu/_resources/files/news-and-announcements/2017-2018/robert-underwood-the_changing_american_lake-111617.pdf

USCC (US–China Economic and Security Review Commission) 2018. 2018 Report to Congress. Washington, DC: US–China Economic and Security Review Commission, November. www.uscc.gov/annual-report/2018-annual-report-congress

US Government (Department of Defense) 2019. *Indo-Pacific Strategy Report: Preparedness, Partnership, and Promoting a Networked Region.* Washington DC: Department of Defense, 1 June. media.defense.gov/2019/Jul/01/2002152311/-1/-1/1/DEPARTMENT-OF-DEFENSE-INDO-PACIFIC-STRATEGY-REPORT-2019.PDF

Walt, S. 2018. What Sort of World Are We Headed For? *Foreign Policy*, 2 October. foreignpolicy.com/2018/10/02/what-sort-of-world-are-we-headed-for/

Watts, J. 2018. We Have 12 Years to Limit Climate Change Catastrophe, Warns UN. *The Guardian*, 8 October. www.theguardian.com/environment/2018/oct/08/global-warming-must-not-exceed-15c-warns-landmark-un-report

WEF (World Economic Forum) 2020. *The Global Risks Report 2020.* 15th edition. Geneva: WEF. www.weforum.org/reports/the-global-risks-report-2020

Wesley-Smith, T. 2013. China's Rise in Oceania: Issues and Perspectives. *Pacific Affairs* 82(2):351–72. doi.org/10.5509/2013862351

Wesley-Smith, T. 2016. Geopolitics, Self-Determination, and China's Rise in Oceania. In M. Ishihara (ed.), *Self-Determinable Development of Small Islands.* Singapore: Springer, 85–99. doi.org/10.1007/978-981-10-0132-1_5

White, H. 2017. Without America: Australia in the New Asia. *Quarterly Essay* 68:1–81. www.quarterlyessay.com.au/essay/2017/11/without-america

White, H. 2019. Can the US Win the New Cold War with China? Not without Risking a Nuclear War. *South China Morning Post*, 6 March. www.scmp.com/comment/insight-opinion/united-states/article/2188648/can-us-win-new-cold-war-china-not-without

Woodward, J. 2017. *The US vs China: Asia's New Cold War?* Manchester: Manchester University Press.

Wroe, D. 2018. Australia Will Compete with China to Save Pacific Sovereignty, Says Bishop. *The Sydney Morning Herald*, 18 June. www.smh.com.au/politics/federal/australia-will-compete-with-china-to-save-pacific-sovereignty-says-bishop-20180617-p4zm1h.html

Wyeth, G. 2018. Is China Building Roads to Nowhere in the Pacific? *The Diplomat*, 17 January. thediplomat.com/2018/01/is-china-building-roads-to-nowhere-in-the-pacific

Xi, J. 2018. Jointly Charting a Course Towards a Brighter Future. Speech at APEC CEO Summit, Port Moresby, Papua New Guinea. *Xinhua*, 17 November. www.xinhuanet.com/english/2018-11/17/c_137613904.htm

Yale News 2018. We May Be Underestimating Future Economic Growth, and its Potential Climate Effects. 14 May. news.yale.edu/2018/05/14/we-may-be-underestimating-effects-economic-growth-climate-change

Zhang, D. 2018. China, India and Japan in the Pacific: Latest Developments, Motivations and Impact. DPA Discussion Paper 2018/6. Canberra: ANU. dpa.bellschool.anu.edu.au/sites/default/files/publications/attachments/2018-09/dpa_dp2018_6_zhang_final.pdf

3

Australia's Response to China in the Pacific: From Alert to Alarmed

Merriden Varrall

Introduction

Australia has moved from a position of alert to one of alarm regarding China's growing presence in the Pacific. As one security analyst explains, 'Canberra is increasingly concerned about Beijing's intensified interest in the Pacific islands, including efforts to sway political elites and targeted pursuit of transportation infrastructure projects in locations across Melanesia' (Graham 2018a). This viewpoint is based on the combination of two main factors: Australia's concerns about China and Australia's understandings of the vulnerabilities of the Pacific. Australia increasingly sees China as a strategic threat at global, regional and national levels, while at the same time it is closely tied to the Chinese economy. Concomitantly, Australia functions on a deeply held assumption that Pacific Island countries (PICs) are in no position to resist China as its presence grows. This chapter will examine the multifaceted aspects of Australia's strong and growing concern about China, including views that China is a revisionist country determined to rewrite the rules of the global order and apprehension about the impact of a rising China on Australia's national interests. It will also look at Australia's concerns about China's impact on the Pacific Islands region and how a stronger China in the Pacific could negatively affect Australia. The chapter will then look at how Australia understands the Pacific Islands region—its needs and interests—and discuss Australian perceptions of how capable, or otherwise, the Pacific is to resist China, comparing these with the views from PICs. It will examine how the combination of these concerns results in a sense of alarm regarding China's intentions and behaviours in the Pacific, as they affect Australia, the region and the international system. Australia's recent Pacific 'Step-Up' policy is a major element of an effort to counteract these concerns, looking to ensure that Australia is the region's preferred partner. Ultimately, this chapter will ask whether Australia's approach to ameliorating its concerns about China in the Pacific Islands is likely to achieve the desired goals.

Australia's understanding of China's rise

For at least a decade, Australia has been observing China's increasing presence on the global stage, in the region and, more recently, within Australia itself with considerable interest. However, in recent years, there has been a distinct shift from observation to anxiety. Australia's foreign policy White Paper of 2003 described China as an economic opportunity, with the focus of the bilateral relationship on engagement and building a strategic economic partnership (Australian Government 2003:5). Then, Australia did not fear the demise of the US's role in global or regional security, confident that no country or group of countries would be able to challenge the US's capacity to shape the global environment. However, by 2017, the central security concern in the new foreign policy white paper was the challenge posed to Australia by China's expanding role in international affairs, occurring at the same time as the US's apparent withdrawal. The 2017 White Paper focused on the changing power balance in the Indo-Pacific, noting that 'the United States has been the dominant power in our region throughout Australia's post–World War II history. Today, China is challenging America's position' (Australian Government 2017:1). The white paper advocates that the US should maintain its commitment and encourages China to operate according to the existing rules.

Likewise, the Australian Government's *Strong and Secure: A Strategy for Australia's National Security* (Australian Government 2013b), the country's first, refers to the risk of another state seeking to influence Australia or its regional and global partners by economic, political or military pressure. It stops short of naming China, but the implication is clear (Hayward-Jones 2013:5). Recent defence white papers also note

Australian concerns about China. The *2009 Defence White Paper* made clear that Australia viewed China as a security challenge for the regional order. While somewhat more moderate in tone, the *2013 Defence White Paper* warned of the danger of a 'major power with hostile intentions' establishing bases 'in our immediate neighbourhood from which it could project force against us' (Australian Government 2013a:25). In its *2016 Defence White Paper*, the Australian Government criticised China directly in some places, as well as referring obliquely to 'newly powerful countries' that 'want greater influence and to challenge some of the rules in the global architecture established some 70 years ago … leading to uncertainty and tensions'(Australian Government 2016:45).

In recent years, many prominent Australian politicians and commentators have taken the stance that China is a revisionist power that seeks to undermine or reinvent the existing structures of the international order. This narrative is widespread across media as well as policy and political circles. For example, then minister for foreign affairs Julie Bishop and prime minister Malcolm Turnbull made a number of high-profile public remarks regarding their concern about China's role in the international system, which were reported across the Australian media. In 2017, Turnbull gave a keynote address at the Shangri-La Dialogue in Singapore that warned of the dangers of Chinese aggression and the importance of maintaining the 'rules-based order', highlighting unilateral actions to militarise or create territory. He advised China to respect others' sovereignty (see, for example, Harvey 2017; Smethurst 2017; Farrow 2017; SBS News 2017). Bishop backed Turnbull's strong line, saying that China had acted in 'direct disregard' of the international order (see, for example, Riordan 2017). Nick Warner, the Director General of newly formed intelligence agency the Office for National Intelligence (ONI), argued that the rules-based order is under threat by countries who prefer to use strength rather than abide by existing rules and norms, alluding— if not referring directly—to China (ABC Radio National 2019). Many public intellectuals and think tank analysts have made similar comments (see, for example, Bisley and Schreer 2018; Chellaney 2018; Graham 2018a; Medcalf 2015).

Impact on Australia's national interests

There are several aspects to how this broader concern about China's rise is seen to be impacting Australia's national interests. One element is the growing anxiety about China's influence on Australian politics, public debate and freedom of speech (see, for example, Chen 2017; Grattan 2017; Smith 2017). Intellectual-about-town Clive Hamilton also weighed in on the debate with his high-profile book *Silent Invasion: China's Influence in Australia* in which he paints China very clearly as 'Australia's enemy', determined not only to control Chinese at home but to dominate the world, including Australia, by whatever means (Hamilton 2018; for a review of the book, see Podger 2018).

The question of Chinese influence in Australia became a heated public debate after the ABC's *Four Corners* program and Fairfax Media released a joint investigation into China's power and influence in Australia in June 2017, dramatically labelling it a 'tale of secrets, power and intimidation' (ABC News and Fairfax 2017). In the program, journalists 'uncover[ed] how China's Communist Party (CCP) is secretly infiltrating Australia' in order to undermine Australian interests and promote the CCP's agenda (ibid.). The concern around Chinese influence centres on the growing role and power of China's United Front Work Department (UFWD) and its agenda to strengthen the authority and legitimacy of the CCP both in China and abroad (see Groot 2015). The UFWD works to convince those who are not the CCP's natural allies that China and the CCP do not pose any kind of threat. It is not easy to be clear about who may be working for the UFWD and, as a result, many Chinese individuals have come to be suspected of promoting the UFWD agenda in Australia. For example, over the past several years, papers and articles have proliferated around the potential role of Chinese students in influencing debates and views in Australia (see, for example, among many others: Garnaut 2017; Gill and Jakobson 2017; Joske 2017; Laurenceson 2017; Seo 2018; Varrall 2017). Chinese media in Australia has also been viewed as a source of concern (see Birtles 2017; Lim and Bergin 2018). Some Chinese businesspeople came under suspicion of disloyalty to Australia because of connections with the United Front or CCP. Connections between Australian politicians and Chinese businesspeople with CCP or UFWD links were closely scrutinised and, in some cases, this scrutiny led to political resignations such as that of former Australian Labor Party (ALP) senator Sam Dastyari (see, for example, Brophy 2019). In response, new national security and foreign interference laws were introduced in 2018, generally accepted as being long overdue (Douek 2018).

Australia is also worried about China choking off economic ties should it decide to do so. Australia is acutely sensitive to the risk that it may experience 'sanctions with Chinese characteristics', as Gavekal

Dragonomics described it in an internal note to clients (Xie and Cui 2017). The Australian economy is closely linked to China—China is Australia's largest trading partner and has been for some years. The economic relationship is broadening and deepening across many areas, particularly in services such as tourism and education. For many educational institutions, international students, of which Chinese students make up a large proportion, are an important source of fee revenue (RBA 2018; see also Smith and Lim 2018). There is considerable concern around what a government-encouraged downturn of Chinese students could mean to the viability of Australian universities, given that they represent around 30 per cent of the international student population and a considerable proportion of funding in some universities (see, for example, White 2018). Linda Jakobson from *China Matters* notes that a warning issued by the Chinese embassy in December 2017 could be read as 'the very first small step in the use of economic coercion' (Smith and Lim 2018). Around the same time, an op-ed article in Chinese newspaper *The Global Times,* titled 'Australia must do more for Chinese students', argued that Australia was not an ideal destination for Chinese students (Wang 2017). Interestingly, this article appeared in the English-language version of the paper, suggesting it was a message intended for Western rather than Chinese readers. There are indications that these signals are having some impact. For example, Australian Department of Education and Training data suggests that while the number of Chinese students to Australia continued to increase in 2018, the rate of growth has dropped by 7 per cent (Australian Government 2018). Coinciding with the most heated discussions about Chinese influence, Australia found its beef exports stranded in Chinese ports and there was also a similarly unexplained slowdown in clearance times for Australian wine and cheese.[1] In early 2019, Australian coal exports were blocked or slowed in ports in northeast China (Walker 2019). Despite Beijing denying any official ban, it was speculated that this slowdown could be retaliation against Australia's ban on Chinese telecommunications company Huawei from bidding on Australia's 5G network (Bloomberg News 2019). At the time of going to press, the China's embassy in Australia had taken the unusual step of releasing a list of 14 grievances, including the Huawei and ZTE ban, and 'incessant wanton interference in China's Xinjiang, Hong Kong and Taiwan affairs', but also concerns that went well beyond

---

1   Australian business representatives, December 2018. Conversations with author.

China's core interests, including funding of an 'anti-China' think tank and 'spreading disinformation imported from the US' about COVID-19 (Kearsley et al. 2020).

China has in the past responded to South Korea's announcement that it would host a US missile-defence system in 2017 by cancelling group tours and closing some local operations of Korean businesses, hurting the South Korean economy for several months. In November 2016, China imposed fees on Mongolian imports after Mongolia hosted a visit from the Dalai Lama. In May of that year, group tours and agricultural imports to Taiwan were cut after President Tsai Ing-wen omitted the One China principle in a speech. In 2012, the Philippines attempted to arrest Chinese fishermen in disputed waters; China suspended imports of Philippine bananas and issued a travel alert. In 2010, China cut imports of Norwegian salmon after Chinese political activist Liu Xiaobo was awarded the Nobel Peace Prize. Also in 2010, after Japan arrested a Chinese fisherman in disputed waters, China blocked exports of rare earths to Japan (Xie and Cui 2017).

In addition to these concerns about Chinese political influence and potential economic leverage in Australia, Australia is also highly alert to the challenge of China as a strategic military threat. This is particularly true of China's increasing role in the Pacific Islands region, as will be explored in more detail in the following section.

China's impacts on and influence in the Pacific Islands region

With these broader concerns about China's increasing global role in mind, Australia has for many years been observing China's activities in the Pacific Islands region with some unease. Over the past 15 years, a number of scholarly and policy-focused papers have drawn policymakers' attention to the topic. For example, in 2003, an article titled 'Dragon in Paradise: China's Rising Star in Oceania' appeared in *The National Interest,* in which authors John Henderson, Benjamin Reilly and Nathaniel Peffer warned of the 'important long-term consequences' of China's growing role in Oceania (2003:1). In 2006 the Australian Parliament's Senate Standing Committee on Foreign Affairs, Defence and Trade released a report on Australia's relationship with China, Chapter 10 of which was dedicated to understanding China's relationship with countries in the Southwest Pacific and the implications for Australia (Parliament of Australia 2006). In 2007, Terence Wesley-Smith published a paper on China as a new force in Pacific politics (Wesley-Smith 2007). In the past several years this interest has noticeably increased and expanded—from discussions in academic and policy circles to numerous articles on the topic of Chinese influence in the Pacific Islands region in Australian think tanks and media. Articles decrying China's 'mighty orbit' in the Pacific (Saunokonoko 2018), its foreign influence as 'offensive' and a danger to Australia, appear regularly (see Brady 2017; Brook 2018; Dobell 2018 and others).

There are a number of recurring themes in the Australian literature about China in the Pacific Islands. In particular, many commentators raise concerns about Chinese aid, including its developmental effectiveness, its labour and environmental standards, links to local corruption, its potential military presence and its potential for creating debt burdens that could be utilised for political purposes. Here I examine those that are of the most concern to Australia.

Developmental effectiveness

Australian government aid officials have long been concerned that Chinese development interventions in the region not only had few sustainable development impacts, but also actually undermined the efforts of traditional donors like Australia.[2] Chinese aid to the Pacific was in Australian headlines again in 2018 when former Australian minister for international development and the Pacific Concetta Fierravanti-Wells described it as 'useless', with few economic or health benefits (Graue and Dziedzic 2018). These concerns reflect a long tradition of criticism of Chinese aid globally, including an influential piece by Moses Naim in 2009 that described China as a 'rogue donor' providing 'very, very toxic' loans to developing countries. Including China with Iran, Saudi Arabia and Venezuela, Naim argued that 'their goal is not to help other countries develop ... Rogue aid providers couldn't care less about the long-term well-being of the population of the countries they "aid"' (Naim 2009). However, more recent analyses suggest that while the developmental effectiveness of Chinese aid in the Pacific is mixed, results are 'dependent in large part on the actions of Pacific Island governments' (Dornan and Brant 2014; see also Smith 2018).

---

2   AusAID (Australia's former Australian international aid agency) and Department of Foreign Affairs and Trade (DFAT) officials in Beijing 2011–14. Conversations with author. AusAID was merged with DFAT in late 2013.

Corruption

Putative connections between an increased Chinese presence and corruption have been a source of concern around the world. Research undertaken in Africa suggests that there is an increase in local corruption around active Chinese project sites, which lingers after the project implementation period has ended. In Africa at least, this effect does not seem to be because of the increase in economic activity per se, but rather because the Chinese presence has an impact on local norms. These impacts do not occur with other bilateral donors or multilateral donors like the World Bank (Isaksson and Kotsadam 2016). The broader picture around the relationship between aid and corruption is inconclusive, so it would be premature to conclude that there is a simple causal connection (ibid.).

However, Chinese investment and the potential it holds for fuelling corruption in the Pacific Islands region is certainly a source of concern in Australia and has been for some years. At the top end of the scale are incidents such as the use of Chinese aid money to make an AU$1 million bribe to the former Papua New Guinea (PNG) prime minister, Sir Michael Somare, as 'part of Beijing's push to exert greater influence in the Pacific' (Grigg and McKenzie 2018). At the more day-to-day level, as Dornan and Brant (2014) note, lack of transparency and an insufficient involvement of the civil service in project selection processes means political leaders can negotiate directly with Chinese contractors. Practices where Chinese construction companies provide benefits such as meals and travel to ministers when lobbying for projects, are described by civil servants as 'corruption', although some argue this is more 'political clientelism' or 'leadership by "big men"', in which gains are received but not necessarily for personal benefit (Dornan and Brant 2014). Dobell noted in 2007 that the competition between Taiwan and the People's Republic of China (PRC) for diplomatic recognition was 'destabilising island states … making Pacific politics more corrupt and more violent' (2007:17).

The issue of Chinese presence and corruption has also been observed by some Pacific Island leaders. For example, Vanuatu Foreign Minister Ralph Regenvanu has argued that policing of local laws and issues around corruption are the biggest problems in dealing with China (Smith and Lim 2019). However, Terence Wesley-Smith (2007) argued that in fact there is little evidence to suggest that China's activities have encouraged corruption and instability in Oceania. The degree and extent of corruption caused by China's increased presence in the Pacific is not clear; however, it continues to be a source of considerable concern for Australia. For Australia, the concern about corruption is not only that it undermines good governance and the effectiveness of aid, but that it is also a particular risk in countries that, in Australian narratives, are often understood as dangerously close to becoming 'failed states'. In 2005, then prime minister John Howard noted that for many 'fragile tiny states' in the Pacific Islands region, 'poor governance, crime and corruption pose a real threat to both economic development and to regional security' (Howard 2005).

Debt

Much of the literature around Chinese interest in PICs discusses the issue of debt burden. Debt is considered to be a burden when a country has trouble paying back the loans it has received, creating pressure on the economy. How much debt a country can manage is usually measured by looking at the ratio of debt to how much the economy is growing (GDP). Chinese bilateral development assistance does not adhere to the OECD's Development Assistance Committee (DAC) guidelines and loans can be provided at whatever concessional interest rate is negotiated between the two parties (for more detailed information on Chinese aid, see Lancaster 2007; Brautigam 2009, particularly Chapters 4, 5 and 6; Dornan and Brant 2014; Varrall 2018; Johnston and Rudyak 2017; Zhang 2017, 2018). Several countries in the Pacific Islands region have high debt-to-GDP ratios and are considered to be in 'debt distress'. The countries in the high-risk category are Kiribati, Marshall Islands, Micronesia, Samoa, Tonga and Tuvalu (Fox and Dornan 2018). Tonga provides an illustration of where Chinese aid practices can result in debt distress with questionable developmental outcomes: 14.5 million Tongan paʻanga (around AU$9 million) in aid money for expanding the royal palace (Dreher et al. 2017, who note that it is unclear whether the funding was a loan or via export credits). However, it is incorrect to assume that all PICs that have high debt are in debt to China or that all countries that have received Chinese loans are in difficult fiscal circumstances. For example, Cook Islands Finance Minister Mark Beer notes that the country is managing its debts well, referring to an Asian Development Bank report that shows the country has a debt-to-GDP ratio of around 25 per cent, well below 'danger' levels (Hill 2018). Importantly, as Fox and Dornan (2018) point out, around half of the countries in the high-risk category do not recognise the PRC, but rather have a diplomatic relationship with Taiwan, so do not have access to Chinese concessional finance. In total,

China holds around 12 per cent of the debt owed by Pacific Island nations and it is only Tonga, Samoa and Vanuatu where Chinese lending makes up more than one-third of total debt. In Samoa, debts to multilateral development banks is higher than debt to China. Vanuatu is not at high risk of debt distress and government statements suggest the country will be working towards lowering levels of debt (Fox and Dornan 2018).

Most recently, Lowy Institute research published in 2019, drawing on data from the International Monetary Fund (IMF) and the Lowy Institute's own Pacific Aid Map, argued that while debt burden is rising in the Pacific, this reflects a confluence of factors and is more closely linked to the region's risk of disaster than excessive Chinese lending (Rajah et al. 2019). The research also records that China is not the dominant financier in the region and, except for Tonga where China holds more than half of public debt, traditional creditors like Japan, the Asia Development Bank and the World Bank play a more significant role. In the case of Tonga, China has twice agreed to defer debt repayments with little apparently in return (ibid.). Additionally, the analysis shows that, in 90 per cent of cases, Chinese loans were made in situations where at the time there appeared to be scope to sustainably absorb the debt, not dissimilar to other official lenders in the region (ibid.).

Strategic military threat

Concerns about China as a strategic military threat are particularly resonant in relation to the Pacific Islands region, based on a long-held view that it is via this route that adversaries could project military power into Australia. Since the 1970s, defence white papers have made clear that the regions near Australia need to be kept secure, stable and able to intercept any adversaries before they reach Australia (Hegarty 2015:8). As Graeme Dobell argues, 'Australia's strategic denial instinct in the South Pacific is a constant, with a 140-year history (it helped drive federation in 1901)' (2017). Similarly, Greg Sheridan and Cameron Stewart (2018) argued in *The Australian* that:

> Australia's intelligence and analysis agencies believe that the South Pacific now presents the greatest strategic threat to Australia, as a result of what they believe is Beijing's intention to establish a military base in the region. This marks the first time since World War II that the South Pacific has been of such intense strategic concern to Canberra.

While this anxiety around the Pacific as an access point for adversaries has been recorded in defence white papers for decades, the current degree of concern has not been seen since World War II and perhaps the Cold War to a lesser extent. Australia's 'vulnerability to threats from hostile powers coming from or through the region' was demonstrated with Japan's advance into Australia during World War II. At that time, as Shadow Defence Minister Richard Marles said in a speech at the Lowy Institute in November 2017, PICs like Kiribati, Solomon Islands and PNG were the scenes of horrific and intense fighting in which thousands were killed. The Bomana War Cemetery in PNG is the largest Australian war cemetery in the world, with around 4,000 Australian defence force personnel buried there (Marles 2017). Concerns were reignited during the Cold War when Libya and the USSR 'made overtures' to countries in the Pacific (Wallis 2017:7).

Now, many in the Australian policy community are convinced that it is China's ambition in the Pacific Islands region to set up one or more military bases as part of a global strategy of force projection. As one security academic explains, it is now becoming a 'settled view' within the Australian Government that 'Beijing has strategic designs on the so-called "second island chain", including ambitions to establish some form of military base, potentially upsetting the Western powers' "traditional" pre-dominance that has existed without serious challenge since 1945' (Graham 2018b). The government's fear is that China is seeking to find a 'malleable country' from which it can begin its 'salami-slicing tactics' in the Pacific Islands region.[3] They foresee that China would pursue a strategy of first setting up something apparently innocuous like a monitoring outpost to police Chinese fishing vessels, followed by the appointment of a defence attaché and then, within 10 years, would install full military facilities.

Reflecting these concerns, reports that China was in discussions with Vanuatu to establish a military base there caused consternation in Australia. Dr Malcolm Davis of the Australian Strategic Policy Institute (ASPI, a think tank funded by the Australian Department of Defence) has noted that Chinese spending in Vanuatu is not just about promoting tourism, arguing that 'they're thinking commercial influence, political influence and ultimately a military presence' (Bilton 2018). China is funding a major new wharf on the island of Espiritu Santo in Vanuatu,

---

3   Australian analyst on the Pacific Islands region, December 2018. Interview with author.

which raised eyebrows in defence, intelligence and diplomatic circles 'because while its stated purpose is to host cruise ships, its size means it also has the potential to service naval vessels' (Jonathan Pryke from the Lowy Institute, as quoted in Wroe 2018). The notion was compared with China's development of a military base in Djibouti and reports that it is considering building military facilities in Sri Lanka and Pakistan, in which China's economic influence appears to be being utilised for strategic purposes. Military experts such as Charles Edel from the United States Studies Centre argue that if a Chinese military base were to be established in Vanuatu, or anywhere in the Pacific, other bases would soon follow, allowing the Chinese military to challenge US and allied access to the region, fundamentally undermining Australia's security (as quoted in Wroe 2018). A proposed Chinese port on Manus Island as well as the possible development of harbours in PNG has also worried Australia, as it could provide 'Beijing with a prime strategic location for projecting military power north towards US forces in Guam, or south towards Australia' (Davis 2018).

Others, however, have argued that despite reports, China has in fact 'not attempted to establish port facilities or military bases anywhere in the vast reaches of Oceania' (Wesley-Smith, 2007:2; see also Hayward-Jones 2013:7). From over a decade ago, researchers of the Pacific Islands region, such as Terence Wesley-Smith and Jenny Hayward-Jones, have observed that analysts who make claims about Chinese military intentions 'offered no proof that China is actually engaged in any military-related activities in Oceania, or has any plans to do so' (Wesley-Smith 2007:15; see also Hayward-Jones 2013:7). Now, despite ongoing concerns, just as argued in this research, China has not established any actual military presence in the Pacific. One possible exception is the Chinese satellite-tracking facility established in Kiribati in 1997. Some suspect this facility was used to monitor US missile-testing activities in the neighbouring Marshall Islands. However, when Kiribati changed its diplomatic recognition to Taiwan in November 2003, China dismantled the tracking station, which does not suggest that it was of critical strategic importance to China (Wesley-Smith 2007:16). Another is the reported approach to the Government of Timor-Leste by Chinese defence firms to establish a radar to monitor shipping and illegal fishing in the Wetar Strait with the condition that the facilities be staffed by Chinese technicians. Then vice prime minister José Guterres contacted the US embassy with concerns that the facilities could be used for other purposes and the project did not proceed (WikiLeaks 2008).

Influence

Australia is particularly concerned about rising Chinese influence in the Pacific Islands region and the implications this may have in the region, globally and directly on Australia's interests. Critics argue that China's propensity to give loans regardless of a country's existing debt burden and repayment capacity is creating a situation in which loan-recipient countries will be so crippled by their debt to China as to be vulnerable to Chinese political influence. That is, they will be economically beholden to China and be in no position to resist China's requests for certain behaviours and positions—for example, regarding China's claims in the South China Sea or the development of military facilities. Commentators point to Hambantota Port in Sri Lanka as an example of the possible result of a debt burden to China. In that case, Sri Lanka was unable to service the loan for the port's construction and the two countries negotiated a debt-for-equity swap accompanied by a 99-year lease for China to manage the port. As one commentator put it, 'China wants to conquer the world, and its sneaky strategy to get there already has several countries in a sticky situation' (Fernando 2018).

The shorthand for this phenomenon is 'debt-trap diplomacy' and it generates great concern in Australia as it suggests China could increase its influence over Pacific Island nations to the detriment of Australia's own influence and interests. In one example, Cameron Hawker, an analyst with the Australian Defence Force Academy (ADFA) and a former adviser to the ruling Coalition government, is quoted in a newspaper article as saying, 'I think we all know now is that [Australia's] role in the Pacific is being challenged by [the fact that] China's frankly cashed up and it's spending its money pretty freely across the South Pacific' (McCarthy 2016). An article in the *Australian Financial Review* (AFR) argued that while Pacific Island countries in general, and PNG in particular, have 'historically been in Australia's orbit', PNG has been 'rapidly taking on Chinese loans it can't afford to pay and offers a strategic location in addition to significant LNG and resource deposits' for China (Kehoe 2018; for similar perspectives on debt distress caused by China, see also Fernando 2018; Garrick 2018; Pryke 2019). A report written by Harvard scholars for the US State Department— classified but a version of it was leaked to the AFR—argued that countries like PNG, Vanuatu and Tonga were at risk of undue Chinese influence because of the unsustainable loans they had received (Parker and Chefitz 2018; discussed by O'Keefe 2018).

The debate around debt and influence has not been clearly resolved. According to Fox and Dornan, Tonga is the only country where the debt-trap diplomacy narrative may have some basis—and even then understanding of how these loans came about makes this unlikely. Based on their analysis, they conclude that while debt is a problem in the region, the Chinese '"debt-trap diplomacy" argument is without foundation' (for an analysis of Pacific Islands region debt, see Fox and Dornan 2018). Rajah, Pryke and Dayant (2019) argue in their research that the most recent evidence suggests that accusations of China using debt-trap diplomacy for leverage are inaccurate, although they emphasise that this could change if current practices continue without substantial restructuring along the lines of formal lending rules similar to those of the multilateral development banks. Smith, however, notes that there are already signs in the Pacific Islands region that the PRC is willing to leverage aid for political advantage, citing examples such as Fiji's closure of its trade and tourism office in Taiwan immediately after Prime Minister Bainimarama attended the Belt and Road Forum in May 2017 (Smith 2018).

Australia's understanding of the Pacific Islands region

Australia has long considered the Pacific Islands region to be 'its backyard', with associated feelings of obligation and managerial responsibility. The perceptions and understandings that underpin the relationship tend to be taken for granted in Australian political, policy and public circles and are rarely interrogated. However, these understandings are not neutral, but constructed and maintained according to particular philosophical and ideological visions of what is and should be happening in the region and have consequences for the policy options Australia considers appropriate or necessary.

Australian commentary on the Pacific Islands region has for some time been founded on the concepts of vulnerability, weakness and the danger of the collapse of the state. These weaknesses are usually ascribed to PICs' small size, low economic growth and general economic strength, and governance challenges. For example, Graeme Dobell (2019) from ASPI argued that 'the familiar list' of challenges facing the Pacific is as cruel as ever—small economies with big challenges, rapid population growth and stretched governments. Plenty of modern ills are arriving, along with climate change to rev recurring natural disasters.

This kind of framing is not new. As Greg Fry observed over two decades ago, prominent Australian images of the South Pacific and Pacific Islanders depicted a 'doomsday' or 'nightmare' scenario (Fry 1997:313). Wesley-Smith argued that the literature around governance in the Pacific Islands region gives the impression that 'all island leaders are corrupt, malleable, self-serving and impulsive' (2007:18). Overall, the picture painted in the great majority of the Australian literature about the Pacific is one of a region and individual countries in multifaceted crisis— economic, governance, health, democratically and security.

Problems and solutions: What does a 'region in crisis' need?

This framing is important because how a 'problem' is constructed and understood serves to allow and disallow certain solutions as seemingly acceptable and appropriate. As Fry argued in 1997, these conceptions 'significantly affect the parameters within which future possibilities are worked out' (1997:313). Over time, and continuing today, the framing of the Pacific Islands as a region in the grip of one or another of multiple forms of crisis allows Australia to conclude that even if certain parties, including the Pacific Islanders themselves, do not like the policy solutions Australia proffers, they are necessary and inevitable. For example, commenting on the *2017 Foreign Policy White Paper*'s policy shift based on Pacific integration with Australia, Dobell (2017) contended that critics will argue that 'integration is colonialism redux, a polite term for dominance'. But, he argued, this does not mean it is a poor policy, rather, the criticisms need to be countered. He stated:

> The rebuttal will require slow persuasion and consistent delivery. The promise of integration with Australia and New Zealand is the offer of a stronger, richer region—because poor and weak states can't be truly independent.

The 'doomsday' Australian discourse continues to result in a perception that Pacific Islanders needed to reinvent themselves—and be reinvented— as rational, liberal, democratic, modern actors in the 'real' world (Fry 1997).

A region in crisis requires a proactive response from Australia

The 'naturally reached' conclusion in Australia has tended to be that the Australian Government must take proactive measures to manage, mitigate, control or prevent weakness becoming a broader problem both for PICs themselves and for Australia's own interests. The Regional Assistance Mission to Solomon Islands (RAMSI) is a good example. First articulated in 2002, the idea of Solomon Islands as a potential failed state was quickly taken up by Australian analysts and commentators (Kabutaulaka 2005:295). In a report with the unequivocal title *Our Failing Neighbour—Australia and the Future of Solomon Islands*, ASPI argued that the imminent risk of Solomon Islands becoming a failed state meant that Australia was obliged to take decisive action in order to prevent 'Solomon Islands becoming a vector in the region for the kind of transnational problems that are so common elsewhere in the world', which would 'make Australia significantly more vulnerable to transnational criminal operations' as well as flowing over to other countries in the region (Wainwright 2003:13–14). The ASPI report's construction of the situation was influential. Then prime minister John Howard used almost exactly the same language in an interview with ABC Radio that same year, and in 2004, RAMSI Special Coordinator Nick Warner used the same reasons to explain the importance of the intervention force in a speech to a national security conference (Warner 2004).

A region in crisis cannot manage external threats without support from Australia

This framing of the Pacific Islands as a region in crisis also underpins how Australia is responding to China's increased presence in the region. The understanding that Pacific Island nations are weak, and governments are overstretched or corrupt, results in the conclusion that they are either incapable of resisting Chinese overtures and influence efforts, or willing to sell themselves cheaply. For example, the aforementioned 2006 Senate Standing Committee's report noted that 'the weakness of Pacific islands make them attractive strategic resources for China', drawing on Henderson, Reilly and Peffer's argument that 'their financial and other problems make the support of Pacific states cheap for Beijing to buy' (Parliament of Australia 2006, citing Henderson et al. 2003:98).

In this research cited by the Senate, the authors argue that the Pacific Islands'

> utility as … possible sites for port facilities or even military bases, means that relatively small investments in these countries can have major longer-term payoffs for countries like China.

Likewise, Susan Windybank from the influential Australian think tank Centre for Independent Studies (CIS) argued in 2005 that Pacific Island countries were vulnerable to what she termed 'The China Syndrome', in which China works to cultivate new friends and allies while others such as the United States are distracted elsewhere (Windybank 2005:28). She raised concerns that the Pacific could 'become a testing ground for China's growing power' (ibid.:29; see also Wallis 2017).

A region in crisis—what did Australia do wrong before and what should Australia do about it now?

With these fundamental assumptions about the Pacific settled into concrete fact, the issue for Australian analysts and policymakers is then framed as a simple technocratic question of 'what did Australia do wrong before and what should Australia do about it now?' (For example, see Dobell 2019; Firth 2018; Hegarty 2015;Wallis 2018).

The question of 'what Australia should do about the Pacific' has been fraught for decades. Australian engagement with, and approaches to, the Pacific Islands region have fluctuated greatly over time, often reflecting events in the region, the advocacy of 'policy entrepreneurs' and the personal interest of the Australian foreign minister of the time. Jonathan Schultz noted in his research that Australia's approach to the Pacific Islands region can be characterised into key periods. He describes 1988–93 as 'constructive commitment'; 1993–96 as focused on economic reform and resource management; 1996–2000 as a period of 'confidence and neglect'; a 'brief and glorious period' from 2000–03; and 'intervention and confrontation' from 2003–07 (Schultz 2012, 2014).

Again, events in Solomon Islands in 2003 provide a good example of the mercurial nature of Australia's approach to the region. In that year, the government switched from adamant rejection of intervention in the Solomon Islands crisis, to full support. In January, then foreign minister Alexander Downer (2003) argued that:

> Sending in Australia troops to occupy the Solomon Islands would be folly in the extreme. It would be difficult to justify to Australian taxpayers. And for how many years would such an occupation have to continue? And what would be the exit strategy? And the real show-stopper, however, is that it would not work … Foreigners do not have the answers for the deep-seated problems affecting the Solomon Islands.

However, within six months, the Australian Government had made a full about-face. An anonymous letter to the editor of the *Solomon Star* and *Island Sun* newspapers (2016) noted that this shift in approach was 'greeted with some surprise' in the Pacific.

The ups and downs in Australia's attentiveness to the Pacific continued through the Howard, Rudd, Gillard and Abbott governments. Former Liberal prime minister John Howard's policy in the Pacific Islands region was frequently criticised. Pacific Island leaders, such as former PNG prime minister Michael Somare, described his government's approach as 'arrogant and insulting' (SBS News 2013). Kevin Rudd's government (2007–10), from the Labor side of politics, made some positive progress in bilateral relations with PNG and Solomon Islands. Rudd made PNG his first overseas visit as prime minister. Subsequently, however, Liberal prime minister Tony Abbott's attitude was uninterested at best, as illustrated by his decision not to attend the 2014 Pacific Islands Forum (PIF) leaders meeting (Maclellan 2014). In 2009, around 12 per cent of Australia's diplomatic posts were in the Pacific, fewer than the number in Europe (Broadbent et al. 2009). Australian broadcasting services to the Pacific Islands region, through the Australia Network and Radio Australia, were closed, and Australia's voice in the region 'has become little more than a croak into the ether' (Dover and Macintosh 2018; see also Maclellan 2014). Since 2014, Australia has been dramatically cutting its aid budget, including to the Pacific (see, for example, Georgeou and Hawksley 2016; Maclellan 2014; Pryke 2019; Wood 2014).

A region in crisis—Australia steps up

Most recently, late 2018 saw another turnaround when the Australian Government's Department of Foreign Affairs and Trade (DFAT) formally announced the Step-Up initiative in the Pacific, stating that the 'Pacific is one of the highest priorities of the 2017 Foreign Policy White Paper' (DFAT 2018). The Minister for Foreign Affairs Marise Payne (2018) said 'stepping up in the Pacific is not an option, it is an imperative'. The stated goal of the Step-Up is simply to 'support a more resilient region'. The means to achieve this goal is through 'strengthening Australia's engagement with the region' with enhanced partnerships and relationships across economic growth, security and people-to-people ties. The political language around this policy shift strongly emphasises the moral obligation aspect of Australia's engagement with the region, setting it in terms of a 'response to the significant long-term challenges faced by our partners in the Pacific' and a 'new chapter in relations with our Pacific family' (DFAT 2018).

The new Step-Up initiatives fall into three categories.

The first, stronger partnerships for economic growth, includes proposals to support infrastructure development in the region. Two major projects were announced on 8 November 2018: AU$2 billion for a new Australian Infrastructure Financing Facility for the Pacific (AIFPP) and a proposal for the Australian Parliament to approve additional resources and powers for Australia's Export Finance and Insurance Corporation (EFIC). A week later, at the Asia-Pacific Economic Cooperation (APEC) summit in PNG, leaders from Australia, Japan and the United States announced a memorandum of understanding (MOU) on a trilateral partnership for infrastructure investment in the Indo-Pacific region. Also at APEC, the Australian Prime Minister jointly announced the Papua New Guinea Electrification Partnership. With Japan, New Zealand, the US and PNG, the partnership aims to provide 70 per cent of PNG with access to electricity by 2030.

The economic growth proposals also include expanding the Pacific Labour Scheme to all PICs, uncapping the numbers of workers and promoting the Pacific Agreement on Closer Economic Relations (PACER) Plus as a means of better integrating Pacific Island economies, expected to enter into force in mid-2020 when ratified by eight of the signatory countries.

The second category, stronger partnerships for security, intends to reflect concerns raised in the Boe Declaration on Regional Security, signed on 5 September 2018 in Nauru by PIF leaders. The Boe Declaration recognises an expanded concept of security that includes human, cyber and environmental security. The establishment of an Australia Pacific Security College and Pacific Fusion Centre are designed to support the implementation of the Boe Declaration. The purpose of these institutions is to provide training and professional development opportunities for officials across countries and agencies, and aggregate and share security information as a means to support well-informed responses to security challenges across the region. Other projects were also announced in November 2018: a dedicated vessel for support, humanitarian and disaster relief and response; an annual Joint Heads of Pacific Security Forces event; an Australian Defence Force Pacific Mobile Training Team; and a Pacific Faculty of Policing at the Australian Institute of Police Management. In addition, the Australian Government announced AU$9 million over four years for expanding Australia's Cyber Cooperation Partnership with the Pacific. These announcements build on earlier initiatives and programs, such as the bilateral security partnership MOUs with Tuvalu and Nauru; a bilateral security treaty with Solomon Islands; and a commitment of AU$2 billion to the Pacific Maritime Security Program over the next 30 years, among others.

The third category, 'stronger relationships between our people', includes education initiatives such as scholarships for Pacific students to study in Australian secondary schools; an increase to the number of scholarships under the Australia Pacific Training Coalition; and an expansion of the Australia–Pacific BRIDGE School Partnerships for teacher training. This category also encompasses a new Church Partnerships Program announced by the Australian Prime Minister in November 2018 and a new Australia–Pacific sports linkages program. A new Pacific–Australia Card (PAC) will offer eligible applicants priority visa application processing and recognition at Australian airports. These initiatives are in addition to a number of existing programs such as the Pacific Connect Program announced in September 2017 and the three-year AU$10 million Australian Aid: Friendship Grants program.

Structural changes within DFAT were another important element of the Pacific Step-Up policy. As the DFAT website sets out, an Office of the Pacific was established to coordinate 'deepening engagement with the Pacific' through whole-of-government coordination and support for Australia's efforts to develop even closer ties with the Pacific (DFAT 2018). As at the end of 2018, DFAT had established a new Indo-Pacific group, under which falls the Office of the Pacific. It consists of two divisions: the Pacific Strategy Division and the Pacific Bilateral Division. Within these divisions are seven branches dedicated to Pacific Island countries and themes. Themes include Pacific Labour Mobility and Economic Growth; Pacific Regional Engagement and Outreach; Pacific Infrastructure; and Pacific Security—Maritime and Climate Change. Some insiders note that that this kind of 're-tooling' has not been seen for decades, and certainly not for the Pacific. However, this new Office of the Pacific at

DFAT was seen by some Pacific analysts as representing very little in terms of a real shift in conceptualisation of, or approach towards, the Pacific Islands region, given that indications suggested it may largely be staffed by secondees from the Australian Federal Police and departments of Defence, Home Affairs and the Attorney-General, with no mention of, for example, education, health or climate change expertise—all key priority areas for the Pacific.[4]

The view from the Pacific—'anything but tiny'

In general, views from the Pacific Islands region differ markedly from the Australian perspective. As Wesley Morgan argues, 'it is far from certain that Pacific island countries share the same geostrategic anxieties, and diplomatic agendas, of traditional powers on the Pacific-rim' (2018). In a beautiful article written in 1993, Epeli Hau'ofa offers a 'view of Oceania that is new and optimistic', in which the Pacific Islands region is not understood as 'pitiful microstates condemned forever to depend on migration, remittances, aid and bureaucracy, and not on any real economic productivity' and in which Pacific peoples are not belittled, even unintentionally, by often well-meaning external commentators (Hau'ofa 1993:150). Hau'ofa argues that 'the world of Oceania is not small; it is huge, and growing bigger every day' (ibid.:151). He says:

> But if we look at the myths, legends, and oral traditions, and the cosmologies of the peoples of Oceania, it becomes evident that they did not conceive of their world in such microscopic proportions. Their universe comprised not only land surfaces, but the surrounding ocean as far as they could traverse and exploit it, the underworld with its fire-controlling and earth-shaking denizens, and the heavens above with their hierarchies of powerful gods and named stars and constellations that people could count on to guide their ways across the seas. Their world was anything but tiny (1993:152).

He posited that the perspective of Pacific weakness is simply a reflection of neo-colonialist perspectives, convincing people that they 'have no choice but to depend' (ibid.:151). Hau'ofa then argued that:

---

4   Nic Maclellan, February 2019. Conversation with author.

> If this very narrow, deterministic perspective is not questioned or checked, it could contribute importantly to an eventual consignment of groups of human beings to a perpetual state of wardship wherein they and their surrounding lands and seas would be at the mercy of the manipulators of the global economy and 'world orders' of one kind or another (ibid.:151–52).

The strategic priorities of the 'Blue Pacific'

Building on these ideas, in 2017, the notion of the 'Blue Pacific' was articulated by Samoan Prime Minister Tuilaepa Sailele Malielagaoi at the Pacific Islands Forum (PIF) leaders meeting, emphasising Pacific Island states' autonomy, independence and ability to determine and pursue their own strategic interests. The Boe Declaration on Regional Security, released at the leaders meeting in Nauru in 2018, further reiterated this determination. Of particular interest is the expanded definition of what constitutes security and threats to security. Whereas Australia's support for the concept of the 'Indo-Pacific' emphasises ameliorating military security concerns, the Boe Declaration explains that for the Pacific, security includes human security, humanitarian assistance and environmental security. However, it also clearly states that the primary security concern is climate change, which 'remains the single greatest threat to the livelihoods, security and wellbeing of the peoples of the Pacific' (PIF Secretariat 2018).

Climate change was again emphasised as the primary concern for the Pacific at the 2019 PIF in Tuvalu. Host Prime Minister Enele Sopoaga's goal was for leaders to agree to the Tuvalu Declaration, which acknowledged a climate crisis, encouraged countries to revise emissions reductions targets and called for a rapid phase-out of coal use. Despite the then Tuvaluan prime minister's efforts, the declaration was not unanimously endorsed. New Zealand had reservations about financing for the UN's Green Climate Fund, as did Australia, and Australia also expressed concerns about the sections on emissions reductions and coal use. Several Pacific Island leaders expressed strong disappointment about these qualifications, including the Prime Ministers of Fiji and Tonga. Mr Sopoaga said that while Australian Prime Minister Scott Morrison was 'concerned about saving your economy in Australia', he was 'concerned about saving my people in Tuvalu' (Clarke 2019).

Collective identity, collective diplomacy

The Blue Pacific, the Boe Declaration and the Tuvalu Declaration all build on a broader movement of Pacific Islands diplomacy based on a common sense of identity and purpose in overcoming common constraints (PIF Secretariat 2014:1) as a means to reassert Pacific Islands' agency and interests. Collective diplomacy itself is not a new idea in the region. During the 20th century, the 'Pacific Way' of undertaking diplomacy emphasised consensus among Island states (Aqorau 2015; see also Tarte 2014). This approach had a number of successes both regionally and globally, including the Rarotonga Treaty of 1985, which designated the South Pacific as a nuclear-free zone (Naupa 2017:903). The more recent narrative position of PICs is that they are one 'Blue Continent', critical to the effective and sustainable management of a vast swathe of the world's ocean, and the marine resources associated with it, notably the world's largest tuna fishery and seabed minerals and energy supplies (Morgan 2018).

More recently, the region has deliberately begun to reconfigure its identity as a neighbourhood with shared interests rather than a collection of individual states pursuing their own interests (Naupa 2017:904). As Fry and Tarte argue, Pacific Island states have experienced what former president of Kiribati Anote Tong described as a 'paradigm shift', fundamentally changing their approach to engaging with regional and world politics (Fry and Tarte 2015:3). Networked, rather than traditional state-centric 'club' diplomacy, is being adopted as a means to gain access to inner circles of policy negotiation (Naupa 2017:904). Pacific diplomacy aims to interrupt the prevalent international relations discourses that see global affairs through the prism of strategies and interests of powerful Pacific Rim countries and in which Pacific Islands' affairs are viewed as means to broader and greater ends.

Regarding China, Pacific Island leaders, such as PIF Secretary General Dame Meg Taylor and Vanuatu Minister of Foreign Affairs Ralph Regenvanu, argue that the Blue Pacific is aware of and capable of negotiating the challenges arising from China's increased presence in the region (see interview with Smith and Lim 2019; also O'Keefe 2018). Taylor and Regenvanu emphasise that Pacific Island states are not naïve regarding China's interests and approaches. However, both emphasise that the immediate security priority for the Pacific is climate change, not potential development of military bases. As Taylor explained in an interview:

> If you look at the Pacific Rim countries, you've got to ask yourself, who is really committed to the *one* issue, the most important issue that faces this region: climate change? (Smith and Lim 2019)

And in relation to the priorities of large powers with interests in the region, Taylor said, 'they're not prepared to really look at the needs of the region and our young people, then I'd be questioning, "Well, why come back?"' (ibid.).

Conclusion

Australia has long been aware of and uncomfortable about China's presence in the Pacific Islands region. Australia has made it very clear that it wants to be the region's preferred partner, not China. As Graeme Dobell (2019) noted, China's growing presence in the Pacific has prompted a renewed surge of interest in maintaining Australia's preeminent position as the preferred partner of PICs. In recent years, Australia's response to China in the region has shifted from alert to alarm. While carefully avoiding direct references to China, its latest Pacific Islands policy, as laid out in the *2017 Foreign Policy White Paper* and in the 2018 launch of the Step-Up initiative, is—at its heart—concerned with managing and containing China's influence in the region (see, for example, Murray 2018; Whiting and Dziedzic 2019 among many other media stories. See also Dobell 2018 and O'Keefe 2018). Australia's Step-Up initiative reflects this recent dramatic increase in concern about China in the Pacific, although a renewed interest (again) in the Pacific Islands region had been under discussion for several years both in political and bureaucratic circles.[5] It is clear that Australia continues to be extremely anxious that Pacific Island nations cannot, or perhaps will not (or perhaps both), push back against China in the way that most aligns with Australian strategic interests and priorities.

While many consider that it is Australia's neglect of the region that has caused Pacific Island states to 'fall into the arms of China', another way to look at the situation is that it is *because* of how Australia constructs the Pacific Islands region, with corresponding actions, that PICs are open to engaging with other partners, depending on whether what is on offer aligns with their own articulated interests. The 2019 PIF in Tuvalu provides an

---

5   Former senior DFAT official, February 2019. Conversation with author.

illustrative example—much of the English-language analysis of Australia's engagement at the 2019 forum suggests that it has had a detrimental effect on Australia's reputation in the region, damaged its Step-Up goal of being the Pacific's preferred partner and affected the region's relationship with China in ways that do not align with Australia's interests (Clarke 2019). Certainly, the Chinese Foreign Ministry lost no time in arguing that Australia would do well to reflect on its 'condescending and insulting' approach to the Pacific Islands region, contrasting it directly with China, which 'doesn't insult island countries and go down and tell the world that we've given this much money to the Pacific islands' and describing Australia as a 'condescending master' (Geng 2019).

Australia's approach to the Pacific for the past several decades has been inconsistent, oscillating between neglect and intervention. Despite this, certain fundamental assumptions about the region have remained constant over time, particularly around the weakness and incapacity of Pacific Island countries. Over the past several years, the Australian policy and political community has combined this long-held understanding with growing concerns about China's influence in the region, resulting in increased anxiety, if not alarm, about risks to security and a renewed determination to 'step up' and counterbalance. However, the distinctly differing conceptions between Australia and Pacific Island countries about what the ultimate threat to security is means that Australia's approach threatens to undermine the very goals it is aiming to achieve.

References

ABC News and Fairfax Media 2017. Power and Influence: The Hard Edge of China's Soft Power. *Four Corners*, 5 June.

ABC Radio National 2019. Australia's Head of National Intelligence Nick Warner. Interviewed by Geraldine Doogue on *Saturday Extra*, 6 April. www.abc.net.au/radionational/programs/saturdayextra/director-general-of-the-office-of-national-assessments-and-inte/10967168

Aqorau, T. 2015. How Tuna is Shaping Regional Diplomacy. In G. Fry and S.Tarte (eds) 2015, *The New Pacific Diplomacy*. Canberra: ANU Press, 223–36. doi.org/10.22459/npd.12.2015.18

Australian Government 2003. *National Interests, Global Concerns: The 2003 Foreign Affairs and Trade White Paper*. Canberra: Department of Foreign Affairs and Trade. www.aph.gov.au/binaries/library/pubs/cib/2002-03/03cib23.pdf

Australian Government 2009. *Defence White Paper 2009*. Canberra: Department of Defence. www.defence.gov.au/whitepaper/2009/

Australian Government 2013a. *Defence White Paper 2013*. Canberra: Department of Defence. www.defence.gov.au/whitepaper/2013/

Australian Government 2013b. *Strong and Secure: A Strategy for Australia's National Security*. Canberra: Department of Prime Minister and Cabinet. apo.org.au/node/33996

Australian Government 2016. *2016 Defence White Paper*. Canberra: Department of Defence. www.defence.gov.au/WhitePaper/Docs/2016-Defence-White-Paper.pdf

Australian Government 2017. *2017 Foreign Policy White Paper*. Canberra: Department of Foreign Affairs and Trade. www.fpwhitepaper.gov.au/

Australian Government 2018. International Student Enrolments in Australia 1994–2018. Canberra: Department of Education and Training. international education.gov.au/research/International-Student-Data/Pages/International StudentData2018.aspx#Pivot_Table

Bilton, L. 2018. Does China's New South Pacific Mega-Wharf Pose a Risk to Australia? *60 Minutes*, 17 June. www.9news.com.au/national/60-minutes-china-south-pacific-australia-sydney-expansion-investment-debt/e074f394-03f7-4889-a6f0-3190cd1bce6c

Birtles, B. 2017. China's Communist Party Seeks News Influence through Australian Media Deals. *ABC News*, 11 June. www.abc.net.au/news/2017-06-11/china-communist-party-seeks-news-influence-australia-deals/8607754

Bisley, N. and B. Schreer 2018.Will Australia Defend the 'Rules-Based Order' in Asia? *The Strategist*, 18 April. Australian Strategic Policy Institute. www.aspi strategist.org.au/will-australia-defend-rules-based-order-asia/

Bloomberg News 2019. China Slows Australian Coal Imports as Beijing Denies Ban. 22 February.

Brady, A.M. 2017. China's Foreign Influence Offensive in the Pacific. *War on the Rocks*, 29 September. warontherocks.com/2017/09/chinas-foreign-influence-offensive-in-the-pacific/

Brautigam, D. 2009. *The Dragon's Gift*. Oxford: Oxford University Press.

Broadbent, J. W. Maley, B.Orgill, P. Shergold, R. Smith and A. Gyngell 2009. *Australia's Diplomatic Deficit: Reinvesting in Our Instruments of International Policy*. Blue Ribbon Panel Report. Sydney: Lowy Institute. archive.lowyinstitute. org/sites/default/files/pubfiles/BlueRibbonPanelReport_WEB_1.pdf

Brook, B. 2018. Papua New Guinea's 'Road to Nowhere' a Stark Sign of China's Influence in the Pacific. *news.com.au*, 17 November. www.news.com.au/technology/innovation/military/papua-new-guineas-road-to-nowhere-a-stark-sign-of-chinas-influence-in-the-pacific/news-story/40ab2e2e4c59c047d6da28609fbdda66

Brophy, D. 2019. Doubts over Huang Ban and Foreign Influence. *The Saturday Paper*, 16–22 February. www.thesaturdaypaper.com.au/news/politics/2019/02/16/doubts-over-huang-ban-and-foreign-influence/15502356007461

Chellaney, B. 2018. China's South China Sea Grab. *The Strategist*, 17 December. Australian Strategic Policy Institute. www.aspistrategist.org.au/chinas-south-china-sea-grab/

Chen, Y. 2017. Chinese State Infiltration: The Inside Story. *Vision Times*. Special edition. www.visiontimes.com.au/pdf/9.pdf

Clarke, M. 2019. Pacific Leaders, Australia Agree to Disagree about Action on Climate Change. *ABC News*, 16 August. www.abc.net.au/news/2019-08-15/no-endorsements-come-out-of-tuvalu-declaration/11419342

Davis, M. 2018. Going Forward to Manus. *The Strategist*, 21 September. Australian Strategic Policy Institute. www.aspistrategist.org.au/going-forward-to-manus/

DFAT (Australian Government Department of Foreign Affairs and Trade) 2018. Stepping-up Australia's Engagement with Our Pacific Family. dfat.gov.au/geo/pacific/engagement/Pages/stepping-up-australias-pacific-engagement.aspx

Dobell, G. 2007. China and Taiwan in the South Pacific: Diplomatic Chess versus Pacific Political Rugby. Centre for the Study of the Chinese Southern Diaspora (CSCSD) Occasional Paper No 1. chl-old.anu.edu.au/publications/csds/cscsd_op1_4_chapter_1.pdf

Dobell, G. 2017. Foreign Policy White Paper 2017: Integrating the South Pacific. *The Strategist*, 4 December. Australian Strategic Policy Institute. www.aspistrategist.org.au/foreign-policy-white-paper-2017-integrating-the-south-pacific/

Dobell, G. 2018 China challenges Australia in the South Pacific. *The Strategist*, 2 October. Australian Strategic Policy Institute. www.aspistrategist.org.au/china-challenges-australia-in-the-south-pacific/

Dobell, G. 2019. *Australia's Pacific Pivot*. Australia Strategic Policy Institute report, 30 April. www.aspi.org.au/report/australias-pacific-pivot

Dornan, M. and P. Brant 2014. Chinese Assistance in the Pacific: Agency, Effectiveness and the Role of Pacific Island Governments. *Pacific Policy Studies* 1(2). doi.org/10.1002/app5.35

Douek, E. 2018. What's in Australia's New Laws on Foreign Interference in Domestic Politics. *Lawfare*, 11 July. www.lawfareblog.com/whats-australias-new-laws-foreign-interference-domestic-politics

Dover, B. and I. Macintosh 2018. International Broadcasting: Not So Simple as ABC. *The Interpreter*, 6 August. Lowy Institute. www.lowyinstitute.org/the-interpreter/international-broadcasting-not-so-simple-abc

Downer, A. 2003. Neighbours Cannot Be Recolonised. *The Australian*. Quoted on the Nautilus Institute, 8 January. nautilus.org/publications/books/australian-forces-abroad/solomon-islands/australian-government-rationale-for-ramsi/#2003-1

Dreher, A., A. Fuchs, B.C. Parks, A.M. Strange and M.J. Tierney 2017. *Aid China and Growth: Evidence from a New Global Development Finance Dataset.* AidData Working Paper 46. Williamsburg, Virginia: AidData. china.aiddata.org/projects/39232

Farrow, L. 2017. Anxiety Around China Tops Security Talks. *The West Australian*, 3 June. thewest.com.au/politics/pm-rejects-australia-us-deputy-sheriff-ng-s-1732880

Fernando, G. 2018. China Wants to Conquer The World, and Several Countries Are Now Swimming in Debt to It. *news.com.au*, 25 March. www.news.com.au/finance/economy/world-economy/china-wants-to-conquer-the-world-and-several-countries-are-now-swimming-in-debt-to-it/news-story/a8c743bd7021187e73817d59ca48cb6b

Firth, S. 2018. Instability in the Pacific Islands: A Status Report. Sydney: Lowy Institute. www.lowyinstitute.org/sites/default/files/documents/Firth_Instability%20in%20the%20Pacific%20Islands_A%20status%20report_WEB.pdf

Fox, R. and M. Dornan 2018. China in the Pacific: Is China Engaged in 'Debt-Trap Diplomacy'? *Devpolicy Blog*, 8 November. www.devpolicy.org/is-china-engaged-in-debt-trap-diplomacy-20181108/

Fry, G. 1997. Framing the Islands: Knowledge and Power in Australian Images of 'The South Pacific'. *The Contemporary Pacific* 9(2):305–44.

Fry G. and S. Tarte (eds) 2015. *The New Pacific Diplomacy.* Canberra: ANU Press. doi.org/10.22459/NPD.12.2015

Garnaut, J. 2017. Our Universities Are a Frontline in China's Ideological Wars. *Vision Times*. Special edition. www.visiontimes.com.au/pdf/5.pdf

Garrick, J. 2018. Soft Power Goes Hard: China's Economic Interest in the Pacific Comes with Strings Attached. *The Conversation*, 17 October. theconversation.com/soft-power-goes-hard-chinas-economic-interest-in-the-pacific-comes-with-strings-attached-103765

Geng, S. 2019. Foreign Ministry Spokesperson Geng Shuang's Regular Press Conference. Ministry of Foreign Affairs of the People's Republic of China, 20 August. www.fmprc.gov.cn/mfa_eng/xwfw_665399/s2510_665401/2511_665403/t1690301.shtml

Georgeou, N. and C. Hawksley 2016. Australian Aid in the Pacific Islands. *Australian Outlook*. Australian Institute of International Affairs, 26 July. www.internationalaffairs.org.au/australianoutlook/australian-aid-in-the-pacific-islands/

Gill, B. and L. Jakobson 2017. Is There a Problem with … Chinese International Students? *China Matters*, 21 September. chinamatters.org.au/wp-content/uploads/2017/09/China-Matters-Recommends-Sept21-Chinese-international-students.pdf

Graham, E. 2018a. Belt and Road: More than Just a Brand. *The Interpreter*, 14 September. Lowy Institute. www.lowyinstitute.org/the-interpreter/belt-and-road-more-just-brand

Graham, E. 2018b. Mind the Gap: Views of Security in the Pacific. *The Interpreter*, 11 October. Lowy Institute. www.lowyinstitute.org/the-interpreter/mind-gap-views-security-pacific

Grattan, M. 2017. Chinese Influence Compromises the Integrity of Our Politics. *The Conversation*, 6 June. theconversation.com/chinese-influence-compromises-the-integrity-of-our-politics-78961

Graue, C. and S. Dziedzic 2018. Federal Minister Concetta Fierravanti-Wells Accuses China of Funding 'Roads that Go Nowhere' in Pacific. *ABC News*, 10 January. www.abc.net.au/news/2018-01-10/australia-hits-out-at-chinese-aid-to-pacific/9316732

Grigg, A. and N. McKenzie 2018. Chinese Aid Funded Alleged $1 Million Bribe to Former PNG Leader, Somare. *Australian Financial Review*, 3 June. www.afr.com/news/world/asia/chinese-aid-funded-1-million-bribe-to-former-png-leader-somare-20180603-h10we3

Groot, G. 2015. The Expansion of the United Front Under Xi Jinping. *The China Story*. Australian Centre on China in the World. www.thechinastory.org/yearbooks/yearbook-2015/forum-ascent/the-expansion-of-the-united-front-under-xi-jinping/

Hamilton, C. 2018. *Silent Invasion: China's Influence in Australia*. Hardie Grant Books.

Harvey, A. 2017. Malcolm Turnbull Warns Asian Leaders of Chinese Aggression, Says China Should 'Curb' North Korea. *ABC News*, 3 June. www.abc.net. au/news/2017-06-03/china-should-curb-unlawful,-reckless-north-korea:-turnbull/8586008

Hau'ofa, E. 1993, reprinted 1994. Our Sea of Islands. *The Contemporary Pacific* 6(1):147–61.

Hayward-Jones, J. 2013. Big Enough for All of Us: Geo-Strategic Competition in the Pacific Islands. *Analyses*, May. Lowy Institute. www.lowyinstitute.org/ sites/default/files/hayward_jones_big_enough_web_0.pdf

Hegarty, M. 2015. *China's Growing Influence in the South-West Pacific: Australian Policies that Could Respond to China's Intentions and Objectives*. Indo-Pacific Strategic Papers. Canberra: Australian Defence College, Centre for Defence and Strategic Studies. www.defence.gov.au/ADC/Publications/documents/ IndoPac/2015/Hegarty_mar15.pdf

Henderson, J., B. Reilly and N. Peffer 2003. Dragon in Paradise: China's Rising Star in Oceania. *The National Interest* 72:94–104. crawford.anu.edu.au/pdf/ staff/ben_reilly/breilly1.pdf

Hill, B. 2018. China in the Pacific: Concern over Beijing's Influence Ramps Up in Cook Islands Election. *ABC News*, 21 May. www.abc.net.au/news/2018-05-21/chinese-influence-in-pacific-ramps-up-in-cook-islands-election/9775778

Howard, J. 2005. Australian Outlook: Australian Policy Priorities for the Asia-Pacific. Speech to the Asia Society. New York, 12 September. asiasociety.org/ australian-outlook-australian-policy-priorities-asia-pacific

Isaksson, A.S. and A. Kotsadam 2016. *Chinese Aid and Local Corruption*. AidData Working Paper 33. docs.aiddata.org/ad4/files/wps33_chinese_aid_ and_local_corruption.pdf

Johnston, L. and M. Rudyak 2017. China's 'Innovative and Pragmatic' Foreign Aid: Shaped by and Now Shaping Globalisation. In L. Song, R. Garnaut, C. Fang and L. Johnston (eds), *China's New Sources of Economic Growth*. Canberra: ANU Press. doi.org/10.22459/cnseg.07.2017.19

Joske, A. 2017. End the Isolation of Chinese Students in Australia. *The Sydney Morning Herald*, 4 September.

Kabutaulaka, T. 2005. Australian Foreign Policy and the RAMSI Intervention in Solomon Islands. *The Contemporary Pacific* 17 (2):283–308.

Kearsley, J., Bagshaw, A. and Galloway, A. 2020. 'If you make China the enemy, China will be the enemy': Beijing's fresh threat to Australia. Sydney Morning Herald. November 18. www.smh.com.au/world/asia/if-you-make-china-the-enemy-china-will-be-the-enemy-beijing-s-fresh-threat-to-australia-2020 1118-p56fqs.html

Kehoe, J. 2018. US Report: China 'Debt Trap' on Australia's Doorstep. *Australian Financial Review*, 14 May. www.afr.com/news/politics/world/us-secret-report-china-debt-trap-on-australias-doorstep-20180513-h0zzwd

Lancaster, C. 2007. The Chinese Aid System. *Center for Global Development essay*, June. www.cgdev.org/publication/chinese-aid-system

Laurenceson, J. 2017. Chinese Students in Australia: Do We Protest Too Much? Australia-China Relations Institute, 21 September. www.australiachina relations.org/content/chinese-students-australia-do-we-protest-too-much

Lim, L. and J. Bergin 2018. Inside China's Audacious Global Propaganda Campaign. *The Guardian*, 7 December.

Maclellan, N. 2014. Abbott's First Year: Nowhere to Be Seen in the Pacific. *The Interpreter*, 10 September. Lowy Institute. www.lowyinstitute.org/the-interpreter/abbotts-first-year-nowhere-be-seen-pacific

Marles, R. 2017. Australia's Approach to the Pacific. Speech by the Hon Richard Marles MP, Shadow Minister for Defence. Sydney: Lowy Institute, 21 November. www.lowyinstitute.org/publications/richard-marles-australia-pacific

McCarthy, J. 2016. China Extends its Influence in the South Pacific. *Pacific Beat* program. *ABC News*, 10 September.

Medcalf, R. 2015. Don't 'Contain' China, But Australia Must Push for Rules-Based Security Order. *Australian Financial Review*, 11 September. www.afr.com/opinion/dont-contain-china-but-australia-must-push-for-rulesbased-security-order-20150910-gjjp0v

Morgan, W. 2018. The Indo-Pacific and the Blue Pacific. *Devpolicy Blog*, 22 August. www.devpolicy.org/the-indo-pacific-and-the-blue-pacific-20180822/

Murray, L. 2018. Australia's Pacific Play is All About China. *Australian Financial Review*, 8 November. www.afr.com/news/policy/foreign-affairs/australias-pacific-play-is-all-about-china-20181108-h17nff

Naim, M. 2009. Rogue Aid. *Foreign Policy*, 15 October. foreignpolicy.com/2009/10/15/rogue-aid/

Naupa, A. 2017. Indo-Pacific Diplomacy: A View from the Pacific Islands. *Politics and Policy* 45(5):902–17. doi.org/10.1111/polp.12226

O'Keefe, M. 2018. Why China's 'Debt-book diplomacy' in the Pacific Shouldn't Ring Alarm Bells Just Yet. *The Conversation*, 17 May. theconversation.com/why-chinas-debt-book-diplomacy-in-the-pacific-shouldnt-ring-alarm-bells-just-yet-96709

Parliament of Australia 2006. *China's Emergence: Implications for Australia*. Report from the inquiry by Senate Standing Committee on Foreign Affairs, Defence and Trade. www.aph.gov.au/Parliamentary_Business/Committees/Senate/Foreign_Affairs_Defence_and_Trade/Completed_inquiries/2004-07/china/report02/index

Parker, S. and G. Chefitz 2018. *Debtbook Diplomacy*. Boston: Belfer Center for Science and International Affairs, Harvard Kennedy School. www.belfercenter.org/publication/debtbook-diplomacy

Payne, M. 2018. State of the Pacific 2018 Conference. Welcoming Remarks by the Minister for Foreign Affairs, Senator the Hon. Marise Payne. Canberra: ANU, 10 September. www.youtube.com/watch?v=rRReJzUQEKc&feature=youtu.be

PIF (Pacific Islands Forum) Secretariat 2014. *The Framework for Pacific Regionalism*. www.forumsec.org/wp-content/uploads/2018/02/Framework-for-Pacific-Regionalism_booklet.pdf

PIF (Pacific Islands Forum) Secretariat 2018. *Boe Declaration on Regional Security*. www.forumsec.org/boe-declaration-on-regional-security/

Podger, A. 2018. Book Review — Clive Hamilton's *Silent Invasion: China's Influence in Australia*. *The Conversation*, 21 March. theconversation.com/book-review-clive-hamiltons-silent-invasion-chinas-influence-in-australia-93650

Pryke, J. 2018. The Bad—and Good—of China's Aid in the Pacific. *The Interpreter*, 11 January. Lowy Institute. www.lowyinstitute.org/the-interpreter/bad-and-good-china-aid-pacific

Pryke, J. 2019. Budget 2019: The Race to the Bottom for Foreign Aid. *The Interpreter*, 4 April. Lowy Institute. www.lowyinstitute.org/the-interpreter/budget-2019-aid-downward-trend

Rajah, R., J. Pryke and A. Dayant 2019. Ocean of Debt? Belt and Road and Debt Diplomacy in the Pacific. *Analyses*, 21 October. Lowy Institute. www.lowyinstitute.org/publications/ocean-debt-belt-and-road-and-debt-diplomacy-pacific

RBA (Reserve Bank of Australia) 2018. Australia's Deepening Economic Relationship with China: Opportunities and Risks. Address to the Australia–China Relations Institute by Philip Lowe, Governor of the RBA. 23 May. rba. gov.au/speeches/2018/sp-gov-2018-05-23.html

Riordan, P. 2017. China in 'Direct Disregard' for International Order. *The Australian*, 5 June. www.theaustralian.com.au/news/world/china-in-direct-disregard-for-international-order-bishop-says/news-story/ea5c251d38c392 cd42007a1d89390ad9

Saunokonoko, M. 2018. China's Mighty Orbit in South Pacific Threatens to Leave Australia in a Spin. *news.com.au*, 25 November. www.kanivatonga.nz/2018/ 11/chinas-mighty-orbit-in-south-pacific-threatens-to-leave-australia-in-spin/

SBS News 2013. The Somare Express. M. Davis Interviewing Pacific Leaders on *Dateline*, 23 August. www.sbs.com.au/news/the-somare-express

SBS News 2017. Turnbull Warns Against a 'Coercive' China During Singapore Speech. 3 June. www.sbs.com.au/news/turnbull-warns-against-a-coercive-china-during-singapore-speech

Schultz, J. 2012. Overseeing and Overlooking: Australian Engagement with the Pacific Islands 1988–2007. PhD thesis, School of Political and Social Sciences, University of Melbourne. minerva-access.unimelb.edu.au/bitstream/ handle/11343/37678/287245_SCHULTZ_amended_file.pdf

Schultz, J. 2014. Theorising Australia–Pacific Island Relations. *Australian Journal of International Affairs* 68(5):548–68. doi.org/10.1080/10357718.2014. 917271

Seo, B. 2018. A Study in Controversy: Chinese Students in Australia. *The Interpreter*, 4 June. Lowy Institute. www.lowyinstitute.org/the-interpreter/ study-controversy-chinese-students-australia

Sheridan, G. and C. Stewart 2018. Top Defence Threat Now Lies in the South Pacific from China. *The Australian*, 22 September.

Smethurst, A. 2017. James Mattis Warns Against North Korea's Threat as Malcolm Turnbull Warns Against Chinese Bullying. *news.com.au*, 3 June. www.news. com.au/national/politics/malcolm-turnbull-warns-against-chinese-bullying-in-singapore-speech/news-story/ff5eb2b9a750ea2b7e4155ac0b41c2c1

Smith, G. 2017. Why Is China So Determined to 'Persuade, Manage, Discipline and Control'? *The Sydney Morning Herald*, 6 June. www.smh.com.au/opinion/ why-is-china-so-determined-to-persuade-manage-discipline-and-control-20170606-gwliy3.html

Smith, G. 2018. Is There a Problem With … PRC Aid to the Pacific? *China Matters*, April. chinamatters.org.au/wp-content/uploads/2018/04/China-Matters-Recommends-04-April-2018-PRC-Aid-Pacific.pdf

Smith, G. and L. Lim 2018. Tinker, Tailor, Student, Spy? Inside Australia's Chinese Student Boom. Graeme Smith and Louisa Lim interviewing Linda Jakobson and Fran Martin. *The Little Red Podcast*.

Smith, G. and L. Lim 2019. Step Up or Be Overrun: China's Challenge for the Pacific. Graeme Smith and Louisa Lim interviewing Ralph Regenvanu and Dame Meg Taylor. *The Little Red Podcast*, 5 March. omny.fm/shows/the-little-red-podcast/step-up-or-be-overrun-china-s-challenge-for-the-1#description

Solomon Star and Island Sun 2016. RAMSI A Historical Perspective—Appreciation and Regrets from a Personal Perspective. Anonymous letter to the editor, 27 December.

Tarte, S. 2014. Regionalism and Changing Regional Order in the Pacific Islands. *Asia and the Pacific Policy Studies* 1(2):312–24. doi.org/10.1002/app5.27

Varrall, M. 2017. Chinese Students Aren't Simply Tools of the Party-State. *Vision Times*.

Varrall, M. 2018. Understanding China's Approach to Aid. *The Interpreter*, 12 January. Lowy Institute. www.lowyinstitute.org/the-interpreter/understanding-chinas-approach-aid

Wainwright, E. 2003. *Our Failing Neighbour—Australia and the Future of Solomon Islands*. Australian Strategic Policy Institute report, 10 June. www.aspi.org.au/report/our-failing-neighbour-australia-and-future-solomon-islands

Walker, T. 2019. The Chinese Coal 'Ban' Carries a Significant Political Message. *The Conversation*, 1 March. theconversation.com/the-chinese-coal-ban-carries-a-significant-political-message-112535

Wallis, J. 2017. What Role Can the Pacific Islands Play in Strengthening Australia's Security? *Australian Outlook*. Australian Institute of International Affairs, 17 October. www.internationalaffairs.org.au/australianoutlook/pacific-islands-play-australia-security/

Wallis, J. 2018. Australia Needs to Reset Its Pacific Policy. *East Asia Forum*, 1 June. www.eastasiaforum.org/2018/06/01/australia-needs-to-reset-its-pacific-policy/#more-129171

Wang, L. 2017. Australia Must Do More for Chinese Students. *Global Times*, 5 December.

Warner, N. 2004. Operation *Helpem Fren*: Rebuilding the Nation of Solomon Islands. Speech to National Security Conference by Nick Warner, RAMSI Special Coordinator, 23 March. www.dfat.gov.au/news/speeches/Pages/operation-helpem-fren-rebuilding-the-nation-of-solomon-islands.aspx

Wesley-Smith, T. 2007. *China in Oceania: New Forces in Pacific Politics*. Honolulu: East-West Center. www.eastwestcenter.org/publications/china-oceania-new-forces-pacific-politics

White, H. 2018. Economy Relies on China as International Students Prop Up Our Universities. *news.com.au*, 14 October. www.news.com.au/finance/economy/australian-economy/economy-relies-on-china-as-international-students-prop-up-our-universities/news-story/6bea7fc2c0c7dbd364346b74722c67df

Whiting, N. and S. Dziedzic 2019. Australia Ramps Up Rivalry With China for Influence in the Pacific. *ABC News*, 10 February. www.abc.net.au/news/2019-02-10/australia-ramps-up-its-rivalry-with-china-over-pacific-influence/10792848

WikiLeaks 2008. Chinese Inroads into Timor-Leste: High Visibility, Low Cost, Few Strings Attached. Dili: US Embassy cable. 20 February. wikileaks.org/plusd/cables/08DILI56_a.html

Windybank, S. 2005. The China Syndrome. Centre for Independent Studies. *Policy* 21(2):28–33. www.cis.org.au/app/uploads/2015/04/images/stories/policy-magazine/2005-winter/2005-21-2-susan-windybank.pdf

Wood, T. 2014. Beyond the Pale? Australia's Aid Cuts in International Comparison. *Devpolicy Blog*, 18 December.

Wroe, D. 2018. China Eyes Vanuatu Military Base in Plan with Global Ramifications. *The Sydney Morning Herald*, 9 April. www.smh.com.au/politics/federal/china-eyes-vanuatu-military-base-in-plan-with-global-ramifications-20180409-p4z8j9.html

Xie, Y. and E. Cui 2017. Sanctions with Chinese Characteristics. Gavekal Dragonomics' internal note to clients, 23 March.

Zhang, D. 2017. Why Cooperate with Others? Demystifying China's Trilateral Aid Cooperation, *The Pacific Review* 30(5):750–68. doi.org/10.1080/09512748.2017.1296886

Zhang, D. 2018. Diplomacy Will Have More Weight in China's Foreign Aid Program. *Devpolicy Blog*, 2 May. www.devpolicy.org/diplomacy-more-weight-chinas-foreign-aid-program-20180502/

4

China's Impact on New Zealand Foreign Policy in the Pacific: The Pacific Reset

Iati Iati

Introduction

This chapter examines New Zealand's 'Pacific Reset' (Reset) policy to determine whether it is a response to anxieties about China's growing presence in the Pacific Islands region. In March 2018, New Zealand's Minister of Foreign Affairs and Trade Winston Peters announced the Reset and its significant policy shift, both financially and diplomatically. The Reset includes a NZ$714.2 million allocation to New Zealand's Official Development Assistance fund, with the Pacific as the major recipient, and 14 new diplomatic posts. On its face, this is a significant change in New Zealand's foreign policy in the Pacific. Intriguingly, Peters' announcement was made the day after former United States secretary of state Hillary Clinton, in a visit to New Zealand, warned of China's soft power push into the Pacific. It also came amidst concerns expressed by New Zealand and Australian officials about China's chequebook diplomacy in the region. Despite this seemingly obvious reason for the Reset, the New Zealand Government insists it was not prompted by China's activities in the region.

This chapter argues that the Reset is intended to address concerns about China's increasing presence in the Pacific and is a result of the perspective New Zealand has adopted about China's place in the region. This perspective has largely been influenced by years of neglect of the region by Western powers, a point that has often been stressed in New Zealand foreign policy circles, but usually by those not directly involved in the decision-making processes. These years of neglect were accompanied by the use of aid as a political tool, often as leverage over Pacific Island countries, a point not lost on foreign policy observers, particularly those in the region. New Zealand's perspective has also been influenced by the rise in the number of external actors in the region, giving the impression of a more contested Pacific geopolitics. While these external actors pose no real rivalry to the incumbents, they raise interesting possibilities, which are influencing how New Zealand views the region. For a country that has since World War II taken strong measures to provide a security architecture in the region, both for itself and its allies, these possibilities can appear threatening.

Whether New Zealand's perspective about China is accurate is another matter. Though New Zealand has always welcomed Chinese money, it has been more ambivalent about its political presence in the Pacific. On this front, New Zealand has clearly taken the position that China's activities, as it perceives them in the context of regional geopolitics, are troubling and warrant a response of the magnitude of the Reset. This chapter examines various statements and arguments contained in speeches about the Reset, the policy context in which the Reset was formulated and the most recent document produced by the New Zealand Ministry of Defence, which complements the Reset. These strongly suggest China is the focus of the Reset.

What is behind the Pacific Reset?

The Reset was announced in March 2018 by New Zealand's Deputy Prime Minister, the Honourable Winston Peters, at a speech delivered at the Lowy Institute (Peters 2018a). According to Peters, there were several reasons for the Reset. First, the Reset is part of a 'dramatic' change in both the domestic and foreign policies of the coalition government, which came into power in late 2017. The coalition is made up of three political parties: the Labour Party (one of the two major parties), New Zealand

First and the Greens. Notably, both the Minister of Foreign Affairs and Trade and the Minister of Defence are from New Zealand First, a party that sits on the centre-right of New Zealand politics. Second, the Pacific is facing 'social and environmental problems', which are 'attracting an increasing number of external actors and interests'. According to Peters, these problems are prompting changes that, at times, are not ideal for the Pacific Island countries, because the 'need and temptation often leads to greater risk than prudence would suggest'. In response, New Zealand wants to be a good neighbour and assist Pacific Island countries in addressing these challenges in a way that preserves their autonomy. Third, the Pacific is becoming more important to international relations. Fourth, stability in the Pacific is critical to New Zealand's national security. Peters noted that these reasons needed to be understood, in particular the following geographical, historical and social facts about New Zealand: it is a Pacific country, historically, culturally, politically and demographically, and 'the Pacific is where New Zealand matters more, wields more influence and can have a more positive impact'. In other words, New Zealand is a small player in international relations, but in the Pacific region, constituted primarily by microstates, it has and wields considerable influence. While it is not a 'big power', it can act like one.

Is the Reset aimed at countering the influence of China in the Pacific? The New Zealand Government has not directly said that this is the Reset's purpose; in fact, Peters has stringently denied that the Reset is 'specifically to counter China' and instead explained in a 2018 Radio New Zealand interview that it is designed:

> to ensure that the shape and character of our neighbourhood maintains the level of influence of countries who believe in democracy … who believe in sovereignty and countries who have got the best interest of the neighbourhood in mind, not some wider and larger purpose (Radio New Zealand 2018f).

Although a number of commentators have inferred a link between the Reset and increasing Chinese influence (Novak 2018; Reuters 2018; Walters 2018b), they provide no direct evidence.

However, there is considerable circumstantial evidence that the purpose of the Reset is to counter China. A report by Stanford University's Hoover Institution, *Chinese Influence and American Interests: Promoting Constructive Vigilance*, argues that New Zealand is 'vulnerable to Chinese influence' and that 'China appears ready to exploit' New Zealand's pursuance of closer ties with it 'to subvert New Zealand's continued ability to independently shape its policy priorities' (Diamond and Schell 2018:169). In the aforementioned radio interview (Radio New Zealand 2018f), Peters was asked to respond to the following comment:

> It [the report] goes on to say that New Zealand has long pursued ties with China but what is changing is the willfulness with which China appears to exploit the dynamic with New Zealand and to subvert New Zealand's continued ability to independently shape its policy priorities. What are you doing as foreign minister to counter that?

Peters replied:

> You know what I'm doing to counter that. The first thing we did when we became a government and I became foreign minister was set out to evaluate what had gone on and that's why we've got the Pacific Reset, which is a huge turnaround in our approach to our neighbourhood and our engagement with it, and our engagement in it, and our engagement with each … every government in the Pacific and also those other players such as Japan, Australia, the European Union, the UK, France (ibid.).

At the very least, Peters' conflicting statements suggest that China is a factor in the Reset.

A critical analysis of Peters' Lowy Institute speech and subsequent rhetoric and actions sheds further light on this issue. Specifically, Peters stated that the Pacific:

> has also become an increasingly contested strategic space, no longer neglected by great power ambition, and so Pacific Island leaders have more options. This is creating a degree of strategic anxiety (Peters 2018a).

Arguably, China is the great power New Zealand is strategically anxious about. China, the US and perhaps France are the only great powers active in the region, and, of these, China is the relative newcomer. France and the US have long histories as colonisers in the Pacific and continue to control their dependencies and, in the case of the US, Compact of Free Association states. As such, it is nonsensical to believe that France and the US are the ones Peters referred to as having 'great power ambition' in the Pacific, even taking into consideration the recent inclusion of the French dependencies in the Pacific Island Forum (PIF). Further, it would be surprising if New Zealand was becoming strategically anxious about the actions of the US in the region after both countries signed the Wellington and Washington declarations in 2010 and 2012, respectively. Both declarations, but especially the first, commit each country to enhancing their partnership in the Pacific, particularly in addressing security issues. Of the great powers in the Pacific (the UK effectively departed after the Cold War and is only now reestablishing ties), China is the only one whose ambitions would cause New Zealand strategic anxiety.

However, anxieties about the increasing presence of China in the Pacific must be understood in context. If New Zealand had retained its traditional influence in the Pacific, a response to China's increasing influence in the magnitude of the Reset might not have been required. Instead, it is the relative demise of New Zealand's, and its allies', influence that is causing consternation in Wellington and gave rise to the Reset. One area where this is particularly noticeable is in Pacific regionalism, or regional cooperation between Pacific countries, including former colonial powers. New Zealand's and Australia's domination of Pacific regionalism is no secret. Initially, regionalism served the interests of the metropolitan powers, and it was not until the 1960s that 'Island leaders began to challenge this biased regional framework' (Tarte 1989:183). Even then, because these powers provided the bulk of the funding to the main regional organisations—the Pacific Community and the PIF (New Zealand and Australia for the PIF)—they were best positioned to control the regional agenda in pursuit of their interests (Bryant-Tokalau and Frazer 2006:2). Nevertheless, the Western powers', particularly Australia's and New Zealand's, domination of Pacific regionalism is waning. Led primarily by Fiji, Pacific Island countries are gaining greater control over the regional agenda, not only with the formation of new organisations such as the Pacific Islands Development Forum, but also in determining the agenda of the premier regional organisation, the PIF (Fry and Tarte 2015).

Does the Reset entail a new direction in New Zealand foreign policy?

The policies that constitute the Reset lift New Zealand–Pacific relations to a different level, and appear to push them in a different direction. According to Peters, the Reset has two distinct strands: 'back-to-basics' diplomacy and an increase in assistance. The first involves engaging Pacific countries with New Zealand's views of the 'strategic environment facing the Pacific, including the proliferation of external actors' (Peters 2018a). This follows five principles approved by the New Zealand cabinet:

1. Demonstrate understanding of the Pacific shaped by government and non-government actors.
2. Exhibit friendship through more interaction, in particular frank conversations at the political level, which also entails a greater focus on the Pacific than previously.
3. Strive for solutions of mutual benefit.
4. Achieve a collective ambition, whereby New Zealand and its allies would work together with Pacific countries and other external actors to achieve common aims.
5. Seek sustainability.

The second involves a budgetary increase, which had not been done since 2008, and a rise in New Zealand diplomatic expertise, particularly in the Pacific. According to Peters, this will demonstrate New Zealand's commitment to the region, allowing New Zealand to do more in relation to issues such as climate change, good governance, human rights and women's political development, as well as give more funding to multilateral institutions. Overall, New Zealand seeks 'leadership diplomacy', in conjunction with Australia, that goes beyond the 'donor/ recipient interaction and into genuine, mature political partnerships' that involve 'understanding, friendship, mutual benefit, and collective ambition, to achieve sustainable results' (ibid.).

The two most important changes in the Reset are the level of investment in the diplomatic core that engages on Pacific issues and the change from a donor–recipient model to one of partnership. As noted, one of the glaring deficiencies or issues with New Zealand's previous Pacific engagement was its relative lack of attention to diplomatic integrity; while professionals designated to regions such as Asia and Europe were equipped with relevant language and cultural training, the same was not expected of those sent to the Pacific. This is not to say that those deployed to the Pacific were not well versed in Pacific languages or cultures, or were not genuinely focused on the region. However, according to Powles and Powles (2017), New Zealand diplomats to other regions are expected to have greater expertise than those sent to the Pacific. In most other regions, it is usual practice to appoint 'senior New Zealand diplomats with training and professional experience in the field of diplomacy' (Powles and Powles 2017:20). In many cases, these diplomats will have been trained in local languages by the Ministry of Foreign Affairs and Trade. By comparison, New Zealand has a much lower proportion of professional diplomats heading its Pacific posts (ibid.). Peters implicitly hints at this phenomenon, stating that the Reset is a 'strategy based on mutual respect' (Peters 2018a). If the Reset entails a radical change, was there a lack of mutual respect previously?

New Zealand's Pacific identity came to the fore of its foreign policy in the early 1970s, particularly with the Kirk Government. However, whether New Zealand was seeking a partnership with the region, or regarded their relationship as something less, is questionable. Gerald Hensley, a New Zealand diplomat and head of the prime minister's department under two administrations, notes that during the early years of the Pacific-focused foreign policy approach, New Zealand demonstrated a lack of genuine and meaningful engagement:

> The new emphasis on the South Pacific, however, was no more than a polite fiction … Revealingly, politicians and diplomats who carried the message of NZ's Pacific identity to foreign governments rarely confirmed their words by wanting a posting there (Hensley 2013:307–8).

The Pacific was a convenient (or inconvenient) means to an end: 'The stress on the South Pacific was a fig leaf to cover a more fundamental withdrawal from the world' (ibid.).

Rightly or wrongly, New Zealand has also used its aid to the Pacific as a tool to control, or at least influence, the region to advance its own interests. For the past several decades, New Zealand has dedicated the majority, approximately 60 per cent, of its overseas development assistance to the Pacific, but not for altruistic reasons. John Henderson, who served as the head of the prime minister's office under David Lange, noted:

> A 1989 audit report of MERT [Ministry of External Relations and Trade] identified foreign aid as a 'principal tool in our foreign policy' in the South Pacific. It noted the importance of aid for providing access to key decision makers at both the political and official levels. While the report also emphasised the role of aid in developing island state economies, it linked this to reducing the scope for outside 'undesirable influences' to meddle in the region. … Political outcomes were more important than the economic

and humanitarian reasons for providing the aid. Aid was an important instrument of foreign policy. As the 1990 policy review put it: 'Our mana as a people of the Pacific is maintained through our ODA because it gives substance to our relationships' (1999:287–88).

Pacific leaders and other commentators on Pacific geopolitics have long known the inequity of this relationship, as well as New Zealand's, and its closest ally Australia's, condescending and overbearing approach. The PIF (formerly the South Pacific Forum) was specifically formed to give Pacific countries more autonomy from the regional influence of metropolitan powers, including New Zealand. New Zealand, along with Australia, was associated with the colonial approach to regionalism and, understandably, was not initially included as a full member of the PIF; they were observers (Tarte 1989:184). Regional leaders such as Fiji's first prime minister Ratu Sir Kamisese Mara expressed concerns about New Zealand's and Australia's dominance of the regional agenda (Bryant-Tokalau and Frazer 2006:3). These concerns were later echoed by other leaders and commentators. Bryant-Tokalau and Frazer noted:

> For inter-governmental organisations in particular, the funding and involvement of Australia and New Zealand has meant a striking asymmetry of power in the running of those organisations and in the settling of regional policy (ibid.).

They conclude that while it would be going too far to say that Pacific countries 'have completely lost control of the regional agenda … it is not very clear just how much control they have left' (Bryant-Tokalau and Frazer 2006:20). Winston Peters' rhetoric suggests that New Zealand is finally acknowledging the asymmetrical power relationship between it and Australia on the one hand, and the Pacific Islands on the other, and is prepared to treat the Pacific Island countries as equals and partners.

New Zealand's back-to-basics diplomacy, which kicked off with a tour of the region in 2018 and a plan to 'spend considerable time' there (Peters 2018a), suggests a new-found emphasis on relationship building. The five principles of the Reset indicate not only the policy areas of future focus, but also past neglect. Notably, there is an emphasis on engaging the Pacific as equals, something that was obviously lacking previously. Peters' rhetoric is telling. He noted that exhibiting friendship includes 'honesty, empathy, trust and respect', which 'means staying in frequent touch at a political level' (ibid.). He also noted, in reference to Australia, that 'I suspect our two countries … have been preoccupied with other parts of the world when building on our own borders are matters of concern' (ibid.). His last statement speaks to Hensley's point.

New Zealand has neglected the Pacific, but Peters underestimates the extent to which and ways this has been done. He is correct that New Zealand has not devoted as much financial resources to its relationship with the region as other Pacific partners, such as Australia and China, and that, diplomatically, New Zealand has not paid enough attention to Pacific Island countries' perspectives. New Zealand has treated the region as a recipient, a tool in its broader foreign policy objectives. However, Peters fails to appreciate, or at least express, that New Zealand's and Australia's overbearing and neo-colonial approaches have resulted in a failure to recognise that these countries are not just sovereign, but autonomous. Not only do many have legal standing in the international community as sovereign nation-states, they also have been striving, as independent countries, to control their affairs without undue influence from abroad, particularly from their previous colonisers, of which China is not a part. Peters' Lowy Institute speech betrays a foreign policy attitude not dissimilar from the past. On the one hand, he stated that 'Pacific countries want to stand on their own two feet as equals, make their own choices and have their distinctive voices heard on the global stage', and the Reset 'will be a strategy based on mutual respect' (Peters 2018a). On the other, he stated:

> New Zealand's view is that we must be respectful of Pacific Island countries' clear wish to manage their own international relations while at the same time retaining New Zealand's traditional emphasis on human rights, the rule of law, transparency, good governance and the promotion of democracy (ibid.).

And then, 'But make no mistake. Isolation and a lack of size is no excuse for failing to strive for the best of standards' (ibid.). This is somewhat reminiscent of the hermeneutic rule: forget the nonsense before the 'but'. Aid conditionality based on what New Zealand considers 'good governance' appears to be as firm a part of New Zealand's foreign policy approach as it has always been.

To what extent has the Pacific become a more contested geopolitical space?

More external actors are seeking diplomatic relations with Pacific Island countries. Aside from the usual suspects, such as the US, China, Taiwan and Japan, a number of other external governments are entering or reentering the Pacific geopolitical scene. Britain, whose presence in the region waned in the 1990s, is officially back. In early 2018, it announced a major reengagement with the Pacific, involving, among other things, the reopening of embassies in Tonga, Samoa and Vanuatu. This could be an inconsequential development. According to Fraenkel, 'I don't really see the connections with the Island states figuring in a major way in British foreign policy in the future. It's too far away and its interests aren't there' (Radio New Zealand 2018a). However, the fact that Britain reopened only nine diplomatic posts around the world, and three are in the Pacific, suggests something more significant.

Among the new or newer actors are Indonesia, India, Russia and, most recently, Israel. Although their contributions and influence in the region pale in comparison with established Pacific hegemons, their presence makes the geopolitical scene interesting, if for no other reason than that they are giving Pacific Island countries more options for assistance, however little it might be relative to that provided by the traditional benefactors. Nevertheless, there may be other reasons to take these actors seriously.

Russia, though far from being a player in the Pacific, is appearing on the region's geopolitical radar. Russia has been actively seeking to build ties with countries in the Asia-Pacific region, including Fiji (Muraviev 2018). In 2012, Russian Minister of Foreign Affairs Sergey Lavrov became the first senior Russian government official to visit Fiji. This was reciprocated a year later when Fijian Prime Minister Voreqe Bainimarama made an official state visit to Russia. In January 2016, Russia donated approximately 20 containers carrying weapons and military hardware to Fiji. Russian military personnel were then sent to train the Fijian military on their use. Fijian government officials said the weapons were to be used to rearm Fijian peacekeepers serving in United Nations missions (Doherty 2016). In 2017, Russia based 100 personnel in West Papua and flew two nuclear-capable Tu-95 bombers over the South Pacific in late 2017, taking off from airfields in Indonesia (Knaus 2017). In May 2018, a Russian training warship arrived in Papua New Guinea (PNG) and was welcomed by PNG officials. Interestingly, the visit was termed by PNG's minister for foreign affairs and trade Rimbink Pato as a 'pre-APEC gesture of friendship' (Riordan 2018), even though APEC was scheduled for November. Peters' concerns about the Pacific being a contested geopolitical space are well-founded.

Is China's presence posing a threat to New Zealand?

Since China entered the Pacific in 1975, signing diplomatic agreements with Fiji and Samoa, its presence and influence have risen dramatically, particularly in the post–Cold War era when powers like the US and Britain visibly withdrew. By the 2000s, it was not uncommon for Pacific Island countries to espouse 'Look North' policies (Crocombe 2007; Henderson and Reilly 2003). Though China's purpose was initially to counter Taiwan's efforts to gain diplomatic recognition as the official government of China, this has morphed into something larger, especially in past two decades.

China's increasing presence threatens the influence that the Western allies, particularly the US, have enjoyed in the Pacific for much of the 20th century. Whether China is seeking to become the regional hegemon, and in particular challenge and perhaps supersede the US, is not known. On the one hand, it could be argued that China uses the Pacific to test its power against the US and its allies as part of its global aspirations for hegemony (Henderson and Reilly 2003). On the other hand, China's rise in the region could be seen as typical for a rising global power, and it possibly has no specific intention to challenge the US or any of its allies (Crocombe 2007). Regardless of the viewpoint taken, there is no doubt that New Zealand and its allies view China as a threat to their interests, especially if its growing influence is not made to conform to the rules-based international order they largely created.

China's initial move into the Pacific was welcomed by New Zealand's allies, in particular the US, as a way to counterbalance Russia. New Zealand also welcomed China's engagement in the region, but probably more for the possible increased economic and trade opportunities. As a small and isolated country, New Zealand places a high value on trade. Since the 1970s, when Britain, then its largest export market, joined the EEC (European Economic Community, now the European Union), New Zealand has had to seek trade opportunities elsewhere, particularly Asia. As such, China has been a focal point for trade relations. This was exemplified when New Zealand became the first OECD (Organisation for Economic Co-operation and Development) country to sign a free trade agreement (FTA) with China. The FTA was enacted despite New Zealand having a reputation for being a moral foreign policy actor, and despite China's human rights record. For these reasons, New Zealand remains supportive of China's presence in the Pacific.

However, New Zealand is more ambivalent about China when it comes to security and strategic issues. In April 2018, media reports suggested that China had military ambitions in the Pacific. One report claimed that China had approached Vanuatu about a military buildup, though no formal proposals were made (Wroe 2018). Australia's *9News* network 'confirmed' that the Australian Defence Force was aware that China had 'sounded out Vanuatu about increasing its military engagement' (Uhlmann 2018). In response, New Zealand Prime Minister Jacinta Ardern noted that she could not comment on the validity of the report, but that New Zealand is 'opposed to the militarisation of the Pacific' (Walters 2018a). Deputy Prime Minister and Foreign Affairs Minister Winston Peters stated the militarisation of the Pacific is 'something New Zealand had been "seriously concerned about" for a while now' (ibid.). Though he did not specifically mention China, Peters did note:

> There were a number of players doing certain things in the Pacific that are not good for the peace and security, long-term, of the Pacific, or for the growth of democracy itself.

Apart from New Zealand's allies, China is the only other big player that can affect regional peace and security. Importantly, Peters' statements came one month after his announcement of the Reset, where he predicated the change on 'strategic anxiety' about the Pacific becoming 'an increasingly contested strategic space, no longer neglected by great power ambition' (Peters 2018a). Unless New Zealand was strategically anxious about the actions of the US, Australia or Japan, China is the only other option. New Zealand wants Chinese money, but fears Chinese political and military influence.

Since the Reset was announced, New Zealand has ramped up its Pacific engagement. It announced 14 new diplomatic posts as part of the Reset, 10 in the Pacific, including Hawai'i, and four Tokyo, Beijing, Brussels and New York, 'to co-ordinate development policy and partnerships for the Pacific region' (Radio New Zealand 2018g). Notably, the New Zealand Ministry of Defence's Strategic Defence Policy Statement 2018

(New Zealand Government 2018), released shortly afterwards, indicated a closer intertwinement of foreign affairs and defence priorities. A 2019 New Zealand Ministry of Defence publication, *Advancing Pacific Partnerships*, has a section entitled 'Defence's Pacific Reset', which makes it clear that Defence's strategic policy settings are aligned with the Reset (New Zealand Government 2019).

The Strategic Defence Policy Statement 2018 (Statement) sets out the principles that guide New Zealand's defence policies. China is, again, treated with ambivalence. On the one hand, New Zealand recognises China's importance to the region and world affairs, particularly in relation to what it perceives as the international rules-based order (IRBO). On the other, it explicitly and implicitly expresses concern about China's pursuit of its interests internationally, including in the Pacific. It notes that Washington and Beijing are in competition with each other, and that this has consequences for other countries. Importantly, it notes that China does not promote, or adopt, similar values to the order's 'traditional leaders', including around governance, human rights, development and economic liberalism. Further, it argues that, in some instances, particularly in military affairs, China is challenging the IRBO. It is within this context that China's increasing presence is discussed. Although the Statement does not specifically mention the Pacific, it states that the challenges posed to the rules and norms by countries that are in pursuit of 'spheres of influence', 'is a risk for open societies, including New Zealand'. China is one of the countries (Russia is the other) that is specifically identified as pursuing 'spheres of influence' (New Zealand Government 2018:17). China's influence internationally and in the Pacific is prompting new narratives about New Zealand defence.

Notably, the Statement also expresses concern about Russia. It notes that, in integrating into the IRBO, Russia, like China, has not always done so in accordance with the values and principles of the traditional leaders. Indeed, Russia has gone further. It 'has attempted to discredit Western democracy by challenging its "internal coherence", leveraging information operations, and exploiting existing fissures with Western societies' (ibid.). Though Russia is not mentioned in relation to the Pacific, two factors connect it to the region. First, Russia is viewed as an ally of China. Second, Russia is making its presence felt in the Pacific. While China and Russia are not acting in concert in the region, at least not explicitly, the possibility that they may in the future cannot be ruled out.

China's rising presence in the Pacific can easily be construed as a threat to New Zealand's interests in the region. First, it gives Pacific countries an alternative source of financial assistance, giving them more leverage when engaging with traditional benefactors, and arguably more autonomy. Whereas New Zealand's attaches conditions to its aid, China does not, although recipient countries are expected to adhere to its One China policy. Often, recipient countries have more discretion in how Chinese grants and soft loans are used as opposed to aid from New Zealand. In fact, China provides financial assistance for specific projects requested by Pacific Island countries, such as funding for new infrastructure, swimming pools, parliament buildings, wharfs and the like. The China alternative reduces New Zealand's ability to use aid as a political tool in the Pacific.

China's policies, and the way it engages Pacific Island countries, often do not support New Zealand policies, not that they should. For example, China does not promote good governance or human rights. New Zealand has and continues to promote these and similar norms; according to Peters, these are non-negotiable parts of the Reset (Peters 2018a). From a New Zealand perspective, China also follows an alternative model of development, which the Statement conceptualises as 'a liberalising economy absent liberal democracy' (New Zealand Government 2018:17). These threats to New Zealand's interests are not new, and analysts such as Henderson and Reilly (2003) have examined them. However, they appear relevant to the current government's view of China.

Newer concerns involving security matters are also emerging. The first is the possibility of a Chinese military presence in the Pacific Islands region. Aside from rumours, this concern also springs from a belief that Chinese economic policies are intertwined with their military ambitions. China's economic growth has been accompanied by an increase in its military power (Robertson and Sin 2017:91) and there is speculation from the US, at least, that the two go hand in hand. With reference to both Asia and the Pacific, former deputy assistant secretary of defence for South and Southeast Asia Joseph Felter claimed that China was aiming to establish 'dual-use' facilities, such as commercial ports, that could be converted to military bases (Radio New Zealand 2018c). This should not be a surprise; as China's economic power increases it will expect a role in the Asia-Pacific commensurate with its rise (Mapp 2014:2).

The intertwinement of Chinese economic and military goals has been associated with the debt-trap narrative. China's economic plans, known popularly as the Belt and Road Initiative (BRI) include 'Pacific pathways' (Garrick 2018), and seven Pacific countries have signed up for it: PNG, Samoa, Fiji, Niue, Cook Islands, Tonga and Vanuatu (Radio New Zealand 2018e). According to Garrick (2018), the fear is that China will use the loans associated with its BRI as leverage to expand its military footprint.

The debt-trap narrative was most prominently deployed at the Asia-Pacific Economic Cooperation meeting held in PNG in 2018 by US Vice President Mike Pence, who accused China of luring developing countries into debt traps through infrastructure loans. China, in return, rejected the accusation, highlighting the fact that no country in the world had fallen into a 'so-called debt trap because of its cooperation with China' (The Economic Times 2018). However, China's promised US$4 billion of finance to build PNG's first national road network (Global Construction Review 2017) does prompt questions about PNG's debt situation and the implications of China's financing.

Pence was not the first to use the debt-trap narrative. In early 2018, US Pacific Fleet commander Admiral Scott Swift warned that China would increase debt in a given country and then ask for something in return that was not part of the original deal (Parker and Chefitz 2018). Parker and Chefitz argued that Pacific countries should be included in those that could be affected by China's debtbook diplomacy, particularly Tonga, Vanuatu and PNG. They noted that China is 'positioning itself to capitalise on the impending fiscal distress of Pacific Island countries' (Parker and Chefitz 2018:41). Since that 2018 report, the narrative has gained traction. Former Australian foreign minister Julie Bishop noted, 'We want to ensure that they [Pacific Island countries] retain their sovereignty, that they have sustainable economies and that they are not trapped into unsustainable debt outcomes', and that 'the trap can then be a debt-for-equity swap and they have lost their sovereignty' (Power 2018). Seidel (2018) argued, 'Debt-trap diplomacy is behind a new land grab'. Rightly or wrongly, New Zealand has been implicated as one country that is countering the possibility of debt traps through an extensive campaign of aid, trade and diplomacy (Lintner 2018; Kehoe 2018; Wu 2018).

Not all are convinced of the debt-trap argument. According to Fox and Dornan (2018), this argument is predicated on 'anecdotal evidence' rather than 'hard data'. Using international debt data, Fox and Dornan argued that, although debt is a problem in the Pacific Islands region, the 'debt distress' is not a result of lending by China. They note that 'Chinese lending comprises less than half of lending in any single country' and makes up around 12 per cent of the total debt owed by Pacific nations, even though China is the largest bilateral lender. Notably, 88 per cent of the total owed by Pacific nations is comprised of debts by PNG and Fiji. However, in both countries, 'domestic debt dominates government borrowing'. Further, 'it is only in Tonga, Samoa and Vanuatu that Chinese lending comprises over one-third of total debt', and the debt-trap only has basis in relation to Tonga, where there is a 'high level of debt distress, and Chinese lending dominates'. Fox and Dornan concluded that the debt-trap argument 'is without foundation'.

The potential problem of Pacific Island countries falling into significant debt is a concern to New Zealand. Deputy Prime Minister Peters cautioned Pacific governments about walking into debt traps (Walsh 2018), and Japan has expressed interest in cooperating with New Zealand to resolve the Pacific Island debt problem (Radio New Zealand 2018d). New Zealand has good reason to be concerned about the possibility of debt traps. The problem with Fox and Dornan's argument, and conclusion, is that it is predicated on the debt level of the region as a whole. Clearly, China does not need to have the entire region in a high-debt ratio to itself in order for the debt-trap narrative to have basis. The region does not act as a single entity, but as independent, sovereign countries. China only needs at least one country in the region to be in a debt-trap scenario in order for the narrative to make sense. It is akin to arguing that there was no debt-trap problem in Asia before Sri Lanka gave up its port to Chinese control. Even if only Tonga and/or PNG and Fiji gives up control of its ports, or some other strategically important asset, the debt-trap narrative could make sense. Further, the level of debt does not have to be the key issue in this narrative. Instead, it is the extent to which debt would allow China to have undue influence on the recipient countries in question (O'Keefe 2018). China does not need to be the biggest creditor to these countries in order to achieve this. Nevertheless, it is one of the biggest creditors in some cases, like Vanuatu, where about half of the country's foreign debt is owed to China, and Tonga, where 60 per cent of the country's foreign debt is owed to China (Klan 2018). China does not need control of strategically important assets in every Pacific Island country.

If debt issues can pave the way for increased Chinese military presence in the region, as aforementioned, this would be problematic for New Zealand's interests in the Pacific and threaten what has long been the Western allies' security control over the region. Before New Zealand took over some of the German colonies in the region on behalf of Britain at the beginning of World War I, it had long held aspirations to project military might in the Pacific. The opportunity to do so arose post–World War II. As the victorious great powers (US, Great Britain and China) planned the division of Japan's Pacific territories, New Zealand and Australia made their own play for strategic control of the region through the Canberra Pact (or the ANZAC Pact) (McIntyre 1995:227). The pact continues to inform New Zealand defence and security policy through the present (New Zealand Government 2018). It provides for a 'permanent machinery for collaboration and cooperation' between the two countries in all defence matters of mutual interest, to the extent that they are acquainted with each other's mindset, so that there will be 'the maximum degree of unity' in the presentation of their views 'elsewhere' (Vandenbosch and Vandenbosch 1967:21). The pact is important to the principle of New Zealand and Australia being a 'single strategic entity' (McKinnon 1998). The US, for its part, has had control over the Micronesian region's security issues, particularly through its compacts of free association with Palau, Marshall Islands and the Federated States of Micronesia, for the better part of the 20th century to the present.

The Australia, New Zealand and United States Security Treaty (ANZUS Treaty) has played an important role in the collective security policies of those countries in the Pacific. Though the 1984 Lange Government's nuclear-free policies caused the cessation of the ANZUS Treaty commitments between New Zealand and the US, relations have largely been restored by the Wellington and Washington declarations. Notably, the Wellington Declaration commits the two countries to a strategic partnership in the Pacific. Further, these declarations were signed around the same time the US made a visible return to the region. In 2009, in response to the Australian *2009 Defence White Paper*, then US secretary of state Hillary Clinton stated, 'We want Australia, as well as other nations, to know that the United States is not ceding the Pacific to anyone' (Davies 2009). She was referring to the broader Asia-Pacific region, but the Pacific was a key consideration. In 2011, the US built one of its largest embassies in Australasia in Suva. In 2012, it sent Clinton, still secretary of state, to the PIF, a first in the history of the organisation. Arguably, these actions were done in response to China's increasing presence in the

Pacific. The rising power of China in the region was clearly the context for Clinton's 2009 comments and subsequent rhetoric associated with president Obama's Asia-Pacific pivot (Clinton 2011; Eckert 2011).

China could pose a strategic challenge and security risk to New Zealand's and its allies' domination of the Pacific. Despite President Trump undoing many of Obama's international commitments, including the Pacific pivot, the Trans-Pacific Partnership Agreement and the Paris Agreement on climate change, not much appears to have changed in the US's view of the Pacific. Vice President Pence's pre-APEC comments warning China about seeking undue influence, clearly referencing the Pacific, shows that the US continues to take the region seriously. In 2019, when Solomon Islands renounced its diplomatic recognition of Taipei in favour of Beijing, Pence cancelled a scheduled meeting with Prime Minister Sogavare, which was to have taken place on the sidelines of a United Nations General Assembly meeting in New York. According to Rampton (2019), a senior US official claimed the cancellation was due to the switch. If true, it is quite ironic; the US recognises Beijing, not Taipei.

Nevertheless, it shows the US's concern with China's increasing influence in the region.

However, perhaps more important are the broader implications of China's rising influence in the region. The Ministry of Defence's Strategic Defence Policy Statement 2018 identifies three key threats to the IRBO: spheres of influence, challenges to open societies and complex disruptors. China is important in relation to the first. Although New Zealand recognises that 'China is deeply integrated into the rules-based order', it believes China has 'not consistently adopted the governance and rules championed by the order's traditional leaders' (New Zealand Government 2018). In particular, China's positions on human rights and freedom of information are different from New Zealand's. Further, China does not follow the same 'model of development' as the West, preferring 'a liberalising economy absent liberal democracy' (ibid.). In terms of military power, New Zealand is concerned with the expansion of China's military presence in the Asian region, at times in contravention of conventional practices regarding sovereignty. While none of these issues are prominent in the Pacific, there is the odd sign that something of a similar nature might emerge.

From a New Zealand perspective, Western allies need to retain control of security issues in the Pacific, and a Chinese military presence, should it eventuate, would threaten that control. This priority is somewhat evident in the Reset and related policies. In his Lowy Institute speech, Peters stated that national security was one of three reasons the Pacific was important for New Zealand. Though he did not mention China's rising influence, he did warn of great power ambitions in the region. In noting that the US was 'grappling' with the same realities as New Zealand, it is obvious he was not referring to the US itself. That leaves China. Notably, Peters urged Australia, the European Union and the US 'to better pool our energies and resources to maintain our relative influence' in the Pacific (Peters 2018a). Before attending a regional forum that included a meeting with US Secretary of State Mike Pompeo, Peters spoke of the need for those in the Western camp to address 'the new ball game' in the Pacific (Radio New Zealand 2018b). He did not clarify what the new ball game was. However, given his statements at the Lowy Institute and the 'spheres of influence' discussion in the Defence Statement, it is arguable that China is the focus. In November 2018, Peters announced the Pacific Enabling Fund as part of the Reset and stated that 'the coalition government is committed to rebuilding New Zealand's standing in the Pacific' and that the fund would allow engagement with Pacific partners on a range of activities that sit outside New Zealand's formal aid funding arrangements, including military cooperation activities (Peters 2018b). Steff (2018) notes:

> Ultimately, balancing China in the South Pacific will require greater coordination with Australia—still the Pacific's largest donor—and reading out to other states. Japan, South Korea and the United States share concerns about China chipping away at their relative influence.

After decades of relative neglect, New Zealand recognises the need to reset its policies and reassert it and its allies influence in the region, with a focus on defence and security issues.

Conclusion

Whatever China's activities in the Pacific, whether building dual-purpose infrastructure or enticing countries into debt traps, it is clear that New Zealand has adopted the view that they warrant a considerable shift in its foreign policy approach, and this is manifest in the Reset. To be sure, this view is not explicit in New Zealand's statements concerning the Reset, and the New Zealand Government fervently denies that it is intended to counter China. Nevertheless, an analysis of related rhetoric and policy documents by the New Zealand Government indicate that the anxieties behind the Reset could not have been caused by any other actor in the region except China.

This view or representation of China must be understood in context. It comes after decades of neglect and a neo-colonial approach to the region, the result of a miscalculation on the part of New Zealand and its allies; they assumed the Pacific was under their control. Pacific loyalty was probably taken for granted. After decades of using aid as a political tool to leverage New Zealand's interests vis-à-vis those of the Pacific Island countries, the latter discovered a new source of power. With the rise in the number of external actors in the Pacific, particularly China, New Zealand's pride of place in the region, which it had developed through various security arrangements, is vulnerable. Regional geopolitics is changing, and China's growing presence is the key contributing factor. Compounding New Zealand's anxieties is the apparent vulnerability of Pacific Island countries to Chinese aid, giving rise to the debt-trap narrative. In the context of New Zealand's, and its allies', history in the region, China's presence has caused consternation to the extent that a policy like the Reset is warranted.

References

Bryant-Tokalau, J. and I. Frazer 2006. *Redefining the Pacific? Regionalism Past, Present and Future*. Farnham: Ashgate Publishing, Ltd.

Clinton, H. 2011. America's Pacific Century. *Foreign Policy*, 11 October. www.foreignpolicy.com/2011/10/11/americas-pacific-century/

Crocombe, R. 2007. *Asia in the Pacific Islands: Replacing the West*. Suva: IPS Publications, University of the South Pacific.

Davies, A. 2009. US Not 'Ceding the Pacific': Clinton. *The Sydney Morning Herald*, 20 May. www.smh.com.au/world/us-not-ceding-the-pacific-clinton-20090520-bei8.html

Diamond, L. and O. Schell 2018. *China's Influence and American Interests: Promoting Constructive Vigilance*. Stanford: Hoover Institution Press.

Doherty, B. 2016. Secret Russian Arms Donation to Fiji Raises Concerns of Bid for Pacific Influence. *The Guardian*, 22 January. www.theguardian.com/world/2016/jan/22/secretive-shipment-of-arms-donated-by-russia-to-fiji-raises-concerns

Eckert, P. 2011. Clinton Declares 'America's Pacific Century'. *Reuters*, 12 November. www.reuters.com/article/us-apec-usa-clinton-f/clinton-declares-americas-pacific-century-idUSTRE7AA2S120111111

Fox, R. and M. Dornan 2018. China in the Pacific: Is China Engaged in 'Debt-Trap Diplomacy'? *Devpolicy Blog*, 8 November. www.devpolicy.org/is-china-engaged-in-debt-trap-diplomacy-20181108/

Fry, G. and S. Tarte 2015. The 'New Pacific Diplomacy': An Introduction. In G. Fry and S.Tarte. *The New Pacific Diplomacy*. Canberra: ANU Press. doi.org/10.22459/NPD.12.2015.01

Garrick, J. 2018. Soft Power Goes Hard: China's Economic Interest in the Pacific Comes with Strings Attached. *The Conversation*, 17 October. theconversation.com/soft-power-goes-hard-chinas-economic-interest-in-the-pacific-comes-with-strings-attached-103765

Global Construction Review 2017. China to Build Papua New Guinea's First National Road System. 24 November. globalconstructionreview.com/news/china-build-papua-new-guineas-first-national-road-/

Henderson, J. 1999. New Zealand and Oceania. In B. Brown (ed.), *New Zealand in World Affairs 1972–1990*. Auckland: New Zealand Institute of International Affairs.

Henderson, J. and B. Reilly 2003. Dragon in Paradise: China's Rising Star in Oceania. *The National Interest* Summer(72):94–104.

Hensley, G. 2013. *Friendly Fire: Nuclear Politics and the Collapse of ANZUS, 1984–1987*. Auckland: Auckland University Press.

Kehoe, J. 2018. US Report: China 'Debt Trap' on Australia's Doorstep. *Financial Review*, 13 May. www.afr.com/news/politics/world/us-secret-report-china-debt-trap-on-australias-doorstep-20180513-h0zzwd

Klan, A. 2018. Pacific Nations Drowning in Chinese Debt. *The Australian*, 29 January. www.theaustralian.com.au/nation/politics/pacific-nations-drowning-in-chinese-debt/news-story/082de1ecc957c9c4380bb9cb8555fa95

Knaus, C. 2017. Australian Air Force Put on Alert after Russian Long-Range Bombers Headed South. *The Guardian*, 30 December. www.theguardian.com/world/2017/dec/30/australian-military-alert-russia-bombers-indonesia-exercises

Lintner, B. 2018. China Advances, West Frets in South Pacific. *Asia Times*, 25 April. www.asiatimes.com/2018/04/china-advances-west-frets-in-south-pacific/

Mapp, W. 2014. *The New Zealand Paradox: Adjusting to the Change in Balance of Power in the Asia-Pacific over the Next 20 Years*. Lanham: Rowman and Littlefield.

McIntyre, W.D. 1995. *Background to the ANZUS Pact: Policy-Making, Strategy and Diplomacy, 1945–1955*. Christchurch: St Martin's Press, Canterbury University Press.

McKinnon, D. 1998. *Australia–New Zealand Defence Ministerial Talks*. New Zealand Government, 27 March. www.beehive.govt.nz/feature/australia-new-zealand-defence-ministerial-talks

Muraviev, A. 2018. Russia Is a Rising Military Power in the Asia-Pacific, and Australia Needs to Take It Seriously. *The Conversation*, 31 October. www.abc.net.au/news/2018-10-31/russia-is-a-rising-military-power-in-the-asia-pacific/10447190

New Zealand Government 2018. *Strategic Defence Policy Statement*. Wellington: Ministry of Defence.

New Zealand Government 2019. *Advancing Pacific Partnerships 2019*. 29 October. Wellington: Ministry of Defence. www.defence.govt.nz/assets/publication/file/5f6dd307e7/Advancing-Pacific-Partnerships-2019.pdf

Novak, C. 2018. New Zealand's China Reset? *The Strategist*, 20 December. Australian Strategic Policy Institute. www.aspistrategist.org.au/new-zealands-china-reset/

O'Keefe, M. 2018. Why China's 'Debt-Book Diplomacy' in the Pacific Shouldn't Ring Alarm Bells Just Yet. *The Conversation*, 17 May. theconversation.com/why-chinas-debt-book-diplomacy-in-the-pacific-shouldnt-ring-alarm-bells-just-yet-96709

Parker, S. and G. Chefitz 2018. *Debtbook Diplomacy China's Strategic Leveraging of its Newfound Economic Influence and the Consequences for US Foreign Policy*. Cambridge: Belfer Center for Science and International Affairs.

Peters, W. 2018a. 'Shifting the Dial': Eyes Wide Open, Pacific Reset. Speech at the Lowy Institute, Sydney, 1 March. www.lowyinstitute.org/publications/winston-peters-new-zealand-pacific

Peters, W. 2018b. Pacific Reset Picks Up Pace. News release, 8 November. www.beehive.govt.nz/release/pacific-reset-picks-pace

Power, J. 2018. China: The Real Reason Australia's Pumping Cash into the Pacific? *South China Morning Post*, 28 July. www.scmp.com/week-asia/geopolitics/article/2157169/china-real-reason-australias-pumping-cash-pacific

Powles, A. and M. Powles 2017. New Zealand's Pacific Policies—Time for a Reset? *New Zealand International Review* 42(2):16–21.

Radio New Zealand 2018a. Academic Questions Significance of UK's Pacific Ramp Up. 20 April. www.radionz.co.nz/international/pacific-news/355609/academic-questions-significance-of-uk-s-pacific-ramp-up

Radio New Zealand 2018b. Peters Says World Needs to Address 'New Ball Game' in the Pacific. 31 July. www.radionz.co.nz/international/pacific-news/363062/peters-says-world-needs-to-address-new-ball-game-in-the-pacific

Radio New Zealand 2018c. US Calls Out China on 'Debt-Trap' Diplomacy. 5 October. www.radionz.co.nz/international/pacific-news/367997/us-calls-out-china-on-debt-trap-diplomacy

Radio New Zealand 2018d. Japan and NZ Join Forces to Help Pacific. 15 October. www.radionz.co.nz/international/pacific-news/368699/japan-and-nz-join-forces-to-help-pacific

Radio New Zealand 2018e. Tonga and Vanuatu Join China's Belt and Road. 20 November. www.radionz.co.nz/international/pacific-news/376372/tonga-and-vanuatu-join-china-s-belt-and-road

Radio New Zealand 2018f. Government Has Its 'Eyes Wide Open' on China: Winston Peters. 4 December. www.radionz.co.nz/news/political/377436/government-has-its-eyes-wide-open-on-china-winston-peters

Radio New Zealand 2018g. NZ Ups Its Diplomatic Presence in Pacific. 4 December. www.radionz.co.nz/international/pacific-news/377458/nz-ups-its-diplomatic-presence-in-pacific

Rampton, R. 2019. Exclusive: Pence Rebuffs Solomon Islands PM After Nation Cuts Ties with Taiwan. *Reuters*, 18 September. www.reuters.com/article/us-taiwan-diplomacy-pence-exclusive/exclusive-pence-rebuffs-solomon-islands-pm-after-nation-cuts-ties-with-taiwan-idUSKBN1W22WK

Reuters 2018. NZ Ramps up Diplomatic Presence in Pacific Where China Influence Rising. 4 December. www.reuters.com/article/us-newzealand-pacific/nz-ramps-up-diplomatic-presence-in-pacific-where-china-influence-rising-idUSKBN1O3094

Riordan, P. 2018. Russian Warship Due to Dock in Port Moresby. *The Australian*, 14 May. www.theaustralian.com.au/nation/defence/russian-warship-due-to-dock-in-port-moresby/news-story/dfd439d2e840f23139558e61181f5dd4

Robertson, P.E. and A. Sin 2017. Measuring Hard Power: China's Economic Growth and Military Capacity. *Defence and Peace Economics* 28(1):91–111. doi.org/10.1080/10242694.2015.1033895

Seidel, J. 2018. China Almost Has Australia Surrounded. But Its Debt-Trap Diplomacy Has Been Exposed. *news.com.au*, 25 September. www.news.com.au/world/pacific/china-almost-has-australia-surrounded-but-its-debttrap-diplomacy-has-been-exposed/news-story/3f8d390e8c8e3b5158214836ee412aee

Steff, R. 2018. New Zealand's Pacific Reset: Strategic Anxieties about Rising China. *The Conversation*, 1 June. www.theconversation.com/new-zealands-pacific-reset-strategic-anxieties-about-rising-china-97174

Tarte, S. 1989. Regionalism and Globalism in the South Pacific. *Development and Change* 20:181–201.

The Economic Times 2018. China Slams Mike Pence; Says No Country in Debt Trap Because of BRI. 18 November. economictimes.indiatimes.com/news/international/world-news/china-slams-mike-pence-says-no-country-in-debt-trap-because-of-bri/articleshow/66679080.cms

Uhlmann, C. 2018. PM Warns China Not to Consider Building Naval Base in the South Pacific. *9News*, 10 April. www.9news.com.au/world/australian-defence-force-china-will-upset-power-balance-in-south-pacific-vanuatu-naval-base/34d9bc89-fa7a-49c9-9985-34c17163d68c

Vandenbosch, A. and M.B. Vandenbosch 1967. *Australia Faces Southeast Asia: The Emergence of a Foreign Policy*. Lexington: University of Kentucky Press.

Walsh, M. 2018. Pacific Leaders More Questioning of Chinese Influence. Radio New Zealand, 24 November. www.radionz.co.nz/news/world/376732/pacific-leaders-more-questioning-of-chinese-influence

Walters, L. 2018a. PM Opposes Pacific Militarisation As China Eyes Vanuatu Military Base. *Stuff*, 10 April. www.stuff.co.nz/national/politics/102971730/pm-opposes-pacific-militarisation-as-china-eyes-vanuatu-military-base

Walters, L. 2018b. New $180m Fund to Help Counter NZ's 'Decreasing Influence' in Pacific. *Stuff*, 3 July. www.stuff.co.nz/national/politics/105183983/new-180m-fund-to-help-counter-nzs-decreasing-influence-in-pacific

Wroe, D. 2018. China Eyes Vanuatu Military Base in Plan with Global Ramifications. *The Sydney Morning Herald*, 9 April. www.smh.com.au/politics/federal/china-eyes-vanuatu-military-base-in-plan-with-global-ramifications-20180409-p4z8j9.html

Wu, W. 2018. Beyond the 'Chinese Debt Trap'. *The Interpreter*, 30 May. Lowy Institute. www.lowyinstitute.org/the-interpreter/beyond-chinese-debt-trap

5

Associations Freely Chosen: New Geopolitics in the North Pacific

Gerard A. Finin

A new era

For the first time since the collapse of the Soviet Union, America's global leadership is being directly challenged. In Asia, blunt trade policies imposed upon China by the Trump administration had raised the spectre of a trade war. United States' withdrawal from the critically important Paris Climate Agreement during the Trump years prompted widespread condemnation by the global community, particularly from Pacific Island nations. President Trump's advocacy of unabashed US unilateralism also generated tensions with European allies, including close partners that for generations cooperated with the US in maintaining stability.

In contrast, the 2020 election of President Joseph Biden is all but certain to usher in a return to the Obama administration's emphasis on multilateralism to advance peace and stability, consciously avoiding the hairpin policy turns, contradictions and befuddlement evident over the last four years. One of the Obama administration's flagship foreign policy initiatives was its 'rebalance' or 'pivot' towards the Asia-Pacific, a decision that reflected long-term economic and demographic trends. The historically robust US military presence across the Asia-Pacific region was balanced by multinational military exercises, the proposed Trans-Pacific

Partnership trade agreement and enhanced public diplomacy. Although the rebalance was clearly articulated during the Obama administration's first term by secretary of state Hillary Clinton, there were in retrospect insufficient concrete actions to impart real credibility. At best, the pivot remained largely aspirational, and never gained traction as a true transformation in US foreign policy. With many of the same individuals who initially conceived the 'rebalance' now back in government, analysts are asking whether the 'rebalance' will in some form be resurrected?

Despite stark differences in approach and style compared to his predecessors, the Trump administration continued to pursue US power projection across this vast area—a pillar in America's westward strategy with roots dating back to the late 19th century (Anderson 2015). What distinguished the Trump administration was its sharp focus on potential threats from China as it attempted to amplify the US's profile and presence across the renamed Indo-Pacific region. However deep the contemporary political divisions with the US may be, there is broad agreement that China cannot be left unchallenged. China's increasingly authoritarian state is viewed as an aggressive threat to the regional order that must be confronted. The Biden administration's change in tone and policy branding will do little to alter the Trump administration's deployment of the full array of US government departments and agencies operating under the loosely constructed, and at times contradictory, Free and Open Indo-Pacific Strategy (Roy 2019).

Consistent with this new thinking about China's motivations in Oceania are New Zealand's Pacific Reset and Australia's Pacific Step-Up initiatives, both designed to counter the People's Republic of China's (PRC) desire to play a larger role in the Pacific Islands region. And even if the US has yet to clearly define what it is now calling the 'Pacific Pledge', there can be little doubt that this is a transformational moment in the Pacific region, with Australia, New Zealand and the US anticipating a much more highly competitive era. While slow in gaining full momentum, the new 'whole of government' responses to China's rise by Western powers are increasingly evident in Oceania as well as across the Indo-Pacific more broadly. The Biden administration's National Security Council point person for Indo-Pacific strategy advocates 'the need for a balance of power; the need for an order that the region's states recognize as legitimate; and the need for an allied and partner coalition to address China's challenges to both' (Campbell and Doshi 2021:1).

Evidence of this change has been apparent in Washington well before the 2020 presidential election. For instance, in March 2019 senior White House staff, including the senior director for Asian affairs and the director for Oceania and Indo-Pacific Security on the National Security Council visited Vanuatu and Solomon Islands for meetings with top officials. Other indications of intensifying US focus in the region in 2019 include a sharp uptick in funding for public diplomacy programs, new military to military initiatives between the Pentagon and Fiji's armed forces and visits to the region by US congressional delegations. New Pacific Island activities among Washington-based research and educational institutions such as the Hudson Institute and Georgetown University's Center for Australian, New Zealand and Pacific Studies suggest interest is by no means limited to government.[1]

High-level North Pacific engagement

The effort to stem Chinese influence in the North Pacific was evident in a February 2019 statement by US Secretary of State Mike Pompeo addressing the foreign policies of two North Pacific nations that have a special 'free association' agreement with the US. Both the Republic of the Marshall Islands (RMI) and the Republic of Palau (Palau) were commended for positions clearly at variance with US policy regarding official recognition of Taiwan. Quoting the US vice president, Secretary Pompeo said:

> America will always believe Taiwan's embrace of democracy is an example to be internationally supported. We respect and support the decision those of you have made to continue to support Taiwan.

Left completely out of the statement was any mention of the Federated States of Micronesia (FSM), the largest nation in Free Association with the US, and the only North Pacific Island nation that, like Washington, recognises the PRC. Shortly thereafter, however, a senior delegation of US

---

1   These activities include seminars and roundtable dialogues focusing on Oceania's evolving strategic position. Similarly, the DC-based Center for Strategic and International Studies recently convened a Strengthening the US–Pacific Islands Partnership workshop in Fiji that brought together a who's who of Oceania's regional organisations. An example of the increase in Pacific-focused publications is a recent Hudson Institute paper on the use of foreign aid to counter China's Djibouti Strategy (Lee 2019). Additional evidence of US military activity is the deployment of some 200 US troops to Palau for an exercise known as Pacific Pathways.

military, coast guard and Department of the Interior officials travelled to meet with leaders of the FSM (as well as FSM's Chuuk State Government) before also visiting Palau and the RMI (Radio New Zealand 2019).

President Donald Trump subsequently convened an unprecedented working-level meeting at the White House on 21 May 2019 with Presidents Hilda Heine of the RMI, David Panuelo of the FSM and Tommy Remengesau of Palau. The brief Oval Office discussion and photo opportunity was intended to advance Compact of Free Association economic support renewal negotiations before the 2023–24 deadlines. Just a few days prior to the White House event, President Remengesau, in an op-ed article published by *The Hill* (2019), noted how China 'has risen as a serious challenge to US dominance of the Pacific Ocean today'. While in Washington, President Heine similarly focused her remarks on Chinese pressure, including incursions within the RMI's Exclusive Economic Zone related to the illegal entry of fishing vessels.

Since re-establishing diplomatic relations with Beijing in 1979, Washington has kept Taiwan at arm's length politically, as it saw far greater prospects for advancing US interests through relations with the PRC. However, China's rapid rise as a global power intent on charting its own course has in more recent years created a range of diplomatic and economic frictions. This includes its renewed emphasis on reincorporating Taiwan into its body politic as part of the One China principle. Under President Xi Jinping, it is clear that of the thousands of islands across the Indo-Pacific, the Austronesian island state that matters most to Beijing is Taiwan. Few scholars dispute that the PRC is resolute in its determination to bring Taiwan within Beijing's direct control. Standing in opposition to Beijing's plans are four sovereign Pacific Island nations, including the RMI and Palau, that at least for now appear unwavering in their recognition of Taiwan.[2] This support for Taiwan, coupled with plans announced by the US in 2004 to greatly reduce economic support to the FSM and the RMI, has encouraged Beijing to increase diplomatic and economic activities in the North Pacific.

---

2   Early in 2019, President Xi made this clear to officials and military leaders seated in the Great Hall of the People when he stated, 'The country is growing strong, the nation is rejuvenating and unification between the two sides of the strait is the great trend of history'. Later in the address he asserted, 'We make no promise to abandon the use of force and retain the option of taking all necessary measures' (Buckley and Horton 2019).

While some analysts may see US–PRC competition in the Pacific Islands region as a mere replay of the Cold War, when Soviet diplomatic and naval activities prompted a sharp US reaction, the dynamics of the US–China relationship are far more complex. To better understand the larger geopolitical developments across Oceania, this chapter explores how US–China relations are evolving in the three Freely Associated States (FAS) of the North Pacific and suggests how and why US policy in the FAS reflects larger trends in US–China relations.

Background

America has not been overtly challenged militarily in the Pacific Islands region since the US concluded World War II. US activities in the North Pacific were especially free of geostrategic constraints because of large US military installations in Hawai'i, Guam and the Philippines. Under United Nations (UN) auspices, in 1947 the Trust Territory of the Pacific Islands (TTPI) was created where Japan had once ruled (Hezel 2003). The UN gave exclusive authority for governing the TTPI to the US. In time, nearly all of this island constellation would become the three FAS, each having a treaty-like agreement or 'compact' with the US guaranteeing unilateral and unfettered US military access. During the post-war decades, the RMI was the site for 67 nuclear tests, while the Northern Marianas reportedly served as a counter-insurgency training location for missions in Southeast Asia and for support of the Chinese Nationalist Party based in Taiwan. With the US represented in the South Pacific by American Samoa, as well as close bilateral ties with Australia, Britain, France and New Zealand, the entire Pacific Islands region during the post-war decades came to be seen by many US policymakers as an 'American lake' (Underwood 2017).[3]

The slow pace of TTPI economic development and Cold War pressures during the 1960s and 1970s brought about a dramatic per capita increase in US funding for the TTPI. Historian David Hanlon assessed the failures of these financial infusions when he observed:

---

3   In the words of former US congressman Robert Underwood (2017), 'The absolute arrogance of these activities was given various justifications at the time. It was classic imperialist exploitation papered over with the flimsiest of authority. As we look at those days, the old saying in the Trust Territory comes to mind. The islanders had the trust and the Americans had the territory'.

> The messy entanglements that marked efforts at economic development by the mid-1970s resulted in part from Trust Territory government offices, federal bureaucracies and international aid agencies working at cross-purposes or against one another in institutionally prescribed ways in the development game (1998:237).

If the initiatives to stimulate economic development fell short of stated goals, the US-led efforts to establish vibrant democratic institutions with elected representative bodies met far greater success. Similarly, the establishment of public educational institutions (from primary through community colleges) and cultural exchanges (e.g. the Peace Corps) saw significant gains (Stayman 2009).

A UN-monitored vote in the late 1970s subsequently offered TTPI residents the opportunity to formally become an unincorporated part of the US. This was rejected by most of the TTPI districts (Levy 2008). Therefore, during the mid-1980s and through the early 1990s, the TTPI structure transitioned to a new arrangement wherein three new nation states and one commonwealth were created. The Northern Mariana Islands chose to become a commonwealth of the US, with a legal status similar to that of Puerto Rico. The RMI and Palau, each embracing considerable cultural homogeneity, voted to become sovereign unitary republics. The more culturally diverse FSM was created by establishing four state governments within one country: Chuuk, Kosrae, Pohnpei and Yap.

What is distinctive about the US's relationships with these three countries is the special bilateral agreements that were created to maintain close and mutually beneficial ties. The idea of free association was first established between New Zealand and two neighbouring South Pacific nations, Cook Islands (1965) and Niue (1974). Self-government in free association provided greater sovereignty and independence for the smaller developing nations without hindering visa-free movement to the larger nation for residency, employment or education.[4] With some modifications, this served as the model for the three newly established nations in the North Pacific.

---

4   While Cook Islanders and Niueans elect their own parliaments and national leaders, they travel internationally with New Zealand passports. This has complicated their desire to have UN representation.

Following independence, the FSM, the RMI and Palau, despite initial US reluctance, joined the UN and other international institutions with full membership rights and responsibilities. At the same time, the compacts of free association in the North Pacific provided for continued US economic assistance and exclusive US military access. Importantly, in keeping with the principles of sovereignty and self-government, each party retains the right to unilaterally withdraw from the free association agreement (Stayman 2009:9). Despite the obvious asymmetries between the interactions of a continental power and smaller states, the basic US relationship with the three FAS advances the national interests of each of the parties to the compacts. Over some three decades, none of the signatory nations have ever taken steps indicating they wish to abrogate their respective free association agreement.

Early years of nationhood

The first compacts of free association were signed by the US with the FSM and the RMI in 1986. An impasse over proposals to make Palau nuclear free delayed its independence until 1994. US budgetary and program support to the FSM and the RMI from 1987 through 2003 is estimated to have totalled US$2.1 billion. For a total population of less than 160,000, this represented approximately US$900 per capita basis on an annual (Finin 2013:24).

The success of the FAS in developing vibrant democratic political institutions contrasts with the ongoing challenges of creating more self-reliant economies, particularly in the FSM and the RMI. A number of post-independence initiatives to stimulate these economies, such as the establishment of domestic fishing fleets, fared poorly (Hezel 2006). An in-depth assessment of the economic support provisions of the FSM and the RMI compacts by the US General Accountability Office (US GAO) in 2003 found that:

> many Compact-funded projects in the FSM and RMI experienced problems because of poor planning and management, inadequate construction and maintenance, or misuse of funds. Further, the US, FSM, and RMI provided little accountability over Compact expenditures and have not ensured that funds were spent effectively or efficiently (2018:1).

The initial 15 years of the FSM's and the RMI's independence (often termed Compact I) demonstrated the complexities of island development in an environment with limited capacities and young institutions. At the same time, it underscored the need make development investments more effective. Following prolonged negotiations focusing on mechanisms to ensure greater accountability of US funds, Compact II (2004–23) created a new structure for US economic support with an emphasis on the health and education sectors.

Under the new Compact II arrangement, five-person economic management committees were established for each country. Membership in the FSM's Joint Economic Management Committee (JEMCO) and the RMI's Joint Economic Management and Financial Accountability Committee (JEMFAC) was composed of three US members and two from each of the respective countries. This imbalance in JEMCO and JEMFAC representation, seen by many as a neocolonial imposition, was described by former US congressman Robert Underwood of Guam as 'less free and more compact' (2003). From the perspective of the FSM and the RMI, there were perhaps fewer anxieties about the stricter process of review and approval for the expenditure of compact funds (US$3.6 billion in economic assistance 2004–23) than were concerns regarding deep infringements of national sovereignty. To many observers, the JEMCO and JEMFAC structures suggested less collegiality and amity in working toward common development goals, reintroducing a process more akin to pre-independence TTPI-style budgetary rule.

Furthermore, Compact II required the establishment of trust funds for each nation. The trust funds were strongly suggestive of US thinking about its future relationships with the FSM and RMI. Widely interpreted as an economic exit strategy for the US, Compact II specified a schedule of reduced annual US treasury flows (called decrements) for recurrent government expenditures (e.g. public worker salaries, government program budgets) and an increase in funds deposited annually into the trust funds' accounts. These accounts were intended to create an investment pool sufficient to generate the income needed to sustain the FSM's and the RMI's fiscal requirements after the economic support provisions of the compacts expire. The yearly decrements in US funding for recurrent expenditures soon forced the FSM and the RMI to attempt budget cuts while simultaneously seeking alternative sources of revenue and economic support.

An analysis of the trust funds by the US GAO published before the 2008 global economic crisis foresaw management challenges and market volatility that would call into question projected revenue streams (US GAO 2007). A subsequent 2018 US GAO analysis of actions needed to prepare for the post-2023 transition to trust fund income concluded that 'the trust funds are increasingly likely to provide no annual disbursements in some years and to not sustain their value' (2018:1).

Even before this most recent report, however, both the FSM and the RMI sought assistance from other countries. For instance, in 2008 and 2010 FSM reportedly deposited US$1 million from Chinese grants in the FSM Trust Fund. The RMI established its own trust fund under an agreement with Taiwan wherein US$10 million was contributed as an initial corpus. By 2017, this fund had grown to US$15.1 million (US GAO 2018:79–80).

In light of the looming scheduled deadline for major US economic support to end, the FSM and the RMI have explored new economic development opportunities. For example, in 2018 the RMI took preliminary steps to embrace digital currency as a way to attract more economic activity, pulling back only when International Monetary Fund officials warned of significant dangers (Baraniuk 2018). Although it is highly likely that agreement with the US will be reached, both countries have carefully assessed what the potential vacuum in economic support could mean for their future bilateral relationships with the US and other nations.

In contrast to its neighbours, the Republic of Palau has a record of strong economic growth and fiscal performance that places it as one of the Pacific Islands' only upper middle–income countries. Its per capita gross national income of US$13,950 (2017) is more than three times that of FSM's and more than twice that of the RMI's.[5] Its trust fund, established at the time of independence in 1994, was valued at an estimated US$184 million in 2015. The extended eight-year delay in the passage of US congressional legislation providing economic support, initially promised in 2010, has been resolved. This has once again set the relationship between the two countries on solid footing for renewal prior to the 2024 deadline.

---

5   See pacificaidmap.lowyinstitute.org.

Viewed as a whole, the bilateral ties between the US and the three countries with free association relationships are generally positive, with US embassies in each of the capitals facilitating regular communication and monitoring the work of numerous US federal agencies. Still, there can be little doubt that the eventual withdrawal of major US funding to the FSM and the RMI creates uncertainty about the future and encourages both nations to explore new forms of engagement with existing allies or potential new partners.

Current US security interests

For well over seven decades, the Pacific has been seen as critical to US national security and other core US interests in the region. The compacts of free association in the northwest Pacific provide for exclusive US access to the waters, land and airspace over an area of more than 5,590,460 square kilometres, an expanse nearly as large as the continental US.[6] Catalysed by China's ambitions, as well as the changing geostrategic environment across the Pacific generally, the US is currently reassessing its relations with the FAS. To a greater extent than ever before, these three sovereign island nations are gaining both voices and negotiating leverage with some of the world's most powerful nations (Wesley-Smith and Porter 2010).

The US views the FAS as peaceful, stable democracies that regularly hold free and fair elections and maintain commendable human rights records. There has never been civil unrest or disruptions of the constitutional processes comparable with those of some neighbouring allies such as the Philippines. Within the UN, the voting records of the FSM, the RMI and Palau are ranked as being among the most consistent with positions taken by the US. Citizens of the FAS value their visa-free access to the US for purposes of study, work or residency without time limitations. In light of the US taking responsibility for their national defence, the FAS are able to focus on domestic issues such as health and education. Qualified citizens of the FAS are eligible to join the US military, with increasing numbers serving in all branches of the armed forces stationed around the globe.[7]

---

6   CIA World Factbook. See also, www.seaaroundus.org.
7   See, for example, Nathan Fitch's 2018 documentary about the FSM's citizens in the US military, *Island Soldier.* www.islandsoldiermovie.com

Though all three countries have some similarities, it is important to distinguish analytically between the FSM, the RMI and Palau, as the strategic importance of each to the US must be seen through a separate lense. There is little doubt, for example, that the major billion-dollar investments in US military assets in the RMI's Kwajalein are unrivalled in the region. Similarly, the economic trajectories of the three FAS are distinctive, with Palau having developed a thriving private sector fuelled by its tourism industry. Foreign policies and diplomatic relations also vary. As noted previously, only the FSM formally recognises China, while Palau and the RMI both have long-standing diplomatic relations with Taiwan. However, to a greater degree than ever before, China seeks enhanced engagement with the FSM and is simultaneously pushing to advance its One China policy in the RMI and Palau.

Critical to understanding the dynamics that underlie contemporary developments are two separate but related issues, both concerned with US security interests. With the current economic support arrangements between the US and the FSM and the RMI set to expire in just three years, there are major economic uncertainties. FSM compact sector and supplemental education grants ending in 2023 comprise 33 per cent of the government's total expenditures. The RMI compact sector and supplemental education grants ending in 2023 constitute 25 per cent of the government's total expenditures (US GAO 2018:20–22). Such a significant reduction in US budgetary support to the FSM and the RMI, if matched by a proportionate reduction in government services, has the potential to disrupt social and political stability.[8]

At the same time, the US is currently seeking to bolster its military capabilities in the FAS through new infrastructure and signals installations. Such enhancements to the strategic posture of the US, particularly in relation to the PRC's island-building activities in the South China Sea, are of increasing priority. Palau's President Remengesau unequivocally welcomed a larger US military presence, stating that all three Freely Associated States are 'natural allies in the Pentagon's new Indo-Pacific strategy' (2019).

---

8   Moreover, both countries may lose population. The visa-free access to the US provided by the compacts of free association could, in the face of diminished public services and economic uncertainty, lead to increased out-migration, especially among those citizens with marketable skills. Over time, the majority of the FSM's and the RMI's citizens may choose to reside in the US, conceivably prompting the two island governments to adopt policies that encourage more skilled in-migration from other Asia-Pacific nations. This is already the case for Cook Islanders and Niueans in the South Pacific, where there is a free association structure with New Zealand.

As the US confronts a fast-changing geopolitical environment across the Indo-Pacific, it is clear that 2023–24 represents a significant juncture. This date offers policy options for economic decoupling with the FAS or, alternatively and more likely, opportunities to bolster bilateral relations through new economic support structures. It appears highly probable that the once-heralded plans for significant decreases in US economic support to the FSM and the RMI will be cast aside in favour of realpolitik. This new environment offers the FAS unprecedented opportunities to advance their respective national interests.

Overseas development assistance in the Freely Associated States

After more than a decade of implicit agreement by China and Taiwan to maintain the status quo in terms of diplomatic ties, changes in Taiwan's internal political dynamics, reflected in the 2016 national elections, resulted in renewed competition for official recognition. The decisions by Kiribati and Solomon Islands in September 2019 to recognise China further altered the geostrategic currents. This strategic competition for the FAS is evident in aggressive diplomacy as well as expanding overseas development assistance (ODA). Concurrently, the increasingly competitive dynamic between China and the US has altered how US policymakers are thinking about future economic support in the North Pacific as well as new opportunities for cooperation with Taiwan.

Competition between Beijing and Taipei for diplomatic recognition has brought about intensified outreach efforts, such as aid project ribbon-cutting visits by Taiwan President Tsai Ing-wen to Palau and the RMI. This has been accompanied by other relationship-strengthening measures, including the signing of a visa-free entry agreement for the RMI's citizens (Radio New Zealand 2018a). Taiwan has also attempted to garner broader support within the region by demonstrating greater inclusiveness than China in education and training programs that allow individuals from all Pacific Island developing states to participate.[9]

---

9   This is seen, for example, in the scholarship program for the University of the South Pacific funded through the Pacific Islands Forum.

The tension between Taiwan and China was evident in recent years during the Pacific Islands Forum meetings hosted by Palau in 2014 and the RMI in 2013. From the perspective of the Pacific Island nations, however, it is not the diplomatic skirmishes but the annual flows of ODA that are of far greater significance.

Neither China nor Taiwan participated in the 2009 Cairns Compact on strengthening ODA coordination and transparency in the Pacific. Both countries have eschewed collaborating with Western development initiatives in favour of charting their own independent courses in the Pacific (Finin 2011). Still, there is little doubt among Pacific Island aid specialists that Taiwan's overall aid program pales in comparison to China's. For China, the principles of South–South cooperation— equality, mutual benefit, common development and non-conditionality—have long been articulated as the basis for their ODA globally, and the Pacific is no exception (Kato et al. 2016:144).[10]

It is estimated by the Lowy Institute that in recent years China has spent nearly five times as much as Taiwan in the region. The most comprehensive estimates suggest China has expended US$1.26 billion, while Taiwan has allocated US$224.03 million. Moreover, China's projects are reported to be some nine times larger on average. Yet, from another perspective, Lowy's analysis found that because the countries that recognise Taiwan have much smaller populations, when viewed on a per capita basis, Taipei spends US$237 to Beijing's US$108 (Nguyen and Pryke 2018). Among the Pacific countries having smaller populations, such calculations may play a role in policymakers' decisions.

Participation in China's massive Belt and Road Initiative has been extended to each of the eight Pacific nations that recognise Beijing. However, the Beijing-based Taihe Institute recently warned that a number of Pacific Island nations would be bad or risky investments for Belt and Road projects (China Economic Review 2018). The possible leverage associated with such debt, as well as the burdens of debt service payments, has the potential to limit Pacific governments' future expenditures on basic needs. In the North Pacific, it appears the FSM has thus far resisted major loans from China (Greenfield and Barrett 2018).

---

10   Concessional and non-concessional financing by China, sometimes in cooperation with state-owned enterprises providing loans and investments, makes it difficult to distinguish what qualifies as ODA (Asplund and Soderberg 2017:108–14).

President Xi Jinping's visit to Port Moresby for APEC's November 2018 meeting and his special side gathering with the leaders of Pacific Island countries that recognise Beijing allowed China to emphasise how potentially transformational Belt and Road Initiative projects could be for its diplomatic allies. Meanwhile, at the same APEC gathering, the US vice president appeared to depend heavily on Australian goodwill to announce 'joint cooperative' aid initiatives for the Pacific, suggesting USAID was not prepared to offer any major new projects to the region. From the perspective of numerous Pacific Island policymakers, Taiwan and other metropolitan donors will have to redouble their efforts as China becomes an increasingly influential Pacific power, both militarily and economically. Based on the recent decisions by Kiribati and Solomon Islands to recognise Beijing, it remains an open question whether Taiwan's intensified diplomatic efforts will continue to dissuade its remaining four Pacific allies from concluding that the current momentum and tide of history favours China.

Despite increasing activity by both China and Taiwan in the North Pacific, it is important to underscore that within the FAS, the US and the Western multilateral development banks it heavily supports remain by far the largest contributors to national development. Multilateral institutions appear more eager than ever before to broaden and deepen activities in Oceania. The Asian Development Bank (ADB) has announced plans to set up seven new offices around the region: Cook Islands, the RMI, the FSM, Palau, Nauru, Tuvalu and Kiribati will all are slated to have an ADB mission by the end of 2022. The ADB's portfolio of work in the region has doubled every five years since 2005. It currently stands at $US2.9 billion, with total assistance expected to surpass $US4 billion by 2020 (Radio New Zealand 2018b).

The World Bank's offices in Washington DC and Sydney both have growing programs with the FAS. A major region-wide research and publication effort focusing on 'Pacific Possible' includes an optimistic vision through 2040 for endeavours such as tourism, fisheries and labour mobility (World Bank 2017). Major World Bank investments are being made in information and communications technology, specifically the installation of fibre optic cables for broadband connectivity. By 2020, for instance, a US$63.5 million connectivity project in FSM had connected Chuuk and Yap. The second phase of the project includes cables that will connect the republics of Nauru and Kiribati, and additional funding from the ADB will connect Kosrae (World Bank 2018). Considered as a whole, these recent developments suggest that there is more new development partner engagement in the North Pacific than at any time since the Cold War.

Still, it is widely acknowledged that the process of getting Western-funded projects off the ground in the FAS can at times be delayed by years. In some cases the delays are well justified, while in others it appears the approval process may be overly bureaucratic. For example, in 2016, US$40 million in US compact fund expenditures for the RMI was approved, a reflection of the fact that from 2012–15, most compact infrastructure money was on hold. It was only with the aid of New Zealand–based engineers that dozens of stalled projects were finally launched (The Marshall Islands Journal 2017).

In contrast, there is a perception by many Pacific Island policymakers that China and Taiwan are both adept at fast-tracking priority projects. In the case of large infrastructure endeavours funded by China, this sometimes means that all materials and labour are shipped in for a project, allowing only minimal local input. But there is little doubt that the project will proceed without delay and be completed on schedule. A recent comparative study of ODA in Tonga and Vanuatu found that China's diplomats do not obscure the transactional nature of their relationship with the Pacific (Cheng and Taylor 2017). Moreover, compared to traditional ODA partners, there is ordinarily little conditionality and only minimal reporting requirements. Interestingly, it was noted that both China's and Taiwan's ambassadors appear to have greater discretionary spending authority than the ambassadors representing traditional aid donors such as the US, Australia, Japan and New Zealand (Funaki 2017). Close examination of specific activities within the three FAS helps illuminate the dynamics of diplomatic and economic relations on the ground.

Federated States of Micronesia

The FSM (population 103,000) established formal diplomatic ties with China in 1989. Since then, the relationship has grown, including the 2014 creation of the commission on economic trade cooperation. FSM's presidents have all consistently articulated adherence to the One China policy. In advancing their strategic goals, it is notable how China and Taiwan have gone beyond ODA chequebook diplomacy. Both have worked equally hard to cultivate Pacific Island leaders through official state visits featuring ceremonies that bestow status and prestige. The extensive formal protocol and high-level access to leaders during official visits by Pacific Island leaders to Beijing and Taipei is carefully observed across the region and is consistent with the practices often reserved for larger nation states.

Indicative of the level of attention China accords Pacific countries that maintain formal diplomatic relations was the March 2017 official state visit of FSM's then president Peter Christian. The well-planned event included a welcome ceremony at the Great Hall of the People with a full military review. A photograph showing both presidents being warmly greeted by flag-waving school children as they walked down a red carpet was widely broadcast on social media. President Xi Jinping personally invested a significant amount of time in one-on-one discussions related to economic development, including the Belt and Road Initiative.[11] On the subject of tourism, it was noted that China has endorsed the FSM as an officially sanctioned tourist destination and announced its support for a range of infrastructure projects related to growing the FSM's fledgling tourism industry. The release of small block grants for each of the four states, as well as the gifting of a new inter-island aircraft, provided media headlines that substantially bolstered China's standing within FSM (Kaselehlie Press 2017). The December 2019 state visit by current FSM President David Panuelo followed a similar formula.

Neither the modest deliverables nor the public respect conveyed through such high-profile visits obscure China's strategic interests in the region. The Pacific's political leadership has a clear understanding of China's desire for strong bilateral relationships that will increase its influence. At the same time, official state visits like that of FSM's president provide a basis for comparison with Washington's overall lack of high-level attention to the FAS, and the Pacific region more generally. Indeed, while on some rare occasions Pacific Island leaders have had working meetings in the West Wing, there has never been a formal state visit to the White House for a Pacific Island leader or group of leaders. Over the last three decades, the US president has engaged with the Pacific Island leaders as a regional group on only four occasions, with each of these events taking place in Honolulu, Hawai'i.

---

11   Another recent example of this personal engagement by China's leadership is Samoan Prime Minister Tuilaepa Sailele Malielegaoi's participation in the Davos Forum in Northern China. While in Beijing, he held talks with President Xi Jinping, who promised to work with Samoa on climate change issues and deepen ties between the two countries.

Since establishing diplomatic ties with the FSM, China has undertaken a wide range of ODA projects. Chinese embassy discretionary grants frequently provide much-needed equipment. Larger infrastructure projects are funded from time to time and may, in some cases, be built by local construction companies. These include constructing official residences for government officials at the national and state levels, as well as providing ships for inter-island transport. Block grants for purposes specified by state governments are also a regular element of Chinese involvement. Educational institutions have benefited from high-profile projects, such as the popular FSM–China Friendship Sports Centre gymnasium built at the College of Micronesia in Pohnpei. Initially structured as a US$3.8 million interest-free loan, it was subsequently announced as a grant. Other small grants and gifts are frequently noted in media accounts, such as solar streetlights for state capitals and library book donations covering a wide range of subjects on China.

Official contact between China's diplomats and state government officials and direct aid to local governments is valued because it bestows prestige on local officials, some of whom in time are elected to national offices. In 2016, for instance, the Chinese embassy donated US$277,844 for the construction of a new gymnasium complex in Madolenihmw. In Pohnpei State alone, China has launched a pilot farm in Pohnlangas, constructed a greenhouse, initiated biogas projects as well as a mushroom demonstration farm (Peterson 2018).

The most ambitious Chinese investment proposal in FSM to date has been the plan to build a 10,000-room holiday resort and casino complex in the state of Yap, accompanied by direct airline connections to facilitate ease of travel for vacationers.[12] Announcement of the endeavour in 2011 surprised Yap's citizenry and gave rise to considerable debate regarding the wisdom of building such a massive resort in a location with a population of some 11,000 on a relatively small island (Anderson 2011; Radio Australia 2012). In 2015, Yap's governor and a 12-member delegation made a 10-day trip to China. A reciprocal visit to Yap was made the same year by representatives of the Guangdong Friendship Association.

---

12   University of Guam Professor Donald Rubinstein at a public seminar on 8 May 2014 indicated that Chengdu Century City New International Exhibition and Convention Center Company Ltd's (better known as ETG) proposed Paradise concept plan consisted of the construction of an oceanfront resort complex including artificial offshore islands and bungalows built over the lagoon, golf courses, expanded airport and seaport facilities, 'an immense water reservoir system' and native towns where displaced Yapese would be relocated (Villegas Zotomayor 2014).

With the neighbouring Republic of Palau having attracted nearly 90,000 Chinese tourists in 2016, Yap's potential for increased tourism presents an attractive business opportunity. However, the image of hordes of tourists adversely changing Yap's highly valued culture and traditions, as well as other potential environmental impacts, has resulted in the temporary shelving of the project. To the extent that most FSM citizens do not distinguish between official Chinese Government assistance and private sector initiatives, the controversial proposal seemingly undermined diplomatic efforts by China to demonstrate that it is a responsible and culturally sensitive Pacific development partner.[13] Still, the foregoing experiences exemplify China's interest in expanding its economic footprint in the FSM.

China's desire to foster enhanced engagement with FSM is also reflected in a pronounced increase in diplomatic activities. In August 2017, for example, Vice Minister of Foreign Affairs Zheng Zeguang visited Pohnpei with a high-level delegation and spoke to the FSM's political leaders. A central topic of the dialogue was the FSM Trust Fund that the government of the FSM may rely on, in conjunction with the Compact Trust Fund, if US economic assistance is not extended after 2023. It was noted that China has already made significant contributions to the FSM national trust fund in recent years and might be willing to further supplement the fund to help the FSM achieve greater self-reliance.

The vibrant diplomatic linkages between the FSM and China are likewise reflected in numerous 'people-to-people' programs. Mechanisms such as 'sister city' agreements are being established to strengthen relationships and promote investment. For example, the FSM's Sokehs Municipal Government and Zhongshan City recently signed a document designed to foster better relations and understanding between citizens of both countries. A similar relationship has been announced with Heilongjiang province, facilitated by a large visiting delegation that requested a reciprocal visit by the FSM's officials and entrepreneurs.

China has provided a steady stream of opportunities for young people. For many years, the FSM's students have availed of scholarship opportunities in China. In 2017, for instance, Yap State and Hainan

---

13   Another point of friction between Yap and a Chinese firm in 2014 centred on the illegal harvesting of sea cucumbers (*beche-de-mer*). It was also found that the company had failed to renew its business licence during the previous year (Yap State Government 2014).

established a new sister province–state relationship, at which time Hainan made a commitment to provide 50 academic scholarships within the next five years for students from the FSM. In addition, a range of invitations were extended for youth exchanges and technical transfer exchanges. Small grants have been provided on a regular basis for athletic activities, including travel stipends and transit accommodations to fund the FSM's participation in the 2016 Olympics in Rio de Janeiro, Brazil.

An emerging and highly sensitive dimension of the FSM–PRC relationship in the post-2023 period focuses on the role China may play in discussions regarding Chuuk's (the FSM's largest state, population 48,500) interest in changing its political status to become a sovereign nation (Jaynes 2015). Throughout the FSM's history, there has been internal contestation between the four state governments and the national government over how to equitably distribute US Compact of Free Association funding. Chuuk government officials periodically intimate that if they were an independent nation Chuuk would stand to directly receive substantially more overseas development assistance from the US, China and other nations.

The US has consistently maintained that its relationship is with the national government in Kolonia and any movement by a state to secede would, if the state were no longer part of the federation, presumably mean an end to compact-related disbursements. While this understanding has implicitly buttressed national unity, the proposed 2023 reduction of economic support could weaken national cohesion and encourage dialogue with China on this issue. The Chuuk lagoon, one of the Pacific's largest and deepest, is of possible strategic interest to the PRC. It was once a critically important location for the Japanese Navy and remains a potentially important strategic naval asset.

None of the current activities or projects linking China and the FSM are outside the bounds of normal diplomatic and economic engagement. In comparative terms, the US and China have a similar range of cultural and diplomatic activities with the FSM that are intended to bolster bilateral relations. However, any significant diminution of US economic support could erode the strong bonds the US presently shares with the FSM and provide China significant new opportunities.

Republic of the Marshall Islands

The strategic value of the RMI (population 53,000) to the US currently exceeds that of the FSM and Palau due to the long-term lease and major Department of Defense infrastructure investments on Kwajalein. From both historical and contemporary perspectives, the relationship between the two countries is complex.[14] By some estimates, the US provides nearly 80 per cent of the RMI's annual budget. Overall economic support from Washington to the RMI from 2004 to 2023 is estimated to total US$1.5 billion. In addition, the US is committed to paying US$18 million per year in rent to the RMI Government through 2066 for exclusive long-term use of Kwajalein's Ronald Reagan Ballistic Missile Defense Test Site.

The Reagan Test Site is but one component of several critical defence-related activities on Kwajalein (US GAO 2002). Facility investments in excess of US$1 billion there over the past decade are indicative of both the importance of the base as well as the long-range US plans for its use. Current land rental agreements have options for renewal after 2066. There is no other similar type of major facility in the FAS, though there are currently discussions underway about leasing land in Palau for defence-related purposes.

Strong diplomatic ties with the US and Taiwan are central elements of the RMI's foreign policy. In 1991, the RMI initially established relations with the PRC. This changed in November 1998 when formal diplomatic linkages were forged between the RMI and Taiwan, occurring during a period when several other Pacific nations such as the Kingdom of Tonga were dropping Taipei in favour of Beijing. Since that time, the two countries have promoted exchanges and cooperation in the areas of fisheries, agriculture, education, tourism, technology and investment.

Despite the lack of a formal diplomatic presence in Majuro, China has nonetheless launched investment initiatives. Most recently indicative of China's economic involvement in the RMI was the Rongelap Atoll Special Administrative Region (RASA) proposal. Following RASA's unveiling by

---

14   The US nuclear testing program in the Western Pacific detonated 67 blasts between 1946 and 1958. In 1987, the US Congress allocated US$150 million to the RMI as compensation for nuclear radiation claims. Bikini Atoll residents received US$75 million over 15 years with the remainder allocated to trust funds. In 1992, an additional US$90 million was conveyed for the resettlement trust fund. Approximately US$600 million has been paid as compensation and remediation for nuclear testing that occurred between 1946–58 (US Embassy Marshall Islands 2012).

Rongelaps' mayor at the 2018 Asia World Expo in Hong Kong, news reports described the endeavour as a 'utopia for foreign investors featuring relaxed tax and visa requirements' (Smith 2018a). With a vision of making the atolls into a 'Singapore-like hub', Chinese websites reportedly noted as many as 1,000 houses had already been sold.

In November 2018, there was an unusual motion of no confidence against then RMI President Hilda Heine, purportedly based on the government's proposal to introduce a cryptocurrency as legal tender. President Heine narrowly prevailed, but indicated that the real issue was Chinese interests:

> Really the vote of no confidence is about the so-called Rongelap Atoll Special Administrative Region, or RASA scheme, which is an effort by certain foreign interests to take control of one of our atolls and turn it into a country within our own country (Smith 2018b).[15]

While the RASA-enabling legislation has yet to be enacted and appears to face significant domestic and US opposition, this episode suggests how China-financed commercial endeavours may strongly influence domestic politics in small island societies.

China's strategy in the North Pacific has, in recent years, demonstrated an increased willingness to exercise its commercial influence in the form of punitive commercial actions, such as charging vessels flagged with the RMI ship registry higher fees when they enter Chinese ports. The RMI's vibrant ship registry program (second only to Panama) may face a significant loss of revenue if China continues this practice.[16] As is detailed in the following, China has also sought to disrupt Palau's tourism-based economy by restricting its citizens' travel to Palau for holidays.

Although the US's ODA to the RMI is by far the largest, Taiwan has been effective in using instruments of soft power to advance its relationships with both Washington and Majuro. Taiwan's activities complement US activities in a manner that deftly helps to maintain amicable relations on all sides. Both grants and soft loans are included in Taiwan's RMI portfolio. For example, in 2016 the International Cooperation and Development Fund provided a US$4 million loan for a new Home Energy Efficiency and Renewable Energy Project encouraging local residents to embrace renewable energy (The Marshall Islands Journal 2016).

---

15   See also Lorennij (2018).
16   US Department of State official, 22 April 2019. Interview with author.

Similarly, Taiwan allocates discretionary funds to support many small but highly visible projects, such as the construction of outdoor multipurpose courts for sports and the installation of solar streetlights (The Marshall Islands Journal 2018). In partnership with the Bank of the Marshall Islands, Taiwan underwrites a popular micro-loan program. Since its inception in 2006, the program has issued some US$4 million in loans to over 1,000 customers (ibid.). The Taiwan-supported Laura Farm is an experimental agriculture and aquaculture facility where pilot projects are tested for applicability to local atoll conditions.

Taiwan and the RMI have frequently highlighted the cultural ties between the two nations in terms of sharing a common Austronesian heritage and the socioeconomic benefits associated with the relationship. In recent years, Taiwan has also stressed its ability to provide high-quality specialised medical care through periodic in-country clinics as well as educational programs in Taipei. The I-Shou School of Medicine for International Students was established in 2013 as part of Taiwan's goal to increase local medical capacities among its diplomatic allies. There are presently 25 Marshall Islands students pursuing degrees in a variety of fields at universities in Taiwan.

As is true for citizens of the FSM and Palau, the RMI has benefited from visa-free entry to the US. It is thought that approximately 1,000 Marshall Islanders emigrate to the US each year, a significant feature of the RMI–US bilateral relationship that neither Taiwan nor China can easily replicate (Hezel 2013). As an increasing number of Marshall Islanders leave for employment in the US, the RMI 2011 Census of Population and Housing documents an increase in international migration to the RMI (Economic Policy, Planning, and Statistics Office 2012). Between 2006 and 2011, 1,434 individuals entered as migrants, with 80 per cent residing in the capital of Majuro. An estimated 43 per cent were from the US, while 9.6 per cent were from the PRC.

In light of the overwhelming long-term US presence in the RMI, it is unlikely that China will secure a diplomatic foothold. High economic dependency on the US suggests the RMI is unlikely to see a plausible alternative to maintaining its current diplomatic relationships. The most significant threat facing US military facilities in Kwajalein and the RMI as a whole is vulnerability to the effects of climate change.

Republic of Palau

Palau is distinguished by its upward economic trajectory, having become one of the most successful economies in the Pacific. With the smallest population of the three FAS (approximately 22,000), Palau's pristine natural environment and favourable geographic location for East Asian visitors has been used to good advantage in building a dynamic tourism industry. Its success as an international visitor destination has also made Palau the most globalised North Pacific nation. By numerous measures it is among the most prosperous of the Pacific Island nations, with a gross national income per capita of approximately US$13,000. Palau is ranked 60 out of 186 countries on the 2017 Human Development Index, the highest of any developing country in the Pacific. (In contrast, the FSM is ranked 131 and the RMI is ranked 106.) At the same time, however, Palau's tourism industry is vulnerable on two fronts: heavy reliance on tourists coming from a single country and dependence on foreign labour in the private sector.

Like the RMI, Palau since 1999 has maintained diplomatic relations with Taiwan. The evolution of Palau's foreign policy began in the early 1990s. Prior to independence, policymakers accepted invitations from China and Taiwan for informal talks. Decisions regarding its bilateral relationships were well considered and included extensive internal debate.[17] Since that time, Palau has taken a leading regional role in promoting Pacific Island nations' relations with Taiwan, such as hosting the Taiwan–Pacific Allies Summit. During such occasions, Taiwan's sovereignty has been endorsed by the Pacific governments in attendance. The summit declarations have regularly underscored Taiwan's impressive achievements in political democratisation and called for Taiwan's participation in international organisations such as the UN and the World Health Organization.

Palau receives substantial ODA, primarily from the US, Japan, Taiwan and Australia. For fiscal years 2011–24, direct US funding support will total US$229 million, as well as an estimated US$36 million in other US federal programs and services. Total US support, including both direct economic assistance and projected discretionary program assistance, may by 2024 approach a total US$427 million (Lum and Vaughn 2017). Estimates suggest Palau receives more than US$10 million annually in

---

17   See Mita (2010).

aid from Taiwan, often indicated by signs announcing infrastructure, agricultural or training projects funded by grant money from Taipei (Lyons 2018).

Among Palau's largest infrastructure projects since independence has been the circumferential road around Babeldaob, at a cost of over US$144 million (US GAO 2008). US funding for the project was limited to 53 miles, with Taiwan funding completion of the ring. The US$25 million Japan–Palau Friendship Bridge completed in 2001 is one of Japan's most visible aid contributions to Palau, connecting Koror to Babeldaob. Another major endeavour is the Taiwan-funded agricultural technical mission intended to advance Palau's commercial agricultural production and thereby reduce food imports. Israel has assisted Palau in a similar manner with projects focusing on fish farming, as well as in the field of medicine.

Yet it is the vibrancy of Palau's private sector that sets it apart from the FSM and the RMI. Drawing on historical linkages and investments from Japan, Palau constructed its first luxury resort in 1985. After independence, efforts were made to diversify the tourism market to include not only Japanese but also Koreans and Taiwanese. Palau's diplomatic relations and geographic proximity to Taiwan steadily increased the visitor flows from Taipei, which by 2012 had reached 39,695 annually. However, it was not long before Taiwanese travel agencies realised the potential for working with travel firms in mainland China to send even larger numbers of tourists (Hezel 2017).

Although the Chinese Government never designated Palau as an approved destination status (ADS) country, it allowed China-based tour agencies to promote group package tours there via commercial and charter flights. These tour groups rapidly came to constitute the largest share of Palau's tourism industry. Between 2011 and 2015, the number of Chinese tourists surged from 1,699 to 86,850 per year, or more than 50 per cent of annual visitor arrivals. Based on 2013 figures, the US$41.4 million collected from gross revenue business taxes, personal income taxes, general import taxes and airport departure green fees were nearly equal to the total grant (US$42 million) money received from the US, Taiwan and multiple other sources.[18] In November 2017, however, the Chinese Government, without advance notice, ordered tour operators to stop selling package tours to Palau. Travel agencies in China were warned that sending package tour groups to

---

18   See Hezel (2017:39).

locations without ADS status could lead to substantial fines.[19] The sudden drop in revenues from Chinese tourists has severely hurt Palau's public and private sectors. Not unexpectedly, restoring outbound plane loads of tourists from China hinges on Palau establishing formal relations with Beijing and acceding to the One China policy.[20] The foregoing suggests that Palau may in the future conclude that its relationship with Taiwan is not sustainable. With interest being shown by major Chinese investors, Palau could, in the absence of significant new US military and ODA investments, begin to seriously consider a change in diplomatic recognition.[21]

Conclusion

Washington appears to be gaining a new appreciation of the FAS's largely successful nation-building efforts, which have produced political and social stability. US plans to end major US economic support for basic services to the FSM and the RMI in 2023 are increasingly viewed by Department of Defense policy analysts as imperilling the returns on this long-term strategic investment. In light of the special relationship between the US and the FAS, as well as increasingly vigorous efforts by Western nations to restrain China globally, it is not surprising to observe the US taking measures to curtail China's drive to establish a more significant North Pacific presence.

Concurrently, there is a clear awareness by policymakers in the FSM, the RMI and Palau of the need for long-term strategic thinking. Recent actions suggest all three nations are open to a significant expansion of international engagement to advance their respective national interests. While the innovative compact relationships between the FAS and the US have clearly established mutually beneficial partnerships, this does not preclude forging closer alliances with other countries.

---

19 This development was reported in Lyons (2018).
20 A second potential area of vulnerability for Palau that may indirectly be subject to China's economic leverage focuses on Filipino 'guest workers'. Despite a rapidly expanding economy over the past two decades, there is an increasing dependence on foreign guest workers in Palau (including approximately 4,000 Filipino workers and approximately 1,000 Chinese workers). Of the approximately 5,000 non-Palauan workers in Palau, some 75 per cent are from the nearby Philippines, suggesting a level of self-imposed dependency on guest workers that is unknown in other Pacific Island nations (Alegado and Finin 2000). If China were to convince the Philippine government to reduce the number of overseas Filipino workers deployed to Palau, this contraction of the labour force could potentially be highly disruptive to Palau's tourism industry.
21 For a fuller explanation of the secretary of state's trip to Cook Islands, see Myers (2012).

Despite the 2020 election of President Biden, a return to earlier US policies that were more accommodating to China's rise is highly unlikely. Similarly, other metropolitan countries in Oceania are also recalibrating their policies to more firmly contain Chinese expansionism through stronger coalitions and more deliberate shaping of the regional order. In particular, Australia and New Zealand's important economic ties with China will require both nations to hedge their Pacific stratagems vis-à-vis the PRC. At the same time, the strong Australia and New Zealand linkages with the US are all but certain to endure. Emboldened by recent developments, the FAS can be counted upon to deepen their engagement with the US while adroitly managing their respective relationships with Taiwan and China.

References

Alegado, D. and G. Finin 2000. Exporting People: The Philippines and Contract Labor in Palau. *The Contemporary Pacific* 12(2):359–70. doi.org/10.1353/cp.2000.0039

Anderson, J.A. 2011. Chinese Investors Plan Major Hotel in Yap. *Pacific Islands Report*, 5 October. www.pireport.org/articles/2011/10/05/chinese-investors-plan-major-hotel-yap

Anderson, P. 2015. *American Foreign Policy and Its Thinkers*. London: Verso.

Asplund, A. and M. Soderberg M. (eds) 2017. *Japanese Development Cooperation: The Making of an Aid Architecture Pivoting to Asia*. New York: Routledge. doi.org/10.4324/9781315407746

Baraniuk, C. 2018. Marshall Islands Warned against Adopting Digital Currency. *BBC News*, 11 September. www.bbc.com/news/technology-45485685

Buckley, C. and C. Horton 2019. Xi Jinping Warns Taiwan That Unification Is the Goal and Force Is an Option. *The New York Times*, 1 January. www.nytimes.com/2019/01/01/world/asia/xi-jinping-taiwan-china.html?searchResultPosition=2

Campbell, Kurt M. and R. Doshi 2021. How America Can Shore Up Asian Order. *Foreign Affairs*, 12 January. www.foreignaffairs.com/articles/united-states/2021-01-12/how-america-can-shore-asian-order

Cheng, Z. and I. Taylor 2017. *China's Aid to Africa: Does Friendship Really Matter?* New York: Routledge.

China Economic Review 2018. Beijing Told to "Assess and Prevent Risks" in New Belt and Road Projects. 27 December. www.chinaeconomicreview.com/beijing-told-to-assess-and-prevent-risks-in-new-belt-and-road-projects/

Economic Policy, Planning, and Statistics Office 2012. RMI 2011 Census of Population and Housing. www.doi.gov/sites/doi.gov/files/migrated/oia/reports/upload/RMI-2011-Census-Summary-Report-on-Population-and-Housing.pdf

Finin, G.A. 2011. Power Diplomacy at the 2011 Pacific Islands Forum. *Asia Pacific Bulletin*, No. 136. Washington DC: East-West Center. www.eastwestcenter.org/publications/power-diplomacy-2011-pacific-islands-forum-pif

Finin, G.A. 2013. Envisioning the North Pacific Economies Post 2023. *ADB Pacific Economic Monitor* July:22–26.

Funaki, K. 2017. Official Development Assistance: Exploring Priority, Disbursement, Dependency and Leverage from the Perspectives of Three Pacific Island Countries. PhD thesis, Ritsumeikan Asia Pacific University.

Greenfield, C. and J. Barrett 2018. Payment Due: Pacific Islands in the Red as Debts to China Mount. *Reuters*, 31 July. www.reuters.com/article/us-pacific-debt-china-insight/payment-due-pacific-islands-in-the-red-as-debts-to-china-mount-idUSKBN1KK2J4

Hanlon, D. 1998. *Remaking Micronesia: Discourses over Development in a Pacific Territory 1944–1982*. Honolulu: University of Hawai'i Press.

Hezel, F.X. 2003. *Strangers in Their Own Land: A Century of Colonial Rule in the Caroline and Marshall Islands*. Honolulu: University of Hawai'i Press.

Hezel, F.X. 2006. *Is That the Best You Can Do: A Tale of Two Micronesian Economies*. Pacific Islands Policy, No. 1. Honolulu: East-West Center.

Hezel, F.X. 2013. *FSM Micronesians on the Move: Eastward and Upward Bound*. Pacific Islands Policy, No. 9. Honolulu: East-West Center.

Hezel, F.X. 2017. *On Your Mark, Get Set…Tourism's Takeoff in Micronesia*. Honolulu: East-West Center.

Jaynes, B. 2015. Chuuk State to Hold Secession Vote in March. *Pacific Islands Report*, 6 February. www.pireport.org/articles/2015/02/06/chuuk-state-hold-secession-vote-march

Kaselehlie Press 2017. Chinese-Made Aircraft Delivered to FSM. 1 December. www.kpress.info/index.php?option=com_content&view=article&id=800:chinese-made-aircraft-delivered-to-fsm&catid=8&Itemid=103

Kato, H., J. Page and Y. Shimomura (eds) 2016. *Japan's Development Assistance: Foreign Aid and the Post-2015 Agenda.* New York: Palgrave Macmillan.

Kuttner, R. 2018. *Can Democracy Survive Global Capitalism?* New York: W.W. Norton.

Lee, J. 2019. *The Use of AID to Counter China's 'Djibouti Strategy' in the South Pacific.* Washington: Hudson Institute.

Levy, J. 2008. *Micronesian Government: Yesterday, Today and Tomorrow.* Pohnpei: Micronesian Seminar.

Lian, Y-Z. 2019. Xi Jinping Wanted Global Dominance. He Overshot. *The New York Times*, 7 May.

Lorennij, K. 2018. Heine Survives Confidence Vote. *The Marshall Islands Journal*, 15 November. marshallislandsjournal.com/?p=6399

Lum, T. and B. Vaughn 2017. *The Pacific Islands: Policy Issues. Congressional Research Service Report.* Washington DC: Library of Congress, Congressional Research Service, 10.

Lyons, K. 2018. 'Palau Against China!': The Tiny Island Standing up to a Giant. *The Guardian*, 8 September.

Mita, T. 2010. Changing Attitudes and the Two Chinas in the Republic of Palau. In T. Wesley-Smith and E.A. Porter (eds), *China in Oceania: Reshaping the Pacific?* Brooklyn: Berghahn Books, 180–81.

Myers, S.L. 2012. Clinton Begins Asia Trip, Trying to Ease Tension with China. *The New York Times*, 1 September. www.nytimes.com/2012/09/02/world/asia/clinton-tries-to-ease-tension-with-china-on-asia-trip.html/

Nguyen, M. and J. Pryke 2018. Exploring Taiwan's Aid to the Pacific. *The Interpreter*, 25 September. Lowy Institute. www.lowyinstitute.org/the-interpreter/exploring-taiwan-s-aid-pacific

Peterson, M. 2018. State of the State. Address to the Pohnpei State Legislature, Pohnpei, 6 March 2018.

Pompeo, M.R. 2019. Statement from Secretary Pompeo to the Micronesia Presidents' Summit. Speech at the Micronesia Presidents' Summit, Koror, 19 February. fj.usembassy.gov/statement-from-secretary-pompeo-to-the-micronesia-presidents-summit/

Radio Australia 2012. Large-Scale Yap Tourism Development Halted in FSM. *Pacific Islands Report*, 5 September. www.pireport.org/articles/2012/09/06/large-scale-yap-tourism-development-halted-fsm

Radio New Zealand 2018a. Marshall Islands Goes Visa-Free with Taiwan. 30 July. www.rnz.co.nz/international/pacific-news/362982/marshall-islands-goes-visa-free-with-taiwan

Radio New Zealand 2018b. Asian Development Bank Scales up Pacific Presence. 20 September. www.radionz.co.nz/international/pacific-news/366926/asian-development-bank-scales-up-pacific-presence

Radio New Zealand 2019. Senior US Officials Visit Three Micronesian Countries. 22 February. www.radionz.co.nz/international/pacific-news/383102/senior-us-officials-visit-three-micronesian-countries

Remengesau, T., Jr. 2019. Pacific Defense Pact Renewal Vital to the US Amid Rising Tension with China. *The Hill*, 17 May. www.thehill.com/blogs/congress-blog/foreign-policy/444291-pacific-defense-pact-renewal-vital-to-the-us-amid-rising

Roy, D. 2019. *Taiwan's Potential Role in the Free and Open Indo-Pacific Strategy: Convergence in the South Pacific*. NBR Special Report #77. Washington: The National Bureau of Asian Research.

Smith, M. 2018a. Remote Marshall Islands Atoll Plans to Become the 'Next Hong Kong'. Radio New Zealand, 21 September. www.rnz.co.nz/international/pacific-news/366965/remote-marshall-islands-atoll-plans-to-become-the-next-hong-kong

Smith, M. 2018b. 'It Is Baseless' - Marshalls President, Facing Ouster, Blames Chinese Influence. Radio New Zealand, 9 November. www.radionz.co.nz/international/pacific-news/375519/it-is-baseless-marshalls-president-facing-ouster-blames-chinese-influence

Stayman, A. 2009. *US Territorial Policy: Trends and Current Challenges*. Pacific Islands Policy, No. 5. Honolulu: East-West Center.

The Marshall Islands Journal 2016. ROC Backs Energy Loan Fund. 25 November. www.marshallislandsjournal.com/roc-backs-energy-loan-fund/

The Marshall Islands Journal 2017. US-Funded Jobs Get Moving. 13 January. www.marshallislandsjournal.com/us-funded-jobs-get-moving/

The Marshall Islands Journal 2018. Let There Be Light at Night. 12 April. www.marshallislandsjournal.com/?p=5644

Underwood, R. 2003. *The Amended US Compacts of Free Association with the Federated States of Micronesia and the Republic of the Marshall Islands: Less Free, More Compact*. East-West Center Working Papers. Pacific Islands Development Series No. 16, September. www.eastwestcenter.org/system/tdf/private/PIDPwp016.pdf?file=1&type=node&id=31948

Underwood, R. 2017. The Changing American Lake in the Middle of the Pacific. Paper presented for the Peter Tali Coleman Lecture on Pacific Public Policy at the Georgetown University Center for Australian, New Zealand and Pacific Studies, 16 November.

US Embassy Marshall Islands 2012. The Legacy of US Nuclear Testing and Radiation Exposure in the Marshall Islands. mh.usembassy.gov/the-legacy-of-u-s-nuclear-testing-and-radiation-exposure-in-the-marshall-islands/

US GAO (US Government Accountability Office) 2002. *Kwajalein Atoll Is the Key US Defense Interest in Two Micronesian Nations.* Washington DC: GAO. www.gao.gov/new.items/d02119.pdf

US GAO (US Government Accountability Office) 2007. *Compacts of Free Association: Trust Funds for Micronesia and Marshall Islands May Not Provide Sustainable Income.* Washington DC: GAO. www.gao.gov/products/GAO-07-513

US GAO (US Government Accountability Office) 2008. *Palau's Use of and Accountability for US Assistance and Prospects for Economic Self-Sufficiency.* www.gao.gov/assets/280/276299.pdf

US GAO (US Government Accountability Office) 2018. *Compacts of Free Association: Actions Needed to Prepare for the Transition of Micronesia and the Marshall Islands to Trust Fund Income.* Washington DC: GAO, 18–415.

Villegas Zotomayor, L. 2014. Mega-Casino Resort Project Reportedly 'Still on the Table' in Yap. *Pacific Islands Report,* 5 June. www.pireport.org/articles/2014/06/05/mega-casino-resort-project-reportedly-%E2%80%98still-table%E2%80%99-yap

Wesley-Smith, T. and E. Porter (eds) 2010. *China in Oceania: Reshaping the Pacific?* New York: Berghahn Books.

World Bank 2017. *Pacific Possible: Long-Term Economic Opportunities and Challenges for Pacific Island Countries.* Washington DC: International Bank for Reconstruction and Development/The World Bank. documents.worldbank.org/curated/en/168951503668157320/Pacific-Possible-long-term-economic-opportunities-and-challenges-for-Pacific-Island-Countries

World Bank 2018. Micro Connections: Connecting the Federated States of Micronesia. www.worldbank.org/en/news/feature/2018/06/11/micro-connections-connecting-the-federated-states-of-micronesia

Yap State Government 2014. Chinese Firm Has Licenses Revoked for Illegal Sea Cucumber Harvesting. News release, 14 July. www.pireport.org/articles/2014/07/22/chinese-firm-has-licenses-revoked-illegal-sea-cucumber-harvesting

6

Stable, Democratic and Western: China and French Colonialism in the Pacific

Nic Maclellan

Introduction

In the 21st century, France remains a colonial power in the Pacific Islands, administering three non-self-governing territories—New Caledonia, French Polynesia and Wallis and Futuna—as well as the uninhabited Clipperton Island. At a time when China is expanding its trade, investment and political relationships with independent nations like Fiji, Samoa and Papua New Guinea, Chinese corporations have had relatively limited engagement with the three Francophone territories. However, this is steadily changing. Chinese companies have expressed interest in resource and aquaculture projects in the French Pacific dependencies. At the same time, Pacific Island leaders in Noumea and Papeete are looking to increase Chinese tourism and expand trade with China.

In response, Western allies are reinforcing their security engagement with Pacific Island nations in an attempt to blunt growing Chinese influence. Alongside Australia's 'Step-Up', New Zealand's 'Pacific Reset' and the US's 'Pacific Pledge', the ANZUS (Australia, New Zealand and US) governments are also seeking to mobilise strategic partners like France in the Pacific Islands region. Australian politicians, media and think tanks have welcomed any signs that allies like France and the United Kingdom will play a greater role in the Pacific Islands, presenting these partners as 'stable, democratic and Western' (Maclellan 2012, 2020). In most cases, however, this support comes without analysis of the implications for local populations, especially those seeking political independence from colonial rule.

This tension between the Western security agenda and the development needs of small island developing states is a central contradiction that will only be exacerbated in coming years. Australia's former consul-general to New Caledonia Denise Fisher has argued that new geopolitical complexity creates significant challenges for the French Government:

> France is now one of many more players with interests in the South Pacific and must compete with them for the attention of the small island countries, and even for the attention of the local authorities in France's own collectivities … The entry of numerous new players, particularly China with its strategic and economic weight, lends a geo-strategic edge even to aid cooperation. Some offer new and different models of economic development, not necessarily compatible with that of France's collectivities in the Pacific (Fisher 2015:30).

The French state has its own strategic interests in the region, both military and economic, that seek to assert sovereignty over the vast 7 million square kilometre exclusive economic zone (EEZ) in the South Pacific (Maclellan 2018d). The governments of New Caledonia, Wallis and Futuna and French Polynesia have their own agenda around the oceans, climate change and resource management, but lack control over key legal and administrative powers because of France's ongoing colonial authority.

Even so, governments in Noumea and Papeete are extending their engagement with non-traditional partners like China. Speaking at a seminar on China's Maritime Silk Road in November 2019, the President of French Polynesia Edouard Fritch saw little difference between investors from China and other nations:

> It's the common interest shown by private investors from China and successive French Polynesian Governments that has led to China including French Polynesia in its Silk Road initiative … We are open to Chinese private investors, just as we were to American, French, European, Samoan or New Zealand investors, in key economic sectors that open up our markets, such as tourism or

aquaculture. I don't see a difference between an American investor and a Chinese investor. If they are honest, they are all worthy of our friendship, whatever their nationality (Fritch 2019:4).[1]

This chapter begins by discussing French President Emmanuel Macron's promotion of an India–Australia–France axis to contribute to strategic containment of China in the Indo-Pacific region. It then presents four examples where France's Pacific dependencies are, in contrast, looking to greater engagement with China. Their means for increasing engagement include increasing trade with China, attempts to increase Chinese tourism, the establishment of a Chinese fishing enterprise on Hao Atoll in French Polynesia, and Chinese involvement in New Caledonia's nickel industry.

Each case study discusses the successes and failures of the engagement and tensions between Chinese corporate and Pacific government agendas, highlighting the lack of nuance and evidence in much media discussion of China in the Pacific.

France and the rise of the Indo-Pacific

France as a Pacific power

Philippe Gomès is president of the anti-independence party Calédonie Ensemble and serves as one of New Caledonia's two representatives in the French National Assembly. In an interview, Gomès argued that France's ongoing presence in the South Pacific serves as protection against rising Chinese power:

> China is an exceptional financial power, which allows them to invest widely and heavily, wherever they want and notably in the Pacific. With China in the region, we're like flies; they'll swat us just like that. To leave the French Republic is to leave us at the mercy of the Chinese. Frankly, to replace France with the Chinese is not on. This would be the exact opposite of independence.[2]

---

1   All translations from French by the author.
2   Philippe Gomès, President of Calédonie Ensemble and deputy to the French National Assembly, 17 October 2018. Noumea. Interview with author.

At a time of geopolitical tensions between China and the US, regional interventions are increasingly framed by the concept of the Indo-Pacific rather than Asia-Pacific. In much academic and media debate over France's role, however, Indo-Pacific is conflated with the South Pacific, even though the strategic and economic dynamics of India and East Asia are fundamentally different from those facing small island developing states. As noted by the Prime Minister of Samoa Tuilaepa Sailele Malielegaoi:

> The renewed vigour with which a 'Free and Open Indo-Pacific strategy' is being advocated and pursued leaves us with much uncertainty. For the Pacific, there is a real risk of privileging Indo over the Pacific (Malielegaoi 2018:6).

The Indo-Pacific framework was used by French President Emmanuel Macron when he visited Australia and New Caledonia in May 2018:

> France is a great Indo-Pacific power, and it has great power in the Indo-Pacific region through its territories New Caledonia, Wallis and Futuna and French Polynesia, as well as Mayotte and Reunion ... [The Indo-Pacific region has] more than 8,000 of our military personnel who project our national defence, our interests, our strategy; the region has more than three quarters of the vast maritime zone—that makes us the second largest maritime power in the world (Macron 2018).

In an interview, France's then ambassador to the South Pacific Christian Lechevry argued that 'the notion of the Indo-Pacific may be new for you [Australians], but not for France, given our long-standing presence in both the Indian and Pacific Oceans'.[3]

A 2018 publication on Indo-Pacific security by the French Defence Ministry highlights France's interests in both the Indian and Pacific Oceans based on its colonial possessions, where 'permanent military basing allows France to fulfil the security responsibilities of a resident power of the Indo-Pacific' (Ministry of Defence 2018). During President Macron's visit, officials argued that ongoing French colonial control in New Caledonia was crucial to France's Indo-Pacific strategy. This was echoed in media coverage:

---

3   France's then ambassador to the South Pacific Christian Lechevry, 5 September 2018. Pacific Islands Forum, Nauru. Interview with author.

In terms of geo-politics, losing control over New Caledonia's foreign affairs and defence would undermine Macron's strategy, of which Australia is a stated ally, to strengthen or protect France's influence in the Indo-Pacific region—presumably as a hedge against China (Patrick 2018).

For this reason, France has been extending its diplomacy with Pacific regional networks. In 2016, after extensive French lobbying, the Pacific Islands Forum (PIF) leaders meeting in Pohnpei 'accepted French Polynesia and New Caledonia as full members of the Pacific Islands Forum' (PIF Secretariat 2016:5).

This decision makes them full participants in the regional body, but has raised concern about France's increased influence over PIF policymaking. Former Fiji foreign minister Kaliopate Tavola (2019:26) has noted:

> How can FICs [Forum Island countries], for example, persist at the UN [United Nations] to push for decolonisation when the prospects of increased French influence as a development partner are increasingly being programmed into regional activities?

PIF membership for the two dependencies further integrates France into regional security policy, given that Paris retains sovereign control over their defence, military forces, policing and many aspects of foreign policy. It also amplifies the capacity of the French Republic to intervene in regional debates about the Blue Pacific and ocean policy (Maclellan 2018d).

France is already a member of the Quadrilateral Defence Coordination Group alongside the three ANZUS allies. Under the March 2017 Statement of Enhanced Strategic Partnership between Australia and France, the relationship is increasingly global rather than regional, focused on North Korea, the South China Sea and the Middle East. However, as then prime minister Malcolm Turnbull welcomed President Macron to Australia in May 2018, he made it clear that he sees France as a long-term ally in the South Pacific:

> France is a Pacific power. It is a Pacific nation and its significant presence in the region can only bring benefits to Australia and to the region more broadly. We welcome that and we'll continue to work closely with France in our region (Turnbull and Macron 2018).

This partnership is dominated by Australia's purchase of submarine technology from France in an AU$80 billion deal with France's Naval Group (Carroll and Ell 2017). After a decade of negotiation, the two countries also signed a new Mutual Logistics Support Agreement in 2018 to allow French and Australian naval and air units to use each other's ports, fuel and logistics in the Pacific (Maclellan 2009).

During their 2018 visit, Macron and Turnbull signed a new Vision Statement on the Australia–France Relationship, extending an agreement first signed by former prime minister Kevin Rudd of the Australian Labor Party (ALP) in 2012. In Australia, support for France's colonial presence in the Pacific region is bipartisan, with leading ALP politician Richard Marles stating:

> France is a stable and strong democracy which projects the values of democracy within a region where democracy is young and we can't take it for granted … France is a very positive player within the Pacific, and we very much welcome France's ongoing role in the Pacific (Maclellan 2012; Marles 2012).

Strengthening the quad against China

During his 2018 visit to Australia, President Macron welcomed China's economic growth and engagement with world markets. However, he stressed that the Chinese Government must operate within the trade and security framework established by the Western allies:

> What's important is to preserve a rule-based development in the region and especially in the Indo-Pacific region. It's to preserve the necessary balances in the region (Turnbull and Macron 2018).

In its *2017 Foreign Policy White Paper*, Australia highlighted this 'rules-based order' as a central pillar of regional policy (DFAT 2017). To maintain this order, it promotes 'the quad'—a structure to increase quadrilateral coordination between Australia, the US, Japan and India to contain China—even though successive Australian governments have denied that containment is the objective of these strategic partnerships.

The French state is eager to engage with this quad network. During a 2016 visit to Canberra, then defence minister Jean-Yves Le Drian promoted an Australia–France–India axis as the basis of strategic cooperation in the region, saying, 'We need to think of a three-way partnership that includes India if we want security in the Indo-Pacific region' (Nicholson 2016).

During his 2018 visit to Australia and New Caledonia, President Macron again highlighted France's connection to both India and Australia, two countries where the French Government is actively promoting arms sales:

> Our shared priority is to build this strong Indo-Pacific axis to guarantee both our economic and security interests. The trilateral dialogue between Australia, India and France has the possibility to play a central role in this (L'Express 2018).

Some French commentators have suggested that this axis relies on Paris maintaining colonial rule in New Caledonia, 'given the new strategic ambition—Noumea is the bridgehead for France in its axis with New Delhi and Canberra, through which it hopes to block Chinese expansion in the Pacific' (Hacquemand 2018).

During a March 2018 trip to New Delhi, President Macron signed a Joint Strategic Vision of India–France Cooperation in the Indian Ocean Region to reinforce France's strategic partnership with India. France is also looking to extend bilateral security agreements with Japan and other East Asian and Southeast Asian nations on defence policy (Rigaud 2016).

French military (in)capacity in the South Pacific

In recent years, successive French defence ministers have announced that France would coordinate naval patrols with the United Kingdom in the South China Sea in support of freedom of navigation (Panda 2016). In June 2018, Defence Minister Florence Parly noted that British withdrawal from the European Union after Brexit would not affect their ongoing defence cooperation:

> When we meet here in Asia, we may no longer be part of the same European club, but we still share something of very deep significance: vision, strength, values and a willingness to protect them (Brattberg et al. 2018).

This increasing strategic cooperation is targeted at China, but is being used to justify French colonialism in the Pacific Islands (Vandendyck 2018). During his May 2018 visit to Noumea, President Macron reaffirmed the notion of France as a mid-sized global power that would be weakened by the loss of its overseas colonies:

> What I would like to say from the bottom of my heart, and in my role as President of the Republic, is that France would not be the same without New Caledonia … France would be less beautiful without New Caledonia, because New Caledonia is part of this global France, the France which exists in this region of the world, tens of thousands of kilometres from Paris. At heart, France's very purpose is to shine across all continents and all oceans (Macron 2018).

Despite this, the conflation of Indo-Pacific security with France's colonial presence in the South Pacific is misleading. The notion that the French Pacific collectivities are a bulwark against Chinese expansionism is undercut by the reality that France deploys very few military assets in the South Pacific. After the 2007–08 global financial crisis, there was a significant draw down of French forces based in the region, including a 50 per cent reduction in French Polynesia (Maclellan 2009).

France's regional naval headquarters, ALPACI, are located in Tahiti, but there is a vast distance between there and potential conflict zones in East Asia. A quick look at the map shows that Papeete is 11,587 kilometres, or 6,256 nautical miles, from Beijing. Even adding new scheduled deployments, France's two frigates, three patrol boats and five surveillance aircraft based in Noumea and Papeete have very limited firepower. This limited capacity is acknowledged by the French Defence Ministry, which notes that these French military assets are focused on humanitarian and disaster response (Ministry of Defence 2018:12).

Pacific Island governments are also seeking to broaden the dominant narrative of security in the region. Alongside traditional notions of state-centred security and transnational threats (drug smuggling, illegal fishing, organised crime), PIF members increasingly address the issue through the prism of human security, encompassing the oceans, climate change and the management of maritime resources. The 2018 PIF leaders meeting in Nauru issued the Boe Declaration, which reaffirms that 'climate change remains the single greatest threat to the livelihoods, security and wellbeing of the peoples of the Pacific and our commitment to progress the implementation of the Paris Agreement' (PIF Secretariat 2018).

However, key development partners do not prioritise funding on climate change and security, focusing instead on more traditional threats. This tension was highlighted in an interview with French Polynesian President Edouard Fritch at the 2018 PIF:

The discussions we had this morning with our partners showed that the Indo-Pacific framework is one that everyone is using, guiding their interventions in the Pacific. Within this Indo-Pacific framework, there is certainly the problem of global warming, but there are other problems that are just as important: the security of populations, maritime security, national security for each country and also regional security. Today, Pacific countries want more security and so are looking to all their partners, whether it's China or the United States.[4]

This perspective of China as a development partner equivalent to the US clashes with the dominant ANZUS narrative of China as a regional security threat. Tahitian desires to increase engagement with China are in tension with Western policies of strategic denial, as France and its Anglophone partners seek to halt supposed Chinese 'debt-trap diplomacy' or the potential deployment of Beijing's military assets to assist the Chinese diaspora in the Pacific in times of conflict (Connolly 2016; Maclellan 2018b).

China and the French Pacific dependencies

The purported role of France as a bulwark against Chinese influence in the Pacific Islands is undercut by the reality that local governments and businesses in France's non-self-governing territories are actively seeking more engagement with China.

Despite this, the extent of Chinese influence in the Francophone Pacific should not be exaggerated. It's growing, but Chinese policy is marked by contradictions and setbacks.

Diplomacy in the Francophone Pacific is complicated by bureaucratic structures within China's Ministry of Foreign Affairs. China's relationship with France and its overseas dependencies is managed by the Department of European Affairs. In contrast, China's diplomacy with Australia, New Zealand, the US and the 10 China-aligned PIF countries comes under the Department of North American and Oceanian Affairs. Unlike

---

4   President of French Polynesia Edouard Fritch, 5 September 2018. Pacific Islands Forum, Yaren, Nauru. Interview with author.

independent PIF countries, the French dependencies are not eligible for grants from China or programs under the new China International Development Cooperation Agency.

There is evidence of varying capability among Chinese diplomats, who—often to impress superiors at home—exhibit bullying behaviour that offends the dignity of Pacific Island leaders (Maclellan 2018c). The clumsiness of Chinese diplomacy in French Polynesia is symbolised by a long-running dispute between the Chinese consulate and local landowners in Tahiti over the ownership of the consulate building first established in Punaauia in September 2007 (Brady 2018; Radio New Zealand 2018).

A significant problem in the Francophone Pacific is China's ambivalent attitude towards decolonisation. In their long struggle for self-determination and independence, the Kanak people and the Maohi people are seeking international support (Maclellan 2015a). The historic support shown by the Chinese Communist Party (CCP) for the struggles of oppressed and colonised peoples has largely dissipated. Since the capitalist roaders took power in Beijing in the late 1970s, the CCP has rejected 'interference in internal affairs' that might raise parallels with Beijing's ongoing dilemmas over Tibet, Hong Kong, Taiwan and Uighur nationalism (Anonymous 2010). The Chinese Government is reluctant to criticise French colonialism, valuing France as an ally against the US in global trade and climate debates.

The Chinese Government also faces complex interactions between 'new Chinese' migrants and the long-established Chinese diaspora in the Pacific. In this regard, French Polynesia is different to the settler colonial state of New Caledonia or the smaller Wallis and Futuna. In Tahiti, Chinese migrants have long intermarried into the local elite and dominate Tahiti's business sector (Burns 2000). In New Caledonia, where a majority support ongoing ties to France, Chinese businesses often face hostility from the European, Javanese and Vietnamese communities. Chinese labourers deployed for mining construction in New Caledonia faced hostility from local unions, as they were employed outside local norms of industrial relations (Smith 2013).

Finally, analysis of China's rising influence in the Pacific Islands needs to be tempered by an understanding of the interplay between the many diverse players in the region (Maclellan 2015b; Zhang 2018a). France and the Anglosphere powers are dealing not only with China's competition with Taiwan, but also with new activity from a number of emerging Asian players—India, Korea and Indonesia. Major powers like France, India and Japan have their own global relationships (and tensions) with China, which complicate their interactions in the Pacific Islands region.

The following section presents four examples of the shifting relationship between China and the French Pacific dependencies: increasing exports to China from New Caledonia and French Polynesia; attempts to increase Chinese tourism by the HNA Group; the establishment of a Chinese fishing enterprise on Hao atoll in French Polynesia; and Chinese involvement in New Caledonia's nickel industry.

Trade with China

As the administering power, the French state contributes significant funding to its three Pacific dependencies, amounting to nearly €2.5 billion per annum. However—as with Australia and the independent island states—this financial support has not guaranteed that France remains their primary partner for trade.

Analysts Matthew Dornan and Sachini Muller (2018) note that Australian–Pacific Island trade is stagnating, at a time when:

> trade between China and Pacific Island countries has grown rapidly, assisted by China's growing economic clout … Since 2000, there has been a twelvefold increase in the value of Chinese exports to the region. Over the same period, imports from Australia have remained stagnant, with their value in 2017 lower than that in 2004.

This pattern can be seen with New Caledonia and French Polynesia. In 2018, China was the number one export destination for New Caledonia with 31.7 per cent of trade—due to nickel ore exports—followed by Korea (15.5 per cent) and Japan (14 per cent). Between 2017 and 2018, New Caledonia's trade balance with China doubled due to exports of nickel ore and ferronickel metal (ISEE 2019). Close neighbour Australia had been a primary export market for ore until the 2016 closure of the Yabulu nickel smelter in Townsville by rogue politician and entrepreneur Clive Palmer (Maclellan 2016). In 2018, Australia ranked number 11 as an export destination, receiving just 1 per cent of New Caledonian exports.

For imports in 2018, China was the third-ranked source for New Caledonia with 9.0 per cent, after France (23.8 per cent) and Singapore (14.3 per cent). Once again, neighbouring Australia ranked lower for imports at just 7.5 per cent (ISEE 2019).

In October 2012, a Chinese business delegation visited Tahiti led by Li Xiaolin, President of the Chinese People's Association for Friendship with Foreign Countries (and the daughter of China's former prime minister Li Peng). The delegation looked at opportunities to invest in transport and tourism infrastructure as well as agriculture.

By 2018, Hong Kong and China ranked first in French Polynesia's principal export destinations (with 14.2 per cent of trade), while Australia was ranked 15th with just 0.2 per cent (ISPF 2019). In 2018, China ranked third (7.9 per cent) in the sources of imports for French Polynesia, following France (25.2 per cent) and the US (20.6 per cent). Australia again lagged at eighth position with just 2.7 per cent.

French Polynesian entrepreneurs of Chinese heritage are looking to China to expand their existing operations. Beyond agricultural products, businessman Robert Wan hopes to expand the export of cultured pearls to China beyond long-standing sales in Hong Kong. His brother Louis Wane is also seeking Chinese investment in his diverse businesses (travel, hotels, supermarkets and beverages) that already make up 12 per cent of French Polynesia's GDP (Polynésie la 1ère 2017). As detailed below, Louis Wane has already had some success in the tourism sector.

Wooing Chinese tourists to the Francophone Pacific

In 2018, Chinese travellers made nearly 150 million trips abroad (an increase of 14.7 per cent on 2017) and spent US$115 billion during their travels (Xinhua 2019). Pacific Island countries have long worked to tap into this tourism market, seeking approved destination status from the Chinese Government. In 2004, China joined the South Pacific Tourism Organisation as the its first member state from outside the region, contributing funding previously provided by Taiwan.

French Polynesia and New Caledonia are now following the path to increased Chinese tourism set by their independent neighbours, but the lack of direct flights from Beijing to Tahiti and Noumea has limited access to this lucrative market. Local governments are testing the waters but face significant constraints because of France's ongoing control over visas. With a policy promoting regional economic integration, the government of New Caledonia has been working to boost the number of Asia-Pacific tourists, especially from China. William Le Grand, deputy director of New Caledonia's international airline Aircalin, notes:

> China is clearly a very important market with nearly 130 million tourists in 2018 around the world. That's a market to explore and we're working on it with a clear desire to investigate the possibilities there (LNC 2018b).

Despite this, the number of Chinese visitors arriving in New Caledonia will be relatively small at first. The national airline, together with hotel groups and tourist authorities, proposed a goal of just 700 tourists in 2018, another 1,000 in 2019 and rising to 6,000 by 2025. With the establishment of a direct air route to China, tourism authorities eventually hope for 20,000 Chinese tourists a year, comprising 15 per cent of the local market (at time of writing, however, the COVID-19 (coronavirus) epidemic may complicate strategic planning for tourism industries around the Pacific).

Aircalin has begun organising charter flights from China to test the market. In February 2018, a preliminary charter with 260 Chinese tourists travelled from Hangzhou for a week-long visit to New Caledonia. In June 2018, New Caledonian authorities signed an agreement with Chinese tour operator Caissa International Travel Service, a subsidiary of Hainan Airlines (LNC 2018a). The agreement allows for three more charter flights to New Caledonia from Tianjin, a city of 15 million people located near Beijing. With two of these flights arriving in September and October 2018, the Chinese tourists were targeted with 'upmarket' services, including a visit to the outlying beaches on the Isle of Pines, a cultural 'bush visit' to the rural town of Bourail and accommodation in five-star hotels (LNC 2018d). Another 258 tourists arrived from Hangzhou in February 2019, with Aircalin's William Le Grand noting, 'With this full flight, we have the confirmation that our destination is attractive to Chinese tourists' (LNC 2019a).

Dominique Michaud, the director general of the Marriott hotel chain in New Caledonia, noted:

> We are just beginning. There is real potential but as long as there are not direct connections, the market will be limited. These facilities have been partly sorted out, as has the need to accept different types of Chinese credit cards. Chinese payments are often virtual. They pay more and more with a telephone and China is one of the most advanced countries in this manner, unlike us (LNC 2018c).

With the delivery of two new Airbus A330 aircraft during 2019, Aircalin director general Didier Tappero announced that the airline was looking to cities in China as potential regular routes, saying, 'China is an option being considered very seriously by Aircalin. Destinations like Shanghai and Hong Kong are being studied' (LNC 2019b).

Similar efforts are underway in French Polynesia. Islands like Tahiti and Bora Bora have long served as destinations for luxury tourism from the US and Europe, but tourism from Australia, New Zealand and Japan has fallen in 2017–19. According to French researcher Sebastien Goulard (2017):

> Tourism has been a major economic sector for French Polynesia, comprising more than 12 per cent of its GDP. But unlike Palau and Fiji, French Polynesia has failed to become a popular destination for Chinese travellers. With less than 6,000 visitors in 2017, Chinese tourists in French Polynesia rank only eighth.

In response, French Polynesia is restructuring its tourist facilities to tap the Chinese market. Shen Zhiliang, China's consul-general in French Polynesia, agreed that Tahiti remains a luxury destination for Chinese tourists, but argued, 'You must take account of the cultural differences, the eating habits and the high cost of the trip. There is still no direct flight between China and French Polynesia' (TNTV News 2019).

Because of France's ongoing control of immigration and customs in Tahiti, Chinese tourists find it difficult to quickly organise visas for holidays there, or arrange a last-minute stopover, even though French Polynesia has held Chinese approved destination status since 2008. In an interview, French Polynesia's independence leader Oscar Temaru highlighted this ongoing colonial control of immigration as a roadblock to expanded tourism from China:

> The real problem for tourism in Tahiti is the visas. There are over a hundred countries that have to get a French visa to come and visit us, so that doesn't interest many people. You can go to lie on a beach in the sun in Fiji, in Samoa or in Vanuatu without a visa. But that's the way France wants it—they want to control everything.[5]

The French Polynesian Government has sought support from successive French governments in Paris for changes to French laws that could facilitate travel in larger numbers from China. They want Paris to approve short-term transit visas that could be issued to Chinese tourists on arrival at Faa'a international airport in Tahiti to increase the chance of a stopover en route to South America. The French Polynesian Government has also hoped that Paris would authorise longer-stay visas for Chinese tourists to make the long trip to Tahiti worthwhile. Currently, visa-free entry to French Polynesia for Chinese citizens can only be provided if they meet an onerous list of bureaucratic requirements (French High Commission 2019).

Gaston Flosse is a leading anti-independence politician in French Polynesia. But this long-time loyalist to the French Republic is one of the leading boosters for improved relations and economic ties with China. As president in 2004, Flosse attempted to set up a French Polynesian office in Beijing, but this attempt was overruled by the French Constitutional Court. After nine years out of office, Flosse briefly won the presidency again in 2013 and actively encouraged Chinese investment in Tahitian tourism.

Flosse led a large delegation to China in December 2013, visiting Beijing, Chungking and Haikou (the capital of the southern-most province of Hainan). During the trip, he held a series of meetings with Chinese officials, including newly elected then vice president Li Yuanchao and the chairman of the China Development Bank Hu Huaibang. Flosse held talks with Chinese civil aviation authorities and the management of Hainan Airlines to discuss the possibility of increased flights from Beijing and Haikou to Tahiti (Maclellan 2014a).

---

5   Former president of French Polynesia Oscar Manutahi Temaru, 30 October 2018. Ponerihouen. Interview with author.

Over two decades, Hainan Airlines has morphed into HNA Group. The company's fortunes illustrate the challenge of boom-and-bust capitalism for Chinese companies. Between 2014 and 2017, the Chinese conglomerate took significant stakes in Hilton hotels, Swissport, Ingram Micro and Germany's Deutsche Bank. This multibillion-dollar global spending spree even extended to French Polynesia. On 28 August 2014, HNA Aviation signed a development cooperation agreement with the government of French Polynesia. This opened the way for another subsidiary of the Hainan-based corporation, HNA Tourism Company Ltd, to buy two companies belonging to prominent French Polynesian businessman Louis Wane: the SA Moorea Lagoon Resort, owner of the Hilton Moorea Lagoon Resort and Spa in Moorea, and the SARL Société Hôtelière Motu Ome'e, owner of the Hotel St Régis in Bora Bora (Tahiti Infos 2016b).

From 2017, through their subsidiary Deer Jet, HNA began offering a 'Hong Kong to Tahiti dream journey' for wealthy Chinese tourists. This trip to paradise involved a non-stop flight on a private 787 Dream Jet and a week-long stay at the presidential suite of the St Regis Bora Bora resort. Then French Polynesian tourism minister Nicole Bouteau, greeting the first flight at the airport, said, 'The Asian market, from China, is under development. It's important for us that a company like Hainan is interested in our country' (Tahiti Infos 2017).

French Polynesia has long sought Chinese investment in its ailing hotel sector, after numerous luxury resorts have closed in recent years due to high costs and a lack of Western patrons. Successive administrations have sought out Chinese investors to buy into the Mahana Beach tourism project, a planned US$2.5 billion luxury beach resort and spa complex first proposed by Gaston Flosse.

Though he was removed from office in 2014 after convictions for corruption, Flosse opened the way for a Hong Kong–led consortium to bid for a 70-year contract to build and operate the Mahana Beach project. The consortium included the real estate firms Recas Global and R&F Properties, together with the Chinese state-owned corporation China Railway International. In December 2015, the Chinese consortium signed a preliminary agreement with the new government of French Polynesia led by Edouard Fritch to proceed with the project. Even with the government committing to provide 53 hectares of public domain to the project, it was clear by the scheduled contract date of 30 June 2016 that the Recas Group could not commit the financing to proceed to a full 70-year contract, and the bid was withdrawn. Then French Polynesian tourism minister Jean-Christophe Bouissou noted:

> We have avoided running aground on a hidden reef by signing a leasing contract with the Recas Group without knowing if this consortium had the capacity to develop the project or not (Tahiti Infos 2016a).

The integration of Chinese corporations into global systems of production and capital accumulation has meant they must ride the boom and bust that is a central feature of capitalist markets. The July 2018 death of HNA co-chair Wang Jian in France disrupted the company's share price. The debt crisis facing the company since 2018 has limited further expansion of global operations, including in French Polynesia. The Bora Bora property was advertised for sale in October 2018 as the HNA Group sought to sell off some of its global property holdings, reducing its stake in Hilton hotels and Deutsche Bank (Zhou 2018).

Facing collapse, the HNA Group sold nearly US$45 billion worth of assets in 2018. However, analysts cited by the US media have raised suspicions that the company, with very deep pockets, has state backing in China (Barboza 2017; Bloomberg News 2018). In December 2019, HNA Group was granted a US$568 million loan by Chinese state-owned banks to bail out its troubled airline subsidiaries in Hong Kong and provincial China. The bailout consortium includes the China Development Bank, China Exim Bank, Industrial and Commercial Bank of China, Bank of China Hong Kong, China Construction Bank and Agricultural Bank of China (Richter 2019).

Fisheries on Hao atoll, French Polynesia

Facing a massive trade deficit and high levels of unemployment, French Polynesia President Edouard Fritch is eager to promote investment from Chinese state-owned and private corporations in agriculture, tourism and infrastructure. In an interview, Fritch said:

> China is present to support countries through investment and the technical assistance that they bring. Today, French Polynesia is certainly a country that is looking for finance and investment to support economic development. Around the Pacific, China has shown that it is making significant efforts to reduce greenhouse

gas emissions at home, but also to provide assistance and funding to support the countries of the Pacific zone. I think that we must say that today, China is the country that is the most present in these smaller island states.[6]

One major investment proposal is a US$300 million Chinese fisheries project on Hao atoll, to be operated by the Chinese corporation Tianrui Group Co. Ltd. Despite the commercial nature of the investment, Australian media have reported that the Hao project may lead to greater Chinese strategic influence. Some even suggest the project opens the way for a Chinese military facility in the French Pacific dependency. A May 2018 article in *The Sydney Morning Herald* stated:

> The massive fish farm project on Hao atoll has raised eyebrows in Canberra because it will sit next to the airport the French military previously used to carry out nuclear tests in the Pacific … Concerns in Canberra focused on speculation Tianrui could seek a lease on their airport, giving Beijing a strategic foothold 11,000 kilometres into the Pacific Ocean (Wroe 2018d).

The article, citing US and Australian security analysts, followed similar articles by the same journalist the previous month that raised concerns about a purported Chinese military base in Vanuatu (Wroe 2018a, 2018b, 2018c). The claims that China and non-aligned Vanuatu were planning a military facility in Luganville were quickly denied by Vanuatu Prime Minister Charlot Salwai and Foreign Minister Ralph Regenvanu (Maclellan 2018b:18). The French Government too is unlikely to welcome a Chinese military base in its Pacific dependency.

It's ironic that Western security analysts are only now expressing concern about the militarisation of Hao atoll. For decades, Hao was used by the French military as a forward base for the Centre d'Expérimentation du Pacifique (Pacific Testing Centre). Located in the Tuamotu Archipelago, Hao's 3,420-metre military airstrip is one of the longest in the Pacific. With a population of around 1,700 people, Hao served as a staging post between France, Papeete and the nuclear test sites at Moruroa and Fangataufa atolls, where France conducted 193 nuclear tests between 1966 and 1996.

---

6   President of French Polynesia Edouard Fritch, 5 September 2018. Pacific Islands Forum, Yaren, Nauru. Interview with author.

Hao lagoon—one of the largest in French Polynesia—was used to decontaminate aircraft, ships and personnel exposed to radioactive contamination at the CEP. A number of studies have investigated potential nuclear contamination on the atoll (Barrillot 1996; CRIIRAD 2006). In 2006, the French Delegate for Nuclear Safety and Radiation Protection for Defence Activities revealed that large amounts of radioactive material were simply dumped in the ocean after the end of testing in 1996, including 2,656 tonnes at two sites off Moruroa atoll and 532 tonnes at Hao (DSND 2006:20–22). Worried by evidence of asbestos and other toxins on the airbase, local environmental groups have questioned whether the atoll is suitable for a fish farming project.

Given this polluted legacy, the government of French Polynesia has been trying for decades to lure investors to Hao atoll. In 2000, the Flosse Government urged foreign corporations to invest in Hao, 'a genuine tax haven in the heart of the Pacific!' Advertisements in *The Economist* (2000) magazine stated that Hao atoll offers 'exemption from corporate taxes, exemption from registration and property taxes, exemption from custom duties and no personal income tax'. The ad also highlighted the potential to repurpose the airstrip and facilities left behind by the French armed forces, including: 'a communication satellite network; international airport runway; wharf for deep sea ships; desalination unit; nautical base; power plant; hospital' (ibid.).

With little interest from Western corporations, the search for investors extended to China. In December 2016, Tahiti Nui Océan Foods presented a proposal for a major fisheries project on Hao. Established in 2014, Tahiti Nui Océan Foods is a subsidiary of the Tianrui Group Co. Ltd. Chaired by billionaire Li Liufa, the parent company operates from Ruzhou City, Henan Province, with investments in cement, foundry, tourism, mining, trade and logistics, finance and other industries.

In August 2017, the government of French Polynesia met with Wang Cheng, CEO of Tahiti Nui Océan Foods, and the project design was finalised on 1 February 2018. Tahiti Nui Océan Foods announced plans to build 2,800 cages in Hao's lagoon to farm fish, prawns and sea cucumbers for export. To woo the investors, the Fritch Government passed legislation in December 2017 allowing for fiscal incentives that encourage major investments in French Polynesia, followed by a decree on 8 March 2018 to create a priority development zone on Hao atoll (Government of French Polynesia 2017, 2018a).

Early publicity in 2016 stated that up to 10,000 jobs would be created, but the scale and cost of the project have been downsized several times and the start of construction regularly delayed. Early company propaganda suggested would make a US$1.5 billion investment and, years later, security analysts and journalists continue to recycle this figure without investigation (see, for example, Wroe 2018d). This comes despite a publicly available French Polynesian Government decree that shows Tahiti Nui Océan Foods will only invest CFP32 billion (French Pacific francs), equivalent to US$300 million (Government of French Polynesia 2018b:6192).

Desperate to generate employment on the atoll, the French Polynesian Government has wooed Tahiti Nui Océan Foods CEO Wang Cheng, even presenting him with the honorific of *Commandeur dans l'ordre de Tahiti nui* in May 2018. But the delay in construction and the likelihood that local jobs will be numbered in the hundreds, not thousands, is causing political problems for local boosters of the project. Seeking reelection in March 2020, Hao Mayor Théodore Tuahine complained that his constituents were originally promised 10,000 jobs. He was also concerned that the island cannot train local workers for the project without knowing the types of positions that will be available for Polynesians rather than Chinese staff:

> There is a lack of detailed information on the project. They talk about the need for workers and their preparation, which we're ready to do. But we don't know what are the technical specialities that they want us to prepare! (Tahiti Infos 2019).

The Hao project highlights the reality that initiatives in the Pacific are often driven by the commercial interests of private or state-owned corporations, rather than overarching government plans. Chinese diplomats are often reliant on the Chinese company for information about progress or the contents of deals struck with the host government. In an interview in early 2019, China's consul-general in French Polynesia Shen Zhiliang reaffirmed his belief that the Hao project will eventually begin:

> In May 2018, there was an inauguration ceremony on Hao and in August a delegation from the China Development Bank came to inspect the works and for deeper discussions. The two parties are both in contact. Polynesian engineers will soon be sent to Shanghai [for training]. I think the project is still on track. Neither of the two parties has indicated to me an intention to abandon the project (TNTV News 2019).

This project is often presented in the Western media as an example of Chinese debt-trap diplomacy, but any debt will rest with the Chinese corporation. Indeed, the agreement signed by the Fritch Government on 29 March 2018 shows that the government has agreed to exempt Tahiti Nui Océan Foods from any tax for 30 years on the importation of materials and fuel. It has also agreed to several other tax holidays for a period of 10 years after construction has been completed (Government of French Polynesia 2018b). In mid-2019, the Fritch Government granted the Chinese corporation a further year to build a 1.2 million litre fuel tank for the project.

On the basis of public documents, neither the Chinese company nor the Chinese state retains control over the airstrip on Hao atoll. With the French Government in Paris signing off on the project, eager to reduce its own state revenues flowing into French Polynesia, there is little evidence that the project gives 'Beijing a strategic foothold 11,000 kilometres into the Pacific Ocean' (Wroe 2018d).

In the future, however, other Chinese corporations may express interest in the vast maritime zone around Clipperton and French Polynesia's five archipelagos. In June 2017, under China's vision of a 21st-century Maritime Silk Road, Beijing proposed three 'blue economic passages' (including a China–Oceania–South Pacific passage) to focus on 'sharing blue space and developing the blue economy' (Xinhua 2017). The University of French Polynesia hosted a seminar on the Maritime Silk Road in November 2019.

There is also growing interest in deep-sea mining from the China Ocean Mineral Resources Research and Development Association (Zhang 2018b). The sector, however, is still governed by the French State—under French Polynesia's current autonomy statute, control of 'strategic metals' on the ocean floor rests with Paris rather than Papeete (Blue Ocean Law et al. 2019; Maclellan 2018d). France is firmly focused on controlling the vast 7,000,000 km² exclusive economic zones (EEZs) surrounding its Pacific colonies, as a French Senate report has highlighted:

> Thanks to its overseas possessions, France is one of the countries affected—indeed the most affected—by this revolution in sharing the oceans. Its EEZ is in fact the second largest behind that of the United States and beyond this, the most diverse. Present in both hemispheres and at all points of the compass, the French EEZ is the only one on which the sun never sets (Senate 2014:13).

Questioned about potential Chinese interest in fisheries during a February 2016 visit to Tahiti, then French president Francois Hollande stressed the importance of ongoing French state sovereignty over French Polynesia's 5,000,000 km² EEZ (Hollande 2016). However, France's sovereignty over EEZs pits the French state against the leading independence party in French Polynesia, which is actively asserting local rights over marine resources under international law. Former senator for French Polynesia Richard Ariihau Tuheiava has argued:

> We have continually emphasised the critical nature of the resource question as a core issue for our future development. Whether or not these resources are considered in Paris to be 'strategic' is irrelevant to the applicability of international legal decisions which place the ownership of natural resources with the people of the non-self-governing territories (Tuheiava 2017).

Exporting nickel from New Caledonia

At current estimates, the Melanesian nation of New Caledonia holds more than 25 per cent of global nickel reserves. The main island Grande Terre is bisected by a massive mountain range filled with vast ore bodies. New Caledonia is often called Le Caillou, an ironic reference to the French word for pebble.

Conservative anti-independence politicians have argued that China's global efforts to access natural resources pose a particular challenge for New Caledonia due to its strategic mineral reserves. Philippe Gomès, leader of Calédonie Ensemble, a major conservative party in New Caledonia and a strong opponent of independence, argued that China is more interested in New Caledonia than other member countries of the Melanesian Spearhead Group (though this may come as a surprise to Papua New Guineans and Fijians). In an interview, the anti-independence leader said:

> On the need for raw materials, who has the greatest demand for nickel on a global scale? The Chinese! We have the second largest reserves of nickel in the world. If they colonise Solomon Islands, Fiji or Papua New Guinea, they'll get beaches and coconut palms. But New Caledonia is le Caillou—the largest rock of nickel in the world. So, they're eyeing us with a hundred, a thousand, times more interest that any atoll in the world with their coconut trees.[7]

---

7 Philippe Gomès, President of Calédonie Ensemble and deputy to the French National Assembly, 17 October 2018. Noumea. Interview with author.

In contrast, members of the independence movement Front de Libération Nationale Kanak et Socialiste (FLNKS) have been eager to break the French monopoly over the smelting of nickel in New Caledonia. They have looked beyond traditional markets in France, Japan and Australia to new partners in China and South Korea to add value to New Caledonia's vast natural resources.

New Caledonia's Northern Province administration is controlled by the FLNKS independence movement under provincial President Paul Neaoutyine. Following the armed conflict of the 1980s, the provincial administration established a development arm, Société de Financement et d'Investissement de la Province Nord (SOFINOR), to expand economic opportunities in the rural north, where the population is majority indigenous Kanak. In 1990, SOFINOR bought the mining company Société Minière du Sud Pacifique (SMSP).

Following the 1969 Billotte laws, a monopoly over nickel smelting was guaranteed to the French-controlled corporation ERAMET and its local subsidiary Société le Nickel (SLN), which operates the Doniambo smelter in Noumea. The French Government has used its Strategic Investment Fund to maintain a 25 per cent holding in ERAMET. French taxpayer funds have often been used to bail out SLN as nickel prices fluctuate on the international market.

After New Caledonia's violent conflict of the 1980s, Kanak independence leaders sought to open the nickel sector to foreign competition. The signing of the Noumea Accord in May 1998 was only possible because contending parties had come to an agreement over the *préalable minière* (mining precondition) posed by the independence movement. The February 1998 Bercy Accord allowed the transfer of strategic deposits of high-grade nickel ore to SMSP and SOFINOR, opening the way for the construction of the Koniambo nickel smelter in the north of the country.

In his role as a New Caledonian Deputy in the French National Assembly, Philippe Gomès accompanied President Macron to Australia in May 2018. During the trip, Gomès said that New Caledonia 'could fall into Chinese hands' if people voted for independence in the territory's November 2018 referendum on self-determination (Higgins 2018). Ironically, at that time it was the government of New Caledonia, led by a member of Gomès' own party, that played a crucial role in opening the way for greater Chinese involvement in New Caledonia's nickel industry.

Government policy since 2009 has tried to add value to the country's vast nickel reserves by expanding the amount of smelted metal rather than exporting raw saprolite or laterite ores. Despite this, ore exports grew by 24 per cent between 2013 and 2015, with the growth focused on China, Japan and Korea. Though New Caledonia has long looked to Japan and Australia for exports, for many years it resisted sales of high-grade ore directly to China in hopes of protecting metal production in local smelting plants.

In March 2016, Queensland Nickel's Yabulu smelter, owned by flamboyant entrepreneur and novice politician Clive Palmer, went into liquidation, even as ships bearing ore were on the water between New Caledonia and Australia (Maclellan 2016). Small mining companies, known as *petits mineurs*, lost their export market. Faced with the threat of strikes and blockades by subcontractors, the New Caledonian Government buckled. In a new plan, then president Philippe Germain announced that his government would grant temporary permits for the export of nickel ore to China. In an interview, Germain said:

> Our mining framework has always prioritised traditional partners like Australia and Japan. But if Australia can no longer buy the same levels from us, we need an alternative in the current circumstances, because we have mines, miners and sub-contractors who are dependent on this activity.[8]

In 2018, New Caledonia exported 6.8 million tonnes of ore, including 3.3 million tonnes to South Korea, nearly 2 million to Japan and 1.5 million to China. However, this tonnage to China is only half the 3 million tonnes authorised for export each year. A number of mining companies are now eager to expand into this market. Thibaut Martelin, president of the minerals export council Syndicat des Exportateurs de Minerai, has stressed the long-term importance of China over traditional export destinations like Japan and Australia:

> China effectively serves as a complete substitute for Australia … The current Chinese market is a huge advantage in comparison to the Australian market because it is open to export from a number of smelters and with a greater range of minerals (content of nickel, amount of nickel in ferronickel, etc). Today, we face less constraints

---

8   Then president of New Caledonia Philippe Germain, 8 March 2016. Noumea. Interview with author.

within the Chinese market. There's a larger pool of clients who will adapt their operations to the ore that's available, rather than the mine having to adapt its operations to the customer (LNC 2019c).

The biggest beneficiary of the opening of export to China has been the Northern Province's SMSP, which has expanded access to the Chinese market as part of a broader development strategy.

Over the last three decades, SMSP has grown into a major nickel producer. The driving force behind the company is New Caledonian entrepreneur Dang Van Nha, known as Andre Dang. His parents arrived in New Caledonia from French Indochina in 1935, working as indentured labourers in the Koniambo Massif mines owned by SLN. His father died in an industrial accident when Dang was just 17 months old, and the family moved to Noumea, where Dang became an accountant, manager and then leading businessman (Maclellan 2014b).

During New Caledonia's armed conflict of the 1980s, Dang was driven into exile in Australia, with the colonial right perceiving him as too close to the FLNKS independence movement. However, he returned to New Caledonia in 1990 to assist the Northern Province in managing its mining and smelting operations.

Begun in 1990 as a mining transport company with 120 employees, SMSP started exporting nickel ore in 2007. SMSP's strategy has been to retain high-value saprolite ore from the Koniambo Massif for domestic use. This ore, with 2.3 per cent nickel content, is being supplied to a new smelter established in the Northern Province: the US$5.3 billion plant at Vavouto operated by Koniambo Nickel SAS (KNS), a joint venture between SMSP and the transnational conglomerate Glencore. In an unprecedented arrangement, Dang persuaded the Anglo-Swiss financial conglomerate to grant SMSP 51 per cent controlling interest in KNS.

This chapter cannot detail the full range of social, environmental and economic impacts of the Koniambo project, but it has been a fundamentally transformative project in the Northern Province and a crucial pillar of the 'economic rebalancing' required under the 1998 Noumea Accord (Grochain 2013; Sourisseau et al. 2017).

To generate funding for its share of Koniambo finances, SMSP developed a strategy to export lower-grade nickel ore to Korea and China, once again using joint ventures controlled 51 per cent by SMSP. The company has two joint ventures with the Korean corporation Posco: the Nickel Mining

Company (NMC) and the nickel processing company Société du Nickel de Nouvelle-Calédonie et Corée (SNNC). In 2009, SNNC began smelting nickel at the company's plant at Gwangyang, South Korea, producing 261,469 tonnes of nickel metal between 2009 and 2017. In the same period, SMSP's subsidiary NMC exported nearly 20,000,000 tonnes of ore to the Gwangyang plant, which uses lower-grade saprolite ore with an average of 1.98 per cent nickel content.

The next challenge was to export even lower-grade ore, with an average nickel content of 1.65 per cent, to a joint-venture smelter in China. On 18 October 2017, SMSP signed a memorandum of understanding (MOU) with Yangzhou Yichuan Nickel Industry Co. Ltd to develop a joint project in China. This MOU was expanded on 22 March 2018 when Andre Dang met Yichuan CEO Zhang Jianguo to finalise a memorandum of agreement (MOA).

These preliminary agreements were designed to test export systems to China before finalisation of a full contract, under which SMSP agrees to deliver 600,000 tonnes of nickel ore to Yichuan each year for the next 25 years, after the Chinese corporation agrees to sell 51 per cent of its share capital to SMSP. The full contract was finalised in 2020, though exports were slow to expand due to the coronavirus pandemic.

In an interview, SOFINOR's chief financial officer Karl Therby explained that Yichuan's pyro-metallurgical smelter at Yangzhou began production in 2012:

> The Chinese had been purchasing nickel ore from Indonesia, but they had a range of concerns about the quality, the humidity of the ore and of the reliability of delivery. So SMSP was able to say to them that, through our Korean operation, we have shown our capacity and reliability to export ore of higher quality than can be found in the Indonesian market. So, by signing the contract with us, they've guaranteed supply—but we retain 51 per cent of the operation.[9]

The decision to operate offshore was driven by domestic politics as well as market realities. Conservative anti-independence parties in Noumea are fiercely opposed to Chinese investment in New Caledonian enterprises,

---

9   Karl Therby, chief financial officer of Société de Financement et d'Investissement de la Province Nord (SOFINOR), 7 November 2018. Noumea. Interview with author.

so SOFINOR and SMSP have developed new ways of working without Chinese companies operating in New Caledonia. SOFINOR's Therby explained:

> In our political context, with referendums on independence and public concern about Chinese influence, we don't want them to operate here. We've seen what has happened in Papua New Guinea, we've seen what has happened in Vanuatu and we want to protect the territory from all that. So, they have no actual investment in our mines; instead, we just have a contract to supply them.[10]

In an interview, Andre Dang explained that this strategy is based on an unprecedented corporate structure that gives majority control to SMSP rather than its Chinese partner:

> The corporate structure is a real innovation and it's the first time in the world that it's been used, above all in China. The structure of 51 per cent/49 per cent—the Chinese have never before accepted this. The Chinese Government was obliged to change a law and it took seven years to allow SMSP to start operations there. We've just taken one small step into the Chinese market. After that we'll see, because the Chinese are very intelligent. We have to be very careful, because they can be terrible! The Chinese aren't here, they've stayed at home! Instead, we've gone over there and have taken possession of a small piece of their country, through our 51 per cent control of the smelter. The cost of operations will be paid for by the profits from the smelting.[11]

In 2018, after striking an agreement with SMSP, Yangzhou Yichuan Nickel added a second production line to its Yangzhou smelter, increasing potential annual production capacity of ferronickel. The metal is then sold to stainless steel producers in China. In July 2018, Northern Province President Paul Neaoutyine paid an official visit to China to meet with officials from Yangzhou City and major shareholders from Yangzhou Yichuan Nickel (SMSP 2018).

The first shipment to China under the MOA, departing Noumea in July 2018, revealed some early tensions with the Chinese corporate partner. The Yangzhou port, in a shallow river channel, only has capacity for vessels weighing 45,000 tonnes, but the first shipment of ore from

---

10   Karl Therby, chief financial officer of Société de Financement et d'Investissement de la Province Nord (SOFINOR), 7 November 2018. Noumea. Interview with author.

11   Andre Dang Van Nha, 7 November 2018. Noumea. Interview with author.

New Caledonia amounted to 62,500 tonnes. Without informing SMSP or the New Caledonian mining directorate, Yinchuan unloaded 16,006 tonnes at Lianyungang port rather than deliver the full load to the Yangzhou smelter.

To assert SMSP's rights as controlling partner, Dang halted further shipments until the Chinese company apologised and agreed to bear the costs of transhipment to smaller vessels. This ensured all the ore was used at the Yangzhou smelter, thereby generating maximum returns to SMSP as controlling partner. New shipments recommenced in January 2019, with ore loading through the Bay of Téoudié at Kaala-Gomen. By May 2019, there had been three shipments, with plans to ramp up to a vessel every month.

For Dang, this strategy of maintaining majority control over operations avoids many of the problems that independent Pacific countries have faced with Chinese mining investments. He contrasts the SMSP strategy with the US$1.4 billion Ramu Nickel project in Papua New Guinea, which has been plagued by the overuse of Chinese labour, poor environmental standards and pressure on local politicians (Smith 2013). Now in his 80s, Dang will be a hard man to replace as a negotiator of unprecedented deals with China. He is, however, grooming successors to implement the vision already laid out:

> As long as I'm at the company, I will never allow it to sell nickel ore directly to China. I only want our resource to be used in New Caledonian plants or those that will be owned by New Caledonia in the future and that will supply benefits to our country. We're going to shoot ourselves in the foot if we simply provide raw minerals to our competitors. That's been going on for 140 years, ever since colonisation.

> We want to ensure the continued existence of our mines, because nickel is not a renewable resource. Once you've exhausted it, bit by bit, that's the end. We don't want New Caledonia to end up like Nauru. They were a world leader in phosphate mining, but they abused it and used it all up. They are a sad country. So, our strategy is to add value to the resource which can generate funds for use in sectors beyond the nickel industry, which will benefit the country and future generations.[12]

---

12 Andre Dang Van Nha, 7 November 2018. Noumea. Interview with author.

Conclusion

As a key member of the European Union (EU), France is well positioned for a new post-Brexit relationship with the Pacific Islands. But, at this time of geopolitical change, governments in Noumea and Papeete are eagerly seeking Chinese grants and investment in tourism, fisheries and infrastructure, as well as export markets for New Caledonia's nickel industry and French Polynesian pearls. As yet, there are only a small number of direct investments by Chinese corporations, but trade relations are shifting rapidly from Europe to Asia, for the French dependencies as well as independent PIF countries.

These changes come at a time when PIF member states have begun to reposition themselves with other European powers. For many years, France and the United Kingdom have contributed significant development assistance to the Pacific through the EU's European Development Fund (EDF). However, the future of EDF funding is in flux in the aftermath of the June 2016 Brexit referendum, Boris Johnson's December 2019 electoral victory and the looming renegotiation of the 2000 Cotonou Treaty between the EU and the Organisation of African, Caribbean and Pacific nations.

The election of Emmanuel Macron as President in 2017 highlighted the crisis facing France's traditional centre-right and centre-left parties. But Macron's République En Marche movement is facing its own crisis, with popular rioting around the country in 2018–19 by the *gilets jaunes* (yellow vests) and massive public service strikes in late 2019.

France's strategic role in the Pacific has support within the French state, given the costs and benefits of empire are unevenly shared. Most metropolitan citizens have limited awareness of the overseas collectivities, so institutions that benefit from the maintenance of colonialism play a disproportionate role in policy formulation. Most politicians and officials in Paris still believe that the costs of maintaining a colonial empire are ones that must be borne, with a report from the French Senate noting:

> The exercise of our sovereignty over these vast stretches and the international competition we face are certainly a difficult cost to bear in this period of crisis. But this is an investment for the future, an historic opportunity for growth and expansion. France, with its overseas territories on the front rank, must seize this opportunity and bet on the blue economy (Senate 2014:13).

Will this gamble pay off, or will France be unable to finance its multibillion-euro commitment in the South Pacific well into the 21st century? And will China be willing to step up to plug the development gap?

References

Anonymous 2010. China and the Principle of Self-Determination of Peoples. *St Antony's International Review* 6(1):79–102.

Barboza, D. 2017. A Chinese Giant Is on a Global Buying Spree. Who's Behind It? *New York Times*, 9 May.

Barrillot, B. 1996. Contamination et État de Pollution à Hao. In B. Barrillot. *Les Essais Nucléaires Français 1960–1996*. Lyon: CDRPC, 263–70.

Bloomberg News 2018. HNA Is Victim of Conspiracy Against China: Co-Chairman. 7 February.

Blue Ocean Law, the Pacific Network on Globalisation and the International Justice and Human Rights Clinic at Allard Law School, University of British Columbia 2019. *Enduring Colonization—How France's Ongoing Control of French Polynesia Resources Violates the International Law of Self-Determination*. Guahan: Blue Ocean Law.

Brady, A-M. 2018. Trouble in Paradise: A Chinese Occupation in Tahiti. *The Diplomat*, 20 April.

Brattberg, E., P. Le Corre and E. Soula 2018. Can France and the UK Pivot to the Pacific? Carnegie Endowment for International Peace, 5 July.

Burns, M. 2000. The Chinese Community in French Polynesia: Scholarly Sources of Understanding. *China Review International* 7(1):28–35. doi.org/10.1353/cri.2000.0008

Carroll, J. and T. Ell 2017. More Than Submarines: New Dimensions in the Australia–France Strategic Partnership. Strategy Paper, Australian Strategic Policy Institute, Canberra.

Connolly, P. 2016. Engaging China's New Foreign Policy in the South Pacific. *Australian Journal of International Affairs* 70:5:484–505. doi.org/10.1080/10357718.2016.1194805

CRIIRAD (Commission de Recherche et d'Information Indépendantes sur la Radioactivité) 2006. Compte Rendu de la Mission Préliminaire de Contrôles Radiologiques sur l'Ile de Mangareva et les Atolls de Tureai et Hao (Polynésie Française). *CRIIRAD Rapport N° 05-49 V3*.

DFAT (Department of Foreign Affairs and Trade) 2017. *2017 Foreign Policy White Paper: Opportunity Security Strength*. Canberra: Government of Australia.

Dornan, M. and S. Muller 2018. The China Shift in Pacific Trade. *Devpolicy Blog*, 15 November.

DSND (Délégué à la Sûreté Nucléaire et à la Radioprotection pour les Activités Intéressant la Défense) 2006. *Les Essais Nucléaires Français dans le Pacifique: Mission du délègue à la Sureté Nucléaire et à la Radioprotection pour les activités et Installations Intéressant la Défense*. Paris: Ministère de la Défense.

Fisher, D. 2015. One Among Many: Changing Geostrategic Interests and Challenges for France in the South Pacific. *Les Études du CERI* 216.

French High Commission 2019. Dispense de Visa pour les Ressortissants de Certains Pays pour Entrer et Séjourner en Polynésie Française, pour Une Durée Inférieure à 15 Jours. Regulations issued by French High Commission in French Polynesia, Papeete, 22 October.

Fritch, E. 2019. Route de la Soie/Axe Indo-Pacifique. Speech at the University of French Polynesia, Tahiti, 5 November.

Goulard, S. 2017. French Polynesia at the Chinese Crossroads. *The Diplomat*, 7 September.

Government of French Polynesia 2017. Loi du Pays N° 2017-43 du 22 Décembre 2017 Portant Incitations Fiscales à la Réalisation de Grands Investissements en Polynésie Française. Conseil des Ministres.

Government of French Polynesia 2018a. Arrêté N° 315 CM du 8 Mars 2018 Portant Création de la Zone de Développement Prioritaire de Hao, Situé sur le Territoire de la Commune de Hao, dans l'Archipel des Tuamotu. Conseil des Ministres.

Government of French Polynesia 2018b. Arrêté N° 500 CM du 29 Mars 2018 Portant Agrément de la Société Tahiti Nui Océan Foods et de Son Projet d'Implantation et d'Exploitation d'une Ferme Aquacole sur l'Atoll de Hao, au Dispositif de la Loi de Pays N° 2017-43 du 22 Décembre 2017 Portant Incitations Fiscales à la Réalisation de Grands Investissements en Polynésie française. Conseil de Ministres. *Journal Officiel de la Polynésie Française* 6192–93.

Grochain, S. 2013. *Les Dynamiques Sociétales du Projet Koniambo*. Noumea: Editions IAC.

Hacquemand, E. 2018. En Nouvelle-Calédonie, la Méthode Macron à l'œuvre. *Paris Match*, 10 May.

Higgins, E. 2018. New Caledonia 'Could Fall into Chinese Hands' If It Votes for Independence. *The Australian*, 4 May.

Hollande, F. 2016. Press conference, Tahiti, French Polynesia, 22 February.

ISEE (Institut de la Statistique et des Études Économiques) 2019. *Commerce Extérieure 2018*. Noumea: Institut de la Statistique et des Études Économiques.

ISPF (Institut de Statistiques de la Polynésie Française) 2019. *Le Commerce Extérieur en Polynésie Française*. Papeete: Institut de Statistiques de la Polynésie française.

L'Express 2018. Emmanuel Macron Souhaite un 'Nouvel axe Indo-Pacifique' avec l'Australie. 2 May.

LNC (Les Nouvelles Calédoniennes) 2018a. Aircalin Signe pour Trois Nouveaux Vols Charters en Provenance de Chine, 1 June.

LNC (Les Nouvelles Calédoniennes) 2018b. Le Tourisme Local Rapporte Plus de 5 Milliards, 4 June.

LNC (Les Nouvelles Calédoniennes) 2018c. Pour Tout Projet, Rien Ne Se Fait sans une Adhésion Fortement Majoritaire, 1 October.

LNC (Les Nouvelles Calédoniennes) 2018d. Un Deuxième Charter Chinois Accueilli à La Tontouta, 28 September.

LNC (Les Nouvelles Calédoniennes) 2019a. Arrivée d'un Troisième Charter de 258 Touristes Chinois, 5 February.

LNC (Les Nouvelles Calédoniennes) 2019b. Bienvenue à Bord du Nouvel Avion d'Aircalin, l'A330neo Kanuméra, 2 August.

LNC (Les Nouvelles Calédoniennes) 2019c. Le Marché Chinois a Cet Immense Avantage d'Être Ouvert sur Plusieurs Usines, 17 April.

Maclellan, N. 2009. The Australia–France Defence Co-Operation Agreement: Implications for France in the South Pacific. *Austral Policy Forum* 09-19A. Nautilus Institute.

Maclellan, N. 2012. Partenariat Stratégique Renforcé entre la France et l'Australie. *Tahiti-Pacifique Magazine* 254 (August).

Maclellan, N. 2014a. Flosse Taps Beijing–Tahiti Connection for Increased Tourism. *Islands Business*, 13 February.

Maclellan, N. 2014b. Mr. Nickel—SMSP's Andre Dang Transforms New Caledonia's Nickel Industry. *Islands Business*, 20 June.

Maclellan, N. 2015a. Pacific Diplomacy and Decolonisation in the 21st Century. In G. Fry and S. Tarte (eds), *The New Pacific Diplomacy*. Canberra: ANU Press. doi.org/10.22459/NPD.12.2015.21

Maclellan, N. 2015b. Transforming the Regional Architecture: New Players and Challenges for the Pacific Islands. *Asia-Pacific Issues* 118. Honolulu: East-West Center.

Maclellan, N. 2016. Palmer's Folly and the Road to New Caledonian Independence. *Inside Story*, 26 May.

Maclellan, N. 2018a. Operation South Pacific? *Inside Story*, 29 March.

Maclellan, N. 2018b. Vanuatu Dismisses China Base Claim. *Islands Business*, May.

Maclellan, N. 2018c. Chinese Walkout. *Pacnews*, 4 September.

Maclellan, N. 2018d. France and the Blue Pacific. *Asia and the Pacific Policy Studies* September 5(3):426–41. doi.org/10.1002/app5.228

Maclellan, N. 2020. Global Britain's Frayed Edges. *Inside Story*, 7 February.

Macron, E. 2018. Speech, Noumea, New Caledonia, 5 May.

Malielegaoi, L.S.M. 2018. Speech at 73rd Session of the United Nations General Assembly, New York, 28 September.

Marles, R. 2012. Interview with then ALP Parliamentary Secretary for Pacific Island Affairs Richard Marles on *Pacific Beat* program. *ABC News*, 10 September. Radio Australia.

Ministry of Defence 2018. *France and Security in the Indo-Pacific*. Paris: Ministry of Defence.

Nicholson, B. 2016. French Call for Defence Ties across Oceans. *The Australian*, 2 March.

Panda, A. 2016. French Defence Minister to Urge EU South China Sea Patrols. *The Diplomat*, 6 June.

Patrick, A. 2018. Emmanuel Macron is More Worried about New Caledonia than Australia. *Australian Financial Review*, 2 May.

PIF (Pacific Islands Forum) Secretariat 2016. Final Communiqué. Forty-Seventh Pacific Islands Forum. Pohnpei, Federated States of Micronesia, 8–10 September.

PIF (Pacific Islands Forum) Secretariat 2018. Boe Declaration. Attachment to Final Communiqué. Forty-Ninth Pacific Islands Forum. Boe, Nauru, 5 September.

Polynésie la 1ère 2017. Combien Pèse le Groupe Wane en Polynésie? 12 August.

Radio New Zealand 2018. Chinese Consulate Renews Tahiti Rental Amid Controversy. 26 April.

Richter, W. 2019. HNA Gets Chopped Up, Its Many Airlines Buckle and Get Bailouts to Dodge Messy Collapse, But Its Hong Kong Airlines? *Wolf Street*, 3 December.

Rigaud, N. 2016. France and Security in the Asia–Pacific. *ASPI Strategic Insights* 112. Canberra: Australian Strategic Policy Institute.

Senate 2014. Rapport d'Information Fait au Nom de la Délégation Sénatoriale à l'Outre-Mer, sur *Zones Économiques Exclusives des Outre-mer: Quels Enjeux?* Senat N° 430 (2013–14).

Smith, G. 2013. Spare a Nickel? On the Trail of Chinese Resource Investment in the Pacific. *The China Story*. The Australian Centre on China in the World, College of Asia & the Pacific, The Australian National University.

SMSP (Société Minière du Sud Pacifique) 2018. President Paul Néaoutyine Visits China, 30 July.

Sourisseau, J-M., S. Grochain and D. Poithily 2017. From Anticipation to Practice: Social and Economic Management of a Nickel Plant's Establishment in New Caledonia's North Province. In C. Filer and P.-Y. Le Meur (eds), *Large-Scale Mines and Local-Level Politics: Between New Caledonia and Papua New Guinea*. Canberra: ANU Press, 61–98. doi.org/10.22459/LMLP.10.2017.02

Tahiti Infos 2016a. De Nouveaux Investisseurs Intéressés par le Projet Tahiti Mahana Beach, 5 July.

Tahiti Infos 2016b. Le Chinois Hainan Airlines Group Rachète deux Hôtels du Groupe Wane, 20 April.

Tahiti Infos 2017. Hainan Airlines à la Conquête du Ciel Polynésien, 20 October.

Tahiti Infos 2019. Projet Aquacole de Hao : Près de 240 Containers Attendus en Avril, 16 January.

Tavola, K. 2019. 'Enduring Colonialism' Raises Vexatious Questions for Pacific Islands Forum. *Islands Business*, 30 August.

The Economist 2000. Government of French Polynesia Advertisement. April.

TNTV News 2019. Bateaux de Pêche, Hao, Tourisme: Entretien avec le Consul de Chine en Polynésie, 30 March.

Tuheiava, R. 2017. Speech to the Pacific Regional Seminar of the UN Special Committee on Decolonisation, Nicaragua, 24 June.

Turnbull, M. and E. Macron 2018. Press conference with Prime Minister of Australia Malcolm Turnbull and President of the French Republic Emmanuel Macron, Kirribilli House, Sydney, Australia, 2 May.

Vandendyck, B. 2018. Le Développement de l'Influence Chinoise dans le Pacifique Océanien. *Revue Juridique, Politique et Économique de la Nouvelle-Calédonie* 2018/1(31):199–209.

Wroe, D. 2018a. China Eyes Vanuatu Military Base in Plan with Global Ramifications. *The Sydney Morning Herald*, 9 April.

Wroe, D. 2018b. Chinese Wharf in Vanuatu Raising Eyebrows across the Pacific. *The Sydney Morning Herald*, 12 April.

Wroe, D. 2018c. Vanuatu PM Defends China Deals But Vows to Oppose Any New Foreign Base. *The Sydney Morning Herald*, 12 April.

Wroe, D. 2018d. China Casts Its Net Deep into the Pacific with $2b Fish Farm. *The Sydney Morning Herald*, 18 May.

Xinhua 2017. China Proposes 'Blue Economic Passages' for Maritime, 21 June.

Xinhua 2019. Chinese Tourists Make Nearly 150 Million Outbound Trips in 2018, 14 February.

Zhang, D. 2018a. China, India and Japan in the Pacific: Latest Developments, Motivations and Impact. DPA Discussion Paper 2018/6. Canberra: The Australian National University.

Zhang, D. 2018b. China's Growing Interest in Deep Sea Mining in the Pacific. *DPA In Brief* 2018/11. Canberra: The Australian National University.

Zhou, E. 2018. HNA Adds Nine Overseas Properties to Fire Sale. *Mingtiandi*, 14 October.

7

A Reevaluation of China's Engagement in the Pacific Islands

Zhou Fangyin

In the past few years, the development of relations between China and the Pacific Island countries has attracted the attention of some Western countries. To avoid taking a superficial view of the relationship between China and the Pacific Island countries, this chapter will analyse the development of and changes in their relations over the past decade and the driving forces behind these changes. The chapter discusses the development direction of China's policy towards the Pacific Islands in the future and how China will seek balance in its relations with the Pacific Island countries and Australia and New Zealand.

Have there been significant changes in China's policy towards Pacific Island countries in the past several years?

Since 2014, Chinese leader Xi Jinping has visited the Pacific Islands region twice and held two collective meetings with the leaders of the island countries that have established diplomatic ties with China. This is an unusual phenomenon in China's relations with the Pacific Islands. The unprecedented frequency of visits by Chinese leaders to the Pacific Islands, as well as China's rising presence in this region, has led some to believe that China's interest in the Pacific Island countries has increased significantly. Some Australians and New Zealanders believe that their countries' influence in the Pacific region has been challenged and a prompt response is needed (Colton 2018; Dornan 2018; Mitchell 2018).

Have there been significant changes in China's relationship with the Pacific Island countries and, if so, in what ways? In order to reliably assess this issue, this chapter will make a judgement based on analyses of high-level visits between the countries and China's trade, investment and aid to the Pacific Islands.

Changes in the frequency of high-level visits between China and the Pacific Islands

Due to the asymmetry in the size and strength of China and the Pacific Island countries, this chapter mainly focuses on two aspects of data. The first is the number of visits to China by Pacific Island leaders between 2012–18 (at the level of president, prime minister and governor), as well as the number of visits to China by Pacific Island leaders over the preceding period of time (2005–11).

Table 1. Visits to China by leaders of Pacific Island nations during two seven-year periods

	Visits to China by Pacific Islands leaders, 2005–11	Visits to China by Pacific Island leaders, 2012–18	Change in frequency
PNG	**3 times in total** 1 time for governor: 10/2006 2 times for prime minister: 04/2009, 09/2010	**7 times in total** 1 time for governor: 09/2015 6 times for prime minister: 09/2012, 11/2013, 11/2014, 07/2016, 12/2017, 06/2018	+4
Fiji	**6 times in total** 2 times for president: 09/2010, 08/2011 4 times for prime minister: 2005, 2008, 2010, 2011	**5 times in total** 1 time for president: 2014 4 times for prime minister: 2012, 05/2013, 07/2015, 05/2017	-1
Vanuatu	**6 times in total** 3 times for president: 07/2007, 08/2008, 10/2010 3 times for prime minister: 02/2005, 08/2008, 04/2010	**4 times in total** 3 times for prime minister: 09/2013, 08/2014, 09/2015, 09/2016	-2
The Federated States of Micronesia	**4 times in total** 4 times for president: 04/2006, 12/2007, 08/2008, 04–05/2010	**3 times in total** 3 times for president: 09/2012, 11/2013, 03/2017	-1

	Visits to China by Pacific Islands leaders, 2005–11	Visits to China by Pacific Island leaders, 2012–18	Change in frequency
Tonga	**4 times in total** 2 times for the king: 04/2008, 01/2011 2 times for prime minister: 04/2007/, 08/2008	**3 times in total** 1 time for the king: 03/2018 2 times for prime minister: 07/2013, 11/2013	-1
Samoa	**5 times in total** 1 time for the head of state: 08/2008 4 times for prime minister: 2005, 03/2007, 09/2008, 08/2010	**3 times in total** 3 times for prime minister: 11/2013, 04/2015, transit, 09/2018	-2
Cook Islands	**3 times in total** 3 times for prime minister: 11/2005, 09/2007, 09/2011	**1 time in total** 1 time for prime minister: 11/2013	-2
Niue	**3 times in total** 3 times for prime minister: 06/2007, 11/2008, 10/2010	**1 time in total** 1 time for prime minister: 11/2013	-2

Source: Collated according to the website of the Ministry of Foreign Affairs of China.

As can be seen from Table 1, the number of visits to China by Pacific Island leaders was 34 during the seven years 2005–11, and 27 during the seven years 2012–18, a reduction of 20 per cent overall. With the exception of the number of visits by PNG leaders to China, which rose from three to seven, the number of visits to China by leaders of all other Pacific Islands decreased.

This study found that Pacific Island leaders make more intensive visits to China around major foreign-related events held in China. Such activities include the first China–Pacific Island Countries Economic Development and Cooperation Forum in 2006, the 2008 Olympic Games, the 2010 World Expo, the second China–Pacific Island Countries Economic Development and Cooperation Forum in 2013, the APEC annual conference in 2014, the '9-3' military parade in 2015, and the Belt and Road Forum for International Cooperation summit in 2017. It is worth noting that visits to China by Pacific Island leaders have not become more frequent since 2013, while China's home-court diplomacy has become more frequent.

The second area of concern is the high-level visits of the Chinese Government to the Pacific Island nations. The frequency of visits by Chinese officials at the ministerial level and above to the Pacific Islands constitutes an effective indictor of the importance China attaches to this region. The scope of statistics analysed were limited to the members of the standing committee of the political bureau, the vice-premiers, the state councillors (at the rank of vice-premier), the ministers for foreign affairs, the head of the International Department of the CPC Central Committee, the minister of commerce, minister of defence and chief of general staff. The results are shown in Table 2.

Table 2. Visits to Pacific Island countries by senior Chinese officials at or above the ministerial level during two seven-year periods

	Number of high-level visits by the Chinese Government to Pacific Island countries, 2005–11	Number of high-level visits by the Chinese Government to Pacific Island countries, 2012–18	Change in frequency
PNG	**3 times in total** Wang Jiarui, head of the International Department of the CPC Central Committee (2005); Li Zhaoxing, minister for foreign affairs (2006); Chen Bingde, member of the central military commission and chief of the general staff of the Chinese People's Liberation Army (2009)	**2 times in total** President Xi Jinping (2018); Wang Yi, State Councilor and Minister for Foreign Affairs (2018)	-1
Fiji	**5 times in total** President Xi Jinping (transit in 2009); Jia Qinglin, member of the standing committee of the political bureau, chairman of the National Committee of the Chinese People's Political Consultative Conference (transit in 2005); Zeng Qinghong, member of the standing committee of the political bureau, vice-president (transit in 2005); Hui Liangyu, vice premier (transit in 2011); Liu Yandong, state councilor (2010)	**3 times in total** Wu Bangguo, member of the standing committee of the political bureau and chairman of the standing committee of the National People's Congress (2012); President Xi Jinping (2014); Wang Yi, State Councilor and Minister for Foreign Affairs (2018)	-2
Vanuatu	**2 times in total** Zeng Peiyan, vice premier of the state council (2007); Li Zhaoxing, minister for foreign affairs (2006)		-2
The Federated States of Micronesia	**1 time in total** Li Zhaoxing, minister for foreign affairs (2006)		-1

	Number of high-level visits by the Chinese Government to Pacific Island countries, 2005–11	Number of high-level visits by the Chinese Government to Pacific Island countries, 2012–18	Change in frequency
Tonga	**1 time in total** Li Zhaoxing, minister for foreign affairs (2006)	**1 time in total** Wang Jiarui, head of the International Department of the CPC Central Committee (2014)	unchanged
Samoa	**3 times in total** Li Changchun, member of the standing committee of the political bureau of the Central Committee (2007); Wu Guanzheng, member of the standing committee of the political bureau of the CPC Central Committee (transit in 2007); Li Zhaoxing, minister for foreign affairs (2006)	**2 times in total** Jia Qinglin, chairman of the national committee of the Chinese People's Political Consultative Conference (2011); Chen Deming, minister of commerce (2012)	-1
Cook Islands	**1 time in total** Li Zhaoxing, minister for foreign affairs (2006)		-1
Niue	**1 time in total** Li Zhaoxing, minister for foreign affairs (2005)		-1

Source: Collated according to the website of the Ministry of Foreign Affairs of China.

As can be seen from Table 2, during the seven years 2005–11, the number of visits to the Pacific Island countries by senior Chinese government officials within the scope of the statistics was 17, and during the seven years 2012–18 the number dropped to eight. In the earlier period, the minister for foreign affairs of China visited seven of the eight Pacific Island countries establishing diplomatic relations (with the exception of Fiji). In the latter period, the minister for foreign affairs of China visited two of the eight island states establishing diplomatic relations: PNG and Fiji. While President Xi Jinping's state visits to Fiji in 2014 and Papua New Guinea (PNG) in 2018 represent the highest level of visits by Chinese leaders, there has been no significant increase in visits to Pacific Island countries by other senior Chinese government officials.

China's trade with Pacific Island nations

Since the beginning of the 21st century, China's trade with Pacific Island countries has experienced relatively rapid growth. However, this growth was from a low starting point, and the total volume of this trade was still limited until 2017.

Table 3. The volume of import and export trade between China and selected Pacific Island countries since 2000 (US$ million)

	PNG	Fiji	Vanuatu	The Federated States of Micronesia	Samoa	Tonga	Cook Islands
2000	225.59	15.43	1.51	1.65	2.04	1.64	0.25
2001	141.51	26.63	1.47	1.87	2.32	1.18	0.38
2002	186.92	31.97	1.67	1.30	2.79	4.84	0.19
2003	292.03	31.32	3.08	2.74	3.19	2.10	0.58
2004	296.37	38.71	7.49	7.45	6.86	6.28	0.91
2005	376.05	45.27	8.27	2.44	5.98	2.94	5.92
2006	518.27	69.23	19.38	2.95	12.96	3.75	2.02
2007	680.98	66.26	21.35	9.49	11.85	7.36	2.98
2008	858.31	90.36	34.67	4.01	27.71	7.29	2.67
2009	885.91	97.13	48.80	8.59	44.87	8.05	7.30
2010	1129.98	128.58	23.26	6.68	70.07	9.76	4.89
2011	1265.27	172.42	136.25	5.02	37.85	13.32	5.70
2012	1282.35	236.18	136.03	15.00	71.77	20.16	5.05
2013	1352.58	303.88	382.73	14.92	54.48	38.51	20.49
2014	2051.24	340.19	187.13	14.78	56.06	23.98	21.12
2015	2797.58	350.28	84.50	15.84	65.68	30.48	17.33
2016	2279.14	400.53	68.72	21.07	70.36	30.31	4.39
2017	2835.78	382.99	79.77	37.94	64.41	28.53	13.19
2018	3615.59	482.05	79.03	40.40	70.32	25.07	7.69

Source: Data from 2000–13 is from China Business Yearbook Editorial Board 2001–17. Data from 2014–18 is from General Administration of Customs, China (www.customs.gov.cn/customs/302249/302274/302277/index.html).

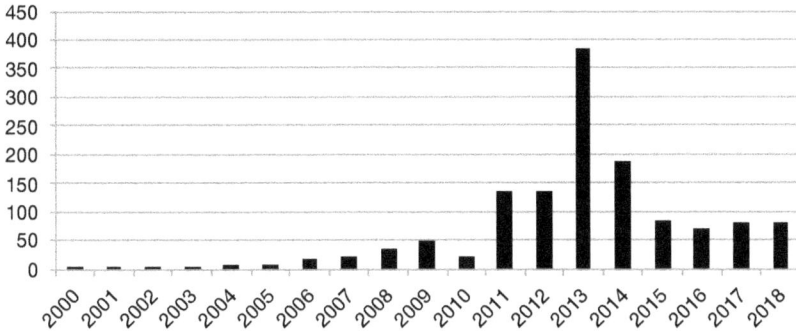

Figure 1. Trade between China and Vanuatu, 2000–18 (US$ million)
Source: Data from 2000–13 is from China Business Yearbook Editorial Board 2001–17.
Data from 2014–18 is from General Administration of Customs, China (www.customs.gov.
cn/customs/302249/302274/302277/index.html).

Of the eight Pacific Island countries with which China had diplomatic relations until the end of 2018, PNG had the largest trade volume with China, followed by Fiji. Vanuatu's trade with China has increased dramatically since 2000, but has fluctuated considerably over the past decade. Trade with Samoa and Tonga has not grown rapidly since 2012. Trade between China and the Cook Islands declined sharply in 2016 and 2018, and was lower in 2018 than in 2013. Trade between China and Samoa was lower in 2018 than in 2012, and trade between China and Tonga was lower in 2018 than most years from 2013 to 2017. With the exception of PNG, Fiji and the Federated States of Micronesia, there has been no notable increase in trade relations between China and other Pacific Island nations since 2013, and some of them decreased during this period. Trade between China and Vanuatu has shown large fluctuations.

As can be seen from Figure 1, trade between China and Vanuatu maintained steady growth from 2000 to 2009, with significant increases in 2011 and 2013. Since then, however, trade between China and Vanuatu fell sharply two years in a row, from 2013 to 2015, by 51.1 per cent and 54.8 per cent, respectively. Trade between China and Vanuatu in 2018 was less than one-quarter of that in 2013.

In 2000, China's total merchandise trade was US$474 billion. In 2018, China's total merchandise trade was US$4,623 billion, about 9.8 times that of 2000 (World Bank 2019). Given the rapid growth of China's overall foreign trade over the past 18 years, the pace of growth in China's trade with Pacific Island countries is not abnormal.

China's investment in Pacific Island countries

In addition to trade, the international community is also concerned about China's investment in Pacific Island countries. From 2016 to 2018, Huawei, a Chinese telecommunications giant, launched a national broadband transmission network project in PNG and an undersea optical cable project to connect Solomon Islands to Australia (ABC News 2017; Huawei 2016, 2017). These two projects garnered a lot of attention in Oceania (Smyth 2017; Wroe 2017). In one sense, investment can bring China's influence more quickly and directly to the Pacific Islands and make China's presence there more perceptible to local people. While there is a perception that China's investment in the Pacific Islands has risen rapidly over the past several years and that China's presence in the Pacific Island countries has increased substantially, this perception may be overstated in terms of the actual amount of Chinese investment in the Pacific Islands.

Table 4. China's investment flows to selected Pacific Island countries since 2006 (US$10,000)

	PNG	Fiji	Cook Islands	The Federated States of Micronesia	Samoa	Tonga	Vanuatu	Total
2004	10	-	-	-	-	-	-	10
2005	558	25	-	16	-	-	-	599
2006	2862	465	-	-	-	-	-	3327
2007	19681	249	-	625	-12	-	-	20543
2008	2992	797	-	−16	-	-	-	3773
2009	480	240	-	-	63	-	-	783
2010	533	557	-	-	9893	-	-	10983
2011	1665	1963	-	−289	11773	-	79	15191
2012	2569	6832	12	341	4759	-	293	14806
2013	4302	5832	17	46	−7793	-	-	2404
2014	3037	−3716	−27	339	3484	10	604	3731
2015	4177	1240	-	355	9586	98	2245	17701
2016	−4368	4461	0	0	10924	35	542	11594
2017	10161	1706	-	−1474	12840	112	2532	25877

Source: China Business Yearbook Editorial Board 2001–17.

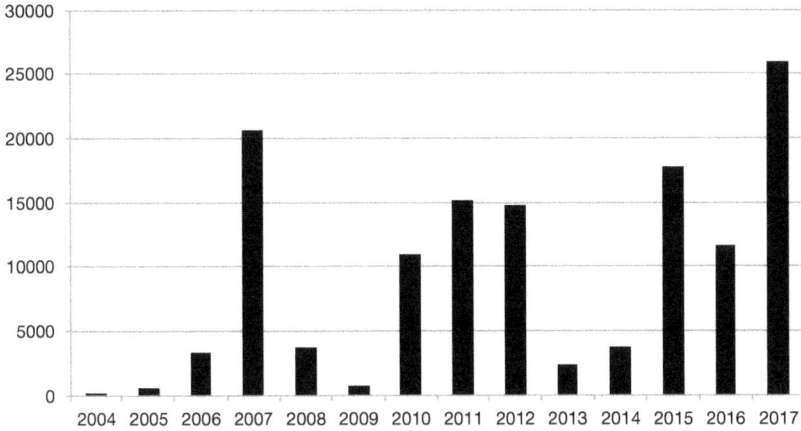

Figure 2. Chinese investment in selected Pacific Island nations (US$10,000)
Source: China Business Yearbook Editorial Board 2001–17.

According to Table 4 and Figure 2, 2007 was the peak of Chinese investment in Pacific Island countries before 2016, and the flow of Chinese investment in these countries did not exceed the 2007 amount until 2017. Over the past decade, China's investment in Pacific Island countries has fluctuated greatly. This should not have happened if the Chinese Government is trying to increase its presence in Pacific Islands by expanding investment.

Statistically, from 2013 to 2016, Chinese investment in PNG did not increase or even decline. Chinese investment in Fiji fell sharply in 2017, equivalent to only one-quarter of that in 2012. Chinese investment in Samoa has risen rapidly since 2014, but was unstable before 2014, and the flow of investment to Samoa in 2017 was only slightly higher than in 2011.

In the past decade, 2010, 2015 and 2017 were the years in which investment flows increased rapidly, with investment in these three years increasing by US$102 million, US$140 million and US$143 million respectively over the previous year, while investment flows decreased significantly in 2013 and 2016, by US$124 million and US$61 million respectively over the previous year. Judging from the investment data, China's investment flows to Pacific Island countries fluctuated greatly and did not show a steady rise until 2016.

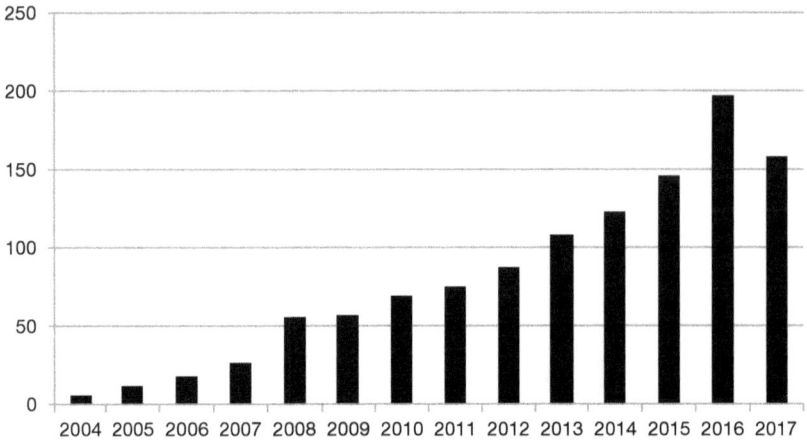

**Figure 3. China's outward foreign direct investment, 2004–17
(US$ billion)**
Source: China Business Yearbook Editorial Board 2001–17.

From a country-specific perspective, China's investment has been most concentrated in PNG, Fiji and Samoa. China's investment in Vanuatu and the Federated States of Micronesia has also increased in recent years.

With the rise of its economic strength, the scale of China's foreign investment has also rapidly increased. In 2004, the amount of China's outward foreign direct investment (OFDI) was US$5.5 billion. In 2016, the amount of China's OFDI reached US$196.4 billion, a remarkable increase of 34.7 times in 13 years. By contrast, Chinese investment in seven Pacific Island countries rose 18.4 times from 2005 to 2016. It was not until 2017 that China's net investment flow to Pacific Island countries exceeded that of 2007. Over the past decade, Chinese investment in Pacific Island countries has grown more slowly than the overall rise in Chinese outbound investment.

Some countries have different interpretations of China's investment in the Pacific Islands. From China's perspective, its flow of OFDI to Pacific Island countries accounted for only 0.16 per cent of its global outward investment in 2017, an almost negligible share for China.[1] But from the point of view of the Pacific Islands, China's investment can have a great impact on the region. Australia and New Zealand, meanwhile,

---

1   Ministry of Commerce, China via CEIC database, www.ceicdata.com.

are more concerned about the possible geopolitical and social impacts of China's projects on the Pacific Islands. Australia's *2016 Defence White Paper* commits Australia to work to 'limit the influence of any actor from outside the region with interests inimical to our own' (Department of Defence 2016:74).

China's aid to the Pacific Islands

China's aid to Pacific Island countries has attracted a lot of attention from the international community in the past several years (Brant 2013; Dornan and Brant 2014; Dziedzic 2018). Some feel that China intends to expand its influence in the Pacific Islands and that China's growing influence has eroded Australia's leadership there; thus, Australia needs to do more to rebalance China's influence (Batley 2017; Hegarty 2015; Riordan 2018). However, judging from the actual amount of Chinese aid to the Pacific Islands, China's intentions are likely exaggerated.

Table 5. Aid delivered to Pacific Island countries (in real terms) (US$100 million)

	Australia	China	EU	Japan	New Zealand	United States
2011	13	0.91	1	1.8	1.9	2.3
2012	12	0.8	0.72	1.5	2.2	2.1
2013	11	2.1	0.87	1.4	2.0	2.2
2014	11	2.5	0.93	1.3	2.5	1.8
2015	10	2.9	1	1.3	2.2	1.3
2016	8.8	1.9	0.66	1.8	2.2	0.66
2017	9.5	1.7	0.95	1.9	2.2	1.6

Source: Lowy Institute (2019).

As can be seen from the data in Table 5, China's aid to Pacific Island countries rose continuously between 2013 and 2015, but declined in 2016 and 2017, with a decline of more than 30 per cent in 2016 compared to the previous year. In 2017, China's aid to Pacific Island countries was lower than that of Australia, New Zealand and Japan and slightly higher than that of the US. China's aid to Pacific Island countries was less than one-sixth of Australia's.

This should not have been the case if China had strategic intentions in the Pacific region. According to data released by the Chinese Government, of the RMB89.34 billion (about US$12.8 billion) China spent in foreign aid from 2010 to 2012, 4.2 per cent, or RMB3.75 billion (about US$536 million), went to Oceania (Information Office of the State Council of the People's Republic of China 2014). Aid to Pacific Island countries accounts for a small proportion of China's foreign aid, and is not rising very fast.

In terms of the amount of aid given, China's position among donors to the Pacific Islands is not prominent. However, China's aid is more focused on infrastructure projects, and the amount of aid given for a single project is often larger than that of other donors, so often attracts more attention. While China's aid program in the Pacific Islands has sparked some criticism from countries such as Australia (Dziedzic 2018), based on the findings of this study, China's aid to this region does not appear to be the result of conscious strategic design (Colton 2018; Connolly 2016).

Dynamics and the sustainability of China's policy towards the Pacific Island countries

The above analysis shows that although trade and investment between China and the Pacific Island countries have been growing rapidly since 2000, and China's aid to the Pacific Island countries is also on the rise, China's relations with the Pacific Islands have not changed dramatically and high-level exchanges have not become more frequent in recent years, despite what officials and the media in countries such as Australia and New Zealand have portrayed (Batley 2017; Dornan 2018; DW News 2018; Peters 2018).

On the other hand, with the improvement of China's overall strength and the development of China's all-round diplomacy,[2] China's national and regional studies underwent a period of relative prosperity. Driven by the 'Going Out' strategy, the Belt and Road Initiative (BRI) and all-round diplomacy, Chinese universities have established a large number of national and regional research centres in a relatively short period of

---

2   In October 2017, the report of the 19th CPC National Congress pointed out that since the 18th CPC National Congress (2012) an important achievement of China's diplomacy has been the in-depth development of all-round diplomacy and the advancing of 'China's diplomatic agenda in a comprehensive, multilevel, multifaceted way' (Xi 2017).

time. In 2017, the Ministry of Education actively promoted national and regional studies, documenting 394 country and regional research centres to achieve full coverage in country and regional studies (Ministry of Education of the People's Republic of China 2017). Against this background, the study of Pacific Island countries in Chinese universities has been promoted. At present, there are two research centres specialising in Pacific Island countries studies: the Research Center for Pacific Island Countries of Liaocheng University and the Center for Pacific Island Countries Studies of Guangdong University of Foreign Studies. This gives the impression that the Chinese Government is paying much more attention to the Pacific Island countries. Such an understanding is somewhat misleading, as it could be merely a reflection of China's generally rising interests in global affairs.

An issue worth paying attention to is whether the rise in China's trade, investment and aid to the Pacific Island countries is a unique phenomenon with these countries or representative of changes in China's foreign relations as a whole.

If we look only at China's trade, investment and aid with the Pacific Islands, it may seem as though China's interest in that region has increased considerably over the past decade. However, a more comprehensive look at the overall transformation of China's foreign trade, investment and aid shows that the Pacific Islands have a limited position in China's overall foreign economic relations. China's investment of resources in this region is not particularly unique.

In the past several years, Australia, New Zealand and some other countries have been quite sensitive to the rise of China's influence in the Pacific Islands region (Colton 2018; Hanson 2011; Hegarty 2015; Lum and Vaughn 2007; Meich et al. 2018; McAslan 2013; Wesley-Smith 2007; Windybank 2005), some believing that China has greater political or strategic intentions and is trying to crowd out the influence of Australia and New Zealand in this region. In this context, Australia and New Zealand have responded with their respective policies, New Zealand launching a principles-based 'Pacific Reset' (Peters 2018) and Australia promoting a security-driven plan to step up its engagement in the region (DFAT 2018).

As countries that have traditionally had influence in the region, Australia's and New Zealand's concerns are understandable. However, it can be hypothetically speculated that if China really has political and strategic intentions in the Pacific Islands region, China's trade, investment and aid to the Pacific Island countries should not have experienced large fluctuations in the past decade, including sometimes notable decreases, as shown in the previous data. Chinese investment in Pacific Island countries, in particular, has fluctuated widely over the past decade. If the trade and investment figures are somewhat coincidental, continued growth is at least achievable if the Chinese Government wants to expand aid to the Pacific Islands. But the reality is that in 2017 China's annual aid to Pacific Island countries had not increased but declined compared to 2013.

One possible conclusion is that the rise of China's influence in the Pacific Islands since 2010 is, to a large extent, a byproduct of the overall rise of China's international influence. It was also influenced by the BRI as well as President Xi Jinping's two state visits to Pacific Island countries. The Chinese Government has not made great efforts to operate in the Pacific Islands region as a key diplomatic direction, nor does it have a comprehensive strategic design related to this region.

The overall growth rate of China's investment in Pacific Island countries has been relatively stable in the past decade, but China's assistance has been noticeable for the following reasons:

1. The relatively limited size of Pacific Island countries, which means that small amounts of aid may bring about major changes in the socioeconomic outlook of the countries.

2. China is a latecomer in providing aid to the Pacific Islands region; under the stable aid structure formed there in the past, the entry of China's aid easily attracts the attention of other donors, especially in the context of the rise of China.

3. China's assistance is more concentrated in areas such as infrastructure construction, where the average amount of Chinese aid to projects is often greater than that of other donors. Roughly speaking, the average size of Chinese aid projects is 10 times that of Australian projects (Dziedzic 2018). Meanwhile, China has a very strong capacity for and high efficiency in infrastructure construction; the existence of China's local infrastructure projects easily gives people an impression of China's national ability (Zhang 2015).

4. As China's aid has no political strings attached, it is different from that of Western countries; this, accompanied by its high efficiency, has prompted Pacific Islanders to compare China's assistance with that of other countries. In the process, there will be a change in Pacific Islanders' attitudes towards different donors (Malielegaoi 2016), which will have a psychological impact on Australia and New Zealand.

On this basis, it is worth discussing how China's economic ties with the Pacific Islands will develop and how China's investment in the Pacific Islands will change over the next five to 10 years. There are four main judgements:

1. The economic capacity and economic structure of the Pacific Islands have restricted the space for economic cooperation between China and the Pacific Island countries. Most of the Pacific Islands are small in size and have a singular economic structure. Most of their consumer and industrial goods need to be imported from abroad. Their human resource base is limited and they lack the capacity for sustainable development. Even in the long run, the market capacity of the Pacific Island countries is limited. In addition, the natural environment of the Pacific Islands is very fragile and the people have a strong sense of environmental protection. Under these circumstances, some of their economies are quite underdeveloped, which reduces the Islands' possible paths for economic development and limits the investment space for Chinese enterprises in the region. Given this, it is unrealistic for China to expand its investment in the Pacific Island countries on a large scale and substantially increase the level of trade between the two sides.

2. What kind of return can China get if it increases its assistance to the Pacific Island countries substantially? Some scholars have tried to explain China's assistance to the Pacific Island countries from the perspective of diplomacy competition between mainland China and Taiwan, as six Pacific Island countries maintained official relations with Taiwan until the end of 2018 (Meick et al. 2018; Yu 2015; Zhang 2015).

Competition with Taiwan for diplomatic recognition is undoubtedly an important factor in the relations between China and the Pacific Islands. However, China's trade, investment and assistance to the Pacific Islands are not mainly subject to diplomatic considerations related to Taiwan, otherwise it would be difficult to explain the increase in Chinese investment and assistance to the Pacific Islands during the 'diplomatic truce'. In explaining China's investment and assistance to the Pacific Island countries in terms of Taiwan-related diplomacy competition, there exists a logic problem. That is, China's assistance to Pacific Islands should be directed more to those countries that have not established diplomatic relations with China, or to countries that lack stability in their relations with China, rather than those that have established diplomatic relations with China, especially those countries maintaining good bilateral relations with China, such as PNG, Fiji and Vanuatu.

Some scholars believe that China is spending more on the Pacific Islands in an effort to compete with Australia for influence in the region. If zero-sum thinking is adopted, it could be argued that the rise of one nation's influence may mean the decrease of another's. Some have suggested the need to find ways to counter China's influence in the South Pacific (Colton 2018; Edel 2018; Hegarty 2015). If the struggle for influence is used to explain China's behaviour in the Pacific region, the questions remain: What does China want that influence for? What benefits can this influence bring to China presently and in the future? And can China gain more influence in the region under the countermeasures of Australia and New Zealand? Is it worth the cost China would need to pay for the influence?

It is a fact that China's influence in the Pacific region is on the rise, but competing for influence with countries such as Australia in the region does not seem to be China's policy goal. For China, there are many more valuable regions in which to gain influence, such as Southeast Asia, Northeast Asia, South Asia, Central Asia, Africa and other places. There is no special necessity for China to compete for influence in the Pacific Islands region.

3. The BRI has not significantly increased China's investment and assistance to the Pacific Islands. The introduction and promotion of the BRI can, to a certain extent, explain China's continued aid and investment in the Pacific Islands region, though the total amount is neither very high nor low. Since the BRI was put forward, China has attached great importance to it at all levels, and the Pacific Island countries are on the Belt and Road route.[3] Additionally, China has a huge economic and social mass with a large number of economic

---

3   On 20 June 2017, the State Development and Reform Commission and the State Oceanic Administration specially formulated and released the Vision for Maritime Cooperation under the Belt and Road Initiative, which mentions 'efforts will also be made to jointly build the blue economic passage of China–Oceania–South Pacific' (Belt and Road Portal 2017).

actors. Under such circumstances, it is natural for some enterprises to respond to the BRI and invest in the Pacific Islands region. The problem with this explanation, however, is that Chinese aid and investment to the Pacific Islands did not rise significantly between 2014 and 2016, the first few years after China proposed the BRI. Though Chinese investment in PNG rose sharply in 2013, this was before the BRI was really put into effect. This shows that although the promotion of the BRI helps maintain the interest of Chinese enterprises and society in the Pacific Islands, it is not as much a boost to China's investment and assistance to the Pacific Island countries as people might think.

In addition to the aforementioned points, the increase in the scale of China's investment and aid to the Pacific Island countries has not been very significant over the past few years. It is also difficult to effectively explain the increase in Chinese investment and aid to the Pacific Islands with a single factor (Hayward-Jones 2013). However, the shift in Chinese investment and aid to the Pacific Islands does not appear to be the result of significant, coherent strategic intention.

In a certain sense, China's assistance to the Pacific Islands is also a means for China to fulfill its international responsibilities, engaging in South–South cooperation with developing countries and jointly responding to the challenge of climate change. For example, Article 4 of the Measures for the Administration of Foreign Aid (for Trial Implementation) promulgated by the Ministry of Commerce (2014) clearly states that:

> Foreign aid shall respect the sovereignty of the recipient country, shall not interfere in the internal affairs of the recipient country, shall strive to alleviate and eliminate poverty, improve the livelihood and ecological environment of the recipient country, promote the recipient's economic development and social progress, and enhance the recipient's capacity for autonomous development, consolidate and develop friendly and cooperative relations with the recipients.

4. The response of countries such as Australia will have some impact on China's Pacific Island policy. Australia has long provided substantial economic assistance to the Pacific Islands. It is difficult for Australia to obtain obvious economic returns from its aid to the Pacific Islands. Providing assistance is an important means for Australia to influence the political situations and policy options of the Pacific Island countries and maintain Australia's dominance in the South Pacific region. The 2017 Foreign Policy White Paper of Australia considers

the Pacific Islands a fundamental strategic interest of Australia and devotes a chapter to its relations with the Pacific Island countries (Australian Government 2017).

Although China believes that the strengthening of its relations with the Pacific Island countries is based on the principle of mutual benefit and win–win cooperation, it also believes that the development of bilateral relations has brought practical benefits to the Pacific Island countries. However, it is also an objective fact that the strengthening of relations between China and the Pacific Island countries will have an impact on China's relations with Australia and New Zealand. One question that arises is whether China is willing to risk damaging its relations with Australia and New Zealand because it wants to strengthen its relations with the Pacific Islands, and to what extent it is willing to take that risk. Relatedly, if Australia and New Zealand put more pressure on some Pacific Island countries to influence their policies towards China, this will affect the attitudes of the Pacific Island countries towards China and thus the relationship between China and the Pacific Island countries.

In the process of developing relations with the Pacific Island countries, China needs to take into account the concerns of Australia and New Zealand. China–Australia relations may deteriorate for other reasons (Beeson 2018), but it is certainly not in China's interests if China's behaviour in the Pacific Islands becomes a major factor in the deterioration of China–Australian relations. This situation should be and can be avoided at the policy level.

Prospects for the development of relations between China and the Pacific Islands

Since 2006, China's trade, investment and aid to the Pacific Islands have greatly increased. President Xi Jinping's visits to Pacific Islands in 2014 and 2018 fully demonstrate the importance China attaches to this region. At the same time, these two visits took place against the background of China's all-around diplomacy in the international arena and President Xi Jinping's participation in the G20 and APEC meetings held in Australia and PNG, respectively. We should not overstate the importance China attaches to the Pacific Island countries.

With regard to the development of relations between China and the Pacific Island countries in the coming years, this chapter makes the following preliminary judgements:

1. Relations with Pacific Island countries are an integral part of China's all-round diplomacy. The development of relations with the Pacific Island countries will not bring China obvious economic and strategic returns, and will even have a certain negative impact on China–Australia and China–New Zealand relations, but China will not stop promoting the development of its relations with the Pacific Island countries because of this. In particular, the Pacific Island countries are an important part of the BRI.

   In terms of China's economic output, which ranks second in the world, the total amount of China's aid and investment to the Pacific Islands, although not low, is not very high. Moreover, its share of China's total foreign aid and outward investment is very low. As a rising power and the world's second largest economy, it is natural for China to maintain relatively good relations with the Pacific Island countries at such a long-term affordable cost. Given Japan and the European Union's long-term investments in the Pacific Islands, China's investment in this region is highly proportionate and reasonable.

2. China's input in the Pacific Island countries will develop steadily, without dramatic rises. When examining the relationship between China and the Pacific Island countries, some Westerners have a feeling that China is entering the Pacific Island countries on a large scale, demonstrating that China attaches importance to the Pacific Islands. They feel there is a strategic design behind this. In fact, what is noteworthy is that although the Chinese president has visited the Pacific Islands twice between 2014 and 2018, the rise in Chinese investment and aid to the Pacific Islands has not been remarkable. With China's size, and considering China's investment in Southeast Asia and Africa in the name of the BRI, China's input in the Pacific Islands could have risen much faster if it had the will, without much economic burden on China.

   Given leaders' visits, the implementation of the BRI and China's attempt to enhance its influence in the international community, China's investment in the Pacific Islands is not rising very fast. This means that even if China's investment in Pacific Island countries rises in the future, it will do so steadily. In fact, over the past several years, the Chinese Government can be said to have shown considerable restraint in increasing input in the Pacific Island countries. If the Chinese Government is more active in encouraging Chinese companies and tourists to visit the Pacific Islands, the resulting Chinese presence in the region may be quite different from what we see now. Considering that Chinese nationals now make more than 120 million international trips a year,[4] and that a small island country like the Maldives receives more than 200,000 Chinese tourists a year, it can be said that the presence of Chinese companies and tourists in the Pacific Islands is relatively not as strong. An important consideration behind this is to avoid too many businesses and tourists going to island countries in a short period of time, thus imposing a burden on the island nations' environments and social economies.

On one hand, China maintains a good relationship with the Pacific Island countries at the current level of resource input, so there is no need for China to increase its input by a large margin. On the other hand, investment and aid to the Pacific Islands is not a big burden for China, so there is no reason for China to lower its input in the region. As a result, in the future, China's input in the Pacific Islands region will likely remain relatively stable. Due to the small size of the Pacific Island countries, the promotion and implementation of individual projects cannot be ruled out as bringing about relatively large fluctuations in the amount of funds invested, but the political significance of such fluctuations should not be exaggerated.

3. China's investment in the Pacific Islands will highly respect the wishes of the island countries. China neither seeks to nor has the ability to establish a sphere of influence in the Pacific Islands region.

China's interest in the Pacific Islands will help improve the strategic position of island countries relative to Australia and New Zealand, enabling them to face Australia and New Zealand more equally. From this perspective, the Pacific Islands' demand for Chinese input will last a long time. On the other hand, geographically, culturally and economically, the Pacific Island countries cannot escape the influence of Australia and New Zealand. The Pacific Island countries do not want to see tensions with Australia and New Zealand caused by their relations with China. The Pacific Island countries have strong tactical

---

4   In 2018, the number of Chinese citizens travelling abroad was 149.72 million and, in 2017, 130.51 million. See the website of the Ministry of Culture and Tourism of the Peope's Republic of China, www.mct.gov.cn/whzx/whyw/201902/t20190212_837270.htm; zwgk.mct.gov.cn/auto255/201802/t20180206_832375.html?keywords.

considerations in developing their relations with China. They will likely try to maintain a balance in their relations with China, Australia and New Zealand.

Due to their small size and relatively limited strength, the Pacific Island countries do not have great international aspirations, lack the ability to withstand the pressure of major power competition, will attach more importance to the acquisition of practical interests and do not want to become bargaining chips in the games of major powers. It is not in the interests of Pacific Island countries to be involved in strategic competition that will cost them a lot.

On the whole, even if China increases investment in the Pacific Island countries, China's influence on them can hardly be greatly enhanced. In relations between the two sides, China lacks the means to effectively restrict the behaviour of the Pacific Island countries. The Pacific Island countries can maintain a great degree of policy freedom in the course of their exchanges with China. In the process of investing resources, China will highly respect the willingness of the Pacific Island countries and avoid the negative consequences of resource input in the Pacific Island countries.

4. China will further understand the importance of respecting the concerns of Australia and New Zealand in developing relations with the Pacific Island countries in the future. Although China will not act in full accordance with the wishes of Australia and New Zealand, it will take into account some of their concerns.

In the trilateral relations among China, Australia and New Zealand and the Pacific Island countries, if China unilaterally increases its investment of resources to the Pacific Island countries, it will stimulate counteraction from Australia and New Zealand. The countermeasures taken by Australia and New Zealand will make China's investment in the Pacific Island countries fail to achieve an ideal outcome. As a result, such an investment increase would have a negative effect on China's relations with Australia and New Zealand, as well as its relations with the Pacific Island countries. This is certainly not a situation China would like to see.

If China and Australia adopt an approach of breaking up each other's influence in the Pacific region, the result will be a lose–lose situation between China and Australia in the region at the expense of China–Australia relations. Chinese investment in the Pacific Island countries is unlikely to yield a reasonable return on its own, and countermeasures taken by Australia will further reduce the long-term return of Chinese investment. From this point of view, China does not want its activities in the Pacific Islands to cause much agitation in the region. China hopes to promote the steady development of its relations with the Pacific Island countries when the overall situation in the region is stable. The idea that China has a comprehensive strategic plan in the Pacific Islands is logically untenable and lacks factual support.

References

ABC News 2017. Undersea Cable Deal with PNG Inked amid Concerns over Chinese Influence in the Pacific. 14 November. www.abc.net.au/news/2017-11-14/png-to-get-new-australia-funded-undersea-internet-cable/9146570

Australian Government 2017. *2017 Foreign Policy White Paper*. Canberra: Commonwealth of Australia. www.dfat.gov.au/publications/minisite/2017-foreign-policy-white-paper/fpwhitepaper/pdf/2017-foreign-policy-white-paper.pdf

Batley, J. 2017. Keep Calm and Step Up: The White Paper's Message on the Pacific. *The Interpreter*, 27 November. Lowy Institute. www.lowyinstitute.org/the-interpreter/keep-calm-and-step-white-paper-message-pacific

Beeson, M. 2018. Calculating Cooperation: Appraisal of China's Influence on Australia [Hezuo de gusuan: pinggu zhongguo dui aodaliya de yingxiangli]. *Journal of Strategy and Decision-making [Zhanlue Juece Yanjiu]* 9(2):68–81.

Belt and Road Portal 2017. Vision for Maritime Cooperation under the Belt and Road Initiative. eng.yidaiyilu.gov.cn/zchj/qwfb/16639.htm

Brant, P. 2013. Chinese Aid in the South Pacific: Linked to Resources? *Asian Studies Review* 37(2):158–177. doi.org/10.1080/10357823.2013.767311

China Business Yearbook Editorial Board 2001–17. *China Business Yearbook*. Beijing: China Commerce and Trade Press.

Colton, G. 2018. Stronger Together: Safeguarding Australia's Security Interests through Closer Pacific Ties. *Analyses*, 4 April. Lowy Institute.

Connolly, P.J. 2016. Engaging China's New Foreign Policy in the South Pacific. *Australian Journal of International Affairs* 70(5):484–505. doi.org/10.1080/10357718.2016.1194805

Department of Defence 2016. *2016 Defence White Paper*. Canberra: Commonwealth of Australia. www.defence.gov.au/WhitePaper/Docs/2016-Defence-White-Paper.pdf

Department of Foreign Affairs and Trade (DFAT) 2018. *Stepping-Up Australia's Pacific Engagement with Our Pacific Family*. www.dfat.gov.au/geo/pacific/engagement/Pages/stepping-up-australias-pacific-engagement.aspx

Dornan, M. 2018. Australia's Pacific Island Myopia. *The Diplomat*, 13 July. thediplomat.com/2018/07/australias-pacific-island-myopia

Dornan, M. and P. Brant 2014. Chinese Assistance in the Pacific: Agency, Effectiveness and the Role of Pacific Island Governments. *Asia & the Pacific Policy Studies* 1(2):349–63. doi.org/10.1002/app5.35

DW News 2018. Australia to Spend Billions to Counter China in Pacific Islands. 8 November. www.dw.com/en/australia-to-spend-billions-to-counter-china-in-pacific-islands/a-46202867

Dziedzic, S. 2018. Which Country Gives the Most Aid to Pacific Island Nations: The Answer Might Surprise You. *ABC News*, 9 August. www.abc.net.au/news/2018-08-09/aid-to-pacific-island-nations/10082702

Edel, C. 2018. How to Counter China's Influence in the South Pacific: The US and Its Allies Need to Coordinate Their Efforts. *Foreign Affairs*, 13 November. www.foreignaffairs.com/articles/china/2018-11-13/how-counter-chinas-influence-south-pacific

Hanson, F. 2011. China in the Pacific: The New Banker in Town. *Policy Brief*. Sydney: Lowy Institute for International Policy.

Hayward-Jones, J. 2013. Big Enough for All of Us: Geo-Strategic Competition in the Pacific Islands. *Analyses*, 11 May. Lowy Institute. www.lowyinstitute.org/publications/big-enough-all-us-geo-strategic-competition-pacific-islands

Hegarty, M. 2015. China's Growing Influence in South-West Pacific: Australian Policies that Could Respond to China's Intentions and Objectives. *Indo-Pacific Strategic Papers*. Canberra: Centre for Defence and Strategic Studies, Australian Defence College.

Huawei 2016. Huawei Marine Helps Papua New Guinea Build a National Broadband Transmission Network. 11 October. www.huawei.com/en/press-events/news/2016/10/Huawei-PapuaNewGuinea-Broadband-Transmission-Network

Huawei 2017. Huawei Marine Signs Submarine Cable Contract in Solomon Islands. 7 July. www.huawei.com/en/press-events/news/2017/7/Huawei Marine-Submarine-Cable-Solomon

Information Office of the State Council of the People's Republic of China 2014. *China's Foreign Aid (2014) (White Paper)*. Ministry of Foreign Affairs of China. www.fmprc.gov.cn/ce/cohk/chn/xwdt/jzzh/t1173111.htm

Lowy Institute 2019. Pacific Aid Map. pacificaidmap.lowyinstitute.org

Lum, T. and B. Vaughn 2007. The Southwest Pacific: US Interests and China's Growing Influence. *CRS Report for Congress*, Order Code RL34086, Congressional Research Service.

Malielegaoi, T.L.S. 2016. Opening Address. In M. Powles (ed.), *China and the Pacific*. Wellington: Victoria University Press, 25–27.

McAslan, H.R. 2013. China's Increasing Influence in Oceania: Implications for the United States. *USAWC Strategy Research Project*. Carlisle Barracks: US Army War College.

Meick, E., M. Ker and H.M. Chan 2018. China's Engagement in the Pacific Islands: Implications for the United States. *Staff Research Report*. US–China Economic and Security Review Commission, 14 June.

Ministry of Commerce of China 2014. *Measures for the Administration of Foreign Aid (for Trial Implementation)*. Ministry of Commerce of China, 15 November. yws.mofcom.gov.cn/article/m/a/201411/20141100803904.shtml

Ministry of Education of the People's Republic of China 2017. Data to See Changes in Education: Opening to the Outside World. 28 September. www. moe.gov.cn/jyb_xwfb/xw_fbh/moe_2069/xwfbh_2017n/xwfb_20170928/ sfcl/201709/t20170928_315527.html

Mitchell, T.E. 2018. Protecting the South Pacific. *The Strategy Bridge*, 27 February. thestrategybridge.org/the-bridge/2018/2/27/protecting-the-south-pacific

Peters, W. 2018. Shifting the Dial. Speech to Lowy Institute, 1 March. www.bee hive.govt.nz/speech/shifting-dial

Riordan, P. 2018. Coalition Attack on China over Pacific Aid. *The Australian*, 10 January.

Smyth, J. 2017. Huawei's Undersea Cable Project Raises Red Flag in Australia. *Financial Times*, 28 December. www.ft.com/content/96513f58-d959-11e7-a039-c64b1c09b482

Society in All Respects and Strive for the Great Success of Socialism with Chinese Characteristics for a New Era. Delivered at the 19th National Congress of the Communist Party of China, Beijing, 18 October. www.xinhuanet.com/english/special/2017-11/03/c_136725942.htm

Wesley-Smith, T. 2007. China in Oceania: New Forces in Pacific Politics. *Pacific Islands Policy*. Honolulu: East-West Center.

Windybank, S. 2005. The China Syndrome. *Policy* 21(2):28–33.

World Bank 2019. World Bank Open Data. data.worldbank.org

Wroe, D. 2017. Solomon Islands Undersea Cable Red-Flagged by Australia's Spy Agencies Dogged by Donation Allegations. *The Sydney Morning Herald*, 19 August. www.smh.com.au/politics/federal/solomon-islands-undersea-cable-redflagged-by-australias-spy-agencies-dogged-by-donation-allegations-2017 0818-gxzlgd.html

Xi, J. 2017. Secure a Decisive Victory in Building a Moderately Prosperous Society in All Respects and Strive for the Great Success of Socialism with Chinese Characteristics for a New Era. Delivered at the 19th National Congress of the Communist Party of China, Beijing, 18 October. www.xinhuanet.com/english/download/Xi_Jinping's_report_at_19th_CPC_National_Congress.pdf

Yu, C. 2015. Pacific Islands in China's Strategy in the 21st Century. In C. Yu (ed.), *Annual Report on Development of Oceania (2014–2015)*. Beijing: Social Sciences Academic Press, 1–14.

Zhang, J. 2015. China's Role in the Pacific Islands Region. In R. Azizian and C. Cramer (eds), *Regionalism, Security & Cooperation in Oceania*. Honolulu: The Daniel K Inouye Asia-Pacific Center for Security Studies, 43–56.

8

Domestic Political Reforms and China's Diplomacy in the Pacific: The Case of Foreign Aid

Denghua Zhang

Introduction

China's rise in the Pacific[1] is in the spotlight and provoking growing concern from traditional powers. Beijing has substantially increased its engagement with the region since 2006. Chinese President Xi Jinping paid his first official visit to Papua New Guinea (PNG) in November 2018. On the sidelines of APEC held in Port Moresby, he also met with leaders of the eight Pacific Island countries (PICs) that have diplomatic relations with China. The leaders agreed to elevate the China–PICs relationship to a comprehensive strategic partnership of mutual respect and common development (China MFA 2018), although China uses this term loosely in diplomacy and the meaning remains ambiguous. To push back against China's influence in the region, US Vice President Mike Pence announced at the APEC CEO summit that the US would partner with Australia and PNG to develop Lombrum Naval Base on PNG's Manus Island and

---

1   In this chapter, the Pacific region refers to the 14 Pacific sovereign states.

jointly 'protect sovereignty and maritime rights of the Pacific Islands' (Pence 2018). Competition between China and traditional powers will most likely continue and intensify in the Pacific.

At the domestic level, the Xi Jinping administration has been conducting political reforms that could have a significant impact on China's engagement with other countries including Pacific Island states. China's diplomacy is becoming more proactive and assertive. Since March 2018, Beijing has been implementing a new round of government restructuring, much of which is closely linked to its diplomacy. For example, in April 2018 China established its first stand-alone aid agency: the China International Development Cooperation Agency (CIDCA). This vice-ministerial organisation, designed to strengthen the planning and monitoring of Chinese aid, has been placed under the supervision of top Chinese diplomats Yang Jiechi and Wang Yi. In addition, the Office of Overseas Chinese Affairs under the State Council, which is responsible for liaising with the Chinese diaspora, has been merged into the United Front Work Department, a powerful organisation of the Chinese Communist Party.

This chapter aims to add a new perspective to the literature on China in the Pacific. By adopting Anthony Giddens' theory of structuration on structure and agency, the chapter aims to analyse how China's recent domestic political reforms will affect its engagement with PICs, which is rarely touched on in the literature. As foreign aid is a crucial element of China's growing outreach in the Pacific and has been in the spotlight due to accusations such as ineffectiveness and the use of debt-for-equity swaps, this chapter will examine three questions through the prism of Chinese foreign aid: (1) What are China's national interests in the Pacific? (2) How have China's evolving national interests guided various Chinese actors' work on aid and informed structure changes? (3) In what ways have these actors reshaped China's national interests and the bureaucratic structure? The impact of CIDCA on China's aid program in the Pacific will be included in the discussion. I will argue that different Chinese actors have been involved in a fierce competition for influence in decision-making on aid, and that diplomacy will have more weight in a CIDCA-led Chinese aid system—with a consequent impact on the Pacific region.

Structure and agency theory

The relationship between structure and agent is a recurrent theme in social sciences. According to the theory of structuration developed in the 1980s by Anthony Giddens, a prominent British sociologist, structure refers generally to rules and resources, and agency is defined as actors' capability to do things in the first place (1984:9, 24). The constitution of agents and structures represent a duality as structure is both constraining and enabling, while the activities of agents constitute and reconstitute social systems (ibid.:25). Constructivists in international relations take the discussion further. For example, Alexander Wendt argues that structure is not static and predetermined but subject to actors' mutual interaction (1992).

Based on Giddens' theory of structuration, a state's national interests inform the creation of its norms and allocation of resources, and form the bureaucratic structure. The bureaucratic structure conditions the actions of actors. However, purposeful actors are not passive but active. They use their agency to alter the state's national interests and transform/reshape the structure. It is noteworthy that the structuration theory is not without criticism, such as it is an analytical rather than substantive theory and does not generate hypothesis (Wendt 1987). This chapter does not intend to engage in these debates or make theoretical contributions, but rather aims to use Giddens' theory as a new approach to analyse China's diplomacy and aid program in the Pacific. Data sources for the research comprise existing scholarly works, interviews and the author's own observation of China–PICs relations as a researcher and former practitioner.

China's national interests in the Pacific

Pacific states are not in the top tier of China's foreign policy agenda. Chinese diplomats categorise the Pacific as part of the broad developing world that China is keen to align with. To be more specific, Pacific states are referred to as part of China's 'greater periphery' (*da zhoubian,* 大周边), a term first used loosely to label China's neighbouring Asian countries and then extended to include the Pacific (Zhang 2017:45). Nonetheless, China's national interests in the Pacific region are multifaceted and evolving.

The diplomatic competition between China (referred to as the People's Republic of China (PRC) or mainland China in China's official discourses) and Taiwan (or the Republic of China) has dominated China's diplomacy in the Pacific. The Chinese Government defines it as an issue of paramount importance to China's territorial integrity and national reunification (Yang 2011). Obtaining Pacific states' support of the One China policy has remained a central task of the Chinese Government since the 1970s when China started to establish official relations with Pacific states such as Fiji and Samoa. Although most of the 14 sovereign Pacific countries are small states and have limited influence in international affairs, they have an equal vote to large states at the UN. Most Pacific states are also highly dependent on foreign aid. These two factors have made PICs important players that both China and Taiwan try to court in the diplomatic wrestling. As Table 1 shows, this battle has been tense and some Pacific states have switched their positions back and forth but, globally, the number of Taiwan's diplomatic allies is decreasing. Since February 2016, another eight countries (Gambia, Sao Tome and Principe, Panama, the Dominican Republic, Burkina Faso, El Salvador, Solomon Islands and Kiribati) moved their recognition to China, reducing Taiwan's diplomatic allies to 15. Among them, four were from the Pacific; the sheer number of PICs now supporting China gives the Pacific region more importance in China's diplomatic competition with Taiwan in the future.

Table 1. Diplomatic landscape for China and Taiwan in the Pacific

Pacific country	Taiwan	PRC	Taiwan	PRC
Fiji		5 Nov. 1975		
Samoa	29 May 1972	6 Nov. 1975		
PNG		12 Oct. 1976	5 July 1999	21 July 1999
Vanuatu		26 Mar. 1982	3 Nov. 2004	11 Nov. 2004
Federated States of Micronesia		11 Sept. 1989		
Cook Islands		25 July 1997		
Tonga	10 Apr. 1972	2 Nov. 1998		
Niue		12 Dec. 2007		
Solomon Islands	24 Mar. 1983	21 Sept. 2019		
Kiribati		25 June 1980	7 Nov. 2003	27 Sept. 2019
Pacific states that recognise Taiwan				
Tuvalu	19 Sept. 1979			
Nauru	4 May 1980	21 July 2002	14 May 2005	
Palau			29 Dec. 1999	
Marshall Islands		16 Nov. 1990	20 Nov. 1998	

Source: Compiled by author.

More broadly, it is wise to position the Pacific states in China's overall diplomacy towards the developing world (Wesley-Smith 2013). The huge differences in political systems and values and the 'century of humiliation' (1840–1949) have made the Chinese Government distrustful of developed countries at a deep level and created a strong sense of insecurity (Callahan 2012; Gries 2004), which forced China to seek support from developing countries. The need to develop a unifying identity with other developing countries has been a fundamental principle in China's foreign policy since the establishment of the PRC by the Communist Party in 1949. Beijing believes that the common identity of being developing countries and a shared history of being victims of colonisation will draw China and these countries together. China also considers developing countries to be a reliable resource that China can call upon for support when needed, such as the PRC's admission to the UN Security Council in November 1971 and after Tiananmen Square in 1989 when developed countries imposed sanctions on China. This strategy is a crucial reason why China sticks firmly to its identity as a developing country despite the fact that it is now the world's second largest economy and the largest emerging donor. It also explains why Chinese leaders have repeatedly highlighted that 'both China and Pacific island countries are developing countries' in meetings with their counterparts from the Pacific. In a recent example, in his group meeting in November 2018 in Port Moresby with the leaders of the then eight PICs that had diplomatic relations with China, Xi Jinping began by emphasising that 'China and Pacific island countries are all developing countries in the Asia Pacific region, they have been good friends … good partners … and good brothers' (China MFA 2018). Relations with Pacific states also enables China to demonstrate that big and small countries are equal partners. China has lavished red-carpet treatment on Pacific leaders during their visits to China.

Guided by this policy of fostering closer relations with developing countries, China has intensified its engagement with the military government in Fiji since the coup in 2006 while the latter was under severe sanctions from traditional powers, especially Australia and New Zealand. Fiji has become the regional hub and one of China's main diplomatic, trade and aid partners in the region. In February 2009, when he was China's vice president, Xi Jinping paid a stopover visit to Fiji despite open opposition from Australia and New Zealand. China has also substantially increased its assistance and financial support to Fiji. As the Lowy Institute (2019) in Sydney estimates, between 2011 and 2017, China's total aid committed and spent in Fiji exceeded US$379.2 million and US$316.7 million respectively, making China the second largest donor behind Australia.[2] Chinese ambassadors dispatched to Fiji are more seasoned career diplomats compared with those assigned to other Pacific states.

China's economic interest in the Pacific region is minimal in the context of its overall global trade. In 2017, China's exports to and imports from the 14 PICs, as well as French Polynesia and New Caledonia, constituted 0.21 per cent and 0.19 per cent of China's global merchandise trade (Pacific Trade and Investment Office 2018:5). China's economic activities have largely focused on extractive industries in resources-rich PICs, with the PNG Ramu nickel mine China's largest single investment in the region (US$1.4 billion). In 2017, fuels represented 43.4 per cent of China's imports from PNG and 25.8 per cent of China's total imports from the region (ibid.:3–4). Since December 2014, China has committed to purchasing 2 million tonnes of PNG liquefied natural gas (worth US$1 billion) per annum for 20 years. In 2017, China also imported wood products from Solomon Islands to the value of US$483.2 million, accounting for 13.9 per cent of China's total imports from the Pacific (ibid.).

China's military ambitions in the Pacific are limited at present but may grow in the near future. Using the 'three island chains' theory adopted by China's People's Liberation Army Navy (PLAN) as the benchmark—although Chinese interpretations are diverse and multifaceted (Erickson and Wuthnow 2016; Pedrozo 2010)—the Pacific region is an important part of the second and third island chains. At present, China's PLAN has been preoccupied with maritime disputes along the first island chain in the South and East China seas and it has not given much attention to the Pacific. PLAN's engagement with PICs is still superficial, consisting of donations of non-combatant vehicles and uniforms, construction/upgrade of military hospitals and visits from PLAN medical ships (the *Peace Ark*). However, there are signs that things are changing and that the Pacific may occupy a more significant position in China's military strategies. Since Xi Jinping took power in 2013, the Chinese Government has apparently started to move away from 'hiding the capacity and keeping a low profile' (*taoguang yanghui*, 韬光养晦), a principle that had guided China's diplomacy since the 1990s. China's diplomacy has become more

---

2   Over the same period, Australian total aid committed and spent in Fiji was about US$551.8 million and US$408.5 million respectively.

ambitious and assertive (Brady 2017:239–40). China PLAN has also stepped up efforts to move from a green-water navy to a blue-water navy with notable progress. It has had two aircraft carriers constructed and a third is under way. In April 2018, President Xi Jinping, who is also Chairman of the Central Military Commission, reviewed China's PLAN in the South China Sea, the largest of its kind in PLAN history. He called on PLAN to build a 'world first-class navy'. PLAN leadership's response to this call casts some light on their strategic thinking:

> From the geo-strategic perspective, China is placed in a disadvantaged oceanic environment, with coastal waters semi-enclosed and separated by island chains, and access to the sea blocked by other powers … Our country has entered into a crucial stage of moving from a land power to both a land and sea power … PLAN is the most appropriate and needed strategic force within PLA to go global (*zou chuqu*) (PLAN Party Committee 2018).

With increased long-range projection capabilities and heightened US–China strategic competition in the Indo-Pacific region, it is likely that PLAN will develop substantial engagement with Pacific states in the future. However, whether and to what extent China can successfully build a closer strategic and defence relationship with these Pacific states is questionable. The 2018 announcement by the US to build the Lombrum Naval Base in PNG with Australia and PNG, and speculation around China's intention to build a naval base in Vanuatu, reveal traditional powers' growing concerns about China's military ambitions in the Pacific.

China's diaspora might be caught in social unrest in some Pacific countries in the future. If this happens, it is more likely that China would arrange charter flights rather than use military forces to evacuate affected Chinese citizens. The Chinese Government adopted this approach during the riots in Solomon Islands and Tonga in 2006. Compared with Africa and Asia, Chinese diaspora and companies, especially state-owned enterprises, in the Pacific are much smaller in number.

The role of structure

The first half of this section will examine how China's national interests in the Pacific have shaped its bureaucratic structure for foreign aid work in the region. The second half discusses some new changes, especially CIDCA's impact on Chinese aid in the Pacific.

Chinese aid to Pacific states consists of grants, interest-free loans and concessional loans. Before the establishment of CIDCA, the Ministry of Commerce (MOFCOM) managed grants and interest-free loans. The China Export-Import Bank (Exim Bank) managed concessional loans, subject to the approval of MOFCOM as the supervisor. Established in 1994 as a vice-ministerial level agency, China Exim Bank is the only policy bank to provide concessional loans and has about 600 staff. The Corporate Business Department, which is in charge of commercial loans and especially export buyers' credits, and the Concessional Loan Department are the two most important sections of the bank and each has about 100 staff.[3]

When MOFCOM was in charge of Chinese aid, the State Council required that it consult China's Ministry of Foreign Affairs (MFA) on aid allocation. MFA is responsible for China's bilateral relations with partner countries including in the Pacific. Based on the needs of China's diplomacy, MFA provided advice to MOFCOM on whether China should provide aid to the targeted recipient country. To secure diplomatic support from Pacific states on the One China policy, MFA encouraged MOFCOM to deliver more aid to the region, as well as favouring debt relief[4] for Pacific states. About five to six officials in the Division of South Pacific and Canada under MFA's Department of North American and Oceanian Affairs manage China's bilateral relations with the Pacific.

Provincial-level aid complements Chinese aid from the central government to the Pacific. In recognition of its close diaspora links with the Pacific, Guangdong Province is tasked with engaging Pacific states and providing provincial-level aid. The vast majority of Chinese diaspora in Fiji and Samoa are from this province and, in recent years, Guangdong's engagement with PICs has increased. The main activities include short-term medical tours (*song yi shang dao*, 送医上岛) and visits by acrobatic/arts troupes for celebrations. The medical tour program started in 2012. It consists of medical specialists of different types selected from hospitals in Guangdong and are led by a senior official from the foreign affairs office or health department of the province. Between 2012 and 2016, the medical tours went to all eight Pacific states with diplomatic relations with China, except Niue (Wang and Yu 2017:201–03).

---

3   Former China Exim Bank official, July 2018. Interview with author.
4   Debt relief means partial or total remission of debt.

Given the critical importance of decreasing Taiwan's influence in the Pacific, foreign aid is the main component of China's engagement with Pacific states. As noted earlier, MOFCOM had been China's central organisation tasked with managing foreign aid until the establishment of CIDCA in April 2018. MOFCOM's Department of Foreign Aid, and more specifically the Division of South Pacific, was responsible for Chinese aid to Pacific states. Within this department, three divisions focused on Africa, two divisions worked on Asia while one each managed Chinese aid in West Africa, North Africa and Europe, Latin America and South Pacific (China MOFCOM 2015). This structure alone is a telling sign that Africa and Asia receive most of China's attention in the area of aid; the Pacific does not receive particular attention.

By providing aid to Pacific states, the Chinese Government also aims to safeguard its growing economic interests in the region. A good bilateral relationship provides a supportive environment for Chinese trade and investment activities in these countries. Moreover, the agreements for Chinese concessional loans require that the project be awarded to Chinese contractors, especially state-owned enterprises. This is a crucial step for Chinese companies to establish themselves in the Pacific market, which is new to them, before they move on to commercial projects.

Military aid is a key tool for China to strengthen military ties with counterparts in the region and protect its strategic interests, which are likely to grow in the near future. Similar to Chinese military aid to other regions, the PLA manages the budget for Chinese military aid to the Pacific and is deliberately non-transparent. It is even more opaque than Chinese aid managed by MOFCOM. Although China's current military aid to PICs is limited in value and scope, Chinese universities are training military officers from the region through scholarship programs and short-term training. For example, in September 2018, Esita Batiniqila became the first female officer from the Fiji Navy to be awarded a four-year Chinese scholarship to study navy ship service command and navy military science at China's Dalian University (Kumar 2018). Such training could have a long-term impact on China–Pacific military relations.

China has also increased its engagement with Pacific media, expecting outlets to portray a benign image of China to the public. This engagement is part of a move to 'tell China's stories well, present a true, multi-dimensional, and panoramic view of China', as envisaged by Xi Jinping when he addressed the 19th National Party Congress (Xinhua 2017).

Since the establishment of a branch of China's official news agency, Xinhua, in Suva in September 2010—the first in the Pacific—China has funded a growing number of Pacific journalists to visit China or attend professional training in China. For example, the MFA's Information Department organised tours for Pacific Island journalists in China in 2013 and 2017. Another delegation of Pacific media visited Beijing and Fujian Province (the main source of Chinese diaspora in Tonga) in 2015 at the invitation of the All-China Journalists' Association, an organisation led by the Chinese Communist Party. Yet, these efforts are compromised by other activities; in November 2018, Pacific journalists were denied entry to report on the meeting between leaders of China and Pacific states in Port Moresby in November 2018.

Recent changes

The Xi Jinping administration has been tightening the Chinese Communist Party's control on government policies including foreign policy. At the 19th Party Congress held in October 2017, which approved his second term, Xi announced that his administration would 'ensure Party leadership over all work' and 'the Party exercises overall leadership over all areas of endeavor in every part of the country' (Xinhua 2017), a lexicon used by former leader Mao Zedong during the Cultural Revolution. Although the Communist Party has already been leading Chinese foreign aid work, even more control could ensue in the future.

The newly established CIDCA will have a significant impact on Chinese aid to the Pacific. In March 2018, China's State Council announced the plan to establish this agency, which is designed to 'do overall planning and coordinating on major foreign aid issues, offer advice and advance the country's reforms in matters involving foreign aid … identify major programs, supervise and evaluate implementation of such programs' (Y. Zhang 2018). The implementation of aid projects was left with the existing executing agencies. These include three agencies affiliated to MOFCOM: the Executive Bureau of International Economic Cooperation (responsible for complete projects—turnkey projects or *chengtao xiangmu,* 成套项目—and technical cooperation projects); China International Centre for Economic and Technical Exchanges (responsible for in-kind donations); and the Academy for International Business Officials (responsible for training programs). Other line ministries such as the ministries of agriculture and education continue to provide foreign aid in their specialised areas. China Exim Bank remains responsible for concessional loans.

The Belt and Road Initiative (BRI) will be a significant factor in Chinese foreign aid in the region; indeed, CIDCA is largely designed to facilitate the implementation of BRI, a signature project of Xi Jinping and his diplomatic legacy. Xi has relentlessly promoted this initiative during his official meetings with leaders from other countries. As of January 2020, all 10 partner countries in the Pacific had signed up to BRI (see Table 2), with PNG the first in the region to sign on. In November 2018, cooperation under BRI featured in the bilateral and group meetings between Xi and Pacific leaders in Port Moresby, with incentives offered to attract Pacific states' participation in BRI. For example, Vanuatu and China signed the MOU on BRI cooperation on 9 November 2018; Xi then announced the MOU during his bilateral meeting with Vanuatu's Prime Minister, Charlot Salwai, a week later in Port Moresby. China also signed a further six agreements with Vanuatu, including economic and technical cooperation (grants provision); a framework for concessional loans; a protocol on debt relief; three MOUs on human resource development cooperation; exchanges between China's Guangdong Province and Vanuatu; and the establishment of a joint economic and trade commission between China's MOFCOM and Vanuatu's Ministry of Foreign Affairs (Vanuatu Daily Post 2018). Similarly, prior to the bilateral meeting between Xi and Cook Islands Prime Minister Henry Puna, China signed the MOU on BRI with Cook Islands and provided a grant of US$6.8 million to the Pacific state (Radio New Zealand 2018).

BRI is even contributing to China's debt relief for Pacific countries. Tonga has linked its participation in BRI to the debt relief offered by China. On the margins of APEC in 2018, Tonga entered into BRI and received a five-year extension for repayment of debts owed to China.[5] In stark contrast, Tonga's requests in recent years for debt relief had failed to gain any traction. Tonga's then prime minister, 'Akilisi Pohiva, had attempted to unify Pacific states to press Beijing for loan forgiveness and was openly mocked by Chinese official media, *The Global Times*, as a greedy move amounting to 'asking for the cow when milk is given' (Liu and Zhao 2018).

---

5   A similar five-year extension was granted in 2013.

It is most likely that China will continue to frame its cooperation with PICs under BRI, as it has done in other regions—and Pacific states that extend more support to BRI could receive more Chinese aid.

Table 2. PICs signing up to the Belt and Road Initiative

PICs	Time, Venue and Occasion
PNG	June 2018, Beijing, during former prime minister Peter O'Neil's visit to China.
Niue	July 2018, Niue, signed by the Chinese ambassador to New Zealand (also accredited to Niue) and Prime Minister Sir Toke Talagi.
Samoa	September 2018, Beijing, during Prime Minister Tuilaepa Malielegaoi's visit to China.
FSM	November 2018, Port Moresby, during the meeting between former president Peter Christian and Chinese President Xi Jinping.
Vanuatu	November 2018, Port Vila, signed by the Chinese ambassador to Vanuatu and the Government of Vanuatu.
Fiji	November 2018, Suva, signed by the Chinese ambassador to Fiji and the permanent secretary of the Office of the Prime Minister of Fiji.
Cook Islands	November 2018, Wellington, signed by the Chinese embassy in New Zealand with the Government of Cook Islands.
Tonga	November 2018, Port Moresby, during the meeting between former prime minister 'Akilisi Pohiva and Chinese President Xi Jinping.
Solomon Islands	October 2019, Beijing, during Prime Minister Manasseh Sogavare's visit to China.
Kiribati	January 2020, Beijing, during President Taneti Maamau's visit to China.

Source: Compiled by author.

A heightened geopolitical competition between traditional powers and China will also affect China's aid program in the Pacific. China's rise in the region has triggered grave concerns about China's intentions and the erosion of traditional powers' interests. In response, traditional powers have embarked on a mission to contain China's influence. In November 2017, the Trump administration introduced its Indo-Pacific strategy, which largely targets China. As part of the effort to implement the strategy, the US Government has merged its Overseas Private Investment Corporation and USAID's Development Credit Authority to facilitate provision of loans and compete with China in the infrastructure sector in developing countries.

In Australia, both the Coalition Government and the opposition Australian Labor Party endorsed in 2019 a plan to provide loan facilities to Pacific Island states for infrastructure development. Similarly, the New Zealand Government is reenergising its regional approach and increasing technical and financial assistance to PICs. Clearly, these decisions have been taken in response to China's growing presence in the region. Powers outside the immediate region, such as Japan and India, are also devoting more resources to the Pacific amid China's rise. At the eighth Pacific Islands leaders meeting in May 2018, Japan committed US$515.8 million (55 billion yen) to the region over three years, and funds for more than 5,000 Pacific Islanders through human resources development and people-to-people exchanges (Japan MOFA 2018). Although India's aid program is small in the Pacific, it is increasing notably. The Indian Government increased its annual grant aid to each of the 14 Pacific states from US$100,000 to US$125,000 in 2009, and further to US$200,000 in 2014 (D. Zhang 2018:7). In November 2014 and April 2016, India also pledged two lines of credit, worth US$75 million and US$100 million, for Fiji and PNG respectively (ibid.).

In the near future, the dynamics of geopolitical competition in the Pacific coupled with China's growing strategic ambitions, could force China to increase its diplomatic and economic engagement with Pacific Island states to protect China's national interests. Geopolitical competition with traditional powers could gain more significance in China's diplomacy towards the region, making it another primary factor after the status of Taiwan. The weight of Pacific Island states in China's overall diplomacy could increase in the long term.

Actors and their agency

Actors involved in China's aid activities in the Pacific are active implementers. While their actions are shaped by China's bureaucratic structure and driven by their own interests, they also help define Chinese national interests and reshape the structure. The Party has the final say, but different ministries and other actors compete with each other for power and resources, and wield influence in aid policymaking and implementation.

Competition between MOFCOM and MFA is prominent in this game. As the two most important ministries in China's aid program, their competition for control of Chinese aid resources has persisted since the 1950s when China started to provide foreign aid. In August 1952, China set up the Ministry of Foreign Trade, the predecessor of MOFCOM, to manage Chinese foreign aid, which was then mostly in the form of in-kind donations. Compared with MFA, the Ministry of Foreign Trade was in a better position to deliver aid because it could instruct its subordinate export and import companies to purchase materials for provision to recipient countries. From this point, MOFCOM remained the main custodian of the Chinese aid program until the establishment of CIDCA. Another reason for MOFCOM's control of Chinese aid is that former MOFCOM ministers were promoted to higher positions in the State Council or the Party than their counterparts from MFA. As a result, despite MFA's occasional proposals that it take control of the aid program, the central government has always ruled in MOFCOM's favour (Zhang and Smith 2017:2336).

Chinese embassies overseas, including in the Pacific, provide a new window to observe the subtle battle between MFA and MOFCOM on aid management. Normally the ambassadors are career diplomats selected within MFA.[6] Officials in the Economic and Commercial Counsellor's office come from MOFCOM or subordinate agencies at provincial/city levels. In principle, commercial officials need to receive the political leadership of the ambassador, report to the latter on aid issues and take into account his/her advice on aid delivery. Differences may arise, as commercial officials tend to consider economic benefits for China while the ambassador places greater weight on China's diplomatic interests. These two types of interests can be in conflict on some occasions. For example, provision of substantial loans to a resource-low country may not produce tangible economic returns for China, but is conducive to China's diplomatic objectives such as winning support for China on Taiwan or the South China Sea. Where such conflict arises, the Economic and Commercial Counsellor's office will wait for final instructions from MOFCOM rather than MFA, although MOFCOM and MFA may consult

---

6   In recent years, the Chinese Government has selected a growing number of senior officials from other ministries and provinces to serve as ambassadors in Chinese embassies overseas. In the Pacific, current Chinese ambassadors to Samoa and Vanuatu used to work in China's Communist Youth League and Heilongjiang province respectively. The impact of non-MFA ambassadors on Chinese diplomacy and aid in the Pacific is unclear.

each other in Beijing. Also, the commercial offices will report directly to MOFCOM and only copy MFA in. These offices in large countries have more budget and autonomy and have separate office buildings from the embassies. In the Pacific, China's Economic and Commercial Counsellor's office in PNG has its own office building.

Other line ministries in China have different organisational interests from those of MFA and MOFCOM. These ministries are responsible for aid delivery in their own areas and have specialised budgets, which represent a small proportion of Chinese total foreign aid spending. Their main interest is to deliver their aid to Pacific states well and maintain this business. Through providing foreign aid, the line ministries are keen to increase professional engagement with Pacific states in areas such as agriculture, health and education. For example, China's medical cooperation with PNG on malaria control presents an opportunity for Chinese experts to test and apply malaria technologies in a new environment.[7] The implementation of line ministries' aid projects are shaped directly by the agency of the Chinese experts involved, as they are motivated by a variety of factors to work overseas. Some of the motives include a sense of glory as aid workers, economic benefits (the salary overseas is a few times higher), less family burden (for senior level experts), career bottleneck at home, and vision expansion (Lu et al. 2015:17–18). The agency of these aid experts can be constrained by other factors. For example, the tenure for Chinese agricultural aid experts in the Pacific is normally two years, which is too short a period to gain familiarity with the local agricultural situation and apply their skills.

China Exim Bank has played a growing role in Chinese aid in the Pacific. Since 2006, concessional loans have become China's largest aid component in the region. The Chinese Government committed concessional loans to Pacific states to the value of US$463.1 million (RMB3 billion) at the first China–Pacific Economic Development and Cooperation Forum in Fiji in April of that year, which marks the beginning of China's concessional loans to the region. A similar US$1 billion loan facility was announced in November 2013. China Exim Bank officials on the ground enjoy plenty of autonomy on loan implementation.[8] The bank has closer relations with MOFCOM than with MFA. The approaches of Exim Bank, MOFCOM and MFA to debt relief requests from recipient countries can also differ.

---

7   Chinese medical aid scholar and practitioner, August 2015. Interview with author.
8   Former Chinese aid official, July 2018. Interview with author.

In recent years, the rapid growth of Chinese concessional loans in PICs has triggered debt-for-equity concerns—that is, that China may seek to control strategic assets in recipient countries when they default on loan repayment. MOFCOM and China Exim Bank, in particular the latter, require recipient countries to honour loan repayment. The careers of bank officials who approved the loans in the first place would be damaged if recipient countries defaulted on repayment. MFA officials, however, are inclined to support repayment extension or even loan forgiveness for the sake of China's bilateral relations with the recipient country. Currently, it is more likely that China will allow Pacific countries to postpone loan repayment rather than write the loans off.

The role of Chinese enterprises as aid contractors in the Pacific deserves greater analysis than is currently discussed in the literature. Chinese enterprises are attracted to the Pacific market, which is under-explored compared to other regions. State/province/city-owned enterprises have implemented Chinese aid projects in PICs and through those projects established themselves. Examples include the:

- China Civil Engineering Construction Corporation (Fa'onelua International Convention Centre in Tonga)
- China Rail First Group (Nabouwalu highway project in Fiji)
- China Harbor Engineering Company (National Capital District Commission road upgrade in Port Moresby)
- Guangdong Foreign Construction Company (University of Goroka dormitory project phase 2–4)
- China Jiangxi Corporation for International Economic and Technical Cooperation (International Convention Centre in Port Moresby).

Such companies operating in the Pacific receive political guidance from Chinese embassies. They engage principally with the Economic and Commercial Counsellor's office to whom they report. Companies working on Chinese concessional loan projects also need to report to China Exim Bank. In 2017, Economic and Commercial Counsellor's offices in the Pacific recorded a total of 53 Chinese enterprises operating in PNG, Fiji, Vanuatu, Tonga and FSM (see Table 3), with PNG home to the largest number of Chinese companies in the region. About 70 per cent of them are operating in the engineering/construction sector.

Table 3. Sample of Chinese enterprises in the Pacific

PIC	Total number	Breakdown by sectors
PNG	24	Engineering/construction: 17 Building materials/equipment: 4 Mining and metallurgy: 2 Information technology: 1
Fiji	12	Engineering/construction: 6 Investment: 3 Fisheries: 2 Building materials/equipment: 1
Vanuatu	11	Fishery: 6 Information technology: 2 Building materials/equipment: 1 Manufacturing: 1 Investment: 1
Tonga	4	Engineering/construction: 3 Manufacturing: 1
FSM	2	Fisheries: 1 Hotel: 1

Note: This sample refers to Chinese companies registered with the Economic and Commercial Counsellor's offices in the Pacific. Data on Chinese companies in Samoa, Cook Islands and Niue is unavailable.

Source: Compiled by author from MOFCOM website data.

While commercial interest is the principal driver for Chinese enterprises, they have an impact on the Chinese aid system in three ways. First, in the past decade, a growing number of Chinese enterprises have moved into the Pacific, which forces the Chinese Government, especially MOFCOM, to devote more attention to the region. Second, these enterprises are contractors for the majority of Chinese aid projects. Their performance directly affects the implementation and image of China's aid. Project quality, cost and use of local labour are the main challenges. Substandard quality of construction has been found in some Chinese aid projects such as the Police, Justice and Sports complex in Cook Islands. Some Chinese contractors, such as China Harbour Engineering Company, have been slammed for inflating the project cost after they win the bidding with an intentionally lower quote. Insufficient use of local labour has provoked growing concerns about opportunities for the recipient countries. Chinese contractors do have agency on how to handle these concerns. In addition, there are complex relations between large Chinese state-owned enterprises, as the main contractor for Chinese aid projects, and other sub-contractor Chinese enterprises (see also Smith 2013), which often affect the progress of projects.

Chinese contractors can also wield influence on Chinese aid through a bottom-up approach. By using their close relations with Pacific Island governments, Chinese enterprises, on some occasions, have actively pushed those governments to approach the Chinese Government to request aid. In this process, they use their local insight to provide assistance—ranging from policy advice to project designs—to help these countries get the aid projects. As a reward, the Chinese enterprises then become the project contractors. Some contractors tend to bypass normal bureaucratic procedures in Pacific states and approach individual politicians, which breeds corruption.

CIDCA

The roles of MFA and MOFCOM in Chinese aid management are changing since the establishment of CIDCA in April 2018. As the Xi Jinping administration expects the Chinese aid program to play a more important role in supporting China's big power diplomacy and the BRI, MFA has been given greater power than MOFCOM in this new agency, which reports to Yang Jiechi and Wang Yi. Yang is director of the Party's Office of Foreign Affairs, the top decision-making organ overseeing China's diplomacy, and former minister of foreign affairs (April 2007 to March 2013). Wang is the incumbent Minister of Foreign Affairs (since March 2013) and State Councilor (vice premier level, since March 2018).

The change will have a significant impact on Chinese diplomacy in the Pacific and the competition between MOFCOM and MFA. To date, and compared with Africa and Asia, this competition in the Pacific has been less notable as most PICs are small and have limited natural resources except fisheries. For the most part, MFA has dominated the agenda due to the paramount importance of managing Taiwan in China's diplomacy in the region. However, foreign aid, which had been controlled by MOFCOM, is China's most important tool to gain support from Pacific states, which gives MOFCOM weight in this game. Foreign aid has dominated China's pledges to deepen China–Pacific cooperation since the visit of former premier Wen Jiabao in 2006 (coinciding with the first meeting of the China–Pacific Islands Economic Development and Cooperation Forum in April 2006), the second Forum meeting in November 2013 and the visit of President Xi Jinping in November 2014.

However, with the creation of CIDCA, MFA and Chinese embassies in the Pacific will have more influence over Chinese aid. In particular, more aid projects will be framed within BRI. BRI dominated Xi Jinping's meetings (group meeting and bilateral meetings) with leaders of the eight PICs in November 2018, where Xi repeatedly called for Pacific states to focus on BRI cooperation. MFA's growing influence will also affect China's arrangement of debt payments for PICs as they need to start repaying Chinese concessional loans in the next few years.[9] Relative to MOFCOM and China Exim Bank, the MFA will be more supportive of debt relief efforts in exchange for Pacific states' support of the One China policy and China's rise in the region. These efforts include the forgiveness of interest-free loans and extension of concessional loans, as the Tonga case suggests.

Embassy staffing also affects China's diplomacy and aid delivery in the Pacific. The Chinese ambassador to New Zealand is concurrently accredited to Cook Islands and Niue. China has resident embassies in PNG, Fiji, Vanuatu, Tonga, Samoa and FSM, and it will soon open embassies in Solomon Islands and Kiribati. There are more MFA officials working in the embassies than their counterparts from MOFCOM. The Economic and Commercial Counsellor's offices in China's embassies in PNG and Fiji have four staff each while the offices in Vanuatu, Tonga, Samoa and FSM have two staff each. Understaffing is a serious problem, as these officials need to work on trade, investment and aid. Moreover, trade and investment attract more of their attention as they have more weight than aid in the officials' annual performance evaluation.

The establishment of CIDCA will not solve understaffing unless more aid staff are allocated to the Economic and Commercial Counsellor's offices, which is unlikely in the near future, as these offices in other regions and CIDCA face similar, if not more serious, challenges. CIDCA has about 90 staff assigned from three sources.[10] The primary source is MOFCOM's Department of Foreign Aid. The whole department of about 60 staff has relocated to CIDCA, except for a small number of retiring officials who preferred not to move. This is the largest concentration of aid technocrats in CIDCA. The second main source is MFA, where about 20 officials transferred to CIDCA of their own choice. China's National Development and Reform Commission is the third source with a small number of staff (mainly in the sections of personnel and logistics) moved to CIDCA with

---

9   The grace period is five to seven years.
10 Chinese aid official and scholar, July 2018. Interviews with author.

Wang Xiaotao. Wang was a former deputy director of the commission and was appointed CIDCA's first director in April 2018. With Wang's extensive experience in policy planning and the commission's leading role in coordinating BRI among China's ministries, it is not surprising that CIDCA will largely focus on Chinese aid planning and BRI overseas, including in the Pacific.

CIDCA has three deputy directors. Zhang Maoyu is the most senior deputy director in rank. His appointment could be perceived as a political decision as his previous three-decade career in the China National Intellectual Property Administration is unrelated to Chinese aid or diplomacy. The other two deputy directors, Zhou Liujun and Deng Qingbo, have a strong background in China's Communist Youth League, a previously powerful party organisation that contributed a number of top echelon leaders, but the league's prominence has declined significantly in the Xi Jinping era. Between 2010 and 2018, Zhou was director-general of MOFCOM's Department of Trade in Services and Commercial Services and the Department of Outward Investment and Economic Cooperation. As CIDCA's deputy director, he will be likely to show strong interest in China's trade and investment activities in the Pacific. In contrast, Deputy Director Deng has nearly two decades of experience in the MFA since 2000. He was China's former ambassador to the Dominican Republic and Nigeria, and director-general of the Department of Party Related Affairs (also known as Department for Diplomatic Missions Overseas). Deng is likely to focus CIDCA's work in the Pacific more on China's diplomatic interests as identified by MFA.

The appointment of these senior officials as CIDCA's senior management reflect fierce competition between Chinese government agencies, especially MFA and MOFCOM for control of China's aid program, which is likely to continue. Wang Xiaotao's appointment as CIDCA director was a big surprise to many observers of Chinese aid and even MOFCOM officials. It could be interpreted as a compromise—a balance between MFA and MOFCOM interests. Internally, CIDCA has set up seven departments, focusing on general affairs, policy and planning, regional affairs (divided between two departments), supervision and evaluation, international cooperation, and party-related affairs (also in charge of personnel) (CIDCA 2018). This arrangement aligns with its intended objectives of prioritising Chinese aid planning and monitoring.

Conclusion

Structure and agents are interdependent. This chapter analyses China's national interests in the Pacific, main actors and their nuanced interactions around Chinese diplomacy and aid in the Pacific region. As the discussion shows, China's national interests inform the work of these actors while the latter take agency to affect the structure. In particular, MFA and MOFCOM have competed to prioritise China's diplomatic and economic interests respectively. The creation of CIDCA will give MFA more influence in the formation of aid policy. The objective of support for China on Taiwan and the role of Pacific Island countries in China's overall diplomacy towards the developing world, as well as in China's geostrategic competition with traditional powers, could receive more attention from China in the future. The research also suggests that China will frame much of its aid program in the Pacific within the BRI.

Compared with previous administrations, the Xi Jinping administration has greater ambitions for China as a rejuvenating superpower in the world. China's diplomacy is becoming more proactive and assertive. China is expected to devote more resources to the Pacific, leaving China's mark and complicating regional dynamics. As traditional powers, such as the US and Australia, pledge to increase their engagement with Pacific states, more open competition between China and these powers is likely to take place in the region. This competition could motivate China to provide more aid to the region.

As a new agency, the impact of CIDCA on the Pacific, including in the sectors of Chinese aid planning, implementation and monitoring, needs to be observed into the future. How China and Pacific Island countries will develop their cooperation under the Belt and Road Initiative also deserves attention.

References

Brady, A. 2017. *China as a Polar Great Power*. New York: Cambridge University Press. doi.org/10.1017/9781316832004

Callahan, W. 2012. Sino-speak: Chinese Exceptionalism and the Politics of History. *The Journal of Asian Studies* 71(1):33–55. doi.org/10.1017/S00219 11811002919

China International Development Cooperation Agency (CIDCA) 2018. Departments, 15 August. en.cidca.gov.cn/2019-08/02/c_262719.htm

China Ministry of Commerce (MOFCOM) 2015. *Neishe jigou* (Internal Structure). Department of Foreign Aid, MOFCOM, 30 June. yws.mofcom. gov.cn/article/gywm/201506/20150601028591.shtml

China Ministry of Foreign Affairs (MFA) 2018. China, Pacific Island Countries Lift Ties to Comprehensive Strategic Partnership. 16 November. www.fmprc. gov.cn/mfa_eng/zxxx_662805/t1615484.shtml

Erickson, A. and J. Wuthnow 2016. Barriers, Springboards and Benchmarks: China Conceptualizes the Pacific 'Island Chains'. *The China Quarterly* 225:1–22. doi.org/10.1017/S0305741016000011

Giddens, A. 1984. *The Constitution of Society: Outline of the Theory of Structuration.* Cambridge: Polity Press.

Gries, P.H. 2004. *China's New Nationalism: Pride, Politics and Diplomacy.* Berkeley: University of California Press.

Japan Ministry of Foreign Affairs (MOFA) 2018. The Eighth Pacific Islands Leaders Meeting (PALM8) Leaders' Declaration. www.mofa.go.jp/a_o/ocn/page4e_000825.html

Kumar, A. 2018. First Navy Woman Gets Chinese Scholarship in the Officer Ranks. *Fiji Sun*, 11 September. fijisun.com.fj/2018/09/11/first-navy-woman-gets-chinese-scholarship-in-the-officer-ranks/

Liu, T. and J. Zhao 2018. *Yao le niunai haiyao nainiu? Tang Jia shouxiang 'yao Beijing mianchu zhaiwu' tiyi tai ganga* [Asking for the Cow After Milk Is Given? The Proposal of Tongan Prime Minister for China's Debt Relief is Embarrassing]. *Global Times*, 21 August. world.huanqiu.com/exclusive/2018-08/12778826.html

Lowy Institute 2019. Pacific Aid Map. pacificaidmap.lowyinstitute.org

Lu, J., Q. He and X. Li. 2015. *Zhongguo yuanfei nongye zhuanjia paiqian xiangmu de kechixuxing chutan* [A Feasibility Study on China's Dispatching of Agricultural Aid Experts to Africa]. *World Agriculture* (4):16–20.

Pacific Trade and Investment 2018. *Trade Statistical Handbook 2017 between China and Forum Island Countries.* Beijing: Pacific Trade and Investment Office.

Pedrozo, S.A. 2010. *China's Active Defense Strategy and Its Regional Impact. Testimony Before the House of Representatives US–China Economic and Security Review Commission.* New York: Council on Foreign Relations. www.cfr.org/report/chinas-active-defense-strategy-and-its-regional-impact

Pence, M. 2018. Remarks by Vice President Pence at the 2018 APEC CEO Summit, Port Moresby, Papua New Guinea. The White House, 16 November. china.usembassy-china.org.cn/remarks-by-vice-president-pence-at-the-2018-apec-ceo-summit-port-moresby-papua-new-guinea/

People's Liberation Army Navy (PLAN) Party Committee 2018. *Nuli ba renmin haijun quanmian jiancheng shijie yiliu haijun* [To Strive to Develop the People's Navy into a World First-class Navy]. *Qiushi Magazine*, 31 May. www.qstheory.cn/dukan/qs/2018-05/31/c_1122897922.htm

Radio New Zealand 2018. China Grants Cook Islands $US6.8 Million in Aid. 22 November www.radionz.co.nz/international/pacific-news/376532/china-grants-cook-islands-us6-point-8m-in-aid

Smith, G. 2013. Beijing's Orphans? New Chinese Investors in Papua New Guinea. *Pacific Affairs* 86(2):327–49. doi.org/10.5509/2013862327

Vanuatu Daily Post 2018. 7 MOUs and Cooperation Agreements with China. 20 November. dailypost.vu/news/mous-and-cooperation-agreements-with-china/article_f2cb8ae5-fe7b-5ede-8683-fb263390917b.html

Wang, X. and F. Yu 2017. China Health Aid to the Pacific Island Countries. In Yu Changsen (ed.), *Annual Report on Development of Oceania (2016–2017)*. Beijing: Social Sciences Academic Press (China):229–49.

Wendt, A. 1987. The Agent-Structure Problem in International Relations Theory. *International Organization* 41(3):335–70.

Wendt, A. 1992. Anarchy Is What States Make of It: The Social Construction of Power Politics. *International Organization* 46(2):391–425. doi.org/10.1017/s0020818300027764

Wesley-Smith, T. 2013. China's Rise in Oceania: Issues and Perspectives. *Pacific Affairs* 86(2):351–72. doi.org/10.5509/2013862351

Xinhua 2017. Report Delivered at the 19th National Congress of the Communist Party of China. *China Daily*, 6 November. www.chinadaily.com.cn/interface/flipboard/1142846/2017-11-06/cd_34188086.html

Yang, J. 2011. *The Pacific Islands in China's Grand Strategy: Small States, Big Games*. New York: Palgrave Macmillan. doi.org/10.1057/9780230339750

Zhang, D. 2017. China's Diplomacy in the Pacific: Interests, Means and Implications. *Security Challenges* 13(2):32–53.

Zhang, D. 2018. China, India and Japan in the Pacific: Latest Development, Motivations and Impact. DPA Discussion Paper 2018/6. Canberra: ANU. dpa. bellschool.anu.edu.au/experts-publications/publications/6388/dp-201806-china-india-and-japan-pacific-latest-developments

Zhang, D. and G. Smith 2017. China's Foreign Aid System: Structure, Agencies, and Identities. *Third World Quarterly* 38(10):2330–346. doi.org/10.1080/01436597.2017.1333419

Zhang, Y. 2018. New Agency to Guide Nation's Foreign Aid. *China Daily*, 14 March. www.chinadaily.com.cn/a/201803/14/WS5aa85af7a3106e7dcc1416dc.html

9

A Search for Coherence: The Belt and Road Initiative in the Pacific Islands

Henryk Szadziewski

Introduction

In the summer of 2017, I sat down for a conversation with Zhang, a Chinese businessman, at his family-owned restaurant in Nadi, Fiji. Over lunch, I asked him to talk about his time as a migrant to Fiji since the mid-2000s. He explained how he had built successful restaurant and retail businesses and discussed his appreciation for the opportunity to create a life in Fiji. 'The good relations between Fiji and China helped me get started here', he said. Taking note of my interest in his comment, Zhang pressed on, 'Of course, it took a lot of my hard work to make it all happen, but I wouldn't be here without the support of family and the new policy to find opportunities abroad'. Changing the topic toward the future of Chinese investment in Fiji, he added: 'It will be different, you watch, there will be more people looking for openings and all of it will be Belt and Road'.

The Belt and Road Initiative (BRI) incorporates over 60 countries in a transnational network of anticipated trade routes centred on China. Comprising land- and ocean-based infrastructure corridors, the BRI connects China with Europe and Africa through the subregions of Asia. The inclusion of Oceania appears as an anomaly, as the region is not usually thought of as a direct thoroughfare to the ports and cities of Europe and Africa. The growing scholarly literature on the BRI, particularly in political geography, has defined the BRI as anything from China's spatial fix for overcapacity in the domestic economy, to no less than a bid for global hegemony to sometimes both at the same time. In Pacific Island Studies, the discussion of the BRI's arrival in Oceania has revolved around the intervention as either an expression of Beijing's ascendency in a region long influenced by Australia and the US or an opportunity for Pacific Island governments to assert agency over these traditional partners with China as the enabling factor (Fry and Tarte 2015).

In this chapter, using a variety of media articles and government statements, I argue that the BRI is a marker for a new discursive phase of Chinese activity in the Pacific Islands region. In addition to its often-stated material outcomes, the BRI is also a narrative vehicle that attempts to bring international and domestic coherence to China's overseas political and economic engagement. In the Pacific Islands region, the notion of a harmonising BRI counters claims, frequently emanating from Australian legislators and media, of China's erratic approach to economic interactions with the Pacific Islands. As a domestic instrument, the BRI harmonises and makes legible a variety of Chinese state and nonstate actors in Oceania under a single policy. This attempt at legibility not only captures Chinese political and economic activity in the region, but also exposes the actors involved to possible state discipline. As Smith et al. (2014) note in the context of China's aid programs in Pacific Island countries (PICs), perceptions of Chinese communities overseas have a bearing on the image of China. Conversely, Chinese officials have built BRI coherence on a broad interpretation of what the initiative constitutes, giving rise to the labelling of all manner of Chinese endeavours as under the BRI.

This 'flexible coherence' offers distinct advantages in creating an umbrella for the variety of activities Chinese actors undertake in the Pacific Islands region. Not all Chinese actors desire state legibility and many employ strategies of evasion or display indifference to state disciplining; however, some private actors have attached the Belt and Road label to their projects seeking political endorsements for their investments. Furthermore, an opaque BRI also opens opportunities for PICs to interact flexibly with the initiative and present the intervention as consistent with Pacific Island interests. Through visit diplomacy, memoranda of understanding, project branding, integration with Pacific Island government development strategies and membership in alternative financing mechanisms, the BRI is increasingly defining Sino–Pacific Island engagement. In a section examining Fiji's relations with China from the 'Look North' to the BRI, this chapter shows how Sino–Fijian discourses have become increasingly entangled through a co-constructed discourse that establishes continuity between the two countries' frameworks. As a result, I argue that while attempting to convey a coherent global, regional and bilateral vision to the world, the BRI also presents opportunities for some governments, such as those of the Pacific Islands, to co-define the terms of their relationships with China, offering leverage and alternative options to traditional regional powers.

Incoherent, erratic, short-term: Chinese presence 2000–15

The presence of the People's Republic of China (PRC) is now an indisputable aspect of political and economic life in the Pacific Islands region. From 2006 to 2016, Chinese aid to Oceania totalled US$1.8 billion (Brant 2016) and China is the region's second largest trading partner (Zhang 2015). Migrants from China to the Pacific Islands region are more visible in PICs; nevertheless, Chinese people constitute less than 1 per cent of the population in any one PIC (D'Arcy 2014). The current engagement between China and Pacific Island governments and peoples fits in to a longer arc of Chinese presence in Oceania. Scholars have identified staged migrations traceable to the 19th century of Chinese traders, indentured workers and political refugees settling in the Pacific Islands (Willmott 2007).

The historical context of Pacific Island and Chinese relations is important to consider, as it demonstrates that exchanges are not only long-standing, but also evolving with political and economic conditions. With contemporary Chinese presence in the Pacific Islands region as his focus, D'Arcy (2014) provides a useful guide to understanding the current stage and its roots in the past. He wrote that the Chinese Government's 1999 'Going Out' policy (走出去战略), encouraging Chinese companies and individuals to invest overseas, initiated a new phase in relations given increased opportunities for aid, trade and mobility. D'Arcy added that analyses, generally external to the region, of this post-1999 phase have clustered into two narratives: fear and agency. Fear discourses characterise

China's economic and political interventions as potentially destabilising, while a somewhat contrasting body of literature has sought a more nuanced analysis reflecting the ways in which these interventions enable Pacific Island government agency. Both discourses suggest that Chinese presence has been neither coherent, consistent nor long-term. I use D'Arcy's post-1999 framework to critique fear and agency discourses to 2015 and suggest that the BRI presents a successor narrative indicating the Chinese state's push for a discourse of coherence.

Discourses of fear

The literature on China's post-1999 presence in the Pacific Islands region initially leant toward emphasising the threats posed by a 'new' power to the established economic and political interests of the US and Australia. Emanating from influential think tanks and a loud media, particularly in Australia, fear narratives singled out Chinese aid as a notable disruptive factor to these interests. Chinese largesse through unconditional loans and grants, primarily for infrastructure projects, undermined the long-term Australian goal of building good governance through conditional assistance. The 2006 Australian Senate's inquiry into Australia's relationship with China included testimony from several researchers, including Susan Windybank, Ron Crocombe, Benjamin Reilly and John Henderson, who would go on to write and speak about the negative aspects of renewed Chinese state interest in Oceania. Taking broad characterisations as a basis for analysis, the Committee on Foreign Affairs, Defence and Trade noted:

> Being relatively poor and tending to lack the appropriate institutional mechanisms to ensure political and bureaucratic accountability, many Pacific Islands are vulnerable to financial influence and corruption (Senate Foreign Affairs, Defence and Trade References Committee 2005:175).

Furthermore, the committee highlighted how 'funds provided to local politicians or government officials without proper conditions attached can encourage fraudulent behaviour and undermine political stability' (ibid.:179).

Following the 2006 inquiry, two reports from the Lowy Institute also proved influential in circulating a narrative of Chinese aid as a disturbance to regional order. The first, published in 2009, stressed China's lack of coordination with in-country funding priorities and the so-called excessive secrecy of Chinese aid financing. In addition, maintenance or repair budgets were frequently not included in loans and grants, and these costs ended up placing Pacific Island governments further in debt (Hanson 2009). The 2009 report concluded that embedded conditions, such as the procurement of labour and materials for infrastructure projects from China, encouraged anti-Chinese sentiments among Pacific Islanders due to the denial of employment opportunities (ibid.). The second Lowy Institute report, published in 2011, upped the risks facing Pacific Island governments who had accepted Chinese aid. Increasing levels of debt to China, especially in Samoa and Tonga, opened the possibility of political and economic pressure or demands from Beijing in exchange for debt forgiveness. The report added that the growing lawlessness of Chinese migrants needed to be addressed if the Pacific Islands were not to become incorporated into the territories of Chinese criminal gangs (Hanson and Fifita 2011). Crocombe (2007) arrived at a similar conclusion, voicing concern over how Chinese migrants were introducing startling levels of criminality to Pacific Island states through illegal gambling, prostitution and drug dealing; nevertheless, like Hanson and Fifita, Crocombe is unable to parse the Chinese state from Chinese migrants, simply labelling all Chinese presence as destabilising. Seib (2010) likewise conflated the Chinese state and migrants into a monolithic entity, claiming Chinese aid has opened the region to 'streams of migrants' who deny locals economic opportunities.

Chequebook diplomacy between China and Taiwan is often cited as a further source of inconsistent and opportunistic aid and investment. Since the 1949 Chinese Communist Party (CCP) victory in the Chinese Civil War and the Nationalist retreat to the island of Taiwan, the two administrations have sought legitimacy through diplomatic recognition. Beijing's and Taipei's search for diplomatic partners has fluctuated between contest and truce, leading to accusations of waning interest during times of détente.

Atkinson (2010) wrote of the incoherence and unscrupulousness of China's and Taiwan's assistance to the Pacific Islands, emphasising a lack of monitoring procedures and adding that 'involvement is primarily due to the capacity of the Pacific Islands to accord diplomatic recognition, and only to a lesser extent the region's economic and strategic characteristics'. He claimed that local elites tend to be the chief beneficiaries of chequebook diplomacy, describing kickbacks such as luxury cars and travel expenses. Falling back on a narrative strongly asserted in the Australian Senate inquiry, he concluded that 'diplomatic competition between China and

Taiwan is destabilising island states in the South Pacific, making Pacific politics more corrupt and more violent'. However, there is little analysis of the strategic advantages China's interventions offer Pacific Island governments regarding leverage over traditional partners.

Discourses of Chinese presence in Oceania as part of a grand hegemonic strategy also mark the post-1999 period and illustrate how some scholars view Beijing's interest in the region as little more than an exploitative opportunity (Henderson 2001; Henderson and Reilly 2003). Aid and investment are not only tools to win diplomatic partners, but also means to achieve political influence regionally or globally. Chinese assistance is not coordinated with domestic priorities and PIC agency is relegated to irrelevance. Windybank (2005) wrote: 'The expansion of Chinese influence reflects more than a benign attempt to gain access to the region's abundant minerals, timber and fisheries. Strategic issues often have economic faces'. Shie (2007) took the logics of this argument further, adding that China's economic interventions will convert to military dominance in the Pacific Islands, an eventuality enabled by the 'passive' interest of the US and Australia in addressing this geopolitical shift.

Discourses of agency

In response to discourses of fear, a group of scholars emphasise the 'disingenuous' character of these analyses (Wesley-Smith 2007). China's augmented presence is neither a grand strategy nor imposed. Discourses of agency emphasise how PICs as sovereign entities are free to choose alternative economic partners, and rightfully so, given the damaging effects of neoliberal conditionality attached to aid from traditional donors in the 1990s. It was not that Australia and the US were passive in the Pacific Islands region, but rather that their harmful insistence on privatisation and deregulated markets opened new opportunities for China. Traditional donors' concern over the nature of relations between PICs and China as part of their own strategic fears also tend not to play well in Pacific Island capitals.

However, discourses of agency also underscore the lack of a systematic Chinese approach to political and economic engagement in Oceania. Chinese presence in the Pacific Islands is merely a byproduct of Beijing's increasing interests across the globe and the need for natural resources to drive its domestic economy (Yang 2009, 2011). In a sharp and justifiable critique, Wesley-Smith and Porter (2010) wrote that fear discourses tend to concentrate on the supposed loss of Australian or US influence and 'it is apparent that the condition of island states or the welfare of Pacific Islanders are, at best, of secondary concern'. Pacific Island governments' positive responses to China's interest have been driven by pressing contemporary needs such as upgrading or building infrastructure, the financing of which is unavailable in Australian social aid programming. In addition, evidence supporting the notion that traditional powers have lost significant soft or hard power in Oceania is lacking. Therefore, China's predominant interests in the Pacific Islands region are quite modest: seeking new markets and opportunities for muting Taiwanese diplomatic initiatives, both of which mean Chinese officials pay significantly less attention to Oceania than other regions (Wesley-Smith and Porter 2010).

Discourses of agency challenge the myth of Chinese aid driven by a quid pro quo for resources and argue that the Chinese state was brought to the Pacific Islands region by Chinese contractors and Pacific Island governments seeking financing for infrastructure projects (Brant 2013). This practice does not indicate a long-term strategy, aid effectiveness or a systematic approach to development planning. Dornan and Brant (2014) make the important point that the responsibility for aid effectiveness sits not only with donors, but also recipients. In a comparison of Chinese interventions in Tonga, Vanuatu, Samoa and Cook Islands, Dornan and Brant found that 'the way in which governments have pursued, overseen and implemented projects has differed considerably, and is an important determinant of the effectiveness and developmental impact of Chinese assistance'. Consequently, if projects should not (or even should) meet expectations, the Chinese actors involved are not the only accountable parties. Nevertheless, Sullivan and Renz (2012) showed the influential role of Australia's and New Zealand's media in promoting a narrative of Chinese presence in Oceania as offering little of lasting value, especially its aid assistance, noting: 'China is seen as the cause of numerous ills affecting the island Pacific and unlikely to contribute to their solution' (Sullivan and Renz 2012:388). Their examination of press coverage since 1999 concluded that the China-as-destabilising force discourse was linked to security anxieties in Canberra and Wellington rather than any alarm for Island societies. As Sullivan and Renz suggested, these findings reveal more about the self-interests of former and current colonial powers than the aspirations of the Pacific Islands region and its residents, as well as a retreat to well-trodden 'yellow peril' narratives, adding: 'China and the homogenised Chinese people are represented as operating in an alien moral universe'.

Towards coherence: The BRI

In 2012, Wang Jisi, a professor at Beijing University, suggested a shift in China's foreign policy towards Eurasia. According to Wang, a 'march west' would offer China political and economic advantages as the US scaled back its presence in Central Asia and the Middle East and embarked on an Asia-Pacific pivot in 2011 (Wang 2012). Wang considered his proposal a transcontinental successor to the state-led development campaigns in China's northwest, such as 'Open Up the Northwest' (1992) and 'Western Development' (2000). This intellectual antecedent of the BRI is important to note because the initiative not only built on the Going Out policy of 1999, but also was driven by domestic development campaigns built on infrastructure construction and mobility. In 2013, Chinese President Xi Jinping first proposed the 'One Belt, One Road' (一带一路) policy, officially renamed in 2016 as the Belt and Road Initiative. The BRI planned to reconfigure global trade and the governance of international finance through China. Encompassing the land-based Silk Road Economic Belt (丝绸之路经济带) and the ocean-based 21st-century Maritime Silk Road (21世纪海上丝绸之路), the initiative would link China with Europe and Africa through infrastructure corridors across subregions of Asia.

The principal financing agency for the BRI is the multilateral Asian Infrastructure Investment Bank (AIIB) founded in 2013. Over 90 nations are currently members of the AIIB and initial capital was established at US$100 billion, of which China provided 50 per cent. China holds the largest voting share in the AIIB at 28.7 per cent; the second largest voting member, India, holds 8.3 per cent. Given this dominance, some analysts claim the AIIB is an attempt to rebalance the limited influence Beijing exercises over the Bretton Woods institutions (Subacchi 2015). Other funding mechanisms for the BRI include the Silk Road Fund, a US$40 billion investment fund created by Beijing, as well as other bilateral-lending entities, such as the Export-Import Bank of China and the China Development Bank.

China's purpose in initiating the BRI has not been fully articulated; however, the literature can be broadly divided into accounts offering internal motivations or overseas motivations. The BRI is mooted as a solution to an overheated domestic economy or as a geoeconomic strategy to confirm China's place as a global power. A more critical body of research has examined the discursive aspects of the BRI, especially its comparisons with the Silk Road, through which internal and domestic motivations flow. The range of these analyses clearly indicates a lack of consensus on the motivation for and the goal of the BRI. However, this ambiguity of purpose is advantageous if viewed from the perspective of coherence building across the broad scope of China's overseas political and economic engagements. In sum, the assortment of ventures (infrastructure and social programming), financial mechanisms (multilateral, bilateral and, at times, private investment) and discourses form a catch-all project defying specific definition. As Shepard (2017) noted:

> The vagueness, lack of institutionalisation, and very broad definition of the China's Belt and Road [sic] is probably one of its greatest strengths … the initiative can be whatever China says it is in any given circumstance as they devise and adapt policies and trade deals to fit any given country, in any given situation, at any given time. Within this open framework, inconsistencies and even outright contradictions are not theoretical problems but standard operating procedures.

The open-ended character of the BRI has confounded some observers. One Center for International and Strategic Studies analyst called Beijing's BRI statements akin to 'Delphic utterances' (Clover and Hornby 2015). Graham (2018), however, while acknowledging the enigma of the BRI, claims 'it is also possible to see in BRI the clear contours of a thought-through, full-spectrum grand strategy for China, straddling economic, political, military and even psychological domains'. I argue differently. While the BRI certainly expands China's presence in regions and states across the globe through infrastructure projects, enhanced trade and alternative financing mechanisms, its discursive power also captures an array of domestic actors, state and nonstate, engaged in current and future enterprises with bilateral partners. It is not so much a blueprint for a grand strategy as it is a means of harmonising overseas relations with China's protagonists.

Overseas Chinese and coherence

Taking a discursive view of the BRI, Ferdinand (2016) reasons the initiative is a project of Chinese national rejuvenation. As such, it is an expression of President Xi Jinping's China Dream to harness the Chinese peoples' material and intangible aspirations into state revitalisation, albeit encouraged through overseas economic cooperation. The 2015 Chinese Government white paper *Vision and Actions on Jointly Building Silk Road Economic Belt and 21st-Century Maritime Silk Road* mentions people-to-people contact five times as one of the integral aspects of the BRI. At the 2017 Belt and Road Forum, President Xi underscored how the human dimensions of the BRI are just as relevant overseas, claiming person-to-person relations as a cornerstone of BRI connectivity. At the opening ceremony to the forum, Xi remarked that '"moving closer towards a community of shared future for mankind" is the ultimate goal of the Belt and Road Initiative' (D. Zhang 2018:196). Ferdinand (2016) concluded that the success of a transnational BRI meant the China Dream must become that of the world. As such, mobility of not only Chinese capital, but also Chinese citizens would play an integral role in China's revitalisation. Muttarak (2017:2) wrote that 'the impacts of China's growing presence … go beyond the macro-economic effects … Along with investments and trade—either state-owned or private—comes movement of labour, entrepreneurs, accompanying family members'. In a 2018 speech, Xu Yousheng, the Deputy Director of the United Front Work Department, outlined how overseas Chinese could as serve as facilitators for Chinese companies looking to start businesses outside of China, as well as, critically, 'active promoters of mutual political trust and mutually beneficial relations between China and neighbouring countries' (Lo 2018).

James To (2014) argued that there is little doubt over the Chinese state's desire to exercise influence over diaspora communities. Through a study of the policies of Beijing's Overseas Chinese Affairs Office (侨务), since merged into the United Front Work Department and a key indicator of strengthening coherence between China's overseas agencies, To proposed the Chinese Government is purposefully organising new migrants (新侨) and established diasporas (老侨) to promote China's political and economic interests overseas. The main objectives of this strategy are to secure resources for continued domestic economic growth and to improve China's image with governments and people abroad. To supports this thesis with evidence of Chinese embassy support for community-driven Chinese cultural events and outreach into the organisations of established Chinese migrants. The purpose of the latter is to offer new migrants social support and financial capital, as well as encourage older generations to restore ties to China. To also claimed that China disciplines migrants once they are overseas and seeks to enhance their 'quality' (素质) through education campaigns to represent China positively. Edney (2014) wrote that this process exemplified the Chinese state's aim to create cohesion, even in civil society, between domestic and overseas state narratives.

In sum, state and nonstate voices unify through rearticulating Chinese Government discourses. The umbrella of the BRI reterritorialises a diverse set of investors and labourers beyond China's borders as legible to the Chinese state and harnesses individual and collective enterprise under the China Dream toward national revitalisation. As such, the people-to-people discourses and the state promotion of investment outside of China under the BRI framework enmesh with the state disciplining of new overseas Chinese and existing diaspora communities to stage the BRI as a unifying project for an assemblage of Chinese presence abroad.

Liu and van Dongen (2016) challenge James To's top-down flow of relations between the Chinese state and overseas Chinese. The notion that migrants, new or old, are co-opted into state priorities does not present a complete understanding of the state–migrant interface. Chinese migrants are empowered in this relationship and frequently lead policy formation in state entities charged with overseas Chinese work (ibid.). In a study of the 'five overseas Chinese structures' (五侨) within the government apparatus, especially the Overseas Chinese Affairs Office, Liu and van Dongen found that Chinese officials incorporated the recommendations and concerns of overseas Chinese into policy. Alternatively, Ong (1999) suggested the acquisition of second or third citizenships as a means by which Chinese migrants evade the state as an individual response to Chinese Government reterritorialising processes. Despite the Chinese Government's nonrecognition of dual citizenship, through naturalisation overseas, migrants not only open new commercial opportunities in host countries, but also circumvent the disciplining projects of the Chinese state. Though still disciplined by 'markets and families' (Ong 1999), Chinese migrants leverage citizenship toward personal, rather than state, benefit. As noted, interactions with the BRI's flexible coherence is contingent on position. The amorphous BRI framework offers advantages (or disadvantages) to a variety of Chinese state and nonstate actors. The following section examines the increasing dominance of the BRI as the basis of Sino–Pacific Island relations, demonstrating the harmonisation of China's regional approach at the state-to-state level. After this appraisal, the chapter surveys Fiji to highlight the capture of Chinese activity under the BRI umbrella, as well as how the Fijian state has developed the flexible coherence of the BRI to co-construct its own narrative of state revitalisation.

The BRI in the Pacific Islands

The People's Republic of China maintains diplomatic relations with 10 PICs: Fiji (since 1975), Samoa (1975), Papua New Guinea (1976), Vanuatu (1982), Micronesia (1989), Cook Islands (1997), Tonga (1998), Niue (2007), Solomon Islands (2019) and Kiribati (2019). Aid and investment to the region have notably grown in the post-Going Out policy period. Between 2006 and 2016, China dedicated an estimated US$1.8 billion in loans and grants to its partners in the Pacific Islands (Brant 2016). This placed China as the third largest donor in the region after Australia (US$7.7 billion) and the US (US$1.9 billion). China committed US$632 million to Papua New Guinea, the largest recipient, and US$360 million to Fiji, the second largest. Aid was disbursed as grants, interest-free loans or concessional loans across a wide range of sectors, including education, transport and agriculture (Brant 2016). At the second meeting of the China–Pacific Island Countries Economic Development and Cooperation Forum in 2013 China pledged US$2 billion in commercial and concessional loans (Ministry of Commerce People's Republic of China 2013). Between 2000 and 2012, trade between China and its diplomatic partners in the region increased from US$248 million to US$1.77 billion with zero tariffs levied on 95 per cent of products from the Pacific Islands region (Taylor 2016).

At a 2014 meeting in Nadi between Xi Jinping and political leaders from the then eight PICs recognising China, the Chinese president welcomed the dignitaries to 'take a ride on the Chinese "express train" of development' under the framework of the Maritime Silk Road (Xinhua 2014). In the 2015 government white paper, *Vision and Actions on Jointly Building Silk Road Economic Belt and 21st-Century Maritime Silk Road*, China included the Pacific Islands region in the BRI network of trade corridors with the addition of the southern leg Maritime Silk Road (National Development and Reform Commission 2015). Maps displaying the BRI show the incorporation of the region with a line either south or north of Papua New Guinea. The addition was warmly received by regional leaders, leading to an outburst of BRI enthusiasm in 2017. In March of that year, then Pacific Island Forum (PIF) deputy secretary general Andie Fong Toy called the BRI 'a contribution to global economic leadership' (Pacific Islands Report 2017), and at the May 2017 Belt and Road Forum in Beijing, PIF representative in China David Morris noted the 'great potential of the Maritime Silk Road' to build regional infrastructure (ABC News 2017). Fijian Prime Minister Bainimarama, Pacific Islands Development Forum Secretary General

François Martel, as well as delegations from Tonga, Samoa and Vanuatu also attended the forum (Pacific Islands Development Forum 2017). In the same year, China took the BRI to its diplomatic partners in the region with a series of regional meetings, including the Belt and Road International Financial Exchange Cooperation Seminar in June and the Post-Forum Dialogue in Apia in September. According to the Chinese Foreign Ministry report on the latter event, Chinese Special Envoy Du Qiwen introduced 'China's policies toward Pacific Island countries and the "Belt and Road" initiative', and PIC attendees 'expressed their willingness to actively participate in the "Belt and Road" cooperation' (Ministry of Foreign Affairs of the People's Republic of China 2017). At meetings with PIC leaders prior to the 2018 Asia-Pacific Economic Cooperation summit in Port Moresby and in an op-ed published in the PNG press, Xi made the case for the BRI, writing:

> I am convinced that the BRI will open up new pathways for Pacific island countries to enhance business ties and connectivity with China, among themselves and with the rest of the world, and for the island countries to take a greater part in economic globalization (Xi 2018).

Despite these impressive official declarations, observers have scaled the importance of this rhetoric. As a region representing only 0.12 per cent of China's global trade volume, the Pacific Islands are of minor importance to China's BRI priorities (Dornan and Muller 2018; Zhang, D. 2017). However, these observations have not prevented a renaissance in grand-strategy narratives. For example, in a 2018 report, the US–China Economic and Security Review Commission wrote:

> Although the Pacific Islands receive less of China's attention and resources compared to other areas of the world, Beijing includes the region in its key diplomatic and economic development policy—the Belt and Road Initiative (BRI)—which suggests China has geostrategic interests in the region (Meick et al. 2018:1).

The geostrategic intent behind the BRI is understood in the context of Beijing's desire to establish a presence in the Pacific Islands in order to break free from containment on its eastern seaboard. To this end, Oceania will not be as peripheral as some observers argue (Lanteigne 2017). As one argument claims:

> Inclusion within BRI of a maritime corridor through Oceania speaks to strategic intent, because there is no convincing economic case for China to invest in 'connectivity' infrastructure for small Pacific island states (Graham 2018).

However, such discourses dismiss Island agency in participation and the flexible interpretation of the Chinese state's opaque BRI narratives. Less dystopian analyses advance the possibilities the BRI offers in terms of infrastructure construction and greater access to markets through connectivity (Hannan and Firth 2016). Given the difficulties in participating in markets in the Asia-Pacific, the BRI makes sense to Pacific Islanders long restricted to trade with Australia, New Zealand and other Pacific states. Access to BRI financing mechanisms is critical in taking advantage of BRI opportunities. Fiji, Papua New Guinea, Samoa, Tonga, Cook Islands and Vanuatu are all members or prospective members of the AIIB as of 2019.

Papua New Guinea

Bilaterally, BRI discourses have been enacted among PICs either through visit diplomacy, memoranda of understanding (MOU) or the development of material projects. In a November 2014 Beijing meeting, then Papua New Guinea Prime Minister Peter O'Neill and Chinese President Xi Jinping declared the opening of a strategic partnership between the two states. Such arrangements are usually a means to demonstrate wide-ranging bilateral engagement; yet, on O'Neill's 2016 return visit to China, bilateral relations were staged under the BRI umbrella. In addition to signing concessional loan agreements for a variety of infrastructure projects, the leaders agreed to synergise the BRI with Papua New Guinea's Development Strategic Plan 2010–2030 (Ministry of Foreign Affairs of the People's Republic of China 2016). A year after the November 2016 meeting, a third visit to Beijing saw Papua New Guinea formally sign on to the BRI and the announcement of a new round of Chinese-financed projects. These projects included a significant upgrade to the road systems on the mainland, New Britain and New Ireland, the construction of a US$ 4 billion industrial park in Sandaun Province and the improvement of the water supply to Eastern Highlands Province. The US$3.5 billion road project was penned with China Railway Group, a private entity whose major shareholder is the state-owned, and stock exchange–listed, China Railway Engineering Corporation. The Sandaun deal was agreed with China Metallurgical Group, the controversial majority investor in the Ramu Nickel mine. As Smith (2017) noted, these projects, especially the overhaul of the road network, could transform Papua New Guinea's economy and delivery of social services, all of which he called 'PNG's Belt and Road dream'.

Former prime minister O'Neill said these deals were the result of Papua New Guinea's new status as a location on the Maritime Silk Road, and talked up the benefits of market access through the BRI in April 2018 as then foreign minister Rimbink Pato was in Beijing to discuss the feasibility of a free trade agreement (Radio New Zealand 2018a). Two months later, O'Neill was in China for his sixth visit since assuming office and signed an MOU confirming Papua New Guinea's ties to the BRI and membership in the AIIB, calling the initiatives 'crucial to lifting the standard of living for our people' (ABC News 2018a). However, the lucrative and ambitious nature of Chinese projects in Papua New Guinea also points to corporate incentives for Chinese companies to interact with the BRI in the Pacific Islands region. In an interview with Xinhua, Wu Dongzheng, a senior official at China Railway International Group's South Pacific branch, stated that he had invited the Papua New Guinea Government to join the BRI (Parsons 2018). In a meeting with then prime minister O'Neill, Zhang Zongyan, President of China Railway Group, discussed how China Railway would:

> actively implement the national 'Belt and Road' initiative, give full play to its advantages in capital, technology, talents and management, and contribute more to the economic and social development of Papua New Guinea (CREC 2018).

Smith reminded us that these corporate incentives do not always fit with the 'strategic designs of the Chinese central government' (2013:349).

Samoa

In 2017, Chinese and Samoan officials elevated BRI discourses into their bilateral relationship, beginning in May with a visit to Samoa by China's Vice Foreign Minister in charge of Oceania Affairs Zheng Zeguang and continuing in September through Samoan Minister of Commerce, Industry and Labour Lautafi Fio Purcell's presence at the China–Pacific Economic Cooperation Forum. At the latter meeting, Purcell highlighted the role of Guangdong Province in facilitating BRI cooperation, and the visit of a Samoa parliamentarian delegation to Fujian underscored the importance of China's provincial governments in leveraging BRI financing (Government Press Secretariat of Samoa 2018; Purcell 2017). Samoan Prime Minister Tuilaepa Sailele Malielegaoi's September 2018 trip to China strengthened Samoa's commitment to the BRI. The prime minister met with President Xi Jinping and Premier Li Keqiang and signed an MOU agreeing to conduct future economic cooperation with China under the BRI framework, as well as a pledge to synergise Samoa's national development strategy with the BRI (Government of Samoa 2018; Ministry of Foreign Affairs of the People's Republic of China 2018d; Xinhua 2018e). Samoa's prime minister told the Chinese media that Samoa's interest in the BRI was principally about market access (Global Times 2018). Discussions in the Samoan media indicate contrasting opinions on this positive-outcomes note. Mata'afa Keni Lesa, editor of the *Samoa Observer*, argued that the lack of alternatives to the financing opportunities available through the BRI means Samoa should make itself 'China ready' (Lesa 2018). In the same publication, journalist Alexander Rheeney (2018), mindful of Samoa's debt burden, tempered BRI expectations by stating the initiative represented a 'step into the deep unknown', especially since other countries are beginning to question participation in the initiative.

Tonga

Tonga's initial engagement with the BRI arose in October 2015 when a CCP delegation introduced the initiative's trade and financing benefits to then Tongan prime minister 'Akilisi Pōhiva and members of parliament. As in the case of Samoa, it took a visit by the nation's head of state to China to mainstream BRI discourses into the bilateral relationship. At a March 2018 Beijing meeting between Xi Jinping and Tongan King Tupou VI, the two leaders underscored the BRI as the basis for infrastructure construction financing in Tonga (Ministry of Foreign Affairs of the People's Republic of China 2018a; Xinhua 2018b). At a subsequent meeting, King Tupou VI and Chinese Premier Li Keqiang agreed to integrate Tonga's development strategy with the BRI, a now familiar policy outcome in the visit diplomacy to China of Pacific Island leaders (Y. Zhang 2018). Though Tonga did not sign up to the BRI, it was accepted as a member of the AIIB (Ministry of Foreign Affairs of the People's Republic of China 2018b). However, in December 2018, prior to the APEC summit in Port Moresby, Tonga formally committed to the BRI through an MOU and received a five-year deferment on concessional loans (ABC News 2018b).

Federated States of Micronesia

Visit diplomacy also dominates Micronesian engagement in the discourses of the BRI. In March 2017, Federated States of Micronesia President Peter M. Christian travelled to China and met Xi Jinping, with Xi extending an invitation for Christian to participate in the BRI (Xinhua 2017a). Following up on the visit a month later, Li Zhanshu, Chairman of the National People's Congress, noted Micronesia's interest in joining the BRI and AIIB, however, no formal application to the AIIB had been made by 2019. Within the nuances of diplomatic protocol, and conceivably as an effect of the Federated States of Micronesia's status as a freely associated state of the US, Micronesia's engagement with the BRI initially appeared less enthusiastic than other PICs, and the possibility of an MOU on economic cooperation under the BRI framework was discussed with Chairman Li in May 2018 (Kaselehlie Press 2018). As if to press the issue, the offer to participate in the BRI was again extended to Micronesia in July 2018 by Huang Zheng, Chinese Ambassador to the Federated States of Micronesia (Ministry of Foreign Affairs of the People's Republic of China 2018c), and once more by the ambassador in September 2018 at a region-wide seminar. On the latter occasion, the ambassador eagerly stated:

> Let's hand in hand, work hard together, jointly pursue the Belt and Road international cooperation and the building of a community with a shared future for the humanity and jointly create a better future! (Ministry of Foreign Affairs of the People's Republic of China 2018e).

By November 2018, the Federated States of Micronesia and the PRC entered into an MOU on BRI cooperation, an event noted by the Chinese ambassador to Micronesia in a commentary piece for the local press (Embassy of the People's Republic of China in the Federated States of Micronesia 2019). In December 2019, the then new president of the Federated States of Micronesia David Panuelo visited China, calling Beijing Micronesia's key economic partner and Washington DC Palikir's leading security partner, an indication of how PICs balance the reintroduction of great power politics into the region (Tobin 2019).

Vanuatu

Vanuatu's engagement with the discourses of the BRI have been overshadowed since the 2018 uproar over the Shanghai Construction Group's construction of the Luganville wharf. In April, media articles circulated in Australia, and then globally, that claimed Canberra had raised alarm over a possible agreement the facility could be used for Chinese military purposes, an allegation denied by Vanuatu Prime

Minister Charlot Salwai (Bohane 2018). Salwai stressed that China's assistance was not imposed and was instead a response to requests from the Vanuatu Government. Nevertheless, the incident displayed regional sensitivities and the difficulties PICs are beginning to experience in managing competing bilateral economic partners.

Prior to the controversy, Vanuatu's attendance at the Belt and Road Forum in May 2017 was pitched at the ministerial level and Port Vila joined the AIIB on 6 March 2018 (Daily Post 2017). Johnny Koanapo Rasou, Member of Parliament for Tanna, captures the pragmatic view of the BRI in Vanuatu, writing:

> We in Vanuatu must also be able to navigate in this policy and see what legislations and policy we need to have in place to take advantage of the opportunities that China has to offer and where we need to avoid and give opportunities for our own people to prosper (Koanapo 2017).

On the sidelines of the APEC summit in Port Moresby in November 2018, Vanuatu formally signed on to the BRI through one of seven MOUs signed with China (Radio New Zealand 2018e). Vanuatu Minister of Foreign Affairs Ralph Regenvanu underscored the open-endedness of BRI agreements, telling the media: 'It's very vague, and it doesn't really commit us to anything except cooperation. And that's fine by us' (Radio New Zealand 2018f). However, the MOU does contain some significant commitments—for example, that the resolution of conflicts should be conducted between the two parties without the possibility of an outside arbitrator (McGarry 2018).

Niue and Cook Islands

The two self-governing states in free association with New Zealand have also engaged with the BRI, which has generated some debate in Wellington about Chinese influence. Niue announced a US$14 million road reconstruction project financed by China in 2017, and the following year Premier Toke Talagi signed an MOU with China on BRI cooperation (Embassy of the People's Republic of China in New Zealand 2018). However, despite Premier Talagi's subsequent statement that he 'was not in any rush for projects under the strategy' (Radio New Zealand 2018b), media in New Zealand have raised the spectre of Niue coming under China's political influence through the BRI. As a reflection of this, and in perhaps the world's first example of 'dumpling diplomacy', the Chinese ambassador cooked for Premier Talagi and locals on Niue's Constitution Day celebrations, at which 'the New Zealand flag, controversially, was not raised' (Rosenberg and Rutherford 2018).

On 27 December 2017, Cook Islands joined the AIIB, with Finance Minister Mark Brown stating it could provide an alternative to financing infrastructure development (Harwood 2017). An announcement that Cook Islands would join the BRI followed in November 2018 (Radio New Zealand 2018d). In the same month, Cook Islands also attended the first China International Import Expo in Shanghai, a BRI mechanism to bring overseas companies to China to meet with domestic buyers (Radio New Zealand 2018c). New Zealand media alleged that China was offered a contract to construct a deepwater port on Penryhn in exchange for participation in the BRI. According to the government source in Wellington, Cook Islands would be 'the next Pacific domino to fall' (Scott 2018). The story drew a complaint from New Zealand's Office of the Prime Minister (ibid.).

Solomon Islands and Kiribati

In September 2019, Solomon Islands and Kiribati switched diplomatic recognition from Taipei to Beijing. The move signalled a swing towards regional alignment with the PRC, leaving Taiwan with four Oceanic partners (Nauru, Tuvalu, Palau and Marshall Islands). In the case of Solomon Islands, the switch involved a drawn-out fact-finding process in Oceania and China to assess the potential benefits and drawbacks of recognising Beijing. Once Solomon Islands made the decision to switch on 21 September 2019, Kiribati soon followed on 27 September. By October, both states had signed on to the BRI following a state visit by Solomon Islands Prime Minister Manasseh Sogavare and an announced visit of Kiribati's President Taneti Maamau to China in January 2020. In a post-recognition round of investment enthusiasm, China and Solomon Islands announced the initiation of several projects, including the multimillion-dollar revival of the Gold Ridge mine and construction of facilities for the Pacific Games. An attempt by a consortium of Chinese interests to lease development rights for the island of Tulagi was stymied by the Solomon Islands' attorney general, indicating not only limits to China-takeover narratives, but also how the exercise of Oceanic sovereignty remains a consideration for new Chinese economic interests.

The BRI in Fiji

The Look North and the BRI

The government of Fijian Prime Minister Bainimarama has been active in diversifying Suva's economic partners. The 2006 coup prompted the adoption of a Look North policy that aimed to attract investment from nontraditional bilateral partners, as Australia and the US imposed economic sanctions on the new administration. Prime Minister Bainimarama branded the Look North as an expression of Fijian agency shaped by Fijians for Fijians in a bid to link state and individual aspirations. Because of this policy setting, Chinese economic interventions and people have become more visible across the Fijian islands. By 2017, China was the largest bilateral aid donor and source of foreign direct investment to Fiji (Pacific Islands Report 2016).

On 12 November 2018, Suva inked a long-hinted-at MOU with China on cooperation with the BRI framework following an enthusiastic exchange of BRI participation pledges between Fijian President Jioji Konrote and Chinese Foreign Minister Wang Yi the previous month (Xinhua 2017b, 2018f, 2018g). Since the introduction of the BRI into the Pacific Islands region, the Fijian and Chinese states have co-constructed a discourse of the Look North and the BRI as mutually compatible projects. This shift from a singular Look North narrative to an integrated discourse does not signal an overwrite of an indigenous policy framework; the thematic continuity from the Look North to the BRI indicates how some PICs are adapting the new paradigm to local conditions. This integrative process is also noted in the previous individual country profiles, as PICs combine the priorities of national development plans with the BRI, giving an impression of coherence between the BRI and domestic priorities.

In an analysis of Fijian and Chinese media and official texts on the Look North and the BRI, the integrative shift in Sino–Fijian economic relations began as early as 2015 (Szadziewski 2020). Clearly, this date overlaps with the formal announcement of the Pacific Islands region as a Maritime Silk Road corridor, as well as Prime Minister Bainimarama's Beijing meeting with President Xi Jinping in July of the same year. Prior to 2015, Look North narratives dominated media and official discussion of Sino–Fijian relations; however, by 2017, the swing toward the BRI framework appears absolute, with Look North mentions barely registering in Chinese and

Fijian sources. That year also coincided with Prime Minister Bainimarama's attendance at the Belt and Road Forum as the only PIC state leader. There is continuity in the claims officials make in both projects, including the creation of investment opportunities (potentiality) and the movement toward shared prosperity (mutuality) (Embassy of the People's Republic of China in the Republic of Fiji 2017a; Q. Zhang 2017). The BRI has not displaced Look North narratives, just repackaged them and underscored its integration and coherence with Fijian interests as articulated by Fijians in the Look North framework.

State legibility

The China–PICs economic relationship includes a range of Chinese actors, such as private investors, state contractors, state-owned enterprises, provincial and central government agencies, media outlets, academic institutions, community associations, migrants and labourers. Brant (see Wesley-Smith 2016) suggested the Chinese state is brought into the region by contractors responding to Pacific Island governments' requests for infrastructure project funding. I argue this is still the case, as more financing options are made available under the BRI; however, the Chinese state is not passive in these processes. The range of Chinese projects and activities labelled as Belt and Road in Fiji demonstrates a broad capture of Chinese actors under the BRI umbrella. Emblematic of the BRI's visibility in Suva is the construction of the Wanguo (WG) Friendship Plaza, which will house retail, hotel and office units. The project has been described as an 'inspiration from China's "One Belt and One Road"' and has visible symbolic value, as it is set to become the tallest building in the country (Bolanavanua 2017). The private investment of approximately US$75 million is the first by WG International through a locally registered company. At the August 2017 groundbreaking ceremony, former Chinese ambassador to Fiji Zhang Ping told assembled dignitaries that the construction of the building 'reflects the confidence that Chinese companies have in the future of our bilateral relations' (ibid.).

Near Komave, 90 kilometres west of Suva, private Chinese investors have proposed a resort complex with a value of US$240 million. Conditions for securing the land lease included financial aid to Komave residents and employment once the facility opens. The Silkroad Ark Fiji Hotel was announced as one of the first BRI projects in Fiji and construction was scheduled for 2018 using Chinese labour. However, on a visit to the site in 2018, there was no visible sign of work underway and the project appears to have come to an end. In conversations with residents of Komave in 2017 and 2018, I documented conflicting responses to the intervention, especially concern over the import of Chinese labour for construction. As a goodwill gesture, the investors offered a scholarship for a Fijian scholar to study at Jinan University, and even though sponsorship came from the Silkroad Ark Investment Company, the award was labelled a Belt and Road enterprise (Kalouniviti 2017). The broad labelling of tourist visits from China to Fiji and the funding of students from Fiji to China as BRI activities is also evident in announcements made in 2017 and 2018 (Tuimasala 2018; Wang 2017).

Notable BRI-labelled construction projects involving state contractors include:

1. the US$9.5 million redevelopment of the Suva Civic Centre under an agreement between Guangdong Province and Suva City Council, with the work contracted to the Nam Yue Group (Xinhua 2018d)

2. the US$6 million construction of the Stinson Parade and Vatuwaqa bridges in Suva under a grant. China Railway 14th Bureau Group undertook the project, and its executive director told Xinhua upon completion of the project in January 2018:

    > As [a] Chinese company, we are proud of doing something like building the bridges to help promote the friendship between the two peoples and make contributions to the Belt and Road Initiative (Xinhua 2018a)

3. the completion of a US$6 million medical training centre and emergency centre at Navua Hospital, as well as the handover of medical equipment donated by Guangdong Province. Construction was financed under a grant and contracted to the Yanjian Group. At the July 2017 opening ceremony, Zhang Ping said:

    > The cooperation between Guangdong and Fiji responds to the ideas of the 'Belt and Road' Initiative … The B&R Initiative not only emphasises on infrastructure connectivity, but also on people-to-people bond (Embassy of the People's Republic of China in the Republic of Fiji 2017b)

4. the upgrading of the Nabouwalu/Dreketi Road on Vanua Levu. The project was funded with a US$135 million concessional loan and work undertaken by the China First Railway Group

(CRFG) (Xinhua 2018c). CRFG are also contracted to build the new Fijian Holdings Limited Tower in Suva, another BRI-inspired project (Chanel 2018)

5. and the construction of the Panda Power Plant. Prime Minister Bainimarama proposed the deal at the 2017 Belt and Road Forum when he met with Su Huaisheng, the deputy general manager of Panda Green Energy Group. The prime minister situated the BRI and the project as potential measures in tackling the PIC priority of climate change (Panda Green 2017).

As an indicator of provincial authorities in China taking BRI opportunities to the region, in May 2017, the China Council for the Promotion of International Trade Guangdong Committee displayed in Suva over 30 companies specialising in manufacturing, tourism and real estate (CCPIT 2017). At the community level, the Belt and Road label has been applied to any number of events and projects, from art displays at the Chinese Cultural Centre in Suva to communal celebrations of the Mid-Autumn Festival (Vakaema 2018). Similarly, local groups such as the Chinese Association and state-linked entities such as the Confucius Institute at the University of the South Pacific's Laucala Campus have enacted the discourses of the BRI in their community engagement (China Daily 2018). In December 2018, the Chinese embassy held a symposium on its overseas Chinese work with over 40 representatives from the Chinese community in Fiji. The meeting indicated a readiness to harmonise state messaging with nonstate actors. Then Chinese ambassador Qian Bo explained new reforms in the government's administration of overseas Chinese affairs and commended the delegates on their role in 'promoting China–Fiji exchanges and cooperation' as well as the embassy's commitment to 'protect the legitimate rights and interests of overseas Chinese in Fiji' (Embassy of the People's Republic of China in the Republic of Fiji 2018). Then ambassador Qian also encouraged the community representatives to participate in the BRI as a means of realising their 'personal dreams' (ibid.).

Conclusion

China's bid for coherence in its approach to the Pacific Islands regions through the BRI is as much a domestic as an international project. The flexible coherence of a vaguely defined BRI not only counters narratives external to the Pacific Islands over China's so-called erratic interactions with the region, but also harmonises a range of Chinese activities within the BRI framework. However, this discursive process has not put to rest questions, in some cases justifiable, over how projects play out on the ground and the seemingly strategic intent of the capture of Chinese economic activity under a singular state policy. Some familiar criticisms persist. Wallis (2017) argued that unmanageable debt to China may bring regional instability, and Pryke (2018) noted the lack of transparency in Chinese interventions. Drawing on extensive research of the finer details of Chinese economic interventions, Smith (2018) commented that 'most large Chinese aid projects in the Pacific are reverse-engineered by a Chinese contractor and their Pacific partners, then presented to China Exim Bank as local initiatives'. The debate over Chinese influence that blew up in Australia in 2018 prompted an examination of increased Chinese presence in the Pacific Islands region, including accusations of projects as 'white elephants' and 'roads to nowhere' (AFP 2018; Wyeth 2018). The rhetoric of legislators and alarmist media in Australia indicates the arrival of the BRI in the Pacific has not dispelled fear discourses. In sum, while state discourses make for clean analyses for the purposes of this chapter, the ground-level outcomes are much messier, a theme widespread in analyses of Chinese interventions in Africa and Latin America (Narins 2016; Power and Mohan 2010). As such, the flexible coherence of a policy in which states and China can co-construct development narratives is a considerable advantage in building a 'community of common destiny' through the BRI (D. Zhang 2018). Discourses often cleanse untidy ground-level implementation of aid and investment projects. As a result, the urgency is clear for research into ground-level impacts of BRI projects and activities in Oceania to demonstrate the kinds of material, rather than discursive, changes that are in process through China's BRI projects and to challenge the sweep of coherence narratives.

It is also important to emphasise that the BRI is not the only anticipatory geography currently on offer in the Pacific Islands region. The Pacific Islands Forum's Blue Pacific framework, Australia's Pacific Step-Up, New Zealand's Pacific Rest, the US's Pacific Pledge, Indonesia's Pacific Elevation, the Republic of Korea's New Southern Policy, Taiwan's New Southbound Policy and Austronesian Forum, the UK's Pacific Uplift and various iterations of the Indo-Pacific concept emanating from Washington DC, Canberra, New Delhi, Paris and Tokyo offer competing geopolitical futures. The emerging complexity of Oceania's geopolitical map raises the critical issues of Pacific Island agency and where Pacific Island governments and Pacific Islanders exert their own vision of a regional future. Even though, as Zhang, the Chinese entrepreneur in Nadi, stated, the BRI will come to define Sino–PIC engagement, this chapter concludes that it is not an imposed project and some of the narratives of its introduction to the region are co-constructed. Furthermore, China represents one of several bilateral engagements between Pacific Island governments and other states. While the BRI may represent Beijing's proposal to the world on how it will conduct its global presence, it may also embody how the Pacific Islands intend to manage their interests on the regional geopolitical stage with many suitors.

References

ABC News 2017. PIF Says the Pacific Can Take Advantage of China's Maritime 'Silk Road' Plan. *Pacific Beat* program, 15 May. www.abc.net.au/radio-australia/programs/pacificbeat/pif-says-the-pacific-can-take-advantage-of-chinas/8528180

ABC News 2018a. PNG Becomes First Pacific Nation to Sign onto China's One Belt, One Road. *Pacific Beat* program, 25 June. www.abc.net.au/radio-australia/programs/pacificbeat/png-china-trip/9905346

ABC News 2018b. Tonga Gets Five Years' Grace on Chinese Loan as Pacific Nation Joins Belt and Road Initiative. 19 November. www.abc.net.au/news/2018-11-19/china-defers-tongas-loan-payments-as-nation-signs-up-to-bri/10509140

AFP (Agence France-Presse) 2018. China Funding White Elephant Infrastructure Projects in The Pacific, Says Australian Minister. *South China Morning Post*, 10 January. www.scmp.com/news/china/diplomacy-defence/article/2127626/china-funding-white-elephant-infrastructure-projects

Atkinson, J. 2010. China–Taiwan Diplomatic Competition and the Pacific Islands. *The Pacific Review* 23(4):407–27. doi.org/10.1080/09512748.2010.495998

Bohane, B. 2018. South Pacific Nation Shrugs Off Worries on China's Influence. *The New York Times*, 13 June. www.nytimes.com/2018/06/13/world/asia/vanuatu-china-wharf.html

Bolanavanua, S. 2017. Tallest Building in the Islands to Open in 2019: Developer. *Fiji Sun*, 15 August. www.fijisun.com.fj/2017/08/15/tallest-building-in-the-islands-to-open-in-2019-developer/

Brant, P. 2013. Chinese Aid in the South Pacific: Linked to Resources? *Asian Studies Review* 37(2):158–77. doi.org/10.1080/10357823.2013.767311

Brant, P. 2016. Chinese Aid in the Pacific. Lowy Institute for International Policy. www.chineseaidmap.lowyinstitute.org/

CCPIT 2017. 2017 Road Show of Guangdong Premium Products in Pacific Islands-Suwa Successfully Held. China Council for the Promotion of International Trade Guangdong Committee, 8 May. www.gdefair.com/news_detail/20175/lb123xl020175815185276620.htm

Chanel, S. 2018. China Railway First Group Ink Big Suva Tower Contract. *Fiji Sun*, 20 September. www.fijisun.com.fj/2018/09/20/crfg-ink-big-suva-tower-contract/

China Daily 2018. Belt and Road Initiative Provides Opportunities for Cooperation: Experts. www.chinadaily.com.cn/a/201808/29/WS5b866894a310add14f3887d6.html

Clover, C. and L. Hornby 2015. China's Great Game: Road to a New Empire. *Financial Times*, 12 October. www.ft.com/content/6e098274-587a-11e5-a28b-50226830d644

CREC (China Railway Engineering Corporation) 2018. 张宗言会见巴布亚新几内亚总理 [Zhang Zongyan Meets the Papua New Guinea Prime Minister]. www.crec4.com/content-1107-26579-1.html

Crocombe, R. 2007. *Asia in the Pacific Islands*. Suva: IPS Publications, University of the South Pacific.

D'Arcy, P. 2014. The Chinese Pacifics: A Brief Historical Review. *The Journal of Pacific History* 49(4):396–420. doi.org/10.1080/00223344.2014.986078

Daily Post 2017. Finance Minister Attends China's Belt and Road Initiative. 1 June. www.dailypost.vu/news/finance-minister-attends-china-s-belt-and-road-initiative/article_0d23e8a3-9090-56b4-82d3-f1e66eb04170.html

Dornan, M. and P. Brant 2014. Chinese Assistance in the Pacific: Agency, Effectiveness and the Role of Pacific Island Governments. *Asia & the Pacific Policy Studies* 1(2):349–63. doi.org/10.1002/app5.35

Dornan, M. and S. Muller 2018. The China Shift in Pacific Trade. *DevPolicy Blog*, 15 November. www.devpolicy.org/china-in-the-pacific-australias-trade-challenge-20181115/

Edney, K. 2014. *The Globalization of Chinese Propaganda: International Power and Domestic Political Cohesion*. New York: Palgrave Macmillan.

Embassy of the People's Republic of China in the Federated States of Micronesia 2019. Kaselehlie Press Publishes Ambassador Huang Zheng's Article on Belt and Road Initiative. 28 May. fm.china-embassy.org/eng/xwdt/t1667106.htm

Embassy of the People's Republic of China in New Zealand 2018. China and Niue Sign Memorandum of Understanding on Cooperation within the Framework of the Silk Road Economic Belt and the 21st Century Maritime Silk Road Initiative. 27 July. www.chinaembassy.org.nz/eng/gdxw/t1582729.htm

Embassy of the People's Republic of China in the Republic of Fiji 2017a. The Fiji Sun Published a Signed Article by Ambassador Zhang Ping Entitled 'Closer Co-Operation Under Belt and Road Win-Win for Fiji, China'. 17 May. fj.china-embassy.org/eng/gdxw/t1462444.htm

Embassy of the People's Republic of China in The Republic of Fiji 2017b. Speech by Ambassador Zhang Ping at the Unveiling Ceremony for Guangdong Aid Program in Navua Hospital. 19 July. fj.china-embassy.org/chn/sgxx/dsjh/t1478683.htm

Embassy of the People's Republic of China in The Republic of Fiji 2018. 驻斐济使馆举办侨务工作座谈会 [Embassy in Fiji Held a Symposium on Overseas Chinese Affairs]. 4 December. fj.china-embassy.org/chn/xw/t1618749.htm

Ferdinand, P. 2016. Westward Ho—the China Dream and 'One Belt, One Road': Chinese Foreign Policy under Xi Jinping. *International Affairs* 92(4):941–57. doi.org/10.1111/1468-2346.12660

Fry, G. and S. Tarte 2015. *The New Pacific Diplomacy*. Canberra: ANU Press. doi.org/10.22459/NPD.12.2015

Global Times 2018. China-Proposed Belt and Road Initiative Provides Opportunities for South Pacific Island Nations: Samoan PM. 14 October. www.globaltimes.cn/content/1122827.shtml

Government Press Secretariat of Samoa 2018. Fujian to Help Samoa. *Samoa Observer*, 23 April. www.samoaobserver.ws/en/24_04_2018/local/32503/Fujian-to-help-Samoa.htm

Government of Samoa 2018. Remarks by China's Ambassador to Samoa Wang Xuefeng at the Reception to Celebrate the 69th Anniversary of the Founding of the People's Republic of China. Speech at the Chinese embassy, Vailima, 28 September. www.facebook.com/samoagovt/posts/speechremarks-by-chinas-ambassador-to-samoa-wang-xuefeng-at-the-reception-to-cel/2053037731393905/

Graham, E. 2018. Belt and Road: More Than Just a Brand. *The Interpreter*, 14 September. Lowy Institute. www.lowyinstitute.org/the-interpreter/belt-and-road-more-just-brand

Hannan, K. and S. Firth 2016. 'One Belt One Road': China's Trade and Investment in Pacific Island States. Paper presented at the ISA Asia-Pacific Conference 2016, City University of Hong Kong, Hong Kong, June 25–27.

Hanson, F. 2009. China: Stumbling Through the Pacific. *Policy Brief.* Sydney: Lowy Institute for International Policy. doi.org/10.1142/9789814304399_0004

Hanson, F. and M. Fifita 2011. China in the Pacific: The New Banker in Town. *Policy Brief.* Sydney: Lowy Institute for International Policy.

Harwood, J. 2017. Cook Islands to Join Chinese-Led Bank. *Cook Islands News*, 22 December. www.cookislandsnews.com/item/67069-cook-islands-to-join-chinese-led-bank/67069-cook-islands-to-join-chinese-led-bank

Henderson, J. 2001. China, Taiwan and the Changing Strategic Significance of Oceania. *Revue Juridique Polynesienne* 1(1):143–56.

Henderson, J. and B. Reilly 2003. Dragon in Paradise: China's Rising Star in Oceania. *The National Interest* 72(Summer): 94–104.

Kalouniviti, M. 2017. Sagar off to China under the 'Belt and Road' Initiative. *The Fiji Times*, 25 July. www.fijitimes.com/sagar-off-to-china-under-the-belt-and-road-initiative/

Kaselehlie Press 2018. Speaker Simina Meets with Leadership of China Parliament. 31 May. www.kpress.info/index.php?option=com_content&view=article&id=972:speaker-simina-meets-with-leadership-of-china-parliament&catid=8&Itemid=103

Koanapo, J. 2017. China's Diplomacy in the Pacific. Government of Vanuatu, 15 May. web.archive.org/web/20191130104336/https://www.gov.vu/en/public-information/196-china-s-diplomacy-in-the-pacific

Lanteigne, M. 2017. China's Expanding Belt and Road Policies: Challenges for Oceania. *Line of Defence Magazine* Winter 2017. www.defsecmedia.co.nz/international-security/winter-2017-belt-road/

Lesa, M.K. 2018. Talofa Lava and Welcome to 'China Ready' Samoa." *Samoa Observer*, 9 August. www.samoaobserver.ws/en/10_08_2018/editorial/35804/Talofa-lava-and-welcome-to-%E2%80%9CChina-ready%E2%80%9D-Samoa.htm

Liu, H. and E. van Dongen 2016. China's Diaspora Policies as a New Mode of Transnational Governance. *Journal of Contemporary China* 25(102):805–21. doi.org/10.1080/10670564.2016.1184894

Lo, K. 2018. Overseas Chinese 'Have Role to Play' in Building Political Trust Abroad for Belt and Road. *South China Morning Post*, 24 August. www.scmp.com/news/china/diplomacy-defence/article/2161062/overseas-chinese-have-role-play-building-political

McGarry, D. 2018. Belt and Road Details. *Daily Post*, 27 November. www.dailypost.vu/news/belt-road-details/article_1528d7dc-ac31-5f98-8c36-433f8b0e2403.html

Meick, E., M. Ker and H.M. Chan 2018. China's Engagement in the Pacific Islands: Implications for the United States. *Staff Research Report*. Washington DC: US–China Economic and Security Review Commission. www.uscc.gov/sites/default/files/Research/China-Pacific%20Islands%20Staff%20Report.pdf

Ministry of Commerce People's Republic of China 2013. Address of Wang Yang at the 2nd China–Pacific Island Countries Economic Development and Cooperation Forum and the Opening Ceremony of 2013 China International Show on Green Innovative Products & Technologies, Guangzhoum, 8 November. english.mofcom.gov.cn/article/newsrelease/significantnews/201311/20131100386982.shtml

Ministry of Foreign Affairs of the People's Republic of China 2016. Joint Press Release Between the People's Republic of China and the Independent State of Papua New Guinea. 8 July. www.fmprc.gov.cn/mfa_eng/wjdt_665385/2649_665393/t1378713.shtml

Ministry of Foreign Affairs of the People's Republic of China 2017. Special Envoy for China–Pacific Islands Forum Dialogue Du Qiwen Attends 29th Post Forum Dialogue of the Pacific Islands. 9 September. www.fmprc.gov.cn/mfa_eng/wjbxw/t1492101.shtml

Ministry of Foreign Affairs of the People's Republic of China 2018a. Xi Jinping Holds Talks with King Tupou VI of Tonga the Two Heads of State Agree to Push China–Tonga Strategic Partnership for New and Greater Development. 1 March. www.fmprc.gov.cn/mfa_eng/wjb_663304/zzjg_663340/bmdyzs_664814/xwlb_664816/t1539432.shtml

Ministry of Foreign Affairs of the People's Republic of China 2018b. Joint Press Communiqué between the People's Republic of China and the Kingdom of Tonga. 1 March. www.fmprc.gov.cn/mfa_eng/wjdt_665385/2649_665393/t1538747.shtml

Ministry of Foreign Affairs of the People's Republic of China 2018c. Ambassador Huang Zheng Hosting Reception for His Assumption of Office. 10 July. www.fmprc.gov.cn/mfa_eng/wjb_663304/zwjg_665342/zwbd_665378/t1575617.shtml

Ministry of Foreign Affairs of the People's Republic of China 2018d. Chinese Premier Eyes Closer Friendship with Samoa. 19 September. www.fmprc.gov.cn/mfa_eng/zxxx_662805/t1597124.shtml

Ministry of Foreign Affairs of the People's Republic of China 2018e. Speech by H.E. Huang Zheng Ambassador Extraordinary and Plenipotentiary of the People's Republic of China to the FSM at the Seminar on Marine Economic Cooperation between China and Pacific Island Countries. 9 October. www.fmprc.gov.cn/mfa_eng/wjb_663304/zwjg_665342/zwbd_665378/t1602697.shtml

Muttarak, R. 2017. Moving Along the Belt and Road: Implications of China's 'One Belt, One Road' Strategies on Chinese Migration. *Translocal Chinese: East Asian Perspectives* 11(2):312–32. doi.org/10.1163/24522015-01102007

Narins, T. 2016. Evaluating Chinese Economic Engagement in Africa Versus Latin America. *Geography Compass* 10(7):283–92. doi.org/10.1111/gec3.12270

National Development and Reform Commission 2015. *Vision and Actions on Jointly Building Silk Road Economic Belt and 21st-Century Maritime Silk Road*. Ministry of Foreign Affairs and Ministry of Commerce, People's Republic of China. www.fmprc.gov.cn/mfa_eng/zxxx_662805/t1249618.shtml

Ong, A. 1999. *Flexible Citizenship: The Cultural Logics of Transnationality*. Durham: Duke University Press.

Pacific Islands Development Forum 2017. China Hosts Belt and Road Forum for International Cooperation High-Level Dialogue. 5 July. www.pidf.int/china-hosts-belt-and-road-forum-for-international-cooperation-high-level-dialogue/

Pacific Islands Report 2016. China Is Biggest Source of Foreign Investment, Tourists to Fiji. 29 November. www.pireport.org/articles/2016/11/29/china-biggest-source-foreign-investment-tourists-fiji

Pacific Islands Report 2017. Pacific Islands Forum Welcomes China's Plan for 'Maritime Silk Road.' 28 March. www.pireport.org/articles/2017/03/28/pacific-islands-forum-welcomes-chinas-plan-maritime-silk-road

Panda Green 2017. The Prime Minister of Fiji Expecting Panda Power Plant to Land in Fiji. 17 May. www.pandagreen.com/show-351.html

Parsons, L. 2018. Roundup: Friendship between Chinese Enterprise, PNG People Deepened after Years of Cooperation. China.org.cn, 7 June. www.china.org.cn/world/Off_the_Wire/2018-06/07/content_51766897.htm

Power, M. and G. Mohan 2010. Towards a Critical Geopolitics of China's Engagement with African Development. *Geopolitics* 15(3):462–95. doi.org/10.1080/14650040903501021

Pryke, J. 2018. The Bad—and Good—of China's Aid in the Pacific. *The Interpreter*, 11 January. Lowy Institute. www.lowyinstitute.org/the-interpreter/bad-and-good-china-aid-pacific

Purcell, L.F. 2017. Opportunities for Trade with China. Remarks at the China-Pacific Economic Cooperation Forum, Apia. *Samoa Observer*, 14 September. www.samoaobserver.ws/en/14_09_2017/local/24319/Opportunities-for-trade-with-China.htm

Radio New Zealand 2018a. PNG and China Approach Free Trade Deal. 16 April. www.radionz.co.nz/international/pacific-news/355190/png-and-china-approach-free-trade-deal

Radio New Zealand 2018b. Niue Mulls Chinese Shipping Tax Scheme under Belt and Road. 3 October. www.radionz.co.nz/international/pacific-news/367801/niue-mulls-chinese-shipping-tax-scheme-under-belt-and-road

Radio New Zealand 2018c. Cook Islands Minister Attends China Trade Expo. 5 November. www.radionz.co.nz/news/pacific/370268/cook-islands-minister-attends-china-trade-expo

Radio New Zealand 2018d. Cook Islands to Join China's Belt and Road. 9 November. www.radionz.co.nz/international/pacific-news/375548/cook-islands-to-join-china-s-belt-and-road

Radio New Zealand 2018e. Tonga and Vanuatu Join China's Belt and Road. 20 November. www.radionz.co.nz/international/pacific-news/376372/tonga-and-vanuatu-join-china-s-belt-and-road

Radio New Zealand 2018f. Pacific Leaders More Questioning of Chinese Influence. 24 November. www.radionz.co.nz/news/world/376732/pacific-leaders-more-questioning-of-chinese-influence

Rheeney, A. 2018. Taking a Breather on China's Belt and Road Initiative. *Samoa Observer*, 16 October. www.samoaobserver.ws/en/16_10_2018/editorial/37633/Taking-a-breather-on-China%E2%80%99s-Belt-and-Road-Initiative.htm

Rosenberg, M. and H. Rutherford 2018. Government Blindsided as Niue Signs up to Chinese Blandishments. *Stuff*, 4 November. www.stuff.co.nz/national/108331406/government-blindsided-as-niue-signs-up-to-chinese-blandishments

Scott, C. 2018. Penryhn Story Draws Formal Complaint from OPM. *Cook Islands News*, 6 November. www.cookislandsnews.com/item/71259-penryhn-story-draws-formal-complaint-from-opm

Seib, R. 2010. China in the South Pacific: No New Hegemon on the Horizon. *PRIF-Reports* No. 90. Frankfurt: Peace Research Institute Frankfurt.

Senate Foreign Affairs, Defence and Trade References Committee 2005. *Opportunities and Challenges: Australia's Relationship with China*. Canberra: Commonwealth of Australia. www.aph.gov.au/Parliamentary_Business/Committees/Senate/Foreign_Affairs_Defence_and_Trade/Completed_inquiries/2004-07/china/report01/index

Shepard, W. 2017. Why the Ambiguity of China's Belt and Road Initiative Is Perhaps Its Biggest Strength. *Forbes*, 19 October. www.forbes.com/sites/wadeshepard/2017/10/19/what-chinas-belt-and-road-initiative-is-really-all-about/#61e228cde4de

Shie, T.R. 2007. Rising Chinese Influence in the South Pacific: Beijing's 'Island Fever.' *Asian Survey* 47(2):307–26. doi.org/10.1525/as.2007.47.2.307

Smith, G. 2013. Beijing's Orphans? New Chinese Investors in Papua New Guinea. *Pacific Affairs* 86(2):327–49. doi.org/10.5509/2013862327

Smith, G. 2017. Dreams of Prosperity in Papua New Guinea. In J. Golley and L. Jaivin (eds), *China Story Yearbook 2017: Prosperity*. Canberra: ANU Press, 130–37. doi.org/10.22459/CSY.04.2018.04A

Smith, G. 2018. The Belt and Road to Nowhere: China's Incoherent Aid in Papua New Guinea. *The Interpreter*, 23 February. Lowy Institute. www.lowyinstitute.org/the-interpreter/belt-and-road-nowhere-china-s-incoherent-aid-papua-new-guinea

Smith, G., G. Carter, M. Xiaojing, A. Tararia, E. Tupou and X. Weitao 2014. *The Development Needs of Pacific Island Countries*. Beijing: UNDP China. www.cn.undp.org/content/china/en/home/library/south-south-cooperation/the-development-needs-of-pacific-island-countries-report-0.html

Subacchi, P. 2015. The AIIB Is a Threat to Global Economic Governance. *Foreign Policy*, 31 March. www.foreignpolicy.com/2015/03/31/the-aiib-is-a-threat-to-global-economic-governance-china/

Sullivan, J. and B. Renz 2012. Representing China in the South Pacific. *East Asia* 29(4):377–90. doi.org/10.1007/s12140-012-9177-0

Szadziewski, H. 2020. Converging Anticipatory Geographies in Oceania: The Belt and Road Initiative and Look North in Fiji. *Political Geography* 77(March 2020). doi.org/10.1016/j.polgeo.2019.102119

Taylor, M. 2016. China's Growing Impact on the Regional Political Order. In M. Powles (ed.), *China and the Pacific: The View from Oceania*. Wellington: Victoria University Press, 41–45.

To, J. 2014. *Qiaowu: Extra-Territorial Policies for the Overseas Chinese*. Leiden: BRILL.

Tobin, M. 2019. China's 'Great Friendship' with Micronesia Grows Warmer, Leaving US with Strategic Headache in Pacific. *South China Morning Post*, 23 December. www.scmp.com/week-asia/politics/article/3043152/chinas-great-friendship-micronesia-grows-warmer-leaving-us

Tuimasala, L. 2018. Two Fijians Graduate from China University. *Fiji Sun*, 14 July. www.fijisun.com.fj/2018/07/14/two-fijians-graduate-from-china-university/

Vakaema, S. 2018. Traditional Celebrations Excellent Opportunity for Intercultural Exchange and Understanding—Vuniwaqa. *Fiji Village*, 26 September. www.fijivillage.com/news/Traditional-celebrations-excellent-opportunity-for-intercultural-exchange-and-understanding---Vuniwaqa-5rk92s/

Wallis, J. 2017. *Crowded and Complex: The Changing Geopolitics of the South Pacific*. Barton: The Australian Strategic Policy Institute.

Wang, J. 2012. 王缉思: '西进', 中国地缘战略的再平衡 ['Go West,' China's Geostrategic Rebalance]. *Global Times*, 17 October. opinion.huanqiu.com/opinion_world/2012-10/3193760.html

Wang, K. 2017. Belt and Road Initiative Gives Fiji a Tourism Boost. Cgtn.com, 13 May. news.cgtn.com/news/3d41544f31677a4d/share_p.html

Wesley-Smith, T. 2007. *China in Oceania: New Forces in Pacific Politics*. Honolulu: East-West Center.

Wesley-Smith, T. 2016. The China Alternative: Geopolitics, Islander Agency, and Changing Regional Order in Oceania. Paper presented at The Pacific Islands in Transition: Opportunities and Challenges, Center for Pacific Island Countries Studies, Guangdong University of Foreign Studies, 17 June.

Wesley-Smith, T. and E.A. Porter 2010. *China in Oceania: Reshaping the Pacific?* New York: Berghahn Books.

Willmott, B. 2007. Varieties of Chinese Experience in the Pacific. In P. D'Arcy (ed.), Chinese in the Pacific: Where to Now? *Centre for the Study of the Chinese Southern Diaspora Occasional Paper* 1, 35–42. Canberra: CSCSD, Research School of Pacific and Asian Studies, ANU.

Windybank, S. 2005. The China Syndrome. *Policy* 21(2):28–33.

Wyeth, G. 2018. Is China Building Roads to Nowhere in the Pacific? *The Diplomat*, 17 January. thediplomat.com/2018/01/is-china-building-roads-to-nowhere-in-the-pacific/

Xi, J. 2018. Set Sail on a New Voyage for Relations Between China and Pacific Countries. *Post-Courier*, 14 November. postcourier.com.pg/set-sail-new-voyage-relations-china-pacific-island-countries/

Xinhua 2014. China, Pacific Island Countries Announce Strategic Partnership. *China Daily*, 23 November. www.chinadaily.com.cn/world/2014xiattendg20/2014-11/23/content_18961677.htm

Xinhua 2017a. China, Micronesia to Cooperate on Belt and Road. 27 March. www.xinhuanet.com//english/2017-03/27/c_136161549.htm

Xinhua 2017b. Fiji Lauds China-Proposed Belt and Road Initiative. 12 October. www.xinhuanet.com/english/2017-10/12/c_136675215.htm

Xinhua 2018a. Feature: China-Aided Bridges open in Fijian Capital, Cementing Bilateral Friendship. 11 January. www.xinhuanet.com/english/2018-01/11/c_136888833.htm

Xinhua 2018b. China, Tonga Agree to Promote Strategic Partnership. 2 March. www.xinhuanet.com/english/2018-03/02/c_137009307.htm

Xinhua 2018c. Feature: China Helps Build Roads in Fiji to Common Development. 9 May. www.xinhuanet.com/english/2018-05/09/c_137166911.htm

Xinhua 2018d. Newly Redeveloped Suva Civic Center Wins Praise from Fiji. 13 September. www.xinhuanet.com/english/2018-09/13/c_137465871.htm

Xinhua 2018e. Chinese President Pledges Support for Samoa's Economic Development. 18 September. www.xinhuanet.com/english/2018-09/18/c_137477072.htm

Xinhua 2018f. China, Fiji Vow to Further Step up All-Round Practical Cooperation. 30 October. www.xinhuanet.com/english/2018-10/30/c_1375 69386.htm

Xinhua 2018g. China, Fiji Ink MoU on Belt and Road Initiative Cooperation. 12 November. www.xinhuanet.com/english/2018-11/12/c_137601722.htm

Yang, J. 2009. China in the South Pacific: Hegemon on the Horizon? *The Pacific Review* 22(2):139–58. doi.org/10.1080/09512740902815292

Yang, J. 2011. China in Fiji: Displacing Traditional Players? *Australian Journal of International Affairs* 65(3):305–21. doi.org/10.1080/10357718.2011.563 778

Zhang, D. 2017. Pacific Island Countries, China & Sustainable Development Goals. Part 2: The Belt and Road Initiative. *DPA In Brief* 2017/18. Canberra: The Australian National University.

Zhang, D. 2018. The Concept of 'Community of Common Destiny' in China's Diplomacy: Meaning, Motives and Implications. *Asia & the Pacific Policy Studies* 5(2):196–207. doi.org/10.1002/app5.231

Zhang, J. 2015. China's Role in the Pacific Islands Region. In R. Azizian and C. Cramer (eds), *Regionalism, Security and Cooperation in Oceania*. Honolulu: Daniel K. Inouye Asia-Pacific Center for Security Studies, 43–56.

Zhang, Q. 2017. B&R Initiative Brings New Opportunities for the South Pacific: Fiji PM. *China Plus*, 12 May. chinaplus.cri.cn/news/china/9/20170512/ 4484.html

Zhang, Y. 2018. Premier Li: China Open to More Cooperation with Tonga. *China Daily*, 1 March. www.chinadaily.com.cn/a/201803/01/WS5a97ed6da 3106e7dcc13ef58.html

10

Solomon Islands' Foreign Policy Dilemma and the Switch from Taiwan to China

Transform Aqorau

Introduction

In September 2019, Solomon Islands severed its diplomatic relations with the Republic of China (Taiwan) and recognised the People's Republic of China (China). This followed months of public discussions about the Solomon Islands Government's proposal to 'switch', illustrating the uncertain nature of its relationship with Taiwan, which was established in 1983. However, this is not unique to Solomon Islands; it characterises Taiwan's diplomatic relations around the world. As China's global influence grows, Beijing has been able to persuade a number of countries to abandon Taiwan. Central to this are Beijing's One China policy and its claim that Taiwan is a renegade province. In 2017, Panama severed relations with Taiwan, followed by El Salvador, the Dominican Republic and Burkina Faso in 2018. In September 2019, Solomon Islands and Kiribati switched relations from Taiwan to China. This leaves only 14 countries, plus the Holy See, that continue to have diplomatic relations with Taiwan, including four Pacific Island countries: Palau, the Republic of the Marshall Islands (RMI), Tuvalu and Nauru.

This chapter examines the nature of the diplomatic relationship between Solomon Islands and Taiwan and discusses the factors underlying the Solomon Islands Government's decision to sever that relationship. It asserts that the decision to switch was influenced largely by the increase in trade between China and Solomon Islands over the past two decades. It also discusses how the relationship has been influenced by a new wave of Chinese migrants who dominate the retail sector in Honiara and, increasingly, the provinces. It also highlights how these new Chinese migrants have had a negative influence on the quality of governance in Solomon Islands. It then discusses issues the Solomon Islands Government should be cognisant of in its new relationship with China. The government should be conscious of the fact that it does not currently have the resources, moral fortitude and knowledge capital to effectively manage this relationship, a relationship that will be characterised by Beijing's assertive influence, an increase in the number of Chinese companies in the country, especially with investments in natural resource–extractive industries and the potential for a continuing increase in the Chinese migrant population and their dominance in retail businesses. The chapter proposes that the Solomon Islands Government should work on building knowledge capital about the Chinese state, corporations and peoples. This will enable it to best manage the relationship and ensure that there is mutual benefit between the two countries. The chapter concludes by reflecting on the future implications of Solomon Islands' diplomatic relationship with China.

The underlying questions of this chapter are: What were the factors that influenced Solomon Islands' relationship with Taiwan? What were the rationales for the switch to China? What are the implications of the switch for Solomon Islands? What can and should Solomon Islands do to ensure that it benefits from its relationship with China?

Taiwan or China? Solomon Islands' foreign policy dilemma

Following independence in 1978, the Solomon Islands Government contemplated establishing diplomatic relations with China. In April 1982, the then minister of foreign affairs and international trade Ezekiel Alebua visited China for talks that were expected to lead to the establishment of diplomatic relations. On his return, Alebua said that 'a good diplomatic foundation has been laid for future sound diplomatic and trade relations between both countries' (Solomon Islands Government Monthly Magazine 1982). But the Solomon Islands Government was at the same time warming up to Taiwan, sending officials to Taipei. So, the battle between China and Taiwan for diplomatic relations with Solomon Islands started at the dawn of independence. In 1983, Honiara established diplomatic relations with Taiwan, beginning a 36-year relationship (Kabutaulaka 2010).

At various times in the past three decades, prominent Solomon Islanders have flirted with the idea of abandoning diplomatic relations with Taiwan and switching to China. As recently as 24 January 2019, for example, the Democratic Alliance Party (DAP) of then prime minister Ricky Houenipwela announced at their convention that they would review Solomon Islands' diplomatic relations with Taiwan if they were reelected to government in the April 2019 national general elections. Prime Minister Houenipwela noted: 'The possibility of actively pursu[ing] opportunities on South–South cooperation[1] and partnership is one of the DAP international affairs policy' (Fanasia 2019). These sentiments cannot be underestimated, as they came from the party of the incumbent prime minister whose government had courted and enjoyed a long relationship with Taiwan. As far as I am aware, this was the first time that any political party had made the issue of the country's diplomatic relationship with Taiwan part of its political platform. It was also a reflection of China's growing importance to Solomon Islands.

By the eve of the April 2019 elections, Solomon Islands was at a diplomatic crossroads. The reasons that had led other countries to sever relations with Taiwan since its pro-independence Democratic Progressive Party (DPP) won the presidential elections in 2016 could not be ignored. Since the end of the DPP's informal diplomatic truce with Taiwan's other major political party—the nationalist Kuomintang Party—even more countries have left Taiwan for China. This partly reflects these countries' desire to go along with the global trend, wherein the majority of countries recognise China, an economic and political superpower that cannot be ignored.

This trend also impacted Solomon Islands. Following the April 2019 elections, Manasseh Sogavare was elected prime minister and formed the Democratic Coalition Government for Advancement (DCGA). In its

1   China regards itself as a developing country and hence frames its development assistance as South–South cooperation rather than aid, which implicitly requires a donor and recipient.

First 100-Days Policy Framework, the DCGA stated that it would review its development partners and engage in a 'comprehensive assessment on the China question' (DCGA 2019:7). In the months that followed, the DCGA Government unveiled its policy to switch diplomatic relations to China and began an assertive campaign to implement it. A bipartisan task force was established to 'assess the gains of the current bilateral relations with ROC and to provide a strategy for the government to counter any positive and negative impacts of a potential switch' (Solomon Islands Government 2019:5). The task force visited Vanuatu, Fiji, Tonga, Samoa and China, then wrote and submitted its report to caucus. At the same time, the Solomon Islands parliamentary Foreign Relations Committee was tasked to:

> initiate this inquiry to examine, observe and make recommendations on the question of severing existing ties with the Republic of China (Taiwan) and the conduct of government's foreign policy in light of the same (National Parliament of Solomon Islands Foreign Relations Committee 2019:15).

The following discusses in some detail the debates surrounding the switch. Even the contemplation of a switch was a major blow to Taiwan, especially given the fact that Solomon Islands was the largest, and perhaps most important, of the six Pacific Island countries that had diplomatic relations with Taiwan at the time. It was also one of three Pacific nations, along with Tuvalu and Palau, that had never had diplomatic relations with China. The other three—Marshall Islands, Nauru and Kiribati—previously had diplomatic relations with China, but later switched to Taiwan. Nauru provides an interesting example of a country that switches to whoever writes it a cheque. It initially had diplomatic relations with Taiwan, switched to China in 2002, then reestablished ties with Taiwan in 2005 when it discovered that China was not going to subsidise their national airline, which had been declared bankrupt by the courts in Australia. Taiwan's method of keeping Nauru members of parliament in line was simple. According to a 2010 report published in *The Australian*:

> The Taiwanese money man comes once a month. An official from the local embassy, he doles out $US4000 in Australian currency to every one of Nauru's 18 members of parliament (Maley 2010).

In keeping with this practice of chequebook diplomacy, Nauru was one of the few nations to recognise the Russian proxy states of Abkhazia and South Ossetia (Wyeth 2017).

In the past decade, there has been renewed interest in China's aid and investment in the Pacific Islands region and the alleged security threat this poses (Smith 2018). It is interesting to see how this attention has transformed to be characterised in negative terms, as if aid from other donors has not also created a dependency syndrome amongst Pacific Island countries. These security threats are largely manufactured, fuelled-up fears led mainly by some in the Australian media (Wroe 2018) and think tanks (Dobell 2018), stoking fear amongst the Australian, New Zealand and broader Western security axis. This fear is not for the safety and security of the people of the Pacific Islands. The Pacific Islands are important from a traditional security perspective because they provide a buffer against a forward attack on Australia and New Zealand, as well as because Chinese engagement in the Pacific Islands region is increasingly viewed as a threat to historical Western dominance. This powerplay between the Western axis and China in recent years has resulted in increased support to the Pacific Islands region, most notably in infrastructure and military aid. All of the Western Axis countries have increased their engagement; even Great Britain has reopened diplomatic posts in Tonga, Vanuatu and Samoa (Bourke 2018). Australia, New Zealand, France and the US have all increased their aid and propped up their security apparatus, arguably increasing the aid dependency of Pacific Island countries at a time when they need to reduce their dependency and become more self-reliant in terms of their economic and social wellbeing.

It was against this backdrop that Solomon Islands confronted the choice between Taiwan and China. Like other Pacific Island countries, Solomon Islands is seeking a sense of purpose, wanting to become more self-reliant, especially after the departure of the Regional Assistance Mission to Solomon Islands (RAMSI), a regional intervention that was deployed from mid-2003 to 2017 following civil unrest in Solomon Islands that led to the near collapse of the state, the deterioration of the country's economy and the death of about 200 people (Hameiri 2009; Moore 2004). The country is confronted with security issues born not out of external threats from war or terrorism, but from internal threats ranging from a lack of employment opportunities to a lack of entrepreneurial skills that would allow people to participate effectively in the global trading system; the loss of biodiversity and ecosystems through changes in the climate; the loss of habitat and arable land from rising sea levels; and the devastating health effects of noncommunicable diseases brought by changes in diet and lifestyle. These are some of the challenges Solomon Islands faces, which it has to navigate in its relations with other countries, including China.

In addition to these issues is, as mentioned previously, the increasing population of new Chinese migrants who dominate the retail sector, especially in the urban areas. The only provinces that have so far been able to withstand the wave of Chinese migration and the takeover of their retail sector are Choiseul, Temotu, Isabel and Makira/Ulawa. It is not clear whether they will be able to withstand pressure from other growing businesses, especially in the mining sector, which might become the dominant natural resource sector as the forestry industry winds down.

While the wave of new Chinese migrants seeking to establish retail shops may be limited to urban centres, the presence of Malaysian Chinese–owned logging companies is widespread throughout the country. To that extent, the level of integration between ethnic Chinese-owned businesses and the Solomon Islands society is almost complete, with the exception of remote places such as Tikopia and Anuta in the east. The major provinces of Guadalcanal, Malaita and Western have been unable to withstand the migration of Chinese nationals who have established retail shops and dominated the retail sector. In Honiara, these migrants—largely from Guangdong province (Smith 2012)—have already taken most, if not all, of the capital's commercial sites. This migration is enabled by a combination of domestic factors, most notably the corruption of government officials; the corrosion of state institutions, particularly the departments of immigration and labour; and the crowding out of Solomon Islanders from the financial sector, which has encouraged them to sell their land to new arrivals because they have not been able to secure funds to develop it. While the switch in diplomatic relations from Taiwan to China was determined largely by trade and investments, Solomon Islands needs to carefully consider the underlying contributing issues.

Now that Solomon Islands has made the switch, there is a need to learn from the Pacific Islands countries that appear to be struggling with the debts they owe to China. Solomon Islands needs to reassess its governance capacities to see how it can best manage this new relationship. As it is, Solomon Islands does not have the wherewithal to manage the trade-offs that will be required to handle the links between a sudden influx of no-strings-attached development finance and the further opening up of its natural resources. Since the departure of RAMSI, and despite the exorbitant investments it made to the machinery of government and the control of public finances, Solomon Islands public service and institutions have become weaker and tainted by a level of corruption never before seen. The government is therefore in a weak position to manage this new relationship that will require trade-offs for grants and loans. Currently, the Solomon Islands Government is unable to properly manage its natural resources sector effectively. Consequently, having state-backed Chinese companies exploiting the mineral, forestry and fisheries resources of Solomon Islands with in-country support from a new embassy could prove disastrous for the people of Solomon Islands. In order to save the country from itself and possible exploitation, Solomon Islands should carefully consider how it will manage this new diplomatic relationship.

Taiwan–Solomon Islands relations: An unstable ship?

Prior to the switch, Solomon Islands Government officials typically described their country's relationship with Taiwan as strong. I would argue, however, that it was an uneasy and unstable relationship at best. Invariably lurking in the background was China, threatening to lure Solomon Islands to switch. This was a factor that some government officials and politicians in Solomon Islands took advantage of. While the Solomon Islands Government had not officially considered a switch prior to 2019, some government officials and politicians had at least considered it, especially as China's trade and investments increased. For example, former prime minister Gordon Darcy Lilo, who contested the April 2019 election, commented that 'sooner or later, when we see our country hasn't been able to grow out of this relationship [with Taiwan], we are at liberty to review our relations and to explore other avenues' (Greenfield and Westbrook 2019). Taiwan and China have often taken advantage of their respective vulnerabilities at the highest political level. It was initially the government of Taiwan that propped up the discretionary funds— the Rural Constituency Development Fund (RCDF)— controlled by politicians. These funds have transformed Solomon Islands' political landscape by shifting the political power base away from voters and government bureaucracy and into the hands of politicians. Though there has been a decline in the level of Taiwan's contribution to the RCDF in recent years to around 20 per cent, and the Solomon Island Government's contribution has risen sharply, there is still a perception amongst urban elites that Taiwan has contributed to their funding and created a system that entrenches the power of politicians. The RCDF has caused controversy, especially amongst the urban elite and the Solomon Islands diaspora, because it is viewed as supporting political corruption and giving incumbent MPs undue advantages in elections. Regardless of the accuracy of this view, it has coloured people's views of Taiwan.

The relationship between Taiwan and Solomon Islands is not one based on mutual trust and goodwill, but one Solomon Islands politicians have used to gain political mileage, often at the expense of good governance and the social and economic wellbeing of the people. Solomon Islands politicians have played on this relationship and used it to support their political base. Criticisms of the RCDF have been elitist, urban-based and largely focused on the ineffectiveness of the fund as a mechanism for rural development. This is particularly important given the fact that the RCFP represents around one-third of the government's development budget and between 10 and 15 per cent of overall budget outlays (Wiltshire and Batley 2018). However, it is also important to note that the RCDF has helped some people and served its purpose. But in a Least Developed Country like Solomon Islands, there are better ways of ensuring a more equitable delivery of health, education and other social services. The government of Taiwan has been complicit in the way the national parliamentarians have undermined the budgetary and development processes. This perception is borne out by Taiwan's initial support for the RCDF, and it is felt that Taiwan is always ready to help Solomon Islands at any costs.

However, beyond the urban centres, most rural people have no particular view of Taiwan's support for the RCDF and are probably grateful for whatever materials they have received through Taiwan's support. Some of the most popular Taiwanese projects channelled through the RCDF are the rural solar lighting programs, administered by the MPs. There has been no evaluation of the ways in which solar lighting projects have impacted Solomon Islanders' livelihoods. The quality of the products used, however, is poor, and most of the solar panels, batteries and lights do not have long life spans. But most people who receive these projects do not care about the quality of the solar panels or batteries and are only too happy to receive a free gift. This dependency mentality cultivated through the RDCF and the wasteful allocation of limited resources has led to criticism of Taiwan's laissez-faire approach to aid in Solomon Islands.

No other country with which Solomon Islands has diplomatic relation has generated this level of controversy. Once again, only educated elites have expressed disquiet about the way Taiwanese aid supports a mechanism that is, in effect, a slush fund for national parliamentarians. Consequently, the widespread view among the general public in Taiwan that their aid to Pacific Island nations is wasted (Huang 2017) seems well-founded in Solomon Islands. The relationship between Taiwan and Solomon Islands has changed over the years; while it has been based on mutual trust, respect and support for Taiwan's independence, the emergence of the RCDF has changed the nature of the relationship.

In 1983, four years after gaining independence, when Solomon Islands chose to establish relations with Taiwan, the world was very different. The Cold War was still the major international influence that polarised the world between capitalism and communism, and China was only starting its 30-year journey of economic transition. Cold War dynamics drove the Solomon Islands Government to establish relations with Taiwan. They were attracted to the idea that Taiwan was a democratic country and not part of communist China, even though Taiwan no longer represented China at the United Nations. The international order at that time was clearly demarcated between the West, led by the US, and the communist countries, led by the Soviet Union. China was not the economic force it is now, and Solomon Islands leaders were sensitive to the communist regime in China. Taiwan was more influential and had diplomatic relations with many more countries, so it was not a difficult decision for the Solomon Islands Government to establish diplomatic ties with Taiwan.

Solomon Islands did not immediately establish full diplomatic relations with Taiwan, however, first going through a period during which Taiwan had only consular-level representation. The geopolitical dynamics of the region were tense, as Kiribati had just entered into a fisheries agreement with the Soviet Union. US purse seine fishing vessels were fishing illegally and there were uncertainties over fishing rights. Biddick provides insight into the rivalry between China and Taiwan over Solomon Islands in the early 1980s, and suggests why Solomon Islands established diplomatic ties with Taiwan:

> The continuing competition for political influence was particularly evident in the Solomon Islands, as suggested by the contretemps surrounding Prime Minister Alebua's participation in the launching ceremony for a PRC-funded ship in Honiara on October 12, 1988.

The launching ceremony, just two days after Taiwan's 'Double Ten' celebration in Honiara, symbolised the sister province relationship between China's Guangdong Province and Guadalcanal Province in the Solomon Islands. Guangdong officials had earlier signed a memorandum of understanding for development of a joint venture fishery project, reportedly to include Chinese technical assistance and funding for development of shipbuilding and tuna processing operations in Guadalcanal. Taiwan's ambassador apparently took exception to Alebua's participation in the ship-launching ceremony, and on October 14 the Solomon Islands Ministry of Foreign Affairs and the Taiwan embassy issued a joint statement clarifying that Alebua had participated in a private capacity and reiterating that the two countries remained committed to maintaining 'warm, cordial and friendly' diplomatic relations. In fact, this was but the most recent episode of a protracted triangular drama dating from Alebua's trip to Beijing in 1982 as foreign minister of the Mamaloni government. He had publicly indicated at that time that establishment of diplomatic relations with the PRC was imminent. Instead, the Mamaloni Government ultimately decided to recognise Taipei, apparently in response to inducements offered by the Taiwan authorities (1989:807).

It would not be surprising if Solomon Mamaloni's government did make the decision based on an inducement from Taipei. As chief minister, Mamaloni was forced to resign in 1975 when it was discovered that he agreed to receive funds in return for having his face on Solomon Islands coins. The scandal was known at the time as the Letcher Mint Affair, named for the US company that tried to get a favour in return for an inducement offered to Mamaloni. That a political relationship should be defined by its origins arising from an inducement perhaps reflects the uncertainties that plagued this relationship and the vulnerabilities that can arise from weak states led by corrupt leaders. It is no surprise that the RCDF was initiated when Solomon Mamaloni served as prime minister from 1989 to 1993, and that he asked Taiwan to fund it. Understanding the backdrop of the decision that led to the establishment of political ties with Taiwan helps explain why Taiwan has been willing to support the RCDF and prop up the Solomon Islands political establishment, thereby defining to some extent the nature of the relationship between the two countries, which also influences the contest between China and Taiwan. Graeme Dobell, writing soon after the 2006 Honiara riots, quoted former head of Australia's Department of Foreign Affairs and Trade Stuart Harris, who testified to an Australian Senate Foreign Affairs Committee that the diplomatic contest is dangerous because it can easily tear at the structure of a weak Island government:

> We found this in the Solomons, where governments are totally disorientated—in fact just about destroyed—by interventions of this kind. You can disorient a government in the Pacific Islands with a very limited amount of money—just a few bribes to the right people at the top and you have undermined the whole governing system (Dobell 2007:11).

Despite these challenges and negative perceptions about the debilitating effect of the relationship with Taiwan on the quality of governance, it is precisely because of Taiwan's support to the RCDF that the Solomon Islands–Taiwan relationship may be described as healthy and stable at the political level. Indeed, former prime minister Ricky Houenipwela reversed his intent to review the relationship only two weeks after announcing the DAP would do so. However, those who deal closely with Solomon Islands foreign relations were not surprised by the DAP's desire to review the relationship. A Ministry of Foreign Affairs official stated that the Solomon Islands–Taiwan relationship, while strong and enduring, should be broadened to the general community to include people-to-people contacts.[2] The strength of the relationship was based largely on the contacts Taiwan had with political leaders and government officials, and the various visits and exchanges that often took place at the highest political level reflected this. This observation is surprising as it ignores the support the Taiwan Agriculture Technical Mission gives to farmers, not only through spending time at the farms providing training on vegetable farming, piggery and poultry, but also through workshops it runs in the provinces for agriculture extension officers and farmers. One of the successful aspects of the Solomon Islands–Taiwan relationship is the Taiwan Agriculture Technical Mission, because it aims to both support the government's agricultural assistance to farmers and, more importantly, reach ordinary farmers throughout the country. The success of the program can be seen in the improved quality and variety of vegetables sold in the main market in Honiara, reflecting the training farmers have received.

---

2   Acting High Commissioner to Australia, 26 January 2019. Canberra. Personal communication.

Taiwan's relationship with Solomon Islands was shaped around influencing the political leadership and supporting state institutions. There is limited evidence of investment in areas that influence the daily lives of Solomon Islanders in the same way the Chinese have done through Chinese migrants and their stranglehold on the retail sector. Taiwan's development assistance to Solomon Islands has focused around a number of areas, such as support for scholarships for Solomon Islanders to study in Taiwan, including support for the regional scholarship scheme administered by the Pacific Islands Forum Secretariat. In addition to agriculture, they also support the health sector. Their best-known project was the construction of the National Referral Hospital. Though the same level of daily interaction might not be seen as between the Chinese retail shop owners and Solomon Islanders, there are important people-to-people links through the exchange of specialist doctors and visits by Taiwanese health teams in the provinces.

There was generally a lot of goodwill at the highest political level in Solomon Islands towards Taiwan, and there should have been, because the political elites had found a partner who largely had a more-willing ear to lend than other countries, who were less likely to support the political elites. It came as no surprise when, at the 2018 Taiwan Double Ten celebrations, then prime minister Rick Houenipwela said the government 'remained very optimistic about the positive direction which Solomon Islands and Taiwan is heading as is shown in the increasing number of high-level visits made by both government representatives' (Kekea 2018). Other than political convenience, another reason for enduring strong political links was a little-known fund administered personally by the prime minister. In 2008, while president of the Kossa Football Club (FC), I approached the ambassador of Taiwan in Honiara to see if they were able to assist Kossa FC. As reigning club champions, they were to represent Solomon Islands in the FIFA Oceania Football Confederation Club championship. The ambassador told me that they did not have any funds he had discretion over, but advised me to approach then prime minister Dr Derek Sikua. He said there was a fund only the prime minister could authorise the use of, through which they would be able assist Kossa. Few people knew of the existence of this fund. The ambassador said the funds could be released by Taiwan only if a request was personally signed by the prime minister. The next day, I saw Dr Sikua and asked if he could make a request to the government of Taiwan to use this fund, as our club was representing Solomon Islands and our pride and national interest was at stake. He liaised with the secretary to the prime minister's office, who at the time was Jeremiah Manele. I drafted the required letter and the prime minister duly signed it. The request was to fund the team to play in Vanuatu and Fiji in the last leg of the championship, which Kossa FC eventually lost in the final to Waitakere FC of New Zealand. US$30,000 was released by the government of Taiwan to the Solomon Islands Football Federation to enable Kossa to meet all its travel expenses. I was surprised by the existence of this fund, as I had no idea there was such a fund that could be used at the discretion of the prime minister. This illustrates the comfortable relationship between Taiwan and the political leaders of Solomon Islands. It is not hard to imagine that this fund could have been used to persuade MPs against a switch to China. No other country with whom Solomon Islands has diplomatic relations would agree to provide such funds. This supports the view that Taiwan's aid fuelled bad governance.

There is also a regional dimension to Solomon Islands' relationship with Taiwan. The six Pacific Island countries that previously had relations with Taiwan would hold the Taiwan–Pacific Islands Forum Dialogue on the margins of Pacific Islands Forum leaders meetings. One of the features of these dialogues was the announcement of projects to be funded by Taiwan. Representatives from the various regional agencies who submitted bids through the Pacific Islands Forum Secretariat took a keen interest in the dialogue. Taiwan's overseas development assistance (ODA) to the region, including Solomon Islands, between 2011 and 2016 is provided below (Table 1). Solomon Islands was the largest recipient of funding support from Taiwan, which was the fourth largest donor to Solomon Islands.

Table 1. Taiwan's support for the Pacific, 2011–16

Country	Amount	Donor Ranking	Aid Share
Kiribati	$45,451,985	4	10%
Marshall Islands	$44,591,120	3	10%
Nauru	$4,111,000	5	2%
Palau	$3,590,000	6	2%
Solomon Islands	$76,387,935	4	5%
Tuvalu	$73,394	20	0.04%
Total	$174,205,436	5	6%

Note: Despite having a high donor ranking, aid share remains relatively low because aid in the Pacific is often heavily concentrated in a select number of donors, usually either Australia or the US, or Japan in the case of Palau.

Source: Dayant and Pryke (2018).

An important feature of the relationship between Solomon Islands and Taiwan was that during the ethnic tensions in Solomon Islands between 1998 and 2003, it was Taiwan's ODA that kept Solomon Islands foreign reserves intact. Atkinson states that:

> as the crisis developed and international donors began withholding aid due to serious governmental irregularities, the Solomon Islands' leadership turned to Taiwan to meet the spiraling compensation demands of the conflicting parties. The Chen Shui-bian Government, elected in March 2000, aimed to improve Taiwan's tarnished donor image, but was unable to resist being pulled deeper into the crisis. In June 2001, Taiwan's state-owned EXIM Bank agreed to a US$25 million loan after the Solomon Islands Government threatened to switch diplomatic recognition to China. The package was used to finance hundreds of payouts routed through Allan Kemakeza's Ministry of National Unity, Reconciliation and Peace. Kemakeza himself was at the top of the list, and was later sacked for embezzlement over the issue. Parliament nonetheless elected Kemakeza prime minister following the 5 December 2001 elections. The final tranche of the EXIM loan arrived in September 2002, and as the money ran out the crisis reached its nadir, with Cabinet and the Finance Ministry invaded by armed men, including police, demanding money (2009:50).

In an analysis of Taiwan's overall approach to the Pacific, Michael Nguyen and Jonathan Pryke (2018) argued that Taiwan attempted to offset China's appeal by working with Pacific partners in different ways. It recognised that it could not exceed the monetary value of Chinese aid and thus identified areas of Pacific development where its smaller contributions could still be effective. Nguyen and Pryke contend that Taiwan's 'projects targeting sectors such as agriculture, health and industry … emphasise Taiwan's advantage: people-to-people relationships'. An example is Taiwan's horticultural projects. These sought to increase the sustainable productive capacity of local populations through training workshops, internships and extended foreign missions by envoys. Increased exposure of local Pacific communities to Taiwanese experts was a key element driving Taiwanese aid. The working relationships that arose created goodwill and fealty that can only come about through prolonged cooperation. I have argued previously that this aspect of the relationship was highly visible and successful.

Observers invariably contextualise Taiwan's political relations in terms of the tussle it has with China and compare the aid both countries give to the Pacific Islands region. In an analysis of the impact of Taiwan's aid to the region, Jonathan Pryke and Alexander Dayant (2018) said this of its assistance to Solomon Islands:

> That isn't to say Taiwan's engagement has been unnoticed. It has significantly impacted lives of those in the Pacific, in some cases profoundly. The clearest case of this is in Solomon Islands. The primary mechanism for Taiwanese support to Solomon Islands comes in the form of supporting 'Constituent Development Funds'—a discretionary fund that is allotted to each of the country's 50 MPs for investing in their electorates (with minimal oversight). Taiwan has provided close to $90 million to these funds between 2011 and 2018. Solomon Island politicians like these funds so much that they have allocated around one-third of the development budget, or between 10 and 15 per cent of the total budget, to these funds. In this regard, Taiwan's aid program has contributed to profoundly changing, and perhaps undermining, public financial management in its largest supporter in the Pacific. (For a more nuanced discussion on the challenges of being an MP in Solomon Islands, take a look at now Prime Minister Rick Hou's reflections for the Department of Pacific Affairs in 2016).

Underscoring the fickleness of the Solomon Islands–Taiwan relationship, in 2018 the then prime minister Rick Houenipwela 'hailed' Solomon Islands bilateral relationship with Taiwan as 'growing steadily' (Radio New Zealand 2018). Even though a number of other countries had switched relations from Taipei to Beijing, prime minister Houenipwela said 'his government was committed to maintaining and further consolidating relations … [and that] Taiwanese funding had helped with agricultural programmes, medical assistance and the fight against climate change'.

Solomon Islanders as well as outside observers have always questioned the future of Solomon Islands relations with Taiwan. Australian diplomat James Batley (2018), for example, observed that:

> Taiwan faces a number of challenges in shoring up its links with Solomon Islands. For the past couple of decades, Taiwan has invested heavily in Solomon Islands' political elite through its support for the notorious 'constituency development funds', which is the discretionary funds provided for members of parliament to spend in their own constituencies.

In some respects, though, Taiwan has become a victim of its own success in supporting these schemes: as the size of these programs has grown, the Solomon Islands Government itself has picked up ever more of the tab, to the point where Taiwan is now funding under 20 per cent of the total, down from 50 per cent less than 10 years ago. So the relative importance and impact of Taiwan's contribution has shrunk.

Even more worrying from Taiwan's point of view, China is far and away Solomon Islands' largest export market. The most recent figures (for 2016) from the Department of Foreign Affairs and Trade in Australia state that over 62 per cent of Solomons' exports go to China. (This is virtually all logs.) By contrast, Taiwan takes around only one per cent of exports from Solomon Islands.

Such a level of economic dependence on China leaves Solomon Islands highly vulnerable to economic pressure—should this be exercised. Senior Solomon Islanders will be aware of claims made earlier this year that Palau, another of Taiwan's Pacific allies, has been the victim of economic pressure with China essentially turning off the tap of a lucrative flow of Chinese tourists to the small northern Pacific country.

Given the importance of Solomon Islands' trade with China, in the past few years Taiwan's relations with Solomon Islands went through periodic waves of unease, with visits by government officials and politicians to China. I have described how Solomon Islands politicians view their relationship with Taiwan, to some extent taking advantage of Taiwan's vulnerabilities. In return for flexible funding arrangements, and perhaps the discretionary funds the prime minister has access to, Solomon Islands has always used its statement to the annual general meeting of the United Nations General Assembly to call for the reinstatement of Taiwan as a full member of the United Nations and its various organs.

There is never going to be any support for Taiwan's reinstatement in the United Nations. But this never stopped Solomon Islands from staging the theatre of appeals to the international community to allow Taiwan to rejoin. This was a small trade-off for the aid that was administered through the prime minister's office. It gave Taiwanese officials a sense of lien, a right of access other diplomatic missions do not have. My conversations with senior officials indicate that staff at the Taiwanese embassy felt they could meet with the permanent secretary and Minister of Foreign Affairs at any time, even though they were not at the ministerial level and protocol dictates they should meet with relevant officers in the Ministry of Foreign Affairs before accessing more senior staff. They were also the only diplomatic mission in Honiara that had the keys to the VIP lounge at the airport and could use it without necessarily going through the Protocol Department of the Ministry of Foreign Affairs. This shows that money can buy access.

The China factor

Hovering in the background of the Solomon Islands–Taiwan relations was China. This is the unavoidable, and almost inconvenient, truth of the relations Taiwan enjoys with any country, including Solomon Islands, and perhaps explains why the number of countries that have diplomatic relations with Taiwan is heading rapidly towards single figures. China is a global economic and political power and Solomon Islands' largest trading partner. These are important considerations and must have been playing in the minds of current and aspiring MPs. However, there are broader policy issues the government must canvass when viewing its relations, as trade is only one factor. Table 2 shows the trade data for Solomon Islands. It is evident that China is an important actor in the economic affairs and interests of Solomon Islands, while Taiwan does not make the top 10.

Table 2. Top 10 export destinations for Solomon Islands

Country	Export US$
China	$325,830,017
Italy	$38,695,793
Switzerland	$19,335,916
India	$18,192,934
Philippines	$17,583,591
Netherlands	$15,005,260
Malaysia	$7,553,025
Hong Kong	$6,436,486
Thailand	$6,331,429
Vietnam	$4,920,341

Source: Global Edge (2019).

Tables 3 and 4 show the bilateral trade between Solomon Islands and Taiwan. China's trade with Solomon Islands dwarfs that of Taiwan, reflecting the strong commercial ties Solomon Islands has with China.

Table 3. Solomon Islands–China bilateral trade (SB$ million)

	2013	2014	2015	2016	2017	Average
Balance	1,344	1,502	1,451	1,634	2,000	1,586
Exports	1,600	1,944	1,842	2,169	2,566	2,024
Imports	256	441	390	535	566	438

Source: Central Bank of Solomon Islands (2019).

Table 4. Solomon Islands–Taiwan bilateral trade (SB$ million)

	2013	2014	2015	2016	2017	Average
Balance	51	26	30	28	33	33
Exports	95	40	45	53	59	58
Imports	44	14	16	25	27	25

Source: Central Bank of Solomon Islands (2019).

Table 5 shows how imports from China compare with those from Taiwan and the rest of the world from 2007 to 2017. Over a 10-year period, imports from China far surpassed those from Taiwan, underlining the importance of China to the Solomon Islands economy.

Table 5. Percentage of Solomon Islands imports from China and Taiwan

	2017	2016	2015	2014	2013	2012	2011	2010	2009	2008	2007
China	13%	15%	11%	12%	1%	8%	11%	15%	10%	6%	5%
Taiwan	1%	1%	0%	0%	1%	1%	1%	0%	1%	0%	1%
Rest of the world	87%	85%	89%	88%	98%	91%	89%	85%	89%	94%	94%

Source: Central Bank of Solomon Islands (2019).

Table 6 illustrates the percentages of Solomon Islands' exports and imports with its major trading partners. Taiwan does not feature in the statistics, but China features quite prominently, once again underscoring the importance of China to the Solomon Islands economy.

Table 6. Solomon Islands major trading partners, exports and imports, 2013–17

	% of exports*	Commodity		% of imports*	Items
China	58	Logs	Australia	30	Food, mixed
Australia	7	Timber, mixed	Singapore	14	Fuel
Italy	7	Fish	China	11	Household, mixed
UK	5	Palm oil	Japan	8	Machines, cars
Philippines	3	Copra	New Zealand	7	Food, mixed
Total SB$m	**3,506**		**Total SB$m**	**3,864**	

* 5-year average.

Source: Central Bank of Solomon Islands (2019).

Three aspects pertaining to China are important to Solomon Islands. The first is the volume of trade and the size of the trade surplus with China in contrast to the large trade deficits run with Australia and Singapore (the main source of fuel imports). However, most, if not all, of the exports to China are round logs from unsustainable commercial logging. Foreign logging companies that control the industry have been responsible for the corrosion of good governance and extremely poor environmental practices for logging. There is a lot of controversy surrounding this industry and China's demand for round logs is exacerbating the deforestation of Solomon Islands (Global Witness 2018). The bribery of officials, politicians and villagers by the logging industry has led to a culture of corruption that is pervasive throughout Solomon Islands society (Aqorau 2008).

Solomon Islands' trade surplus with China, impressive as it is, remains tied to an industry that has undermined good governance and degraded the natural environment. Despite the RAMSI intervention, corruption by government officials has become more pervasive. Parliament passed anticorruption legislation in 2018, which provides a framework to address the problem. However, is not clear if the government has the resources to make the legislation effective. According to Transparency International, Solomon Islands dropped two points in the 2019 Corruption Perceptions Index, from 44 points in 2018 to 42 points (Radio New Zealand 2020). The weak state institutions that characterise the Solomon Islands Government have thus far been incapable of addressing the impact of the exploitation of Solomon Islands forests. Mining represents the extraction of another natural resource that Chinese businesses have shown an interest in, and, like the forestry sector, the mining sector has suffered from weak compliance stemming from weak state institutions.

The second factor is the migration of new Chinese, who now dominate the retail sector. Most, if not all, the prime retail sites in Honiara are owned by these new arrivals, creating increasing levels of animosity towards them from locals. They are known to bribe their way through government offices to secure licences, work and residential permits and planning permissions, further exacerbating the level of corrosion in the public service. Despite the Honiara riots in 2006, which saw many of the new Chinese businesses burnt and looted, their presence has increased and expanded to the provinces as well. The dominance of Chinese businesses in the retail sector has firmly entrenched Chinese interests, and arguably integrates Solomon Islands' economy, jobs, trade and businesses with China. In contrast, Taiwan's relationship with Solomon Islands is not integrated across the business sector.

To provide a long-term perspective on the new Chinese arrivals, I interviewed John Leong, a Chinese Solomon Islander from Malaita. His father Leong Kee married a woman from Langalanga in Malaita, and he grew up knowing both his mother's Solomon Islands culture and his father's Chinese culture. When he was small, he was sent to stay with his grandmother in Hong Kong and they would visit their relatives in Guangdong in mainland China. He returned to Solomon Islands after completing secondary schooling in Hong Kong. He explained that many of the new Chinese immigrants were not interested in investing in the country to help the Solomon Islands economy, but were really there to do business for themselves and then move to the US, Australia or New Zealand. Most have no particularly strong feelings for the country, unlike many older Chinese who initially immigrated to Solomon Islands, settled down and have family who have taken over their shops. Most, if not all, of the newly arrived Chinese retain strong links back to their homeland and families.

The third factor is Guadalcanal Province's sister relationship with Guangdong Province in China, which has allowed provincial government officials and politicians to engage with the Chinese in a deeper and more integrated way than is the case with Taiwan. The Overseas Chinese Affairs Office of Guangdong Province, now subsumed by the United Front Work Department, is responsible for the Chinese community in

Solomon Islands (this includes all people of Chinese descent, even those from Taiwan and Hong Kong—including John Leong). For Solomon Islanders, the most important factor is their public presence in the shops, on the road driving vehicles, in the rural areas working in the logging camps and in the warehouses. They have a noticeable presence in the community that allows Solomon Islanders to interact with them on a daily basis. Even if they have brought some practices that have corroded good governance within the public sector, their involvement in the community is providing employment opportunities for Solomon Islanders. Moreover, the corruption occurs because local conditions encourage it.

In an article published in the *Solomon Star* on 28 January 2019, former immigration officer Richard Mana claimed that he had witnessed extensive corruption in the government system. He said:

> Between 2009 and 2011, three Asian girls were deported after they were caught engaging in an underground prostitution ring. 'These girls were brought in by those running the ring and entered the country on tourist visas', Mana said. He said the girls were then used to serve customers of the prostitution ring, which operates from a well-known commercial establishment in town. 'There were locals involved in the organisation to bring the girls over. They are those in authority who I believe were paid to assist organisers of the ring'. He also claimed that a lot of foreigners have overstayed their visas. Mana said that in cases like this, they should be fined but due to leniency from authorities, the country loses much-needed revenue. He said he was also aware of top public officers who accepted gifts of cars from foreign business people in return for their favours when it comes to matters like visas and licenses. Mana said that as a junior officer, they were left at the mercy of their bosses, who dictated decisions on issues from the top. He stated government officers were easy prey because they worked for very small salaries so it is easy for them to be manipulated. He further claimed that junior officers knew what the bosses are doing but they were powerless to do anything. 'An example is the issuing of work permits to foreigners just within days after arrival. Some of these foreigners, especially those working in the logging industry, should not be issued with work permits because they are not qualified. Yet they were given work permits to go and drive log trucks, operate chainsaws, and do other jobs that could be easily filled locally. That's the kind of corruption going on within our system' (Babasiana 2019).

Interactions with Chinese and other foreign nationals have introduced a level of corrosion to good governance and the government machinery, highlighted by the former immigration officer, that should also have some bearing on the way in which Solomon Islands will be able to conduct its relations in the future. But the interactions with the new Chinese provide an economic pathway for Solomon Islanders to learn from the entrepreneurialism of the Chinese. This is perhaps something the Solomon Islands Government can do through a program of affirmative support for indigenous Solomon Islanders to participate in business, not as bystanders but as drivers. It is not hard to imagine a policy of affirmative support for indigenous Solomon Islanders through a program that guarantees loans for them to construct buildings, which they can then rent to the Chinese. There is no reason for indigenous Solomon Islanders to sell their land because they are unable to develop it because they lack the capital to build retail space. This is one path the Solomon Islands Government can pursue, rather than complaining about the influx of new Chinese migrants who are buying land from indigenous Solomon Islanders and developing it for their own benefit.

The China switch

Following Solomon Islands' national general election in April 2019, Manasseh Sogavare was elected prime minister, making it his fourth stint as the country's leader. He subsequently formed a coalition government dubbed the Democratic Coalition Government for Advancement. One of the new government's most prominent policies was the review of the country's relationship with Taiwan and the exploration of the possibility of switching relations to China. Discussions about the China switch, especially amongst MPs and their associates, started prior to the election and intensified following it. Not long after his election as prime minister, and in referring to Solomon Islands' relationship with Taiwan, Sogavare acknowledged that 'we are under a lot of pressure to rethink this relationship' (Dziedzic 2019). This was fanned largely by the anticipation that diplomatic relations with China would attract greater financial assistance, particularly for infrastructure development and the RCDF.

In Solomon Islands, there were mixed reactions to the proposal. Many entrepreneurs of Chinese descent supported the switch. This included people like Tommy Chan, a former MP and well-known businessman, and owner of the Honiara Hotel. For him and other Chinese and indigenous Solomon Islander entrepreneurs, diplomatic relations with China could potentially improve trade and investment opportunities, which would be good for business. This was a sentiment held by many politicians and their supporters. For example, in an interview with ABC News, former prime minister Gordon Darcy Lilo asked:

> What is wrong for this country to consider the opportunities that can come out from a China that is a reformed China and a China that can offer a better economic opportunity? (Dzeidzic 2019)

This was partly a reaction to concerns expressed by traditional partners such as Australia, New Zealand and the US. While acknowledging that this was a sovereign decision for Solomon Islands, there was disquiet in Canberra about the switch. In June 2019, following his election as prime minister of Australia, Scott Morrison's first official visit was to Honiara, where he pledged AU$250 million worth of Australian assistance to Solomon Islands (The Guardian 2019). Even the US weighed in, offering to assist Solomon Islands in light of growing Chinese influence. When the Solomon Islands Government cut ties with Taiwan, the US subsequently reassessed its proposed aid to the country (Reuters 2019).

Other Solomon Islanders were opposed to the proposal largely due to concerns about Chinese domination of businesses; allegations that Chinese citizens and their money have corrupted Solomon Islands politics and public service; and fears that Chinese Government assistance could lead to increasing national debts. There were also concerns about the lack of consultation in the decision-making process on the matter. Then opposition leader Matthew Wale, for example, accused the Sogavare Government of rushing the issue and argued that:

> there's been no discussion at all about what are our national interests. What are we trying to achieve? What are we looking for? Are we just looking for more money? At the moment it seems that's the driving force (Dziedzic 2019).

For many Solomon Islanders, their opposition to the switch was influenced by the fact that their encounters with China had mostly been with Chinese shopkeepers, loggers, fishermen, etc. As discussed previously, these Chinese were largely seen as unscrupulous individuals with a no-care attitude towards the place and its people. That is the lens through which most Solomon Islanders see, interact with and understand China.

While public debates were still ongoing and the Foreign Relations Committee still carrying out its assessment, the Solomon Islands Government in September 2019 severed its 36-year diplomatic relations with Taiwan. The decision was based on the report of the bipartisan task force, which recommended the switch. The issue was never debated in parliament. In fact, the report of the Foreign Relations Committee, which was released in November 2019, criticised the switch and recommended that the government 'should deepen its relationship with the Republic of China (Taiwan) instead of severing existing ties' (National Parliament of Solomon Islands Foreign Relations Committee 2019:11). It was obvious, however, that most MPs wanted to see a deeper engagement in their foreign relations and were therefore attracted by the potential for increased Chinese investments. They had seen and were lured by the Chinese investments in the other Pacific Island countries they have diplomatic relations with. It was also obvious that China already had a strong informal presence in the country through its citizens, its trade and ongoing investments from Chinese-owned businesses. The potential for greater investment and trade was a major driver to switch to China. It was anticipated that China would bring additional resources to facilitate much-needed infrastructure to foster rural development so that Solomon Islands' untapped natural resources, including its wealth in minerals, could be explored and developed.

But while the relationship with China is sealed, Beijing has not yet won over the entire country. As Zhang and Futaiasi point out:

> Although China presently has an upper hand in the diplomatic wrestle with Taiwan in Solomon Islands, the controversies surrounding the switch suggests it is too early for Beijing to claim victory. The challenges are serious, whether they are objections from politicians or grassroots in Solomon Islands (2020:5).

The most vocal challenge to the switch was from the Malaita provincial government. In October 2019, a Malaita Communiqué was published, 'stating that the province "rejects the Chinese Communist Party-CCP and its formal systems based on atheist ideology", and pledged to prevent "willful and exploitative investors"' (ibid.). More concerns emerged when, a month after the switch, the government of the Central Province signed an agreement with China Sam Enterprise Group Ltd for a long-term lease of the island of Tulagi. The agreement was later nullified by the attorney general, but it illustrated how Chinese companies could bypass the national government and target subnational governments, which 'are a softer target for influence operations, being subject to less media oversight and scrutiny by civil society' (Foukona and Smith 2019).

In this discussion, it is important to consider what Solomon Islands will likely lose as a result of the switch to China. One of the key features of this new relationship is the potential for flexibility. There is a perception that Taiwan meddles in the political affairs of Solomon Islands by supporting the provision of funds, which politicians use as RCDF. There is also the discretionary fund administered within the Solomon Islands prime minister's office that requires only the prime minister's signature for funds to be provided from Taiwan. However, there are broader policy issues that need to be canvassed. China's global power and outreach is a matter of interest for politicians who want to see the villages in their constituencies connected with roads and electricity. China's Belt and Road Initiative (BRI) offers possibilities that are more difficult to obtain from other donors, though Taiwan recently signed an MOU to provide US$30 million in 'strategic loans', including support for Solomon Islands to host the 2023 South Pacific Games (Yeh 2019).

Solomon Islands does not have a clear foreign policy framework, and the dilemma of whether or not to switch offered an opportunity to reshape their foreign relations. There were—and still are—concerns about the trade-offs that would be made with its natural resources if Solomon Islands were to receive substantial loans from China. Solomon Islands may be expected to further open its mineral, forestry and fisheries resources to Chinese businesses. There are important lessons to be learned from the impact of the loans taken out by Sri Lanka and Zambia, and how these countries have had to give up the management of state assets to Chinese state-owned enterprises.

As discussed previously, there are elements of the Solomon Islands' relationship with China that are a cause for concern. Arguably, the new Chinese migrants have contributed to the corrosion of the quality of governance in Solomon Islands. Having diplomatic ties with the Chinese Government will enable it to provide consular protection and may put stress on the already weak institutions of the Solomon Islands Government. It is also possible that some of the worst excesses of Chinese businesses— at least in Honiara—may be curbed with the arrival of Chinese officials charged with managing the diaspora. Under the BRI, a major priority of China's Ministry of Foreign Affairs is to improve China's international image, and new migrants from Guangdong have done little to aid that cause. Previous research indicates a less-than-harmonious relationship between Chinese officials and China's economic migrants to the Solomon Islands (Smith 2012).

Conclusion

The previously mentioned concerns raise questions about whether or not Solomon Islands rushed into making a decision, and perhaps the timing was not right to switch. Solomon Islands had not fully explored the range of its relationship with Taiwan. Perhaps it should have pushed to have a more structured relationship with Taiwan that extended beyond the narrow confines of the political establishment and government institutions. There should have been more people-to-people interactions and more Taiwanese investments in technology and other areas where jobs can be created for Solomon Islanders.

How the decision was made and the personalities involved cannot be underestimated as a reason for the outcome; there were influential Solomon Islanders working behind the scenes to facilitate the switch to China. Former prime ministers Sir Francis Billy Hilly and Danny Philipp are known to support the switch, as does Sir Tommy Chan. The decision to switch was influenced largely by the business and personal connections of former politicians and certain local Chinese business houses. Though it was a political decision determined by the cabinet, the influence of powerful individuals was paramount. Whilst there was broad public debate about the switch, the decision was ultimately made by a few men: members of caucus and cabinet. There is much to suggest that Solomon Islands is not ready; rather, it should have looked to augment its relations with Taiwan. Now that China has established diplomatic relations with Solomon Islands, Beijing must carefully consider whether or not it wants to contribute to the RCDF or other discretionary funds administered by politicians. Supporting such funds is not the way a normal diplomatic relationship should be conducted. Furthermore, doing so could exacerbate corruption and damage this new relationship between Solomon Islands and China.

Economics and trade are the major factors that influence Solomon Islands foreign policy. With the predicted decline of the logging industry, it is not clear whether this dominant influence will be maintained. They are, however, important considerations for now. However, it is respectfully argued that Solomon Islands should be conscious of the cost of Chinese aid. It will not be free. As the example of Papua New Guinea suggests, China's funding support may come at the cost of further opening up natural resources to Chinese companies. Given the poor quality of government—worsened in part by Taiwan's support for the RCDF—and the poor track record of natural resource management, it is argued that the switch will only exacerbate the already weak governance settings in Solomon Islands.

References

Aqorau, T. 2008. Crisis in Solomon Islands: Foraging for New Directions. In S. Dinnen and S. Firth (eds), *Politics and State-Building in Solomon Islands*. Canberra: ANU E Press, 246–68. doi.org/10.22459/PSBS.05.2008.10

Atkinson, J. 2009. Big Trouble in Little Chinatown: Australia, Taiwan and the April 2006 Post-Election Riot in Solomon Islands. *Pacific Affairs* 82(1): 47–65. doi.org/10.5509/200982147

Babasiana, C. 2019. 'Immigration Corrupt': Former Officer Cries Foul. *Solomon Star Newspaper*, 28 January. www.solomonstarnews.com/index.php/news/national/item/21302-immigration-corrupt

Batley, J. 2018. Will Solomon Islands Abandon Taiwan? The *Interpreter*, 4 September. Lowy Institute. www.lowyinstitute.org/the-interpreter/will-solomon-islands-abandon-taiwan

Biddick, T.V. 1989. Diplomatic Rivalry in the South Pacific: The PRC and Taiwan. *Asian Survey* 29(8):800–15. doi.org/10.1525/as.1989.29.8.01p0298d

Bourke, L. 2018. UK to Open Diplomatic Posts in the Pacific, Citing Security Concerns. *The Sydney Morning Herald*, 20 April. www.smh.com.au/world/oceania/uk-to-open-diplomatic-posts-in-the-pacific-citing-security-concerns-20180419-p4zan2.html

Central Bank of Solomon Islands (CBSI) 2019. *Annual Report 2018*. Honiara: CBSI.

Dayant, A. and J. Pryke 2018. How Taiwan Competes with China in the Pacific. *The Diplomat*, 9 August. thediplomat.com/2018/08/how-taiwan-competes-with-china-in-the-pacific/

DCGA (Democratic Coalition Government for Advancement) 2019. *First 100-Days Policy Framework.* Honiara: DCGA.

Dobell, G. 2007. China and Taiwan in the South Pacific: Diplomatic Chess versus Pacific Political Rugby. *CSCSD Occasional Paper* No. 1. Canberra: Centre for the Study of the Chinese Southern Diaspora, ANU. chl-old.anu.edu.au/publications/csds/cscsd_op1_4_chapter_1.pdf

Dobell, G. 2018. Awkward Alarum: China, Vanuatu and Oz. *The Strategist*, 16 April. Australian Strategic Policy Institute. www.aspistrategist.org.au/awkward-alarum-china-vanuatu-oz/

Dziedzic, S. 2019. Diplomatic battle underway in the Solomon Islands over China recognition. *ABC News*, 13 June. www.abc.net.au/radio/programs/am/diplomatic-battle-underway-in-solomon-islands/11204750

Fanasia, A. 2019. Shaky Ties: Democratic Alliance Party to Review Relationship with Taiwan. *Solomon Star*, 24 January. www.solomonstarnews.com/index.php/news/national/item/21288-shaky-ties

Foukona, J. and G. Smith 2019. Rumblings Along the Federal Fault Line in Solomon Islands. *The Interpreter*, 21 October. Lowy Institute. www.lowyinstitute.org/the-interpreter/rumblings-along-federal-fault-line-solomon-islands

Global Edge 2019. Solomon Islands: Trade Statistics. www.globaledge.msu.edu/countries/solomon-islands/tradestats

Global Witness 2018. *Paradise Lost: How China Can Help the Solomon Islands Protect its Forests*. London: Global Witness. www.globalwitness.org/en/campaigns/forests/paradise-lost/

Greenfield, C. and T. Westbrook 2019. Solomon Islands Look Beyond Taiwan Alliance as Election Looms. *Reuters*, 21 March. www.reuters.com/article/us-pacific-china-solomonislands/solomon-islands-look-beyond-taiwan-alliance-as-election-looms-idUSKCN1R12TR

Hameiri, S. 2009. State Building of Crisis Management? A Critical Analysis of the Social and Political Implications of the Regional Assistance Mission to Solomon Islands. *Third World Quarterly* 30(1):35–52. doi.org/10.1080/01436590802622276

Huang, K-B. 2017. Taiwan and Its South Pacific Allies. *The Interpreter*, 11 December. Lowy Institute. www.lowyinstitute.org/the-interpreter/taiwan-and-its-south-pacific-allies

Kabutaulaka, T. 2010. Milking the Dragon in Solomon Islands. In T. Wesley-Smith and E.A. Porter (eds), *China in Oceania: Reshaping the Pacific?* New York: Berghahn Books, 136–50.

Kekea, G. 2018. PM Hou Congratulates Taiwan on 107th National Day. *The Island Sun*, 10 October. www.theislandsun.com.sb/pm-hou-congratulates-taiwan-on-107th-national-day/

Maley, P. 2010. If You're Willing to Pay, Nauru Can be Amazingly Accommodating. *The Australian*, 14 August. www.theaustralian.com.au/national-affairs/if-youre-willing-to-pay-nauru-can-be-amazingly-accommodating/news-story/849d6b8 eafa27aa86b2dcff0d697f559

Moore, C. 2004. *Happy Isles in Crisis: The Historical Causes for a Failing State in Solomon Islands, 1998–2004.* Canberra: Asia Pacific Press.

National Parliament of Solomon Islands Foreign Relations Committee 2019. Committee Report: Report on the Inquiry into the Question of severing existing ties with the Republic of China (Taiwan). *NP-Paper* No. 21/2019. Honiara: National Parliament Office.

Nguyen, M. and J. Pryke 2018. Exploring Taiwan's Aid to the Pacific. *The Interpreter*, 25 September. Lowy Institute. www.lowyinstitute.org/the-interpreter/exploring-taiwan-s-aid-pacific

Radio New Zealand 2018. Solomons' PM Hails Relationship with Taiwan. 15 October. www.radionz.co.nz/international/pacific-news/368662/solomons-pm-hails-relationship-with-taiwan

Radio New Zealand 2020. Solomons Drops Two Points in 2019 Corruption Perceptions Index. 27 January. www.rnz.co.nz/international/programmes/datelinepacific/audio/2018731251/solomons-drops-two-points-in-2019-corruption-perceptions-index

Reuters 2019. US Reassessing Aid to Solomon Islands after Taiwan Ties Cut. 19 September. www.reuters.com/article/us-taiwan-diplomacy-usa-solomons/u-s-reassessing-aid-to-solomon-islands-after-taiwan-ties-cut-idUSKBN1 W32RL?rid=88752

Smith, G. 2012. Chinese Reactions to Anti-Asian Riots in the Pacific. *The Journal of Pacific History* 47(1):93–109. doi.org/10.1080/00223344.2011.653482

Smith, G. 2018. Duchesses and Overlords. *Inside Story*, 18 January. www.inside story.org.au/duchesses-and-overlords/

Solomon Islands Government 2019. *Report of the Bi-Partisan Task-Force: Review of Solomon Islands Relations with People's Republic of China and Republic of China*. Honiara: Office of the Prime Minister and Cabinet.

Solomon Islands Government Monthly Magazine 1982. Relation with China Nearer. *Solomon Islands Government Monthly Magazine* 1(4):1.

The Guardian 2019. Australia Pledges $250m to Solomon Islands as China's Influence in Pacific Grows. 3 June. www.theguardian.com/world/2019/jun/03/australia-pledges-250m-to-solomon-islands-as-chinas-influence-in-pacific-grows

Wiltshire, C. and J. Batley 2018. Research into Constituency Development Funds in Solomon Islands. *DPA In Brief* 2018/4. openresearch-repository.anu.edu.au/bitstream/1885/141950/1/ib2018_4_wiltshire_and_batley.pdf

Wroe, D. 2018. China Eyes Vanuatu Military Base in Plan with Global Ramifications. *The Sydney Morning Herald*, 9 April. www.smh.com.au/politics/federal/china-eyes-vanuatu-military-base-in-plan-with-global-ramifications-20180409-p4z8j9.html

Wyeth, G. 2017. The Sovereign Recognition Game: Has Nauru Overplayed Its Hand? *The Diplomat*, 17 May. thediplomat.com/2017/05/the-sovereign-recognition-game-has-nauru-overplayed-its-hand/

Yeh, J. 2019. Ties with Solomon Islands Stable: Deputy Foreign Minister. *Focus Taiwan*, 21 March. focustaiwan.tw/news/aipl/201903210007.aspx

Zhang, D. and D.G. Futaiasi 2020. China Has Honiara Onside But Hasn't Yet Won Over Solomon Islands. *The Interpreter*, 23 January. Lowy Institute. www.lowyinstitute.org/the-interpreter/china-has-honiara-onside-hasn-t-yet-won-over-solomon-islands

11

'We're Not Indigenous. We're Just, We're Us': Pacific Perspectives on Taiwan's Austronesian Diplomacy

Jessica Marinaccio

Introduction

In the 1970s, when the People's Republic of China (PRC) initially established diplomatic relations in the Pacific, it was motivated mainly by competition with Taiwan (the Republic of China) (Yang 2011:51–52). This was because, until the late 1980s, both Taiwan and the PRC claimed to exclusively represent the Chinese Government and accumulating diplomatic allies was seen as bolstering this assertion (Hu 2015; Wesley-Smith 2016). Overt competition for allies slowed in 2008 with Taiwan's election of then president Ma Ying-jeou, who was friendly to the PRC. However, since the 2016 inauguration of President Tsai Ing-wen, who represents an independence-leaning party, the PRC has again moved to openly forge ties with Taiwan's allies, this time to mute Taiwan's sovereignty claims.

As Taiwan has sought to cultivate alliances in this fraught context, it has adopted numerous discourses to differentiate itself from the PRC and highlight its status as the superior ally. Early on, Taiwan's anti-communist stance was undoubtedly persuasive diplomatic rhetoric (see Aqorau, Chapter 10, this volume; Government of Tuvalu 1979). However, given economic reforms in the PRC, Taiwan now emphasises its democratic government and strong human rights record to distinguish itself and encourage and reinforce ties with like-minded nations. These discourses are clearly compelling, even to Taiwan's unofficial partners like the US (Hu 2015; Office of the President, ROC [Taiwan] 2002, 2013, 2017a; van der Wees 2018).

In addition, Taiwan has established a special discourse for relationship-building with the Pacific: Austronesian diplomacy. Because the languages of Taiwan's indigenous populations and numerous Pacific peoples all belong to the Austronesian language group, these linguistic similarities are used to strengthen diplomatic ties while simultaneously asserting Taiwan's innate difference from the PRC (Blundell 2011; Ciwidian 2018; Guo 2017). This strategy is akin to the anticipatory geographies and mapping exercises described by Henryk Szadziewski in Chapter 9 and Tarcisius Kabutaulaka in Chapter 1.

Unfortunately, however, the term 'Austronesia(n)' is understood differently from the perspectives of both Taiwan and the Pacific nations represented in Taiwan as of August 2019. These nations include Taiwan's Pacific allies: Tuvalu, Palau, the Marshall Islands and Nauru; two allies that broke relations in September 2019: Solomon Islands and Kiribati; and one non-ally: Papua New Guinea (PNG), which has a trade office in Taipei. These multiple understandings of Austronesia(n) lead to conflicting perspectives on how Austronesian diplomacy should be implemented and whether it is a persuasive diplomatic tool. This suggests that, although Taiwan pursues creative strategies to maintain alliances in the independent Pacific, the effectiveness of these strategies in deflecting PRC encroachment is debatable.

From the perspective of previous work with Tuvaluan diplomatic communities in Taiwan and doctoral research on Tuvaluan–Pacific diplomacy, in this chapter, I explore the effectiveness of Taiwan's Austronesian diplomacy from Tuvaluan and other Pacific perspectives.[1] The first section discusses the background of Taiwan's Austronesian diplomacy, positing Taiwan's focus on diplomacy with the Pacific as

---

1   Information for this chapter is derived from semi-structured interviews conducted in Taiwan and Tuvalu between 2017 and 2018. Interviewees included Taiwanese diplomats, officials and indigenous and non-indigenous participants in cultural diplomacy projects; Tuvaluan diplomats, officials and students/trainees with experience in Taiwan; and diplomats from all other Pacific nations with embassies/representative offices in Taiwan at the time, except the Nauru embassy.

partially embodied in the rise of Austronesian discourse and indigenous rights movements. It also examines conflations of the terminology involved in Taiwan's official promotion of Austronesian diplomacy, specifically the conflation of the terms Austronesian, Pacific and indigenous. This merging of terminology demonstrates the complexities of Austronesian diplomacy and suggests that Taiwan maintains greater conceptual affinity with non-allied Pacific settler colonies than with its Pacific allies (or other independent Pacific nations represented in Taiwan). The second section considers how Austronesian diplomacy links Pacific allies to Taiwan's indigenous peoples, sometimes leading to demeaning views of these allies in Taiwan's mainstream Han Chinese society rather than empowering Pacific relations in Taiwan. These trends indicate how Taiwan's settler colony status colours its imaginings of the Pacific and suggest that, even domestically, Austronesian diplomacy is far from convincing.

The second half of the chapter outlines how Pacific diplomats in Taiwan, as well as Tuvaluan diplomats, officials, students and trainees, interact with Taiwan's Austronesian diplomacy. It focuses on the seven Pacific nations represented in Taiwan in 2017–18, before Solomon Islands and Kiribati severed ties in September 2019. Consequently, the third section considers interviews with Pacific diplomats, outlining their understandings of Austronesian diplomacy and their opinions on whether this discourse has fortified Pacific–Taiwan relations. It argues that Pacific ideas of the term Austronesia(n) do not align with those forwarded by Taiwan and that Pacific diplomats are divided as to whether Austronesian diplomacy is effective. The fourth section uses Tuvalu as a case study to explore how a range of Tuvaluan citizens engage with Taiwan's indigenous/Austronesian discourse. Generally, the Tuvaluan case dovetails with that of Pacific diplomats. However, it also shows how Austronesian diplomacy affects numerous Tuvaluans beyond diplomats and has even been appropriated in Tuvalu's official government discourse.

Finally, the conclusion argues that Taiwan's conflation of terms such as Austronesia(n), Pacific and indigenous is misinformed and insufficient to preserve diplomatic ties in the face of PRC pressure, except when Pacific allies use Taiwan's discourse to assert the cultural/ethnic legitimacy of relations. It also addresses Austronesian diplomacy as it relates to the decisions by Solomon Islands and Kiribati to break relations with Taiwan in September 2019 and discusses the role Taiwan's indigenous peoples play in Austronesian diplomacy, as well as their agency in Pacific–Taiwan relations.

'This person isn't Austronesian, but [her artwork is] extremely Pacific, extremely ocean': Austronesian diplomacy and understandings of the term Austronesia(n) in Taiwan

This section outlines what the term Austronesia(n) entails from an academic perspective before examining how its meanings have both expanded and contracted in Taiwan. While the term Austronesia(n) refers to a linguistic group encompassing languages from Madagascar to Rapa Nui, including the languages of Taiwan's indigenous peoples, discourse of Austronesian diplomacy in Taiwan has expanded the meaning of the term so that it refers to linguistic, cultural and ethnic ties. However, this expansion has emphasised links between Taiwan and countries in the Pacific rather than the entire Austronesian region. Thus, as the similarities shared by Austronesian peoples expand to the ethnic level, the Austronesian language group contracts to include only the Pacific and Taiwan. This phenomenon also creates conflations where the sociocultural situations of Taiwan's indigenous populations, which are most like those of Pacific settler colonies such as New Zealand and Hawai'i, are taken to represent those of all Pacific nations.

The Austronesian language group was first identified in the 19th century, but the 'overarching term … Austronesian [was applied to the] language family' only in the late 19th and early 20th centuries. Austronesian 'languages number about 1,200 [and] are spoken by 270 million to 300 million people' in a region extending from Rapa Nui in the east to Madagascar in the west and from Taiwan in the north to New Zealand in the south (Blundell 2011:77–79). Due to work by linguist Robert Blust and archaeologist Peter Bellwood in the 1980s and 1990s, Taiwan's indigenous languages have been promoted as the possible origin of all Austronesian languages (Blundell 2011:77; Everington 2017; Munsterhjelm 2014:28).

Because Taiwan's indigenous languages are included in and the potential source of the Austronesian language group, in the 1990s, the term Austronesia(n) was adopted in Taiwan. Austronesian linguistic connections were first mobilised by indigenous peoples to contest the erasure of their languages and cultures by the Kuomintang (KMT), a ruling party that moved from mainland China to Taiwan in the 1940s, imposed martial law and saw Taiwan as the legitimate seat of the Chinese Government and nothing more (see Dvorak and Tanji 2015; Munsterhjelm 2014:28). When martial law ended in 1987, official opposition parties emerged to challenge the KMT, and groups like the Democratic Progressive Party (DPP) that champion Taiwanese independence (but not necessarily indigenous sovereignty) have co-opted the Austronesian concept to highlight Taiwan's innate difference from the PRC and develop connections with the Pacific (Dvorak and Tanji 2015; Munsterhjelm 2014; Wang 2013).[2] Taiwan's participation in Festival of Pacific Arts, which is an important indicator of the unique status of Taiwan's indigenous peoples but which was also initially facilitated by a DPP government, is demonstrative of this discursive confluence/appropriation.[3]

In 2007, indigenous scholar Awi Mona termed Taiwan's use of Austronesian discourse 台灣的南島民族外交 (Taiwan's Austronesian ethnicity diplomacy), and, as of 2017 and 2018, the Taiwan Government and Taiwanese scholars have referred to this practice as 南島外交 (Austronesian diplomacy) (Ciwidian 2018; Guo 2017; Office of the President, ROC [Taiwan] 2017b). Yet, Mona's use of the phrase Austronesian ethnicity diplomacy suggests tension in how the term Austronesia(n) has been adopted to conceptualise relations with the Pacific. As numerous Taiwanese interviewees noted, although the term Austronesia(n) is consistently used in Taiwan Government and media discourse, its original academic meaning is not necessarily apparent to the public or even the government.[4] Consequently, though Blundell cautions that Austronesia(n) refers to a language family not a group of people (2011:81), the term is used flexibly in Taiwan to suggest that linguistic similarities necessarily imply cultural and ethnic ties. Thus, while Mona referred to 'Austronesian *ethnicity* diplomacy' in 2007, in

2   Staff at Taiwan's National Museum of Prehistory, 30 September 2017. Taitung. Interview with author; Former Mayor of Taitung City, 23 October 2017. Taipei. Interview with author; Head of the Amis Kakeng Musical Group, 16 November 2017. Taitung. Interview with author; Anonymous, 22 November 2017. Kaohsiung. Interview with author; Officials from Taiwan's Council of Indigenous Peoples, 29 November 2017. New Taipei City. Interview with author; Ambassador for Taiwan Embassy in Tuvalu, 25 April 2018. Funafuti. Interview with author.

3   Former Mayor of Taitung City, 23 October 2017. Taipei. Interview with author; Head of the Amis Kakeng Musical Group, 16 November 2017. Taitung. Interview with author; Officials from Taiwan's Council of Indigenous Peoples, 29 November 2017. New Taipei City. Interview with author; Indigenous Amis singer-songwriter, 19 December 2017. Taipei. Interview with author.

4   Chairman of the Formosa Indigenous Song and Dance Troupe, 10 November 2017. Taipei. Interview with author; Head of Amis Kakeng Musical Group, 16 November 2017. Taitung. Interview with author; Anonymous, 22 November 2017. Kaohsiung. Interview with author; Officials from Taiwan's Council of Indigenous Peoples, 29 November 2017. New Taipei City. Interview with author.

2017, Taiwan's vice president urged that 'Austronesian *culture* [be used] to explore the present and future prospects of indigenous peoples' (Office of the President, ROC [Taiwan] 2017c) (emphasis added). This flexible linking of the term Austronesia(n) to language, culture and ethnicity alters the power of the term, as a shared Austronesian culture/ethnicity indicates affinities that linguistic similarities may not. An indigenous choreographer contested the level of rapport the term Austronesia(n) now implies between indigenous Taiwan and other Austronesian language-speaking nations, explaining that '[other countries in the language group] are different from us. Only some words are [the same]'.[5]

However, while the term Austronesia(n) has been expanded within Austronesian diplomacy to suggest cultural and ethnic connections, it has also been contracted, so that instead of indicating all countries in the language group, it often only refers to Pacific nations and Taiwan. For example, a 2007 *Taiwan Today* article referred to 'Austronesian communities' as 'the indigenous peoples of the Pacific region' (Tsai 2007). Furthermore, the Kaohsiung Museum of Fine Arts, a major exhibitor of contemporary Pacific art in Taiwan, has hosted exhibitions featuring Pacific artists and indigenous artists from Taiwan for which the Mandarin exhibition title includes the term 南島 (Austronesian), but translates it into English as 'Pacific' (KMFA 2017). A researcher involved in these exhibitions explained that she knows the Austronesian language group and the Pacific region are different, and 'Pacific' was only used in the English translations because the term Austronesian is unfamiliar to native English speakers. However, later in the interview, she directly conflated Austronesian and Pacific by describing a Caucasian artist as follows:

> This person isn't Austronesian, but [at] that time, I was collaborating with another colleague. He thought [that artist's] works were extremely Pacific, extremely ocean, so, no matter what, he definitely wanted to include her.[6]

Thus, in Taiwan, the Austronesian language group is removed from its original academic contexts, and the shape this removal takes suggests that fostering ideas of Austronesian culture and ethnicity focuses more on ties between Taiwan and the Pacific than with other countries in the

---

5   Member of Tai Body Theatre, 24 November 2017. Hualien. Interview with author.

6   Anonymous, 22 November 2017. Kaohsiung. Interview with author; Former mayor of Taitung City, 23 October 2017. Taipei. Interview with author; Head of Amis Kakeng Musical Group, 16 November 2017. Taitung. Interview with author.

Austronesian group. However, compared to previous administrations, President Tsai Ing-wen's Government (2016–present) has promoted the economically oriented 'New Southbound Policy', which sometimes highlights Taiwan's Austronesian connections with Southeast Asia at the expense of Pacific ties;[7] Taiwan's Austronesian links with the Pacific are still strongly emphasised throughout the government (Office of the President, ROC [Taiwan] 2017b).[8]

Finally, conflation of the Austronesian language group and the Pacific region (plus Taiwan) has led to a second phenomenon that is particularly troublesome for Taiwan's Pacific allies (and other independent Pacific nations represented in Taiwan). That is, in Taiwan, the peoples of all countries included in Taiwan's Austronesian conception are considered indigenous peoples who see themselves as indigenous and encounter problems similar to indigenous peoples in settler colony Taiwan. In an interview with Taiwan's Council of Indigenous Peoples (CIP), three officials explained that because indigenous peoples constitute the majority of the populations in Taiwan's Pacific allies, 'they don't have a concept of "indigeneity"' and 'we don't specifically emphasise that they also have indigenous peoples'. However, during the same interview, the officials referred to Pacific allies as 南島原住民族的國家 (Austronesian indigenous countries). Additionally, CIP representatives explained that it was not until 2016, during a workshop for indigenous students and students from Pacific nations studying in Taiwan, that they even realised that the problems of indigenous students in Taiwan differed from those of Pacific students in their home countries.[9]

In Taiwan, this conflation of Austronesian language, culture and ethnicity, as well as the terms Austronesia(n), Pacific and indigenous, emerges from a realisation that locations such as New Zealand, Guam and Hawai'i, all settler colonies like Taiwan where 'there is articulation of …

---

7   Deputy Chief of Mission for Marshall Islands embassy in Taiwan, 4 December 2017. Taipei. Interview with author; Ambassador for Palau embassy in Taiwan, 1 March 2018. Taipei. Interview with author.
8   Though Austronesian languages are spoken in Madagascar, Taiwan rarely extends its Austronesian diplomacy into the Indian Ocean. This may be because Madagascar is neither an ally nor a settler colony, and because Taiwan has no representation in the country (Ministry of Foreign Affairs, ROC [Taiwan] 2000), but it also seems that, in Taiwan, Madagascar is less intelligible as an Austronesian space than other countries in the language group (Anonymous, 22 November 2017. Kaohsiung. Interview with author).
9   Officials from Taiwan's Council of Indigenous Peoples, 29 November 2017. New Taipei City. Interview with author.

Pacificness and indigeneity' (Te Punga Somerville 2018:102), possess similar institutions to Taiwan; similar concepts of indigeneity;[10] and even shared ancestral ties (CIP 2016:37; Sissons 2005:11–25).[11] Thus, Taiwan's Austronesian diplomacy, though broadly applied to all Pacific countries, is most relevant to non-allied Pacific settler colonies. This suggests that even for diplomatic strategies ostensibly targeted at Pacific allies, these allies are only a secondary focus, which raises questions regarding the efficacy of Austronesian diplomacy in strengthening diplomatic ties.

'They lead lazier lives … [Maybe] that's just the nature of the Austronesian people': Marginalisation of Pacific peoples through Austronesian diplomacy

Besides revealing Taiwan's conceptual affinity with Pacific settler colonies, Austronesian diplomacy has also had negative domestic consequences where portions of the Taiwanese population have disparaged Pacific peoples. This phenomenon demonstrates the domestic tension in which Austronesian diplomacy and, by extension, Taiwan's Pacific partners are implicated in Taiwan and further suggests questions regarding the potency of Austronesian discourse.

Rather than cultivating affinity for Pacific partners, Austronesian diplomacy has sometimes promoted negative ideas of Pacific peoples among Taiwan's Han majority. This is because, though some people in Taiwan now claim to embrace indigenous cultures/concepts (e.g. Dvorak and Tanji 2015; Lai 2017), indigenous populations in Taiwan are still marginalised (Munsterhjelm 2014:1–30)[12] and comparisons between

---

10   Though conceptualisations of indigeneity are more prevalent in Pacific settler colonies than independent nations, acceptance, use and definitions of indigeneity are not identical within either category. These diverging ideas undoubtedly influence different Pacific framings of identity vis-à-vis indigeneity in Taiwan.

11   ANZTEC, a 2013 free trade agreement signed by Taiwan and New Zealand that includes a chapter on indigenous issues, is demonstrative of this trend (New Zealand Commerce and Industry Office Taipei 2019). Staff at Taiwan's National Museum of Prehistory, 30 September 2017. Taitung. Interview with author; Chairman of the Formosa Indigenous Song and Dance Troupe, 10 November 2017. Taipei. Interview with author; Member of Tai Body Theatre, 24 November 2017. Hualien. Interview with author.

12   Indigenous Taiwanese activist, 6 December 2017. Taipei. Interview with author.

indigenous and Pacific peoples under the umbrella term Austronesia(n) allow for a similar marginalisation of Pacific partners.[13] For example, when discussing Tuvalu, a Taiwanese medical volunteer said:

> Now, about the people … [they] lead lazier lives. For example, you don't see many people fishing … If you said—a hypothetical, if *Taiwanese people* lived here, they would definitely always be fishing, but you don't see the people here fishing. Instead, they sell their EEZ to other people. So, maybe that's just the nature of the *Austronesian people* (emphasis added).[14]

Here, the interviewee separates the industrious Taiwanese from the lazy Austronesians, marginalising Taiwan's indigenous peoples by intimating that they are not Taiwanese. The quote also demonstrates how the term Austronesia(n) is used to simultaneously stereotype indigenous and Pacific peoples.

Furthermore, the Taiwan Government's international application of Austronesian diplomacy has led to backlash from conservative portions of Taiwan's Han population. For example, during President Tsai Ing-wen's 2017 visit to the Marshall Islands, Tuvalu and Solomon Islands (which was an ally at the time), official references to the trip as a 尋親之旅 (search for relatives) (Cui 2017) generated intense debate regarding Tsai's attempt to de-Sinicise Taiwan. An editorial from the time captures the major concerns of the debate:

> What relatives are we searching for? … [Whether] from the perspective of race, blood, language, culture, or other aspects, Taiwan's majority [population] moved from mainland China to Taiwan and has been Han Chinese for generations … Tsai Ing-wen can say this is [a trip] to search for the relatives and roots of Taiwan's indigenous peoples but cannot purposefully expand and mislead so that it becomes a search for the relatives of all people in Taiwan … If, to achieve the political goal of shaping a 'new Taiwan ethnicity' and the 'historical perspective of an independent Taiwan', only … Austronesian culture is presented, how can we look the twenty-three million people of Taiwan in the face? … That [Tsai Ing-wen] has … traveled far across the·ocean to find a disproportionate and distant relative … sends the wrong signal (China Times 2017).

---

13 In Taiwan, there are also negative feelings toward Pacific allies separate from Austronesian diplomacy (Huang 2017). Nevertheless, Austronesian diplomacy may compound these feelings or create new negativity or ambivalence.
14 Taiwanese medical volunteer, 14 April 2018. Funafuti. Interview with author.

More inflammatory reactions to Tsai's 'search for relatives' trip included that by a Taiwanese actor/singer who proclaimed that Tsai, who is a quarter indigenous, 'is perhaps an aborigine of the South Seas and wants to go [there] to search for relatives, but this has nothing to do with us! We are Chinese!' (Liberty Times 2017).

Consequently, Austronesian diplomacy sometimes incites negative feelings toward Pacific partners because ambivalent or adverse views of Taiwan's indigenous populations are linked to Pacific peoples when both groups are categorised as Austronesian. Additionally, when Austronesian diplomacy is seen by certain portions of Taiwan's Han population as reconfiguring Taiwanese culture and ethnicity, indigenous and Pacific peoples are further ostracised.

Austronesian diplomacy indicates that Taiwan's settler colony status affects its relations with the Pacific in two ways: (1) it shows that Taiwan imagines all Austronesian-language speakers as Pacific peoples who are similar to Taiwan's indigenous peoples, regardless of whether indigenous peoples are viewed positively or negatively; and (2) it demonstrates that portions of Taiwan's settler population are uncomfortable with diplomacy that might privilege indigenous peoples or increase their international visibility by connecting them to broader networks. Thus, even domestically, the efficacy of Austronesian diplomacy is debatable both because it is not adequately structured to promote ties with Pacific allies (and other independent Pacific nations) and because it involves divisive issues regarding Taiwan's ongoing colonisation.

Yet, as complex as Austronesian diplomacy is from a domestic perspective, Taiwan's Pacific allies/Pacific nations represented in Taiwan have also developed their own extremely varied perceptions of this diplomatic discourse. The next section explores how Pacific diplomats in Taiwan understand Austronesian diplomacy.

'They say "Austronesian" and "indigenous", and it's all foreign concepts to me': Pacific diplomats and their understandings of Austronesian diplomacy

Austronesian diplomacy is also open to interpretation by Pacific diplomats stationed in Taiwan, at whom this diplomatic discourse is most regularly targeted. However, Pacific diplomats typically engage with Austronesian diplomacy differently than the government and people of Taiwan do. Rather than immediately accepting Austronesian ties between the Pacific and indigenous Taiwan, Pacific diplomats focus on ascertaining the meaning of Austronesia(n) (a term not widely used in the Pacific), determining whether there are ties between Taiwan's indigenous peoples and Pacific peoples and examining Taiwan's application of the term indigenous to Pacific contexts.

During interviews conducted in 2017 and 2018, many Pacific diplomats noted that they were unfamiliar with the term Austronesia(n) before travelling to Taiwan. For example, the Palau ambassador and PNG trade representative explained that:

> **Palau ambassador:** I first heard about … the term when I came here before I became ambassador. So, then I went back and I searched for it, and there's really a term used, you know, but it's not really familiar.[15]

> **PNG trade representative:** Yeah, so, [Austronesian] may have come out of some terms, but I heard it here, because I'm more used to like Melanesia, Polynesia, Micronesia.[16]

Furthermore, when Pacific diplomats were familiar with the term Austronesia(n), they often developed meanings for it that did not overlap completely with either academic or Taiwanese conceptions. The Marshall Islands deputy chief of mission (DCM) posited that, within Taiwan's population, indigenous and Austronesia(n) did not necessarily refer to the same groups of people:

---

15   Ambassador for Palau Embassy in Taiwan, 1 March 2018. Taipei. Interview with author.
16   Representative for the PNG Trade Office in Taiwan, 21 November 2017. Taipei. Interview with author.

> [Sometimes] I forget that there's the indigenous and the
> Austronesian and then the Taiwanese. [To] play it safe, I just say
> Austronesians—or indigenous, I like to use indigenous, because
> [it's a] better way to say it, because I don't know who classifies
> themself as Austronesian.[17]

In contrast, a Solomon Islands student[18] noted that Austronesia(n) referred
only to Pacific Islanders and excluded indigenous Taiwanese:

> That [television] program that they ask all the Pacific Islanders
> to go and dance and to showcase the traditional food is just us
> Austronesians. That's what we were called. I recall that program.
> So, it was only the Pacific Islanders … So, there wasn't any
> aboriginal Taiwanese.[19]

Clearly, because it is unfamiliar, the word Austronesia(n) is subject to
interpretations from Pacific Islanders that reshape the term, and this
process often involves definitions different from those posed by Taiwan.

Even when Pacific diplomats did understand Taiwan's conception of
Austronesia(n), only some were persuaded by Austronesian diplomacy.
Those who were persuaded had typically attended events (often in
unofficial contexts) that involved Taiwan's indigenous peoples and
confirmed to them the validity of their mutual connections. Thus, the
Solomon Islands ambassador and the PNG trade representative used
personal experiences to advocate for Austronesian diplomacy and the
value of Pacific–indigenous links:

> **Solomon Islands ambassador:** [This is] a bamboo raft … that
> belongs to the Fara'ngau tribe in [Taitung, Taiwan] … [A] couple
> of years ago, they decide to revive [the raft] as part of the …
> Austronesian Studies program … but they had problems with the
> sail [of their raft] … [Then], they heard about this group from
> Duff Islands in Solomons: the Taumako Group … [So,] end of
> this July this year, I took my holiday, went home to Solomons.
> I didn't realise, in my absence, they were already communicating,
> and, lo and behold, by the time I got back here … they've gone
> to Taitung … [So, we] took [the boat] to this artificial lake and

---

17　Deputy Chief of Mission for Marshall Islands embassy in Taiwan, 4 December 2017. Taipei.
Interview with author.

18　Though this quote is from a Pacific student and not a diplomat, it is cited here to demonstrate
conflicting views on the term Austronesia(n) that emerge among Pacific peoples in Taiwan.

19　Solomon Islands student who formerly studied on scholarship in Taiwan, 27 August 2017.
Skype. Interview with author.

launched [it], and, then, they took the—oh, there was a ceremony. They did a ceremony and we also did our ceremony—and launched, took the sail, hoist it on. Then, everybody stood quiet, and there was no wind … This elder—from Taiwan, he just said something, he talked in their language, and the next thing is I heard everybody whistling … It's like they were chanting—it's unbelievable, but, you know, my hairs actually grew … and the breeze came … So, that to me was the expression of this is culture at its liveliest form … So, suddenly, this tend to be the binding over everything else, the politics, the economic dialogue, the trade (Everington 2017).[20]

PNG trade representative: I mean, the difference between Chinese and Taiwanese is the Taiwanese aborigines. I think we have a better connection in terms—culturally, that's what I see because looking at some of their dances and even dressings, they are more related to some of our Islanders … [There] was another [indigenous] Amis Festival [in 2016], and my first secretary and the driver actually attended … [So], my first secretary came back and then said, 'Oh, well, it's like our dance. So, it was comfortable for me to join in!' … So, coming here was a big eye opener, you know. You could see that, no, these people are totally different. They're not Chinese, you know, they are Pacific.[21]

However, other Pacific diplomats found Taiwan's Austronesian diplomacy far from compelling. For example, the Kiribati ambassador saw Taiwan's claims of Pacific–indigenous links as highly unconvincing:

I don't feel that connection because … [Taiwan's Council of Indigenous Peoples (CIP)], they are more focused on New Zealand, you know, the Māoris and probably the ones in American territories and they don't really go out of their way to—so, they don't know our islands, they don't know. They know more about the Māoris and Guam … [Because], for us, there's really no other race to say that we are the indigenous people, you know? So, our experiences are very different.[22]

---

20 Former ambassador for Solomon Islands embassy in Taiwan, 20 October 2017. Taipei. Interview with author.
21 Representative for the PNG Trade Office in Taiwan, 21 November 2017. Taipei. Interview with author.
22 Former ambassador for Kiribati Embassy in Taiwan, 12 October 2017. Taipei. Interview with author.

This quote highlights a concern raised by several Pacific diplomats and discussed in previous sections: while linking terms like Austronesia(n), Pacific and indigenous might be effective for Pacific settler colonies like Taiwan, Pacific allies/independent Pacific nations often have different concepts of indigeneity.

Taiwan's Austronesian diplomacy reveals tension between Taiwan and its Pacific partners over ideas of indigeneity and whether using indigeneity to strengthen relations is appropriate. Both the Marshall Islands DCM and the Palau ambassador discussed how their national or ethnic identity was challenged within Austronesian diplomacy:

> **Marshall Islands DCM:** [The Taiwan Government says] 'Austronesian' and 'indigenous', and it's all foreign concepts to me because we're Marshallese. I mean, there's not a certain … group of Marshallese that are not considered … Yeah … we have some similarities, and I think we value the same things, but we don't have the same challenges.[23]

> **Palau ambassador:** [Taiwan's CIP] wanted to know about our issues as indigenous people. I'm like, 'You know, we're not indigenous. We're just, we're us, and we rule our country'. [So,] our issues—we don't have issues like you … I just want to speak on what is the culture, and … what our youth are going through … but issues fighting with the government and that—you know, no. It's so different.[24]

Austronesian diplomacy is a unique layer in Taiwan's Pacific relations and highlights conflict not only within Taiwan's domestic population but also in Pacific–Taiwan relations. Domestically, Austronesian diplomacy incites discord over the identity and place of indigenous peoples in foreign affairs, revealing how Taiwan's settler colony status influences its imaginings of and interactions with the Pacific. Multilaterally, Pacific understandings of Austronesian diplomacy and diverging opinions of its efficacy indicate that this diplomatic discourse clashes with how some Pacific diplomats identify themselves.

---

23   Deputy Chief of Mission for Marshall Islands embassy in Taiwan, 4 December 2017. Taipei. Interview with author.
24   Ambassador for Palau embassy in Taiwan, 1 March 2018. Taipei. Interview with author.

The next section explores how various Tuvaluan citizens have engaged with Taiwan's discourse on Pacific–indigenous links, as well as their views on Austronesian diplomacy. This discussion dovetails with the current section but also shows how widely Taiwan has promoted Austronesian diplomacy and how different Tuvaluan citizens interact with this discourse.

'[People] ask us why Tuvalu still sticks with ROC … I mean … we have some … ethnic connections': Tuvaluan engagement with Austronesian diplomacy

This section outlines how Tuvaluan diplomats, officials, students and trainees engage with Austronesian diplomacy. It first discusses how the Taiwan Government and other Taiwanese institutions have successfully inserted ideas of similarity between Tuvalu and indigenous Taiwan into interactions with various Tuvaluan citizens. Subsequently, it demonstrates that this 'success' does not indicate the ultimate triumph of Austronesian diplomacy. Because the potential for ancestral links between Tuvalu and Taiwan's indigenous populations is not clearly explained to all Tuvaluans who engage with indigenous Taiwanese peoples, Tuvaluans define Austronesia(n) in multiple ways, and Taiwanese claims of indigenous/ Austronesian ties are not entirely persuasive. However, the end of the section examines how the Tuvalu Government now appropriates Austronesian diplomacy when dealing with Taiwan and even uses this discourse to assert cultural or ethnic links that naturalise its choice of Taiwan as an ally. Thus, though Austronesian diplomacy is contested, both the Tuvalu and Taiwan governments recognise it as beneficial to official diplomatic rhetoric.

In interviews, not all Tuvaluan citizens discussed similarities between Tuvalu and indigenous Taiwan. However, relevant concepts had been introduced to diplomats, officials, students and trainees by the Taiwan Government, Taiwanese universities, Mandarin-language training centres and indigenous and non-indigenous Taiwanese citizens. For example, in 2017, the Tuvalu ambassador to Taiwan explained her knowledge of the term Austronesia(n) as coming directly from the Taiwan Government.[25]

---

25 Ambassador for Tuvalu embassy in Taiwan, 10 November 2017. Taipei. Interview with author.

Similarly, during short visits to Taiwan, Tuvaluan officials and their spouses were introduced to Tuvalu–indigenous commonalities by the Taiwan Government, and some officials who had not visited Taiwan were informed of these connections by the Taiwan embassy in Tuvalu or even by other Tuvaluan officials:

> I was privileged to be part of the prime minister's delegation to the state visit to Taiwan. We visited the … eastern part of Taiwan … [We] were welcomed by the traditional—there was a tribe … [And] I was surprised too because we [both] said 'lima': 'lima' for figure five and 'lima' for hand … I've heard of Tuvaluans, maybe our ancestors came from Taiwan. So, I was thinking, maybe we are part of that.[26]

> [The] first time I knew about that we had ties [with Taiwan's indigenous peoples] was because my mom [another official's spouse] said it … Because they had a visit, and she was telling me how the dance was similar to fatele [a Tuvaluan performative/ dance form] … [So], I heard first from my parents because they had [a] foreign-service background … Yes [Taiwan's embassy in Tuvalu also brings up indigenous ties].[27]

Tuvaluan students who were studying or had previously studied for tertiary degrees under Taiwan Government scholarships were also aware of similarities between Tuvalu and indigenous Taiwan. However, their information was derived from more diverse sources that included the Taiwan Government, their educational institutions and indigenous and non-indigenous friends or acquaintances:

> I just had a meeting … with the big boss for the indigenous people in the government … Because of my [academic] advisor … [The indigenous official] told me he wanted me to … tell him one, two, three in my language, so I told him 'tahi,' 'lua'—and, then, he also told me the similar thing in—up to ten. And, then, he said, 'Oh. We are the same'. 'Cause the counting, it's very similar.[28]

---

26 Anonymous, 30 May 2018. Funafuti. Interview with author.
27 Foreign affairs official for the Tuvalu Government, 20 April 2018. Funafuti. Interview with author.
28 Former scholarship student in Taiwan from Tuvalu, 30 October 2017. Taipei. Interview with author.

I mean, some of [the indigenous] performances are similar …
Yeah. I saw them in the mountain … And, I mean, the costumes
are different, but the way they move their body is the … same with
us. It's a school trip. Yeah. For Ming Chuan [University].[29]

I was playing for the university's volleyball team, and, then …
a teammate, he's actually indigenous. So, we went up to where he
lives. Surprisingly, you know, some of the words they are using,
like the fish, 'ika', you know, the nose, you know … I got surprised
because it's very similar to … Tuvaluan.[30]

Even Tuvaluans involved in short-term leadership or vocational training
programs in Taiwan developed similar ideas based on trips arranged by
the Taiwan Government or their training institutions:

Well, it was really nice my experience in Taiwan [during the
leadership program] 'cause I get to see that, in Taiwan, the villages
that we visited, they were similar with our Tuvaluan culture, and
even their language … [The] counting is similar with us, and even
with [a] few words[:] your ear, for us is 'taliga' and for them is
'taliga'. So, it's really similar.[31]

We went to Sun Moon Lake [with our vocational training
program] … Yeah, yeah. [I saw aboriginal dancing there] … Yeah.
It's good. I asked my friends—nearly the same as ours, eh?[32]

Consequently, Taiwan's discourse on Pacific–indigenous similarities is
not only being successfully disseminated to various Tuvaluans in Taiwan,
but even to Tuvaluans, especially officials, who have not visited Taiwan.
This suggests that the Taiwan Government sees Austronesian diplomacy
as a powerful tool in fortifying Pacific–Taiwan relations while also
showing how, in Taiwan, ideas of Austronesian diplomacy reach beyond
the government and structure how other institutions and citizens engage
with Tuvaluans.

However, Taiwan's success in promoting Pacific–indigenous similarities
among Tuvaluans is not indicative of the ultimate effectiveness of
Austronesian diplomatic discourse. For example, interviewees who
identified commonalities between Tuvalu and indigenous Taiwan were

---

29   Former scholarship student in Taiwan from Tuvalu, 15 April 2018. Funafuti. Interview with author.
30   Former scholarship student in Taiwan from Tuvalu, 24 May 2018. Funafuti. Interview with author.
31   Former scholarship student in Taiwan from Tuvalu, 21 May 2018. Funafuti. Interview with author.
32   Former vocational trainee in Taiwan from Tuvalu, 3 May 2018. Vaitupu. Interview with author.

not always provided enough information to fully contextualise indigenous peoples in Taiwan's multicultural society (see Damm 2012). Thus, some interviewees mistakenly referred to one of Taiwan's Han minorities, the Hakka, as an indigenous group (see Leo 2015).[33] Additionally, several Tuvaluan students who had been exposed to Taiwan's indigenous cultures during school field trips explained that it was not until their interviews that they learned the Tuvaluan language may have originated in Taiwan.[34] Finally, though the Tuvaluan citizens interviewed detected similarities between Tuvaluan language and culture and the languages and cultures of Taiwan's indigenous peoples, none used the term Austronesia(n) to discuss these similarities. Thus, Taiwan's promotion of Pacific–indigenous commonalities does not elicit well-formed Tuvaluan understandings of these ties and Austronesian discourse is not a prevalent talking point among Tuvaluans.

Furthermore, like Pacific diplomats, when Tuvaluan citizens did address the term Austronesia(n), they often adopted definitions different from those used in Taiwanese discourse. They also frequently focused on linking Austronesia(n) to more common (if not equally problematic) terms used to delineate the Pacific, such as Polynesia(n), Micronesia(n), and Melanesia(n). The former Tuvalu ambassador to Taiwan described Austronesia(n) as mainly meaning Polynesia(n):

> [Taiwan is] trying to prove the fact that we have a trace from Taiwan or from the Philippines to come this way … [But] the trace here is more or less to do with Polynesian, not the Melanesian and the Micronesian.[35]

In contrast, a Tuvaluan student explained that he thought Austronesia(n) referred only to Melanesia(n):

> [When] I hear 'Austronesian', I don't take into consideration Polynesia or Micronesia. I just think Melanesia and Australia, like—Aboriginal, like the Solomons, Vanuatu. I wouldn't think Taiwan.[36]

---

33   Former scholarship student in Taiwan from Tuvalu, 14 October 2017. Hualien. Interview with author; Former scholarship student in Taiwan from Tuvalu, 24 May 2018. Funafuti. Interview with author.

34   E.g. former scholarship student in Taiwan from Tuvalu, 15 April 2018. Funafuti. Interview with author.

35   Former ambassador for Tuvalu embassy in Taiwan, 20 May 2018. Funafuti. Interview with author.

36   Scholarship student in Taiwan from Tuvalu, 19 October 2017. Taipei. Interview with author.

Even when Tuvaluan citizens engaged with Taiwanese understandings of Austronesia(n), they were not necessarily persuaded by Austronesian diplomacy, especially its reliance on concepts of mutual indigeneity. This is again consistent with the perspectives of Pacific diplomats. For instance, three Tuvaluan students expressed doubt regarding arguments that intimate ties existed between Tuvaluans and Taiwan's indigenous peoples and were concerned by Taiwan's attempts to classify Tuvaluans as indigenous/aboriginal:

> [This] is what [the Taiwanese volunteers in Tuvalu] said, 'We also have aborigines in our country'. They're like super excited to tell me. 'Ok'. I didn't understand what that meant at the time because I'd never been to Taiwan … I think someone just asked me that. Yeah, someone just asked me that a couple days ago. 'Do you guys have aborigines in Tuvalu?' … We wouldn't think of [being aborigines]. We think of things like, 'Oh. Now we have Chinese in Tuvalu' … It's not really a thing for us. I don't know. 'Do you guys have aborigines there?' 'What?'.[37]

> When I was in Taiwan—yes, I attended that indigenous workshop thing [hosted by the government] … [The language] was written up on—so, 'taliga', 'lima', some words—the counting even [was similar] … [But] there are questions they give us. [They] put us in these groups, and I forgot what our topic was, but mainly our topic referred to [the] losing of our mother tongue. [What] can they [indigenous students in Taiwan] do in order not to lose the language and all? And us [Pacific students] sitting there were like, 'There are many ways, and how can these people lose their language when everyone's still here and all?' … You should have asked [another Tuvaluan student]. She thought that thing was a waste of time.[38]

> We [the Pacific Island Students Association (PISA) in Taiwan] are trying to also reflect members of the Forum … [so that we don't … give a wrong perception of what the Pacific Islands is like … So, we did invite them [the indigenous Taiwanese] to come. It's not a problem. [Interviewer: But just maybe not as, like, a full—] A full member, yeah. Because we know very well that if we invite them, I think we might as well just change [our name to] Pacific Indigenous Students Association (PISA Facebook Post 2009).[39]

---

37   Scholarship student in Taiwan from Tuvalu, 19 October 2017. Taipei. Interview with author.
38   Former scholarship student in Taiwan from Tuvalu, 11 May 2018. Funafuti. Interview with author.
39   Former scholarship student in Taiwan from Tuvalu, 24 May 2018. Funafuti. Interview with author.

Obviously, the Taiwan Government and other Taiwanese institutions have successfully introduced indigenous languages and cultures to Tuvaluan citizens and indicated their relevant similarities. However, Austronesian diplomacy is not ultimately effective, both because this diplomatic discourse is not clearly explicated and because Taiwan's conflation of Austronesia(n), Pacific and indigenous unravels when Taiwan imagines Tuvaluan citizens as identical to Taiwan's indigenous peoples. Rather than supporting Austronesian diplomacy, Tuvaluan citizens who have interacted with Taiwan's indigenous peoples and conceptions of indigeneity actually undermine this diplomacy, asserting that Tuvaluans are not indigenous, that indigenous concerns are different from their own and that indigenous Taiwan is not part of the Pacific.

Yet, it is critical to note that despite contested Tuvaluan views of Austronesian diplomacy, at the official level, the Tuvalu Government clearly sees Austronesian diplomacy as a powerful tool for communicating/ negotiating with the Taiwan Government. In 2013, then Tuvalu prime minister Willy Telavi highlighted Austronesian ties when he opened the Tuvalu embassy in Taiwan (Telavi 2013:2). Furthermore, the Tuvalu Government now uses Austronesian diplomacy as a cultural/ ethnic rationale to explain why it maintains relations with Taiwan and undercut analysis attributing the country's diplomatic decisions to greed or corruption (see Hu 2015; Langa'oi 2010). A Tuvaluan foreign affairs official used Austronesian discourse to justify Tuvalu–Taiwan relations as follows:

> Yes [Taiwan's Embassy in Tuvalu brings up indigenous ties.] [And] we also bring it up because when President Tsai Ing-wen came, she brought a minister of indigenous who was actually also indigenous, and the president is also—they made a comment that she's actually … [a] quarter Polynesian … So, yeah, they really tried to reinforce that, that connection, which is good in any diplomatic relationship … 'Cause people ask us why Tuvalu still sticks with ROC and not with mainland China. I mean, we've been with them since independence, and we have the same principles, and same—we have some cultural, you know, ethnic connections.[40]

---

40   Foreign affairs official for the Tuvalu Government, 20 April 2018. Funafuti. Interview with author.

This discursive strategy is by no means isolated to Tuvalu. Other Pacific diplomats similarly asserted the advantages of using Austronesian discourse when communicating/negotiating with Taiwan,[41] or when delineating cultural/ethnic links that justify maintaining separate relationships with Taiwan and the PRC.[42]

Conclusion

Since DPP President Tsai Ing-wen's inauguration in 2016, the PRC has exerted increased pressure on Taiwan, and between 2016 and 2018, a number of Taiwan's allies in Africa and Central America severed relations, forging ties instead with the PRC. Taiwan's Pacific allies appeared secure in their commitment to Taiwan until September 2019, when Solomon Islands and Kiribati broke relations in the same week. Though Austronesian diplomacy is one aspect of Taiwan's official diplomacy unique to the Pacific, I contend that Taiwan's use of Austronesian diplomacy does not explain why Taiwan's Pacific allies began severing ties later than other allies. Furthermore, this form of diplomacy has clearly not dissuaded Pacific allies from switching to the PRC. From a domestic Taiwanese perspective, the term Austronesia(n) is not clearly defined and even elicits backlash from conservative portions of the population. From a Pacific perspective, contested understandings of Austronesia(n) exist among Pacific diplomats and citizens, and they often feel that Taiwan's categorisation of them as indigenous requires that they demonstrate differences from (rather than similarities to) indigenous Taiwan.

Though the Taiwan Government is now cultivating more nuanced understandings of divisions in the Pacific, especially between settler colonies and independent nations,[43] the implementation of Austronesian diplomacy has been disorganised and inconsistent. For Taiwan, enhanced success of this discourse requires recognition that simply including the term Austronesia(n) in speeches and event titles does not immediately inspire Pacific affinity for Taiwan. It also requires the commitment of greater human and financial resources to understanding, coordinating

---

41   Deputy Chief of Mission for Marshall Islands embassy in Taiwan, 4 December 2017. Taipei. Interview with author.
42   Representative for the PNG Trade Office in Taiwan, 21 November 2017. Taipei. Interview with author.
43   Officials from Taiwan's Council of Indigenous Peoples, 29 November 2017. New Taipei City. Interview with author.

and developing Pacific–indigenous ties with and in the Pacific. Moves in 2018 and 2019 to (re)open an Austronesian Forum headquarters in Palau, a plan forwarded by Taiwan, Taiwan's Pacific allies and the Philippines in 2007 but abandoned shortly thereafter, signal new possibilities for Pacific–Taiwanese co-constructions of Austronesian discourse (Ciwidian 2018; Formosa News 2019; Liberty Times 2018). Additionally, I would argue that, as of 2019, the advantage of Austronesian diplomacy lies not in how the Taiwan Government implements it but rather in how Pacific governments and officials appropriate it to negotiate queries regarding their decisions to ally themselves with Taiwan and how long their alliances will last. As seen in the Tuvaluan case, Taiwan's Austronesian discourse acts much like Taiwan's democratic government or human rights record, allowing Pacific officials to assert the legitimacy of relations with Taiwan and discursively bypass arguments that their foreign policy is motivated by avarice or malfeasance.

Finally, another group that must be mentioned vis-à-vis Austronesian diplomacy is the indigenous population in Taiwan, which does not necessarily share the same views as the Taiwan Government on whether or how Austronesian diplomacy should be implemented. Based on interviews with indigenous Taiwanese people who have participated in official and unofficial cultural exchange in the Pacific, it is clear that the settler colony bent of official Austronesian diplomacy is shared by the general indigenous population of Taiwan, which highlights close ties with New Zealand, Guam, Hawai'i, Tahiti and New Caledonia. What also emerges from these interviews, however, is that indigenous populations in Pacific settler colonies tend to reciprocate ideas of shared identity and kinship with Taiwan.[44] This suggests that while Austronesian diplomacy is not highly effective for Pacific allies, it is more compelling to non-allied settler colonies. Though not beneficial to maintaining official diplomatic ties, this phenomenon can allow Taiwan and its indigenous peoples to strengthen unofficial links in ways that increase visibility and empathy throughout the Pacific.

---

44 Staff at Taiwan's National Museum of Prehistory, 30 September 2017. Taitung. Interview with author; Indigenous Taiwanese participant in a Taiwan Government cultural diplomacy program, 9 November 2017. Taipei. Interview with author; Head of Amis Kakeng Musical Group, 16 November 2017. Taitung. Interview with author; Member of Tai Body Theatre, 24 November 2017. Hualien. Interview with author; Indigenous Amis singer-songwriter, 19 December 2017. Taipei. Interview with author.

References

Blundell, D. 2011. Taiwan Austronesian Language Heritage Connecting Pacific Island Peoples: Diplomacy and Values. *International Journal of Asia-Pacific Studies* 7(1):75–91.

China Times 2017. *Mili de xunqin, cuowu de zhengzhi xunhao* [*A Bewildering Search for Relatives and Mistaken Political Signals*]. 11 November. opinion.chinatimes.com/20171111002772-262101

CIP (Council of Indigenous Peoples) 2016. *Di12jie taipingyang yishujie* [*12th Festival of Pacific Arts in Guam*]. Taipei: Council of Indigenous Peoples.

Ciwidian, S.M. 2018. *Nantai waijiao? Yihuo shi nandao waijiao? Taiwan yuanzhumin de nandao jingyan yu xiangxiang* [*South Pacific Diplomacy or Austronesian Diplomacy? The Austronesian Experiences and Imaginings of Taiwan's Indigenous Peoples*]. Paper presented at the 2018 Annual Conference of the Taiwan Society for Anthropology and Ethnology, Taitung, 6–7 October.

Cui, C. 2017. Yongbao nandao qunuan, cai han zhuigen suyuan [Embracing Austronesia, Tsai Calls for a Search for Roots and Origins]. *China Times*, 5 November. www.chinatimes.com/newspapers/20171105000274-260118

Damm, J. 2012. Multiculturalism in Taiwan and the Influence of Europe. In J. Damm and P. Lim (eds), *European Perspectives on Taiwan*. Wiesbaden: Springer VS, 84–103. doi.org/10.1007/978-3-531-94303-9_5

Dvorak, G. and M. Tanji 2015. Introduction: Indigenous Asias. *Amerasia Journal* 41(1):ix–xxvi. doi.org/10.17953/aj.41.1.v

Everington, K. 2017. Birthplace of Austronesians Is Taiwan, Capital Was Taitung: Scholar. *Taiwan News*, 6 September. www.taiwannews.com.tw/en/news/3247203

Formosa News 2019. 11 Years on, Austronesian Forum Reopens in Palau. 1 October. englishnews.ftv.com.tw/read.aspx?sno=2FD9B3F89CCA27E371B6F33EA4684FCE

Government of Tuvalu 1979. *Tuvalu Parliament Official Report, December Session 1979*. Funafuti: Government of Tuvalu.

Guo, P. 2017. Shilun 'nandao waijiao': Yige dayangzhou renleixuejia de guandian ['Austronesian Diplomacy' from the Perspective of an Anthropologist of Oceania]. *Guava Anthropology*, 8 May. guavanthropology.tw/article/6590

Hu, S. 2015. Small State Foreign Policy: The Diplomatic Recognition of Taiwan. *China: An International Journal* 13(2):1–23.

Huang, K-B. 2017. Taiwan and Its South Pacific Allies. *The Interpreter*, 11 December. Lowy Institute. www.lowyinstitute.org/the-interpreter/taiwan-and-its-south-pacific-allies

KMFA (Kaohsiung Museum of Fine Arts) 2017. *WAWA nandao dangdai yishu* [*WAWA, Art in the Contemporary Pacific*]. www.drive.google.com/file/d/16e BHQa_XUNHXxxsqUKiP7Qy1cdqEY_CQ/view? usp=sharing

Lai, V. (J.L.) 2017. 'Yuanzhumin shi shidayun kaichang de shenjiuyuan', lian jingyu ye you geng! ['Indigenous Peoples Are the Heroes of the Opening of the Summer Universiade': Even the Whale is Symbolic!]. *Mata Taiwan*, 20 August. www.matataiwan.com/2017/08/20/indigenous-in-world-university-games/

Langa'oi, P. 2010. China's Diplomatic Relations with the Kingdom of Tonga. In T. Wesley-Smith and E.A. Porter (eds), *China in Oceania: Reshaping the Pacific?* New York: Berghahn Books, 164–78.

Leo, J. 2015. *Global Hakka: Hakka Identity in the Remaking*. Leiden: Brill. doi.org/10.1163/9789004300279

Liberty Times 2017. Chufang nantai youbang ye neng ma, huang'an suan caiyingwen: Zuxian shi tuzhu [Even Scolding a Visit to South Pacific Allies, Huang An Remarks Sourly That Tsai Ing-wen's Ancestors Were Aborigines]. 15 October. ent.ltn.com.tw/news/breakingnews/2223114

Liberty Times 2018. Nandao minzu luntan chongqi, zongbu she boliu [Austronesian Forum Re-Opens, General Headquarters to be Established in Palau]. 2 August. news.ltn.com.tw/news/focus/paper/1221379

Ministry of Foreign Affairs, ROC (Taiwan) 2000. *Wo zhu madajiasijia daibiaochu daibiao liushi xiang lutoushe biaoshi maguo zhengfu sanshiri yaoqiu taiwan guanbi banshichu … bingfei shishi* [*It is Untrue that the ROC Representative to Madagascar Liu Shi Told Reuters that the Madagascar Government Requested that Taiwan Close its Mission on 30 November*]. 2 December. www.mofa.gov.tw/News_Content_M_2.aspx?n=FAEEE2F9798A98FD&sms=6DC19D8 F09484C89&s=36A979DE63F5BF38

Mona, A. 2007. Taiwan de nandao minzu waijiao [Taiwan's Austronesian Foreign Affairs]. *Taiwan International Studies Quarterly* 3(3):161–86.

Munsterhjelm, M. 2014. *Living Dead in the Pacific: Contested Sovereignty and Racism in Genetic Research on Taiwan Aborigines*. Vancouver: UBC Press.

New Zealand Commerce and Industry Office Taipei 2019. About ANZTEC. www.nzcio.com/en/anztec/about-anztec/

Office of the President, ROC (Taiwan) 2002. *Zongtong jiejian tuwalu zongli taolekai* [*President Receives Tuvalu's Prime Minister Talake*]. 18 April. www.president.gov.tw/NEWS/1557

Office of the President, ROC (Taiwan) 2013. *Zongtong jiejian nuolu zongtong waka (Baron Divavesi Waqa) kangli fanghuatuan* [*President Ma Meets President of Nauru Baron Divavesi Waqa*]. 6 December. www.president.gov.tw/NEWS/18232

Office of the President, ROC (Taiwan) 2017a. *Zongtong yi guoyan kuandai tuwaluguo suobenjia zongli kangli ji junli huansong* [*President Tsai Holds State Banquet and Military Send-Off for Tuvalu Prime Minister Sopoaga*]. 13 October. www.president.gov.tw/NEWS/21679

Office of the President, ROC (Taiwan) 2017b. '*Yongxu nandao, xieshou gonghao—2017nian taipingyang youbang zhilv*', *zongtong chufang zengli shuoming jizhehui* [*Presidential Office Showcases Indigenous Culture in Gifts for Diplomatic Allies*]. 26 October. www.president.gov.tw/NEWS/21720/

Office of the President, ROC (Taiwan) 2017c. *Fuzongtong chuxi '2017nian nandao minzu guoji huiyi'* [*Vice President Attends the '2017 International Austronesian Conference'*]. 13 November. www.president.gov.tw/NEWS/21790/

PISA Facebook Post 2009. Suggestions for PISA New Name. 6 April. www.facebook.com/groups/56755729747/permalink/10150554526124748/

Sissons, J. 2005. *First Peoples: Indigenous Cultures and Their Futures*. London: Reaktion Books.

Te Punga Somerville, A. 2018. Searching for Trans-Indigenous [Review of *Trans-Indigenous: Methodologies for Global Native Literary Studies* by Chadwick Allen]. *Verge: Studies in Global Asias* 4(2):96–105.

Telavi, W. 2013. Statement by the Prime Minister of Tuvalu, Honourable Willy Telavi, at the Opening Ceremony of the Embassy of Tuvalu in the Republic of China (Taiwan), Taipei, 14 March. static1.squarespace.com/static/53089893e4b09a0716b753ae/t/53ca7b64e4b076d747f8f5d6/1405778788520/2013+0314th+PM+Speech+for+Opening+of+Tuvalu+Embassy+in+Taiwan.pdf

Tsai, J. 2007. Austronesian Forum is Created. *Taiwan Today*, 10 August. www.taiwantoday.tw/news.php?unit=10,23,45,10&post=14553

van der Wees, G. 2018. The Taiwan Travel Act in Context. *The Diplomat*, 19 March. thediplomat.com/2018/03/the-taiwan-travel-act-in-context/

Wang, C. 2013. Academic Proposes 'Pacific Identity'. *Taipei Times*, 23 September. www.taipeitimes.com/News/taiwan/archives/2013/09/23/2003572809

Wesley-Smith, T. 2016. Reordering Oceania: China's Rise, Geopolitics, and Security in the Pacific Islands. In M. Powles (ed.), *China and the Pacific: The View from Oceania*. Wellington: Victoria University Press, 98–110.

Yang, J. 2011. *The Pacific Islands in China's Grand Strategy: Small States, Big Games*. New York: Palgrave Macmillan. doi.org/10.1057/9780230339750

12

Building a Strategic Partnership: Fiji–China Relations Since 2008

Sandra Tarte

Introduction

Fiji and China celebrated a 'double anniversary' in 2015. It was the 40th anniversary of the establishment of diplomatic ties between the People's Republic of China (PRC) and Fiji and 160 years since the arrival of the first Chinese settlers in Fiji. This milestone was commemorated by the exchange of congratulatory letters between the two governments and declarations highlighting their close and mutually beneficial relationship. The then Fijian foreign minister described engagement with China as forming 'a fundamental part of our government's Look North Policy' and 'crucial to Fiji's economic development' (Kubuabola 2015). Meanwhile, the Chinese ambassador to Fiji described the China–Fiji relationship as 'a model of friendly cooperation between China and island countries in the South Pacific'. He also later referred to China's policy towards Fiji as 'an epitome of China's foreign policy towards the South Pacific countries' (Zhang 2015, 2016).

Relations between China and Fiji have strengthened considerably over the past decade. As the Chinese ambassador to Fiji commented in 2018, 'China has had a very good relationship with Fiji, particularly after 2006' (Kumar 2018b). By 2016 China had become Fiji's largest aid donor and its largest source of foreign investment. Politically China established itself as a close and valued partner on both regional and global issues, in the context of Fiji's more assertive and independent foreign policy after 2009 (Komai 2015). For China, Fiji has long held a special place in its Pacific regional diplomacy. In part this stems from the strategic location of Fiji at the centre of the Pacific Islands region, making it a hub for regional diplomacy as well as a communications crossroads. Fiji has also played an increasingly influential role in regional affairs. Moreover Fiji is home to an influential and growing Chinese population, now numbering about 10,000, and has thus been a focal point for both Taiwan's and China's regional engagement (Tarte 2010a; Yang 2011).

As these developments have taken place, concerns have been voiced both domestically and beyond about China's growing influence in Fiji, in particular the perceived loss of influence of traditional Western partners and the impact of Chinese aid and investment on Fiji's sovereignty, security and development. These concerns echo those voiced about China's influence in the region more broadly and which have become more heightened in recent times (see 60 Minutes 2018; Brady 2015; Chang 2018).

This chapter surveys developments in the Fiji–China relationship over the past decade (2008–18) in order to highlight the way the relationship has strengthened in that time politically, economically and culturally. It will locate these developments within two broad frameworks: Fiji's new foreign policy after 2009 and China's new strategic initiative—the Belt and Road Initiative (BRI)—since 2013. This will not only show the convergence of Fiji's and China's interests that helps to underpin the relationship, but will also highlight the extent to which the Fiji Government has been instrumental in driving and shaping this relationship. Contrary to concerns about China's increasing influence in Fiji, the analysis suggests that Fiji has proactively exploited opportunities within this partnership, while maintaining and exercising its autonomy and agency. Moreover, the return of traditional partners in recent years (Australia and New Zealand) appears to have diluted China's influence, as Fiji has taken advantage of a growing range of foreign policy and defence options. These developments underscore the point made by Wesley-Smith (2013:369) about Pacific Island leaders 'making rational decisions about what they see as their best interests in the face of changing opportunities in the external environment'.

Evidence of a growing relationship

While 2015 was an auspicious anniversary year for China–Fiji relations, it was in fact 2014 that marked a highpoint in bilateral ties, when the relationship was elevated to a 'Strategic Partnership of Mutual Respect and Cooperation'.[1] This was a year marked by intensifying diplomatic activity culminating in a two-day state visit to Fiji in November by Chinese President Xi Jinping. As the first such visit to the region by a Chinese head of state, the Fiji Government hosted other Pacific Island leaders (those with diplomatic ties with China) in a collective meeting with the Chinese leader, as well as a series of bilateral meetings. According to China's ambassador to Fiji, the goal of the visit was 'to exchange opinions on the development of China–Pacific relations and to promote practical cooperation and friendly communication of both sides' (Tarte 2014).

The backdrop to the state visit was a series of high-level political meetings between Fiji and China in 2014. The foreign ministers of China and Fiji met on the sidelines of the UN General Assembly in New York in September, the first meeting following the Fijian election on 17 September, and reaffirmed the close relationship between the two states. As the Fijian Minister for Foreign Affairs stated: 'Fiji will not forget that when other countries were quick to condemn us following the events of 1987, 2000 and 2006, China and other friends in Asia demonstrated a more understanding and sensitive approach' (Tarte 2014).

Another high-level meeting took place in August 2014, when the then president of Fiji, Ratu Epeli Nailatikau, met President Xi in Nanjing, while attending the second Summer Youth Olympic Games. President Xi used the opportunity to describe the 'development of China–Fiji relations' as being in the 'fundamental interests of both peoples and conducive to peace, stability and development of the region' (Tarte 2014). He foreshadowed the visit to Fiji and other Pacific Island countries of the *Peace Ark*, a Chinese naval hospital ship. The Fijian president responded with a call for more Chinese investment in Fiji as well as more exports (of agricultural and fishery products) to China. There has also been a longstanding view that Fiji could reap some benefits from the growth

---

1   According to official Chinese sources, the term Strategic Partnership for Mutual Respect and Cooperation connotes a relationship that is experiencing 'long-term growth'. Designating the Fiji–China partnership in this way indicated a 'step forward' in the relationship (Embassy of PRC in Fiji, March 2019. Personal communication with author).

of Chinese tourism to the region. In order to give weight to this declared goal, the Fijian president officiated at the opening of Fiji's consulate general in Shanghai (the Fijian embassy in Beijing opened in 2001).

High-level political visits between China and Fiji reflected a pattern of so-called 'visit diplomacy' that had emerged over the previous decade and underscored the increasing priority both sides accorded the relationship (Tarte 2010a). These visits provided opportunities to promote and advance key diplomatic, economic and strategic objectives of both states.

President Xi's 2014 state visit was not his first visit to Fiji. He also visited in February 2009, as the then vice president of China. While the visit was described by Chinese media sources as a 'transit stopover' it served to reaffirm China's appreciation of Fiji's 'adherence to the one-China policy' (Smith 2015).[2] The visit also appeared to be a significant show of support for the Bainimarama Government at a time when Fiji was under pressure from the Pacific Islands Forum (PIF) to hold elections by May 2009.

As president, Mr Xi first welcomed Prime Minister Bainimarama to Beijing in May 2013—once again stating that China appreciated Fiji's support on issues 'related to China's core interests', that being Fiji's support for the One China policy. The Fijian prime minister also held meetings with his counterpart, Premier Li Keqiang, who supported an agreement on visa exemption between the two countries. He also pledged China's support for increased coordination with the Pacific on climate change.

The bilateral visa exemption arrangement was implemented in 2014 and sought to further boost visitor arrivals from China. These have been steadily increasing—from 4,000 in 2009 to 48,796 in 2017 (Meick et al. 2018),[3] aided by the launch by Fiji's national airline of direct flights between Fiji and Hong Kong in 2009. Chinese investment also increased and in 2016 a China Chamber of Commerce in Fiji (CCCF) was established. By 2019 it had 40 member companies, and was chaired by China Railway First Group, with China Railway Fifth Group, Shanghai Deep Sea Fisheries and Ge Zhou Ba Group as vice chairs. According to its Secretary General, Zhou Yang, in the two years since its inception, CCCF member companies had invested US$100 million in Fiji (Chambers 2019).

---

2   The One China policy declares the People's Republic of China as the sole legal government and sovereign state of China, with Taiwan Province an inalienable part of its territory.
3   Fiji's total tourist arrivals in 2017 reached 772,013. Arrivals are dominated by visitors from Australia and New Zealand (Meick et al. 2018:23).

Meanwhile, Fiji benefited from concessional loans, scholarships, professional training and agricultural and green energy assistance, offered as part of aid packages announced by China at the second China–Pacific Economic Development and Cooperation Forum held in Guangzhou in November 2013, and subsequently by President Xi during his state visit to Fiji in 2014. Infrastructure funded by Chinese loans and grants included roads, bridges, a hydropower project and public rental board housing. (P. Zhang 2015; then Chinese vice premier Wang Yang, cited in J. Zhang 2015:49). According to the Lowy Institute, aid to Fiji from China (between 2006 and 2016) amounted to AU$485 million, compared to AU$408 million from Australia for the same period (Chang 2018).

Fiji reciprocated by cooling its relations with Taiwan. There was some suggestion that this may have been at the initiative of the Taiwanese Government—a response to Fiji's post-2006 coup isolation by 'important' Western countries and the 'diplomatic truce' between China and Taiwan after 2008 (Yang 2011). However, Taiwan had long enjoyed a good relationship with Fiji (predating Fiji's diplomatic ties with China) as well as good relations with the local Chinese community in Fiji. Nor had it shied away from capitalising on previous post-coup crises that forced Fiji to search for new friends and partners. Indeed, following the 2000 coup, when Fiji reached out to China under its 'Look North' policy, it also strengthened ties with Taiwan. This invariably prompted protests and pressure from China to desist from these links, but to no avail (see Tarte 2010a:124–25).

Since 2006, however, there has been a gradual distancing and downgrading of the relationship. Taiwanese representatives have been left out of key events (such as the Fijian-hosted summits of the Pacific Islands Development Forum from 2013–15). High-level visits have ceased. In 2017 Fiji closed its Trade and Tourism Representative Office in Taipei (that had been established with Taiwanese Government funding). A Taiwanese politician claimed the move was 'orchestrated by China to embarrass Taiwan', but from the Fijian Government's perspective the decision was in line with its commitment to the One China policy (Meick et al. 2018). Significantly, the closure of the Taipei office coincided with Prime Minister Bainimarama's visit to Beijing to attend the Belt and Road Forum for International Cooperation hosted by President Xi. In a further downgrading of the relationship in 2019, the Fijian Government directed that the Taiwan Trade Mission in Fiji be renamed the Taipei Trade Office in Fiji. This move coincided with the 70th anniversary of the founding of the PRC and the diplomatic switch by Solomon Islands and Kiribati from Taiwan to the PRC.

Alongside the strengthening of bilateral ties (and commensurate cooling of Fiji's relations with Taiwan), the Fiji Government has also welcomed more 'people-to-people ties' and cultural diplomacy with China. China's stepped-up efforts in this area may be viewed as a way to counter the negative perceptions and stereotypes of China and Chinese immigrants that prevailed in Fijian public opinion (for examples see Tarte 2010a; also J. Zhang 2015). A Fiji–China Friendship Association was launched in 2012 as a branch of the Pacific China Friendship Association, aiming to strengthen 'bilateral exchanges in the area of poverty reduction, culture, sports and women's involvement in trade and investment' (PCFA n.d.). In 2015 its interim president was the Fijian Minister for Women, Children and Poverty Alleviation. There have been two visits by the People's Liberation Army (PLA) hospital ship, *Peace Ark*, providing free medical care to thousands of local patients. A Confucius Institute was established at the Suva campus of the University of the South Pacific in 2006 and a China Cultural Centre was opened in the Fijian capital (announced by President Xi during his 2014 state visit). Scholarships for study in China expanded and were increasingly utilised by Fijian students who in the past had appeared reluctant to take up these opportunities (Tarte 2010a). In 2018, 23 Fijians graduated from various universities in Beijing alone. Fijians receive between 30 and 40 scholarships a year for study in China. Senior public servants regularly receive leadership training at the China Executive Leadership Academy in Pudong.

Perhaps most significant, however, has been the effort by the Chinese Government, through its embassy in Suva, to cultivate the local (Cantonese-speaking) Chinese community, including by regular invitations to conferences and cultural events in China. In the past, this community, comprising the descendants of original Chinese settlers, was more closely associated with Taiwan, while Beijing focused its attention on the more recent arrivals from mainland China. Now the embassy 'gives equal attention to the Cantonese and Mandarin speakers',[4] according to community representatives, making inroads in what was previously Taiwan's stronghold. The next section explores the drivers behind Fiji's shift towards closer ties with China.

---

4   Interview with Chinese community leader, December 2018. Personal communication.

Fiji's new foreign policy orientation

The 2009 abrogation of the Fijian constitution (which deferred for five years the holding of fresh elections following the coup of 2006) triggered the unprecedented suspension of Fiji from the PIF in May 2009 and its subsequent suspension from the Commonwealth in December. These events, coupled with existing sanctions and censure from traditional partners, were the catalyst for a major reorientation of Fiji's foreign policy, beginning in 2010. This in turn formed an integral part of the Bainimarama Government's Strategic Framework for Change, the set of reforms that Bainimarama was committed to implementing before Fiji returned to elected government in 2014. A number of strategies were put in place, aimed at not only countering Fiji's diplomatic isolation but also enhancing Fiji's overall standing in international affairs.

A key component of this reorientation was a revamped Look North policy. Like the earlier versions of this policy (initiated in 1987 and 2000) the Look North policy aimed to diversify Fiji's foreign relations, primarily economic partners (Tarte 2010a). But unlike its antecedents, this was not limited to new markets and donors in Asia. In fact, the foreign policy trend from 2010 onwards was an 'open door' policy of engaging with 'all members of the international community'. The Fijian Minister for Foreign Affairs Ratu Inoke Kubuabola explained the policy to an Australian audience in 2013:

> Jolted from our complacency by the doors that were slammed in our faces, we looked north—to the great powers of Asia, especially China, India and Indonesia and more recently to Russia. We looked south to the vast array of nations, big and small, that make up the developing world … And we looked to our Melanesian neighbours, to forge closer ties with them and use our collective strength to make our voices heard in global forums and secure better trading deals for us all (quoted in Komai 2015:13).

In line with this more activist foreign policy, in 2010 Fiji sought membership of the Non-Aligned Movement. It announced new embassies in South Korea, Indonesia, Brazil and South Africa. It hosted a visiting delegation from Russia, led by the resident ambassador in Canberra (Tarte 2011). At the United Nations, Fiji was instrumental in boosting the role of Pacific Small Islands Developing States group as an alternative caucus to the PIF group and successfully lobbied for the renaming of the Asia group to Asia-Pacific Small Islands Developing States group. This name change was more than cosmetic. It became the springboard to greater Pacific representation in the group and within the UN and was instrumental in Fiji being elected Chair of the Group of 77 plus China, in 2012 (Komai 2015).

Within this evolving foreign policy context, relations with China assumed an especially prominent place. It was the most frequent foreign destination for Fiji's leaders in 2010, including the prime minister, foreign minister and president—the latter at the invitation of the Governor of Ningxia Hui Autonomous Region, thus not a state visit. Prime Minister Bainimarama chose to mark the 40th anniversary of Fiji's independence in China, attending the World Expo in Shanghai. Although these visits were mainly exploratory and few concrete outcomes were announced, a number of future deals were mooted, including new arms procurement (to support Fiji's peacekeeping operations) and Chinese investment in the expansion of the government shipyard and slipway in Suva (Tarte 2011).

A key motivation for Fiji in building new partnerships, and strengthening those with China, was to 'fill the gaps' left by Australia, New Zealand and others in the aftermath of the coup of 2006. Nowhere was this more apparent than in the area of defence and law enforcement cooperation. This was evident as early as 2007 when Bainimarama declared, 'We have to talk to China about continuation of military courses which have been stopped by Australia and New Zealand'. He went on to explain:

> We have always had close ties with Beijing. I have already made one official visit there at the invitation of the People's Liberation Army and we have had two senior officers at China's defence college since 2000 (quoted in Tarte 2010a:124).

Fiji actively pushed for closer military ties with China after the 2006 coup, although China did not always appear willing to reciprocate. Significantly, Chinese authorities did not approve the accreditation of a defence attaché to the Fijian embassy in Beijing. Despite this, defence links have grown stronger since President Xi took office in 2013, including bilateral meetings of senior military officers and a biannual forum hosted by the PLA for senior defence officials from the Caribbean and Pacific (Meick et al. 2018:17). The Fijian navy has also benefited from training opportunities for its officers (including scholarships for degree studies in China) and, most significantly, the donation of a hydrographic vessel in 2018. According to the Commander of the Fiji Navy, Captain Tawake, the new vessel would assist the Fijian navy in the 'measurement and description of the physical features of the coastal areas' as well as assist with maritime surveillance (Qaranivalu 2018).

In 2011 Fiji and China signed a memorandum of understanding (MOU) on the enhancement of bilateral law enforcement cooperation, especially targeting transnational crime. Since then the Fiji Police Force and China's Ministry of Public Security have developed what has been described as 'a close working relationship', with Fijian police officers undertaking training in China on tackling cybercrime, drugs and corruption, as well as receiving equipment. According to the Fijian Police Commissioner, 'When other countries had closed their doors on us, China had stood by us and continued with their assistance to the Fiji Police Force' (Kumar 2018a).

This collaboration came to the fore in 2017 when a joint operation between the Fijian police and their Chinese counterparts led to the deportation (under somewhat dramatic circumstances) of 77 Chinese nationals from Fiji. According to a joint statement from the Chinese embassy in Fiji and the Fiji Police Force, the deportees were suspected of telecom and online fraud in China worth FJ$1.1 million and had breached their visa conditions.

While there was media speculation about the actual nature of the criminal activity, the operation appeared very similar to those China had conducted in other countries, including Kenya, Indonesia and Cambodia, where Chinese nationals suspected of telecom and cyber fraud were deported to China. It has been claimed that China has become 'increasingly assertive' in extraditing suspected cyber criminals targeting victims in China (Agence France-Presse 2017).[5]

There has been a longstanding (popular) perception in Fiji of China 'as a country that produces criminals' and of links between recent Chinese arrivals and organised crime (Tarte 2010a:127). While the above operation may have served in part to demonstrate the Chinese state's determination to deal with such activities, it also fuelled concerns in Fiji about the impact of the visa waiver agreement on the country's border control. According to the Fijian Leader of the Opposition, 'This may be

---

5   I am grateful to Dr Nicola Baker for these insights.

just the tip of the iceberg … People are just moving in and out [of Fiji] and involved in all sorts of criminal activities, which we only get to hear about after the fact' (Hill 2017).

The government of Prime Minister Bainimarama weathered the adverse international environment following the 2006 coup (and subsequent political events of 2009) through implementing a proactive and innovative foreign policy. It has been argued that China, in turn, strengthened 'Bainimarama's hand' and 'he was able to afford to ignore economic and political sanctions imposed by New Zealand and Australia' (Brady 2015). China has become an increasingly important trade, investment and aid partner of Fiji (Meick et al. 2018). It also stood by Fiji in international forums. Significantly, China refused to support a move led by Australia and New Zealand to 'shut Fiji out of peacekeeping duties'. This move had been strongly condemned by Prime Minister Bainimarama, as it targeted a cornerstone of Fiji's international role as well as a longstanding approach to nation-building.[6] A resolution to the UN Security Council against Fiji's peacekeeping participation in 2010 was subsequently withdrawn (Komai 2015:115).

The following section examines China's reasons for supporting Fiji at this time and the motivations behind its steadily increasing engagement with Fiji, especially since 2013.

China's evolving regional strategy

Following the December 2006 coup in Fiji, some commentators predicted that the 'hostile reaction' of traditional partners (particularly Australia and New Zealand) provided China with 'its best chance yet of gaining a more substantial presence in Fiji and the surrounding region' (journalist Graham Davis quoted in Tarte 2010a:128). A dominant argument (propagated by the Fijian Government as well as by observers) has been that Australia (and others) left an opening that China stepped into.[7] China's policy of non-interference in the internal affairs of states has been highlighted as facilitating this growing relationship. As Prime Minister Bainimarama

---

6   Between 1978 and 2008, over 25,000 Fijians served in overseas peacekeeping missions. It has long been a source of national pride that, on a population basis, 'no nation can approach Fiji's peacekeeping performance' (Tarte 2010b:81).

7   See, for example, comments by the Fijian Attorney General, Aiyaz Sayed-Khaiyum (60 Minutes 2018).

stated in 2009, 'The Chinese authorities are very sympathetic and understand what's happening here—the fact that we need to do things our own way' (quoted in Komai 2015:113). It is significant perhaps that this comment was made after the abrogation of the constitution and just prior to Fiji's suspension from the PIF.

Evidence of China's 'sympathy and understanding' can be found in the lack of criticism of the coup in 2006—it instead expressed the hope that 'all parties involved resolve their problems for the sake of economic development, political stability and people's harmonious life' (Embassy of the PRC in Fiji statement, December 2006, quoted in Tarte 2010a:130). In 2007 the Chinese Government accepted a Bainimarama appointee as Fiji's new ambassador to China. As noted above, in early 2009 then vice president Xi Jinping made a two-day visit to Fiji, pledging to enhance Sino–Fijian cooperation. On subsequent occasions Chinese officials defended Fiji's human rights record, in the face of international criticism, and spoke against the 'imposition of isolation by some countries over Fiji' (Brady 2015).

But in the initial post-coup years (up to 2013) it was not clear that China 'pursued a well calculated strategy of displacing the traditional western players in Fiji' (Yang 2011:318). This reflects a broader point made by Wesley-Smith, 'Most commentators struggle to identify any coherent policy in Beijing regarding Oceania, let alone a grand strategy driven by hegemonic aspirations' (2013:360). China's priorities with Fiji remained centred on the One China policy. This was emphasised by then vice president Xi during his 2009 stopover in Fiji (Smith 2015).

As noted above, China did not respond to Fiji's request to accredit a military attaché to the Fijian embassy in Beijing. According to informed sources, Chinese officials gave no reason for the non-approval; they simply failed to act on the request.[8] This could be interpreted as a sign of caution on China's part, as it sought to navigate competing foreign policy interests in the region. An important consideration in this regard was managing its relations with Australia and New Zealand. It was clear that Australia was 'pressing China to curb its support for Fiji' (Yang 2011:314). According

---

8   Fiji has not pursued this request. At the time of writing, it had deployed only one defence attaché, accredited to Fiji's mission to the United Nations, overseeing peacekeeping operations. Nor is there a Chinese defence attaché accredited to the Chinese embassy in Suva. The only foreign missions with defence or military attachés in Fiji are Australia, New Zealand, the United States and, most recently, Indonesia.

to Yang, 'China has a big stake in a good relationship with Australia and New Zealand', including trade, support for the One China policy and as a conduit to the US on security matters (Yang 2011). It has also been argued that in order to maintain influence in the region, China 'may not want to be too much out of step with the position on Fiji taken by the Pacific Islands Forum' (Tarte 2010a:129).

The beginning of President Xi's first term in office in 2013 and the launch of the strategy of global engagement dubbed the Belt and Road Initiative (BRI) marked the shift towards a more assertive engagement with Fiji. It was on his two-day state visit to Fiji in 2014 that President Xi set out a plan for heightened engagement with the Pacific Islands region, based on five diplomatic priorities. These were to build a strategic partnership; enhance high-level exchanges; deepen economic cooperation, including through the 21st Century Maritime Silk Road Initiative; expand people-to-people exchanges; and increase multilateral cooperation through the PIF and Pacific Islands Development Forum (Meick et al. 2018:16).

President Xi backed up this announcement by restating economic commitments made at the second meeting of the China–Pacific Island Countries Economic Development and Cooperation Forum in Guangzhou in November 2013. At this gathering, then vice premier Wang Yang had 'announced an aid package of $1 billion in concessional loans and promised to set up a $1 billion special loan fund to support infrastructure development in the region' (J. Zhang 2015:49).

The BRI provides the overarching framework for China's enhanced relations with the Pacific Islands region. The 21st-Century Maritime Silk Road Initiative is one component of BRI (Meick et al. 2018:3). While the BRI has been described as 'a gigantic economic belt across Asia, Africa and Europe … [that] carries the spirit of the ancient Silk Road', the 21st-Century Maritime Silk Road is seen as an 'important maritime passage connecting China's coast with Europe through the South China Sea and from China's coast through the South China Sea to the South Pacific' (Tuimaisala 2018).[9]

---

9   According to President Xi, 'BRI aims to achieve policy, infrastructure, trade, financial and people-to-people connectivity, building a new platform for international cooperation and creating new drivers of shared development' (Tuimaisala 2018).

The rolling out of the BRI and Maritime Silk Road Initiative has shaped the narrative underpinning China's relations with the Pacific and with Fiji.[10] BRI is now referred to by China as the 'framework' for building the China–Fiji 'comprehensive strategic partnership' (Xinhua 2018b).[11] In his address on the 40th anniversary of China–Fiji diplomatic ties, the then Chinese ambassador to Fiji, Zhang Ping, linked the BRI with Fiji's national development plan. He declared that 'the two sides should proceed from long-term interests and overall national development goals to find ways to integrate our development strategies' (P. Zhang 2015).

This was reaffirmed during a visit by the Chinese Minister of Foreign Affairs, Wang Yi, in 2018, when he declared that 'China stands ready to step up all-round practical cooperation with Fiji and align the China-proposed Belt and Road Initiative and Fiji's 20-year National Development Plan' (Xinhua 2018a). Prime Minister Bainimarama in turn said, 'Fiji would firmly support and actively take part in the Belt and Road Cooperation between the two countries' (Xinhua 2018a). A Fijian BRI working committee, headed by the Ministry for Foreign Affairs, was tasked to negotiate a BRI MOU with China. The signing of this MOU on 12 November 2018 was described by the Chinese ambassador as marking a 'new chapter' in relations between China and Fiji (Xinhua 2019).

While the narrative has focused on BRI as an economic partnership, from China's perspective the value of the relationship with Fiji goes much beyond that. As the Chinese foreign minister declared in a 2018 meeting with Prime Minister Bainimarama, 'China attaches importance to Fiji's role in the South Pacific island countries' (Xinhua 2018a). The key factor for China is the influential role Fiji plays in regional affairs and as a leading Pacific Island state in the international arena, including at the UN. While Fiji has grown more steadfast on the One China policy in the past decade, it has close and influential relationships with two of Taiwan's remaining allies in the Pacific (Tuvalu and Nauru). It remains an important diplomatic hub in the region (it hosts the secretariats of the PIF and the Pacific Islands Development Forum) and a communications crossroads in terms

---

10   Some accounts of the BRI and Maritime Silk Road fail to include the South Pacific. However, the second edition of China's *Blue Book on Oceania*, released in 2015 and subtitled 'China's 21st Century Maritime Silk Road Initiative and the South Pacific Countries', describes the Pacific Islands as 'the natural extension of China's new Maritime Silk Road Initiative and can be a testing ground for South-South cooperation' (Smith and Zhang 2015).

11   According to Meick et al., the use of the term 'comprehensive strategic partnership' is reserved for China's 'more important partners' (2018:16).

of air and sea connectivity. Fiji is also home (and destination) to a growing number of Chinese migrants and visitors, who in turn provide a vanguard for China's cultural diplomacy and people-to-people links.

But the growing presence and visibility of China in Fiji has also fuelled fear-mongering (in some cases politically motivated) about its impact and intentions. In an Australian television documentary in 2018, the leader of Fiji's main opposition party (former prime minister Sitiveni Rabuka) declared that he was 'not comfortable' with China's involvement in Fiji's affairs. He expressed the view that China planned 'domination' of the region and to take over Fiji's ports and airports (60 Minutes 2018). Other opposition leaders have also indicated their reservations. One of the foreign policy priorities of the National Federation Party in the 2018 general election was to 'reduce our dependence on countries that do not share democratic values and respect for human rights', an oblique reference to China (Nacei 2018).[12]

These concerns have resonated with an environment of heightened anxiety, if not paranoia, surrounding China's regional presence. In 2018, Australian media reported that a Chinese space surveillance ship, on a regular stopover in Suva harbour, was spying on a visiting Australian naval vessel. This prompted the Chinese ambassador to Fiji to denounce the claims as 'sheer fabrication', adding that 'spying is not at all the Chinese technique' (Kumar 2018b).

It is clear that China's growing engagement with Fiji and the region, underpinned by the BRI strategy, has ignited renewed geopolitical rivalry in the Pacific (Morgan 2018). But ironically this has transpired at a time when Fiji's foreign policy was again on the move. As China's interests in building closer relations with Fiji have grown in recent years, so too have the interests of other more traditional partners, willing to reembrace Fiji once it returned to elected government in 2014. This has important implications for the China–Fiji relationship, as discussed in the next section.

---

12   While the government of Prime Minister Voreqe (Frank) Bainimarama, from the FijiFirst party, has appeared uniformly committed to the Fiji–China partnership, it is perhaps significant that the powerful Deputy Prime Minister, Minister for the Economy, Civil Service and Communications, and Attorney General Aiyaz Sayed-Khaiyum has not made an official visit to China.

New dynamics in Fiji–China relations

The adverse international environment facing Fiji after 2006 compelled Fiji to reach out beyond its 'traditional' comfort zone to forge new partnerships and diplomatic strategies. The success of this new foreign policy was perhaps beyond the expectations of the government—as Fiji reached new heights on the world stage. These included being the first Pacific Island state to chair or preside over the Group of 77 plus China, the UN General Assembly and the UN Climate Change conference (COP23). Such achievements have in turn bolstered the confidence of the Bainimarama Government to pursue a foreign policy that is both independent and assertive (Fry and Tarte 2015).

Evidence of this independence in its relations with China came in 2016 in the context of jurisdiction over the South China Sea. Following a meeting in Beijing between the Chinese foreign minister and his Fijian counterpart, a so-called joint press release was issued that claimed— among other things—that 'Fiji supported China's proposition on the issue of the South China Sea'. According to the press release, both sides stressed the right of states to 'independently choose the means of dispute settlement', adding that 'prior consent of parties to the dispute must be sought before proceeding with any third party settlement' (Xinhua 2016). This referred to the arbitration case brought by the Philippines against China under provisions of the United Nations Convention on the Law of the Sea (UNCLOS); an arbitration that China has rejected.

Almost immediately the Fijian Government issued a separate 'clarification', stating that the press release by China 'incorrectly depicts Fijian policy towards China's territorial claims in the South China Sea'. The statement explained that:

> In line with our policy of strict non-alignment, Fiji enjoys friendly relations with all countries bordering the South China Sea, including China. We also believe in the strict adherence to and enforcement of international law. In relation to the South China Sea, Fiji calls on all relevant parties to resolve any territorial disputes by peaceful means under international law (Delaibatiki 2016).

In its jingoistic editorial on this issue, the pro-government daily newspaper *Fiji Sun* declared that 'this emphatic statement sends a clear message to the international community that we will not be forced into a foreign policy position by anyone' (Delaibatiki 2016). It went on to describe the Bainimarama Government as working hard since 2006 'to show that Fiji no longer dances to the Australia/New Zealand/USA foreign policy tunes … The same applies equally to all countries, including our good friends in China' (ibid.). It would also have been pertinent to point out that, as one of the architects of UNCLOS, Fiji was not likely to take a stand that would undermine the authority of the convention in resolving such maritime disputes.

Since Fiji returned to parliamentary rule in 2014, Australia, New Zealand and the United States have resumed their high-level political, diplomatic and military engagement. There has also been a reassertion of traditional economic partnerships. For example, Fiji commissioned a new consulate general and trade commission in Sydney in 2018. Speaking at the opening, Prime Minister Bainimarama declared:

> We're leaving old disagreements in the past, where they belong, and we're writing a new chapter in our partnership— putting Fiji and Australia in a position to take our cooperation to historic heights, particularly when it comes to opening up new and greater flows of trade and investment (Islands Business 2018:32).

But in the context of heightened geopolitical competition, it is the security relationships that have taken on greater significance. The Australian Government has refitted a Fijian naval vessel (which also took part in a naval exercise in Darwin in 2018). Coincidently, the return of the refitted vessel occurred just before the arrival of a new hydrographic vessel from China. Between 2020 and 2022 Australia will deliver two new patrol boats to Fiji's navy. Meanwhile the New Zealand Defence Force has for two consecutive years (2017 and 2018) deployed one of its inshore patrol vessels to Fiji to assist with surveillance of Fiji's exclusive economic zone. The Fiji Navy also received a new hydrographic vessel in early 2019, donated by South Korea.

The US has also stepped up its defence cooperation. In 2018 a US guided-missile destroyer (USS *Shoup*) visited Fiji as part of its Oceania Maritime Security Initiative deployment. In a symbolic gesture, the Fiji naval maritime commander was transferred to the vessel by a US Black Hawk helicopter to welcome the crew. In 2018 Fiji became the 11th Pacific Island state to conclude a 'Shiprider agreement' with the US Government to allow Fijian law enforcement officers to be deployed on US coast guard and naval vessels. In the words of the US chargé d'affaires, the agreement demonstrated that 'the United States is a committed security partner with Fiji and other Pacific island nations' (United States Embassy in Fiji 2018).

These renewed relationships have reduced or diluted China's influence in Fiji, essentially by offering Fiji more options and choices. Nowhere was this more evident than the announcement in June 2018 that the Black Rock military camp in Fiji would be redeveloped by Australia as a regional hub for police and peacekeeping training. According to a Fiji military source, while China had an interest in Black Rock, Australia had offered a more 'holistic' package, providing troop training as well as infrastructure, 'something that China was reluctant to do' (Radio New Zealand 2018). For some commentators, this incident reflected how Australia was willing to 'outbid' China. But there has also been speculation that China is not getting the same attention from Fiji it once enjoyed and that the ball game has now changed.

Conclusion

In the decade since 2008 the Fiji–China relationship strengthened significantly—politically, economically and culturally. This was propelled, on the one hand, by Fiji's own efforts to redefine its foreign policy and place in the world, as it navigated a difficult (if not hostile) diplomatic environment following the political upheavals of 2006 and 2009. On the other hand, the Chinese Government has elevated the relationship to a 'comprehensive strategic partnership', signalling the importance China attaches to relations with Fiji, especially in the context of its evolving strategy of global and regional engagement: the BRI and 21st-Century Maritime Silk Road Initiative.

The evidence suggests that Fiji has benefited from these closer ties with China. On the political and diplomatic front, China has proven to be a close and valued supporter and partner, especially as Fiji sought to define a more independent foreign policy after 2009. On the economic front, Fiji and China have exploited new opportunities, especially in trade and investment. The economic relationship has been increasingly underpinned by the BRI, which is seen as providing the catalyst for rapidly growing Chinese investment in Fiji and for increasing Fiji's 'exposure in the Chinese market' (Fiji Broadcasting Corporation 2017). The BRI has also become the framework for future development cooperation between Fiji and China and for promoting people-to-people ties.

For China, Fiji is crucial to the implementation of the five diplomatic priorities announced in 2014 by President Xi in his policy of heightened engagement with the Pacific Islands region. Relations with Fiji serve to bolster China's credentials as an economic power in the region. They also help to curtail Taiwan's regional influence, which has waned in Fiji over the past decade. But this relationship has not been without its controversies and setbacks. It has been observed that some of the purported investment from China (especially in the tourism sector) has either failed to materialise or encountered major obstacles. These obstacles include alleged violation of environmental laws, sometimes leading to prosecution (such as the Freesoul real estate development on Malolo Island) and conflicts with landowning units (such as the Guangdong Silkroad Ark Investment (Fiji) Company's hotel project on the Coral Coast). Such controversies in turn complicate the political relationship, fuelling criticisms in Fiji of the Chinese connection.[13]

In recent years, Fiji has welcomed the return of traditional partners—especially Australia, New Zealand and the United States; all three motivated by a common interest to counter the perceived influence of China in Fiji (and the region more broadly). This 'changing external environment' has opened up new opportunities for Fiji—economically, politically and strategically. It is clear that the Bainimarama Government (elected for a further four years in November 2018) takes a pragmatic approach to its foreign and defence relations, making decisions based on its calculations of Fiji's national interest. These decisions seem unlikely to privilege relations with China over other foreign relationships. How China responds to these changing dynamics in relations with Fiji remains to be seen.

References

60 Minutes 2018. The China Syndrome: Part Two—Is China Taking Over the South Pacific? 18 June. www.youtube.com/watch?v=Xwk0vZwpPpw

Agence France-Presse 2017. Indonesia to Deport 153 Chinese for US$450m Scam. *The Jakarta Post*, 1 August. www.thejakartapost.com/news/2017/08/01/indonesia-to-deport-153-chinese-for-450-million-scam.html

---

13 There also remains some confusion among business leaders in Fiji, who struggle to understand the relevance of BRI for the region and are wary of formal MOUs governing the relationship.

Brady, A.M. 2015. China Matters in the South Pacific. *The China Story*. Australian Centre on China in the World, 27 February. archive.thechinastory. org/2015/02/china-matters-in-the-south-pacific/

Chambers, C. 2019. Fiji–China Relationship Generates Earnings. *Fiji Sun*, 27 February:13. www.pressreader.com/fiji/fiji-sun/20190227/2825401346 27485

Chang, C. 2018. The Truth about China's Power Play in the Pacific. *news.com.au*, 20 June. www.news.com.au/finance/work/leaders/the-truth-about-chinas-power-play-in-the-pacific/news-story/fb8e8be28d65fd4df0141d59109a230d

Delaibatiki, N. 2016. Clearing the Air on Our Position on the South China Sea. *Fiji Sun*, 16 April. fijisun.com.fj/2016/04/16/clearing-the-air-on-our-position-on-the-south-china-sea/

Fiji Broadcasting Corporation 2017. Fiji's Trade with China Has Grown by 22 Percent over the Last Five Years. 24 September. www.fbc.com.fj/fiji/54862/fiji%E2%80%99s-trade-with-china-grows-by-22, accessed 22 June 2018 (webpage discontinued).

Fry, G. and S. Tarte 2015. The 'New Pacific Diplomacy': An Introduction. In G. Fry and S. Tarte (eds), *The New Pacific Diplomacy*. Canberra: ANU Press, 3–19. doi.org/10.22459/npd.12.2015.01

Hill, B. 2017. Dozens of Chinese Fraud Suspects Deported from Fiji Arrive Handcuffed, in Hoods. *Pacific Beat* program. *ABC News*, 8 August. www.abc. net.au/news/2017-08-08/chinese-suspects-deported-from-fiji-arrive-hooded-and-handcuffed/8786080

Islands Business 2018. New Trade Office in Sydney. November/December:32.

Komai, M. 2015. Fiji's Foreign Policy and the New Pacific Diplomacy. In G. Fry and S. Tarte (eds), *The New Pacific Diplomacy*. Canberra: ANU Press, 111–21. doi.org/10.22459/npd.12.2015.10

Kubuabola, I. 2015. Congratulatory Letter from Hon. Kubuabola to HE Wang Yi, 2 November. fj.china-embassy.org/eng/topic/jjsszn/t1311547.htm

Kumar, A. 2018a. Our Cops to Train in China Regarding Meth, Synthetic Drugs. *Fiji Sun*, 29 April. fijisun.com.fj/2018/04/29/our-cops-to-train-in-china-regarding-meth-synthetic-drugs/

Kumar, V. 2018b. We're Not Spying, Says Chinese Envoy. *The Fiji Times*, 13 June. www.fijitimes.com/were-not-spying-says-chinese-envoy-to-fiji/

Meick, E., M. Ker and H.M. Chan 2018. *China's Engagement in the Pacific Islands: Implications for the United States.* Staff Research Report, 14 June. Washington DC: US–China Economic and Security Review Commission. www.uscc.gov/sites/default/files/Research/China-Pacific%20Islands%20Staff%20Report.pdf

Morgan, W. 2018. *Back on the Map: Pacific Islands in a New Era of Strategic Competition.* School of Government, Development and International Affairs Working Paper No. 5. Suva: University of the South Pacific. www.usp.ac.fj/fileadmin/files/faculties/business/SGDIA/SGDIA_WORKING_PAPER_SERIES_-_No._5_-_Complete.pdf

Nacei, L. 2018. Election 2018 Foreign Policy. *The Fiji Times*, 17 October:3.

PCFA (Pacific China Friendship Association) (n.d.) www.pacificchina.org/fiji-china-friendship-association/

Qaranivalu, T. 2018. Fiji Navy to Receive a New State of the Art Navy Vessel RFNS *Kacau* from People's Republic of China. *Fijivillage*, 10 September. fijivillage.com/news/Fiji-Navy-to-receive-new-state-of-the-art-navy-vessel-RFNS-Kacau-from-Peoples-Republic-of-China-2k59rs

Radio New Zealand 2018. Australian Offer over Fiji Base Beats China's. 13 September. www.rnz.co.nz/international/pacific-news/366386/australian-offer-over-fiji-base-beats-china-s-news/366386/australian-offer-over-fiji-base-beats-china-s

Smith, G. 2015. China in the Pacific: Zombie Ideas Stalk On. *SSGM In Brief* 2015/2. Canberra: ANU. dpa.bellschool.anu.edu.au/experts-publications/publications/1270/china-pacific-zombie-ideas-stalk

Smith, G. and Zhang, D. 2015. China's *Blue Book of Oceania. SSGM In Brief* 2015/70. Canberra: ANU. dpa.bellschool.anu.edu.au/experts-publications/publications/4129/chinas-blue-book-oceania

Tarte, S. 2010a. Fiji's 'Look North' Strategy and the Role of China. In T. Wesley-Smith and E.A. Porter (eds), *China in Oceania, Reshaping the Pacific?* New York: Berghahn Press, 118–32.

Tarte, S. 2010b. Fiji Islands' Security Challenges and Defence Policy Issues. In *Asia Pacific Countries' Security Outlook and Implications for the Defense Sector.* NIDS Joint Research Series No. 5. Tokyo: National Institute for Defence Studies, 67–84. www.nids.mod.go.jp/english/publication/joint_research/series5/pdf/5-5.pdf

Tarte, S. 2011. Fiji's Search for New Friends. *East Asia Forum*, 13 January. www.eastasiaforum.org/2011/01/13/fijis-search-for-new-friends-2/

Tarte, S. 2014. Fiji–China Relations and the Wider Regional Context. Unpublished seminar paper, University of the South Pacific, Suva.

Tuimaisala, L. 2018. Fiji, China MOU 'Sealed Soon'. *Fiji Sun*, 11 June. fijisun. com.fj/2018/06/11/fiji-china-mou-sealed-soon/

United States Embassy in Fiji 2018. Remarks at the Fiji Shiprider Agreement Signing. 12 November. fj.usembassy.gov/remarks-at-the-fiji-shiprider-agreement-signing/

Wesley-Smith, T. 2013. China's Rise in Oceania: Issues and Perspectives. *Pacific Affairs* 86(2):351–72. doi.org/10.5509/2013862351

Xinhua 2016. Fiji Supports China's Proposition on South China Sea Issue: Ministers. Press release, 13 April. Available at english.cctv.com/2016/04/14/ ARTIHU1FeYHJrwOjBdcCAYtT160414.shtml

Xinhua 2018a. China, Fiji Vow to Step Up All-Round Practical Cooperation. 30 October. xinhuanet.com/english/2018-10/30/c_137569386.htm

Xinhua 2018b. Chinese Premier Li Congratulates Fijian PM on Winning Second Term. 26 November. www.xinhuanet.com/english/2018-11/26/c_ 137632686.htm

Xinhua 2019. A New Chapter in the Relations. Special advertising feature for Chinese New Year. *The Fiji Times*, 5 February:9.

Yang, J. 2011. China in Fiji: Displacing Traditional Players? *Australian Journal of International Affairs* 65(3):305–21. doi.org/10.1080/10357718.2011.563778

Zhang, J. 2015. China's Role in the Pacific Islands Region. In R. Azizian and C. Cramer (eds), *Regionalism, Security and Cooperation in Oceania*. Hawai'i: Asia-Pacific Center for Security Studies, 43–56.

Zhang, P. 2015. To Create a New Splendid Future of China–Fiji Relationship. Speech by Ambassador Zhang Ping at the Symposium Commemorating the 40th Anniversary of the Establishment of Diplomatic Ties between China and Fiji. Embassy of the People's Republic of China in the Republic of Fiji website, 6 November. fj.china-embassy.org/eng/topic/jjsszn/t1312572.htm

Zhang, P. 2016. Chinese Foreign Policy and China-Fiji Relationship. Speech by Ambassador Zhang Ping at the University of the South Pacific. Embassy of the People's Republic of China in the Republic of Fiji website, 31 May. fj.china-embassy.org/eng/sgxx/dsjh/t1368452.htm

13

Bridging the Belt and Road Initiative in Papua New Guinea

Sarah O'Dowd

The decision by Papua New Guinea (PNG) to sign on to China's ambitious Belt and Road Initiative (BRI) has reignited concerns regarding the intentions, impacts and long-term sustainability of Chinese financial activities in the Pacific. As one of the first Pacific nations to sign on to the BRI, PNG's decision is a manifestation of increasing engagement with China by Pacific Island countries (PICs). China's relations with PICs were recently scrutinised over allegations that China planned to build a military base in Vanuatu, which was denied by both countries. Though some traditional donors to the Pacific, like Australia, suspect that Beijing aims to become the dominant power in the region, these concerns are likely influenced by Australia's own intentions to incorporate the Pacific within the 'rules-based global order' (Australian Government 2017). Research and media reports on the BRI tend to be dominated by this 'China threat' discourse that envisions the BRI as a monolithic, centralised and primarily strategic policy that exploits partner countries to enable Chinese access to foreign natural resources, markets and critical infrastructure. Some studies, such as the widely cited report by Harvard University researchers, extend this narrative by arguing that unsustainable loans associated with Chinese-funded infrastructure projects render certain PICs vulnerable to Beijing's influence (Kehoe 2018). Through this zero-sum lens, PICs are often envisioned as the passive victims of China's exploitation.

Despite the significant academic and political interest in the BRI's varied impacts, this narrative is rarely interrogated. This focus may lead to scholars overlooking the reasons PICs sometimes select Chinese financing over other sources and the multifaceted nature of Chinese investing entities and projects. Furthermore, the 'debt-trap diplomacy' narrative tends to divert attention away from the more nuanced, and often more immediate, risks that joining the BRI may pose to PNG's environment and governance. These risks may not be due to the Chinese nature of investment, but rather to the inexperienced or unethical character of certain companies, which may be paralleled by similarly damaging behaviour by firms from other nations. While certain Chinese projects in the Pacific do generate negative results for PICs, treating all Chinese financial activities the same may lead to an overly assertive response from countries like Australia that see China as interfering in Canberra's 'backyard' (Wallis 2012). As PNG's involvement in the BRI is likely to intensify these assumptions and the fears that China will entrap PNG in unsustainable debt, this chapter seeks to explore the credibility of popular narratives surrounding the BRI and determine the likely impacts of the BRI in PNG, as well as traditional donors' responses. Though development is a contested concept and aid to the Pacific is increasingly securitised, this chapter attempts to provide an objective view of the likely opportunities and risks PNG faces when engaging in the BRI. Similarly, while the China–PNG relationship is considered in this chapter, it should be noted that the actions of other regional actors, such as Australia, may deliver similarly mixed outcomes for PNG.

This chapter is divided into three sections that each assess one broad perceived risk the BRI presents to PNG: the 'debt-trap diplomacy' theory, the BRI's socioeconomic impacts and the influence of Chinese financing on governance. The first section introduces the BRI and 'debt-trap diplomacy'. It then investigates PNG's current debt situation, the likelihood that the BRI in PNG is a coherent foreign policy manoeuvre by Beijing that aims to erode the influence of traditional regional powers, and the potential threats that Chinese investment poses to PNG's sovereignty. This section argues that Chinese financing in the Pacific is fragmented, which may reduce the likelihood that these funds are part of a deliberate strategic ploy by China to exploit PICs. Nonetheless, PNG's indebtedness does present an economic risk if Port Moresby's revenue crisis continues and the country refrains from adopting fiscal consolidation policies (Pryke 2017). Similarly, a continuation of China's current lending practices, particularly the US$4.1 billion financing for the promised BRI roads project, could imperil PNG's debt sustainability (Rajah et al. 2019).

The second section evaluates the BRI's impact on PNG's economy and environment to argue that PNG and China's current policy frameworks may be unable to ensure that BRI projects are conducted legally, sustainably and with the consent of relevant local stakeholders and landowners. Failure to meet these criteria will reduce the development benefits that accrue to locals. This may spark local protests that are able to delay and, in some cases, even stop foreign investment projects. Using data from the American Enterprise Institute's China Global Investment Tracker, this section argues that large-scale Chinese investments in PNG tend to be concentrated in resource-intensive, extractive and polluting industries. This investment history, coupled with concerns that the BRI may 'lock-in' poor environmental practices in developing nations, raises particular concerns for island states like PNG (Hong and Johnson 2018).

The final section investigates the impact of Chinese financing on governance in PNG and finds that while certain Chinese companies abide by international norms to the extent of winning lucrative contracts from international lending bodies like the Asian Development Bank (ADB), others may engage in corrupt practices that harm governance in PNG. However, this corruption is often believed to be facilitated by PNG partners. This indicates that it is not purely the presence of Chinese investment that harms governance in PNG, but rather the combination of corrupt Chinese and PNG entities, which may complicate reform attempts in PNG. The reaction to PNG's decision to join the BRI by traditional donors like Australia is also considered. The extent to which PNG's decision to join the BRI alters the current regional dynamics may depend on PNG's ability and willingness to exploit Australia and China's competition to access higher-quality or more lucrative financing arrangements.

The BRI in PNG: A debt trap or development opportunity?

An overview of the BRI in PNG

Under President Xi Jinping's leadership, China's international engagement has come to be defined by the US$1 trillion BRI. The aims of the BRI are multifaceted and contentious, with some commentators envisioning the BRI as a purely commercial mechanism while others argue that the BRI has geopolitical dimensions and may undermine the US's post–World

War II global leadership. Announced in 2013 as a means to connect Eurasian markets, the BRI was later incorporated into the Constitution of the Chinese Communist Party during the 19th National Party Congress in 2017 as a method of achieving 'shared growth through discussion and collaboration' (Xinhua 2017). At present, US$4.46 billion is earmarked for three BRI infrastructure projects in PNG: the High Priority Economic Roads Project, the Goroka Town Water Supply Upgrade Project and the PNG–China Integrated Agriculture Industrial Park.

The most significant concern raised by analysts regarding the BRI in PNG is the belief that Beijing aims to entrap partner countries in unsustainable levels of debt. Proponents of this theory argue that Beijing aims to then use this debt as leverage to achieve a combination of commercial and geopolitical aims. These purported objectives include acquiring ownership stakes in debtor countries' natural resources and infrastructure assets (which may allegedly be used for Beijing's military purposes), compelling debtor nations to support China's diplomatic initiatives (particularly as they relate to Taiwan) and transforming debtor nations into 'wholly owned subsidiaries of China' (Chefitz and Parker 2018).

However, PNG's debt-related risks are not primarily driven by Chinese lending but rather ineffective domestic policies. One of the most tangible BRI-related threats to PNG may be the exploitation of natural resources. Yet this risk is not unique to the BRI. Foreign companies from a variety of countries are also accused of exploiting PNG's natural resources. One example is the controversial Exxon-led and partly Australian Government–financed PNG LNG project, which is accused of significantly decreasing economic welfare in PNG across a range of measures, including aggregate employment and household disposable income, while increasing real gross domestic product (GDP) by just 10 per cent instead of the expected 97 per cent (Jubilee 2018). While the risk of exploitation by foreign companies may be intensified by the increased investment associated with the BRI, it can only be resolved by improved domestic regulation and enforcement mechanisms regarding economic and environmental policies.

The China–PNG relationship

PNG's decision to join the BRI is a relatively natural continuation of the dynamic relationship between Port Moresby and Beijing. Though China's aid and trade presence in the Pacific are outstripped by other non-Pacific countries, China is now the region's largest bilateral lender—and PNG is no exception (Greenfield and Barrett 2018). In 2017, China was PNG's fourth largest export and import partner after Australia, Singapore and Japan. From China's perspective, PNG was China's second largest trading partner and largest investment destination in the Pacific (Kenneth 2017a). Though Australia's substantial aid program means that Canberra, rather than Beijing, is the main financial backer in the South Pacific, China is the Pacific's and PNG's largest bilateral creditor.

There is substantial uncertainty regarding PNG's financial reliance on China due to confusion between Chinese investment and debt in PNG as well as a lack of year-on-year official data. According to the Chinese Ambassador to PNG Xue Bing, China had invested US$1.9 billion in PNG by the end of 2017. Media outlets such as the *Asia Times* and *South China Morning Post* have quoted this figure as representing the total volume of concessional loans PNG owes to China. Contrastingly, in 2017, PNG budgetary documents revealed that PNG's debt to China was approximately US$588 million, comprising 23.7 per cent of PNG's total external debt (PNG Department of Treasury 2017a, 2017b). However, it is difficult to update this figure, as PNG's most recent budget refrains from identifying the total amount of debt owed to China. This omission challenges attempts to track variations in PNG's debt to China over time, an important indicator of the sustainability of PNG's debt and the overall nature of the PNG–China relationship. Moreover, in some areas of the 2020 PNG National Budget, data on PNG's debt obligations to China is grouped with PNG's debt obligations to Taiwan, rendering it difficult to track variations in PNG's debt obligations to China specifically over time (PNG Department of Treasury 2019a).

There is no universally accepted formula or debt ratio that can indicate whether foreign debt accumulation is sustainable or unsustainable (Roubini 2001). Moreover, it is not solely the volume of debt accumulation in aggregate or relative-to-GDP terms that presents risks. PNG must also be able to regularly service its debts in order to avoid defaulting on any loans. Most research outputs and media reporting on China's alleged 'debt-trap diplomacy' in the Pacific focus on the total volume of debt owed to China and the associated risks of insolvency. This close scrutiny of PNG's and PICs' total indebtedness to China may, somewhat ironically, lead observers to overlook the significant debt-servicing risks PNG faces. PNG's exposure to the risks of its volume and servicing of debt are assessed individually.

A debt sustainability analysis by the International Monetary Fund (IMF), published in November 2017, calculated PNG's central debt-to-GDP ratio at 33.4 per cent, a relatively low figure within the domestic and regional context. This figure was already higher than the debt-to-GDP ratio of 30 per cent mandated by PNG's Fiscal Responsibility Act (IMF 2017). In October 2019, the PNG parliament reported that PNG's debt-to-GDP ratio had risen to 39.8 per cent, a figure some officials appeared to blame on the 'many, many poor investment decisions' and 'risky and often irresponsible loans' of the previous O'Neill administration (PNG Department of Treasury 2019b). A subsequent report confirmed that PNG's debt-to-GDP ratio rose to 38 per cent in 2018, which the IMF attributed to 'persistent overshoots on personnel costs, together with falling revenues' (IMF 2020). As it appeared unfeasible to lower the debt-to-GDP ratio to below the legally advised level of 30 per cent within the year, the PNG parliament agreed to raise the mandated debt-to-GDP ratio to a maximum of 45 per cent. However, the IMF projects PNG's public debt to reach 45 per cent of its GDP over the medium-term. The 2019 PNG National Budget's goal to reduce the country's debt ratio to 30 per cent of the GDP by 2022 may prove difficult to achieve in this context.

A lingering concern is whether official data captures all outstanding debt owed by the PNG Government and its various statutory authorities and state-owned enterprises (SOEs). Recent research suggests that as much as half of Chinese overseas loans to developing nations may be 'hidden' and not captured in official reporting (Horn et al. 2019). The varying transparency of both PNG and Chinese government data means that PNG's debt situation may become more ambiguous—and potentially more precarious—over time.

PNG's deteriorating debt profile led to Standard & Poor's (S&P) lowering PNG's sovereign credit rating from B+ to B in April 2018—five levels below 'investment grade'. The PNG Secretary for Treasury Dairi Vaele criticised the downgrade and argued that it was based on 'outdated data and failed to comprehend fully the more positive fiscal outturn in 2017 and early 2018' (PNG Department of Treasury 2018). Regardless of whether the S&P downgrade was an accurate reflection of PNG's debt, the situation is likely to worsen unless Port Moresby implements the IMF's recommendations of consolidating its fiscal position through measures that include acquiring more cost-effective and longer-term financing. Whether China is able to offer financing that meets these requirements and partially alleviate PNG's debt situation is uncertain.

The burden of debt-servicing repayments may present a more immediate risk to PNG. Debt servicing is persistently the government's third largest area of expenditure, comprising more than 10 per cent of total expenditure in the past three budgets. Recent estimates suggest that PNG's annual debt repayments to China will increase 25 per cent to approximately US$67 million by 2023 (Barrett and Greenfield 2019). However, these calculations appear to draw on data from the PNG 2020 National Budget that groups China and Taiwan together as a single creditor, making it challenging to identify the proportion of the debt obligations driven by China and the proportion driven by Taiwan. Despite this limitation of the data, two insights can be drawn: China and Taiwan combined represent PNG's largest 'bilateral' creditor, and PNG's debt-servicing obligations will increase notably over the short to medium-term.

The growth of PNG's debt obligations is particularly concerning given PNG's challenges with its 'revenue crisis', which may impede Port Moresby's capacity to address outstanding debts (Howes 2017). In 2017, the PNG Government's revenue declined to 2006 levels. The 2020 budget offers hope that PNG's total revenue will reach its highest levels in the country's recorded history, but expenditure is expected to similarly rise such that PNG is left with a 'historic' budget cash deficit of K4,631.1 million (PNG Department of Treasury 2019c). The previous O'Neill administration refrained from implementing the IMF's recommendations to resolve the revenue crisis by reducing government expenditure on funds for members of parliament and depreciating the kina. However, the current Marape administration has signalled its willingness to consider an IMF bailout, heralding stricter financial measures to improve PNG's economic sustainability.

PNG's level of debt and related solvency and liquidity risks are further obscured by the lack of transparency surrounding Chinese aid. Some observers argue that Chinese aid, when disbursed as a loan, may increase the indebtedness of recipient nations (Var and Po 2017). Attaining an accurate understanding of the impact of Chinese aid on PNG's debt is particularly important, as a single Chinese project in PNG may have both aid and investment aspects, conflating the boundaries, aims and impacts of both sources of funding. One notable example is the US$1.4 billion Ramu Nickel mine, which is among China's largest investment projects in PNG. The exact proportions of aid and commercial funding to Ramu Nickel are uncertain, and made more unclear by contradictory statements by the mine's operating company, the Metallurgical Corporation of

China Ltd (MCC). Given Ramu Nickel's significant size and importance for both PNG and China, it is probable that BRI projects could incorporate similarly blurred boundaries between commercial finance and development aid.

According to the Lowy Institute's Pacific Aid Map, actual Chinese aid spending in PNG peaked in 2014 at approximately US$120 million and declined to US$22 million in 2017 (Lowy Institute 2019). However, Chinese aid spending is likely to increase in PNG over the medium-term as the two countries implement BRI-affiliated aid projects. China's aid commitment to PNG soared to a record-high $4.7 billion in 2017, largely driven by the High Priority Economic Road Project. Analysing the funding composition of spent Chinese aid to PNG reveals that, in aggregate, concessional loans comprised 80.48 per cent of spent funds between 2009 and 2019. The loan composition of Chinese aid funding to PNG rose from 0 per cent in 2009 to a peak of 98.72 per cent in 2016, but then dropped year-on-year to 66.79 per cent in 2017, 14.46 per cent in 2018 and 0 per cent in 2019. In contrast, the loan composition of China's committed aid remains generally high at 99.35 per cent in 2017, 86.87 per cent in 2018 and 0 per cent in 2019. The decline in the loan composition of China's spent aid is a significant reversal, but it is uncertain whether this trend will hold once China begins to realise its BRI-related aid commitments.

Given the burden posed by PNG's existing debts, the likelihood that joining the BRI will be accompanied by further Chinese lending, and Port Moresby's potentially limited capacity to service its debts, it is understandable that some observers are concerned about the economic risks posed by PNG's decision to join the BRI. However, China's ability to exploit this debt for political or strategic purposes is more unclear.

The view from Beijing: The organisation, funding and delivery of the BRI

Contrary to China's centralised government structure, the conceptualisation, funding and implementation of BRI projects exhibit notable decentralisation. President Xi and other prominent Chinese Communist Party (CCP) leaders direct top-level national strategy and rhetoric surrounding the BRI and urge Chinese government agencies to realise BRI goals. Yet there is significant scope for implementing agencies, banks and SOEs to construe Xi's direction in a way that serves the organisation's political or commercial interests. As these substate entities are bound by diverging mandates and interests, different institutions are likely to generate different development outcomes for BRI partner countries like PNG. Thus, recognising the variabilities between the Chinese substate organisations involved in the BRI is crucial to understanding how the BRI may function in PNG and the overarching strategic or commercial intents that drive it. Fundamentally, the impacts of the BRI in PNG are likely to be influenced not only by the combination of Chinese institutions involved but also the ability of these institutions to cooperate with relevant PNG government agencies.

Several Chinese government agencies are involved in the BRI. The National Development and Reform Commission (NDRC) and sectoral agencies appear to provide more policy input for BRI projects than the Ministry of Foreign Affairs (MFA) and Ministry of Commerce (MOFCOM) (Ye 2018). Unlike the MFA and MOFCOM, the NDRC has made several new policy proposals and risen as the central agency guiding the BRI. As the NDRC's mandate relates to domestic economic planning, this indicates that the BRI may be guided more by China's domestic needs rather than its foreign policy.

Some of the most important funding bodies for BRI projects are Chinese policy banks, Chinese commercial banks and multilateral development banks. These institutions often provide 'concessionary loans' with terms that vary widely from interest-free to commercial rates. These terms may be less favourable than funding offered by organisations like the World Bank and the ADB (Slattery et al. 2018). However, given the lack of transparency surrounding most Chinese lending agencies, it is difficult to understand the full scope of PNG's debt obligations to China or the likelihood of renegotiating onerous debt. Tonga's deferment of its US$115 million debt to China suggests that China remains willing to provide debt relief in specific—albeit unclear—situations. Tongan officials denied speculation that China provided debt relief to Tonga in exchange for the country signing on to the BRI (which occurred five days after China provided debt deferment), but the reliability of these claims is uncertain. The modes of financing and types of lending institutions associated with the BRI generate widely different opportunities and risks for debtors, particularly small debtors like PNG that may possess limited negotiating power or leverage over China.

The primary implementing bodies of the BRI are SOEs. Despite their linkage to the state, the motivations of individual SOEs are often a unique combination of political and commercial rationales that may be distinct from similar SOEs and the CCP itself. While Chinese private businesses in PNG abound, particularly in the retail sector, large-scale investment projects are generally driven by SOEs. Indeed, the vast majority of Chinese firms that have made investments of over US$100 million in PNG are SOEs (Appendix 1). This trend reflects the differing preferences of Chinese SOEs and private firms, with SOEs tending to align more closely with Beijing's strategic objectives, prioritise natural resource acquisition and demonstrate neutrality to political and economic risk (Amighini et al. 2013:312–25). However, SOEs are also incentivised to 'brand' their intended projects as being part of the BRI in order to gain easier and greater access to state-backed finance (Financial Times 2017). In contrast to popular conceptualisations of the BRI as a cohesive and pre-determined strategy crafted by the CCP, the commercial motivations of SOEs may fragment the selection and implementation of BRI projects.

In addition, the practice of reverse engineering Chinese aid projects in PNG may herald further fragmentation of China's involvement in PNG and the broader Pacific (Smith 2015). This process refers to Chinese contractors and their Pacific partners developing a project and then misleadingly framing it as a local initiative to Chinese lending institutions. The complexity surrounding the implementation of the BRI generates two key implications for PNG. First, statements regarding a clear Chinese strategy in PNG may be overblown due to the diversity of interests, public agencies and private entities involved. Second, it may fall on the shoulders of PNG officials to ensure that Chinese investment projects are cohesive and work towards PNG's longer-term economic goals, rather than deliver a piecemeal and fractured result.

The complex bureaucratic processes that underlie the BRI suggest that BRI project selection may not always be rational or part of a larger overarching strategy driven by the core CCP leadership. In contrast, the number of Chinese government agencies involved, their competing interests and their unclear hierarchies are all factors that complicate the process of BRI project selection and suggest that the BRI's implementation may be more fragmented than assumed by many foreign commentators. While it is almost certain that many BRI projects are driven by Chinese foreign policy objectives, this cannot be assumed for any or all BRI projects.

Given PNG's late entry to the BRI and the Pacific's somewhat peripheral importance to Beijing, it is unlikely that all Chinese and BRI investment in PNG are driven primarily by Beijing's geopolitical objectives.

The argument that Chinese lending in the Pacific is not driven by strategic means or debt-trap diplomacy is further supported by empirical data. Tonga is the only Pacific nation at 'high risk' of debt distress and where Chinese lending comprise the majority of debt (Fox and Dornan 2018). However, Tonga's debt to China is the result of the 2006 Nuku'alofa riots that damaged Tonga's central business district and political moves by Tongan leaders to direct loan-financed expenditures to their electorates. These loans were enabled by for-profit Chinese construction firms rather than strategic ploys or opportunism by Beijing. Fundamentally, the origins, terms and contractors of BRI projects vary widely. A multiplicity of public and private entities from China and the host country are often involved in delivering BRI projects, and each of these entities is driven by its own unique objective. Even if the CCP desired to exert debt-trap diplomacy in PNG and the Pacific, corralling the various Chinese firms and government agencies involved in the region may prove a difficult task.

Is PNG selling its sovereignty?

The dominance of the debt-trap diplomacy theory raises the questions of why PNG and other debtor nations continue to seek Chinese financing and the extent to which PNG's sovereignty is threatened by Chinese investment. While China has been accused of exploiting PNG's natural resources, projects like the Pacific Marine Industrial Zone (PMIZ) indicate that PNG companies and individuals have also gained significantly at the expense of Chinese interests. Moving beyond such zero-sum dynamics, Chinese and PNG partners have also cooperated to engineer mutually beneficial and successful development projects, such as the dormitories at the University of Goroka (Smith 2012).

While ineffective Chinese projects harm PNG's development outcomes and fiscal space, they do not dissuade PNG from continuing to seek Chinese financing. One reason for PNG's ongoing reliance on Chinese investment and aid is PNG's critical need for infrastructure development. This need may be more easily financed through China's 'flexible' and infrastructure-targeted support than Australian support, which prioritises governance initiatives (Packham 2018). The recently announced AU$2 billion Australian Infrastructure Financing Facility for the Pacific (AIFFP) could see Canberra's priorities shift from governance to infrastructure, but it is currently too early to tell. The ADB estimates that the Pacific needs US$46 billion in infrastructure financing over the period 2016–30. When compared to other parts of the Asia-Pacific, the Pacific Islands region has the highest proportion of investment needs as a percentage of GDP at 9.1 per cent (ADB 2017). The BRI could thus fulfil a crucial need for investment funding in PNG and its PIC neighbours if the funds are used appropriately to finance productive assets.

The focus on China's alleged debt-trap diplomacy may also overlook more tangible threats to PNG's sovereignty. Of particular concern is the fact that PNG has permitted certain concessional loan agreements, such as the agreement for the PMIZ, to be 'governed by and construed in accordance with the laws of China' rather than PNG and 'irrevocably waived any' sovereign dispute for PNG in the event of loan disputes (PNG Exposed 2012). Agreements of this nature are not always adhered to in practice. For example, a PNG court successfully ordered a block on further construction on the PMIZ in October 2012 (ABC News 2012). Yet even if these agreements are not acted upon, PNG's waiving of its sovereign immunity in certain loan disputes is concerning. This practice may carry greater risks under the more ambiguous dispute resolution mechanisms of the BRI, which are alleged to prioritise Chinese over foreign interests.

Fundamentally, while PNG's level of debt may not be ideal, any debt crises are likely to be driven more by domestic mismanagement rather than Chinese strategising. China's ability to capitalise on any debt crises in PNG is constrained by the level of fragmentation inherent in the BRI process. This fragmentation is particularly noticeable in PNG due to the practice of reverse-engineering projects, the country's late entry to the BRI and the region's lesser importance to Beijing. The focus on the debt-trap diplomacy theory of China's geopolitical ambitions may thus overlook threats that are less grand than transforming PNG into a 'tributary state', but of more immediate risk to PNG's economy and sovereignty.

The economic impact of the BRI in PNG

While the quantity of Chinese investment is rising, its quality and spread across PNG's economy are often ambiguous. Certain projects, like the University of Goroka dormitories built by Guangdong Foreign Construction (GFC), are recognised as successful Chinese projects

(Smith 2018). Indeed, the dormitories were so favoured by locals that during the 2009 anti-Asian riots, students from the University of Goroka defended the Chinese GFC workers from rioters. In contrast, some Chinese projects, such as Lae Port and a rice monopoly project in Central Province, attract substantial criticism for overblown budgets, defective workmanship and breaches of customary landowners' rights (Eroro 2012; Papua New Guinea Today 2016). Other projects, like MCC's Ramu Nickel mine, receive both substantial criticism for environmental damages, delayed royalty payments and land ownership issues, and some praise for MCC's provision of 'schools and clinics, business opportunities and roads and bridges' (Joku 2009).

The variable quality of Chinese investment in PNG is likely due to the fact that the investing firms are often highly diverse in size, history, capabilities and organisational and operational culture—all of which influence development outcomes for PNG. However, these firms may be united in their similar levels of inexperience in PNG. As only two Chinese companies have invested in multiple projects worth over US$100 million (Appendix 1), many large-scale investments in PNG are undertaken by Chinese firms with limited to no experience in similarly sized projects within a PNG context. Even Chinese firms with long histories in PNG may not adapt to the local context. For example, though MCC has been involved in PNG through the Ramu Nickel mine since 2005, the firm is still attempting—and struggling—to apply Chinese approaches in a PNG context (Moyle and Dayant 2018). While this inexperience does not characterise all Chinese firms in PNG, it may create challenges for future BRI projects and their Chinese contractors.

In the absence of comprehensive official data, the American Enterprise Institute and the Heritage Foundation's China Global Investment Tracker (CGIT) can be used to evaluate China's history of large-scale investment in the Pacific and identify likely BRI projects (Appendix 1). The CGIT compiles all Chinese foreign investments greater than US$100 million in value from 2005–17. While these figures are unlikely to be precise due to the lack of official government sources, the data provides valuable insights into broad patterns of Chinese investment that are likely to be intensified under the BRI.

Chinese investments in the Pacific worth more than US$100 million were already concentrated in PNG prior to Port Moresby signing on to the BRI. Timor-Leste and Fiji were the only other PICs that received Chinese investments of over US$100 million. The limited sample size of Chinese investment in other PICs makes a cross-country comparison with PNG difficult, but it is interesting to note the role of China Railway Engineering (CRECG). CRECG was responsible for the first and largest-recorded BRI investment in Timor-Leste at US$290 million, and is a major shareholder of China Railway Group Limited—the company that was contracted to build PNG's first three BRI projects, collectively worth US$4.46 billion (Kenneth 2017b).

Only two Chinese companies—China Communications Construction Co., Ltd. (CCCC) and China State Construction Engineering (CSCEC)— have completed multiple US$100 million or more investments in PNG. CCCC is the only Chinese company to pursue investments of more than US$100 million in the same sector multiple times, having invested twice in the PNG transport sector in 2012 and 2013. Out of the 15 listed Chinese investments in PNG, 60 per cent were concentrated in one of three sectors: transport (four projects), real estate (three projects) and metals (two projects). The three sectors that attracted the most Chinese investment were metals (US$930 million), energy (US$880 million) and real estate (US$730 million), cumulatively making up 65 per cent of the total recorded US$3,880 million in Chinese investment. If these trends continue under the implementation of the BRI, PNG is likely to experience an influx of investment bids from new Chinese companies targeting the energy, metals, real estate and transport sectors. The predominance of extractive and polluting industries in China's historical investment portfolio in PNG may threaten environmental sustainability and protections in PNG.

PNG's environment and land tenure

Given PICs' vulnerability to the risks of environmental degradation, pollution and climate change, the allegations that China is using the BRI to exploit foreign natural resources and outsource pollution-intensive production must be examined. Some observers argue that the BRI is partly driven by an attempt to alleviate China's oversupply of steel and cement production and will thus promote carbon- and pollution-intensive development models in host countries (Pike 2017). Indeed, rather than assisting host countries in developing renewable energy sources, the BRI may 'lock-in' their fossil-fuel dependency (Ascensão et al. 2018). China also has significant commercial interests in PNG timber, nickel and natural gas that may be expanded under the BRI.

The PNG–China timber trade reveals that the failure by both the PNG Government and Chinese investors to exert due diligence harms the reputations of both countries and may enrich certain political and economic elites at the expense of PNG citizens. While Chinese firms are not the only foreign entities complicit in illegal logging, they deserve particular scrutiny as PNG is China's largest supplier of tropical logs and PNG exports roughly 80 per cent of its timber to China (PNG Exposed 2010). Illegal logging has been recognised as a problem in PNG since the Barnett commission in 1989. The issue recently received renewed attention due to investigations by the non-government organisation Global Witness and the controversies associated with PNG's Special Agriculture and Business Lease (SABL) licences. In 2017, major Chinese and US hardware companies were forced to halt sales and review their supply chains following a Global Witness investigation that revealed a third of PNG's timber was illegally obtained from land owned by local communities (Global Witness 2017). PNG landowners allege that the government is attempting to 'give away' local land to foreign logging companies, often originating from Malaysia, and that police personnel intimidated protestors (Pacific Media Centre 2017). These observations corroborate the Revenue Watch Institute's finding that resource governance in PNG is 'poor' due to weak government oversight, corruption and opaque data (Papua New Guinea Mine Watch 2014).

Many of these controversies occurred under the widely criticised SABLs, which saw up to 12 per cent of PNG land loaned to foreign entities for up to 99 years. Though the PNG Government claimed to have cancelled the leases following a commission of inquiry and international criticism, illegal logging has continued (Blades 2018). While much of the criticism regarding SABL licences has focused on the complicity of the Department of Lands and the PNG Forestry Authority, it is also speculated that elements of PNG customs contributed to illegal exports of timber to China. The wide variety of government agencies and officials complicit in illegal logging may complicate reforms that aim to eradicate the practice.

The SABL issue may reaffirm PNG landowners' fears that some foreign entities are attempting to alienate customary land. Certain Chinese companies are among the many foreign investors that have allegedly infringed upon landowners' rights. For example, the Basamuk Landowners Association threatened to shut down the MCC-run Basamuk refinery due to MCC's perceived neglect of local landowners and illegitimate use of the land. The association's criticism of the Madang Provincial Government's mismanagement of the dispute raises concerns regarding PNG officials' ability to mediate tensions between locals and foreign investors, and the credibility of government officials in the eyes of local landowners.

It must be noted that Chinese companies are not the only foreign firms to exploit PNG's environmental regulatory system. For example, Australian mining businesses and Malaysian logging entities have been implicated in significant environmental infractions in PNG. This suggests that PNG's current policy and enforcement mechanisms may be unable to prevent foreign exploitation of local resources and land.

As such, it is worth considering the BRI-related regulations that are intended to ensure Chinese investments under the BRI are legal, ethical and green to discern the extent to which PNG's natural resources are vulnerable to further exploitation. Though the Chinese Government has produced numerous policies that call for BRI projects to be environmentally friendly, such as the Guidance on Promoting Green Belt and Road, few of these policies are binding (Zhu 2015:27). Even compulsory policies possess weak enforcement mechanisms and are unevenly implemented. Enforcement mechanisms often rely on the host country reporting environmental infractions, which may be challenging in countries like PNG where accountability mechanisms may be underdeveloped, or local politicians may have stakes in Chinese projects. Despite Chinese and international rhetoric surrounding 'greening' the BRI, there may be little difference between BRI and non-BRI investments in the context of environmental risk in PNG.

The ability of the BRI to destabilise PNG

PNG's decision to join the BRI has reignited concerns that Chinese financing may prove to be a destabilising force in PNG and the Pacific. These arguments do not necessarily rely on assuming the BRI is a strategic ploy by China to control the Pacific, but rather that Chinese assistance adheres to weaker standards than other foreign development partners, contributes to corruption in PNG and threatens the security interests of traditional donors (Wallis 2017:5). This section argues that while certain Chinese investors in PNG are able to meet international standards to the point of winning competitive and lucrative ADB contracts, some Chinese companies and PNG officials exploit PNG's relatively weak regulatory environment for personal and commercial gains and erode good governance in the country. In addition, traditional donors like Australia view Chinese investment in certain PNG industries, such as telecommunications and defence, as a potential security risk and intervene accordingly. PNG may be able to exploit this competition between Australia and China to secure preferable lending arrangements. Fundamentally, joining the BRI may increase the risk of corruption in PNG if the influx in foreign lending is not accompanied by anticorruption measures and improved bureaucratic and enforcement capabilities.

Adherence to international norms

Though Chinese financing may be valued by PNG and other recipient countries for its flexibility, it has often been criticised for failing to adhere to international standards and practices, particularly in regards to transparency and accountability. While China's model of investment does not always reflect international norms, some Chinese companies in PNG play significant roles as contractors in projects funded by multilateral institutions like the ADB. This indicates that a notable proportion of Chinese work in PNG does abide by international standards and suggests that Chinese companies' cooperation with the ADB may inculcate Chinese contractors with more internationally acceptable practices.

From 2011 to 2016, the most significant contractor for ADB projects in PNG was the China Overseas Engineering Group Co. Ltd (PNG), also known as Covec (PNG) Ltd (Appendix 2). Covec is a subsidiary of China Railway Group Limited, which is in turn a subsidiary of the state-owned China Railway Engineering Corporation—the same SOE that was contracted to complete US$4.46 billion in BRI projects in PNG.

Covec is notable not only for ranking first among the ADB's top contractors, but also for the contract amount. In the periods 2011–15 and 2012–16, Covec's ADB contract alone made up the majority of the ADB's total contract funds for PNG at 63 per cent and 56 per cent of total funding, respectively. The US$80–88 million contracts won by Covec are also unusual, with the next highest ADB contract being US$14.17 million, roughly one-sixth of this amount. Another Chinese company, Hunan Lishui Hydro and Port Co. Ltd (JV), became one of the top five most significant ADB contractors in 2012–17 by pursuing a joint venture partnership with UK company AG Investment Limited to deliver the Divune Hydropower Plant (Post-Courier 2016). Combining the contract amounts awarded to Covec and Hunan Lishui reveals that

Chinese companies were awarded 63 per cent, 63 per cent and 26 per cent of total ADB contract funds in the 2011–15, 2012–16 and 2013–17 periods, respectively.

Though Covec has become increasingly well-established in PNG over the past decade, its history in the country is not spotless. In 2017, the PNG National Court ordered Covec to pay US$15.5 million to Kundiawa-based business man Peter Kama and his family for illegally extracting road building materials from Kama's land in 2006 (Pacific Islands Report 2017). This figure was the largest ever awarded by the National Court. Covec's history and more recent relationship with the ADB indicates that while certain Chinese companies may act dubiously, this is not always an indicator of their future behaviour. Some Chinese firms in PNG may be able to progress and deliver improved development outcomes. The cooperation between Chinese contractors and multilateral institutions like the ADB indicates that Chinese organisations in PNG are more diverse in terms of their operations than assumed by some commentators, which is a promising assessment for PNG's ability to ensure that the benefits of the BRI accrue proportionately and transparently to PNG.

Given the recent referendum for independence held by Bougainville, China's ties to the region are worth briefly noting, particularly as Beijing has reportedly offered valuable investments and may support Bougainville's bid for sovereignty diplomatically. Chinese representatives have approached Sam Kauona, a former Bougainville Revolutionary Army general and possible presidential candidate, with a detailed infrastructure plan that Australia and the US have reportedly not matched (Danckert and Bohane 2019). Unspecified Chinese officials also reportedly expressed interest in reopening the controversial US$58 billion Panguna mine, which could be linked to a proposed US$1 billion package for investment in mining, tourism and agriculture to assist Bougainville's transition to independence (Bohane 2019). However, Bougainville has experienced its own challenges with Chinese investment. Attempts to encourage Chinese investment in Bougainville from 2011 onwards resulted in joint venture Chinese–Bougainvillean companies either disappearing, failing to pay local contractors or stifling local competition. An anonymous Bougainville official claimed that the Bougainville Government 'cannot control [the Chinese companies] … they are doing whatever they want on Bougainville' (Roka 2014). In March 2019, the Chinese partners of the Bougainville Import Export General Corporation allegedly disappeared after failing to pay taxes and 'took all the cash [out of the company] and left nothing' (Tseraha 2019). While it is possible that Chinese investment in Bougainville under the BRI would prove to be more organised and reliable, increased involvement by the Bougainville Government seems critical to ensuring that the mistakes of the past are not repeated.

Corruption

Chinese investment may exacerbate PNG's challenges with corruption, public sector mismanagement and poor governance by offering less regulated funding opportunities for projects of dubious development value. Most recently, former PNG prime minister Michael Somare was accused of accepting a US$1 million bribe from Chinese company ZTE (Grigg and McKenzie 2018).

Prior to joining the BRI, the PNG Government vowed to crack down on business dealings with China by mandating local participation in Chinese projects in PNG, among other measures (Kenneth 2018). It is unclear how Port Moresby's promises will be incorporated into BRI projects. Given Port Moresby's history of awarding contracts worth hundreds of millions of dollars to Chinese companies blacklisted by the World Bank for fraud and corruption, PNG may struggle to further regulate its business dealings with China.

In 2012, PNG awarded CCCC's subsidiary China Harbour Engineering Company (CHEC) a US$290 million contract to develop PNG's Lae Port, despite the company being blacklisted by the World Bank for fraud at the time. The PNG Government's response to CHEC's mismanagement may be more concerning than the faulty development itself. Port Moresby refrained from publicly disclosing the results of government inquiries into the Lae Port mismanagement. In addition, though a relevant PNG authority stated that CHEC would fund the repairs, then opposition leader Don Polye alleged that CHEC refused to cooperate with the PNG Government (Papua New Guinea Today 2016). Despite these controversies, the PNG Government attempted to shortlist CHEC as a contractor for the Lae Port's second phase of development prior to the announcement of the tender process. This alleged behaviour may undermine the political will and ability of the PNG Government to further regulate Chinese business dealings in PNG. Indeed, some PNG government officials may be active participants in, rather than the passive victims of, corruption involving Chinese companies. This distinction suggests that attempts to reform governance in PNG that only target Chinese investment are unlikely to be successful, as this would only address one side of the problem. Greater transparency regarding investment deals is necessary to reduce the risk of corruption and improve both commercial assets for Chinese investors and development outcomes for PNG.

Foreign reactions

While Chinese investment in PNG and the broader Pacific is generally viewed with suspicion in foreign policy circles, certain BRI projects are likely to be more controversial than others and may influence PICs' relationships with other countries. The BRI incorporates technology, information and communication projects that, if pursued in PNG or other PICs, may spark security concerns from nations like Australia. For example, Australia intervened to majority fund a US$136 million cable project to PNG and Solomon Islands, planned to be developed by Huawei, due to Canberra's suspicions regarding Huawei's links to the Chinese Government. Canberra controversially announced that it would fund the US$136 million project through the aid budget, which critics argued could reorient Australia's aid spending away from its traditional priorities of governance and towards infrastructure (Graue 2018; SBS News 2018).

While the *Australian Aid Budget Summary 2018–19* does not disclose how the cable project will be funded, infrastructure spending as a percentage of overall official development assistance by investment priority was higher than the Pacific average of 21.7 per cent in both Solomon Islands (42.6 per cent) and PNG (22.5 per cent) (Australian Government 2018). Australia's promise that it will 'compete' with China's infrastructure spending in the Pacific and the establishment of the AIFFP indicate that similar episodes of competition over infrastructure projects in the Pacific—and in PNG in particular—are likely to reignite (Wroe 2018).

PNG may be able to capitalise on this competition to attain more preferable lending arrangements, but whether this would deliver better outcomes for the PNG economy as a whole or solely for certain PNG officials is unclear. On one hand, PNG appeared to benefit from regional competition by securing a US$300 million loan from Australia that 'replaces' a similar loan proposed by the China Development Bank in late 2019, despite claims by the Australian Government that the loan was 'completely unrelated' to China (Clarke 2019). On the other hand, then PNG prime minister Peter O'Neill is accused of using China's and

Australia's regional rivalry to fund the construction of the controversial Western Pacific University in O'Neill's own electorate of Ialibu, Southern Highlands (PNGi 2018). O'Neill's electorate was selected as the location for the new university without any public feasibility study or independent valuation of the land. As PNG's existing universities are in need of funding and repair, the economic benefit the new university may generate is not guaranteed. If the Western Pacific University is indicative of an emerging trend in PNG development, the competition between Australia and China could worsen, rather than improve, economic outcomes in PNG.

It is highly likely that PNG's decision to join the BRI will herald more infrastructure projects that are concerning to traditional partners like Australia, which views the Pacific as its 'part of the world' (The Australian 2018). Hence, Chinese investment in PNG does not only affect the behaviour of Chinese and PNG stakeholders, but also the behaviour of other countries with strategic stakes in the Pacific. The Pacific could stand to gain from the increased foreign attention and investment from China and potential competitors that come with the BRI, but this depends on the ability of PICs' governments to manage these funds appropriately. Without greater transparency and stronger anticorruption measures— both challenging endeavours in their own right—Port Moresby may find it difficult to ensure that BRI projects are sustainable, non-fraudulent and benefit the local and national economies.

Conclusion

Like its Pacific neighbours, PNG is in significant need of infrastructure financing that the BRI could provide. However, the BRI presents a myriad of risks to PNG's economy and governance that may have been overlooked by the current discourse, which tends to focus on the debt-trap diplomacy theory. The ability of PNG to harness the potential development benefits associated with the BRI will depend on the quality of the Chinese contractors involved and the aptitude of the responsible PNG officials. Attempts by traditional donors like Australia to dissuade PNG from relying on China are unlikely to be successful and may entrench the commonly held perception by PNG locals and leaders alike that Australia is a paternalistic force in the region. Accordingly, foreign critics of PICs' debt to China are often met with significant criticism from Pacific leaders, particularly when these critics do not offer alternative funding arrangements. The nascent AIFFP may mitigate these criticisms if Canberra is able to provide more cost-effective loans and fund higher-quality projects than the BRI. The exact impact of the AIFFP is difficult to predict given the lack of clarity regarding the proportion of grants to loans offered, the allotment of financing across the Pacific, the sources of the AIFFP's funds and whether the AIFFP will affect Australia's aid budget for the Pacific.

Current criticisms of China's increased involvement in the Pacific and PNG's decision to join the BRI in particular tend to focus solely on the level of debt owed by PICs to Beijing. In certain cases, such as Tonga, the country's level of debt is likely to be a genuine threat to its economy and, potentially, its sovereignty. The situations of other PICs with relatively lower levels of debt, larger economies and nuanced relations with traditional donors, such as PNG and Fiji, may be more complex. The diplomatic and development efforts of traditional donors may gain greater traction with Pacific leaders if they focus on the specific high-risk elements of PNG's decision to join the BRI that this analysis has identified, rather than solely criticising the overall level of debt. This is particularly relevant when traditional donors offer debt-financing organisations of their own, such as Australia's AIFFP.

Moreover, traditional donors like Australia, New Zealand and France are unlikely to be able to outspend all Chinese investment and aid if Beijing is truly determined to control the region. Identifying and attempting to outbid specific Chinese projects in PNG that represent perceived risks to the region may represent a more realistic and effective strategy for traditional donors concerned about China's growing influence in the Pacific. Australia's outbidding of China to become the only foreign donor for the Fijian Military Forces' Black Rock Camp and the Pacific subsea cable project are two notable examples. Such reactive activity should also be accompanied by improvements in traditional donors' own aid and investment activities in the region, as this engagement is not without its flaws. As observed by a local leader in PNG, like all traditional donors to the Pacific, 'Australia needs to recognise reality: China is rising' (Clarke et al. 2018). Traditional donors like Australia may not be able to stop China's rise—and would incur backlash from Pacific leaders by attempting to do so—but they can prioritise efforts to ensure that Chinese influence in the Pacific leads to improved development outcomes, rather than debt dependency or destabilisation.

References

ABC News 2012. PNG Court Halts Controversial Industrial Project. 24 October. www.abc.net.au/news/2012-10-24/an-png27s-tmiz-put-on-hold/4332016

ADB (Asian Development Bank) 2017. *Meeting Asia's Infrastructure Needs*. Manila: ADB.

Amighini, A.A., R. Rabellotti and M. Sanfilippo 2013. Do Chinese State-Owned and Private Enterprises Differ in Their Internationalization Strategies? *China Economic Review* 27:312–25. doi.org/10.1016/j.chieco.2013.02.003

Ascensão, F., L. Fahrig, A.P. Clevenger, R.T. Corlett, J. AG Jaeger, W.F. Laurance and H.M. Pereira 2018. Environmental Challenges for the Belt and Road Initiative. *Nature Sustainability* 1(5): 206–09. doi.org/10.1038/s41893-018-0059-3

Australian Government 2017. *2017 Foreign Policy White Paper*. Canberra: Commonwealth of Australia.

Australian Government 2018. *Australian Aid Budget Summary 2018–19*. Canberra: Department of Foreign Affairs and Trade.

Barrett, J. and C. Greenfield 2019. Papua New Guinea faces cash crunch as China repayment schedule ramps up. *Reuters*. 29 November. www.reuters.com/article/us-papua-china-debt-idUSKBN1Y30B9

Blades, J. 2018. Loggers Still Operating on PNG Lease Despite Court Ruling. Radio New Zealand, 23 February. www.rnz.co.nz/international/pacific-news/351026/loggers-still-operating-on-png-lease-despite-court-ruling

Bohane, B. 2019. 'Where Is Australia?' China Makes a Bold Play for the South Pacific's 'Treasure Islands'. *The Sydney Morning Herald*, 17 November. www.smh.com.au/world/oceania/where-is-australia-china-makes-a-bold-play-for-the-south-pacific-s-treasure-islands-20191115-p53b4g.html

Chefitz, G. and S. Parker 2018. *China's Debtbook Diplomacy: How China is Turning Bad Loans into Strategic Investments*. Harvard Kennedy School Policy Analysis Exercise. Cambridge: Belfer Center for Science and International Affairs, President and Fellows of Harvard College.

Clarke, M. 2019. Papua New Guinea Budget Reveals Canberra is Spending $440m to Keep China at Bay. *ABC News*, 30 November. www.abc.net.au/news/2019-11-29/png-budgets-reveals-canberra-spending-440million-keep-china-away/11751110

Clarke, M., C. Pan and S. Wilson 2018. Ceding Influence? Consequences of Reducing Australian Aid in the Pacific. Submission to Parliamentary Inquiry into Australia's Aid Program.

Danckert, S. and B. Bohane 2019. This Derelict Mine Caused a Bloody War. Now Aussie Companies are Fighting over It Again. *The Sydney Morning Herald*, 15 November.

Eroro, S. 2012. Ex-Customs Chief Against Rice Monopoly Project. *PNG Exposed*, 18 January. pngexposed.wordpress.com/2012/01/18/ex-customs-chief-against-rice-monopoly-project/

Financial Times 2017. Australia Port Project Highlights Schism over Chinese Investment. 17 July. www.ft.com/content/b4d35440-5a68-11e7-9bc8-8055 f264aa8b

Fox, R. and M. Dornan 2018. China in the Pacific: Is China Engaged in 'Debt-Trap Diplomacy'? *Devpolicy Blog*, 8 November. devpolicy.org/is-china-engaged-in-debt-trap-diplomacy-20181108/

Global Witness 2017. *Stained Trade*. Washington DC and London: Global Witness.

Graue, C. 2018. Budget 2018: Australia to Pay for New High-Speed Internet Cable for PNG and Solomons Using Aid Funds. *ABC News*, 6 May. www. abc.net.au/news/2018-05-06/budget-how-is-australia-going-to-pay-for-the-png-undersea-cable/9727192

Greenfield, C. and J. Barrett 2018. Payment Due: Pacific Islands in the Red as Debts to China Mount. *Reuters*, 31 July. www.reuters.com/article/us-pacific-debt-china-insight/payment-due-pacific-islands-in-the-red-as-debts-to-china-mount-idUSKBN1KK2J4

Grigg, A. and N. McKenzie 2018. Chinese Aid Funded Alleged $1 million Bribe to Former PNG Leader, Somare. *The Sydney Morning Herald*, 3 June. www.afr.com/world/asia/chinese-aid-funded-1-million-bribe-to-former-png-leader-somare-20180603-h10we3

Hong, C.-S. and O. Johnson 2018. Mapping Potential Climate and Development Impacts of China's Belt and Road Initiative: A Participatory Approach. *SEI Discussion Brief* Oct. 2018. Stockholm: Stockholm Environmental Institute.

Horn, S., C. Reinhart and C. Trebesch 2019. *China's Overseas Lending*. Kiel Working Paper no. 2132. Kiel: Kiel Institute for the World Economy, 4–14. doi.org/10.3386/w26050

Howes, S. 2017. Papua New Guinea 2018 Budget Fails to Solve Revenue Crisis. *Devpolicy Blog*, 29 November. devpolicy.org/png-budget-20171129/

IMF (International Monetary Fund) 2017. *Papua New Guinea: Debt Sustainability Analysis*. Washington DC: IMF.

IMF (International Monetary Fund) 2020. *Papua New Guinea. IMF Country Report No. 20/95*. www.imf.org/en/Publications/CR/Issues/2020/04/06/Papua-New-Guinea-2019-Article-IV-Consultation-and-Request-for-Staff-Monitored-Program-Press-49307

Joku, H. 2009. Landowners Urge Ramu MCC to Work. *Post-Courier*, 25 May.

Jubilee Australia 2018. *On Shaky Ground: PNG LNG and the consequences of development failure*. Sydney: Jubilee Australia Research Centre. www.jubilee australia.org/storage/app/uploads/public/5fb/8c6/2dd/5fb8c62dd31d 4510474121.pdf

Kehoe, J. 2018. US Report: China 'Debt Trap' on Australia's Doorstep. *The Australian Financial Review*, 13 May. www.afr.com/world/us-secret-report-china-debt-trap-on-australias-doorstep-20180513-h0zzwd

Kenneth, G. 2017a. China's Investment in PNG at $US1.9B. *Post-Courier*, 3 October.

Kenneth, G. 2017b. Multi-Billion Kina Deal Signed to Strengthen PNG and China Relations. *Post-Courier*, 21 November.

Kenneth, G. 2018. Govt to Tighten Up on Dealings with Chinese. *Post-Courier*, 7 February.

Lowy Institute 2019. Pacific Aid Map. pacificaidmap.lowyinstitute.org/

Moyle, E. and A. Dayant 2018. Reconciling with China in the Pacific. *The Interpreter*, 15 October. Lowy Institute. www.lowyinstitute.org/the-interpreter/reconciling-china-pacific

Pacific Islands Report 2017. PNG Court Orders Chinese Company to Pay $15.5 Million for Illegally Extracting Road Building Materials. 16 January.

Pacific Media Centre 2017. US, Chinese Companies Linked to PNG Land Theft, Deforestation, Says Report. *Asia Pacific Report*, 4 August.

Packham, B. 2018. China's More Flexible Support Better Than Australia's, Says PNG. *The Australian*, 12 June.

Papua New Guinea Mine Watch 2014. Revenue Watch Institute Says PNG Resource Government 'Poor'. 27 January.

Papua New Guinea Today 2016. Chinese Company's Harbour Work Done at Lae Basin is Defective: Opposition. 27 February.

Pike, L. 2017. Explainer: Will China's New Silk Road Be Green? *China Dialogue*, 11 May.

PNG Department of Treasury 2017a. 2018 Budget Estimates of Revenue and Expenditure for Statutory Authorities, Provincial Governments, Debt Services and Trust Accounts.

PNG Department Treasury 2017b. 2018 National Budget: Economic and Development Policies.

PNG Department of Treasury 2018. S&P Global Rating for PNG. Press Release.

PNG Department of Treasury 2019a. 2020 Budget Estimates for Statutory Authorities, Provincial Governments, Debt Services and Trust Accounts.

PNG Department of Treasury 2019b. Amendments to the *Fiscal Responsibility Act 2019*.

PNG Department of Treasury 2019c. 2020 Budget: Take Back PNG.

PNG Exposed 2010. China Has Big Plans in PNG. 14 September. pngexposed. wordpress.com/2010/09/14/china-has-big-plans-in-png/

PNG Exposed 2012. O'Neill Allowing China to Cash in on PNG Resources— and Making Us Foot the Bill! 26 September. pngexposed.wordpress.com/ 2012/09/26/oneill-allowing-china-to-cash-in-on-png-resources-and-making-us-foot-the-bill/

PNGi 2018. China and Australia Encouraged to Pork Barrel in Prime Minister's Backyard. 14 May. pngicentral.org/reports/china-and-australia-encouraged-to-pork-barrel-in-prime-ministers-backyard

Post-Courier 2016. Construction of New Hydro Plant to Start. 24 August.

Pryke, J. 2017. No Course Correction in PNG Budget. *The Interpreter*, 30 November. Lowy Institute. www.lowyinstitute.org/the-interpreter/no-course-correction-png-budget

Rajah, R., A. Dayant and J. Pryke 2019. Ocean of Debt? Belt and Road and Debt Diplomacy in the Pacific. *Analysis*. Sydney: Lowy Institute, 16–20.

Roka, L.F. 2014. Bougainville China Corporation is a Disaster for Bougainville. *PNG Attitude*, 9 December. asopa.typepad.com/asopa_people/2014/12/ bougainville-china-corporation-is-a-disaster-for-bougainville.html

Roubini, N. 2001. *Debt Sustainability: How to Assess Whether a Country is Insolvent*. New York: Stern School of Business, New York University.

SBS News 2018. Contract Signed for Pacific Data Cables. 19 June. www.sbs. com.au/news/contract-signed-for-pacific-data-cables

Slattery, D., M. Dornan and J. Lee 2018. *Road Management in Papua New Guinea: An Evaluation of a Decade of Australian Support*. Canberra: Australian Government Department of Foreign Affairs and Trade.

Smith, G. 2012. Are Chinese Soft Loans Always a Bad Thing? *The Interpreter*, 29 March. Lowy Institute. archive.lowyinstitute.org/the-interpreter/are-chinese-soft-loans-always-bad-thing

Smith, G. 2015. The Six Billion Kina Answer. *Devpolicy Blog*, 8 October. dpa.bell school.anu.edu.au/experts-publications/publications/4110/six-billion-kina-answer

Smith, G. 2018. The Belt and Road to Nowhere: China's Incoherent Aid in Papua New Guinea. *The Interpreter*, 23 February. Lowy Institute. www.lowyinstitute. org/the-interpreter/belt-and-road-nowhere-china-s-incoherent-aid-papua-new-guinea

The Australian 2018. Julie Bishop's Message for China: Pacific is Australia's Patch. 5 June.

Tseraha, P. 2019. Bougainville Govt Takes Back Chinese Company. *Post-Courier*, 1 March.

Var, V. and S. Po 2017. Cambodia, Sri Lanka and the China Debt Trap. *East Asia Forum*, 18 March. www.eastasiaforum.org/2017/03/18/cambodia-sri-lanka-and-the-china-debt-trap/

Wallis, J. 2012. The Dragon in Our Backyard: The Strategic Consequences of China's Increased Presence in the South Pacific. *The Strategist*, 30 August. Australian Strategic Policy Institute.

Wallis, J. 2017. *Crowded and Complex: The Changing Geopolitics of the South Pacific*. Barton: The Australian Strategic Policy Institute.

Wroe, D. 2018. Australia Will Compete with China to Save Pacific Sovereignty, Says Bishop. *The Sydney Morning Herald*, 18 June. www.smh.com.au/politics/federal/australia-will-compete-with-china-to-save-pacific-sovereignty-says-bishop-20180617-p4zm1h.html

Xinhua 2017. 'Belt and Road' Incorporated into CPC Constitution. 24 October. www.xinhuanet.com/english/2017-10/24/c_136702025.htm

Ye, M. 2018. *Economy in Command: Unpacking the Domestic Politics of China's Belt and Road Initiative*. GEGI Working Paper 16 02/2018. Boston: Global Economic Governance Initiative, Global Development Policy Center, Boston University.

Zhu, R. 2015. *Understanding China's Overseas Investments Governance and Analysis of Environmental and Social Policies*. Beijing: Global Environmental Institute.

Appendices

Appendix 1: Chinese investment over US$100 million to the Pacific, 2005–17

Year	Chinese entity	Quantity ($m)	Sector	Subsector	Country
2005	MCC	$670	Metals	Steel	Papua New Guinea
2009	Sinohydro	$150	Energy	Hydro	Fiji
2012	China Communications Construction	$290	Transport	Shipping	Papua New Guinea
2013	China Shenyang International Economic and Technical Cooperation Corp	$100	Agriculture		Papua New Guinea
2013	China Communications Construction	$140	Transport	Autos	Papua New Guinea
2013	Huawei	$200	Technology	Telecom	Papua New Guinea
2013	Sinomach	$170	Transport	Autos	Papua New Guinea
2014	State Construction Engineering	$250	Real Estate	Construction	Papua New Guinea
2015	China Railway Engineering	$290	Transport	Autos	Timor-Leste
2015	Zijin Mining	$300	Metals		Papua New Guinea
2015	China Communications Construction	$100	Transport	Autos	Papua New Guinea
2015	Shandong Gaosu	$270	Utilities		Timor-Leste
2016	State Construction Engineering	$180	Utilities		Papua New Guinea
2016	Jiangsu International	$120	Logistics		Papua New Guinea
2016	China Railway Engineering	$130	Real Estate	Construction	Papua New Guinea
2017	Shenzhen Energy, Power Construction Corp	$880	Energy	Hydro	Papua New Guinea
2017	Minmetals	$350	Real Estate	Construction	Papua New Guinea

Source: American Enterprise Institute and the Heritage Foundation, www.aei.org/china-global-investment-tracker/.

Appendix 2: Top ADB contractors in PNG, 2011–17

Year	Contractor	Contract Amount ($m)	Rank	Sector
2011–2015	Covec (PNG) Ltd	80.27	1	Industry, Trade, Transport
2011–2015	Global Constructions Ltd	14.17	2	Transport
2011–2015	Shorncliffe (1967) Ltd	6.38	3	Transport
2011–2015	Avenell Engineering Systems Ltd	2.98	4	Health
2011–2015	ARPI Ltd	2	5	Energy
2011–2015	**Total**	**127.1**		
2012–2016	COVEC (PNG)	88.34	1	Transport
2012–2016	Global Constructions Ltd	14.07	2	Transport
2012–2016	Ag Investment Ltd	11.52	3	Energy
2012–2016	Hunan Lishui Hydro and Port Co. Ltd (JV)	11.52	3	Energy
2012–2016	Shorncliffe (PNG) Ltd	7.7	5	Transport
2012–2016	**Total**	**158.26**		
2013–2017	Global Constructions Ltd	14.06	1	Transport
2013–2017	Ag Investment Ltd	12.44	2	Energy
2013–2017	Hunan Lishui Hydro and Port Co. Ltd (JV)	12.44	2	Energy
2013–2017	COVEC (PNG)	11.72	3	Transport
2013–2017	Shorncliffe (PNG) Ltd	7.71	4	Transport
2013–2017	Pacific Development Contractors Ltd	5.16	5	Health
2013–2017	**Total**	**91.95**		

Source: Asian Development Bank, www.adb.org/publications/series/fact-sheets.

14

The Shifting Fate of China's Pacific Diaspora

Fei Sheng and Graeme Smith

This chapter attempts to bring into focus one of the more contentious aspects of the People's Republic of China's engagement with the Pacific: migration. Overseas Chinese communities have been both the source and the target of social unrest in Pacific urban centres, and Pacific leaders identify tensions around these communities as one of the major barriers to China's engagement with the Pacific (Little Red Podcast 2019). This chapter will focus on historical trends among the Chinese migrant community in Vanuatu and question a number of concepts that have become accepted in Pacific Studies. In particular, we question the sharp distinction drawn by scholars and media commentators between 'old' and 'new' Chinese communities in the Pacific, even though this shorthand has been adopted by the Chinese communities themselves.[1]

Academic circles in the People's Republic of China (PRC) know almost nothing about the history of Oceania and the overseas Chinese in this region.[2] This is unsurprising. The Pacific was never a major destination

---

1   In Vanuatu, 'old' Chinese are taken to be those from Guangzhou who arrived before 1980, while the 'new' Chinese came after that time and may hail from other provinces.
2   The entire Pacific, including Australia and New Zealand, lacks Chinese-language research on the history and current situation of Chinese migrants. In recent years, a more representative study is Zhang Qiusheng's *A History of Chinese Emigrants to Australia* (1998). Research on the Pacific Islands is even more limited. Chinese literature includes 'Chinese Labor in Oceania', the eighth section of Chen Hanzao's *Compilation of Historical Materials on Overseas Chinese Labor* (1985). There is also Australian scholar Liu Weiping's *A History of the Chinese in Oceania* (2000), published in Hong Kong. See also Fei Sheng, *The Overseas Chinese in the South Pacific Islands* (2014).

for Chinese migration. The absolute number of Chinese migrants remains small and historical ties with the modern Chinese state are limited— Cold War competition in parts of Africa, which saw Maoist China spend close to 3 per cent of its GDP on foreign aid (Kitissou 2007), was largely absent from the Pacific. From a geopolitical perspective, Pacific nations are surrounded by ocean, far from China, and are not crucial to the development of China's foreign relations. From the perspective of the PRC state, Pacific issues are insignificant. However, the Pacific was one of the earliest regions to accept Chinese migrants, it is still absorbing new migrants, and their scale and impact on the changing geopolitics of the Pacific should not be underestimated. While much of the history of Chinese migrants in Australia has been elided in favour of the white settler narrative (Loy-Wilson 2014), Chinese migrant families in the Pacific maintain a strong sense of their history.

With the rising status of the Pacific in China's international strategy—the Pacific was added to the Maritime Silk Road in November 2014 when President Xi Jinping visited Suva—the Pacific Chinese community is not only more influenced by China, but is also an important medium for China to expand its overseas influence, even though the migrants themselves are not encouraged by the Chinese state. The formation and development of Chinese migrant society in Oceania is inseparable from the extension of the ocean network in which an outward-looking and more assertive China is situated. This chapter provides an overview of the evolution of Chinese communities in Oceania and incorporates new findings from archival research, field investigations and interviews in Vanuatu. These will be used to analyse changes in Chinese migrants' livelihoods, complicate the sharp distinction between old and new Chinese that has developed in the literature[3] and provide context for the new forms of migration that are emerging among Chinese communities in the Pacific.

The Asia-Pacific Ocean network and Chinese migrants in the Pacific

China and the Pacific Islands had close ties before the arrival of Western colonial powers, especially in Melanesia due to its proximity to Southeast Asia. These ties can be seen as an extension of China's trade network,

---

3   See, for example, Chin (2008).

which operated alongside many other ethnicities—Malays, Jews, Tamils and Gujartis. With the rise of the pearl, beche-de-mer and, later, sandalwood trades, China and Oceania belonged to the same trading network (Shineberg 2014). The influx of Chinese migrants into Oceania and their impact on the Pacific began with indentured Chinese labourers in 1850. China was dragged into the global colonial system built by European capital. China began to deploy its labour resources according to the needs of the global market. Large-scale Chinese migration to Oceania began in 1848 when about 390 contract workers were transported from Xiamen to the colony of New South Wales in Australia (FitzRoy 1849). However, after the 1851 gold rush, Cantonese people, largely from the Pearl River Delta, became the main drivers of immigration to Australia.

Early Chinese migrants to the Pacific can be divided into two types. The first was individual migrants, largely to Australia. The second type, common from the 1860s and found mainly in the Pacific, was Chinese labourers recruited by colonial labour companies. The cause of the latter was a new regulation that emerged from the treaty signed after the Second Opium War legalising the commodification of Chinese labour. Foreign merchants were no longer prohibited from recruiting workers directly from China. Concurrently, Pacific islands were claimed and developed by European (and later American) powers in the mid-19th century, driving demand for plantation labour. There were, however, significant differences among colonial powers in their attitudes towards recruiting Chinese labour. Germany promoted large-scale labour recruitment in German New Guinea and German Samoa while strongly discouraging any interbreeding between Chinese labourers and the local population (Steinmetz 2007).[4] British and Australian colonial administrators tended to oppose Chinese migration, but would often find the commercial interests of plantation owners in conflict with their sympathy for the racist underpinnings of migration restrictions, which included poll taxes and a restriction on steamers that only one Chinese could be carried for each 100 tonnes of cargo (Fitzgerald 2007:164–66).

Further driving the demand for Chinese labour was the tough natural environment and living conditions on the Islands, which made it difficult to develop a large workforce without the use of contract or forced labour. Spread from German New Guinea to as far as French Polynesia, the

---

4   German administrations were often bent on keeping 'native populations' in a museum-like state—an obsession that extended to prohibiting the use of corrugated iron for roofing.

indentured labourers were geographically isolated. Many of those who survived continued on to Australia and New Zealand, becoming vegetable farmers and small traders (Chen 1984). The spread of Chinese migrants to the Pacific Islands was the result of the Western colonial project and their control of the Pacific exchange network. But Chinese migrants, both forced and free, took advantage of emerging maritime traffic to establish their own transnational networks. Even under the White Australia Policy, retail empires such as Wing On stretched from London to Hong Kong to Fiji (Fitzgerald 2007).

The maritime colonial network dominated by the Western powers broke down in the 1940s and the development of overseas Chinese communities in Oceania entered an important transition period. With the outbreak of the Pacific War, the momentum of Chinese migrants gathering in the Pacific Islands and dominating local economies was curbed as Micronesia and much of Melanesia were occupied by Japan. Many Chinese migrants were forced to relocate to Australia or safer Pacific islands. Chinese workers in then phosphate-rich Nauru were evacuated to Melbourne or the Gilbert Islands. At the end of World War II, the Chinese indentured-labour export system, with its overtones of slavery, was completely abolished in the Pacific. Many Pacific Islands governed by European and American powers also introduced bans on Chinese migrants, often justified in terms of avoiding the mixing of races and social stability. Large-scale, organised Chinese migration to the Pacific Islands ceased.

Chinese migrants intensified their engagement with the Pacific Islands during the post-war years, and the Chinese community dispersed throughout the region. Changes in the international situation, particularly the onset of the Cold War, further encouraged the localisation of Chinese migrants. The first generation of migrants were fully naturalised and married into local communities, bringing them higher social status when their host countries gained independence. Papua New Guinea (PNG), which was home to the largest Chinese community, became, like many island colonies, a trustee of Australia. At the time, the Australian Government (which, along with the British, had opposed Chinese migration to PNG) resolutely maintained the White Australia Policy, which prohibited Chinese from continuing their migration journey to Australia. As a result, the existing Chinese community, predominantly male and with no prospect of finding brides from China, faced the choice of a rapid demise or marriage with the local population.

After the founding of the People's Republic in 1949, the Nationalist Government was defeated and fled to Taiwan. Most Chinese communities in the Pacific were affiliated with the Nationalists and so were forced to interrupt their ties with the mainland, but also did not have the means to return to Taiwan. As a result, the pressure on these communities to integrate with local societies grew. By the end of the 1950s, Australia began to allow Chinese born in the trusteeship to become naturalised. The statistics of the PNG authorities in 1966 showed 2,455 residents were believed to be Chinese. Among them, 566 were born in China, but only 282 retained Chinese nationality (Nelson 2007:2). By the 1970s, the Chinese community in the Pacific was no longer in close contact with the regimes on either side of the strait, and its Chinese identity was weakening. In 1971, PNG had 50,000 expatriates, including 3,500 Chinese; however, almost none of them still had Chinese nationality or had been born in China. By 2000, the census no longer counted whether people were of Chinese descent—almost all Chinese populations identified as Papua New Guinean or Australian (Nelson 2007:4). Many localised migrants and their descendants gained prominence; PNG's second prime minster Sir Julius Chan is an obvious example.

Between 1960 and 1980, most of the island nations of Oceania achieved independence or autonomy, leading to the adjustment of their immigration policies. Although former colonial powers such as Australia and New Zealand supported the island countries through development assistance, the burden of self-reliance for remote island nations was considerable. The leaders of many countries regarded the development of foreign trade and the attracting foreign investment as means of building modern nation-states, which gave the populations of neighbouring Asian countries an opportunity to expand their trading networks. At the same time, the White Australia Policy was abandoned in 1972 and under the Hawke–Keating Government (1983–96) Australia promoted a national development strategy of engagement with Asia, which encouraged Pacific countries to relax controls on Asian immigration. This saw a spike in Chinese migrants to the Pacific from neighbouring Asian countries such as Malaysia and Indonesia. From the early 1990s, migrants came directly from mainland China, largely from Fujian and Guangdong provinces. This has seen the emergence of a new group of Chinese in the Pacific: the 'new Chinese migrants'. Within the Chinese community in Vanuatu, the dividing line between 'new' and 'old' is understood to be 1980, a less complex division than that required in PNG (Chin 2008:119–24).

In migration history, scholars usually divide immigrants into two categories: 'sojourners' and 'settlers'. The former emphasises the roots of immigration from China as either a result of migrant preference or differential exclusion (Castles 2003:11), while the latter emphasises the establishment of migrants in local communities. Over the past three decades, these categories have coexisted in the emerging Chinese immigrant groups in the Pacific Island countries, but the former predominates. There are four sources of emerging Chinese immigrant groups. One is the resource-development activities of Southeast Asian Chinese enterprises in the Pacific Island countries since the 1980s, especially deforestation activities in PNG and Solomon Islands (Global Witness 2018; Nelson 2007:6). The second is Chinese project labour since the 2000s—that is, the large number of workers brought by Chinese companies to develop local mineral resources and infrastructure, some of whom seek further commercial opportunities when the project finishes (Smith 2013a:184–85; Smith and Dinnen 2015).[5] The third is migrants who acquire nationality through legal procedures, mainly through marriage or investment migration; these migrants dominate the retail trade in many Pacific nations (Firth 2006; Smith 2016). The fourth source is middle-class migrants relocating to the Pacific for health or lifestyle reasons; these will be described briefly in this chapter.

When discussing emerging Chinese migrant groups in the Pacific, it is difficult to apply the usual concept of immigration that implies a long-term commitment to a new country. Since few Pacific Island countries have elements that attract ordinary Chinese people, particularly in terms of personal safety and the standard of schooling available (Smith 2013b), a large number of new migrants are simply 'passing through'. In an era of continued facilitation of the trans-Pacific transportation network and China's growing influence in the Asia-Pacific, their mobility is remarkable and their livelihoods closely tied to Chinese society and domestic markets.

---

5   Ramu Nickel remains the largest Chinese-owned mining company in the Pacific, but they have been joined by other state-owned enterprises, including Zijin (China's largest gold mining company) in partnership with Barrick at the Porgera gold mine and Guangdong Rising Asset Management at the Freida River copper mine in partnership with Australian mining company Highlands Pacific.

The rise of the Chinese business community in Vanuatu

Among Chinese communities in the Pacific, the number of people who identify as Chinese in Vanuatu is relatively small. Official PRC statistics put the number at 2,000 legal settlers, estimating that more than half of them are new migrants who have arrived in the past 10 years (Guillain 2018). However, as of 2018, local sources say the number is between 4,000 and 5,000, though the extreme mobility of the population makes a reliable estimate difficult.[6] The political situation in Vanuatu is relatively stable, there is no history of anti-Chinese riots and Chinese in Vanuatu are concentrated in Port Vila and Luganville, the capital of the largest island. Over the past century, Chinese traders in Vanuatu have not closely integrated with the broader population. This is in contrast to other Pacific nations—such as Tonga and PNG—where Chinese settlement now reaches into the hinterlands.

The emergence of Chinese migrants in Vanuatu was initially the result of colonial expansion by Britain and France into a country of extraordinary linguistic and cultural diversity (Bedford and Spriggs 2014). Due to this unusual joint colonial project, Vanuatu was integrated into a regional market that relied on maritime transport links, and this regional market established direct links with China's southeast coast. The first Chinese migrants who appeared in Vanuatu were chefs and carpenters aboard British merchant ships in 1844, but locals knew of no descendants of these early voyagers. The first Chinese who survived and set down roots were Chinese retailers (*huashang* 华商) who appeared in the mid-to-late 19th century.

The Chinese community of Vanuatu can be traced back to Cheung Yabao (张亚宝), widely known as 'Ah Pow', who arrived from Fujian in 1912, having worked as a chef with the merchant vessel *Euphrosyne* (Willmott 2005:7, 2007:37).[7] After he settled in Port Vila, he opened a bakery, importing ingredients from Australia through British merchants. The Cheung family has prospered for four generations, becoming the most powerful merchant family in Port Vila and leaders of the Chinese community there. Cheung Yabao's grandson, Charles Cheung

---

6   Second author's interviews, July 2018. Port Vila.
7   This family will be referred to as the Cheung family in this chapter.

(Cheung Zhali 张查理), is head of the family and, together with his uncle Cheung Lianzhong (张连仲), owns Vanuatu's largest supermarket chain, Au Bon Marché.[8] Charles Cheung is the chairman of the Vanuatu Chinese Club, the largest Chinese community organisation in Vanuatu, and serves as Vanuatu's Consul General in Shanghai. In a country like Vanuatu that lacks industrial diversification, the Chinese business community has significant economic and political influence. The Chinese Association of Port Vila in the capital is registered as a corporate legal entity and has a charter in accordance with company law (Chinese Club 2004).

It is no accident that merchants with strong overseas ties dominate Vanuatu's Chinese society. Vanuatu's economy was born out of a single crop plantation introduced by the colonial powers. From the mid-to-late 19th century, the pillar of the colonial economy was coconut planting. Today, Vanuatu's main exports are copra, which can be used for oil extraction, and medicinal kava. As of 2016, the value of merchandise imports was seven times greater than the value of exported goods, an imbalance partially offset by tourism, which accounts for 80 per cent of service exports (WTO 2018:16–17). French colonists mixed cattle in coconut plantations and established a profitable beef export industry. But until World War II, Vanuatu lacked an industrial base and the proportion of foreign workers was low. This can partly be attributed to a lack of enthusiasm on the part of the colonial powers. In Colonial Office communications, British officials disparaged the climate as unsuitable for white settlers and even attempted to swap their stake in the colony with France in return for French territory in Africa. The French refused. Vanuatu still relies heavily on the import of consumer goods, and early Chinese merchants such as the Cheung family used this to dominate the retail trade and accumulate wealth.

World War II created further opportunities for Chinese businesses. On the one hand, the southwestern Pacific battlefield established by the United States made Vanuatu a military supply base and a defence facility. The US military began the construction of a large-scale infrastructure, altering the local landscape and consumer culture. While the urban population expanded, introduced pests and diseases caused hardship in

---

8   Zhang Yabao had a wide range of operations, including the sale of a small amount of opium, as Zhang Yabao himself had a preference for smoking opium, though he abstained after getting married. Zhang Yabao had three sons: Zhang Lianfang, Zhang Liansheng and Zhang Lianzhong. Charles Cheung is the son of Zhang Lianfang (Zhang Liansheng (the second son of Zhang Yabao), 22 August 2016. Interview with first author; Charles Cheung, 23 August 2016. Interview with first author).

rural areas (Bennett 2004), leading to the near collapse of subsistence economies in the port areas and increasing reliance on export earnings and imports. In the shadow of war, many Chinese in Vanuatu began to invest in Australia and New Zealand while gradually establishing a monopoly over imported consumer goods. After the withdrawal of US troops from Luganville, US military camps became the centre of a new urban area, with Chinese merchants building new shops along the hardened roads. The Huang family drew on their connections in Australia to become the main rice suppliers, establishing exclusive sales rights.[9] Similarly, the Liang family in Luganville established a monopoly over potatoes, onions and non-perishable vegetables from New Zealand. Supply ships regularly visited Luganville to provide fresh vegetables and receive the hospitality of Chinese businessmen.[10]

Chinese business forces not only benefited from wartime conditions, but their identity within colonial society was unique. Unlike other Pacific Island colonies, Vanuatu was under the joint management of Britain and France. The two colonial authorities cooperated, but also displayed mutual restraint and even competition, which Chinese businesses exploited. Due to its large number of colonies in the South Pacific, Britain neglected Vanuatu, while the French focused more resources there.[11] In order to compete with the British, French authorities provided free basic education and limited the penetration of the British forces in various ways, giving Chinese merchants more scope than they enjoyed in neighbouring colonies such as Solomon Islands or PNG, where colonial authorities restricted Chinese merchants to favour British trading companies such as Swires.

Unlike neighbouring New Caledonia, Vanuatu attracted few European migrants. There were missionaries and farmers, but Vanuatu's European population had few industrialists or commercial operators, making it difficult for the colonial authorities to replace or suppress Chinese businessmen. On the contrary, colonial authorities relied on Chinese businessmen to maintain the local private economy, and

---

9   The surname of the merchant has been changed, respecting the interviewee's wishes.
10   Suppliers in New Zealand and Australia regularly visit Vanuatu retailers. After updating or confirming contracts, they often travel the islands with their hosts and attend banquets hosted by local Chinese businessmen.
11   Many Chinese merchants expressed the view that those with high academic qualifications have English and French bilingual ability, while less-educated people only speak French (Liang Wenhua (owner of the Luganville Port Iowa store), 19 August 2016. Interview with first author).

so rarely restricted their activities. Unlike most in Pacific or Southeast Asian countries, there has never been an anti-Chinese movement in Vanuatu, though there are signs of the sentiment emerging in present-day Port Vila. Because the island's pillar industries, coconut cultivation and cattle farming, do not require intensive labour input, the colonists did not introduce a large number of Chinese workers from overseas. The main imported agricultural labour force in Vanuatu were Vietnamese introduced by France. While they largely returned to Vietnam during the first Indochina War, with over 500 current residents they still represent the second largest foreign community in Vanuatu (Willie 2018). The concept of private property in Vanuatu is also weak, making it difficult for local business groups to compete with Chinese businesses.[12] Thus, since World War II, the Chinese community has controlled Vanuatu's economic lifeline.[13] After Vanuatu's independence, local communities took ownership of land, but control was typically concentrated in the hands of the chiefs. Because their sources of monetary income are limited, clan leaders often exchanged land for the Chinese migrants' money and goods, allowing them to advance socially through contact with local elites and commercially by building up holdings of urban and rural land.

The Vanuatu Chinese community in a shifting Asia-Pacific regional network

In the 20th century, especially after World War I, Pacific Island countries were integrated into the colonial system dominated by Britain and France. Under British–French joint management, the Vanuatu Chinese could use both British and French maritime routes built in the Pacific, resulting in strong mobility. For example, before the founding of the PRC, Vanuatu Chinese enjoyed visa-free or loosely reviewed access to the majority of British and French colonies in the Asia-Pacific, allowing Chinese

---

12 Chinese merchants held the belief that the lack of private property ownership means local merchants face filial pressures to extend credit and goods, and in a tight market bankruptcy comes extremely fast. They also frequently expressed the view that the leisurely lifestyle of local people makes them reluctant to engage in regular wage employment (Liang Wenhua and Yaxiu (wife of Liang Wenhua), 19 August 2016. Port Vila. Interview with first author. For privacy reasons, Yaxiu is a pseudonym). These comments echo those by Chinese business owners in PNG in the 1970s, who claimed, 'The native trade store can never survive long simply because it usually is "eaten" by relatives of the storekeeper before he can make any profit' (Wu 1982:106).

13 Other ethnic Chinese businessmen such as Zhang Liansheng and Liang Wenhua agreed with this proposition.

businessmen to travel freely throughout the region. The following case study of the Huang family in Tahiti, French Polynesia and, ultimately, Vanuatu reflects this.

French Polynesia began importing Guangdong Hakka labourers into their sugar cane farming industry via Hong Kong in 1865, and they eventually formed a relatively large community of Chinese traders.[14] In 1911, Huang Cai, a three-year-old Hakka child from Dongguan, accompanied his mother Yumei to Tahiti, joining his father, Huang Jin, who had already settled in the local area. Huang Cai grew up in Tahiti and attended a local Chinese elementary school run by the Chinese Nationalist Party from 1916 to 1922 before making a living from farming for the next 25 years. In 1941, he married across the racial divide, taking E Tama of Tahiti as his wife. At the same time, his younger sister Huang Yajiao married a Frenchman and they moved to Luganville.[15] In 1947, there was a rumour that France wanted to send more troops to Indochina to fight and would recruit from the Asian population of Tahiti, so Huang Cai fled with his wife and two sons to Dongguan, close to the border with Hong Kong. In February 1950, following the fall of the Nationalist Government in China, Huang Cai fled back across the border and worked as a carpenter on Hong Kong Island. However, after three years, he transferred to Kowloon to work on a farm. Since his economic situation was not improving, he returned to the Pacific, joining his sister in Vanuatu in 1958. He started farming with his younger sister Huang Yajiao while his younger brother Huang Yasheng entered the retail industry. Huang Cai died in early 1960. His son, Huang Wan, though born in Tahiti, completed high school in Hong Kong and worked at airport customs. Taking on his father's career, Huang Wan went to Vanuatu in about 1970 and ran the family store with the help of his aunt. He founded Luganville's first commercial cinema and hired local Chinese to serve visiting international sailor consumers. In 1979, on the eve of Vanuatu's independence, Huang Wan decided to sell his assets in Luganville and move to French Polynesia to work with his

---

14 English-language sources on the history of the Chinese diaspora in French Polynesia are limited. The most authoritative source in French is Coppenrath (1967).

15 Huang Wan, 20 August 2016. Port Vila Bakery. Interview with first author. Information from the resume submitted by Huang Wan in 1970 to the Vanuatu Government when applying for citizenship. Held by the Huang family. The name is written like this, but it seems to be transliterated according to his nickname in Hakka dialect, Huang Jiajiao. The latter is also the case for his younger brother Huang Ansheng.

father's old friends, fearing expropriation by the new regime.[16] In 1988, Lena Li, a niece who had married into the Cheung family in Port Vila, invited Huang Wan to come to Vanuatu to settle down again, sponsoring the reopening of the cinema. Huang Wan eventually joined the Cheung family's pastry business.

Immigration and secondary migration caused by changing times increased the international mobility of the Pacific Island–based Chinese. Vanuatu, as an English–French co-managed colony, created new opportunities for the Chinese to establish their status and expand overseas exchanges. Changes in the geopolitics of the Asia-Pacific, including the Pacific War and the Cold War, greatly influenced the Chinese Pacific Island diaspora. Due to the remoteness of the islands, misinformation, rumours and scams frequently affected the life choices of Chinese migrants. However, Huang Cai, Huang Wan and his son were able to shuttle freely between French Polynesia, Vanuatu and China, demonstrating the centrality of the trans-Pacific network to the livelihoods of Chinese people in the Pacific.

China's rising influence and the Pacific Islands diaspora

For the Pacific Island Chinese, the opportunities brought by earlier geopolitical shifts cannot be compared with the changes wrought by the independence of the Pacific Island states and their establishment of diplomatic relations with either the People's Republic of China or the Republic of China (Taiwan). After the establishment of diplomatic relations between Vanuatu and mainland China in 1983,[17] institutional barriers to the flow of people and goods were largely removed. Independence in the 1970s and 1980s coincided with China's own efforts to reform its economy and open up trade, leading to rapid regional integration. It also

---

16   Huang Wan, 20 August 2016. Port Vila Bakery. Interview with first author. He had heard rumours there may be anti-Chinese activities after independence. Because the French colonists resisted Vanuatu's independence, they suffered more hatred from the locals. Chinese who maintained deep ties with French colonists were worried their property might not be protected after losing their British passports.

17   This is aside from a brief interlude in November 2004 when the government of Serge Vohor briefly recognised Taiwan. The Council of Ministers overturned the decision and Vohor, who was accused of assaulting the Chinese ambassador (Chen 2004), was removed the following month in a no-confidence vote. Vanuatu has since remained a diplomatic ally of the PRC, signing on to the Belt and Road Initiative in 2019 and even recognising China's position on the South China Sea.

spurred the development of Vanuatu's foreign trade, which, along with remittances, was a major contributor to Vanuatu's development over the next two decades (Kumar et al. 2011).

In 2006, under the auspices of China, Fiji hosted the first Ministerial Conference of the China–Pacific Island Countries Economic Development and Cooperation Forum in Nadi, attended by state ministers from the eight countries that recognise China, including Vanuatu. Vanuatu's Minister of Trade, Industry and Tourism demonstrated knowledge of both Chinese political slogans of the day and their potential impacts on domestic businesses, arguing that:

> in order to promote this harmonious development in our respective regions we shall ensure to encourage and to undertake foreign trade and investment in an orderly way, as foreign capital enterprises would certainly take the lead and positive role in our region's economic growth and development. We must also ensure that domestic and external capital enterprises develop side by side and in a complementary manner (Bule 2006).

Undoubtedly, increased trade and investment has not only encouraged more Chinese citizens to migrate to Vanuatu, but also created opportunities for the local Chinese community. The impact goes beyond economics. The experience of Liang Wenhua from Luganville illustrates how some of Vanuatu's Chinese residents have seized these new opportunities.

In the 1970s when Huang Wan was running the Luganville cinema, he hired a poor grocery store owner, Liang Wenhua (known to locals as 'Ah Hua'), as a partner and ticket seller.[18] Liang is second-generation Chinese. His father is from Dongguan, but was forced to leave in 1939 and arrived in Vanuatu with his fellow clansmen, finding work as a helper in Chinese shops. After the outbreak of the Pacific War, he went to Sydney to work as a market gardener, returning to Port Vila before moving to Luganville to run a grocery store. Born in 1955, Wenhua was one of eight children—six of them daughters. Because Luganville lacks Chinese men of the right age, four of the daughters remained unmarried. They assisted their parents in running the store and gave up opportunities to make a living in the capital. Wenhua had one sister married in Port Vila who eventually left for Hong Kong. The other sister chose to marry

---

18 Despite sharing a surname, Liang Wenhua is not part of the influential Liang family from Luganville.

into a Vanuatu family and ultimately was ostracised from her Chinese family. Despite this, his father insisted that Wenhua go to Australia to complete secondary education before returning to Luganville. When his father died, the family's economic burden fell on Wenhua. In addition to working with his sisters, he also worked for other Chinese businessmen, including Huang Wan. During the Maoist era, China and the Pacific Island countries had no direct contact. In addition to lacking goods and news, it was difficult for Wenhua to find a Chinese woman to marry.[19]

The establishment of diplomatic relations between China and Vanuatu was crucial for Wenhua. After 1983, news from China increased. Chinese businessmen who visited the Pearl River Delta in southeast China returned with photos of single girls from their hometowns for the consideration of lonely Chinese men in Vanuatu. In 1993, Wenhua, then 38, saw photos of a Dongguan girl named Yaxiu and quickly got in touch. Yaxiu had just suffered a short, failed marriage at a time when divorce was uncommon in China and the economic and social status of divorced women was low (Liu and Chan 1999). She expressed her willingness to leave her hometown and start a new life in Vanuatu. They were married in 1994 and started to run the store together. Yaxiu's previous full-time work was in finance, so she learned the operation of Wenhua's store and established a professional financial system to reduce losses and waste. She used contacts in her hometown to import light industrial products from the Pearl River Delta, changing the tradition of relying on re-export trade between Australia and New Zealand and greatly increasing the profitability of Wenhua's store. The president of the Santo branch of the Chinese Association of Vanuatu said, 'Yaxiu is really capable, not only her business ability, but also her social skills are strong. Unlike the local Chinese, her eyes are open and active'.[20]

Unlike many Chinese born in Vanuatu, Yaxiu frequently travels to wholesale markets in Guangzhou to learn about the latest consumer trends and source goods directly from China. She is also establishing close ties with the Chinese Government's Overseas Chinese Affairs Office (now subsumed by the United Front Work Department) and the Ministry of Foreign Affairs so that she can grasp the latest developments in China's politics and diplomacy. Since the mid-to-late 1990s, Yaxiu has

19   Liang Wenhua, 19 August 2016. Interview with first author.
20   Liang Yuyuan (president of the Santo Vanuatu Chinese Association), 17 August 2018. Interview with first author.

also built wealth by buying land from chiefs in Vanuatu and investing in real estate in Australia. Through the contacts provided by Yaxiu, Wenhua was permitted to open a petrol station adjoining the retail store, which became its main source of profit. In the past two decades, Liang Wenhua has improved his economic state and that of his sisters, building new homes for them. Wenhua's only regret is that, typical of new Chinese traders, Yaxiu is too mobile. She is unwilling to settle in Vanuatu for long periods and is mobile between China, Australia and Vanuatu.[21] Unlike earlier generations of migrants (Wang 1993:927), Yaxiu did not spend time in Hong Kong, Singapore or Taiwan before migrating to the Pacific.

Although the case of Wenhua and Yaxiu is striking, it is by no means a rare example of 'old' and 'new' Chinese migrants benefiting each other. Cheung Yabao, the first Chinese migrant with a known descendant in Vanuatu, once lived with a local Vanuatu woman, but had no children, so returned to his hometown to marry. His son explained, 'The family specifically asked, not to find a virgin, but to find a woman who has already had a child to get married, to ensure Dad can have descendants.'[22] His second son, Cheung Liansheng, was married to a new migrant from Mawei in Fujian province around the age of 45. A number of second-generation Vanuatu Chinese men born in the 1950s were married to Chinese women from China in the mid-to-late 1980s through photos and contact with distant relatives. The brides usually came from poor families or were willing to go abroad for various reasons. The old Vanuatu Chinese families were maintained through the influx of new female migrants. Even if the Pacific network exists, without openness and extensive contacts with China, old Chinese communities are likely to shrink, as in PNG[23] (Nelson 2007:3; Wu 1982), or to marry into the local community, as seen in Samoa and smaller Pacific Island nations (Willmott 2007). As Willmott urged, it is important to recognise:

> the enormous importance of chance in migration: where people end up depends as much on luck as decisions … Professor Wang [Gungwu] would not call them migrants all, but they became such by dint of shipwreck or opportunity grasped (Willmott 1995:131).

---

21 Liang Wenhua and Yaxiu, 19 August 2016. Interview with first author. Port Vila.
22 Zhang Liansheng, 22 August 2016. Interview with first author.
23 The 1933 census found only five Chinese living in PNG.

To this, we should add misinformation, rumors and chance, which are the basis of many migration decisions for the Chinese in the Pacific, a problem that has not improved with the arrival of the internet. This is not a complete break from migration based on false promises, common in the 19th century. While the element of coercion is no longer present, the misinformation obtained by today's Chinese migrants often has a commercial motive, whether it is found in Pacific-focused WeChat groups or a Baidu (China's main search engine) enquiry for 'Vanuatu', which at the time of writing yielded the result 'what are the benefits of having more than one passport? A Vanuatu passport is quickly obtained'.

The strengthening of China's ties with Vanuatu has increased the speed of information exchange within Vanuatu's Chinese community with the introduction of social networking platforms such as WeChat and the spread of officially approved Chinese culture. An early proposal by the Vanuatu Chinese Society (Port Vila) to set up Chinese-language schools gives a flavour of the efforts made to standardise Chinese language and culture in a community where Mandarin ranked far behind Cantonese, English, French and Bislama:

> Going to visit relatives and friends in China and sightseeing has become a dream of many people. But when you enter China, you need to communicate with each other. To communicate, you must use a common language. Mastering Mandarin is the first key to roaming the land of China. To this end, in direct response to the voice of people who want to learn Chinese, under the advocacy of the Chinese Embassy and the Chinese Chamber of Commerce, we decided to 'promote Chinese culture'. For the purpose of hosting a Chinese school in Port Vila that is both Chinese and friendly to Chinese culture (Yuan 1997).

Efforts to promote a 'friendly' version of Chinese culture in Vanuatu have continued, and in February 2015 the University of the South Pacific Emalus Campus in Port Vila opened a Confucius classroom, partnering with Beijing University of Posts and Telecommunication.

The position of many new migrants in relation to the Chinese state is complex. Researchers have argued that the Chinese state 'can be a vocal advocate of the rights of ethnic Chinese in the Pacific, particularly when they are under threat' (Henderson and Reilly 2003:99). While riots against Chinese migrants in the Pacific from 2006 onwards proved the opposite proposition—that the Chinese state and Chinese citizens were indifferent or even hostile to recent Chinese migrants to the Pacific (Smith 2012)—recent rhetoric around 'overseas citizen protection' indicates that the geopolitical calculus around these concerns may also be shifting (Connolly 2016). This is complicated by growing public expectations of what a powerful Chinese state is able to do for them, expectations fostered by a series of popular movies based around the extraction of Chinese citizens from hostile African environments, notably *Wolf Warrior II* and *Operation Red Sea*, respectively the highest and third-highest grossing Chinese films ever made.

A change in the recent geopolitical calculus that has largely gone unnoticed is the arrival of middle-class migrants in the more stable countries of the Pacific—notably Fiji and Vanuatu. Rather than being driven primarily by economic goals, as migrants from Fujian and Guangdong have been, many of these new arrivals are drawn by the slower pace and clean environment offered by the Pacific Island nations. The owner of a small restaurant in Port Vila who had trained as an artist back in China explained her journey to Vanuatu:

> I came to Vanuatu because of illness. The doctor told me I should move to a country where the pace was slower, where there was less pollution, no factories. I did a lot of research and settled on Vanuatu. At first, I wasn't used to it. After less than a month, I fled! They didn't have streetlights; the roads were filled with potholes or gravel. I remember when I arrived thinking, 'I had no idea it would be so poor'. The airport had no air conditioning, not like the huge airports in China. The cars were old and battered. It was a shock. I wondered if I'd got on the wrong plane. But the locals: I saw how happy they were. When I was applying, I knew that of all the developing countries Vanuatu was one of the happiest. Their smiles were a comfort, not like the fake smiles you get in China (*pi xiao, rou bu xiao* 皮笑肉不笑). Even though their shoes and clothes were simple, happiness radiated from them. After a month back in China, I got sick again, I wasn't sleeping, too many obligations (*yingchou* 应酬). It doesn't matter whether you feel like it, friends will take you out for a meal, go for a drink, eat lots of meat, it's how you express affection—no thought of whether it's good for you. Friends, family, relatives, husband, an endless cycle of obligations. I went downhill fast. Now [three years later], I don't even need to take medicine.[24]

---

24 Restaurant owner, 9 February 2019. Interview with second author.

She observed that in Port Vila, while people from Fujian ran shops, most migrants from other parts of China were recovering their health, or that of their children (*liao yang* 疗养). Chinese citizens from other Pacific Island countries were also migrating to Vanuatu because countries like PNG and Tonga felt unsafe. All of this had seen the Chinese population rise from 500 or so in 2014 to more than 3,000 in 2019. Medical teams visiting on the Peace Ark had been told by the Chinese embassy that 4,000 to 5,000 Chinese people lived in Vanuatu (including all people of Chinese ethnicity). The restaurant owner hesitated to call the new arrivals migrants, as it seemed unlikely many would settle in Vanuatu, with most looking to move on to Australia or New Zealand or return to China when their children's schooling required it. Many traders also felt there was no need to get citizenship—which they were eligible for after 10 years—because an investment permit allowed them to do everything required to run a business.

A shopkeeper from Shandong said that the money to be made running a shop in Vanuatu was scarcely worth the effort, with many finding there was more money to be made working off the books on a tourist visa in Australia, a short two-hour flight away. She explained, 'It's Fujian people exploiting other Fujian people'. Aside from exploitation, many migrants were brought to the Pacific by misinformation and outright scams, with some taken in by a promise that migration to American Samoa would enable them to get a US passport. Others were kept hanging for years on the promises of migration agents that Vanuatu could be a 'springboard' to Australia and New Zealand. This shopkeeper knew of one man who had waited nearly 20 years to secure a New Zealand passport, finally managing to do so when he was 60 years old. True to her word about the worsening business environment, she soon returned to China.[25] Sources in the old Chinese community confirmed that some 'Chinese shops' in Port Vila now stand empty, with no one willing to take on the lease.[26] In some ways, this shift reflects the growing prosperity of China—more Chinese migrants, but fewer willing to work long hours in shops and restaurants. As Patrick Matbob notes in Chapter 15, to reduce their workload, some Chinese business migrants in PNG are hiring local workers from an area—Misima—they regard as producing hard workers.

---

25 Shopkeeper, July 2018 and January 2019. Port Vila and on WeChat. Interviews with second author.
26 February 2019. Port Vila. Interviews with second author.

There is a widespread belief in Vanuatu that the sudden spike in the number of Chinese arriving on their shores is the result of Chinese state support, a belief shared by some senior Vanuatu government ministers.[27] While the opposite seems to be true—in conversations with the second author in July 2019, Chinese shopkeepers in Honiara largely did not want Solomon Islands to switch diplomatic allegiance from Taiwan to China (see Aqorau, Chapter 10, this volume)—there is ambition within the Belt and Road Initiative to coordinate and harmonise, or at least ameliorate the impact of, new commercial migrants from China. The second author's interviews with a range of migrants from Fujian and other provinces bring into question the practicality of this approach, at least in the short term. Many of these migrants have enjoyed few, if any, positive interactions with Chinese officials, and their instinct is to steer well clear of the embassy, except when they need to renew their passports. More successful businesspeople and leaders of the Chinese community are more likely to engage with Chinese officials, not least because of the access to information and business opportunities that such networks can bring. However, for ordinary shopkeepers, Chinese officials are best avoided (Smith 2013b).

The recent experience of six Chinese migrants who found that Chinese authorities were able to exercise extra-territorial power in Vanuatu to detain them and remove them from Port Vila without trial—even though four of them had Vanuatu passports—will reinforce sentiment that the PRC state is best given a wide berth (McGarry 2019a). The embarrassment caused to government officials by this case, which included the revelation that Vanuatu's Interior Minister Andrew Napuat did not know which Chinese agency he was liaising with, led to the reporter having his work permit denied and being the subject of a no-fly order, stopping him from rejoining his family in Port Vila (Garrett 2019). This operation echoed the deportation of 77 Chinese nationals from Fiji two years earlier. They were accused of being involved in telephone and online scams targeting China, but an investigation by the Australian Broadcasting Corporation suggested that at least some of them were sex workers (Cohen and Webb 2017).

---

27 July 2018. Port Vila. Interviews with second author.

Further complicating the relationship of Vanuatu's Chinese community with the Chinese state is the increasing popularity of Vanuatu passports as a second passport for Chinese businessmen, particularly those looking to work in the European Union. Strictly speaking, Chinese citizens are not allowed to hold another passport, but the sale of these passports to 'honorary citizens'[28] (US$150,000 for an individual, US$205,000 for a family of four) has reached such a scale—1,800 sold in 2018—that they are now the largest source of Vanuatu Government revenue, outstripping VAT (McGarry 2019b). While it is unclear whether this will result in large-scale migration, the experience of Tonga suggests that at least some passport holders will look to settle in Vanuatu (van Fossen 2007), particularly if China encounters economic or political upheaval.

The evolution of migrant livelihoods in the Pacific

Although the Chinese in the Pacific are a branch of the Chinese family that China has limited awareness of, they are also distinct. A small and scattered population, they are completely dependent on networks of cross-sea exchange, not only between their place of residence and China, but also between different Pacific Islands. The case of Vanuatu indicates that the colonial rule of European powers created opportunities for Chinese settlers in the South Pacific. Dependency, the checks and balances between different colonial powers, and maritime traffic between the Pacific islands improved their economic and social status and shaped their business-led livelihoods. Despite distance, the connection with China is increasingly vital to the Chinese communities in Pacific Island countries. The proliferation of Chinese families and the development of their businesses depend on the use of hometown resources. Especially since the 1980s, the arrival of 'new' migrants allowed the 'old' Chinese community to develop and grow.

China's increasing affluence has changed the nature of the Chinese community in Vanuatu, with the emergence of migrants seeking not just commercial opportunities, but also the health and lifestyle benefits offered by a country free of the stress and pollution that characterises

---

28   Some limits are placed on the rights of these passport holders, such as the ability to run for public office in Vanuatu.

present-day China. While President Xi Jinping's focus on the rejuvenation of the Chinese nation calls for greater coordination of the activities of Chinese overseas, the diversity of Vanuatu's Chinese population and the antipathy of many of its members towards the Chinese state make it unlikely this community will advance the lofty goals laid out under the Belt and Road Initiative.

References

Bedford, S. and M. Spriggs 2014. The Archaeology of Vanuatu: 3000 Years of History Across Islands of Ash and Coral. In E. Cochrane and T. Hunt (ed.), *The Oxford Handbook of Prehistoric Oceania*. Oxford: Oxford University Press, 1–17. doi.org/10.1093/oxfordhb/9780199925070.013.015

Bennett, J.A. 2004. Pests and Disease in the Pacific War: Crossing the Line. In R.P. Tucker (ed.), *Natural Enemy, Natural Ally: Toward an Environmental History of War*. Portland: Oregon State University Press, 217–51.

Bule, J. 2006. Official Statement of the Honorable James Bule. Statement at the Ministerial Conference of the China–Pacific Island Countries Economic Development and Cooperation Forum, Nadi, 5 April.

Castles, S. 2003. Migrant Settlement, Transnational Communities and State Strategies in the Asia Pacific Region. In R.R. Iredale, C. Hawksley and S. Castles (eds), *Migration in the Asia Pacific: Population, Settlement and Citizenship Issues*. Cheltenham: Edward Elgar, 3–22.

Chen, H. (ed.) 1984. *Collection of Overseas Chinese Historical Materials* [*Huaren chuguo shiliao huibian*]. Beijing: Zhonghua Books.

Chen, H. 1985. Chinese Labor in Oceania [Dayangzhou huagong]. In H. Chen (ed.), *Compilation of Historical Materials on Overseas Chinese Labor* [*Huagong chuguo shiliao huibian*]. Vol. 8. Beijing: Zhonghua Book Company [Zhonghua shuju].

Chen, M. 2004. China's Envoy to Vanuatu Says Vohor Punched Him. *Taipei Times*, 6 December. www.taipeitimes.com/News/taiwan/archives/2004/12/06/2003213963

Chin, J.U. 2008. Contemporary Chinese Community in Papua New Guinea: Old Money Versus New Migrants. *Chinese Southern Diaspora Studies* 2:117–26.

Chinese Club 2004. *The Companies Act: Memorandum of Association of the Chinese Club Limited*. Port Vila: Chinese Club.

Cohen, H. and T. Webb 2017. Chinese Nationals Deported from Fiji Were Sex Workers, Not Fraudsters: Source. *ABC News*, 6 October.

Connolly, P.J. 2016. Engaging China's New Foreign Policy in the South Pacific. *Australian Journal of International Affairs* 70(5):484–505. doi.org/10.1080/10357718.2016.1194805

Coppenrath, G. 1967. *Les Chinois de Tahiti: De L'Aversion à L'Assimilation 1865–1966.* Paris: Musée de l'Homme. doi.org/10.4000/books.sdo.180

Fei, S. 2014. The Overseas Chinese in the South Pacific Islands: An Historical Approach [Taipingyang daoguo huaren shehui de fazhan: lishi yu xianshi de renzhi], *Pacific Journal* [*Taipingyang xuebao*] 22:11:55–62.

Firth, S. 2006. *Globalisation and Governance in the Pacific Islands.* Canberra: ANU E Press, Chapter 6. doi.org/10.22459/GGPI.12.2006

Fitzgerald, J. 2007. *Big White Lie: Chinese Australians in White Australia.* Sydney: UNSW Press.

FitzRoy, Governor C.A. to Earl Grey 1849. *Accounts and Papers Session 4, No. 1.* 8 February 1851, Vol. XL.

Garrett, J. 2019. China, Media Freedom in the Pacific, and the Great Australian Silence. *The Interpreter*, 20 November. Lowy Institute.

Global Witness 2018. Paradise Lost: How China Can Help the Solomon Islands Protect Its Forest. www.globalwitness.org/en/campaigns/forests/paradise-lost/

Guillain, E. 2018. The Chinese Community in Vanuatu. Lycée de Port Vila, 17 April. www.lfportvila.edu.vu/?p=4179

Henderson, J. and B. Reilly 2003. Dragon in Paradise: China's Rising Star in Oceania. *The National Interest* 72:94–105.

Kitissou, M. 2007. *Africa in China's Global Strategy.* London: Adonis and Abbey.

Kumar, R.R., V. Naidu and R. Kumar 2011. Exploring the Nexus between Trade, Visitor Arrivals, Remittances and Income in the Pacific: A Study of Vanuatu. *Acta Universitatis Danubius. Œconomica* 7(4):199–217.

Little Red Podcast 2019. *Step Up or Be Overrun: China's Challenge for the Pacific.* 5 March. omny.fm/shows/the-little-red-podcast/step-up-or-be-overrun-china-s-challenge-for-the-1

Liu, M. and C. Chan 1999. Enduring Violence and Staying in Marriage: Stories of Battered Women in Rural China. *Violence Against Women* 5(12):1469–92. doi.org/10.1177/10778019922183471

Liu, W. 2000. *A Collection of Chinese and Western Historical Material of Oceania* [*Dayangzhou huaren shi shicong gao*]. Hong Kong: Tiandi Press.

Loy-Wilson, S. 2014. Rural Geographies and Chinese Empires: Chinese Shopkeepers and Shop-Life in Australia. *Australian Historical Studies* 45:3:407 –24. doi.org/10.1080/1031461X.2014.948020

McGarry, D. 2019a. Six Chinese Deported. *Vanuatu Daily Post*, 6 July.

McGarry, D. 2019b. Passport Sales Out-Earn VAT. *Vanuatu Daily Post*, 22 August.

Nelson, H. 2007. The Chinese in Papua New Guinea. ANU Research School of Pacific and Asian Studies Discussion Paper 2007/3. dpa.bellschool.anu.edu.au/sites/default/files/publications/attachments/2015-12/07_03_dp_nelson_0.pdf

Shineberg, D. 2014 (1967). *They Came for Sandalwood: A Study of the Sandalwood Trade in the South-West Pacific 1830–1865*. St Lucia, Qld: University of Queensland Press.

Smith, G. 2012. Chinese Reactions to Anti-Asian Riots in the Pacific. *The Journal of Pacific History* 47(1) 93–109. doi.org/10.1080/00223344.2011.653482

Smith, G. 2013a. Nupela Masta? Local and Expatriate Labour in a Chinese-Run Nickel Mine in Papua New Guinea. *Asian Studies Review* 37(2):178–95. doi.org/10.1080/10357823.2013.768598

Smith, G. 2013b. Beijing's Orphans? New Chinese Investors in Papua New Guinea. *Pacific Affairs* 86(2):327–49. doi.org/10.5509/2013862327

Smith, G. 2016. The Drivers of Current Chinese Business Migration to the South Pacific. In M. Powles (ed.), *China and the Pacific: The View from Oceania*. Wellington: Victoria University Press, 144–49.

Smith, G. and S. Dinnen. 2015. And Then There Were Three: A New Chinese Miner in Papua New Guinea. *SSGM In Brief* 2015/48. ssgm.bellschool.anu.edu.au/experts-publications/publications/4115/and-then-there-were-three-new-chinese-miner-papua-new-guinea

Steinmetz, G. 2007. *The Devil's Handwriting*. Chicago: University of Chicago Press.

van Fossen, A. 2007. Citizenship for Sale: Passports of Convenience from Pacific Island Tax Havens. *Commonwealth & Comparative Politics* 45(2):138–63. doi.org/10.1080/14662040701317477

Wang, G. 1993. Greater China and the Chinese Overseas. *The China Quarterly* 136:926–48. doi.org/10.1017/S0305741000032392

Willie, G. 2018. Vietnam Community is Second Largest Foreign Community in Vanuatu: New Ambassador. *Vanuatu Daily Post*, 12 September. dailypost.vu/news/vietnam-community-is-second-largest-foreign-community-in-vanuatu-new/article_d4b45b19-066c-52c9-bc90-4208d730a7e0.html

Willmott, W.E. 1995. Origins of the Chinese in the South Pacific Islands. In P. Macgregor (ed.), *Histories of the Chinese in Australasia and the South Pacific*. Melbourne, Vic.: Museum of Chinese Australian History, 129–40.

Willmott, W.E. 2005. *A History of the Chinese Communities in Eastern Melanesia: Solomon Islands, Vanuatu, New Caledonia*. Working Paper no. 12. Christchurch, NZ: Macmillan Brown Centre for Pacific Studies.

Willmott, W.E. 2007. Varieties of Chinese Experience in the Pacific. *Chinese Southern Diaspora Studies Occasional Paper*, 1, Chapter 3. chl-old.anu.edu.au/publications/csds/cscsd_op1_6_chapter_3.pdf

WTO (World Trade Organization) 2018. *Trade Policy Review: Report by the Secretariat, Vanuatu*. www.wto.org/english/tratop_e/tpr_e/s378_e.pdf

Wu, D.Y.H. 1982. *The Chinese in Papua New Guinea: 1880–1980*. Hong Kong: Chinese University Press.

Yuan, T. 1997. *My Opinion on Chinese Schools in Vila* [*Zai Vila juban zhongwen xuexiao zhi wojian*]. Vanuatu Chinese Association's Archives.

Zhang, Q. 1998. *A History of Chinese Emigrants to Australia* [*Aodaliya huaqiao huaren shi*]. Beijing: Foreign Language Teaching and Research Press [Waiyu jiaoxue yu yanjiu chubanshe].

15

On-the-Ground Tensions with Chinese Traders in Papua New Guinea

Patrick Matbob

Introduction

Papua New Guinea (PNG) became the first country in the South Pacific to sign on to China's Belt and Road Initiative (BRI) in June 2018. Former prime minister Peter O'Neill's decision to join the BRI was no doubt driven by his desire for PNG to benefit from China's offer of funding and development opportunities. China's aid has less restrictive conditions than are usually required by PNG's traditional donor Australia, and is seen as attractive despite criticisms and warnings about the risk of falling into China's alleged debt-trap diplomacy (Mantesso 2018). O'Neill rebutted his critics, saying that PNG, like Australia and other countries, wanted to do business with China, the fastest-growing world economic power. O'Neill argued that PNG should have the choice to access China's markets, technology and financing for infrastructure development, reflecting one of the key points of the Blue Pacific approach to development endorsed by Pacific Island Forum (PIF) leaders in 2017. Secretary General of the PIF Dame Meg Taylor has also rejected the dominant narrative in the Pacific region that presents the Pacific nations a choice between traditional donors and the China alternative. Instead, she says that the PIF seeks genuine partnerships with all actors, including China (Taylor 2019). Geopolitics in the Pacific region is largely a matter for those in power, especially in developing countries like PNG. Generally, the people have little say, as the majority are isolated from the major commercial and administrative centres of PNG and affected by increasing poverty and a lack of basic government services. They have little knowledge or concern about PNG's foreign relations, except when they become affected by issues such as the spillover from the West Papuan independence struggle with Indonesia. The country's citizens remain largely spectators to the government's international relationships and dealings.

However, with O'Neill's resignation as prime minister and the election of his former finance minister James Marape as the new prime minister in May 2019, the country's focus has shifted somewhat. Marape is focusing internally with an agenda to fight corruption and ensure his people benefit fairly from their resources, part of his vision to 'take back PNG' and make it 'the richest Black Christian Nation on earth' (Kenneth 2019). Marape has so far kept his word by setting up a commission of inquiry into the UBS loan issue and reactivating the parliamentary Public Accounts Committee to inquire into the operations of government bodies. The inquiry into the AU$1.2 billion loan from Swiss bank UBS is to determine whether PNG leaders, including former prime minister Peter O'Neill and current Prime Minister James Marape, broke the law when acquiring the loan. Marape has not deviated from PNG's foreign affairs policy of 'friends to all, enemies to none' and has welcomed all investors into the country as long as they follow PNG laws—and there will be no favourites, China included. It would be reassuring for many who are wary about PNG's relationship with China that Marape's first international engagement a month after taking office was to visit Australia to reaffirm ties with its former coloniser and seek funding assistance. Australia has since agreed to loan PNG US$300 million (K1 billion) in direct budget assistance to cover its expenses and planned reforms, though details of the loan have not been revealed. Australia denied that the loan was to stop PNG accepting a loan from China. PNG, however, has formal ties with China and the fruits of the relationship are visible on the ground with a number of large infrastructure projects, such as roads, stadiums, conference centres and institutions, as well as China's biggest investment project in the Pacific, the US$800 million Ramu Nickel project. The BRI is the latest initiative in this relationship.

PNG's interactions with China, however, have a long history. Contact began as early as the 15th century with traders hunting birds of paradise and continued when Chinese labourers were brought in to work on

German plantations in 1884. There was a small number of Chinese traders who came and settled around that time, and their numbers and businesses grew over the years, spreading to other towns in PNG. When PNG gained independence in 1975, most of the Chinese took the option of Australian citizenship and moved to Australia. After that, the 'new Chinese', mainly from Malaysia, Indonesia and Singapore, as well as mainland China, began to arrive in PNG. While it is difficult to know exactly how many Chinese are in PNG, the number is generally estimated at around 20,000 (Chin 2008). The Malaysian Chinese were initially associated mainly with the logging industry, but some later became engaged in the retail industry throughout the country.

Other Chinese citizens in PNG are associated with companies like the Ramu Nickel mine and the infrastructure projects aid from China is funding in the country. These Chinese workers are usually flown into PNG to work on the projects and flown out again. Little is known about the arrangements the Chinese corporations have with the workers they bring into PNG. In a court case I attended in Madang, a Chinese construction company worker was charged with dangerous driving that caused the death of his Papua New Guinean passenger. He pleaded with the court to reconsider imposing a fine on him. He told the court that his employer was remitting his pay to his family in China and he therefore was not in a position to compensate the relatives of the victim. Whether PNG's signing on to the BRI will translate into increased engagement between PNG and China remains to be seen.

Countries like Australia and the US are concerned that PNG signing on to the BRI could place the country at risk of debt-trap diplomacy. Broadly defined, debt-trap diplomacy is where a creditor country intentionally lends excessive credit to a smaller debtor country with the intention of extracting economic or political concessions when the smaller country cannot service the loan (Doherty 2019). Yet, there are more pressing issues for PNG to address at home that may impact its future and stability. PNG's unstable political, economic and social situation, its chronic law and order problems and its widespread corruption in all levels of government pose the biggest challenges to its development aspirations. These problems will have an impact on whatever relationships PNG establishes at both regional and international levels. While Australian aid to PNG has mainly concentrated on building the capacity of the country's human resources and strengthening its governance system, China's aid has been geared towards building infrastructure. Politicians favour infrastructure developments as they are more visible and easier to quantify, adding to their portfolio of achievements during their term in parliament. Yet infrastructure development in PNG has its own challenges, including the country's unstable geography, the fact that almost 90 per cent of land remains under customary ownership and a lack of capacity and resources within the government systems to facilitate and process any government plans. In addition, PNG's problems with governance, especially at the subnational level, continue to hinder the effective implementation of projects as well as the delivery of government services to communities in rural areas of the country.

This chapter demonstrates that PNG's internal challenges continue to impact any planned development, creating tensions among the government, developers, landowners and other stakeholders. While the national government and politicians may engage with foreign investors and sign agreements for development projects at the national level, these investments are often stalled and delayed by the government's own incapacity to push the process forward through the bureaucracy at national or subnational levels. If the projects involve landowners, which they often do, that creates another layer of challenge that has to be negotiated, which can further delay and stall investments. Even agreements between project developers, the national government and the landowners made in the past need to be reviewed over periods of time, which can create added tensions. This chapter also details how Papua New Guineans are becoming increasingly aware of the issues created by foreign investments and agreements negotiated by their government and becoming vocally dissatisfied. An example is the PNG LNG project, which is yet to identify and compensate landowners, even though production and exports have commenced. Currently, the landowners of the Porgera and Ramu Nickel mines are demanding, with the support of their governors, that the mine agreements be reviewed. These issues create a complex environment for development in PNG and an unpredictable future for the planning and establishment of new projects. Marape's catchphrase of 'take back PNG' is already seen as an attempt to address these issues, particularly to ensure resource development has significant benefits for resource owners. The Marape Government's review of the new PNG LNG agreement is a move in this direction.

The new Chinese

As PNG was moving towards independence in 1975, many of the 'old Chinese' who had been in New Guinea for nearly 100 years took the option of Australian citizenship and moved south because their future was uncertain in the emerging independent country. In June 1957, the Australian Government made a decision to give Asians who were born in New Guinea or arrived during the Mandated Territory of New Guinea years the opportunity to take up Australian citizenship (Sinclair 2006). The majority became Australian citizens while a few remained to become PNG citizens.

As PNG was moving towards independence, there was a general feeling of uneasiness and people did not know what the future would be like. Papua New Guineans were being prepared to take over jobs held by Australians and other expatriates and there was the expectation for indigenous people to run their own affairs. In Rabaul, where the majority of the Chinese population lived, the tensions created by land disputes between the Tolais and Europeans resulted in the killing of the district commissioner Jack Emmanuel (Goldring 1972), and the administration's introduction of the multiracial councils created fear amongst the Chinese population. There were also increasing law and order problems in parts of the country.

As the old Chinese were leaving along with other Australian and foreign expatriates, a new wave of Chinese migrants moved in to replace them. Chin (2008) categorises these 'new Chinese' into two groups: the Southeast Asian Chinese, who are ethnic Chinese from Malaysia, Indonesia and Singapore, and the mainland Chinese and Taiwanese.

The new Chinese migrants were also seeking economic opportunities, either to work and/or set up and operate their own businesses, or to expand their business empires, as in the case of the Malaysian timber merchants. The most successful of the timber merchants is Rimbunan Hijau, which has grown into a major diversified company. There has also been an increase in Chinese migrants from mainland China as PNG has looked north for aid and to attract Chinese investments in the country. A number of major Chinese state-owned enterprises have invested in PNG, mostly benefiting from China's 'boomerang' concessional loans that restrict the projects to the use of Chinese expertise, labour and equipment. Amongst the Chinese who have come from mainland China, Chin (2008) stated the largest number have done so under the work permit scheme.

This scheme, which was designed to recruit expatriates with specific skills and expertise to be engaged by local companies to train locals workers, has been much abused. Instead, government officials are bribed and in turn have allowed in hundreds of Chinese workers with no skills or knowledge of the English language, an entry requirement under PNG law. Once in the country, these permit holders are employed in or set up small retail operations, mainly kai bars selling food, cheap electronic goods and clothing. A number of these operations have been busted by police and government officials and the owners convicted and deported. However, due to widespread corruption amongst migration officials—including law enforcement agencies—illegal migrants continue to come.

It takes two to be corrupt, yet the Chinese get the bad name

The large number of Chinese from mainland China who bribe their way into PNG and end up doing jobs reserved for Papua New Guineans are viewed with contempt by both fellow Chinese migrants and Papua New Guineans. They are blamed for giving all Chinese migrants a bad name. What is often overlooked is that it takes two parties to initiate a corrupt deal. This group of Chinese would never have set foot in PNG if PNG officials were doing their jobs honestly in the first place. After all, the migrants have to apply for visas and fulfil the requirements, then pass through customs and security checks before entering PNG. The fact that they are able to get visas from PNG officials while still in China proves that PNG officials are also corrupt and easily bribed to break the laws of the country. Yet when Chinese who are involved in any criminal activity or overstay their visas are caught, they appear in the PNG media as criminals who abused PNG laws. Nothing is said about the PNG officials who demand bribes and commissions who are also breaking the laws. They remain faceless and are not investigated or prosecuted for their crimes.

According to Chin, the mainland Chinese who bribe their way into PNG are poorly educated with limited skills and tend to become involved in businesses and employment reserved for local people. This brings them into daily direct contact with ordinary Papua New Guineans on the streets, so when the authorities finally catch up and deal with them, the bad news spreads. The majority of Papua New Guineans today were born well after independence and have had little or no experience of the good relationships that existed with the old Chinese; they form their views of the Chinese from the media and the popular views on the streets.

To add to the problem, the majority of Papua New Guineans do not distinguish the origins of the new Chinese and why they came to PNG. Instead, they identify the Chinese physically and culturally, not by their places of birth or nationalities. Therefore, the well-publicised wrongs of the Chinese who break the laws of the country are often used to judge the rest of the Chinese who are law abiding and innocent. The old Chinese in particular have been critical of the newcomers and have a poor regard for them (Smith 2014). Operating retail outlets has its risks and many Chinese shops, along with other local and expatriate businesses, have been targeted by criminals. The Chinese retailers who are driven by a desire to make a lot of money quickly place themselves at a higher risk because they tend to operate their shops longer hours into the evenings. Over the years, there have been numerous attacks on and killings of the Chinese in PNG, especially those involved in retail businesses. Many of the killings occurred in armed hold-ups by criminals, but some were by disgruntled employees who did not like how their bosses treated them. In 2013, the killing of four Chinese in their shop in Port Moresby made international news (BBC News 2013) and was condemned by then prime minister O'Neill. In Manus Province, the deaths of 10 Chinese retailers who were burnt in their supermarket was investigated by police and arrests were made after the matter was raised in parliament by the local member of parliament.

In a country of more than 800 languages, the names people give to a person or group of people can reveal a lot about how they are perceived. The recent poor relationships between the Chinese and the local people is revealed in the names the local people use to refer to them. In Tok Pisin, a Chinese would be called a *Sainaman* (Chinese man). If the Chinese person is disliked, they are usually referred to using derogatory names such as a *Saiko* or *Kongkong*. *Kongkong* (or *Singapo)* is also the common Tok Pisin name for the Chinese taro that originates from Asia. In his Melanesian pidgin dictionary, Mihalic says the Chinese object to being called *Kongkong* (1971). *Saiko*, on the other hand, is a more recent term used mainly to refer to the new Chinese. Its origin is uncertain, though, like other Tok Pisin words, it likely comes phonetically from the English word 'psycho', which refers to an insane person.

PNG's vibrant media is also responsible for creating the negative perception of the Chinese over time, starting in the late 1970s and 1980s. Soon after independence, one of the major corruption cases investigated by the Ombudsman Commission and widely publicised in the media was the 1981 Diary Affair, which involved Singaporean businessman Tony Loh and the office of the then prime minister Sir Julius Chan (Ombudsman Commission 1982). In this case, officers within the prime minister's department had attempted, without following the due processes of going to a public tender or having funds budgeted, to buy 15,000 diaries from Loh's company for the government. The Central Supply and Tenders Board had three times rejected the application from the government to approve the purchase due to abuse of process, yet the government attempted to force the board's approval. In this case, government officers in the prime minister's department had prior contact and dealings with Loh and his company and thus wanted to give him the contract.

This was soon followed by the Barnett Inquiry, which investigated and reported widespread corrupt practices in the forestry industry involving PNG leaders and Asian businessmen of Chinese origin. The Barnett Inquiry (Barnett 1987) highlighted serious abuses of laws and practices that shook the forestry industry, particularly the use of transfer pricing, declarations of losses by logging companies to avoid paying taxes and the bribing of political leaders. Again, a prominent PNG political leader and public servants were involved. Many of the abuses remain today, and illegal logging continues with exports to China.

The Ramu Nickel project is a recent experience for Papua New Guineans of the way a large Chinese mining company has gone about trying to develop a mine in the country. Papua New Guineans have observed and experienced large mining projects such as Bougainville Copper Limited, Ok Tedi, Misima, Lihir and others where international standards of work practices on the project sites were followed by the companies when developing and operating the mines. The same was expected of the Ramu Nickel project, which began with Highlands Pacific at the exploration stages following the standards set in the country. However, when Highlands Pacific was not able to attract a developer due to low nickel prices at the time, the National Alliance Government of Somare went to the Chinese. It was a completely new experience for PNG learning how the Chinese develop a world-class project. The biggest initial shock was learning how the concessional loans would work, in that the Chinese were going to bring in their own workforce, plant and equipment, and there would be limited opportunities for the local workforce and suppliers to participate in the project. Locals with mining experience who managed to get a job with Ramu NiCo were further dismayed when they saw that the Chinese were not adhering to basic standards required in the operation of such a large-scale project. There were wide-ranging health, safety and pay issues that forced the Department of Labour and Industrial Relations to intervene and close down the project until all the basic requirements under the labour laws were met. The PNG Department of Labour and Industrial Relations issued a detailed list of recommendations in February 2010 for Ramu NiCo Management Limited and ENFI PNG Ltd to comply with.

Another major issue with the Ramu Nickel project was the abuse of PNG laws by allowing Chinese workers who could not speak a word of English or Tok Pisin and who had dubious 'expertise' to enter the country in large numbers. The Department of Labour intervened, arresting 178 illegal migrants and taking them to court. Eventually, then chief magistrate John Numapo found that the workers had not really 'broken' any laws because they were brought into the country under a special state-to-state agreement.

In an interview in 2007, then regional MP for Madang Sir Peter Barter urged the Chinese to understand the seriousness of the situation and begin to improve relations with landowners, the people and their employers:

> They [the Chinese] need to improve their communication, employ responsible liaison officers, abide by labour and industrial laws, conduct regular briefings with the Madang and district administrators and to quickly begin initiating some services for the people.[1]

The latest issue affecting Ramu NiCo is the slurry spill at the Basamuk refinery, which became controversial when locals found dead fish in the area. A group of Swiss scientists independently engaged by the Madang Provincial Government investigated the spill, taking away and testing samples of the water and dead fish. They found toxic levels of heavy metal contamination and accused the company of not managing its waste properly. PNG's Conservation and Environmental Protection Authority said it had not authorised the study by the Swiss scientists and promised to carry out its own. A Provincial Government ban on the consumption

---

1   Sir Peter Barter, 15 February 2007. Regional member of Parliament for Madang. Madang. Interview with author.

of any fish from the area until further tests created hardships for the local fishermen who depend on the sale of fish for their livelihood. The ban was eventually lifted in March 2020 when the Madang National Court declared it 'unenforceable' (PNG Report 2020).

Of course, not all Chinese companies operating in PNG performed as poorly as those that developed Ramu Nickel, and the Western mining companies also had their issues: the first Australian mine in Bougainville caused a civil war that took 20,000 lives; the Anglo-Australian Ok Tedi mine was responsible for polluting the Ok Tedi river; and the North American Porgera mine is still grappling with illegal miners and a host of other issues.

PNG's chronic corruption and law and order issues remain a challenge for investors

PNG has been plagued by rampant corruption for years now, with Transparency International's Corruption Perception Index 2018 placing the country at a low 138 out of 180 countries. Much has been said and written about the issue, which is widespread within the government from the national to the district levels. It is now seen as normal to bribe or pay commissions to get anything done. A lack of capacity, resources and funding has crippled government services, allowed corrupt practices to permeate all sectors of government and is visible and experienced everyday throughout the country. From parents bribing teachers to put their children in school to hospital staff stealing and selling medicines, policemen demanding fuel for their vehicles before they will attend to cases, politicians putting their own people in key government positions so they can divert funds and public servants colluding and misusing funds, the list goes on. The Public Accounts Committee, revived by Prime Minister Marape, held its first inquiry at the end of 2019 into the Department of Health. It found widespread corruption, a lack of accountability in the issuing of contracts to suppliers, officers getting bribes and unlawful appointments of persons to key management and administrative roles. While many political leaders have spoken out against corruption, none were as outspoken as the late former prime minister Sir Mekere Morauta. Sir Mekere, former governor of the Bank of PNG, said that when he was forced to resign in the 1990s, he detected serious signs of wear and tear and a weakening of the structures and processes of government:

Already a culture of political domination of all aspects of the state was developing, undermining the efficiency and profitability of state enterprises and the functioning of important institutions of the state whose independence formed a basic pillar of good governance (Morauta 2010).

The widespread corruption in PNG affects everyone, citizens and foreigners alike, and the Chinese are no exception. It can take the form of the bribes or commissions Chinese retailers pay to police or government officers to obtain protection from criminal elements, gain access to land, property or licences to operate a business or get quick services from government agencies. It can also take the form of paying kickbacks on the supply of equipment and services to government departments or state enterprises.

The PNG Government has strict laws that govern the use of public funds through the provincial and district treasuries. Yet politicians and administration heads continue to find ways to gain access to these funds illegally and do so without fear of being arrested and prosecuted.

After the anti-Asian riots in May 2009, the government at the time set up a parliamentary bipartisan committee to investigate their cause. The key government agency officers who appeared before the committee made revelations not only about the presence of illegal Asian migrants in the country, but that they were protected by top government officials and action could not be taken to deport them (Kolo 2009). Senior foreign affairs and immigration officers said there was 'rampart corruption and bribery' in their department, which was underfunded, understaffed and unable to do its job effectively (ibid.). The officers said they suspected that there were up to 15,000 foreigners living illegally in the country. The Philippines embassy revealed at the time that of the 10,120 Filipinos in PNG, 670 were permanent residents, 6,600 were temporary migrants and 2,850 were 'irregular or undocumented' (Hernandez 2009).

Today, the media continues to report on illegal foreigners who have been caught in the country. In 2017, the media reported four Chinese men had been arrested for illegally entering the country without proper visas. Another Chinese man arrested in Port Moresby after customs authorities discovered K7 million worth of illegal cigarettes being imported admitted to smuggling in a wide variety of goods, including guns, ammunitions, pornographic materials and drugs (Wani 2018). He also admitted bringing in duplicate documents such as blank bank savings cards, driving licences, work permits, passports and motor vehicle registration papers bearing duplicated model numbers. In a more sensational case, a Chinese businessman was arrested by police and charged with attempting to bribe police with K10,000 to stop ongoing investigations and release documents and items seized by police (Tlozec 2018). Police allegedly found the man in possession of 200 common seals belonging to various companies, including 24 owned by the Chinese Government. These companies included China Engineering (PNG) Ltd, China Railway Construction Engineering Group North Project Company PNG Ltd, China Harbour Engineering Company Ltd and Covec (PNG) Ltd, all of whom are working on major infrastructure projects.

Other activities revealed before the parliamentary committee included the booming guns for drugs trade, prostitution involving Asian women, foreigners entering the country illegally by land, sea and 'through the normal process', government agencies such as customs, foreign affairs and immigration lacking the human resources to do their jobs effectively, hundreds of millions of kina being lost through tax evasion, false declarations being made and companies hiding their books from authorities. PNG's Internal Revenue Commission admitted to the committee that it was only able to scrutinise 200 big companies, while the collection of tax from 6,000 smaller operations was unchecked. The committee also heard from customs that at least half or three-quarters of containers coming through the ports each week are unchecked, and that counterfeit and illegal products flood the country. Meanwhile, authorities said they cannot remove the cheap products sold on the streets because of the removal of the anti-dumping law. Unfortunately, the work of the committee ended inconclusively after the chairman, Anglimp-South Waghi MP Jamie Maxtone-Graham, and his deputy were removed by the government after he was accused of doing a radio talkback show about the inquiry while it was still in process and preempting its final report. Their removal prompted the resignation of three other members in protest: Theo Zurecnuoc (Finchhafen), then vice minister of public service Anthony Nene (Sohe) and Bulolo MP Sam Basil. Maxtone-Graham said he was removed because the committee was about to 'expose the involvement of certain politicians in questionable activities with certain people of Asian origin' (Tannos and Eroro 2009). In PNG, the political will and actions to match anticorruption rhetoric are all too often missing.

It is obvious that in order to attract investments and do business, PNG has to address the widespread corruption in government and business as well as minimise law and order problems. Unfortunately, PNG has not been able to effectively achieve this and genuine investors continue to take risks investing in the country and have to beef up their own security throughout their operations. Transparency International, when rating PNG and other Asia-Pacific countries on anticorruption, pointed out that one of the reasons for poor ratings is the overall weakening of democratic institutions and political rights. Investors, whether from China or any other country, have to negotiate the environment of corruption, law and order problems and a lack of effective governance when trying to do business in PNG.

New Chinese and the retail industry

Not all 'new Chinese' have entered PNG illegally; some have come legally and invested in the retail industry throughout the country. They have mainly taken over retail and wholesale businesses that belonged to the old Chinese and other expatriates and locals. In places like Madang, they have actually taken over recently built shopping complexes. The arrival of the new Chinese into the provinces has been received with mixed feelings by the indigenous people, with many expressing the view that the country's retail industry is again being dominated by the Chinese after seeing them depart in the years leading up to and after independence.

'Little by little they are taking slices of our businesses', says PNG activist Martyn Namorong, who campaigns to protect local jobs and communities. 'My people feel we can't compete' (South China Morning Post 2018). Despite their mixed feelings, many locals grudgingly admire the Chinese's strong work ethic and drive to make money. The Chinese also provide employment for many Papua New Guineans and contribute to the country's economy. In fact, a number of indigenous shop owners who had been struggling with their businesses, mainly due to cultural pressures from relatives and kinsmen to share their wealth, have gladly sold or rented out their businesses to the Chinese. The main disadvantage of the PNG *wantok* system (social security network), which is at the heart of the Melanesian cultures that promote communal values and tribal and family allegiance, is that it often works against indigenous businesspeople and prevents them from growing their businesses. While having large number of relatives and tribespeople can guarantee a businessperson cheap labour and security, he/she is expected to reciprocate by contributing to cultural feasts, ceremonies and funeral expenses and support the education and health of relatives. In the coastal areas of PNG, there is jealousy of people doing well in business. Businesspersons are always at risk of having their business assets sabotaged or, worse, being killed. Cultural obligations can affect the success of an enterprise and distract businesspeople from concentrating on their businesses as much as the Chinese would. In turn, local people admire and wonder how the *Sainaman* (Chinese) can sit in a shop from dawn to dusk, seven days a week.

This is not to say that doing retail business in PNG is easy for the Chinese and other expatriates. The risks are equally high for them, as one can see when visiting Chinese retail shops. The small shops on the street fronts are always vulnerable to criminal elements, and many have been held up and money and goods stolen. The Chinese have resorted to constructing steel-grid fences that enclose their shop fronts, sometimes with rolls of razor wire over the top. Grids are also sometimes built around the cash registers in the shops. Guards at the gates strictly control the crowds coming in or leaving with bags and body searches regularly take place. Body searches without authorisation are illegal under PNG criminal laws; however, people have come to accept the practice and often raise their arms above their heads in surrender when leaving the shops so body searches can be done quickly. But the guards are selective, allowing affluent customers to leave without body searches. There have been instances where guards have been assaulted for body searches, and there is at least one successful district court case against a Chinese shop owner in Wewak (*Lapmiemben v Kuso* 2009). In addition to installing CCTV, the Chinese have come up with another way of preventing thefts. They build a raised platform, usually near the checkout, where they can have a bird's-eye view of the shop interior, and also of their checkout cashiers.

Obviously, the Chinese feel they can never trust anyone and are aware that much of the shoplifting is done with the aid of the shop assistants and/or security guards. To prevent this, the Chinese have identified the products targeted by shoplifters and these are sold over the counter in the front part of the shop, in full view of the shop supervisors and guards. One of the old Chinese retailers in Madang complained bitterly, saying she had stopped sponsoring local sports team and assisting the community because customers steal from her shop. Not long after, she began bringing in workers from Nepal to run the supermarket, thus creating a community of Nepalese in PNG. In an interesting twist, a new Chinese retailer who opened a shop in Madang has brought in checkout assistants from Misima Island in Milne Bay. Misima, a historic island that has had gold mine operations since 1900s, has three sizeable supermarkets in its small township, all operated by Chinese. These shops, which sell everything from groceries to electronics, fuel and hardware, were originally owned and run by locals. The Misima economy is largely supported by remittance from the island's workforce, many of whom were trained by Misima Mines in the 1980s and are working in other mining projects in PNG and internationally. Business there is brisk, especially during the end of the year when workers return to the island for Christmas to fulfil their cultural obligations. The Islanders are generally hardworking and reliable, and it seems the Chinese have recognised this.

The wide variety of cheap goods sold by the Chinese are often of poor quality. Many are imitation products of popular international brands, often with slight differences in the spellings of the brand names or in the logo designs that are hard to detect. Imitation products with popular international sports team brands abound, as do shirts with PNG's national colours, flags and souvenirs for independence and provincial days. In fact, in the past, one could not purchase the PNG national flag so easily, but today every Chinese shop has flags of all sizes ready for any occasion.

Illicit trade poses the biggest threat

The anti-Asian riots investigation, while inconclusive, highlighted another problem facing PNG: the incapacity of government agencies to carry out their functions effectively. Where there is a lack of law enforcement, corruption flourishes. Often, government officers collaborate and take advantage of the situation to abuse the system for bribes and favours. Many illegal activities and illicit trades are not done in secret anymore, but quite openly, as there is no longer respect for and fear of the law. An example is the smuggling of firecrackers into PNG, a product that has been banned since the 1970s. Today, firecrackers are smuggled in and openly exploded without fear of prosecution by the authorities. In many cases, police officers themselves are involved in selling the banned product.

The Manufacturers Council of PNG (MCPNG) has warned of rampant illicit trade in PNG despite steps being taken to address it. MCPNG chief executive Chey Scovell said an illicit trade taskforce has been set up by the government but has not been operational, and his biggest concern is public safety, followed by brand damage and loss of business by council members (The National 2018). PNG's popular local beer South Pacific was one of the products to have counterfeits imported and sold in the country, but Scovell said other products like 'biscuits, water, canned foods, bleach, detergents, soap, matches, nails, plywood, cigarettes, tea, coffee and even nails have all been counterfeited over the years' (ibid.).

The Independent Consumer and Competition Commission (ICCC) has also called on retail shops and supermarkets to stop selling counterfeit products, which it described as non-English-labelled products (Kuusa 2017). It identified a popular product in PNG, Indomie Mi Goreng noodles, had been found to have a counterfeit. ICCC commissioner and chief executive officer Paulus Ain said both products look the same except the label of the counterfeit product is not written in English but another language. The ICCC said the English labelling requirement was specific and that the ingredients, distributor, importer, country of origin and net weight needed to be in English.

Even traditional items made by Papua New Guineans have not been spared. Goods including string bags (*bilum*) and *meri* blouses have imitations produced in China and imported and sold cheaply in Chinese shops in PNG. The government has raided Chinese retail shops and confiscated and destroyed such goods. According to Commerce and Industry Minister Wera Mori, *bilum* weaving is a reserved activity as a cottage industry for Papua New Guineans only (Eri 2018). Popular PNG rugby league team the PNG Hunters has also had imitations of its merchandise produced and sold illegally by Chinese shops, resulting in police raids in Port Moresby confiscating and destroying some of the goods. League administrators have called on the authorities to investigate and punish shops that carry out such activities (Badui-Owa 2018).

Another illegal activity by Chinese-owned businesses is the piracy of popular local music, which has widely affected the PNG music industry. Music piracy is a global menace, and PNG has its share of complaints that Chinese shops illegally copy local music onto flash drives and sell them to the public. The practice has severely impacted the fledgling local music industry, with artists and recording studios losing out on revenue from sales of recorded music. Local artists now depend on performances to generate revenue, while recorded music is only used to promote the artist. In 2012, popular local music artist Gedix Atege took a Chinese businessman to court, accusing him of illegally selling his musical works on flash drives to customers (Safihao 2012). National Court judge David Cannings found that while there was sufficient evidence the accused had downloaded songs onto a flash drive and sold them, Gedix had not provided evidence to prove that the downloaded songs were in fact his musical works that he had not authorised the reproduction of; thus, the case was dismissed.

PNG's incapacity to police and protect its borders is giving smugglers of drugs, weapons and other illegal items access to the country and posing security threats to PNG and its neighbours Australia, Indonesia, New Zealand and the Pacific countries. These threats require Australian police and border security to work closely with PNG authorities to secure the borders of both countries, which has been happening for years.

A challenge for investors, including the Chinese

PNG's persisting law and order problems, together with its deteriorating infrastructure and the incapacity of the government to govern and police, will continue to be a challenge to investments in the country. Chinese and other foreign investors, whether in large-scale projects operated by multinational conglomerates or in retail industries in townships, need the guarantee of security for their operations. While big companies provide their own internal security forces that are often backed up by PNG police squads strategically located nearby, independent retailers have to make their own arrangements. Armed police officers are also assigned to investors operating in remote areas such as mining or logging companies. These officers have been known to harass and assault local people who have grievances with the companies. PNG's police force has inadequate human resources, with an ageing force that has not been sufficiently replenished and enlarged to serve the ever-growing population. Assigning officers to provide security for projects patronised by the government and politicians further weakens and undermines the rule of law in the towns and districts. The ratio of police officers to the growing PNG population is one police officer to more than 1,000 people, well above the United Nations recommended ratio of 1:450. Factors such as a lack of police accommodation, as is the case in Madang, has worsened the ratio to 1:3000 people (Shisei 2015). Chinese retailers also have to secure their investments and need to establish relationships with the police, local government officials and local people to guarantee their safety and security. Again, providing fuel money, lunch, beer or other incentives to the police is a common practice. In provincial towns, police officers are mandated to provide security to the businesses, and often this can extend to providing armed escorts for bank runs. A number of Chinese retailers have been killed by criminals when banking. Retailers who move into the rural areas do so at their own risk and a number have become targets from criminal elements.

The integrity of the PNG police was also seriously undermined when the former prime minister O'Neill removed successive commissioners to prevent them from arresting him following investigations into the Paraka case. Paul Paraka is a lawyer whose firm, Paul Paraka Lawyers, was alleged to have been unlawfully paid K71.8 million by O'Neill. Prime Minister Marape has taken steps to restore the force by appointing Madang MP Bryan Kramer, a critic of O'Neill seen as a key architect in engineering his downfall, as Minister for Police. Kramer's first action after taking office was to remove the police commissioner appointed by O'Neill and replace him with a younger officer, David Manning. Kramer has also vowed to keep politics out of the police force and to ensure the police follow up on and investigate the list of complaints against senior PNG leaders, including O'Neill.

The Pacific Marine Industrial Zone in Madang, a major project that was funded by China and to be developed by Chinese companies some 10 years ago, has also failed to get off the ground. The PNG Government spent K30 million (US$9 million) on the project, but there is nothing to be seen for it except a fence covered by bushes and a gate at the site. Money from the Export-Import Bank of China was also supposed to fund the project; however, mounting opposition to the project by local people halted its development. The project was one of the things discussed by former prime minister O'Neill and President Xi Jinping when he went to sign on to the BRI. The Secretary for the Department of Commerce and Industry Andrew Liliura said that the revised Export–Import Bank of China loan will be US$156 million (K484 million), which will be drawn down to start the project (Post-Courier 2018). The money will be used to build the fishing and container wharves. The project was originally planned to house 10 canneries and provide 30,000 jobs.

Conclusion

PNG's development progress to achieve its Vision 2050, a national strategy for the country to become fully developed by 2050, is not on target as its leaders envisioned. Already the country has failed to achieve any of the United Nations millennium development goals it had set (PNG Government 2015). Tensions with Chinese traders and other Chinese investments are not likely to ease in the near future as PNG struggles with its rampant corruption, chronic law and order problems and governance issues affecting the economy, politics and the delivery of services. The change of government in 2019 brings some hope that these issues will be addressed; however, it will require a huge commitment from the government and the people. PNG landowners and stakeholders involved in major investments by the Chinese and other foreign companies continue to have issues that disrupt operations and have to be addressed or dealt with by the government and the investors. As Papua New Guineans become better educated and experienced in dealing with investors, they are questioning and challenging investment agreements, including new ones being planned. Major investments planned for the country such as the Pacific Marine Industrial Zone are yet to get off the ground despite vast amounts of money already spent on them. China is seeking natural resources to feed its massive industries and offering attractive loans in return that allow it to export not only its expertise and technology but plants, equipment and labour as well. While PNG has received some attractive infrastructures that are visible evidence of development, other projects— like the K40 million (US$12 million) six-lane boulevard to the parliament, which was appropriately dubbed the road to nowhere—are useless to the people. The reality is that people are unable to access basic government services, are dying from poor health services and drug shortages, are struggling to educate their children and are deprived of economic opportunities to support themselves. The Marape Government's reactivation of the parliamentary Public Accounts Committee began with an inquiry into the health department that revealed widespread corruption and breaches of process in the acquiring and distribution of medical drugs as well as in appointments to key positions. Institutions that are supposed to serve the people lack the capacity, with shortages of funding, human and material resources allowing corruption to spread as people desperately seek services. PNG's Catholic bishops were scathing when criticising the hosting of APEC (Asia-Pacific Economic Cooperation) in 2018, saying that all it showed was the rich getting richer while the poor were getting poorer:

> APEC seems to be a manifestation of this gap as the whole of PNG watches billions being spent on appearances in Port Moresby while we experience teachers and health workers without pay and health centres without medicine (CBC 2018).

These serious issues are creating tensions every day in PNG, and this is the reality that Chinese traders and investors are both contributing to and being impacted by. If China really wants to help PNG and Pacific countries, it should be critical about whether the aid it is giving is benefiting the people of the country or just creating white elephants. China should be more concerned about what its citizens are doing in PNG and take steps to control their movements and prevent them from breaking the laws. Vanuatu's Foreign Minister Ralph Regenvanu echoed similar sentiments when he recently warned that 'Chinese investment in the region is fuelling corruption and causing resentment among local people' (Packham 2019). Former prime minister O'Neill nurtured a close relationship with China and signed on to the BRI with promises of more Chinese funding for development, but he was forced out of power soon after. If China truly wants to make the world a better place by engaging nations through the BRI to expand trade links, it needs to show more interest in the affairs of the countries it is signing on and make sure the relationship is mutually beneficial.

References

Badui-Owa, J. 2018. Morobe Governor Warns Foreign-Owned Shops Against Selling of Fake Bilums. *EMTV*, 4 July. emtv.com.pg/morobe-governor-warns-foreign-owned-shops-against-selling-of-fake-bilums

Barnett, T. E. 1987. *Report of the Commission of Inquiry into Aspects of the Forestry Industry.* Boroko: Commission of Inquiry into Aspects of the Forest Industry.

BBC News 2013. Four Chinese Killed in Papua New Guinea Knife Attack. 26 June. www.bbc.com/news/world-asia-china-23058550

CBC (Catholic Bishops Conference of Papua New Guinea & Solomon Islands) 2018. The Catholic Church and APEC. www.pngsicbc.com/press-release-4-apec

Chin, J. 2008. Contemporary Chinese Community in Papua–New Guinea: Old Money versus New Migrants. *Chinese Southern Diaspora Studies* 2. chl-old.anu.edu.au/publications/csds/csds2008/117ChinCSDS2008Master.pdf

Doherty, B. 2019. Experts Dispel Claims of China Debt-Trap Diplomacy in Pacific but Risks Remain. *The Guardian*, 21 October. www.theguardian.com/world/2019/oct/21/chinese-loans-expose-pacific-islands-to-risk-of-unsustainable-debt-report-finds

Eri, S. 2018. Ban on Counterfeit Bilums and Meri Blouses. *EMTV*, 15 August. www.emtv.com.pg/ban-on-counterfeit-bilums-and-meri-blouses/

Goldring, J.L. 1972. New Guinea Review. *The Australian Quarterly* 44(1):114–26.

Hernandez, A. 2009. Philippine Embassy Denies 'Aliens' Report. *The National*, 10 November. thenational.com.pg/philippine-embassy-denies-%E2%80%98 aliens%E2%80%99-report/

Kenneth, G. 2019. Eoe Delivers 'Take Back PNG' Policies at UN Meet. *Post-Courier*, 30 September. postcourier.com.pg/eoe-delivers-take-back-png-policies-at-un-meet/

Kolo, P. 2009. Bribery rampant in PNG Foreign Affairs Ministry. *Pacific Islands Report*. 11 June. www.pireport.org/articles/2009/11/06/bribery-rampant-png-foreign-affairs-agency

Kuusa, M. 2017. Non-English Labelled Products a Concern. *Loop PNG*, 31 October. www.looppng.com/png-news/non-english-labelled-products-concern-68781

Lapmiemben v Kuso 2009. PGDC 62; DC932. 30 July. www.paclii.org/pg/cases/PGDC/2009/62.html

Mantesso, S. 2018. Are China's Cheap Loans to Poor Nations a Development Boost or a Debt Trap? *ABC News*, 16 November. www.abc.net.au/news/2018-11-16/are-china-cheap-loans-to-poor-nations-a-debt-trap/10493286

Mihalic, F. 1971. *The Jacaranda Dictionary and Grammar of Melanesian Pidgin*. Port Moresby: Jacaranda.

Morauta, M. 2010. Corruption: Plenty Talk, Little Action. In W. McCarthy and W.M. McManus (eds), *Inclusive Approaches to Good Governance*. Madang: DWU Press, 10–15.

Ombudsman Commission 1982. *Corruption in Government*. Port Moresby: Ombudsman Commission.

Packham, B. 2019. China 'Fuelling Corruption, Resentment in Pacific': Vanuatu Foreign Minister. *The Australian*, 12 March. www.theaustralian.com.au/nation/world/china-fuelling-corruption-resentment-in-pacific-vanuatu-foreign-minister/news-story/3a616846ed88566356748b7ce3874100

PNG Government 2015. *Milennium Development Goals Final Summary Report 2015.* Port Moresby: Department of National Planning and Monitoring, Government of Papua New Guinea. www.undp.org/content/dam/papua_new_guinea/docs/015UNDP%20PNG%20MDG%20Progress%20Report_100216.pdf

PNG Report 2020. Madang Fish Market Reopens. 3 March. www.pngreport.com/fisheries/news/1382031/madang-fish-market-reopens

Post-Courier 2018. Revised PMIZ Loan Confirmed at US$156m. 13 July. postcourier.com.pg/revised-pmiz-loan-confirmed-us156m/

Safihao, J. 2012. Salesman Escapes Copyright Penalty. *The National*, 1 April. www.thenational.com.pg/salesman-escapes-copyright-penalty/

Shisei, R. 2015. Mandang PPC: 33 New Police Recruits, Not Enough for the Province. *EMTV*, 25 September. www.emtv.com.pg/madang-ppc-33-new-police-recruits-not-enough-for-the-province/

Sinclair, J. 2006. *Madang.* Madang: DWU Press.

Smith, G. 2014. Fuqing Dreaming: 'New' Chinese Communities in Papua New Guinea. In P. D'Arcy, P. Matbob and L. Crowl (eds), *Pacific-Asia Partnerships in Resource Development.* Madang: DWU Press, 232–39.

South China Morning Post 2018. 'My People Can't Compete': As China's Influence Grows in Pacific, So Does Local Resentment and International Worry. 18 June. www.scmp.com/news/asia/southeast-asia/article/2151217/my-people-cant-compete-chinas-influence-grows-pacific-so

Tannos, J. and S. Eroro 2009. Asian Riot Probe Team Members Step Down in Protest. *Post-Courier*, 26 November.

Taylor, M. 2019. The China Alternative: Changing Regional Order in the Pacific Islands. Keynote address at the University of the South Pacific, Port Vila, Vanuatu, 8 February. www.forumsec.org/keynote-address-by-dame-meg-taylor-secretary-general-the-china-alternative-changing-regional-order-in-the-pacific-islands/

The National 2018. Rise in Illicit Trade Upsets Council. 17 December. www.thenational.com.pg/rise-in-illicit-trade-upsets-council/

Tlozec, E. 2018. Chinese Businessman Charged with Bribery in Papua New Guinea over Immigration Scheme. *ABC News*, 17 May. www.abc.net.au/news/2018-05-07/chinese-businessman-charged-with-attempted-bribery-in-png/9733708

Wani, D. 2018. Illegal Group Exists. *The National*, 12 February. www.thenational.com.pg/illegal-group-exists/

16

Overseas Chinese, Soft Power and China's People-to-People Diplomacy in Timor-Leste[1]

Laurentina 'Mica' Barreto Soares

Introduction

Over the past decades, people-to-people diplomacy, also known as public diplomacy, has become one of the cornerstones of international relations between countries around the world. Countries often use public diplomacy[2] as a soft power instrument to build relationships with other countries. Joseph S. Nye defines soft power as the ability to get what you want through attraction rather than coercion or payments … Soft power arises from the attractiveness of a country's culture, political ideals and policies' (Nye 2004:256). Conversely, hard power, defined as 'the ability to coerce, grows out of a country's military and economic might' (ibid.). Now enshrined as part of China's Belt and Road Initiative (BRI), people-to-people diplomacy is part of China's soft power toolkit. The Chinese

---

1   This chapter is part of the author's research project for her PhD studies on China–Timor-Leste relations at Swinburne University of Technology, Melbourne. The empirical data used in this chapter derive from the author's fieldwork from 2014 to 2018.

2   Paul Sharp defines public diplomacy as 'the process by which direct relations with people in a country are pursued to advance the interests and extend the values of those being presented' (d'Hooghe 2007:5). This definition suggests a broader interaction beyond the state level, and thus includes non-state actors' involvement in public diplomacy.

Government considers its overseas communities important assets in promoting and strengthening China's presence in and relationships to countries with which it engages. The term 'overseas Chinese' refers to two categories: *huaqiao* and *huaren*. The most widely accepted definitions of these terms by academics and policy circles are *huaqiao* as overseas Chinese who reside outside China and have obtained permanent residency abroad but still maintain their Chinese nationality, and *huaren* as ethnic Chinese who reside in and become nationals of other countries (Tan 2013:311).

In May 2017, China and Timor-Leste celebrated 15 years of bilateral relations. China was the first country to present its credentials and establish diplomatic relations with the newly independent government of Timor-Leste in May 2002.[3] Over the past 15 years, the relationship between the two countries has been cordial, and China's presence in Timor-Leste has been on the rise. Material indications of their close relationship include a series of public buildings in the Timorese capital Dili built with grants from China Aid, as well as technical assistance in the agriculture, health and military sectors. This highly visible support is a cornerstone in China's soft power efforts in Timor-Leste.

While providing development assistance to the country, China also stressed people-to-people relations as a pillar of its foreign relations with Timor-Leste. This was manifested in an April 2014 high-level joint statement by the two countries establishing a 'Comprehensive Partnership of Good Neighbourly Friendship, Mutual Trust and Mutual Benefit' (Timor-Leste Government 2014). A year later, in April 2015, China's Vice Chairman of the Standing Committee of the 12th National People's Congress, Chen Zhu, visited Timor-Leste and reiterated the importance of people-to-people relations as part of China's overall practical cooperation with Timor-Leste towards broadening Beijing's 21st-Century Maritime Silk Road initiative (Xinhua 2015). Though there have been few reciprocal

---

3   Record of the Ministry of Foreign Affairs and Cooperation of the Democratic Republic of Timor-Leste on the Joint Communiqué on the Establishment of Full Diplomatic Relations between the Democratic Republic of Timor-Leste and the People's Republic of China on Monday, 20 May 2002.

visits and exchange programs,[4] a practical manifestation of this diplomacy has been an influx of Chinese migrants to Timor-Leste. It is estimated that between 4,500 and 5,000 recent Chinese migrants currently reside in Timor-Leste.

This chapter argues that the Chinese Government tries to use overseas Chinese in Timor-Leste as public diplomacy agents to promote officially approved narratives of China's cultural values and advocate for Taiwan's diplomatic isolation. As the Chinese in Timor-Leste are known for their entrepreneurial spirit and business acumen, the increased presence of new Chinese migrants has changed Timor-Leste's economic landscape. Thus, China's people-to-people diplomacy may foster good relations between the two countries; however, it is not always mutually beneficial. This public diplomacy predominantly benefits China through its overseas community's engagement as intermediaries between the two countries, which fosters China's economic advancement through access to Timor-Leste's markets, resources and public funds. Such engagement has created tensions, both between the Chinese-Timorese and the new Chinese migrants and between new Chinese migrants and the local community.

This chapter presents an overview of Chinese migration to Timor-Leste. The analysis touches upon the migration history of the overseas Chinese community and the recent influx of new Chinese migrants. The second section examines the role of overseas Chinese as public diplomacy agents in China's strategy for building people-to-people relations and illustrates how the Chinese Government attempts to use overseas Chinese to promote the Chinese state's soft power goals. The third section analyses the overseas Chinese community's engagement in social and economic activities, including Chinese–Timorese interactions. The chapter concludes by highlighting a series of issues that are creating cultural and racial tensions around Chinese migrants and their business interests in Timor-Leste.

---

4   Reciprocal visits involve government officials including military officials, representatives of political parties, and public and private enterprises. There have been frequent visits by the Chinese business community to Timor-Leste. Some have been facilitated through the Macau Forum for Economic and Trade Co-operation between China and Portuguese-speaking Countries. Since 2003, the Chinese Government has dispatched three to five Chinese medical doctors to Timor-Leste on an annual basis to provide medical treatment. The Chinese Government also provides scholarships for Timorese students and short training courses for Timorese government officials in China. As of mid-2017, the total number of Timorese students and public officials, including military officials who have received short training courses, in China is estimated to be more than 1,500 people, 120 of them students.

An overview of overseas Chinese migration to Timor-Leste

China has a long history of contact with Timor-Leste. Previous research suggests that Chinese traders were sporadically visiting Timor long before the first Portuguese in the 16th century to trade in sandalwood, beeswax and honey (Berlie 2015; Durand 2016; Gunn 2016; Pinto 2014a, 2014b; Ptak 1987). Most of these Chinese merchants, like other Asian traders, stayed temporarily, and very few of them settled and established businesses in Dili. By the 18th century, many overseas Chinese arrived from Macau and started to settle in Timor. They initially settled in the Portuguese colony of Lifau, but moved to Dili in 1769 when the capital moved there from Oecussi (Berlie 2015:40). However, it was only in 1906 that the Portuguese colonial government started to facilitate the arrival of a large number of Chinese labourers into the territory. They sought male labour from Guangdong and Fujian provinces in particular, as well as Macau (Kwartanada 2001:7; Telkamp 1979:7). The decline of the Qing Empire's social and economic power led large numbers of Chinese from rural areas to leave in search of a new life (Chew and Huang 2014:306).

The early arrival of Chinese migrants was welcomed by the Portuguese colonial government to help increase local economic activities and fill gaps in local skills such as masonry, carpentry and other trades (Gunn 2010:56; Saldanha 1994 in Kwartanada 2001:4). The Portuguese authorities acknowledged the skills of the Chinese, including their economic entrepreneurship, and encouraged the immigration of Chinese families, not just male labourers (Pinto 2014b:276). The colonial government declared that Chinese migrants were not allowed to be involved in local markets. This policy restriction was designed to reserve opportunities for Timorese vendors to sell local goods and agricultural products such as rice, cassava and beans once a week. In the predominantly Catholic territory, this was usually on Sundays after mass. Conversely, apart from lack of capital to begin with, Portuguese authorities did not encourage Timorese involvement in any large-scale commerce and provided more opportunities for the Chinese and other outsiders such as Arabs and the Portuguese themselves to participate (Kwartanada 2001:4). This policy demonstrated that, unlike in many Pacific colonies, the Chinese community in Timor-Leste was granted privileges under the colonial system. In return, many Chinese businesses became firm supporters of the colonial regime (Wise 2011:147).

As political turmoil in China increased between the Nationalists and the Communists, more people left for Southeast Asian and Pacific countries, including Portuguese Timor (Chew and Huang 2014:306). By 1975, it was estimated that around 25,000[5] overseas Chinese resided in Timor-Leste (Berlie 2015:40). Half of them were Portuguese citizens and the remainder were Taiwanese (Capizzi et al. 1976:385). Despite some being married to local women and settling in different parts of the territory, the Portuguese colonial government had discouraged them from assimilating into indigenous life. This policy was similar to the anti-integration policy pursued in the Dutch East Indies, which was continued after Indonesia gained independence (Turner 2003:340).

Just before the Indonesian invasion in November 1975, the Fretilin[6] government—which the People's Republic of China (PRC) was the first to recognise—promised to give citizenship rights to the ethnic Chinese and allow them to officially become part of Timor-Leste society (Capizzi et al. 1976:385). Prior to Fretilin's declaration of independence, most ethnic Chinese were Taiwanese citizens, and only a few of them held Portuguese nationality. However, in January 1975, the Portuguese Government issued a diplomatic communiqué stating its recognition of Taiwan as part of the PRC (Gonçalves 2003:58). This left the nationality of the ethnic Chinese uncertain. Today, these ethnic Chinese identify themselves as Chinese-Timorese or Timorese-Chinese and Hakka speakers. The common expression for Chinese who arrived before 1975 is *Xina-Timor*. During field research in Dili, however, a respondent of Chinese background strongly defended her social identity as Timorese-Chinese, not Chinese-Timorese. She was third-generation Chinese in Timor-Leste; both her maternal and paternal grandparents came from Canton in the mid-19th century. However, not all Chinese-Timorese share her concerns about this ambiguous term.

Ethnic Chinese in Timor-Leste's homogeneity as Hakka speakers contrasts with ethnic Chinese groups in Indonesia, where Hokkien and Teochew backgrounds predominate (Hoon 2008:4). Chinese-Indonesians are classified as Indonesian citizens, but culturally are divided into *peranakan*, ethnic Chinese who no longer speak Chinese languages or dialects, and *totok*, ethnic Chinese who continue to speak Chinese. The identity of

---

5   Other sources reported that up to 1975 there were around 20,000 Chinese Hakka living in Portuguese Timor—see Chew and Huang (2014). Others still stated there were 13,500 (Kwartanada 2001:5).
6   Fretilin was formed in 1974—originally named the Associação Social-Democrata Timorense or Timorese Social Democratic Association (ASDT)—as an independent movement against Portugal.

ethnic Chinese in Indonesia was severely politicised, with restrictive laws imposed during almost 35 years of the Suharto regime (Koning and Susanto 2008:161; Purdey 2003:425). They were subject to suspicion, particularly by the military, of having a tendency to lean towards the Indonesian Communist Party, which had links to the Chinese Communist Party (CCP). By contrast, Chinese-Timorese ethnic identity was never problematic, neither before nor after independence.

Following the 1975 Indonesian invasion, many Timorese nationalists and Chinese-Timorese were killed by the Indonesian military. Around 700 ethnic Chinese were murdered in 1975 alone (Berlie 2015:40). Over the next few years, many Chinese-Timorese left the territory due to economic hardship and political pressure from the Indonesian Government towards pro-independence groups. A year before the Indonesian invasion, a number of wealthier ethnic Chinese left the territory following the Lisbon revolution of April 1974.[7] By April 1975, around 600 ethnic Chinese had departed Dili with support from the Taiwanese Government. This group dispersed to Taiwan, Hong Kong, Macau and Australia. Dispersal to Australia was largely due to its proximity to Timor-Leste and reflected warnings from the Taiwanese consul Huan Yinchuan not to return to Taiwan due to the sophisticated and competitive business practices there. Most Chinese-Timorese were considered to have limited capacity to do business outside the territory and did not invest their money outside Timor. Taiwan only opened its door to the wealthiest ethnic Chinese (Nicol 2002:61).

In the 1980s, the Australian Government's Special Humanitarian Program also encouraged many Chinese-Timorese to immigrate (Chew and Huang 2014:310). According to the 2011 Census, there were 5,522 Timor-Leste-born ethnic Chinese living in Australia (Australian Government 2014). The departure of Chinese-Timorese from the territory created an economic vacuum in Timor-Leste. The Indonesian Government facilitated the arrival of around 1,000 Chinese-Indonesians with Hokkien origins during the early years of occupation (Kwartanada 2001:5). They were drawn from various urban centres, including Kupang, Surabaya and Jakarta. Along with these Chinese-Indonesians were merchants from Makassar (Sulawesi) and other military-backed Indonesian businessmen.

---

7 The Lisbon revolution is also known as the Carnation Revolution and was led by the Portuguese armed forces in April 1974 to overthrow the dictator regime, or *Estado Novo*/New State, under António de Oliveira Salazar. The fall of the *Estado Novo* also led to the end of Portuguese colonial power in Africa (Angola, Mozambique, Guinea Bissau and São Tomé and Príncipe) and Timor-Leste and only then was Timor-Leste invaded by Indonesia and occupied for 24 years.

These groups formed joint ventures for large-scale business activities such as coffee and sandalwood trading (Dunn 2003:221–22). The arrival of Chinese-Indonesians in Timor-Leste not only filled an economic gap, but they also became intermediaries for the Indonesian Government, similar to the role performed by Chinese-Timorese during the colonial era (Kwartanada 2001:1). Following the 1999 referendum for independence, the Chinese-Indonesian community left with the Indonesian regime. Normalisation of Timor-Leste–Indonesia relations has allowed some to return and resettle in Timor-Leste. This includes the owners of the two largest printing shops in Dili, Sylvia and Xeros. In the post-independence period, some Chinese-Timorese have also returned, mostly from Australia as well as Macau and Hong Kong. The returnees who decided to resettle include families associated with Jape, Lita Store, Leaders and Kathleen Gonçalves. Today, some 4,000 Chinese-Timorese live in Timor-Leste.[8]

During the United Nations transitional administration from 2000 to 2002, few Chinese citizens from mainland China or other Asian countries entered Timor-Leste, apart from a small number of Chinese police officers and sojourners who stayed temporarily. In the post-independence period, following the official establishment of China–Timor-Leste relations in 2002, the number of new Chinese migrants increased, with large numbers arriving from 2004 onwards. This contemporary wave of migration follows the pattern of Chinese migration in other parts of the world since the 'open door' policy was launched by Deng Xiaoping in the late 1970s. Chinese government officials and academics refer to this wave of Chinese migrants as *xin yimin* (new migrants) (Siriphon 2015:148).

The recent migration of overseas Chinese to Timor-Leste is mainly from rural areas of the coastal province of Fujian. Fujian has been a source of overseas migrants for several centuries (Liang and Morooka 2004:145). Most Chinese who migrated to developing countries from the 1990s onwards are from Fujian (Pieke and Speelman 2013:12). Fujian migrants are known for their resilience in the face of hardship, notably being drawn to work in Fukushima, telling Chinese researchers, 'All you need is courage. The one thing the earthquake and radiation zones have is work, and wages are higher' (cited in Smith 2016:147). Despite an interruption during the 2006 political crisis where the Chinese embassy in Timor-Leste evacuated around 250 residents to China, along with a few Chinese-Timorese who

---

8   Fieldwork interview with author, 22 August 2014. Dili.

sought refuge, many elected to stay behind.[9] Those who left went back to Timor-Leste when the security situation returned to normal. Since then, the number of newly arrived Chinese migrants has increased yearly. It is reported that around 4,000–5,000[10] new Chinese migrants currently reside in Timor-Leste, and some of them are married to local women and have children. Their numbers remain relatively small compared to the 7,000 Indonesian citizens currently living and working in Timor-Leste (Aritonang 2015).

Early migration from China to Timor-Leste was mostly driven by political turmoil and economic hardships in China and the colonial government's migration policy. The recent wave of migration from Fujian to Timor-Leste also reflects both push and pull factors (Liang and Morooka 2004; Thuno 2007). These include a desire for a better chance to improve life and easy access to economic opportunities as well as social pressures and rising economic competition in China. The similar experience of other developing countries suggests that some Chinese migrants have used the opportunity as a stepping stone to settle in other developed countries after economic success in the first host country (Zhuang and Wang 2010:177–78). The reality of Timor-Leste as a young country became a pull factor, attracting overseas Chinese to chase new market opportunities, especially for China's cheap products.[11]

Today, the Chinese community in Timor-Leste comprises Chinese-Timorese (or Timorese-Chinese), new Chinese migrants from the mainland and other ethnic Chinese from Macau, Hong Kong, Indonesia, Singapore, Malaysia, Philippines, Thailand and Vietnam. Despite all being considered overseas Chinese, there are complex differences amongst the groups given their very different origins, tenures and ideological and political stances (Liu 2005). For example, the Chinese-Timorese consider themselves to be local and view the new Chinese migrants and other ethnic Chinese as foreigners. They do not share their cultural backgrounds, speak different languages and have different lifestyles. Most Chinese-Timorese

---

9   Chinese-Timorese named Afuk, 28 September 2014. Interview with author.
10   According to a research report conducted by the Office of President in 2014, 1,000 new Chinese migrants arrived in Timor-Leste that year. The Immigration Office reported around 3,000–4,000 new Chinese migrants arriving in Timor-Leste between 2002 and 2014. Some of them left the country after their contracts with Chinese companies terminated. However, the number of new arrivals has continued to increase annually.
11   In an interview with a new Chinese migrant in Dili, the respondent said: 'Timor-Leste has [a] bright future ... the country has great opportunity for conducting business ... it has enormous potential for future market because there is not much economic competition on the ground' (New Chinese migrant, 25 September 2014. Dili. Interview with author).

have adopted some elements of local culture whilst maintaining their Chinese traditions. For the purpose of this chapter, I focus mainly on the new Chinese migrants, or *xin yimin*, and Chinese-Timorese for their historical presence and dynamic involvement in social and economic activities in Timor-Leste.

Overseas Chinese and China's public diplomacy in Timor-Leste

Public diplomacy has become an important part of Beijing's foreign policy and is considered an essential element of state soft power (Manurung and Saudek 2016:4). Over the past three decades, the Chinese Government has regarded overseas Chinese as instrumental to China's public diplomacy to promote China's image around the world (d'Hooghe 2006:26; Ding 2014:9). China's public diplomacy through its overseas community's interactions in Timor-Leste is slowly gaining traction. The Chinese Government views overseas Chinese in Timor-Leste as key advocates for public diplomacy through social and cultural activities. These efforts have been directed principally into three areas of strategic public diplomacy: cultivating a positive image of China abroad through the promotion of officially approved forms of Chinese culture, supporting its political diplomacy to isolate Taiwan and promoting China's economic interests.

To bolster its public diplomacy strategy, one approach China uses is embracing the Chinese-Timorese community. The Chinese embassy in Dili has supported the Chinese-Timorese in the form of in-kind and financial contributions to their social and cultural festivities, such as the Chinese New Year celebration and moonlight festival. The Chinese Government has also built close relations with representatives of the Chinese-Timorese and unofficially considers them to be part of its overseas community[12] at large.

---

12 Kathleen Gonçalves, former president of the Chinese-Timorese Association and third-generation Chinese-Timorese in Dili, confirms that China considers and classifies Chinese-Timorese as part of its overseas community, regardless of how long they have been living in and become part of Timorese society at large. Nevertheless, the Chinese-Timorese community do not share a sense of common identity and cultural values with the new Chinese migrants. Chinese-Timorese are more sensitive to local culture and many of them are well adjusted and have adopted Timorese culture as part of their culture as well. Most Chinese-Timorese consider themselves more Timorese despite their continuous practice of and close attachment to Chinese culture (Fieldwork interview with author, 8 and 22 August 2014. Dili). This continuing strong attachment and holding onto Chinese culture, despite long separations from the mainland and experiencing social and political repression from their host countries, is also very common amongst overseas Chinese elsewhere.

The Chinese Government has capitalised on the Chinese-Timorese's knowledge of the country, social, political and economic networks and language ability to promote its public diplomacy in the territory. Often, the Chinese-Timorese are asked to facilitate relations between the Chinese embassy and local Timorese, between the government of Timor-Leste and new Chinese migrants and between local communities and new Chinese migrants.

As an example of their efforts to be seen as 'honest brokers', the Chinese Government is relying on the Chinese-Timorese community to negotiate an agreement with the government of Timor-Leste to reclaim the Sional building located at the waterfront in Dili. The *Associação Comercial da Comunidade Shinesa Timor-Oan* [Chinese-Timorese Community Business Association] has been the leading negotiator in this matter with support from various Chinese-Timorese associations abroad, including the Chinese-Timorese Association of New South Wales and Victoria, Australia. The Sional building was built by the Chinese-Timorese community and rented to the Taiwanese Government for its consular office until 1975. During the Indonesian period, the building was used as the Indonesian Navy headquarters. It is now occupied by the office of the Secretary of State for Youth and Sports. However, there is an expectation that the premises will be converted into an overseas Chinese centre for social and cultural activities.[13]

China is keen to advance its prestige through cultural promotion and the construction of favourable views of the Chinese presence. Previously, the Indonesian Government had prohibited the PRC's influence in the territory, as well as terminated cultural links with Taiwan (Berlie 2015:40). This was because Chinese–Indonesian diplomatic ties were frozen for almost a quarter century until 1990. Nonetheless, the Chinese-Timorese community in the territory quietly maintained Chinese traditions and cultural practices. Beijing hopes to revitalise and foster Chinese culture in Timor-Leste with the involvement of the overseas Chinese community in establishing a Chinese cultural centre and a school to teach Mandarin Chinese. In the interest of revitalising Chinese culture, the Chinese-Timorese community is also keen to revive an old Chinese school for teaching Chinese language and culture. The Chinese-Timorese Association has been attempting to reclaim the former Chinese high school in Dili

---

13   President of the Chinese-Timorese Community Business Association, 22 September 2015. Dili. Interview with author.

known as *Chun Fá Hok Tong Su Pó Sá*. This school was registered under the Portuguese colonial government in 1960 and is now one of the public primary schools in Dili. During the Portuguese era, there were several Chinese schools in the territory, including a high school, all funded by the Taiwanese Government (Wise 2011:147). Formerly, the Taiwanese Government supported these schools by sending teachers, textbooks and all related learning materials as well as scholarships for Chinese-Timorese students to continue their study at the university level in Taiwan.[14]

In 2019, the Chinese Government announced the establishment of a Confucius Institute[15] in Dili's National University of Timor-Leste to promote Chinese culture (Xinhua 2019). In 2014, China and Timor-Leste agreed to establish a sister city relationship between Dili and Fuzhou, the capital of Fujian province, which aims to facilitate the movement of people. This initiative will attract more new Chinese migrants and Chinese enterprises to Timor-Leste.

Apart from assisting the state's attempt to promote Chinese culture, the ethnic Chinese community also plays an active role in promoting Chinese identity in the Timor-Leste. This can be seen in the continued existence of some Chinese places of worship from the Portuguese era, such as the Chinese Temple (*Kuang Ti Meu*) in Dili and Chinese cemeteries in several districts. The Chinese Temple in Dili was inaugurated in 1931 and has been used as a place for prayer and other ritual observances. It also provides a structure to preserve Chinese cultural tradition.

Despite Indonesian authorities' ban on all public events associated with Chinese tradition, they did not prevent the Chinese community from visiting the Chinese Temple and cemeteries for prayer (*Sambayan*). Thus, the Chinese community has continued to practice Chinese tradition through ritual ceremonies, the celebration of Chinese New Year and the use of Chinese names.

---

14   President of the Chinese-Timorese Community Business Association, 23 September 2015. Dili. Interview with author.

15   Confucius Institutes teach Chinese language and promote officially approved Chinese culture while spreading China's soft power abroad. As of 2019, there were a total of 550 Confucius Institutes installed in foreign universities, in both developed and developing countries, and 1,172 in classrooms for elementary and high school students (Hays 2012; Xinhua 2019).

With the massive influx of the new Chinese migrants into Timor-Leste, the effort to promote the construction of Chinese ethnicity in the country is rising. For example, in the past, there was no 'Chinatown' in Timor-Leste. With the arrival of the Chinese new migrants, there is a concentration of their communities along the street of one of the neighbourhoods in Dili called Hudi-Laran. The locals have named it the slang term *Xina-Laran* (Chinese neighbourhood) and it is possible the neighbourhood will become Dili's 'Chinatown' in the near future. Other visible effects include the ubiquity of Chinese goods and Chinese food, as well as celebration of Chinese traditions such as Chinese New Year and the Tomb Sweeping Festival. For years, the Chinese-Timorese community has been lobbying the Timor-Leste Government to consider Chinese New Year's Day as part of the national holidays and official commemorative dates. In 2018, the Timor-Leste Government finally granted a holiday on 16 February to mark Chinese New Year's Day celebrations (Timor-Leste Government 2018). Both the Chinese-Timorese and the new Chinese migrant communities in Dili welcomed the decision. The day was observed with a number of cultural events, including dragon dance shows in several places in Dili, and a courtesy visit to the Chinese embassy compound in Dili by Chinese Ambassador Liu Hongyang and other Chinese diplomatic officials, who were warmly welcomed for about one hour (Fieldwork observation, Dili, 16 February 2018).

Political diplomacy for China's unification

The question of Taiwan's unification with mainland China has become one of the core principles of China's foreign policy over the past seven decades since Chiang Kai-shek's Nationalist forces fled to the island and declared it the Republic of China in 1949. This leads Beijing officials to define China's key political objectives in the 21st century as reunification and rejuvenation, and overseas Chinese are considered 'potential political assets' to accomplish the tasks (Barabantseva 2010:130). In many countries, China's overseas communities establish branch chapters of the China Council for the Promotion Peaceful National Reunification to facilitate the campaign for China's unification. As of 2016, there are 86 such councils around the world. Though many of these councils claim to be independent non-government organisations, the overseas councils' websites are expected to be linked to the Chinese Government's official agencies, such as the Ministry of Foreign Affairs and the CCP's United Front Work Department (Groot 2017).[16]

In Timor-Leste, however, there has not been any overseas Chinese unification council or other organisation to publicly campaign for Taiwan's unification. The Chinese Government, whilst expecting its overseas Chinese to play a significant role in China's political communication and promoting China's image abroad, is also sensitive to the legacy of Taiwan's influence amongst the Chinese-Timorese community. During the Indonesian occupation, the Taiwan link was sustained through Chinese-Timorese living overseas in places such as Australia and Macau, and this was the reason for the Chinese Government's concern. In Australia, many first-generation Chinese-Timorese have strong attachments to Taiwanese culture and tradition, and some of them have business links with Taiwan. The Taiwanese Government has funded Chinese-Timorese Association activities, such as cultural practices and Mandarin classes for Chinese-Timorese children (Wise 2011:153).

Chinese-Timorese in Timor-Leste, despite echoing the Timor-Leste Government's position in their public acknowledgement of the One China policy, do not lose sight of Taiwan. The Chinese-Timorese's position on this matter is in stark contrast to that of the new Chinese migrants, who recognise the One China policy without reservation.[17] Chinese-Timorese have continued to maintain low-profile communication with Taiwan on trade and investment opportunities in Timor-Leste, despite the absence of Taiwan's official trade office in the country. Since independence, a number of Taiwanese businessmen have been paying frequent visits to

---

16 United Front of the People's Republic of China is a political and popular front under the CCP's leadership. It consists of the CCP itself and eight small political groups (the China Revolutionary Committee of the Kuomintang, China Democratic League, China Democratic National Construction Association, China Association for the Promotion of Democracy, Chinese Peasants' and Workers' Democratic Party, China Zhi Gong Dang, Jiusan Society and the Taiwan Democratic Self-Government League) as well as the All-China Federation of Industry and Commerce. The eight small political groups are not opposition parties to the CCP.

17 In my separate interviews with the new Chinese migrants' coordinator Chenguo Qin and the current president of the Chinese-Timorese Association Lay Siu Pan, the former said: 'We are from the mainland, we have to support the central government's policy and we consider Taiwan is part of China' (Fieldwork interview with author, 4 September 2014, Dili). The latter stated: 'We see China as one … we wanted to see China as one country in the world. We are fully supportive of the Timor-Leste Government's policy in maintaining good relations with China and we respect China's One China Policy … but we are more familiar with Taiwan because of our historical relations' (Fieldwork interview with author, 19 September 2014, Dili).

Timor-Leste on tourist visas looking for business opportunities. Taiwan's link with the Chinese-Timorese business community operates through Taiwan's Trade Center in Jakarta, at one stage covertly inviting Timorese members of parliament to visit Taiwan.[18] Taiwan uses historical ties and economic diplomacy to maintain links with the Chinese-Timorese community. Since 2007, however, due to China's active diplomacy and the Timor-Leste Government's firm commitment to the One China policy, Taiwan's attempts to influence Timor-Leste through the Taiwan Trade Center have declined.

Despite the Chinese-Timorese community's strong attachment to Taiwan, the PRC Government continues to consider the overseas Chinese community in Timor-Leste as an important asset to advocate for Taiwan's unification in the future. Through its embassy in Dili, the Chinese Government communicates with representatives of the overseas Chinese community about the importance national integrity. As Kathleen Gonçalves, former president of the Chinese-Timorese Association, recalled:

> The Chinese Embassy frequently invites us to talk about China's national territory … we discuss the border issue between Taiwan and mainland China and also Tibet. They want to make sure we are aware of the issue and understand their concerns. Every time there is tension that involves China and other countries regarding territorial issues, they always call us for a briefing and emphasise the One China policy. We support the initiative because it is good for us.[19]

The Chinese Government also uses local media to communicate and raise awareness about China's sovereignty. For example, in 2016, as tension in the South China Sea escalated, the Chinese embassy in Dili published Beijing's official statement about China's territorial integrity and historical claim in the South China Sea in a local newspaper for three consecutive days. Despite the absence of any formal unification group in Timor-Leste, the Chinese community's willingness to accept Chinese Government policy indicates their tacit support for Taiwan's diplomatic isolation.

---

18   During my interview with the former president of the Chinese-Timorese Association Kathleen Gonçalves, she said that between 2004 and 2006 the Taiwan Trade Center in Jakarta invited Timorese members of parliament to Taiwan as part of Taiwan's people-to-people relations program (Fieldwork interview with author, 8 August 2014, Dili).

19   Former president of the Chinese-Timorese Association Kathleen Gonçalves, 8 August 2014. Dili. Interview with author.

Promoting China's economic interests

Overseas Chinese have become important economic intermediaries for China's economic development (Pieke and Speelman 2013; Smart and Hsu 2004). Their engagement in economic activities has been closely linked to China's 1990s 'going out' or 'going global' strategy. The strategy encourages Chinese citizens and Chinese enterprises, including both state and non-state-owned companies, to leave China and venture overseas (Xia 2011:214). Overseas Chinese are seen as not only equipped with financial capital and technological skills, but able to access wider business networks. With the current leadership under President Xi Jinping, China expects overseas Chinese to be involved in extending its economic reach in the 21st century and promoting China's economic interests through its Belt and Road Initiative (BRI) (Wijaya 2016).

The recent influx of new Chinese migrants and Chinese enterprises to Timor-Leste is arguably part of China's strategy to expand its economic activities in there. The Chinese Government has been facilitating such migration,[20] with others arriving through informal networks or family links with previous arrivals and through the *Associação Comercial da Comunidade Xinesa Timor-Oan*. The exact number of overseas Chinese enterprises is difficult to determine due to the absence of official statistics. However, some Chinese enterprises, mostly state-owned, are involved in a range of construction projects, including the Chinese Nuclear Industry 22nd (CNI22), China International Construction Cooperation, Fujian International Cooperation, Guangxi International Construction Engineering, China Shandong International Economic and Technical Cooperation Group Co. Ltd and Shun International Economical and Technical Corporation Group Company. The projects are funded by the Chinese Government through grants and compete for public tenders in Timor-Leste.[21]

With regards to the BRI, Timor-Leste is now officially integrated into China's Maritime Silk Road initiative. China considers Timor-Leste its 'traditional friend' and attaches great importance to Timor-Leste's

---

20 According to representatives of new Chinese migrants in Dili, Chinese authorities include staff of the Ministry of Foreign Affairs, the Ministry of Public Security and the Overseas Affairs Office of the State Council, who work collaboratively in facilitating the migration. Some of the new Chinese migrants have been arriving through informal networks and family links.
21 For example, the CNI22 won a more than US$350 million public tender to build power plant in Timor-Leste (La'o Hamutuk 2013).

geographical location within the Southeast Asian region, where Beijing is considered part of the good-neighbour policy. In 2017, the Board of Governors of the Asian Infrastructure Investment Bank approved Timor-Leste's application to become one of the institution's regional prospective members. To date, Timor-Leste has yet to engage actively with the initiative and details about implications on the ground remain limited. However, an interesting strategy of engagement emerged long before the BRI was announced. China has been using Macau as a platform to increase its economic connectivity with Timor-Leste and other Lusophone countries since 2003. The Forum on Economic and Trade Cooperation between China and Portuguese Countries held its first meeting in 2003 and has since been dubbed the Macao Forum (Jansson and Kiala 2009).

But having discussed Chinese economic engagement in the country, it is also important to note that there are many countries competing for economic opportunities in Timor-Leste through public tenders, such as Indonesia, Portugal, Australia, France and South Korea. Indonesian state-owned companies are arguably the biggest beneficiaries of Timor-Leste's public funds, presumably because of their close connections with Timorese businessmen and political elites. There are currently more than 7,000 Indonesians in Timor-Leste. In an interview with *The Jakarta Post*, former prime minister of Timor-Leste Rui Maria de Araújo stated that there were 24 Indonesian state-owned companies and up to 400 Indonesian private companies operating in Timor-Leste (Aritonang 2015). The Indonesian ambassador to Timor-Leste Sahat Sitorus confirmed the dominant presence of Indonesian state enterprises in Timor-Leste (Simorangkir 2017).[22]

Overseas Chinese, economic activities and positive implications

Most overseas Chinese in Timor-Leste are involved in small to medium enterprises. This makes the overseas Chinese community a significant player in Timor-Leste's economy. During Portuguese times, ethnic Chinese monopolised the territory's economy, controlling retail commerce

---

22　Indonesian state-owned enterprises include Hutama Karya, Waskita, WIKA, PT PP and Adhi Karya and are involved in road construction, houses and buildings as well as cinemas (Simorangkir 2017).

and the coffee trade. This, however, does not mean that all ethnic Chinese are affluent: one-fifth of them live in poverty. Nonetheless, out of the 25 largest firms in the Portuguese territory, only two were Portuguese: SAPT and SOTA.[23] Amongst some 400 wholesale and retail commerce businesses in the Portuguese territory, 95 per cent belonged to ethnic Chinese. The largest business during the colonial period was run by the Sang Tai Hoo family—owned by two brothers (Dunn 2003:38–39). The Sang Tai Hoo family extended their business network to other parts of Asia, mainly Hong Kong, Singapore and Macau. Today, amongst the Chinese-Timorese community, the top three business enterprises are AKAM (the owner of Leader, Lita Store and Toyota dealer), the Jape family, which owns Timor-Plaza, and the Star King.

New Chinese traders settle across the country, but mainly concentrate in Dili, the centre of economic activity. Most of these new Chinese merchants occupy strategic locations for easy access along the main roads by renting land and properties from local government and private individuals, usually for minimum periods of 10–20 years.[24] The absence of formal statistics on foreign business enterprises in Timor-Leste makes it difficult to provide accurate figures for new Chinese migrants' businesses. However, it is estimated that there are currently more than 4,500–5,000 new Chinese migrants living in the country and up to 300–400 business enterprises that are currently owned by new Chinese merchants. They are involved in diverse economic activities, from the trading and retailing of cheap goods to the wholesaling of construction materials, hotel businesses, gas stations, restaurants, internet cafes and brothels. Most of the goods and materials sold are directly imported from China, with some from Indonesia.

The increased presence of new overseas Chinese and their involvement in diverse economic activities have prompted conflicting views not only amongst locals and the Timor-Leste Government, but also amongst the Chinese-Timorese community. Some Timorese and the Timor-Leste

---

23   SAPT (Sociedade Agricola Patria e Trabalho, also known as the Sociedade) was a state-owned firm established by Portuguese governor Celestino da Silva towards the end of the 1800s. Meanwhile, SOTA (Sociedade Orientale do Transportes e Armazens) was an investment company controlled by the Japanese before the Portuguese took over after Japanese occupation during World War II. It was a successor to the pre-war Asia Investment Company. These two companies were involved largely in coffee plantations and export/import activities (Dunn 2003:38).

24   Renting costs range from US$300 to more than US$1,000 per month (Zhen Jiang, a new Chinese merchant, 3 September 2014. Dili. Interview with author.).

Government welcome these developments, while others are critical of the new Chinese migrants' presence in the country. On the positive side, the new Chinese migrants' presence helps address local needs and contributes to the social and economic development of Timor-Leste.[25] They provide employment, pay taxes, drive down the price of goods through competition and many Timorese families benefit by leasing private and state-owned lands and properties to them. New Chinese migrants are also known as risk-takers, bringing economic activity to remote villages where other merchants, including Timorese, are hesitant to venture. This not only generates income, especially in the districts, but also improves young Timorese's knowledge of and skills in business development.

Issues and concerns

Despite many positive implications, a number of concerns have arisen about social, cultural, economic and political repercussions. Arguably, certain practices of the Chinese-Timorese and the new Chinese migrants can be considered forms of neocolonialism. This can be observed through the influx of new Chinese migrants and their occupation of strategic economic sectors, as well as domination of a number of key economic activities. The experience of Timor-Leste is not unique, with Ogunrotifa Ayodeji Bayo characterising Africa's recent experience with Chinese migrants as neocolonialism through diverse interventions (Bayo 2011:228).

Many in Timor-Leste have observed that the interactions between new Chinese migrants and locals in certain practices have the perhaps unintended effect of distorting local cultural values. For example, during All Souls' Day in early November (*loron matebian*), Timorese families observe the day solemnly by visiting graves, praying, laying flowers and

---

25 As a former chief of staff of the president's office stated:

I think, like many countries in other part of the world, the influx of new immigrants such as newly arrival Chinese and other foreign workers could recreate and create opportunity in the part of the local economy to grow. Having rather criminalizing immigration is not a solution, or having utterly and strongly xenophobic policy is not a solution either. Timor-Leste is hoping to become a member of ASEAN and ASEAN would soon have its free mobility of its people … more people coming in from the region. The way the Chinese people doing business in Timor-Leste … this is one manifestation of Timor-Leste's integration into regional framework … I think what we have to do, rather than criminalizing that, we have to make sure that our people become more competitive and be more prepared (Fidelis Magalhaes, 2 September 2014. Dili. Interview with author).

lighting candles in honour of dead ones. New Chinese merchants initiated the vending of plastic flowers and candles in front of cemeteries in Dili during the observance day. The practice is considered inappropriate as no merchants, including the Chinese-Timorese business community, have ever done so before. Traditionally, Timorese families prefer to prepare the flowers and candles carefully from home.

Tensions also arise in other ways. Some new Chinese migrants stay illegally after their visas expire. Some have married local women in remote places in order to have easy access to land and other property[26] as a way to circumvent the law that does not permit foreigners to own land and properties in Timor-Leste. Others operate joint venture partnerships using Timorese names for business registration to avoid paying higher taxes.[27]

The involvement of new Chinese migrants in various economic opportunities creates tensions with Chinese-Timorese and locals alike. The Chinese-Timorese feel the new Chinese merchants and other ethnic Chinese are taking over their privileged role as a major economic player in Timor-Leste's economy. New Chinese migrants' encroachment into local markets has influenced traditional market development, which had to date been dominated by locals.[28] New Chinese migrants mainly prefer to remit their profits to China rather than reinvest them in Timor. This is similar to strategies used by the Chinese community during the colonial administration, when substantial remittances were channelled to Taiwan and Macau (Yong and McKenna 1990 in Cheok et al. 2013:76).

---

26 As a Timorese senior scholar noted with concern:

> With many Chinese newcomers coming into Timor-Leste, their relationship with Timorese is also full of risk—they will influence Timorese's social and cultural domain through inter-marriage like Chinese people in the past … I see this phenomenon as natural but it is not normal. It is natural because we see interracial marriage is everywhere but it is not normal because it does not follow Timor-Leste's cultural norms and as a result, things that are supposedly natural become not natural. This will bring risk to Timor-Leste in the future. For example, they get married with Timorese and can buy lots of land and own properties in Timor-Leste—this will create a lot of problem in the future (Lucas da Costa, 2 September 2014. Dili. Interview with author).

27 Local newspaper *Independent* reported information from the Timor-Leste Business Registration Center (SERVE) that local Timorese in Dili have facilitated new Chinese traders by giving their names and properties for new Chinese traders' business registration (Dos Santos 2017). Such practices complicated the Timor-Leste Government's control over foreign businesses' tax payments.

28 In an interview with a Chinese-Timorese, the respondent stated that new Chinese migrants are greedy and very aggressive in doing business—their presence destroyed local market development and has increased prices for renting land and properties (Chinese-Timorese respondent, 8 October 2014. Dili. Interview with author).

New Chinese migrant engagement has also raised environmental and safety issues. The increased presence of new Chinese merchants has forced some Timorese families in the capital to move further inland or into the hills in search of accommodation, as residential density and real estate prices in the city rise. Reports of isolated incidents of fighting involving locals and new Chinese migrants in the capital Dili and districts are attributed to social jealousies. It may be premature to claim that there has been a rise in openly anti-Chinese sentiment in Timor-Leste, but isolated incidents have raised tensions and directed racially motivated sentiments at new Chinese migrants. Some conflicts have forced the Chinese embassy to intervene to protect their nationals. The embassy is also now more preoccupied with the wellbeing and security of its nationals than it has been in the past. As former Chinese consul Chung in Dili stated, 'The growing number of Chinese coming here is really keeping us busy, (as) very often they get into trouble with locals' (Horta 2011).

Some new Chinese migrants may have been involved in illegal activities, including human trafficking, gambling and money laundering. More Chinese-run brothels are now open in Dili with women from China and Southeast Asian countries. According to a former United Nations Police officer who worked in the Investigation Unit, new Chinese migrants have supported black market money lending since 2007, directed mainly to new Chinese migrants but also some ethnic Timorese.[29] On another front, a Chinese company named Fuzhou Hoo Long Ocean Fishing Co. Ltd, which was licensed by the Timorese Government to fish in Timor-Leste seas, was found to be involved in illegal fishing of protected fish species, particularly sharks. The exposure of their activities by *Sea Shepherd Asia* prompted public protests and resulted in the suspension of their fishing licence (James 2017; Lusa 2017).

These diverse concerns involve not only new Chinese migrants and enterprises, but also members of the established Chinese-Timorese community who have been accused of 'land grabbing'. There are accusations that the Jape Kong Su family evicted many Timorese families to build its modern Timor-Plaza. The eviction case prompted tensions among Timor-Plaza developers, local landowners and a local rights

---

29   Former United Nations Police officer Jose Brito, 13 October 2014. Dili. Interview with author.

organisation, which prosecuted the case for evicted families.[30] The Timor-Plaza case also generated public accusations of bribery involving a former minister of justice and the charge that Timor-Plaza was permitted to use the 5 acres of land in Comoro in return for a large private house construction in the Manufahi district. As a top player in property business amongst Chinese-Timorese, in 2013, the Jape family, or the Timor-Plaza company, also reportedly bought more than 50 acres of prime elevated land in eastern Dili at a very cheap price. The land is expected to be rented out for hotels and other businesses.[31]

Conclusion

People-to-people or public diplomacy has become a potent diplomatic tool for many countries' foreign relations. It has served as a soft power tool to advance Beijing's global rise through the engagement of overseas Chinese and provides an important asset to promote China's social, cultural, political and economic interests around the world. So far, China has benefited greatly from its overseas community's interactions in various ways. Beijing's views the role of ethnic Chinese in people-to-people relations, regardless of their nationality, either *huaqiao* or *huaren*, as a strategic tool to gain access to other countries. For example, prior to China's official establishment of diplomatic relations with Timor-Leste, one of former president Jiang Zemin's first questions to Timorese leader Xanana Gusmão upon their first meeting in Beijing in 2001 was about ethnic Chinese life in Timor-Leste (Wise 2011:150). China's presence in Timor-Leste will continue into the foreseeable future, and its overseas community will no doubt become important agents for China's long-term relationship with the country. Timor-Leste has felt the impact of this pattern of Chinese public diplomacy. The relationship has helped promote the international images of both countries, but has also had repercussions that affect the political economy of Timor-Leste and Timorese society. Overseas Chinese have taken advantage of policy

---

30 A local non-government organisation, Matadalan ba Rai-Haburas Foundation, noted:

> In Comoro, a luxury shopping mall called Timor-Plaza has recently been built by a large construction company from Darwin called Jape Construction. Many people cite this shopping mall as the real signal that Timor-Leste is finally developing. The reality is that Timor-Plaza is a business whose objective is wealth accumulation … the project of this private company resulted in the forced eviction of many families (Matadalan ba Rai-Haburas Foundation 2010:73).

31 Timorese worker for the Jape Company, 4 September 2014. Dili. Interview with author.

and regulatory gaps as well as limited institutional capacity to advance their political and economic interests. For many, the vaunted mutually beneficial relationship between China and Timor-Leste remains weighted heavily in favour of China and its citizens rather than Timor-Leste.

References

Aritonang, M. 2015. Discourse: Indonesia, Timor-Leste Have Developed a Mature Relationship: PM Rui Maria De Araujo. *The Jakarta Post*, 31 August. www.thejakartapost.com/news/2015/08/31/discourse-indonesiatimor-leste-have-developed-a-mature-relationship-pm.html

Australian Government 2014. *The Timor-Leste Born Community*. Canberra: Department of Social Services.

Barabantseva, E. 2010. *Overseas Chinese, ethnic minorities and nationalism: De-centering China*. London: Routledge.

Bayo, O.A. 2011. The Chinese in Africa: New Colonialism Is Not a New Deal. *Bostwana Journal of African Studies* 25(2):228–45.

Berlie, J.A. 2015. Chinese in East Timor: Identity, Society and Economy. *HumaNetten* 35(Autumn):35–49. doi.org/10.15626/hn.20153503

Capizzi, E., H. Hill and D. Macey 1976. FRETILIN and the Struggle for Independence in East Timor. *Race and Class* XVII(4):17. doi.org/10.1177/030639687601700403

Cheok, C.K., H.K. Lee and P.P. Lee 2013. Chinese Overseas Remittances to China: The Perspective from Southeast Asia. *Journal of Contemporary Asia* 43(1):75–101. doi.org/10.1080/00472336.2012.735918

Chew, D. and J.S. Huang 2014. The Timorese Hakka in Australia: Community and the Internet. *Global Hakka Studies* 2:301–36.

d'Hooghe, I. 2007. *The Rise of China's Public Diplomacy*. The Hague: Clingendael—The Netherlands Institute of International Relations.

Ding, S. 2014. *Chinese Soft Power and Public Diplomacy: An Analysis of China's New Diaspora Engagement Policies in the Xi Era*. Bloomsburg: University of Pennsylvania.

Dos Santos, H. 2017. SERVE identifika Timoroan backing Xineza loke loja. *Independente*, 29 March. www.independente.tl/tl/ekonomia/serve-identifika-timoroan-backing-xineza-loke-loja?tmpl=component&print=1

Dunn, J. 2003. *East Timor: A Rough Passage to Independence*. Double Bay: Longueville Books.

Durand, F.B. 2016. *History of Timor-Leste*. Chiang Mai: Silkworm Books.

Gonçalves, A.M.A. 2003. Macau, Timor and Portuguese India in the Context of Portugal's Recent Decolonization. In S. Llyod-Jones and A.C. Pinto (eds), *The Last Empire: Thirty Years of Portuguese Decolonization*. Bristol and Portland: Intellect Books, 54–66.

Groot, G. 2017. The Long Reach of China's United Front Work. *The Interpreter*, 6 November. Lowy Institute. www.lowyinstitute.org/the-interpreter/long-reach-Chinas-united-front-work

Gunn, G.C. 2010. *Historical Dictionary of East Timor*. London: The Scarecrow Press, Inc.

Gunn, G.C. 2016. The Timor–Macao Sandalwood Trade and the Asian Discovery of the Great South Land? *Review of Culture* 53:125–48.

Hays, J. 2012. Confucius Institutes and Spreading China Abroad. factsanddetails.com/china/cat8/sub52/item2272.html.

Hoon, C.-Y. 2008. *Chinese Identity in Post-Suharto Indonesia: Culture, Politics and Media*. Brighton and Sussex: Academic Press.

Horta, L. 2011. US, China Build Timor-Leste Soft Power. Pacific Forum CSIS, 26 April. csis-website-prod.s3.amazonaws.com/s3fs-public/legacy_files/files/publication/pac1123.pdf

James, F. 2017. Chinese Fishing Boats with 'Thousands of Sharks' Caught in Timor-Leste Waters. *ABC News*, 15 September. www.abc.net.au/news/2017-09-15/sharks-killed-in-fishing-revealed-by-sea-shepherd-timor-police/8945946

Jansson, J. and C. Kiala 2009. *Patterns of Chinese Investment, Aid and Trade in Mozambique*. Stellenbosch: Centre for Chinese Studies, University of Stellenbosch.

Koning, J. and A. Susanto 2008. *Chinese Indonesians and a Transforming China: Apprehension, Admiration, and Ambiguity*. Institute of China Studies Working Paper 2. Kuala Lumpur, University of Malaya.

Kwartanada, D. 2001. Middlemen Minority in an Isolated Outpost: A Preliminary Study of the Chinese in East Timor to 1945. www.academia.edu/4772157/Middlemen_Minority_in_an_Isolated_Outpost_A_Preliminary_Study_of_the_Chinese_in_East_Timor_to_1945

La'o Hamutuk 2013. LH Protests Contract Award to CNI22. 9 October. www. laohamutuk.blogspot.com/2013/10/lh-protests-contract-award-to-cni22.html

Liang, Z. and H. Morooka 2004. Recent Trends of Emigration from China. *International Migration* 42(3):145–64. doi.org/10.1111/j.0020-7985.2004. 00292.x

Liu, H. 2005. New Migrants and the Revival of Overseas Chinese Nationalism. *Journal of Contemporary China* 14(43):291–316. doi.org/10.1080/10670 560500065611

Lusa 2017. Timor-Leste Suspende Licenças e Retém Navios Chineses Que Pescaram Tubarão. 22 September. www.dn.pt/lusa/timor-leste-suspende-licencas-e-retem-navios-chineses-que-pescaram-tubarao-8789243.html

Manurung, H. and M.I. Saudek 2016. China Public Diplomacy in Asia Pacific. 14 July. SSRN. doi.org/10.2139/ssrn.2821986

Matadalan ba Rai-Haburas Foundation 2010. Community Voices on the Land: Results of the Consultation by Matadalan ba Rai. Matadalan ba Rai–Haburas Foundation, UNDP, Trocaire and Oxfam.

Nicol, B. 2002. *Timor: A Nation Reborn*. Jakarta: Equinox Publishing.

Nye, J.S., Jr. 2004. Soft Power and American Foreign Policy. *Political Science Quarterly* 119(2):255. doi.org/10.2307/20202345

Pieke, F.N. and T. Speelman 2013. Chinese Investment Strategies and Migration: Does Diaspora Matter? *Report for the Migration Policy Centre, European University Institute, Florence*. Leiden: Leiden University, The Netherlands.

Pinto, P.J.d.S. 2014a. Traders, Middlemen, Smugglers: The Chinese and the Formation of Colonial Timor (18th–19th Centuries). In J. V. Serrão, E. R. Bárbara Direito amd S. M. Miranda (eds), *Property Rights, Land and Territory in the European Overseas Empires*. Lisbon: Cehc-Iul, 267–77. doi.org/10.15847/ cehc.prlteoe.945X022

Pinto, P.J.d.S. 2014b. Visitors and Settlers: Notes on Timor and the Chinese as Cultural and Economic Brokers (16th–19th Centuries). *Journal of Asian History* 48(2):139–64.

Ptak, R. 1987. The Transportation of Sandalwood from Timor to Macau and China during the Ming Dynasty. *Review of Culture* 1(April–June):31–39. doi.org/10.13173/jasiahist.48.2.0139

Purdey, J. 2003. Reopening the Asimilasi vs Integrasi Debate: Ethnic Chinese Identity in Post-Suharto Indonesia. *Asian Ethnicity* 4(3):421–37. doi.org/10.1080/1343900032000117231

Simorangkir, E. 2017. BUMN RI Dominasi Pembangunan di Timor Leste. Detik Finance, 20 September. finance.detik.com/berita-ekonomi-bisnis/3650588/bumn-ri-dominasi-pembangunan-di-timor-leste

Siriphon, A. 2015. Xinyimin, New Chinese Migrants, and the Influence of the PRC and Taiwan on the Northern Thai Border. In Y. Santasombat (ed.), *Impact of China's Rise on the Mekong River*. New York: Palgrave Macmillan. doi.org/10.1057/9781137476227_6

Smart, A. and J-Y. Hsu 2004. The Chinese Diaspora, Foreign Investment and Economic Development in China. *The Review of International Affairs* 3(4):544–66. doi.org/10.1080/1475355042000241511

Smith, G. 2016. Drivers of Current Chinese Business Migration to the South Pacific. In M. Powles (ed.), *China and the Pacific: The View from Oceania*. Wellington: VUW Press.

Tan, C.-B. 2013. *Routledge Handbook of the Chinese Diaspora*. Hoboken: Taylor and Francis. doi.org/10.4324/9780203100387

Telkamp, G.J. 1979. The Economic Structure of an Outpost in the Outer Islands in the Indonesian Archipelago: Portuguese Timor 1850–1975. In P. Creutzberg (ed.), *Between People and Statistics: Essays on Modern Indonesian History*. The Hague: Martinus Nijhoff, 71–89. doi.org/10.1007/978-94-009-8846-0_6

Thuno, M. 2007. Introduction: Beyond 'Chinatown': Contemporary Chinese Migration. In M. Thuno (ed.), *Beyond Chinatown: New Chinese Migration and the Global Expansion of China*. Copenhagen: NIAS.

Timor-Leste Government 2014. Joint Statement between the People's Republic of China and the Democratic Republic of Timor-Leste on Establishing Comprehensive Partnership of Good-Neighbourly Friendship, Mutual Trust and Mutual Benefit. Press release. timor-leste.gov.tl/?p=9967&lang=en

Timor-Leste Government 2018. Day-Off on February 16, 2018. Press release. timor-leste.gov.tl/?p=19452&lang=en

Turner, S. 2003. Setting the Scene Speaking Out: Chinese Indonesians after Suharto. *Asian Ethnicity* 4(3):337–52. doi.org/10.1080/1343900032000117187

Wijaya, T. 2016. Can Overseas Chinese Build China's One Belt, One Road? *East Asia Forum*, 3 April. www.eastasiaforum.org/2016/06/02/can-overseas-chinese-build-chinas-one-belt-one-road

Wise, A. 2011. *Exile and Return among the East Timorese*. Philadelphia: University of Pennsylvania Press.

Xia, L. 2011. China's Consular Service Reform and Changes in Diplomacy. In J. Mallissen and A.M. Fernandes (eds), *Consular Affairs and Diplomacy*. Leiden: Koninklijke Bril NV.

Xinhua 2015. China Willing to Expand Practical Cooperation with Timor-Leste: NPC Vice Chairman. 2 April. www.ecns.cn/2015/04-02/160397.shtml

Xinhua 2019. 8 More Countries Set up Confucius Institutes or Classrooms in 2019. 11 December. www.xinhuanet.com/english/2019-12/11/c_138623776.htm

Zhuang, G. and W. Wang 2010. Migration and Trade: The Role of Overseas Chinese in Economic Relations between China and Southeast Asia. *International Journal of China Studies* 1(1):174–93.

Contributors

Transform Aqorau is from Solomon Islands. He studied law in Papua New Guinea and Canada and undertook his PhD in law at the University of Wollongong. He started his career as a legal officer in the Solomon Islands Ministry of Foreign Affairs, where he served for 10 years. He has worked as a legal adviser to the Pacific Islands Forum Secretariat in Fiji, and with the Pacific Islands Forum Fisheries Agency in Solomon Islands, where he served as legal counsel and deputy director-general. He was founding CEO of the Parties to the Nauru Agreement Office in the Marshall Islands and administered the Purse Seine and Longline Vessel Day Schemes. He is CEO of iTuna Intel, a Solomon Islands–based consultancy and research firm specialising in international fisheries law, and the founding director of Pacific Catalyst, a research consortium consisting of Duke University, the University of the South Pacific (USP), the Australian National Centre for Oceans, Resources and Security of the University of Wollongong, the Environmental Defense Fund and iTuna Intel. He is an adjunct fellow in the School of Government, Development and International Affairs at USP and a visiting fellow at the Australian National Centre for Oceans, Resources and Security at the University of Wollongong. He has published on Pacific tuna fisheries and other aspects of development studies. In 2020, he took up the post of Solomon Islands Permanent Representative to the United Nations.

Laurentina 'Mica' Barreto Soares is a PhD candidate at Swinburne University of Technology, Australia. Her research is focused on China–Timor-Leste relations. She earned her master's in international development from Ohio University in 2011. Mica has worked as a senior technical support advisor to the Office of the Commissioner of the Anti-Corruption Commission of Timor-Leste and as a program specialist on governance and public administration to the United Nations Development Program Timor-Leste. A Fulbright scholarship and the Swinburne University Postgraduate Research Award have supported her research. Her work has been published in the *Routledge Handbook of Contemporary Timor-Leste*. She has presented her findings to audiences in China, the United Kingdom, Brazil, Canada, Australia and Timor-Leste.

Fei Sheng is an associate professor in the Department of History at Sun Yat-sen University in Guangzhou, China. He is also the deputy director of the National Center for Oceania Studies sponsored by the Chinese Ministry of Education. He publishes widely on topics including the Chinese diaspora in the Antipodes and the environmental history of modern migration. He received his doctorate at Peking University (Beijing). His dissertation drew on fieldwork in the Victorian goldfields and the National Archives of Australia.

Gerard A. Finin has worked in the Asia-Pacific region for over three decades, with a focus on Oceania and Southeast Asia. He recently joined the faculty of Cornell University's Department of City and Regional Planning. Prior to this, he served as director of the East-West Center's Pacific Islands Development Program in Honolulu, Hawai'i, where he worked with Pacific Island governments on issues of economic development, climate change and sustainability. His research endeavours have been supported by the Asian Development Bank, the United Nations, the Ford Foundation, and the US Department of State. He earned his undergraduate degree from the University at Albany and received his doctorate from Cornell.

Iati Iati is a senior lecturer in the Politics and International Relations Programme and a Pacific security fellow in the Centre for Strategic Studies at Victoria University of Wellington. He teaches international relations and New Zealand foreign policy at the undergraduate level and strategic studies at the master's level. He coedited a 2018 book on *New Zealand and the World: Past, Present and Future*, and has published on various subject matters in relation to Pacific politics, including land reform, regionalism, geopolitics and governance. He was a lecturer and senior lecturer at the University of Otago Politics Department for eight years, and was also codirector for the 48th and 50th Otago Foreign Policy Schools. His current projects include New Zealand foreign policy in the Pacific, the geopolitics of the Pacific and land reform in the Pacific.

Tarcisius Kabutaulaka is an associate professor and director of the Center for Pacific Islands Studies (CPIS) at the University of Hawai'i at Mānoa. He is the editor the Pacific Islands Monograph Series and a member of the editorial board of *The Contemporary Pacific*. Kabutaulaka is a political scientist with research interests in China in Oceania, land and economic development, natural resources and economic development, conflicts and postconflict rehabilitation/peacebuilding, international interventions and political developments in Oceania. He is the coeditor (with Greg Fry) of *Intervention and State-Building in the Pacific: The Legitimacy of 'Cooperative Intervention'* (Manchester University Press, 2008). He has a PhD from The Australian National University and undergraduate and master's degrees from the University of the South Pacific (USP). He joined CPIS in 2009. Prior to that, he was a research fellow at the East-West Center's Pacific Islands Development Program and previously taught at USP. Kabutaulaka comes from Tasimauri on Guadalcanal, Solomon Islands.

Nic Maclellan is a journalist and researcher working in the Pacific Islands. He is a correspondent for *Islands Business* magazine and a regular contributor to *Pacnews, The Contemporary Pacific, Inside Story* and other regional media. He has published widely on French colonial policy in the Pacific and is coauthor of *La France dans le Pacifique—de Bougainville à Moruroa* (La Découverte, 1992) and *After Moruroa—France in the South Pacific* (Ocean Press, 1998). His latest book *Grappling with the Bomb* (ANU Press, 2017) is a history of British nuclear testing in Kiribati.

Jess Marinaccio received her doctorate in Pacific Studies at Victoria University of Wellington, New Zealand, in 2019 and undertook postdoctoral research with the Institute of Ethnology at Academia Sinica, Taiwan. She is currently an independent researcher. She also holds a master's in Chinese literature from National Taiwan University and has worked as a Mandarin–English interpreter for the Tuvalu embassy in Taiwan. Jess's research focuses on Tuvalu–Taiwan cultural diplomacy as well as understandings of diplomacy and indigeneity in Taiwan and its Pacific allies. She has published relevant articles in *Issues & Studies, Asia Pacific Viewpoint, International Journal of Cultural Policy, International Journal of Taiwan Studies* and *The Contemporary Pacific*.

Patrick Matbob teaches communication arts at Divine Word University in Madang, Papua New Guinea (PNG). He formerly worked as a journalist with *Wantok, The Times of PNG* and *Post-Courier* from 1985 to 2000. He joined Divine Word University as a lecturer in the Department of Communication Arts after gaining a master's degree in journalism studies from Cardiff University, Wales. He currently teaches courses in journalism and publishing and assists in supervising students' research. He continues to write news and feature articles for local newspapers and was a correspondent for the regional *Islands Business* magazine in Fiji for some years. His research interests are in journalism, media and communications as well as governance issues, national elections, West Papua and the growth of Chinese influence in PNG. He also has a keen interest in PNG arts, having written about the country's diverse traditional and contemporary arts and music as a journalist. He has published several papers and presented at local and international conferences. He has coedited two books.

Sarah O'Dowd is a research student at The Australian National University in the College of Asia and the Pacific studying economics and Asia-Pacific security studies. She has previously been published by the Development Policy Centre's *Devpolicy Blog*, *East Asia Forum* and the political risk start-up *Foreign Brief*.

Graeme Smith is a fellow in The Australian National University's Department of Pacific Affairs. His research team explores the People's Republic of China's investment, migration, military engagement, technology and aid in the Asia-Pacific, with projects in Papua New Guinea, Vanuatu, Fiji, Timor-Leste, Thailand and Vietnam. He also hosts the award-winning *Little Red Podcast* with Louisa Lim, which covers China beyond the Beijing beltway.

Henryk Szadziewski is a PhD candidate at the Department of Geography and Environment at the University of Hawai'i at Mānoa. He holds a bachelor's (hons) in modern Chinese and Mongolian studies from the University of Leeds and a master's (econ.) in development management from the University of Wales. His research focuses on the local impacts of Chinese state economic interventions in Xinjiang and Fiji.

Sandra Tarte is an associate professor and head of the School of Government, Development and International Affairs, Faculty of Business and Economics at the University of the South Pacific (USP) in Suva, Fiji. She has been a lecturer and senior lecturer at USP since 1995 and held various roles, including head of the School of Social Sciences. Sandra graduated with a PhD in East Asian studies from The Australian National University (ANU) in 1996. Her PhD thesis, Japan's Aid Diplomacy and the Pacific Islands, was copublished by the ANU National Centre for Development Studies and USP's Institute of Pacific Studies in 1998. Sandra specialises in the international politics of the Pacific Islands region. Her publications include *The New Pacific Diplomacy* (ANU Press, 2015), coedited with Greg Fry. She has written widely on regional cooperation in the Pacific, with a focus on fisheries management and conservation and regional security issues. She has also consulted for the Pacific Islands Forum Fisheries Agency, the South Pacific Regional Environment Programme, the International Development Center of Japan and Greenpeace Pacific.

Merriden Varrall holds a PhD in Chinese foreign policy through the Free University of Amsterdam and Macquarie University, Sydney. Chinese overseas aid was an important component of her research and she spent time conducting fieldwork in Madang and Papua New Guinea, as well as elsewhere in the Asia-Pacific. Merriden is a nonresident fellow and former East Asia Program director at the Lowy Institute in Sydney. Before this, she headed the South–South cooperation unit of the United Nations Development Programme in China, where she worked closely with the Ministry of Commerce and Ministry of Foreign Affairs on China's global engagement. Prior to this role, she worked for the Australian Government in Canberra, including in the development banks section of the Department of Treasury. Merriden's work on China, including China in the Pacific, has been published in *The Pacific Review, The Griffith Review, The China Journal* and *The Quarterly Magazine,* as well as in edited volumes, Lowy Institute *Analysis* papers and the *Europe China Research and Advice Network* research series.

Terence Wesley-Smith is a professor in the Center for Pacific Islands Studies (CPIS) at the University of Hawaiʻi at Mānoa, where he has taught courses about contemporary issues in Oceania for many years. He was CPIS director from 2010–18, and edited the centre's interdisciplinary journal *The Contemporary Pacific: A Journal of Island Affairs* from 2008–15. Dr Wesley-Smith coedited (with Jon Goss) *Remaking Area Studies: Teaching and Learning Across Asia and the Pacific* (University of Hawaiʻi Press, 2010), as well as (with Edgar Porter) *China in Oceania: Towards a New Regional Order?* (Berghahn Books, 2010). He has published extensively about the implications of China's rise in the Pacific Islands and other political issues in the region. He is the Principal Investigator of the National Resource Center grant (Pacific Islands) awarded by the US Department of Education and managed by CPIS.

Denghua Zhang is a research fellow in the Department of Pacific Affairs at The Australian National University (ANU). His PhD thesis, completed in 2017 at ANU, examines Chinese foreign aid and trilateral cooperation in the Asia-Pacific. He has developed an active research and teaching profile. His latest journal articles on China's foreign policy, development studies and Pacific Studies are published with *Third World Quarterly*, *The Pacific Review*, *Round Table*, *The Journal of Asia and the Pacific Policy Studies*, *Security Challenges* and *Asian Journal of Political Science*. Denghua's research mainly focuses on international relations, development studies, Chinese foreign policy and foreign aid and China in the Asia-Pacific, especially the Pacific. He has worked on the Pacific region for nearly 20 years and acquired knowledge of Chinese diplomacy, Chinese foreign aid and China in the Pacific.

Zhou Fangyin is dean of the School of International Relations, Guangdong University of Foreign Studies, and director of the Center for Pacific Island Countries Studies. He obtained his PhD from Tsinghua University in 2006, majoring in international relations. He was head of the Department of China's regional strategy at the National Institute of International Strategies, Chinese Academy of Social Sciences from 2011 to 2013. His research interests include Chinese foreign policy, international strategies and East Asian regional cooperation, as well as the study of Pacific Island countries. He is the author of several books, including *East Asian Order: Ideas, Institution and Strategy* (Social Sciences Academic Press, 2012), *Asia-Pacific Strategies of Major Powers* (Social Sciences Academic Press, 2013) and *Development Report on China's Diplomatic Relations with Neighbouring Countries* (Social Science Literature Publisher, 2015), and journal articles in *International Affairs* and *The Chinese Journal of International Politics*.

www.ingramcontent.com/pod-product-compliance
Lightning Source LLC
Chambersburg PA
CBHW040151270326
41926CB00079B/4557